CHINA'S LONG MARCH TOWARD RULE OF LAW

China has enjoyed considerable economic growth in recent years in spite of an immature, albeit rapidly developing, legal system; a system whose nature, evolution, and path of development have been little explored and poorly understood by scholars. Drawing on his legal and business experience in China as well as his academic background in the field, Randall Peerenboom provides a detailed analysis of China's legal reforms, adopting an institutional approach that considers the possibilities for, and obstacles to, reform resulting from the current state of development of Chinese institutions. Questioning the applicability of Western theoretical conceptions of rule of law, Peerenboom develops a new theoretical framework. He argues that China is in transition from rule *by* law to a version of rule *of* law, though most likely not a liberal democratic version as found in certain economically advanced countries in the West. Maintaining that law plays a key role in China's economic growth and is likely to play an even greater role in the future, Peerenboom assesses reform proposals and makes his own recommendations.

In addition to students and scholars of Chinese law, political science, sociology, and economics, this book will interest business professionals, policy advisors, and governmental and nongovernmental agencies, as well as comparative legal scholars and philosophers.

RANDALL PEERENBOOM is a member of the faculty of UCLA School of Law, where he teaches courses on Chinese law and international human rights. His publications include *Lawyers in China: Obstacles to Independence and the Defense of Rights* (1993) and *Law and Morality in Ancient China: the Silk Manuscripts of Huang-Lao* (1993).

CHINA'S LONG MARCH TOWARD RULE OF LAW

RANDALL PEERENBOOM

UCLA School of Law

CAMBRIDGE
UNIVERSITY PRESS

PUBLISHED BY THE PRESS SYNDICATE OF THE UNIVERSITY OF CAMBRIDGE
The Pitt Building, Trumpington Street, Cambridge, United Kingdom

CAMBRIDGE UNIVERSITY PRESS
The Edinburgh Building, Cambridge CB2 2RU, UK
40 West 20th Street, New York, NY 10011-4211, USA
477 Williamstown Road, Port Melbourne, VIC 3207, Australia
Ruiz de Alarcón 13, 28014 Madrid, Spain
Dock House, The Waterfront, Cape Town 8001, South Africa

http://www.cambridge.org

First published 2002

Printed in the United Kingdom at the University Press, Cambridge

Typeface Adobe Minion 10.5/13.5 pt   *System* LaTeX 2$_\varepsilon$ [TB]

A catalogue record for this book is available from the British Library

Library of Congress Cataloguing in Publication data

ISBN 0 521 81649 1 hardback
ISBN 0 521 01674 6 paperback

For Lo, Shirley, and Rayne

CONTENTS

Preface   *page* ix

List of abbreviations   xvi

1   Introduction   1

2   The evolution of rule of law in China: the role of law in historical context   27

3   Post-Mao reforms: competing conceptions of rule of law   55

4   Rule of law and its critics   126

5   Retreat of the Party and the state   188

6   The legislative system: battling chaos   239

7   The judiciary: in search of independence, authority, and competence   280

8   The legal profession: the quest for independence and professionalism   343

9   The administrative law regime: reining in an unruly bureaucracy   394

10   Rule of law and economic development   450

vii

11   Rule of law, democracy, and human rights   513

12   Conclusion: the future of legal reform   558

     References   599

     Index   653

PREFACE

Imagine it's 1978, and you are Deng Xiaoping. Mao Zedong has just died two years earlier. The Cultural Revolution is still fresh in everyone's minds. The economy is in shambles. The legal system has been destroyed. The Ministry of Justice was shut down, along with the Procuracy. Only a handful of law schools are open, though there are few professors around to teach, and no students. No one wants to study law. There are only 2000 lawyers, many of them trained before 1949. You have just ascended to power. What would you do?

Now imagine it's 2003, and you are the successor to Jiang Zemin. Twenty-some years of reforms have resulted in a proliferation of new laws, so many that China's lawyers, now well over 150,000 in number, have begun to specialize. The Ministry of Justice has been reestablished, as has the Procuracy. There are numerous law schools, churning out tens of thousands of lawyers every year – law now being considered a hot, and lucrative, area. For several years, the Chinese Communist Party (CCP) has endorsed the establishment of a socialist rule-of-law state in which the government must act in accordance with law, and the new policy was expressly incorporated via amendment into the Constitution in 1999. Recent years have seen the passage of a Judges Law, Lawyers Law, Procuracy Law, and Police Law, all aimed at raising the level of professionalism of the various branches of the justice system. In addition, the Criminal Law and Criminal Procedure Law have been amended to bring them more into line with international standards. Administrative law reforms have provided citizens with the right to sue the government, and they are increasingly taking advantage of it.

Nevertheless, foreign investors complain bitterly about the lack of rule of law; human rights activists denounce the repeated persecution of political dissidents; citizens continue to complain about judges on the take, notwithstanding the ongoing campaign to root out judicial corruption. Critics note that despite the rapid development of a legal aid system in recent years, indigent defendants often cannot secure the service of a lawyer. In their haste to attract investment, local governments regularly flout national laws and policies, approving projects without authority, and offering tax breaks despite Beijing's repeated warnings not to. What do you do?

China's commitment to a law-based order has deepened in the past two decades since the end of the Cultural Revolution, the death of Mao, and the launching of China's reform and opening policies. At the same time, it is widely acknowledged both at home and abroad that China has encountered numerous problems in the realization of rule of law. What accounts for China's woes? Are the problems ideological? China remains a nondemocratic socialist state dominated to a large, albeit diminishing, extent by the CCP. Historically, socialist legal theory has conceived of law in instrumental terms, as a tool of the "Party-state". Is, then, socialist rule of law an oxymoron? Setting aside the role of the CCP for a moment, does the fault lie with China's constitutional structure, with the lack of the kind of separation of powers found in some Western liberal democracies? Does China lack the proper mechanisms for checking and balancing the CCP and the administrative branch? Or is the problem more at the level of doctrine: does China lack important laws or are there major shortcomings in the laws that do exist? Are there other historically contingent factors, such as China's traditions and culture, the current level of institutional development of the major organs of state power and the legal profession, or the impact of the transition from central planning to a more market-based economy? Are all of the above factors, and if so, what are the implications for reform?

This book examines legal reforms and the efforts to establish rule of law in China. There are a number of possible approaches one could take to such a project. One approach would be to begin with certain predetermined theories and assumptions about rule of law, the necessary institutions for its implementation, and the historically proven path of other countries that have realized rule of law, and then use China to test these predetermined theories and assumptions. One could therefore use China to test Weber's theory of the relation between capitalism, rational bureaucracy, and rule of law; North's theory of the importance of clear property rights for economic growth; modernization theory or some other variant of an evolutionary theory that predicts that legal reforms will produce not only economic development but that legal and economic reforms will lead to political reforms and in particular the establishment of liberal democracy; globalization theories that predict that the rise of global markets will result in the convergence of legal systems toward rule of law and political systems toward pluralist democracies; or cultural theories that claim rule of law is the product of Western enlightenment traditions at odds with China's legal traditions and thus simply not possible, or at least less likely, in China, or alternatively, that predict that any rule of law in China will be rule of law with Chinese characteristics.

Such an approach has obvious advantages. China is an important test case for general theories. It is an authoritarian socialist state rather than a democracy. It is an Asian country rather than a Western one. It is a large, politically significant, developing state rather than a small, politically weak developing state. Certainly the failure of China to develop as a theory would predict would be worthy of attention. Even if the idiosyncratic features of China would ultimately allow one to save the theory by dismissing China as an exception to the general rule, China's failure to conform to the theory would deserve at minimum a rather long footnote.

There are, however, certain costs associated with this approach. Relying in a comparative law context on predetermined theories drawn from the experiences of very different countries is dangerous. All too often, if one approaches the target country with too many expectations of how a legal system is supposed to function, what the role of law should be or where legal reforms will lead, one will end up seeing oneself in the mirror – as Stanley Lubman accurately noted in his highly regarded 1999 study of post-Mao legal reforms, *Bird in a Cage*. As a result, one will miss what is important within the Chinese legal system, and in the process miss opportunities for exploring different roles that law might play given China's particular context and potentially novel institutional arrangements or practices for achieving them.

My approach was somewhat different. I did not expressly start with the objective of testing China against any particular theory. Rather, in 1996 Carine Defoort of Katholiek Universiteit Leuven, Belgium asked me if I wanted to coedit a special volume of *Cultural Dynamics* on the concept and implementation of order in China. After I happily agreed, we narrowed the topic down to "law and order in China." At the time, I had been practicing law in China for several years. I was struck by the manifestly greater reliance on law to govern China than at any time in the past, and the increased role of law in commercial transactions and even daily life. No longer was it the case that China had so few laws that a reasonably diligent lawyer could master them in a fortnight. The regulatory regime was increasingly complicated and sophisticated, with many laws being modeled on laws from Western countries. There were also significant changes in noncommercial areas such as criminal and administrative law. Even more strikingly, the theoretical underpinnings of law appeared to be changing, as China moved away from a purely instrumental conception of law toward a conception of rule of law where law was meant to bind both government officials and citizens alike.

Clearly, law's role in the Chinese polity was changing, in keeping with the dramatic changes in Chinese society, particularly since 1992. Not surprisingly given the rapid pace of change, much of what I read about the legal system was out of date. What I read was often not correct as a matter of law; more importantly, most of the available accounts of the legal system failed to adequately reflect the changes in the actual role of law in Chinese society. Alarmingly, the dramatic theoretical shift toward rule of law and its potential political significance attracted little notice in the Western press and academic literature. When the higher profile of rule of law was mentioned, it was generally dismissed as mere rhetoric. With some notable exceptions, the Western press continued to focus on human rights violations; meanwhile legal scholars and other academics, again with some notable exceptions, emphasized the many deficiencies of the legal system, and the very different social, cultural, political, and economic contexts in which law operated. Undeniably, the legal system suffers from a number of shortcomings, and no one would mistake China for Kansas. Nevertheless, the existing accounts seemed unduly dismissive of the remarkable progress that had been achieved in the relatively short period of twenty-odd years.

I wanted to begin therefore with a thick description (in the Geertzian sense) of what was actually happening on the ground. Accordingly, I began to jot down things that struck me as unusual, either because they represented a significant change from the way law functioned in the Imperial or Mao period, or because they were at odds with at least my initial conception of a law-based order.

A pattern soon emerged. Many of the problems that I identified were "technical" in nature. They fell easily into categories typically cited as part of a "thin" or procedural rule of law, discussed more fully in the following chapters. For instance, whereas a thin rule of law requires procedural rules for law-making and laws must be made by an entity with the authority to make laws in accordance with such rules to be valid, China's legislative system was in disarray. A wide variety of entities had vaguely defined powers to issue various types of legislation whose legal effect was often unclear at best. Similarly, whereas a thin rule of law requires publicly promulgated laws, knowable in advance, that are generally prospective rather than retroactive, relatively clear, consistent, and stable, laws in China were often vague, inconsistent internally and with other laws, and subject to rapid change. To further complicate matters, there was often a wide gap between laws on the books and actual practice. Even when laws were implemented, there were often questions as to the fairness of the way in which they were implemented.

Having taken note of the problems, the next task was to explain them, and to explore their causes. As we shall see, the story that emerges is a complicated one in that there are often multiple, overlapping causes for the dysfunctional features of the PRC legal system. Moreover, in explaining the obstacles to realization of even a thin rule of law in China, it quickly became apparent that I would have to address issues that exceed the boundaries of a thin theory of rule of law – including the social, cultural, political, and economic contexts in which the legal system is embedded.

Put differently, thick description by itself is insufficient. In the end, one cannot avoid confronting the kinds of theoretical issues mentioned previously, such as the relationship between rule of law and economic development; the legal system's role in enforcing property rights in order to ensure economic growth; the relationship between rule of law and democracy and human rights; and the influence of Chinese culture and traditions on the legal system. Yet in theorizing about the role and rule of law in China, we need to avoid simply imposing concepts and categories developed in light of the experiences of other countries. We cannot assume that what works for economically advanced, Western liberal democracies will necessarily work for China. In theorizing about the future of legal reforms in China and the form of rule of law most likely to take hold and flourish in China's different soil, we need to bear in mind the differences in political and economic institutions, differences in the level of development, and differences in cultural practices and values. We need to keep our minds open to the possibility that China may develop an alternative to liberal democratic rule of law – a form of rule of law with Chinese characteristics, as it were.

At the same time, we need to avoid the opposite mistake – that is, treating China as so different from other states that none of the same rules and assumptions apply. As a result of economic reforms, China increasingly has a market-oriented economy. As a result of legal reforms, China has passed many laws and established institutions similar to those in other countries. As result of its policy of opening to the outside world, China's citizens now enjoy a wide variety of cultural products enjoyed by others around the world. In other words, rule of law with Chinese characteristics is still rule of law.

Research for this book has been supported by grants from the Smith Richardson Foundation, UCLA Academic Senate, UCLA International Studies and Overseas Program, and UCLA School of Law. Various draft chapters and articles from which parts of this book have been drawn were presented at conferences and colloquia at the Columbia Law School, Harvard Law School, City University of Hong Kong, Hong Kong University, Van Vallenhoven Institute at Universiteit Leiden, Katholiek Universiteit in Leuven, Southwestern University of Political and Legal Science in Wuhan, UCLA Law School, University of Washington Law School, and Yale Law School. I thank all of those attending for their insights and comments. A "salon" organized by Mike Dowdle in Hong Kong was most enjoyable and informative. I am grateful to all of the attendees for the lively debates and constructive criticisms, including Jean-Piere Cabestan, Albert Chen, Carol Jones, Fu Hualing, Lin Feng, Song Bing, Lutz-Christian Wolf, Wang Shaoguang, and Yu Xingzhong. I am also grateful to many individuals who have read and commented on parts or all of the draft manuscript or earlier versions of chapters, or with whom I have had discussions on these topics, including Bill Alford, Joseph Chan, Don Clarke, Sean Cooney, Mike Dowdle, Paul Gewirtz, Fang Shirong, Hu Yunteng, Jiang Mingan, Liang Zhiping, Stanley Lubman, Herb Morris, Steve Munzer, Arthur Rosett, Richard Steinberg, Wang Liming, Wang Xixin, Calla Wiemer, Margaret Woo, Xia Yong, and Shirley Xu. I also thank several anonymous reviewers for their helpful suggestions. Needless to say, none of these individuals bears any responsibility for the mistakes herein, or necessarily shares my views. In many cases, several rounds of edifying conversation were most helpful in clarifying our positions and bringing the differences in our views into sharper relief, without resulting in either side being persuaded by the other's arguments. Yet the process was invariably both immensely enjoyable and intellectually stimulating, at least for me.

Our superb library team has been invaluable in locating materials. Chen Xia deserves special mention for her efforts in tracking down some obscure Chinese sources. I was also fortunate to work with two very qualified research assistants, Tim Fitzpatrick and Heather Stern.

This book draws in places on previously published works, including *Lawyers in China: Obstacles to Independence and the Defense of Rights* (Lawyers' Committee on Human Rights, 1998); "Globalization, Path Dependency and the Limits of Law: Administrative Law Reform and Rule of Law in the People's Republic of China" (*Berkeley Journal of International Law*, 2001); "Human Rights and Asian Values: the Limits of Universalism," *China Review International* (2000); "The Limits of Irony: Rorty and the China Challenge," *Philosophy East & West* 50: 56–89 (2000); "Ruling the Country in Accordance with Law: Reflections on the Rule and Role of Law in China," *Cultural Dynamics* 11: 315–51 (1999). My thanks to the publishers for permission to quote from these works.

ABBREVIATIONS

ALL	Administrative Litigation Law
ARL	Administrative Reconsideration Law
ARR	Administrative Reconsideration Regulations
ASL	Administrative Supervision Law
BERI	Business Environmental Risk Intelligence
BGB	Bürgerliches Gesetzbuch (German Civil Code)
BPC	Basic People's Courts
CASS	Chinese Academy of Social Sciences
CCP	Chinese Communist Party
CCTV	China Central Television
CIETAC	Chinese International Economic and Trade Arbitration Commission
CIM	contract-intensive money
CRIT(s)	Critical Legal Studies Scholar(s)
CSRC	China Securities Regulatory Commission
DPP	Democratic Progressive Party
FBIS	Foreign Broadcast Information Service
FDI	foreign direct investment
FIE	foreign-invested enterprise(s)
GATT	General Agreement on Tariffs and Trade?
GDP	gross domestic product
HPC	High People's Court
ICCPR	International Covenant on Civil and Political Rights
ICRG	International Country Risk Guide
IPC	Intermediate People's Court
IMF	International Monetary Fund
JV(s)	joint venture(s)
MFN	Most Favored Nation
MOFTEC	Ministry of Foreign Trade and Economic Co-operation

MOJ	Ministry of Justice
NGO(s)	nongovernmental organization(s)
NPC	National People's Congress
NPCSC	National People's Congress Standing Committee
NSC	National Seed Group Corporation
OECD	Organization for Economic Co-operation and Development
PLC	Political–Legal Committee
PRC	People's Republic of China
SAFE	State Administration of Foreign Exchange
SAIC	State Administration of Industry and Commerce
SOE(s)	state-owned enterprise(s)
SPC	Supreme People's Court
SPP	Supreme People's Procuratorate
TLSS	township legal services stations
TVE(s)	township and village enterprise(s)
UCLA	University of California at Los Angeles
UDHR	Universal Declaration of Human Rights
UN	United Nations
USTR	United States Trade Representative
VAT	value-added tax
WFOE(s)	wholly foreign-owned enterprise(s)
WTO	World Trade Organization

1

Introduction

The hallmarks of modernity are a market economy, democracy, human rights, and rule of law. Not surprisingly, China first began to grapple with the need to reform the legal system in earnest during the Qing dynasty as part of its attempt to come to grips with modernity. Although those early reforms could not gain a foothold in the chaotic civil war conditions of the Republican era, and law subsequently took a back seat to politics during much of the Mao period, legal reforms and rule of law again became a hot issue when China emerged from the Cultural Revolution in the late 1970s and Deng Xiaoping announced his ambitious platform to modernize China. Twenty years of economic and legal reforms have only served to raise the temperature.

Nowadays, it is virtually impossible to open any Chinese newspaper without seeing reference to rule of law. Signs painted on buildings in the countryside proclaim the need to act in accordance with law. Flyers posted in cities urge passersby to steadfastly uphold the law. Scholars have produced literally hundreds of books and articles on the topic in the last ten years. And in 1999, the Constitution was amended to expressly provide for the establishment of a socialist rule-of-law state.

On the other hand, the initial reaction of many members of the general public to any attempt to link rule of law to China is one of shock and amusement. The less informed genuinely if bemusedly still question whether China even has laws. Lamenting the absence of rule of law, foreign investors and human rights activists keep up a steady drum beat calling for its realization. Meanwhile, skeptical legal scholars and longtime China observers query whether China actually is, or should be, moving toward rule of law. Some critics dismiss legal reforms as part of a sinister plot to hoodwink foreigners into investing in China or a jaded attempt by senior leaders to gain legitimacy abroad while actually just strengthening the legal system to forge a better tool of repression.

A few minority voices, all but drowned out in the din over the wonders of rule of law, suggest that the economy is doing fine without it, and hence question whether China really needs it. Ironically, although most in China proudly chant the rule-of-law mantra, many Western legal scholars and political scientists dismiss it as a meaningless slogan – "just another one of those self-congratulatory rhetorical devices that grace the public utterances of Anglo-American politicians."[1] Worse yet, some condemn it as a mask for oppression and injustice.[2]

Notwithstanding such reservations about its value and the self-proclaimed failure of earlier efforts to transplant Western liberal democracy and rule of law to developing countries in the 1960s and 1970s, multinational agencies continue to pour millions of dollars into legal reform programs in China.[3] If anything, Russia's collapse and the Asian financial crisis have only increased faith in the importance of rule of law and opened the funding floodgates even wider. Bilateral programs also abound. In 1997, for instance, Presidents Clinton and Jiang signed a broad-ranging agreement widely touted as a rule-of-law initiative in the Western press. Not to be outdone, the EU entered into a Legal and Judicial Cooperation Program in 1998.[4]

What is one to make of such wildly divergent perspectives? Is China in the process of establishing rule of law? If so, is that good or bad? What has prevented China from realizing rule of law? Assuming China does implement rule of law, will rule of law in China differ from rule of law in Western liberal democracies? This book attempts to sort through these and related issues, beginning with the basic question of the meaning of rule of law.

What is rule of law?

Rule of law, like other important political concepts such as justice and equality, is an "essentially contested concept."[5] Yet the fact that there is room for debate about the proper interpretation of rule of law should not blind us to the broad consensus as to its core meaning and basic elements. At its most basic, rule of law refers to a system in which law is able to impose meaningful restraints on the state and individual members of the ruling elite, as captured in the rhetorically powerful if overly simplistic notions of a government of laws, the supremacy of the law, and equality of all before the law.

Theories of rule of law can be divided into two general types: thin and thick. A thin theory stresses the formal or instrumental aspects of rule of law – those features that any legal system allegedly must possess to function effectively as a system of laws, regardless of whether the legal system is part of a democratic or nondemocratic society, capitalist or socialist, liberal or theocratic.[6] Although proponents of thin interpretations of rule of law define it in slightly different ways, there is considerable common ground, with many building on or modifying Lon Fuller's influential account that laws be general, public, prospective, clear, consistent, capable of being followed, stable, and enforced.[7]

In contrast to thin versions, thick or substantive conceptions begin with the basic elements of a thin concept of rule of law but then incorporate elements of political morality such as particular economic arrangements (free-market capitalism, central planning, etc.), forms of government (democratic, single party socialism, etc.), or conceptions of human rights (liberal, communitarian, "Asian values," etc.). Thick conceptions of rule of law can be further subdivided according to the particular substantive elements that are favored.

Thus, the Liberal Democratic version of rule of law incorporates free market capitalism (subject to qualifications that would allow various degrees of "legitimate" government regulation of the market), multiparty democracy in which citizens may choose their representatives at all levels of government, and a liberal interpretation of human rights that gives priority to civil and political rights over economic, social, cultural, and collective or group rights.[8]

In contrast, Jiang Zemin and other Statist Socialists endorse a state-centered socialist rule of law defined by, *inter alia*, a socialist form of economy, which in today's China means an increasingly market-based economy but one in which public ownership still plays a somewhat larger role than in other market economies; a nondemocratic system in which the Party plays a leading role; and an interpretation of rights that emphasizes stability, collective rights over individual rights, and subsistence as the basic right rather than civil and political rights.

There is also support for various forms of rule of law that fall between the Statist Socialism type championed by Jiang Zemin and other central leaders and the Liberal Democratic version. For example, there is some support for a democratic but nonliberal (New Confucian) Communitarian variant built on market capitalism, perhaps with a somewhat greater degree of government intervention than in the liberal version;[9] some genuine form of multiparty democracy in which citizens choose their representatives at all levels of government; plus an "Asian values" or communitarian interpretation of rights that attaches relatively greater weight to the interests of the majority and collective rights as opposed to the civil and political rights of individuals.[10]

Another variant is a Neoauthoritarian or Soft Authoritarian form of rule of law that, like the Communitarian version, rejects a liberal interpretation of rights but, unlike its Communitarian cousin, also rejects democracy. Whereas Communitarians adopt a genuine multiparty democracy in which citizens choose their representatives at all levels of government, Neoauthoritarians permit democracy only at lower levels of government or not at all.[11] For instance, Pan Wei, a prominent Beijing University political scientist, has advocated a "consultative rule of law" that eschews democracy in favor of single party rule, albeit with a redefined role for the Party, and more extensive, but still limited, freedoms of speech, press, assembly, and association.[12]

A full elaboration of any of these types requires a more detailed account of the purposes or goals the regime is intended to serve and its institutions, practices, rules, and outcomes in particular cases, as will be provided in Chapter 3. Nevertheless, this preliminary sketch is sufficient to make the following points. First, despite considerable variation, all forms accept the basic benchmark that law must impose meaningful limits on the ruler and all are compatible with a thin rule of law. Put differently, any thick conception of rule of law must meet the more minimal threshold criteria of a thin theory. Predictably, as legal reforms have progressed in China, the legal system has converged in many respects with the legal systems of well-developed countries; and it is likely to continue to converge in the future.

Second, at the same time, there will inevitably be some variations in rule-of-law regimes even with respect to the basic requirements of a thin theory due to the context in which they are embedded. For example, there may be differences in the way disputes are handled, with some systems relying more on the formal legal system to enforce property rights and resolve social conflicts and other systems relying more on informal and nonlegal means of protecting property rights and resolving social conflicts. Similarly, administrative law regimes will differ in the degree of discretion afforded government officials and the mechanisms for preventing abuse of discretion. Judicial independence will also differ in degree and in the institutional arrangements and practices to achieve it.[13] And differences in fundamental normative values will lead to divergent rules and outcomes. Hence signs of both divergence from and convergence with the legal systems of well-developed countries are to be expected. Indeed, whether one finds convergence or divergence depends to a large extent on the particular indicators that one chooses, the time frame, and the degree of abstraction or focus. The closer one looks, the more likely one is to find divergence. But that is a natural result of narrowing the focus.

Third, when claiming that China lacks rule of law, many Western commentators mean that China lacks the Liberal Democratic form found primarily in modern Western states with a well-developed market economy. Although some citizens, legal scholars, and political scientists in China or living abroad have advocated a Liberal Democratic rule of law, there is little support for liberal democracy, and hence a Liberal Democratic rule of law, among state leaders, legal scholars, intellectuals, or the general public.[14] Accordingly, if we are to understand the likely path of development of China's system, and the reasons for differences in its institutions, rules, practices, and outcomes, we need to rethink rule of law. We need to theorize rule of law in ways that do not assume a liberal democratic framework, and explore alternative conceptions of rule of law that are consistent with China's own circumstances. While the three alternatives to a Liberal Democratic rule of law each differ in significant ways – particularly with respect to the role of law as a means of strengthening the state versus limiting the state – they nevertheless share many features that set them apart from their liberal democratic counterpart.

Given the many possible conceptions of rule of law, I avoid reference to "the rule of law," which suggests that there is a single type of rule of law. Alternatively, one could refer to the *concept* of "the rule of law," for which there are different possible *conceptions*. The thin theory of rule of law would define the core concept of rule of law, with the various thick theories constituting different conceptions. Yet, as I argue in Chapters 3 and 12, from the perspective of philosophical pragmatism, how one defines a term depends on one's purposes and the consequences that attach to defining a term in a particular way. As thick and thin theories serve different purposes, I do not want to privilege thin theories over thick theories by declaring the thin version to be "the rule of law."[15]

Fourth, assuming, as seems likely, that China will ultimately more fully implement some version of rule of law, the realization of rule of law in any form will require significant changes to the present system.

China's march toward rule of law

Although it may be too early to declare definitely that China will succeed in fully implementing rule of law, there is considerable direct and indirect evidence that China is in the midst of a transition toward some version of rule of law that measures up favorably to the requirements of a thin theory. As an official matter, both the Party constitution and the 1982 constitution confirm the basic principles of a government of laws, the supremacy of the law, and equality of all before the law. Moreover, in 1996, Jiang Zemin adopted the new *tifa* or official policy formulation of ruling the country in accordance with the law and establishing a socialist rule-of-law state (*yifa zhiguo, jianshe shuhui zhuyi fazhiguo*), which was subsequently incorporated into the Constitution.[16]

Were the only evidence for the shift toward rule of law mere words, we would be justifiably dubious. However, China has backed up its rhetoric with actions. Decimated by the Cultural Revolution and decades of neglect and abuse, the legal system had to be rebuilt virtually from scratch. One of the first tasks was to start passing laws. Given the heavy reliance on Party policies rather than law during the Mao period, China lacked even the most basic laws such as a comprehensive criminal code, civil law, or contract law. The response has been a legislative onslaught the pace and breadth of which has been nothing short of stunning. Between 1976 and 1998, the National People's Congress (NPC) and its Standing Committee (NPCSC) passed more than 337 laws and local people's congresses and governments issued more than 6,000 regulations. In contrast, only 134 laws were passed between 1949 and 1978, with only one law passed during the Cultural Revolution from 1967 to 1976. Moreover, of the 134 laws passed between 1949 and 1978, 111 were subsequently declared invalid and many of the remaining ones were amended during the post-1978 reform era.[17]

Considerable effort and resources have also been spent on institution-building. The Ministry of Justice, dismantled in 1959, was reestablished in 1979. Law schools were reopened, and a wide variety of legal journals commenced publication. The government has sought to rebuild its legal institutions and promote greater professionalization of judges, procurators, lawyers, and police. The legal profession in particular has made remarkable strides over the last twenty years. While in 1981, there were just 1,465 law offices and a mere 5,500 lawyers, by 1998 there were more than 8,300 law firms and over 110,000 lawyers.[18]

Much time and effort have been spent on legal dissemination and consciousness raising. China is now in its fourth five-year plan to publicize laws. Recently, live trials have been broadcast on television. Every day CCTV broadcasts the half-hour program *Today on Law* where experts discuss the ins and outs of interesting cases.[19] In addition, local stations have been quick to respond to the interest in law by providing a variety of law-related programs.[20] There is also a radio program to inform people about their rights. Judging from the increase in litigation, the efforts are achieving some success. While litigation was virtually nonexistent in 1979, the total number of cases of first instance reached 3 million by 1992, and 5 million by 1996.[21]

Perhaps the best evidence for the contention that the legal system is moving in the direction of greater compliance with the requirements of rule of law is the increasing importance of law in everyday life. Whereas during the Mao period the country was governed mainly on the basis of Party policy and administrative regulations, often passed internally up and down the administrative hierarchy but not made available to the general public, today the country is increasingly governed on the basis of publicly promulgated laws rather than Party policy or internal regulations (*neibu guiding*). Nowadays, lawyers and consultants who dismiss the law and advise their clients that all is possible with the right connections (*guanxi*) are simply guilty of gross malpractice. Moreover, law is beginning to impose meaningful restraints on the ruling regime (which of course is not to claim that law is the only source of restraints on government actors). For instance, Party interference with specific court decisions is the rare exception rather than the rule. Significantly, a number of administrative laws have been passed establishing legal mechanisms for challenging government officials and holding them accountable. Increasingly, citizens are willing to take on the government through administrative reconsideration and litigation. More important, they are often successful. In fact, the plaintiff prevails in whole or in part in some 40 percent of the administrative litigation cases, a rate three times higher than in the USA.[22]

Rule of law or rule by law?

While there is considerable evidence that China is in the midst of a transformation to some form of rule of law, there is at the same time some evidence to support the view that the legal system remains a type of rule *by* law rather than a form of rule *of* law. Whereas the core of rule of law is the ability of law and legal system to impose meaningful restraints on the state and individual members of the ruling elite, rule by law refers to an instrumental conception of law in which law is merely a tool to be used as the state sees fit.[23]

Despite remarkable progress, the reach of the law is still clearly limited. The Party's actual role in governing the country is at odds with or not reflected in the Constitution or other legal documents. In some cases, Party policies continue to trump laws. The nomenklatura system whereby the Party is able to appoint or at least veto the appointment of key members of the people's congresses and courts undermines the legitimacy, independence, and authority of the legislature and judiciary. Senior Party members, moreover, are generally subject to sanctions, if at all, by Party discipline committees rather than the courts, in flagrant violation of the fundamental rule-of-law principle that the law applies equally to rulers and commoners alike. Further, the government continues to limit civil society and political dissidents are denied their rights as provided by law.

Of course, assuming China is in the process of implementing rule of law, one would expect that during the transition period many aspects of the current system would be at odds with rule of law. During this period, some commentators, emphasizing how far China's legal system falls short of the ideal of rule of law and looking back to its rule-by-law past, will insist that China remains fundamentally rule by law. Others, stressing the ruling regime's formal commitment to a system in which law binds the state and state actors and the progress that has been made in promulgating laws and creating institutions to achieve that purpose, may be inclined to describe China's legal system as a fledgling, albeit deeply flawed, form of rule of law.[24] Still others, observing that China's legal system differs significantly from the rule-by-law regime of the Mao era, yet acknowledging that the current system falls far short of the ideal implied by the honorific rule of law, will prefer to describe China's legal system as in transition toward rule of law, as I have here.[25] In any event, while some skeptics may question whether China is moving toward rule of law, everyone agrees that there are many significant obstacles to its implementation. Opinions differ, however, as to the relative weight of the various impediments and their underlying causes.

Why has China not implemented rule of law? An institutional approach

One way to study China's legal reforms is to examine in turn particular areas of law: commercial, family, criminal, administrative, environmental, and so on. The advantage of such an approach is that each area is likely to give rise to its own particular set of issues. China's problems in the environmental area, for example, are due in part to a weak central agency and the desire for economic growth.[26] The Criminal Procedure Law, recently revised to afford greater protection to the accused, falls prey to the public's demand to strike hard at crime and turf struggles between the procuracy and the judiciary.[27] Family laws aimed at curbing domestic violence butt up against longstanding traditions in which wives were subordinate to husbands in the family hierarchy and violence against women was tolerated. The effectiveness of administrative litigation and other means of reining in the bureaucracy is diminished by a low level of legal consciousness among citizens who are unaware of their rights, and the persistent influence of a paternalistic tradition in which the ruled are expected to defer to mother and father officials (*fumu guan*) much as children defer to their parents. Thus, even when citizens do know their rights, they are often reluctant to challenge abusive administrative officials.[28]

At the same time, there are general systemic and institutional obstacles to enforcement that cut across the various areas, albeit with varying degrees of relevance and importance to any given area. A weak judiciary, for example, undermines effectiveness in all areas. Rather than focusing on particular areas of law, this study is organized by institutions, with reference to various areas of law as needed to illustrate specific issues and problems. The advantages of this approach are twofold. Although in-depth studies of specific areas of law are valuable and needed, such studies often run the risk of missing the forest for the trees. Understandably, given their focus, the task of drawing connections to other areas of law is frequently slighted. Moreover, as will be shown throughout this work, the major obstacles to rule of law in China are systemic and institutional in nature. Accordingly, to understand any specific area of law requires that one understand the larger institutional context in which it exists.

The role of the Party

The most common explanation for China's troubles places the brunt of the blame on ideology and the attitudes of China's ruling elite, particularly senior Party leaders.[29] Analyses of China's failures to realize rule of law thus typically begin, and all too often end, by noting that China remains a single party socialist state. Some critics argue that single party socialism is simply incompatible with rule of law and a limited government because the leading role of the Party cannot be reconciled with the supremacy of the law and a system in which law limits Party power.[30] It is standard socialist legal theory dogma that law is a tool of the state and the ruling class. In a Leninist state, the Party is assigned a leading role based on the premise that it knows best what is in the interests of the people. Law then becomes a tool of the Party to be used to serve the interests of the people and to attack the enemy.

Setting aside the theoretical issue of the compatibility of single party socialism and rule of law, cynical realists claim that as a practical matter there is no rule of law in China at least to a considerable extent because senior Party leaders and other interested parties simply do not want it.[31] After all, rule of law implies some degree of separation between law and politics and the imposition of limits on the Party and government authority. While Party leaders are happy to use law as a tool to ensure more efficient implementation of Party policies, the last thing they want is meaningful restraints on their own power.

In contrast, I suggest that single party socialism in which the Party plays a leading role is in theory compatible with rule of law, albeit not a Liberal Democratic version of rule of law. Party members and government officials are required to comply with the law, and in practice their behavior is increasingly constrained by law, especially when compared to twenty years ago. Although the CCP still often fails to abide by the circumscribed role set forth in the state and Party constitutions, on a day-to-day level, direct interference by Party organs in administrative rule-making or specific agency decisions is not common. Increasingly, routine acts of governance are handled by the usual government entities with little or no interference from the Party. As the Party's grip over society loosens, opportunities for conflict between Party policy and law become fewer. While it remains to be seen whether the legal system will be able to impose meaningful restraints on the CCP on issues of major importance, there will be fewer and fewer instances where the will of the Party or individual Party members will be able to trump laws.

The Party's main relevance to realization of rule of law lies in its ability to promote or obstruct further political and legal reforms that would strengthen the legal system but could lead to the demise of the Party or a drastic reduction in its power. Reforms such as the establishment of a more independent and authoritative judiciary, the development of a more robust civil society, the creation of an anticorruption commission, and the holding of higher-level elections of people's congress delegates and government officials all require Party approval. Naturally, given their vested interest in retaining power, some senior leaders may be ambivalent at best about some of these reforms and their implications for the Party.

Nevertheless, the extent of Party ambivalence toward legal reforms and rule of law should not be overstated. First, the CCP is not monolithic; there are different factions within the CCP, and individual Party members hold different opinions on issues, though according to PRC legal scholars there is widespread support for some form of rule of law among senior Party leaders as well as rank-and-file members.[32] Many of the younger members who joined the CCP have done so not for ideological reasons but rather for the perceived economic benefits and career opportunities. Thus, even though the Party is still a force within the Chinese polity, with the power to influence and in some cases determine the outcome on certain key issues, the increased diversity of views within the Party makes it more difficult for Party leaders to rally the necessary support to block reform proposals. More importantly, the Party is not drawing on a blank slate; its choices are constrained by the pressing need to sustain economic growth and attract foreign investment, international pressure, growing discontent over corruption, and the rising domestic demand for rule of law. Hence the future of rule of law in China depends on more than the preferences of senior leaders.

Accordingly, I place less emphasis on socialist ideology and the intent of the leaders and more emphasis on context and the particular problems that China is confronting in establishing a law-based order. The CCP is only one of the obstacles to realizing a law-based order. Even if China's leaders were wholeheartedly committed to establishing a legal order in which the law imposed meaningful constraints on state actors, it could only be imperfectly realized at this point.

China's legal system is beset by a number of problems. As a result of more than a decade of feverish legislating, the legal framework is by and large in place. Although there are still some gaps in the framework and loopholes in the existing laws, tinkering with doctrine or passing more laws and regulations alone will have little impact. At this point, the biggest obstacles to a law-based system in China are institutional and systemic in nature: a legislative system in disarray; a weak judiciary; poorly trained judges and lawyers; a low level of legal consciousness; a weak administrative law regime; the lack of a robust civil society; the enduring influence of paternalistic traditions and a culture of deference to government authority; rampant corruption; large regional variations; and the fallout from the unfinished transition from a centrally planned economy to a market economy, which has exacerbated central–local tensions and resulted in the fragmentation of authority.[33]

The legislative system

The turn away from Party policy to a more law-based order has resulted in a more independent, authoritative, and professional legislature at both the national and local levels. Although delegates from the National People's Congress and local people's congresses are not elected (except at the lowest level) and key appointments are still made in accordance with the nomenklatura system, people's congresses are no longer merely rubber stamps. The institutional capacity of the people's congresses has been enhanced steadily through a variety of measures, including rapid expansion in personnel, the development of subcommittees responsible for specific technical tasks, and efforts to raise the educational level of delegates. The newly minted Legislation Law and other laws have clarified and standardized the law-making process and increased transparency and opportunities for public participation to some degree. Meanwhile, the State Council and local governments have passed a number of regulations to govern administrative rule-making, and legislators are busy working on a draft of a comprehensive Administrative Procedure Law that promises to render the administrative law-making, interpretation, and implementation processes more transparent, accountable, and accessible to the public.

Notwithstanding such positive developments, the legislative system continues to be a major obstacle to the realization of rule of law. For a variety of reasons, laws are often general and vague. Many laws and regulations are poorly drafted, due partly to the lack of practical experience and the low level of competence of the drafters, especially at the local levels. Laws and regulations are subject to frequent change, frustrating investors who find it difficult to develop long-term strategies. On the other hand, China's legislators simply cannot keep up with the pace of reforms. As a result, many laws are out-of-date, at odds with reality and current practices, and in need of amendment. Perhaps most worrisome, however, is the astoundingly high level of inconsistency between lower-level and higher-level legislation and the lack of effective channels to rectify the problem.

Although a number of solutions have been proposed and a number of steps taken to reduce the level of inconsistency, they are not likely to suffice for reasons explained in Chapter VI. In the end, deeper institutional reforms, including judicial reforms to increase the independence and authority of the courts – in particular giving the courts the power to annul administrative regulations – are likely to be required.

The judiciary

China has taken a number of steps to increase the professionalism and authority of the judiciary. The Judges Law raised the standards for becoming a judge. The National Judges Institute and other institutes run extensive judicial training programs, often funded by foreign agencies and involving foreign experts. Specialized courts have been established to handle intellectual property disputes. Nevertheless, the judiciary remains a weak link in the rule of law chain.

Rule of law requires that laws be enforced fairly and impartially. In China, however, judicial corruption and the longstanding practice of judges meeting *ex parte* with litigants and their lawyers undermine the fairness and impartiality of the process. Moreover, despite the efforts to raise the level of competence, many judges remain poorly trained and ill-suited for the job. Indeed, there are still many former military officers with little or no formal training in law serving as judges, though many are set to retire in coming years or are being transferred to posts within the court that do not require them to hear cases.

More fundamentally, the courts lack both independence and authority. Under the nomenklatura system, the Party continues to approve the appointment of senior judges. The president of the court, who has considerable power within the court, frequently lacks formal legal training and has been appointed based on political criteria. To be sure, direct Party interference in specific cases is rare for the simple reason that the Party has no interest in the outcome of most cases other than that it be fair. By far the biggest source of outside interference in court decisions is not the Party but local government officials seeking to protect local interests.

The authorities have attempted to overcome the problem of local protectionism by passing regulations, applicable to particular areas of judicial work such as enforcement, that increase the independence of judges by shifting responsibility for certain personnel decisions to higher-level courts. However, such partial reforms are unlikely to succeed in combating rampant local protectionism and are even more unlikely to succeed in addressing the broader issue of the courts' lack of independence and authority. Ultimately, deeper institutional reforms are necessary. However, the authorities have been reluctant to approve any such reforms, no doubt in part out of fear that a more independent court able to decide run-of-the-mill commercial, criminal, and administrative litigation cases fairly and impartially would also be able to decide politically sensitive cases fairly and impartially. As in other areas, such as propaganda and thought control work, the Party's goals are at odds with each other; and the desire for economic growth is forcing senior leaders to choose between goals and accept compromises, often with irreversible results.[34]

The legal profession

The legal profession has developed rapidly in terms of the numbers of lawyers, their quality and professionalism, and their independence. Today, a growing number of PRC lawyers are able to compete with foreign lawyers for lucrative foreign investment work by taking advantage of their bilingual language skills and knowledge of the local environment to provide superior advice and more effective service. Nonetheless, there are still many problems that plague the legal profession as a whole. The supply of lawyers falls far short of demand, particularly outside of the major commercial centers. Equally important, many lawyers lack the training and skills to provide the quality legal services sought by businesses engaged in increasingly sophisticated transactions or by defendants seeking to take advantage of China's revised criminal procedure laws. Despite efforts to raise the standards for becoming a lawyer, many attorneys have received no formal legal training and some lack even a college education.

Although lawyers are no longer considered "workers of the state" as in the Mao era, the independence and autonomy of the legal profession remains limited. Lawyers are now subject to the dual oversight of the Ministry of Justice (MOJ) and the bar association. However, the national and local bar associations remain closely affiliated with the MOJ and its local counterparts. The relationship between the legal profession and the state is best characterized as a form of corporatism or clientelism. Lawyers seek to establish a close relationship with the MOJ or its affiliates mainly for commercial reasons: either to gain access to business opportunities or simply to stave off excessively predatory rent-seeking by greedy justice bureau officials. Political considerations are rarely a factor, in part because most lawyers much prefer to concentrate on high-paying commercial work rather than politically sensitive cases.

The legal profession also suffers from rampant professional responsibility violations. Many lawyers survive and in some cases thrive based on their *guanxi* (connections) with judges and government officials rather than their legal skills. Given the current environment in which they must operate, including widespread corruption and a poorly trained judiciary, lawyers often feel they have no choice but to rely on *guanxi* as much as on legal arguments.

All in all, the legal profession is still young and immature, both in terms of the average age of lawyers and the profession itself. The lack of professionalism of lawyers contributes to difficulties in implementing the law and establishing a law-based order. Although in time the legal profession will mature and become more professional, there are still likely to be signs of divergence vis-à-vis legal professions in other countries, particularly in common law countries such as the USA. Given China's more civil law system, lawyers are less likely to emerge as major

catalysts for social change. While lawyers are likely to back further legal reforms and press for the implementation of rule of law, whether
they will be ardent champions of democracy and political reforms more
generally is doubtful. Like other entrepreneurs who have benefited from
economic reforms, lawyers on the whole appear to be politically conservative and risk averse. They do not want to rock the boat and risk
instability – and endanger their privileged lifestyles – by hastily moving
toward democracy. Most seem content to focus on accumulating wealth
and all of the perks that go with being a high-paid lawyer, including for
the very elite the latest mobile phone, a new car, a villa in the suburbs,
and vacations abroad.

The administrative law regime

Because administrative law plays a key role in limiting the arbitrary acts
of government, the centrality of administrative law (administration in
accordance with law – *yifa xingzheng*) to rule of law is well accepted both
in China and abroad.[35] Whereas in the past the purpose of administrative law was considered to be how to facilitate efficient government and
ensure that government officials and citizens alike obey central policies,
administrative law is now understood to entail a balancing of government efficiency with the need to protect individual rights and interests.[36]
Moreover, China has established institutions and mechanisms for reining in the bureaucracy similar to those in countries known for rule of
law, including legislative oversight committees, supervision committees
that are the functional equivalent of ombudsmen, internal administration reconsideration procedures, and judicial review. At the level of legal
doctrine, China has passed a number of laws that not only resemble but
are modeled on laws from other countries. Even in the area of outcomes
there are signs of convergence with the legal systems of Western countries, albeit rather limited convergence.[37]

Despite convergence with respect to goals, institutions, mechanisms
for checking administrative discretion, and legal doctrines, China's administrative law regime produces comparatively suboptimal results
because of a variety of context-specific factors. Although some of the
troubles are specific to the administrative law system – such as loopholes or shortcomings in particular laws – most of the problems have
little to do with the administrative law system as such. Rather, the system

is undermined by deficiencies in the legislative system, a weak judiciary, poorly trained judges and lawyers, and general problems such as a relatively low level of legal consciousness among the citizenry, many of whom are afraid to challenge government officials.

Administrative law reformers therefore face a number of challenges. Having concentrated on legislation and the establishment of a regulatory framework for much of the last twenty years, attention must now turn to opening up the law-making, interpretation and implementation processes to greater public participation, as contemplated in the Administrative Procedure Law currently being drafted. However, a more active role for the general public and private interest groups requires a relaxation of the state's grip over civil society. Thus, administrative reforms will continue the shift of power from the state to society that has occurred in the last twenty years as a result of economic reforms. The ongoing separation of government from enterprises and the change in the role of administrative agencies from both regulators and market players to primarily regulators will further enhance the development of the private sphere. As the economy expands and the administration in its role as regulator is responsible for resolving increasingly technical policy issues, the Party's role in the policy-making process is reduced accordingly, shifting the balance of power from the Party to state organs.

But as administrative agencies have assumed more of the responsibility for setting policies and daily governance, the possibility that they will abuse their power has grown. While China currently relies on a variety of mechanisms to check the administration, all are in need of reform. Even though the importance of judicial review is easily overstated,[38] in China's case a stronger judiciary is necessary to combat local protectionism and deal with increasingly recalcitrant local governments.

General obstacles: the path-dependent nature of reforms

In carrying out institutional reforms, China must take into consideration the organizational structure, practices, and culture within the existing institutions and the general context in which the institutions operate. Tradition and culture, corruption, regionalism, the absence of a vigorous civil society, and China's unfinished economic transition are among the most important factors shaping, and in some cases limiting, legal reforms. Simply put, the lack of a culture of legality, a deeply ingrained tradition in which personal relations tend to supplant generally applicable laws, and a relatively low level of legal consciousness among legal actors and consumers make the establishment of a law-based order difficult. Widespread corruption among government officials distorts the law-making and implementation processes, while corruption within the judiciary tarnishes the image and authority of the legal system and deprives the ruling regime of the potential legitimacy benefits to be derived from its efforts to promote rule of law. Large regional differences complicate the law-making and implementation processes. To take account of regional variations, laws are necessarily broadly drafted and local government and administrative officials are given considerable discretion in interpreting and applying national laws. In the absence of effective mechanisms for checking administrative discretion, however, agencies and local governments pass regulations that serve their own interests but contradict national laws both in spirit and letter. Yet the main reason local governments pass such legislation is to promote economic growth in the region. Facing a reduction in state subsidies, local governments depend on economic growth to generate tax revenues to cover the increased welfare costs that they have been forced to bear as part of economic reforms. Predictably, local protectionism is a serious problem. Local governments erect trade barriers to keep out products from other regions, or, as noted previously, pressure courts to find in favor of local companies.

Reformers are not omnipotent – they must play the hand that is dealt them. As a result, reforms are unavoidably path-dependent to some extent. To illustrate with one of many examples discussed at greater length in the following chapters, proposals that call for the immediate elimination of adjudicative supervision committees, which supervise the decisions of the panel of judges that hear cases, are likely to be rebuffed at this stage given the low level of competence of many judges and serious corruption within the courts. A more feasible approach is to revise the procedures to make the process more transparent and to allow the parties to more effectively challenge supervision committee decisions.

Although the path-dependent nature of reforms sets the outside parameters for what is feasible, it also opens up the possibility that China will develop its own institutions and practices in the process of responding to context-specific problems.[39] For instance, China might explore the possibility of controlling administrative discretion and combating corruption through such methods as consultative committees, anticorruption commissions, and an expanded letters and petition system and hot-line network. The authorities might also consider modifying the cadre evaluation system to include a quantifiable rule of law index in the hope that local government officials would be less likely to pass inconsistent local laws or engage in local protectionism if so doing would jeopardize their chance for career advancement. Conceivably, though improbably, China might even consider a constitutionally separate branch of government similar to the control *yuan* envisioned by Sun Yatsen.[40] Ultimately, the possibilities for reform are constrained to a considerable extent by the limits of human imagination.

Does China need rule of law? Rule of law and economic development

Advocates of rule of law and neoclassical economists alike have argued that sustainable economic development requires rule of law and in particular clear and enforceable property rights.[41] Yet at first blush China seems to have had tremendous economic growth without either, leaving economists, political scientists, and legal scholars to puzzle over the success of China's economy despite market and legal imperfections.[42] China's phenomenal growth rate has been attributed to cultural factors,[43] a distinct form of "Chinese capitalism,"[44] a *guanxi*-based rule of relationships,[45] clientelism[46], and corporatism.[47]

   In contrast, I suggest that law has played a more important role in China's economic growth, and in the growth of those Asian countries that have experienced high growth rates over long periods of time, than is usually assumed; and, more importantly, law is likely to play an even greater role in the future in China. As discussed in Chapter X, multi-country empirical studies that test the relationship between "rule of law" and economic growth support the conclusion that rule of law is necessary for sustainable growth.[48] While China has been able to take advantage of several distinctive features to achieve rapid growth, in the mid to late 1990s, foreign investment and growth slowed. Although the Asian financial crisis was a major factor, deficiencies in the legal system have also deterred investors and limited economic reforms, including state-owned enterprise reforms.

   To be sure, rule of law appeals to different sectors of the economy to varying degrees. Foreign investors, particularly large multinational companies, arguably need it the most. But the private sector, township–village enterprises, and even state-owned enterprises and farmers could also benefit from rule of law to one degree or another. On the other hand, not all economic actors will benefit from rule of law – in particular, inefficient companies that now thrive due to their clientelist and corporatist ties will be threatened by rule of law.

Nor is rule of law sufficient for economic growth. Many other factors also play a role, and no doubt a more important role, including sound economic policies. Moreover, no system can rely on compulsory enforcement to ensure that economic actors act rationally, obey the law, honor their contracts and pay their debts. Informal dispute resolution mechanisms play a vital role in complementing the formal court system in all countries. Similarly, market mechanisms that impose discipline on companies without having to resort to the courts are also needed. For example, disclosure rules and commercial associations make it costly for parties to breach their contracts, dodge their debts or misuse funds obtained from public offerings.

In the end, economies, like legal systems, differ in significant ways upon closer scrutiny. As China's economic reforms have progressed, there has been considerable convergence with the economies of well-developed countries. At the same time, there has been considerable divergence. But even if there is sufficient variation to describe the economy in terms of a unique form of Chinese capitalism, the notion that the PRC economy will be able to sustain economic growth without further legal reforms that bring the system into greater compliance with the basic requirements of a thin conception of rule of law is doubtful.

Rule of law and political reform: political reform without democracy

Democracy in the sense of genuine, multiparty elections in which citizens elect officials at all levels of government is not a viable option at present. The Party opposes it. There is little support among intellectuals for genuine elections. Nor is there a hankering for democracy on the part of the general populace. Moreover, even if the Party were willing to endorse democracy and the people did want it, China currently lacks the institutions, including rule of law, to make democracy work.

Rule of law is a desirable alternative in that it allows for political reform without democracy and holds out the promise of a limited government and perhaps some relief from the pervasive corruption that is threatening to destabilize China. On the other hand, rule of law is no panacea and cannot resolve social tensions resulting from deep social cleavages. Normally, such tensions are worked out through the electoral process and the horse-trading that occurs in democratically elected legislatures. Moreover, although rule of law is possible without democracy, the lack of democracy creates certain obstacles to its implementation and raises accountability issues. Accordingly, I suggest in Chapter 11 that in the long run China will most likely become democratic, though probably not a *liberal* democracy.

The organization of this book

In summary, China's legal system is in the midst of a transition to a more law-based system. Assuming, as appears likely, that China is moving toward rule of law, which form is most appropriate for China remains hotly contested.

Chapters 2 through 4 examine the evolution of rule of law in China. I begin in Chapter 2 with a brief overview of early legal theories and the role of law in the Imperial and Mao. I then focus in Chapter 3 on the evolving PRC discourse on rule of law in the wake of the endorsement of the new *tifa* in 1996, and develop the four thick conceptions of rule of law in more detail by taking into account the purposes each is meant to serve and the differences in their institutions, practices, rules, and outcomes. Chapter 4 considers some of the major critiques of rule of law and the concerns on the part of PRC scholars about the possible costs and negative effects of implementing it at this time.

Chapter 5 takes up the role of the Party and its significance in light of its ongoing retreat from day-to-day governance. Chapter 6 examines the legislative system, Chapter 7 the judiciary, Chapter 8 the legal profession, and Chapter 9 the administrative law regime. These chapters explore in detail efforts to strengthen these institutions and the various, often interrelated, problems that limit their effectiveness. I then discuss various reform proposals and add my own thoughts on possible reforms. Chapter 10 turns to the issue of whether China needs rule of law for sustained economic development, and Chapter 11 to whether legal reforms and economic development will lead to political reforms and the establishment of a liberal democracy in China. Finally, Chapter 12 concludes with some reflections on why the efforts to reform the legal system have attracted relatively little attention among scholars and accounts of the system remain so negative despite remarkable improvements. I also provide an overview of a comprehensive reform agenda by synthesizing the discussions of reforms for particular institutions, and then offer some policy recommendations for governments, particularly the United States, that are interested in promoting the implementation of rule of law in China.

Notes

1   Shklar (1987: 1).
2   Unger (1976).
3   deLisle (1999).
4   The program will include training for some 200 lawyers, prosecutors, and officials by the EU over the next four years. In contrast to the US program, which until recently was not funded at all and remains underfunded, the EU dedicated some 13.55 million Eurodollars to the program. See *China Announces Largest Judicial Cooperation Program With EU* (2001).
5   Radin (1989: 791).
6   Raz (1979); Summers (1988); Summers (1993). See also Chapter 3.
7   Although one of the first to spell out the elements of a thin theory of rule of law, Fuller (1976) was uncomfortable with the instrumental aspects of a thin theory and its potential for abuse by authoritarian or fascist regimes, arguing that truly evil regimes would not comply with even a thin theory. For a more complete account of thin theories, see Chapter 3.
8   See, for example, the influential statement of rule of law in the report of Committee I of the International Congress of Jurists at New Delhi, 1959, and the Rule of Law Foundation's statement on their website. See also Chapter 3.
9   Although many East Asian countries are known as "development states" in which the state takes an active and interventionist role in the economy, the nature and degree of intervention differ dramatically across the region. Hong Kong's laissez-faire policies, at least until the 1997 handover, are the antithesis to interventionism.
10 On the Asian values debate, see Kausikan (1995–96); Ghai (1994); Davis (1998); Chan (1995); Bauer and Bell (1999); Peerenboom (2000d).
11 In some cases, the state may give the appearance of allowing genuine multiparty elections at all levels but in fact control the outcome by limiting the ability of opposition parties to campaign as in Singapore.
12 Pan Wei (2001).

13   Shetreet and Deschenes (1985).

14   See Chapter 11 and the polls and articles cited therein.

15   For the concept/conception distinction, see Dworkin (1977: 134–36).

16   For the importance of policy formulations in China, see Schoenhals (1992), who observes Mao once proclaimed "one single [correct] formulation and the whole nation will flourish; one single [incorrect] formulation and the whole nation will decline." For a philosophical account of why Chinese political theory has placed such importance on language dating back to Confucius' emphasis on the rectification of names, see Peerenboom (1998a).

17   Pei (2001a).

18   Peerenboom (1998b).

19   To publicize laws, the Ministry of Justice, All China Lawyers Association, and China Central Television organized national debates among lawyers. More than 6,300 lawyers participated in local contests, leading to a grand finale televised on national networks. See *China to Hold First Televised Lawyers' Debate Contest* (2001).

20   Yuwen Li (2002) notes that there are law-related programs in Beijing, Tianjin, Chongqing, and Hebei among other places.

21   1993 *China Law Yearbook*, at 83; *Zuigao renmin fayuan gongzuo bagao* (1997).

22   See Chapter 9.

23   On the instrumental, rule-by-law nature of the PRC legal system, see Baum (1986); Yu Xingzhong (1989); Potter (1995a: 5–7); Hintzen (1999: 169); Alford (1999). Potter (1999: 672, 674, 683) describes the system as "rule through law" and concludes that rule of law, in the sense of the state being just another actor, remains a distant prospect. Chen Jianfu (1999) suggests that legal reforms are not meant to change the nature of law as a tool but just to make law a better tool. Although Lubman does not use rule by law to characterize his own views, he (1999: 130–35) emphasizes the instrumental nature of law, the primacy of policy, and the deep contradiction between socialist ideology and rule of law. As a result, he is cautiously pessimistic about the future of legality in China. For further discussion of Lubman's views, see below and Chapter 12.

     Of course, law is used instrumentally in every legal system. Thus, a distinction must be made between pernicious instrumentalism and acceptable instrumentalism. Legal systems in which the law is *only or predominantly* a tool of the state are best described as rule by law, whereas legal systems in which the law imposes meaningful limits on state actors merit the label rule of law. Whether a legal system in which as a formal matter the state and state actors are bound by law but that goal is often not realized in practice should be deemed a rule of law, albeit an imperfect one, or rule by law, is discussed in Chapter 3. In a piece that combines a sophisticated theoretical discussion with a wide-ranging account of law in practice, Epstein (1994) described the tension between the instrumental and autonomous aspects of law in China and pointed out that law is becoming increasingly autonomous. For PRC discussions of rule by law, see Chapter 3.

24   This approach was favored by a number of participants on the Chinese Law Net during an on-line discussion that took place during June 2001.

25 See Chapters 4 and 12 for a fuller discussion of these issues.

26 Alford and Shen (1997).

27 The Strike Hard campaign owes its strength in part to the Party's desire to respond to public demand and at the same time to demonstrate that it is still in control and capable of maintaining order.

28 There are of course other reasons why citizens are reluctant to challenge government officials, including fear of retaliation, high costs, and the belief that there are more effective ways to resolve the problem. See Chapter 9.

29 See, for example, Leslie Palmer (1996: 141), who declares that "it is certainly not possible to speak of the rule of law, and not even of the rule by law. It is clear...that the country's rulers, namely the Communist Party, regard such rules as simply Western 'bourgeois' conventions which limit their freedom of action; arbitrary government, which recognizes no restraint, is usual."

30 Lubman (1999: 123) notes that there has been considerable progress in institution-building and yet the legal system continues to suffer from a range of shortcomings. He claims that one of the major impediments to rule of law is the lack of a unifying concept of law resulting from a fundamental ideological struggle: "Two conflicting principles have been bound together at the core of Party policy since legal reform began. Party policy dictates that law must serve the Party-state, but at the same time declares that China must be governed by law and aim to attain the rule of law." In examining the Party's policy toward law, Lubman (1999: 7) also emphasizes "the inescapable contradiction between the avowed goal of attaining the rule of law and the ideological limits that Deng Xiaoping set on attempts to reach that goal, which his successors have maintained." Given that for Lubman a transition to rule of law is possible only if the ideological limits of the ruling regime are overcome, it would seem that the ruling regime must either fall from power or abandon – or at minimum fundamentally revise – its socialist ideology, including the commitment to a leadership role for the Party.

In my view, Lubman places too much weight on ideology as an obstacle to rule of law, for reasons discussed in Chapter 5. It should be noted that the Party, having endorsed rule of law and the principle that the Party and state actors must act in accordance with law, apparently does not consider rule of law to be incompatible with socialist ideology and a leading role for the Party. It also bears noting that while Lubman sides with those who see the development of the NPC not in terms of an evolution to rule of law but as serving the purpose of a heavily instrumental law, he (1999: 141) does allow that China's "legislative institutions are in the midst of an evolutionary process, and may be able to overcome the narrow limits that ideology has imposed on their scope of action." It is not clear why ideological limits are not an insurmountable obstacle to the development of a legislative system compatible with rule of law and yet they supposedly are with respect to legal reforms and rule of law more generally. Lubman does emphasize problems with the judiciary, especially their embeddedness in a "Leninist–Maoist state apparatus." But surely the legislative system is also embedded in the same system. If it can change, why not the judiciary? While Lubman does not expressly address that issue, one possible response might be that the Party sees an independent and assertive judiciary as more of a threat than an independent and assertive legislature. We can only speculate whether that is indeed the case. In any event, as noted in Chapter 7, although many legal scholars acknowledge the need for deep institutional reforms of the judiciary, there are a number of obstacles to such reforms other than ideological opposition on the part of the Party. Not surprisingly, there is considerable debate as to which institutional reforms are necessary and their optimal sequencing and timing.

Like Lubman, PRC scholars have struggled over the issue of the compatibility of socialist ideology and the leading role of the Party with rule of law. See Chapter 5. As Li Shuguang (1998) observes, there is a certain irony in the government leading a rule-of-law movement whose ultimate objective is to restrain the government.

31 See, for example, Corne (1996: 43); Alford (1999). See also Lubman (1999), who portrays the ruling regime's desire to maintain power as a major obstacle to rule of law. Although all note that there are many other obstacles to the realization of rule of law, they appear to claim that a hostile view toward rule of law among the leaders is sufficient to prevent its realization. Alternatively, their claim may be the weaker one that the intent of the leaders is a relevant (important?) factor in determining whether rule of law will be realized in China. If so, then the difference between us may simply come down to a matter of degree as to how important such views are, since I believe the views of leaders are relevant but not determinative.

Significantly, they do not rule out the possibility that China will implement rule of law. For instance, although Lubman (1999: xvi) is cautiously pessimistic about the future of legality in China, he does allow that "China may develop something like the rule of law in the future," and even acknowledges that he perceives "fragile harbingers of that possible future in China today." Similarly, Corne (2001) recently appears to have modified his views and now to accept that China is on its way toward rule of law, though many institutional obstacles remain:

> Considering the enormous strides that China has made since 1979 in the development of its legal infrastructure, its ultimate establishment of a reasonably functional legal system that observes the basic tenants of the rule of law should be achievable. It may be too bold to suggest that the remaining cultural, historical, political, and structural impediments to the establishment of a fully functional legal system will have fallen away by 2020. But by that juncture, the realization of a society and government governed by law should no longer seem like a distant objective.

32 See Keith and Lin (2001: 31). To be sure, just as there are tensions between the central government and local governments, so are there tensions and differences in the incentive structures and agendas between central Party organs and local Party organizations, which could produce varying levels of support for different forms of rule of law.

33 On the fragmentation of authority, see Lieberthal (1995).

34 On the Party's increasingly ineffective struggle to control the thoughts of Chinese citizens and their access to information, see Lynch (1999a).
35 See, for example, *Jiang Zemin's Congress Report* (1997). The report was delivered at the 15th National Party Congress. See also Liu Cuixiao and Wang Jianrong (1998), who report that a 1996 conference on administrative law theory and practice emphasized administration in accordance with law as the heart of ruling the country according to law.
36 Luo (1997).
37 See, for example, Pei (1997a), for a discussion of the outcomes of administrative law cases.
38 See, for example, Cross (1999).
39 See Dowdle (2001a).
40 See Rubin (1997); see also Chapter 9.
41 See, generally, Pistor and Wellons (1999); North (1981, 1990).
42 See Jefferson and Rawski (1995); Putterman (1995); Clarke (1992); David Li (1996); Pei (1998b).
43 See Weitzman and Xu (1994).
44 See, for example, Redding (1990); Ghai (1993a). See also Chapter 10.
45 See Carol Jones (1994); see also Chapter 10.
46 See Wank (1999).
47 Corporatism has been put to three main, quite different uses, in China. Some have used it as has been used elsewhere – as a way of looking at state–society relations and a measure of civil society. See, for example, Unger and Chan (1995). Others have used it as a way of understanding East Asian statist models of economic development. See, for example, Pearson (1997). Jean Oi and others have also used it to explain local forms of government–business relations. See Oi (1999); Walder (1998: 62).
48 These studies do not measure economic growth against all of the criteria of a thin theory of rule of law as defined herein. However, they employ criteria for rule of law that stress consistency and predictability, and are therefore consistent with a thin conception of rule of law.

2

The evolution of rule of law in China: the role of law in historical context

In this chapter, I present a brief and necessarily simplified survey of China's legal theories and systems from the pre-Han era to the beginning of the reform era in 1978.[1] The purpose is threefold. First, for many rule of law *means* a Liberal Democratic rule of law.[2] It is difficult for many modern Westerners in particular to imagine rule of law being embedded in a nonliberal context, and as a result, for law to play a different role in society, such as state-strengthening rather than the protection of individual rights. Yet the logic and appeal of the Statist Socialist, Neoauthoritarian, and Communitarian models are rooted in China's own traditions. By exploring the historical, political, and philosophical backdrop against which reforms are occurring, it is easier to understand how rule of law in China could develop along a different path, and to appreciate why it is unlikely that reforms are likely to lead to a Liberal Democratic rule of law.

Second, some skeptics in China argue that rule of law is the historical product of modern Western capitalist democracies at odds with China's own traditions.[3] Thus, they suggest, it cannot be transplanted to China. At minimum, rule of law will need to be adapted to China's own circumstances. It must develop a rule of law with Chinese characteristics that takes advantage of China's own native resources. To make sense of these arguments requires some understanding of China's legal traditions. Only then can one begin to assess what traditional native resources are available to reformers – and what obstacles they are likely to encounter in trying to establish rule of law given China's past.

Finally, even a cursory review of the Imperial and Mao era legal systems will suffice to demonstrate just how remarkable China's legal transformation has been. Notwithstanding the many shortcomings in the legal system, dramatic progress has been made in creating a viable legal system that increasingly meets the standards of a thin rule of law.

Classical legal theories

Early Chinese theories of law are often classified as *lizhi* (礼治) and *fazhi* (法治). The contrast between *li*, conventionally translated as rites or rituals, and *fa*, conventionally translated as law, marks a distinction in Chinese political theory as to the nature of political order and the preferred means of achieving such order. *Li zhi*, traditionally associated with Confucianism, refers to political order predicated on and achieved primarily by reference to the *li* or rites, that is, traditional customs, mores, and norms.[4] In contrast, *fa zhi*, associated with Legalism, refers to political order attained primarily through reliance on *fa* or laws, that is, publicly promulgated, codified standards of general applicability backed up by the coercive power of the state.

The lizhi of Confucius

The locus classicus for *li zhi* is the *Analects* of Confucius: "Lead the people with government regulations and organize them with penal law (*xing* 刑), and they will avoid punishments but will be without shame. Lead them with virtue and organize them through the *li*, and the people will have a sense of shame and moreover will become humane people of good character."[5] Confucius maintained that to rely solely or even predominantly on law to achieve social order was folly. Laws, backed up by punishments, may induce compliance in the external behavior of individuals, but they are powerless to transform the inner character of the members of society. Confucius' goal was not simply a stable political order in which everyone coexists in relative harmony and isolation from each other, with each afraid to interfere with the other for fear of legal punishment. Rather, Confucius set his sights considerably higher. He sought to achieve a harmonious social order in which each person is able to realize his or her full potential as a human being through mutually beneficial relations with others.

For Confucius, society is the medium through which one becomes a human being. That is, one becomes a human being, a humane person, by virtue of participation in society. Personhood and humanity are functions of socialization. At birth, before the process of enculturation, of becoming humane, humans are not different than the other beasts. If one does not or is not willing to participate in society, to enter into harmonious relations with others, one remains at the level of a beast – of human *qua* member of a biological species. By turning one's back on society, the bestial person (literally "small person" – *xiao ren*) fails to utilize the cognitive, aesthetic, and spiritual powers which distinguish humans from other species. It is just the engagement of these capacities in joining with others to shape a new world, to create a significantly different and better society, to overcome one's natural conditions in achieving innovative resolutions to conflicts which is distinctive about humans. If one cannot overcome the passions, instincts, and desires that one shares with other beasts, if one wars against all and resorts to violence and brute strength to fulfill one's narcissistic wants, then one fails to become truly human, to achieve humanity.

Of course there will always be those who turn their back on society, who refuse to participate in creating a harmonious order and insist on pursuing their narrow self-interest in any manner possible. For such people, law and punishments are necessary. Confucius, ever practical, did not advocate the complete abandonment of laws. Nevertheless, the goal is to foster an environment in which laws need to be imposed as little as possible: "In hearing litigation I am much the same as anyone. If you insist on a difference, it is perhaps that I try to get the parties not to resort to litigation."[6]

Thus for Confucius the ethical and political challenge is to inspire in the many members of society the desire to achieve a humane society and to encourage them to direct their energies toward the attainment of a harmonious social order. What is required is a willingness to participate in collective living, to search for a cooperative solution, to become humane (*ren* 仁).

For Confucius, the codification and public dissemination of laws sends the wrong kind of message. Laws are designed to protect the minimum interests of the members of society and to provide a mechanism for dealing with and removing those individuals who are not only unwilling to participate in fostering a harmonious social order, but whose behavior threatens the well-being of others and the ability of society to function. Making the laws public focuses attention, not on the achievement of the highest quality of social harmony possible, but on the lowest level of participation required by society. Consequently, it may encourage some persons to look only for ways to manipulate the system for their own advantage.

Hence we find Confucius criticizing the state of Jin for publicly promulgating laws: "Jin is going to ruin. It has lost its proper rules . . . But now when those rules are abandoned and tripods with penal laws on them are cast instead, the people will study the tripods, and not care to honor men of rank."[7] The proto-Confucian Shu Xiang adds:

> In antiquity, the former kings considered the particular circumstances in regulating affairs. They did not make public general laws of punishments and penalties, fearing that this would foster a contentious attitude among the people that could not be stopped or controlled. For this reason, they used their discretionary judgment (*yi* 义) to keep the people in bounds . . . and guided them in their behavior through the rites (*li*) . . . [8]

Confucius rejects law as a means for attaining social order because law focuses on external compliance. Since one is merely expected to conform one's behavior to the given legal norm, one is denied the opportunity to fully participate in the creation of a social order more reflective of one's individual character. Laws, as standards of general applicability, do not allow for sufficient individual expression or particularity.

The formal character of a legal proceeding further diminishes the opportunity for a more contextualized justice able to account for the particular circumstances of the individuals involved. By its very nature, a formal legal system elevates procedural justice relative to, if not at the expense of, substantive justice. In fact, one of the motivations for the development of a formal legal system is to provide a procedural means of resolving interpersonal conflicts that cannot be resolved on a more informal, personal level. While substantive justice has always remained the primary goal of the legal system in China, the formal character of the process and the emphasis on predetermined procedures for resolving conflict have often been seen as obstacles to a more personalized and creative approach to interpersonal conflict.

Confucius' politics of harmony requires the voluntary participation of the individuals who collectively comprise society. If conflicts arise, as they inevitably will, each person must evidence a willingness to look for a mutually acceptable solution. Of course a willingness to cooperate is not enough to overcome all conflicts. There must also be sufficient common ground to provide a basis for discussion, understanding, and potential mutually agreeable solutions. The *li* provide this essential communally owned repository of shared meaning and value on which to draw in times of conflict. One is inextricably a part of one's tradition. However different one may be from one's neighbor, there are still deep chords of affinity that bind one to other members of one's community. By tapping the areas of commonality, one may be able to find the ground upon which to build a consensus, to forge a new harmony. It is the *li* that provide this common foundation for Confucius, and it is in this sense that the *li* are, in the apt description of one contemporary philosopher, "schemes of mutual accommodation of differences in attitudes, beliefs and values in social intercourse."[9]

The *li* have often been construed as universal ethical principles.[10] As a result, Confucius' *li zhi* has been depicted as a kind of natural law. However, the *li* are better understood as customary norms that gain favor within a particular historical tradition at a particular time and that constitute not unchanging, determinant rules of behavior but culturally valued, though negotiable, guidelines for achieving harmony in a particular context. There is nothing sacred about the *li* in the manner of the Ten Commandments. The *li* are merely culturally and historically contingent norms. As such, to depict them as eternal, universal norms is to render them unduly static and determinate.

Although the *li* derive their normative force in part from the fact that they have withstood the test of time and as such represent the amassed wisdom of the ages, they nevertheless must be interpreted in light of present circumstances to retain their currency and relevance in shaping behavior. If the *li* are not invested with new meaning and value, if they are not reinterpreted in light of current circumstances, they will degenerate into irrelevant and trivial formal rules of etiquette.

Traditionally, Confucians were members of the *shi* (literati) class, charged with the responsibility of interpreting the *li* and making the *li* applicable to the times. When called on to resolve conflicts, they attempted to interpret and apply the *li* in such a way as to give effect to a particularized justice that was amenable to all parties and thus restored harmony. Accordingly, they had a vested interest in the *li* and the informal system of mediating conflict that relied heavily on their individual wisdom and judgment. Each individual charged with mediation wielded considerable power, a power that could be abused in the absence of the kinds of procedural protections afforded by a formal legal system.

On a grander sociopolitical level, the ruler was charged with generating and maintaining social order. Living as he did during the late Spring and Autumn period when social order had begun to decay, Confucius realized that society was comprised of persons with diverse interests. To bring diverse interests into harmony requires a unifying agent. The ruler was the unifying agent – the Pole Star – responsible for providing the pivotal note.

Yet the Confucian ruler was more of a facilitator of order than a dictator – at least in theory. Using persuasion rather than force he was to inspire in others a willingness to become humane, to put aside narrow self-interest, and form a harmonious society. The ruler was to lead by example. His virtue (*de* 德) was to sweep over the people and transform them just as the wind blowing over long stalks of grass bends them as it passes. Ideally, the ruler would not have to impose his way. Rather, the people would naturally defer to his example, to his superior moral cultivation. With everyone participating willingly in the collective project of creating a humane society, social order was sure to result. There was no need for the heavy hand of the law. The ruler merely set himself aright, assumed his position at the center, and let society follow his lead. This was the ideal of the *wuwei* (无为) ruler: The Master said: "If there ever was a ruler who could be said to have achieved proper order while refraining from actively imposing his way on others (*wuwei*), it was Shun. What was there for him to do? He simply made himself respectful and took up his position facing due south."[11]

While the ideal Confucian ruler at least in theory sought not to impose his way, he nevertheless played a pivotal role in setting a course for society, particularly in times of conflict or trouble. It was his ability to perceive creative solutions to the problems facing society that enabled him to lead.

In the end, the Confucian ruler ruled by virtue of his moral vision. His authority to lead was a function of his ability to know the Way (*dao* 道). *Dao* refers to the patterns in the world, the ways in which things are related and the possible ways in which they might be related. To "know *dao*" is to perceive these patterns and relations. As a moral achievement, knowing the Way requires that one overcome the limited perspective of one's narrow self-interest to see oneself in relation to others. The more truly cultivated one is, the more relations and possible relations one sees. For Confucius, knowing *dao* also meant understanding tradition and how the past informed and shaped the present. Accordingly, knowledge of the *li* was an essential component of the education of the ruling class.

Confucianism is decidedly elitist,[12] and as a result, paternalistic. In theory, the ruler is the one able to see things other people do not, to see a way (*dao*) to bring harmony out of diversity, to turn disorder into order, and to persuade others to join in the realization of that harmonious social order by virtue of his moral vision, character, and the example he sets. But vision is at bottom personal. As a consequence, political order was (and has remained) largely dependent on the quality of those in power. The absence of effective institutional checks on the power of the ruler charged with achieving sociopolitical order on a macro level mirrored the absence of procedural constraints on the Confucian literati charged with resolving conflict on an interpersonal level. The combination of the lack of effective restraints and the elitist assumption that the Confucian literati/sage/ruler possessed superior normative insights left the disempowered largely at the mercy of those in power.

The Legalist response

Not surprisingly, there were those who objected to the power granted the literati (and the ruler) in a Confucian *li*-based order. To the Legalists, the Confucian system of *li zhi* was nothing more than "rule of man" (*ren zhi* 法治).[13] The Confucian sage determined what was best in a given situation based on his own judgment and interpretation of the *li* rather than by appeal to fixed standards or laws of general applicability. Accordingly, *li zhi* strengthened the hand of the elitist class by ceding to the literati the discretionary authority to interpret and apply the *li* as they saw fit. In response, the Legalists advocated clearly codified, publicly promulgated laws applicable to commoner and nobleman alike as a means of undermining the dual class system in which "the *li* do not reach down to the common people; penal law does not reach up to the great official."[14]

While advocating the impartial application of publicly codified laws, Legalism was hardly a "rule of law" which, at minimum, refers to legal limits on the ruling elite. Rather, the Legalist *fa zhi* is better understood as rule *by* law. Law was simply a pragmatic tool for obtaining and maintaining political control and social order. In the Legalist view, humans are self-interested. To avoid conflict and achieve order, they must be manipulated through a reliable and impartial system of rewards and punishments. Clear, codified, public law lets every person know what is expected and what the consequences will be of one's actions.

Law was also a pragmatic tool in the sense that the Legalists understood that reliance on the personal qualities and judgment of the ruler would in many, if not most, instances lead to disarray. According to Han Fei, most rulers are simply average in their abilities: the truly exemplary ruler such as Yao or Shun is as rare as the truly evil and incompetent ruler such as Jie or Zhou. Thus the Legalists sought to design a system that would work even with – or despite – a ruler who is neither exceptionally bright, morally good, nor politically adept. To do this, they had to conceal the weaknesses of the ruler by erecting a screen of institutional mechanisms, political strategies, and techniques (*shu* 术). Law was one such mechanism. Once the system of laws with its attendant punishments was made known, the laws were to be impartially applied. Neither the ruler nor the bureaucrat who applied the law on a daily basis was to allow personal bias or relationships to sway the outcome. In fact, Han Fei encouraged the ruler to remain behind the scenes and allow his ministers to carry out the day-to-day functions of governance. This was the Legalist understanding of *wu wei* – literally, nonaction – that is so central to Laozi's Daoist philosophy.

Nevertheless, the ruler remained the ultimate authority, both in theory and practice. In the final analysis, law was what pleased the ruler. Accordingly, the ruler retained the authority to promulgate and change laws, and remained above and beyond the law.

In sum, Legalist law was positive law, not natural law. It was a pragmatic tool for effecting social order. While law was intended as a means to limit the arbitrary power of the ruling class and the ruler, Legalist *fa zhi* or rule by law ultimately failed, as did Confucius' *li zhi* or rites-based order, to impose effective checks on the ruler. By allowing the ruler the final word, Legalism lent theoretical legitimacy to the excesses of Qin Shi Huang, the first emperor to unite China, whose reign, marked by strict laws and draconian punishments, was short-lived.

Huang-Lao: a natural law alternative

There arose in response to the deficiencies of both Confucianism and Legalism a new school, the Huang-Lao school, which flourished during the early Han period (circa 200 BC).[15] Huang-Lao attempted to limit the power of the ruler and provide a theoretical and moral foundation for a law-based rule by grounding the sociopolitical order in a normatively predetermined natural order. Ultimate authority lies not with the ruler but with the Way (*dao*). The Way/*dao* gives rise to or determines the laws (*dao sheng fa* 道生法); the ruler is merely the medium who by overcoming personal, subjective biases is able to apprehend the objectively given Way.

Laws are therefore determinate normative standards to be discovered by the sage-ruler: "There is a distinction between right and wrong: use the law to adjudicate between them. Being empty, tranquil and listening attentively, take the law as the tally."[16] Just as the sage is responsible for discovering the law but not for creating it, so is he responsible for impartially applying the law but not for interpreting it. In the legal empire of Huang-Lao, the scales of justice are finely calibrated objective standards. Discretion is eliminated. It is neither the sage's duty nor his role to balance the arguments pro and con in light of the particular circumstances or the culturally and historically contingent norms, attitudes, and beliefs of a particular community (i.e., the *li*). Unlike his Confucian (and Daoist) counterpart, the Huang-Lao sage is not called upon to build a consensus out of dissension, to realize a harmony amenable to all concerned parties. He is a judge, not a mediator. His task is to decide who is right and who is wrong, nothing more, nothing less. On one side of the scales of justice goes the deed, on the other the Way. The burden on the sage is to eliminate subjective bias so that he is able to apprehend the deed as it actually is and the Way as it should be.

Thus, like the Legalists and contra Confucius, Huang-Lao advocates an impartial application of publicly promulgated, codified laws of general applicability. However, unlike the Legalists, Huang-Lao attempts to constrain the power of the ruler. Whereas the Legalist ruler was the ultimate authority as to what the law is and how it should be interpreted and thus was above the law, in the Huang-Lao universe the Way is the ultimate authority and thus the ruler, like all others, must abide by the laws. Accordingly, law for Huang-Lao is not merely a political tool to be used by the ruler to further his own ends. The ruler cannot change the law at will. Nor can he circumvent it by issuing pardons.

Whereas law for the Legalists was positive law, a pragmatic means of attaining social order, law for Huang-Lao is natural law, grounded in the normatively predetermined natural order or Way. By grounding law in the Way, Huang-Lao attempted to circumscribe the power of the ruler, and thereby avoid the evils of the despotic first emperor of China, Qin Shi Huangdi. However, while there may have been limits on the ruler in theory, there were no such limits in practice. Given that there is no way to verify the ruler's claim to have discovered the Way and hence the correct laws, the ruler's power remains as unchecked in practice as that of either the Confucian or Legalist ruler. Nor did Huang-Lao propose effective institutions for controlling the ruler or government officials.

The Imperial era

China has had a well-developed legal system for over two thousand years replete with detailed legal codes, procedures for law-making, rules that specified the hierarchy of the different types of legislation, a multi-level court system, and procedural rules covering all aspects of litigation from the filing of a complaint to pretrial investigation, the trial itself, the issuance of the judgment, and appeal.

Although the names and details of the types of legislation varied from dynasty to dynasty,[17] at the top of the hierarchy were codes or laws (*lu* 律), which remained fairly constant from one dynasty to the next. The broadly drafted codes or laws were then kept up to date and applied to particular circumstances through substatutes (*li*) or Imperial edicts, which were specific decisions made on legal points, and prevailed over conflicting generally applicable code provisions.[18] Sometimes they were decided by the emperor himself, while at other times they were suggested by ministers and ratified by the emperor. In addition, there were specific cases that were recognized to have varying degrees of precedential value or importance.[19] There were also official and private commentaries on the codes and substatutes. Although authoritative, the official commentaries were not legally binding.

Bureaucratically, there were four tiers responsible for legal affairs.[20] District (*xian*) courts heard cases in the first instance. The magistrates charged with deciding cases were educated in Confucian classics rather than law, although during the Song dynasty efforts were made to provide magistrates with legal training.[21] However, magistrates were aided by clerks who generally had studied the law. In any event, district-level courts were limited in their authority. The magistrate could only impose light punishment. Sentences calling for more severe punishment required review by higher authorities. The prefect (*zhou*) level, like the district, consisted of several bureaus or departments, the most important for present purposes being the Bureau of Punishments. The head of the Bureau and the subdivisions within the Bureau were all appointed by the central government and were well-versed in law.[22] Above the prefect were the circuit level, responsible for supervision, and the center, where ultimate authority resided.

Cases at the district level generally began with the filing of a complaint, which was frequently prepared by scriveners. Labeled litigation tricksters and pettifoggers, scriveners and other purveyors of legal advice were much vilified. In 1820 the Qing emperor, blaming the rise in litigation on unscrupulous scoundrels who in their quest for profits induced people to bring groundless charges, issued an edict demanding severe punishment of anyone who made a living preparing legal documents for others.[23] As a result, China's early lawyers were at times rewarded with up to three years of penal servitude for their troubles.[24] Notwithstanding the state's negative view, scriveners played a valuable social role, much appreciated by the people, in making the legal system accessible to those who otherwise would not have been able to take advantage of the state's coercive power to obtain justice.[25]

In keeping with the emphasis on substantive justice, considerable attention was paid to fact-finding.[26] Forensics was relatively well developed in China from early on. At trial, the magistrate would ask the parties questions in an effort to ferret out the facts. Lawyers were not involved. Police were also not allowed to attend the trial for fear that they would intimidate the accused into confessing since police received a reward for convictions. During some periods, confessions were generally required for conviction, except in certain cases such as where the defendant was elderly, a juvenile, or a member of the privileged class and hence not subject to torture.[27] Torture was common.[28] Although there were rules limiting the nature and degree of torture and the types of cases in which it was permissible, such rules were often abused in practice. In some dynasties, such as the Song, trials were closed; in others, such as the Ming and Qing, they were open to the public. The trial ended with a written judgment, in which the magistrate was required to cite the code provision on which the case was decided and to note the result and punishment. If the magistrate was not certain of the decision or wanted to increase or decrease the punishment, he had to obtain approval from higher authorities.

One of the most striking aspects of the system is the virtually unlimited ability of parties to appeal.[29] The accused or members of the

accused's family could ask the prefecture or circuit supervisor to reconsider the case. Parties could also appeal to travelling inspectors, and
could even take their case all the way up to the emperor. In addition,
review was obligatory in many instances where the punishment was
severe.[30] Indeed, during some periods, all death sentences had to be
reviewed by the emperor.

The Imperial system showed clear signs of both Legalist and Confucian influence. The former was most apparent in the emphasis on codified laws and punishment. The codes were heavily penal in nature, and
stipulated numerous carefully calibrated punishments. The Legalist concern for constraining the power and discretion of officials is also evident
in the large number of regulations governing the behavior of officials.[31]

On the other hand, the amoral positivism of Legalism was tempered by
the infusion of Confucian mores and values into the codes and the entire
legal process.[32] For instance, the legal system paid particular attention to
familial relations and filial piety. One of the unpardonable "ten offenses"
was unfilial behavior.[33] Another was the murder of one's parents. In
keeping with the deference owed to parents, a son could be punished for
simply accusing his father of a crime. Conversely, sons were allowed to
conceal the crimes of the parent, except in the case of treason, where the
interests of the state prevailed over moral niceties. Children also had a
legal duty to support their parents – as is still true today. The legal codes
even allowed for a reprieve for those sentenced to death if they were an
only child so that they could look after their parents.

The influence of Confucianism and the *li* is also reflected in the hierarchical nature of the legal system. Punishments were meted out in
accordance with one's status and the status of the victim. Officials were
treated more favorably than commoners. They could not be arrested, investigated, or sentenced without permission of the emperor. Some were
exempt from torture for certain crimes. All benefited from sentence reductions, and could redeem certain punishments either by paying a fine
or accepting a demotion. Status was also important for the official *qua*
victim.[34] Generally speaking, the higher the status of the victim and the
lower the status of the offender, the more severe the punishment. In
addition, the legal codes took into consideration gender, age, and moral
character in determining sentences.

As often noted, the formal legal system was complemented by a large
informal system.[35] Disputes were frequently mediated by the clan elders,

guild leaders, or village heads in accordance with clan or guild regulations and communal practices and norms.[36] The heavy reliance on informal or semi-formal means to settle disputes is arguably a product of the Confucian *li zhi* tradition. It is, however, also a product of the harshness of the formal legal system and the economic constraints of the state. State resources were limited. The magistrate received a budget to cover all expenses, including the costs of administering justice. The funds fell far short of the amount required to meet all of the costs of governing. By relying heavily on informal mechanisms to resolve many disputes, magistrates were able to put the available funds to other arguably more productive uses.

More generally, the influence of Confucianism and *li zhi* was evident in the people's attitudes toward law. Many people felt it was a disgrace to be involved in a lawsuit. At trial, even plaintiffs were required to kneel throughout the proceeding, and could be subject to torture.[37] Although litigation fees were not necessarily out of reach of the average person,[38] extra costs arising from the need to pay off court officials often made litigation an expensive proposition, as captured by the Chinese proverb "win your lawsuit but lose your money."[39] Not surprisingly given the costs of litigating and the unpleasantness of the formal legal process, many parties for purely prudential reasons preferred to explore the possibility of informal dispute resolution first and turned to the courts as a last resort.[40]

Another product of the Confucian tradition was the tendency to pursue a particularized substantive justice at the cost of procedural justice and formal equality, as indicated in the emphasis on fact-finding, the use of torture to extract the truth, the importance of confessions and the ready availability of appeal, and arguably in the reliance on discretion-based moral judgments in deciding cases. Until recently, the prevailing view was that magistrates tended to decide cases based on general moral principles rather than strictly in accordance with legal provisions, and in the process used their discretion to mold a judgment that reflected the particular circumstances. In support of this position, Chu notes that magistrates generally did not cite the legal authority for their decisions even though they were required to do so by law.[41] Further, magistrates enjoyed considerable discretion because of the general nature of many laws and the practice of relying on case-specific substatutes to create new precedents. In addition, magistrates were able to take advantage of broad catch-all laws, such as "conduct that ought not be done," and provisions authorizing them to find crimes by analogy, to tailor a decision to the circumstances based on their own sense as to what was appropriate.[42]

Recently, however, Philip Huang has challenged many of the assumptions about the traditional legal system, including that magistrates decided nonpenal cases based on general Confucian moral values and in so doing tended to split the loaf between the plaintiff and defendant. In a survey of some 600 Qing cases, he found that over three-fourths of the civil cases that made it all the way to judgment ended up with one party a clear winner.[43] Moreover, he claims that in deciding cases, judges tended to rely on legal codes, not custom or general moral principles. In support, he notes that one could find a tenable basis for most decisions in the code or substatutes.[44]

On the other hand, in many cases the code and substatutes are very vague, and thus consistent with a variety of outcomes in particular cases, or they call for penal sanctions, which the judges routinely ignored. Indeed, Mark Allee, reviewing some of the same cases, reached a quite different conclusion.[45] He found that magistrates decided cases based on three factors – the code, broad cultural norms, and local customs – and tried to harmonize them. Magistrates appealed to morality in part because moral norms often supported state objectives in maintaining social order. In addition, parties presumably would be more likely to accept the judgment if they felt it was based on moral principles with which they agreed. Satisfied parties would be less likely to appeal, which could result in the judgment being overturned and adverse consequences for the magistrate. Accordingly, magistrates for their own reasons would be expected to appeal to general moral principles to justify decisions to the parties.

Moreover, like Chu, Allee notes that magistrates seldom cited the code – only four times in seventy-seven cases, and even among those four, only two of the citations were on point, and in one case the magistrate proceeded to ignore the prescribed punishments. Huang attributes this tendency not to cite the code to the fact that the court's judgment is directed to the parties, who generally are laypersons of inferior social status. Accordingly, it would not have been appropriate for magistrates in their posture as father–mother officials (*fumu guan*) to cite the code in such a context.[46] Nevertheless, presumably the magistrate has an interest in persuading the parties that the decision is legally justified, if for no other reason than to decrease the possibilities of appeal, and so there would still be value in citing the code.[47]

In any event, although the Imperial legal system was quite well-developed in many respects, it could not be characterized in terms of rule of law if by that one means a system in which law imposes meaningful limits on the rulers. The emperor was not subject to legal limits, though he was subject to normative constraints reflected in the notion of the Way (dao), heavenly principles (tianli 天理), the mandate of heaven (tianming 天命), and practical limits, including the expectation of the people and ministers that the ruler would follow the precedents of earlier rulers.[48] Nevertheless, law was indisputably a tool to serve the interests of the state. As noted, the system was primarily designed to handle criminal cases, with most commercial and civil cases being relegated to the informal resolution sphere. Moreover, while administrative laws have been part of China's legal system since the Han dynasty in 200 BC, the purpose of such laws was to ensure that government officials faithfully implemented the ruler's decrees. The emphasis was on government efficiency rather than protecting individuals against an overreaching government.[49] Further, there was no separation between the judiciary and the state. The courts were simply another branch of the state bureaucracy.

As a synthesis of the Confucian lizhi and Legalist fazhi theories of law, the Imperial legal system reflected their inherent limitations. First, the Imperial system failed to provide effective restraints, particularly institutionalized legal restraints, on the power of the ruler.[50] Second, it failed to adequately address the need to protect individuals against the state. This failure, like the failure to adequately restrain the power of the ruler, can be traced back to certain underlying philosophical assumptions common to both the li zhi and fa zhi traditions. These assumptions include the rejection of three key tenets of the Western liberal tradition: First, that to treat one with respect and as one's equal requires that one refrain from imposing one's view on that person (the toleration or normative equality premise).[51] Second, that each person usually knows what is best for him or herself, and/or people reasonably disagree about what constitutes the good (the epistemic equality premise).[52] And third, that the interests of the individual and state are not always reconcilable.[53]

Chinese philosophical thinking has always been elitist. Few Chinese intellectuals would accept the liberal assumption (the epistemic equality premise) that no person or group possesses superior moral insight. From the prehistorical mythical ancestors of China, Yao and Shun, to the Confucian sage-ruler of the Warring States period to Mao Zedong and Deng Xiaoping today, Chinese leaders have been credited with an uncanny ability to fathom what is in the best interests of society. Indeed, as noted previously, much of their authority to rule is predicated on their claim to special ethical insight and unique political knowledge of the way of rulership.[54]

The rejection of the epistemic equality premise calls into question the normative equality premise (for liberals, the latter also follows as the conclusion of the former): i.e., that to treat someone with respect is to refrain from imposing one's normative views on them. In China, the government has pursued a substantive moral agenda defined in large part by the particular normative vision of the ruler. Chinese governments have been and continue to be paternalistic (much to the dismay of Americans who find, for example, Singapore's public flogging of juvenile delinquents and prohibitions on chewing gum objectionable). The image of the father dominates the political rhetoric of China. To be sure, the specifics of the image vary by school. The Confucian father–ruler is kind and compassionate whereas the Legalist father–ruler is the tough disciplinarian who well understands that to spare the rod is to spoil the child. Today, the Party in its role as vanguard decides what is best for the people and combines tolerance for the people with harsh attacks against the enemy who dares oppose the scientifically correct Party line. Nevertheless, the image remains the same: the father, knowing what is best, takes care of his children.

Paternalism is on the whole antithetical to individual rights. Not surprisingly, individual rights were not a prominent feature of the political landscape of traditional China. To be sure, a strong tradition of individual rights is a singular phenomenon until this century unique to the Enlightenment West. Moreover, there are many reasons why a strong tradition of individual rights did not emerge in China. One such reason is the view that the interests of the state and the individual can be brought into harmony, an assumption particularly prevalent among *li zhi* thinkers but also present in *fa zhi* proponents such as Han Fei. Given this assumption, there is no need for rights to protect the individual against the state, or so it is suggested.

By the Qing dynasty, the inadequacies of the imperial dynastic system gave rise to calls for radical political and legal reforms. China's humiliating loss at the hands of Great Britain and Japan demonstrated that the central kingdom was no longer the most advanced nation in the world and shook the confidence of rulers and citizens alike in the assumed superiority of Chinese civilization. With modernization as their slogan, turn of the century reformers such as Liang Qichao and Sun Yatsen declared ideological war on Confucianism, arguing for *fa zhi* over and against *li zhi* and *ren zhi* (rule by man).[55] Many reformers proposed institutional reforms that would limit the power of the state.[56] Some turned to the West for inspiration, advocating constitutionalism and promoting individual rights.[57] To be sure, the purposes rights were meant to serve and the conception of rights were often quite different than in the West. Some believed rights would strengthen the state by allowing for greater individual initiative.[58] Rights were typically conceived of as grants from the state rather than natural rights which individuals possessed by reason of birth.[59] Justified on utilitarian rather than deontological grounds, rights were not antimajoritarian trumps of collective interests and the social good but another kind of interest, to be weighed against the interests of the group and society as a whole.[60] Ultimately, the hope was that rights would serve as a new means for facilitating social harmony by redrawing to some extent the balance between the individual and the state and making possible a reconciliation of the interests of individuals, society, and the nation.

On a less abstract level, a number of concrete steps were taken to improve the legal system. China drafted its first constitution in the early 1900s. It adopted legal codes modeled on statutes primarily from Germany and Japan, and sought to modernize the judiciary by restructuring the courts (including the establishment of administrative courts) and increasing the professionalism of judges and the newly established private bar.[61] Unfortunately, such reforms could not take root during the turbulent Republic period, and thus the first wave of legal globalization had little lasting impact.

The Mao era

Classical socialist theory takes a dim view of law.[62] Bourgeois law is nothing more than a tool used by the ruling class to protect its privileged position. In the ideal communist society, the state will wither away and law will not be needed. In the interim, law is to serve political ends. In particular, law is to be used by the proletariat as a weapon in class struggles against the enemy in order to realize the people's democratic dictatorship.[63]

While the classical socialist theory of law dominated the Mao period, the status and importance of the legal system rose and fell in accordance with alterations in the official attitude toward the judiciary and law.[64] At times, the government promoted a professionally trained and operated judiciary; at other times, it advocated a "mass line" approach and other legally less formal and specialized means of administering justice. Mao and other leaders were revolutionaries, not lawyers. As remains true today, none of the senior leaders had received any formal legal training.[65] Following Marx and Engels, they viewed law as the superstructure that reflected the underlying economic modes of production. Whereas in capitalist societies, law served the interests of the bourgeoisie, in socialist China, law would serve the interests of the proletariat. Accordingly, laws and the legal process should be kept simple so as to be accessible to laypersons not trained in law. Mao and his revolutionary cohorts were deeply skeptical of the legal professionals who, given their training and expertise, advocated a complex formal legal system.

One of the first acts of the new government upon taking power was to abolish existing laws of the Guomindang government.[66] The Party then set out to establish a new socialist legal system. In the early 1950s, a number of regulations were passed, including laws on marriage, land reform, and corruption. The legal system experienced a brief moment in the sun from 1954 to 1956. A Constitution similar to the 1936 Soviet Constitution was passed that included a bill of rights. Four levels of courts were established in accordance with the Constitution and organic laws – the Supreme People's Courts, Higher People's Courts, Intermediate People's Courts, and Basic People's Courts. As today, courts were subordinate to the National People's Congress (NPC), but of the same rank – at least on paper – as the State Council, military, and procuracy. The courts were to enjoy functional independence. The Ministry of Justice (MOJ) was also created, law schools opened up, and law journals began to appear.

The legal system's brief heyday came to an abrupt end with the anti-rightist movement in 1957. By the mid-'50s, the revolution had begun to lose steam. Faced with the problem of governing a large and developing country, including an increasingly entrenched and inefficient bureaucracy, Mao decided to "let a hundred flowers bloom, a hundred schools of thought contend," and to invite criticism of the government. Judges, lawyers, and legal scholars were at first cautious and guarded in their criticisms. But upon further encouragement, they let loose a barrage of scathing criticisms that took Mao by surprise. Laws were too vague and inconsistent; the emphasis on law as a tool of class struggle was wrongheaded; there was little or no separation between law and politics. Many in the legal community challenged the Chinese Communist Party (CCP) dominance of law. The stress on political criteria ("red") at the expense of legal expertise was undermining the legitimacy of the legal system. The courts were being run by revolutionaries with little or no legal training. Former revolutionaries, used to being decisive and taking bold action, lacked the skills and temperament to succeed as judges and bureaucrats. In Shanghai, 34 percent of cases in the Intermediate Court were wrongly decided.[67] The endless political campaigns to attack counterrevolutionaries regularly resulted in numerous violations of laws. Accordingly, some members of the legal community called for greater judicial independence. Party policies should be transformed into laws. After that, the courts should decide cases on their own without Party interference in accordance with the law.

Mao's response was swift and brutal. Labeled capitalists and rightists, many judges, lawyers, and academics were persecuted, often being sent to the countryside to "learn from the peasants." The pendulum swung back toward red. The MOJ was dismantled in 1959; the procuracy was downgraded, with much of the work for law enforcement turned over to the Public Security. Law schools limped along, with the usual fare consisting more of politics than law. China's once active legal journals ceased to publish or printed heavily politicized articles.

For a brief period during the early 1960s, efforts were made to rebuild the socialist legal system. The drafting of a number of laws, including a criminal law and criminal procedure law, resumed. But this fledgling attempt at legal reform was cut short by the Cultural Revolution. From 1966 to 1976, the legal system was under attack, legal professionals were again persecuted, and law took a back seat to politics as China relied on mass mobilization campaigns, party policies, administrative regulations, and the military rather than laws as sources of order.[68]

Although the legal system reached its nadir during the Cultural Revolution, at no time during the Mao period was the law meant to impose meaningful restraints on the CCP. Law was indisputably a tool to serve the interests of the Party-state. Party policies were enacted as laws or simply trumped laws. The formal penal system was used primarily to attack counterrevolutionaries and enemies of the state, in keeping with Mao's distinction between contradictions among the people, which were to be settled through persuasion and other "democratic" means, and contradictions with the enemy, which required harsher actions.

While the degree of independence and authority of the judiciary varied to some extent depending on the political mood, the courts were always required to follow Party policy. In addition, the CCP regularly determined the outcome in specific cases, and had the final say in judicial appointments. In particular, the CCP made sure senior judges appointed to the adjudicative supervision committee within the court were politically correct. The NPC, and in some instances the procuracy also, were charged with supervising the courts, as is still the case.

During the Mao era, the Party's role in day-to-day governance was extremely intrusive. To ensure control over government operations, the Party established a parallel system of Party organizations mirroring government organizations at all levels. As real authority resided with the Party, government officials answered to their Party counterparts. Party cells were also established within government entities and other work units. The Party placed a great deal of emphasis on thought control and reinforcing the allegedly scientifically correct Party line. The media and other channels of communication were tightly controlled. Individuals were required to attend regular political meetings where they studied the latest pronouncements of Mao reported in the *People's Daily*. Tight restrictions on social groups limited the possibilities for the emergence of a civil society.

Conclusion

Despite their differences, the legal systems during the Imperial dynastic period and during the Mao era shared a number of features antithetical to a Liberal Democratic rule of law and indeed to any form of rule of law. Law was conceived of as an instrument to strengthen a paternalistic state. The purpose of law was to serve the state, not to protect individual rights. There was little if any separation between law and politics. The ruler – whether the emperor or Mao – could make law. In the Imperial era, magistrates who were government officials trained in the orthodox state ideology interpreted and implemented law; in the Mao era, Party cadres interpreted laws in light of the prevailing Party line, or simply ignored laws and applied Party policies directly. There was neither an independent judiciary nor an autonomous legal profession. Most important, there were no effective legal limits on state power, particularly the power of the ruler and the ruling elite. Although a number of laws were administrative in nature, the purpose of such laws was to enhance government efficiency, and to ensure that lower-level government officials obeyed the ruler's orders or central Party dictates, whether in the form of law or policies. There were few legal channels for citizens to challenge government decisions, and there was little opportunity for public participation in the law-making, interpretation, or implementation processes. Nor was there a robust civil society, particularly during the more totalitarian Mao period. During all periods, but even more so during the Mao era, the state emphasized ideology and sought to control the expression of heterodox views, especially views that challenged the authority of the state. Just as the principle of the supremacy of law gave way to the prerogative of the ruler or the leadership of the Party, so was the principle of equality of all before law compromised by the Confucian emphasis on social hierarchies and status, and by the Socialist distinction between the people and the enemy.

Admittedly, there were also significant differences. Although in both periods, law allegedly served the interests of the people, in the Imperial era, its served the dynasty; in the Mao era, it served the Party. The legal system and indeed society as a whole were much more politicized during the Mao era. For instance, while informal dispute resolution played a prominent role throughout, mediation became much more political during the Mao era.[69] The state became more involved, and family, guild, and community leaders played a lesser role. In keeping with Mao's more confrontational belief in unending class struggle, the emphasis of mediation shifted from restoring social harmony to upholding the Party line, inculcating Party ideology and socialist values, and oppressing the enemy.

Whatever their differences, the Imperial legal system and the legal system during the Mao era were embedded in a very different ideological context than that which gave rise to rule of law in the West. There was no social contract theory where atomistic individuals – born into this world with a full complement of natural rights – preceded the state. Further, in some Western traditions, such as Islam and Judaism, natural law and the laws of nature often flow from the same source: a divine lawmaker who made laws for all things to obey. Accordingly, it is not permissible for human law to run contrary to divine law, including the God-given laws of nature. In striking contrast "no one at any time has ever hinted that any kind of written law – even the best written law – could have divine origin" in China.[70] Although there were attempts to ground law in a transcendent normative moral order – whether *tian, tianli* (heavenly principles), or the natural order of Huang-Lao – the transcendent normative dimension of law received relatively short shrift. As a practical matter, these normative concepts played a limited role with respect to particular institutions, rules, or practices.[71] As we have seen, the formal legal system was heavily penal and positivist in nature, and served the interest of the state. To be sure, the concept of *tianming* or heaven's mandate did confer on the people as a group the right to rebel, and provided support for the idea that rulers had a moral if not legal obligation to ensure the material and spiritual well-being of the people.[72] But in reality *tianming* rarely served as the rallying cry for the disgruntled, oppressed masses. Rather, it simply served to legitimate whatever warlord or faction was able to vanquish its rivals and rise to power.

Complicating the task of legal reformers who wish to establish rule of law in China, law has always been held in low esteem as a means of achieving social order. The lack of respect for law is no doubt due to various factors. In traditions where law is the product of a divine lawmaker or grounded in a transcendent religious order, law is (allegedly) sacrosanct. The lack of a divine origin for law in China may explain in part law's lowly status.[73] The Confucian emphasis on character building also played a role, as did the unfortunate association of Legalism with the draconian laws of the short-lived Qin dynasty. Similarly, the limited opportunity for public participation in the law-making, interpretation and implementation processes, the heavily instrumental nature of the law, its statist orientation and the fact that real authority resided not in the law but in the political arena no doubt all further diminished respect for law.

Given the very different historical and institutional context, the likelihood of a Liberal Democratic rule of law taking root in China's very different soil would seem low. Indeed, it may seem unlikely that any rule of law would be able to take root and flourish. It is true that China's traditions do contain certain features that are supportive of rule of law, including the notion that rulers are to ensure the material and spiritual well-being of the people, and thus even if the legal system is a tool of the state, its ultimate purpose is to serve the citizenry. Similarly, although administrative rules were not meant to limit the ruler or to protect individual rights *per se*, they nevertheless did impose limits on government officials. Further, particular rules and practices such as the legal system's emphasis on careful fact-finding and ensuring that the punishment fit the crime may also be pressed into the service of a rule-of-law regime.[74] On the whole, however, China's traditions do not provide a very friendly environment for rule of law to grow in. Ironically, the main contribution of the Mao era may have been to highlight the urgent need for a more law-based order. The disastrous Cultural Revolution made it clear to all that China needed to rebuild its legal system to limit government arbitrariness and provide the predictability and certainty required to attract foreign investors and grow the economy. When China emerged from its lost decade and opened its doors to the outside world in the late 1970s, it quickly became apparent that China had fallen behind many other countries. Accordingly, China's leaders again began to stress the need to modernize. Rule of law being one of the pillars of modernity, the cry rose once more, as in the Qing, to establish rule of law.

Notes

1 For a more extensive discussion of early Chinese theories of law, see, in addition to the works cited herein, Peerenboom (1993a). For a discussion of the legal system during the Han to Qing period, see Hulsewe (1955); MacCormack (1990); McKnight (1987; 1992); McKnight and Liu (1999); Bernhardt and Huang (1994); Huang (1996; 2001). For the Mao period, see Leng (1967); Victor Li (1971; 1978); Tay (1987; 1990). For post-Mao reforms, see Lubman (1999); Alford (1999); Cai (1999).

2 Orts (2001: 49) notes the claim that rule of law may be divorced from democracy provoked considerable controversy at the annual Law and Society meeting in 2000, though numerous scholars supported the proposition that rule of law need not entail democracy.

3 See Chapter 4.

4 Confucianism is a broad and potentially misleading term. There are significant philosophical differences among Confucius, Mencius, and Xun Zi, not to mention later Confucians, Neo-Confucians, turn of the century Confucians, New Confucians, and Western disciples of Confucianism. Accordingly, I focus primarily on the views of Confucius as an archetype Confucian. See, for example, Peerenboom (1990; 1993a; 1998c) for a discussion of differences in the legal

views of Confucius, Mencius, and Xun Zi; see de Bary, et al. (1960a) for a discussion of Neo-Confucianism; for more modern Confucian ideas, see Hall and
Ames (1999); Tu (1993); and Neville (2000).

5 Analects, 2:3.

6 Analects, 12:13.

7 Zuo Zhuan (Legge 1985: 732).

8 Zuo Zhuan (Legge 1985: 609).

9 Cua (1978).

10 See, for example, Needham (1956); Bodde and Morris (1967).

11 Analects, 15:5.

12 Although elitist, Confucianism is also a meritocracy. Confucius, for instance,
   maintained that humans are by nature similar. Each person has the potential
   to become a sage. At the same time, however, he realized that not all people
   will become a sage. As a practical matter, people will achieve different levels
   of cultivation and accomplishment. A properly functioning society recognizes
   excellence and harmoniously integrates the varying roles of its members. Thus
   it was essential for Confucius that each person fulfill one's role, as delineated
   by the *li*: a ruler was to act as a ruler; a minister as a minister; a father as a
   father; a son as a son; a friend as a friend; and so on.

13 For an overview of Legalist thought, see generally, Peerenboom (1993a); Graham
   (1989).

14 Li Ji 1966 [Book of Rites], 1:35a.

15 See generally, Peerenboom (1993a); Turner (1989).

16 Huang-Lao Boshu (1980: 58, 75a).

17 McKnight (1987: 112; 1992: 62).

18 McKnight (1987: 122).

19 MacCormack (1990: 60).

20 Shiga (1974).

21 McKnight (1992).

22 McKnight (1992).

23 Bodde and Morris (1967: 416–17).

24 Bodde and Morris (1967: 415).

25 Macauley (1998).

26 Alford (1984).

27 Conner (1998: 181). Other exceptions include when the co-offenders were at
   large and when the offender's guilt was clear but the defendant still refused to
   confess.

28 Conner (1998: 181).

29 Ocko (1988).

30 As Don Clarke has noted in personal communication, voluntary appeals should
   be distinguished from obligatory review. Particularly in the latter case, the
   emphasis was on a top-down quality control rather than some notion that the
   parties were entitled to demand a just verdict.

31 Hulsewe (1955).

32 Chu (1961).

33 MacCormack (1990).

34 Peerenboom (1993b).
35 Van der Sprenkel (1962); Lubman (1967); Cohen (1968).
36 Van der Sprenkel (1962).
37 Miyazaki (1980).
38 Philip Huang (1996) suggests that the process was not as expensive as often portrayed.
39 Van der Sprenkel (1962).
40 Philip Huang (1996) argues that Chinese citizens were much more likely to litigate than is often suggested. See also Moser (1982). To be sure, in many systems, even the allegedly litigious USA, parties often first prefer to resolve disputes without recourse to litigation. In general, a rational person will be less likely to litigate where the "costs" of litigation are much higher relative to the available alternatives, all else being equal. Comparing the costs – financial and otherwise – of litigating in Imperial China to the costs of litigating today in China or the USA, the former are higher. Accordingly, one would expect lower rates of litigation, all else being equal.
41 Chu (1961).
42 MacCormack (1990) argues that this catch-all clause was invoked during the Qing primarily to punish those who had contributed in some ancillary way to someone else committing a crime. Ocko (1997: 739), however, argues that the clause was used to enforce general ethical obligations.
43 To be sure, the vast majority of cases were resolved through mediation, either informally or through the intervention of the magistrate. Cases that went forward were arguably more likely to result in winner-take-all judgments because if a compromise had been possible, the parties would already have settled, particularly given that the magistrate would often oversee mediation and push the parties toward settlement. As Huang (1996) notes, mediation occurred against the backdrop of the formal legal system. Indeed, parties frequently filed cases and then settled through mediation once the magistrate had reviewed the petition and expressed a preliminary opinion.
44 Philip Huang (1996). McKnight and Liu (1999: 15) argue that it would be a "serious misreading of the record" to claim that Sung judges could decide matters on the basis of their inner conviction. In support, they note that even though judges often fail to cite particular provisions, they frequently state that "the law says ... " when making their judgment. They also suggest that while judges had a certain amount of discretion to adjust sentences to accord with the circumstances, their discretion was limited.
45 Allee (1994).
46 Philip Huang (1996).
47 To sort out this issue requires test cases where the code is at odds with general moral principles and local customs. In most cases, the general legal principles cited by Huang are indistinguishable from widely accepted moral norms and local customs – for example, legitimate market transactions should be upheld and parties should repay their debts. Moreover, in all systems, judges try to reconcile the law with moral principles and local practices, and in some cases – such as runaway juries or civil disobedience – morality trumps the law. Indeed,

Huang's most recent work (2001) discusses the complex interplay between law and custom in the Qing, Republican, and Guomindang eras. He notes that sometimes law conflicted with custom, and in such cases, sometimes law prevailed and sometimes custom prevailed. At times, the code was changed to reflect or incorporate custom. He also concludes that on the whole Guomindang judges were more "legalistic" than Qing magistrates. In short, at present, the empirical basis for broad conclusions, particularly about how the decision-making process compares to that in other systems, is lacking. Moreover, given that in most cases law will be aligned with morality and custom, and we are not likely to find many test cases, the issue of whether magistrates decided based on law *as opposed* to morality seems insoluble. Given the considerable overlap, whether the issue is even significant is debatable.

48   Ocko (2000) notes the role of conscientious officials in attempting to persuade the ruler of the merits of abiding by the law. As one Han official said to Emperor Wendi, "law is held in common by the son of heaven; it is not his alone." Ocko (2000: 69). Other officials resisted the emperor's instructions and refused to deviate from the stipulated punishment in sentencing criminals. As one official explained, it was his duty to follow the law if asked to judge a case, although he acknowledged that the emperor had "the power of life and death" and could give whatever sentence he wanted. Ocko (2000: 78). Indeed, as Turner (2000: 10) points out, the emperor could simply have ignored the officials or even had them killed.

49   William Jones (1994).

50   Wejen Chang (2000: xi).

51   I am indebted to Ron Replogle for suggesting the terminology of normative equality and epistemic equality. The point can be made in terms of normative equality, toleration, or political-legal legitimacy. Habermas (1996: 107) locates the legitimacy of moral principles, political decisions, his elaborately conceptualized legal system and particular legal rules in the possibility of rational consensus: "Just those action norms are valid to which all possibly affected persons could agree as participants in rational discourses." While moral norms require universal assent, certain legal norms may be justified by ethical and pragmatic reasons. Thus, Habermas defines the notion of "rational discourse" broadly to include, with respect to certain legal norms that involve non generalizable interests, fairly negotiated compromises that result in a rational balancing of competing value orientations and interests. Thomas Nagel (1991: 159) puts the issue as follows, combining an appeal to the normative equality premise and political legitimacy: "if you force someone to serve an end that he cannot be given adequate reason to share, you are treating him as a mere means – even if the end is his own good, as you see it but he doesn't. In view of the coercive power of the state, the requirement becomes a condition of political legitimacy." Even most liberals will allow that it is justified to impose views on others in some cases, for example when the person is acting in a clearly unreasonable or irrational fashion (hence the acceptance of criminal laws to control deviant behavior) or perhaps in self-destructive fashion (hence some acceptance of paternalistic rules, though this is more controversial) or where

someone fails to realize one's views on particular issues are inconsistent with one's more fundamental values. Yet the more difficult issue is where people reasonably disagree about fundamental moral issues and conception of the good, such as with respect to religion and abortion. Thus, normative equality assumes epistemic equality. Even where people reasonably disagree, Nagel (p. 168) notes that there are some conceptions of the good that are simply incompatible with liberal toleration and "the ideal of the reasonable unanimity that is the heart of the Kantian position." When respect for the normative equality premise and toleration give way to the imposition of particular conceptions of the good, the commitment to legitimacy is stretched to the breaking point. Given the existence of deeply held but conflicting conceptions of the good, however, Nagel notes that all we are left with is the hope that conflicts capable of undermining democracies will be rare and that the forms of fanaticism that divide states will gradually die out. Nagel (1991: 168).

52 Nagel (1991: 160); Rawls (1987).

53 Mill (1885).

54 The first generation was dominated by the egalitarian and revolutionary beliefs of Mao. The second generation was dominated by the more pragmatic vision of Deng. The third generation is dominated by Jiang Zemin, who has promoted socialist spiritual civilization and endorsed the three represents. See Chapters 4 and 5. Of course the ruler's vision is affected by the views of others. Moreover, it is not the only factor in determining the moral agenda for society. Further, heads of state everywhere are chosen to some extent because of their vision of a good society. Nevertheless, there still remain important differences between traditional Confucian and liberal views on the nature of political order and how to achieve it.

55 Chen (1999: 129); de Bary (1998: 109–17); Li Buyun (1998b: 138–39). Liang's position, however, varied over time. As Li Buyun notes, at times he favored a strong, one-person rule, though with more public participation such that it was a more diversified rule of man (*duoshu renzhi* rather than *shaoshu renzhi*).

56 See, for example, Kang Youwei (de Bary, 1960a). Much earlier, Huang Zongxi (1610–1695) had suggested radical political and legal reforms intended to limit the power of the ruler in order to better protect the interests of the people. See, for example, de Bary (1993).

57 China's experiments with legal reform undoubtedly were spurred on by its confrontation with the West and the promise of Western powers to relinquish their extraterritorial rights and submit their nationals to Chinese courts if China carried out reforms. Nevertheless, reforms were not solely a response to the impact of the West. As Paul Cohen (1970) points out, the impact–response model is oversimplified. There were many responses in China from calls to westernize to conservative reactions to restore the imperial system.

58 Nathan (1986b).

59 Edwards (1986: 44–45).

60 Peerenboom (1995).

61 Ch'ien Tuan-Sheng (1950); Philip Huang (2001).

62 Berman (1963).

63 Mao (1977: 391).
64 Victor Li (1971).
65 We may be seeing the beginnings of change. The so-called fourth generation of leaders includes more lawyers. See Li Cheng (2000). Senior leaders are now also required to attend periodic lectures on the legal system.
66 Common Program of the Chinese People's Political Consultative Conference, adopted September 29, 1949, art. 17.
67 Leng (1967: 59).
68 Leng (1967).
69 Lubman (1999: 65–70).
70 Bodde (1963: 378). See also Needham (1956: 518).
71 Peerenboom (2001c). Yongping Liu (1998: 13) also claims that even in its early days Chinese law was not significantly influenced by religion.
72 Alford (1986: 955) argues that the Mandate of Heaven imposed a fiduciary-like set of obligations on those in power, though he notes that the constraints of the Mandate of Heaven and the *li* were not always observed in practice.
73 Unger (1976: 99).
74 The emphasis on particularism and substantive justice are to some extent at odds with rule of law's emphasis on generally applicable laws, limited discretion, and procedural justice. However, all systems must balance these general goals. A rule-of-law system with Chinese characteristics may draw a somewhat different balance than a Western Liberal Democratic rule-of-law system would.

3

Post-Mao reforms: competing conceptions
of rule of law

With the death of Mao in 1976, China began to steer a new course.[1] Many Party leaders, having suffered personally and severely from the arbitrary and lawless acts of Red Guards during the Cultural Revolution, were eager to advocate greater reliance on law as a means of preventing the reoccurrence of such policy-driven excesses. In addition, legal reforms were seen as a way for the Party, whose image had been badly tarnished, to regain legitimacy both domestically and abroad.

Most importantly, however, Deng Xiaoping and other leaders decided that the major problem confronting China was not class struggle but economic growth. China was declared to be in the primary stages of socialism.[2] Before China could reach the hallowed ideal of a communist society, it would first have to pass through a capitalist phase. One of Mao's mistakes was to try to leapfrog over the capitalist stage. Accordingly, Deng announced that to get rich was glorious and threw open the doors to foreign investment. The success of the reforms, and especially China's ability to attract foreign investment, hinged on improvements to the legal system and greater reliance on law. "A market economy is a rule of law economy" became the rallying cry.[3] At the most basic level, law is necessary to create and maintain a modern market: to establish property rights and a contract regime; ensure market equality and maintain market order by protecting against fraud, unfair competition, and monopoly; separate government from enterprises; establish and regulate financial and capital markets; and so on.[4] Similarly, China could not persuade foreign companies to deliver vitally needed technology without a system of intellectual property that could be implemented in practice.

Despite a consensus as to the need for a more law-based order, there have been considerable differences of opinion as to the merits of rule of law, its compatibility with the leadership role of the Party, its value for China, and its meaning. This chapter examines these debates and traces the evolution of rule-of-law discourse in the PRC. In particular, I develop in greater detail the four thick conceptions of rule of law set out in the Introduction and illustrate how the various conceptions are likely to lead to differences with respect to the purposes of the legal system, the particular institutions, rules and practices adopted, and ultimately to divergent outcomes in specific cases.

Toward rule of law

During the late 1970s and early '80s, legal scholars actively debated the merits of rule of law (*fazhi* 法治) as opposed to rule of man (*renzhi* 人治). Scholars divided into three camps: (i) those who supported rule of law over rule of man; (ii) those who favored a synthesis: no system can operate without human intervention, so rule of law implies a government of both laws and men; in this view, law is a tool that requires someone to choose the ends for which the tool is to be used;[5] (iii) and those who rejected rule of law as an unscientific (*bu kexue*) or incoherent concept or as incompatible with socialism and the leading role of the Chinese Communist Party.[6] There has been little support for a pure form of rule of man. To the extent that the rule-of-man position is advocated, it has been by synthesists who maintain that law alone is insufficient to govern and must be supplemented by morality, education, and Party leadership, and that every system is a combination of laws and human beings in that people are needed to make, interpret, and implement laws.

Both of these points are readily accepted by rule-of-law advocates.[7] However, rule-of-law supporters note that the difference lies in whether to rely on the wisdom and discretion of rulers or laws to rule, and whether law is supreme and the rulers are also bound by laws. Rule-of-man devotees deny that the law is supreme and that government leaders must also act in accordance with law. In contrast, rule-of-law proponents claim that laws are necessary to avoid the arbitrariness of the Cultural Revolution where the views of top leaders and CCP policies trumped laws.[8] Reliance on law rather than policies or the personal views of leaders provides for greater stability. The Party may exercise its leadership role by setting policy, but the policies must be transformed into laws through the legislative process to be effective. Moreover, the Party itself must be subject to law.

The debate ended in a victory for the rule-of-law camp when the 1982 constitution incorporated the basic principles of a government of laws not men, the supremacy of the law, and the equality of all before the law. Article 5 confirms that the state shall uphold the dignity of the socialist legal system; that all state organs, armed forces, political parties, enterprises, and institutions must abide by the law; and that no organization or individual is privileged to be beyond the constitution or the law. Article 33 declares that all citizens are equal before the law. Reflecting the new policy, the 1982 CCP constitution also required the Party to act in accordance with the law.

China did not wait for a resolution to the rule-of-law debate to begin rebuilding the legal system. The pivotal 3rd session of the 11th plenary of the CCP in 1978 did not mention rule of law, focusing instead on the need for socialist democracy and the construction of a socialist legal system. The motto of the day was *youfa keyi, youfa bi yi, zhifa bi yan, weifa bi jiu* – there must be laws to rely on; where there are laws, they must be followed; laws must be strictly enforced; and violations of law must be corrected.[9] The urgent need for laws led Deng Xiaoping to call for experimental and provisional laws and to emphasize timeliness over drafting technicalities.

> There is a lot of legislative work to do, and we do not have enough trained people. Therefore, legal provisions will inevitably be rough to start with, then be gradually improved upon. Some laws and statutes can be tried out in particular localities and later enacted nationally after experience has been evaluated and improvements have been made . . . In short, it is better to have some laws than none, and better to have them sooner rather than later.[10]

Apart from passing numerous laws and regulations, a number of steps were taken to strengthen the legal system. As noted in the Introduction, efforts were made to rebuild the judiciary and legal profession, and law schools were reopened. To prevent the abuses of the rough justice meted out during the Cultural Revolution, the Criminal Procedure Law afforded defendants a number of legal protections. The Administrative Litigation Law was passed in 1989, followed by the Administrative Supervision Regulations and the Administrative Reconsideration Regulations.[11] For the first time, PRC citizens had the legal weapons to challenge state acts.

To be sure, the path of legal reforms has not always been a smooth one. The 1989 Tiananmen incident slowed both economic and legal reform. For a brief period, law journals were once again full of articles discussing the class nature of law and the need to use the law to strike hard at the enemies of the state.[12] But Deng's trip south in 1992 reignited the reform engines, especially with regard to foreign trade and economic investment. Foreign direct investment jumped dramatically.[13] While Deng's trip accelerated reform most noticeably in the economic area, legal reform also benefited from the spirit of openness. The Ministry of Justice (MOJ) started to allow greater independence in the legal profession and to experiment with different types of law firms, including partnerships.[14] This period also witnessed the passage of the Lawyers Law, Judges Law, Procuracy Law, and Prisons Law, all aimed at professionalizing the various arms of the justice system. The arbitration system was overhauled in accordance with the Arbitration Law passed in 1994, which called for arbitration commissions to sever their ties to local governments and reorganize as independent social organizations.[15] In addition, the long process of establishing a legal aid system inched forward.

Although government officials and scholars continued to emphasize the need to pass more laws, particularly in the economic area,[16] the focus in the 1990s began to shift from the quantity of laws to the quality and to the need to ensure that laws are implemented once passed. The emphasis on the quality of laws highlighted the need to amend many of the existing laws – including the Economic Contract Law, Foreign Economic Contract Law, General Principles of the Civil Law, and various intellectual property laws – which were often passed with a centrally planned economy in mind and thus fell out of step with the realities of a more market economy. Criticisms of the failure to implement laws became a regular feature of official reports and stories in the popular press. Many commentators noted the damage to the authority of the legal system and the credibility of the government resulting from a large gap between law on the books and actual practice.

But the biggest event in terms of the evolution of rule of law discourse in the mid-'90s was the official endorsement by the Party of the concept of *yifa zhiguo, jianshe shehuizhui fazhiguo* 依法治国，建设社会主义法治国 – rule the country in accordance with law, establish a socialist rule-of-law state. The notions of *fazhi* and using law to rule the state were not new; they were present in the rule-of-man debate in the late 1970s.[17] However, they had not been picked up and developed by scholars because the time was not ripe. China first needed to rebuild its legal institutions and pass some laws before it would be possible to rely on law to govern. The CCP had also not been ready to endorse the position.

Then in February 1996, Wang Jiafu, former head of the Law Institute of the Chinese Academy of Social Sciences (CASS), gave a speech to top Party and government leaders entitled "The Theoretical and Practical Problems Regarding Ruling the Country According to Law, Establishing a Socialist Rule of Law State."[18] Drawing on the ideas of legal reformers such as Li Buyun, Liang Huixin, and Xia Yong, Wang argued that ruling the country according to law is to use the will of the people manifest in the form of law to rule the country. Rule of law means that the legislature, government, courts, political parties, and all other organizations and individuals are subject to law and must act within the parameters of the law. A socialist rule-of-law state governed in accordance with law was necessary given China's transition to a market economy. It was also necessary to establish and guarantee socialist democracy and protect individual rights, promote spiritual civilization and social progress, ensure peace and political stability, and solve the succession problems that often plagued socialist states. Only rule of law would ensure that major decisions are scientific and democratic and comply with the interests of the people.

Wang denied any conflict between rule of law and the centralization of power and the leading role of the CCP.[19] Rather, rule of law would provide the legal basis for centralized power and CCP leadership and make them more effective. At the same time, Wang noted that power must be subject to restraints and that the government and CCP must act in accordance with the Constitution and laws. The law must be supreme and laws must be implemented in practice. The government and CCP should also accept supervision by the people.

Wang also took a preliminary stab at distinguishing between a capitalist and socialist rule of law. Because political power belongs to the people, socialist rule of law serves the interests of the people rather than the bourgeoisie. In addition, the economic basis is different in that socialist rule of law is predicated on public rather than private ownership.

The day following the speech by Wang both the *Renmin Ribao* (People's Daily) and *Fazhi Ribao* (Legal Daily) ran articles in which

Jiang Zemin proudly declared ruling the establishing a socialist rule-of-law state to be major policies of the CCP and integral parts of Deng Xiaoping's theory of socialism with Chinese characteristics. In March 1996, the National People's Congress (NPC) approved the Outline of the State Economy and Social Development 9th Five Year Plan and 2010 Long Term Target, which incorporated the new policy. Jiang Zemin then reiterated his support in his keynote speech to the 15th Party Congress in the fall of 1997.

Jiang Zemin endorsed rule of law in part because he sees it as a tool for strengthening Party rule.[20] Rule of law is a way to rein in increasingly independent local governments and ensure that central Party and government policies are carried out. It is also a weapon to be used in the fight against corruption and a means of promoting economic development. Curtailing corruption and raising living standards are in turn important means of shoring up the legitimacy of the ruling regime. As the core of the third generation of leadership, Jiang has also been searching for a normative agenda to call his own that would differentiate Jiang from Mao and Deng, provide the moral foundation for his right to rule, and the basis for his future legacy. In that respect, it is interesting that rule of law had initially been associated with Peng Zhen and then Qiao Shi during their tenure as head of the NPC. Qiao was forced out of power in the reshuffling that resulted in Zhu Rongji's promotion to premier and Li Peng's shift to the NPC. With Qiao removed, Jiang Zemin assumed the mantle of champion of rule of law. Prior to backing rule of law, Jiang's main contribution to a vision for a new China was a hodgepodge of nationalism, socialist spiritualization, and revisionist Confucianism.[21]

Whatever the underlying motivations, Jiang's socialist rule-of-law platform includes many of the features that are central to a thin theory of rule of law. Most importantly, it includes the principle that all are equal before the law and no one is beyond the law: in particular, Party members and government officials must act in accordance with the law. It also includes better enforcement of laws; a more independent judiciary; the legislative principle that all major policy decisions should be enacted in laws; an emphasis on more and better legislation, including clearer property rights; intensified efforts to raise legal consciousness among cadres, government officials, and the people; and administrative law reforms, including downsizing of the bureaucracy and separation of government from enterprises.

In March 1999, the constitution was amended to incorporate the new policy formulation. Some commentators have dismissed the 1999 amendment as more symbolic than substantive since the 1982 constitution already incorporated the basic principles of rule of law that all must abide by the law and no one is above the law.[22] The reality has been considerably different, with the CCP often acting in ways that are inconsistent with these basic rule-of-law principles. Furthermore, PRC constitutions have had a tendency to be programmatic in nature, setting out aspirational ideals that cannot be realized in the near future.[23]

Nevertheless, the amendment may turn out to be more significant than the skeptics suggest. Power in a Leninist state tends to concentrate in the central government organs, and ultimately in a core group of senior Party leaders, because of the Party's leading role as the vanguard of society. State power, and ultimately the power of the people, must be subject to the control of the Party. Although some socialist constitutions have incorporated the principle of the supremacy of the law, Leninist socialist states have failed to resolve the tension between the leading role of the Party and the supremacy of the law.[24] As will be discussed in Chapter 5, PRC scholars have struggled to resolve the tension, with some claiming that the leading role of the Party is compatible with the supremacy of the law and rule of law while others claim that it is not. Clearly Jiang and other leaders still see the Party as playing a leading role. Yet they apparently believe that the Party will be strengthened by accepting limits on its power implicit in the notion of rule of law, in part because a more limited role for the Party in day-to-day governance may lead to better results and actually enhance its legitimacy. In particular, the legitimacy of the Party depends to a considerable extent on its ability to sustain economic growth (and appeals to nationalism). Party leaders widely acknowledge that a more law-based order is necessary for economic development. Thus they have little choice but to accept some limits on their powers and a possible shift in the balance of power from the Party to government organs and ultimately to society to ensure growth. Accordingly, the amendment may signal a change in the way senior Party leaders view state–society relations, and that they have come to realize (if not yet fully accept in practice) that the new economic order requires a new role for the private sector and a realignment of the balance of power between the Party, government, and society.

Even if the amendment does not signal a sea-change in attitudes among senior Party leaders as to the role of the Party, at minimum it reaffirms the commitment of Jiang Zemin and the Party to a socialist rule of law in which the CCP and government must act in accordance with law, and does so in a highly visible way. The amendment therefore makes it more difficult for the Party to set aside law whenever it chooses and provides leverage to those who wish to use law as a means to protect individual rights and oppose arbitrary acts of the government.

Further, incorporating the concept of socialist rule of law into the constitution makes it part of the public domain. No longer is the concept simply the policy of the CCP, to be interpreted by Jiang Zemin and other Party leaders as they want. The meaning of socialist rule of law is now a matter of constitutional interpretation, to be debated by the NPC, legal scholars, and the broad public. To be sure, given the current limited level of constitutional development and Party influence over the NPC, courts, and key government organs, there is no entity with the institutional authority to challenge the Party's interpretation in any significant way. Nevertheless, that could change over time. In both Taiwan and South Korea, for instance, the judiciary became increasingly aggressive as reforms progressed in interpreting and applying constitutional provisions that initially were empty promises.[25] Moreover, government officials, academics, and ordinary citizens have engaged in lively debates about the meaning of the new policy. Some PRC scholars, for instance, have already linked rule of law to wide-ranging political reforms – including genuine democracy and expansive civil and political rights of the type enjoyed in Western liberal democracies – that far exceed what Jiang is willing to tolerate at this point.

Although Jiang tied rule of law to democracy and human rights in his speech at the fifteenth Party Congress, political reforms have been subordinated to economic reform and the need to maintain social order and stability. Nonetheless, reformers hope that the adoption of the latest policy formulation will open up new possibilities for reform, much in the way Deng's trip south stimulated economic reform.[26] In a 1999 poll, fifty academics and government officials cited the growing disjunction between the new market-based economic order and old political institutions as the major constraint on economic and social development and a potential cause of instability.[27] Accordingly, many scholars see political reform as the inevitable next phase to follow economic reform.[28] Rule of law is a promising area to begin political reforms. Even if democracy is not a viable option at present, rule of law allows for political reform by shifting control over day-to-day governance from the Party to state organs. Further, because state organs must act in accordance with law, and citizens have greater opportunities to participate in and challenge government decisions, power also shifts from the state to society.

The meaning of rule of law: let a hundred flowers bloom

After the 1996 endorsement of the new policy formulation, a number of major conferences were held to explore its meaning and implications for legal and political reform.[29] In the years that followed, scholars produced hundreds of articles and books discussing the concept of rule of law, its value for China, and the obstacles to and resources for achieving it.[30]

Fazhi (legal system) and fazhi (rule of law)

One early debate that received new attention was the difference between the construction of a legal system (*fazhi* 法制) and establishment of rule of law (*fazhi* 法治). The rhetorical shift away from the legal system to a socialist rule-of-law state made it necessary to distinguish between the two concepts expressed by the homophone *fazhi* (same sound but different Chinese characters).[31] Jiang Mingan, a professor at Beijing University and one of China's leading administrative law experts, pointed out that rule of law is the goal of a legal system; a legal system is a necessary means to rule of law. He also noted that simply emphasizing the legal system is compatible with instrumentalism where the rulers use law to control others but are not themselves bound by law. In contrast, rule of law requires the supremacy of law and that the government be bound by laws.[32]

Like Jiang, Li Buyun, a prominent legal scholar at CASS known for his advocacy of democracy and human rights, observed that it was possible to have a legal system without having rule of law.[33] The reason, in his view, was that rule of law incorporated certain substantive elements. A legal system required laws but not necessarily good laws. Rule of law required good laws that promote democracy, human rights, and justice. Thus, according to Li, Hitler's Germany had a legal system but the system could not be given the honorific label of rule of law.

Fazhi: rule of law or rule by law

Linguistically, the Chinese word *fazhi* (法治) may be translated as either rule of law or rule by law. As noted in the Introduction, the main difference between the two is that rule by law refers to a form of instrumentalism where law is merely a tool to be used by the state to control others without imposing meaningful restraints on the state itself. In such a system, law is not supreme, there is little or no separation between law and politics, and the dictates and policies of the rulers trump laws. Rule of law on the other hand requires at minimum that law impose meaningful restraints on the state and its rulers.

PRC scholars have picked up on the rule of law versus rule by law distinction to argue that an emphasis on rebuilding the legal system (*fazhi*) is consistent with rule by law whereas *fazhi* means rule of law, understood to entail meaningful restraints on government.[34] Others have noted that in the late 1970s, scholars tended to use the phrase *yifa zhiguo* (以法治国) rather than *yifa zhiguo* (依法治国).[35] The former means to use law to rule and hence implies a more instrumental rule by law. In contrast, the latter means to rule the country in accordance with law, implying that the government is also bound by law. Accordingly, scholars favor the latter formulation as it is more conducive to rule of law.

Liu Junning, a political scientist at CASS until his removal in 2000 due to his endorsement of Western liberalism, has argued that the concepts of legal system (*fazhi*), ruling the country according to law (*yifa zhiguo*), and rule-of-law state (*fazhiguo*) are all consistent with the notion of an instrumental rule by law.[36] While these concepts are an advance over rule by man in that they require the rulers to exercise their will through law rather than by simply issuing fiats, they do not, in Liu's view, impose any restraints on the rulers. However, Liu is in the minority in interpreting ruling the country according to law and rule-of-law state as *not* requiring the supremacy of law or imposing restrictions on the rulers.

In sum, although *fazhi* linguistically could be translated as rule of law or rule by law, *yifa zhiguo* entails limits on government actors and thus is consistent with rule of law and at odds with a pure rule by law. Of course, whether as an empirical matter China's legal system is best described in terms of rule of law or rule by law is a separate issue. Moreover, there is more to rule of law than simply the requirement that law impose limits on government actors. Just how much more depends on whether one favors a thin or thick conception of rule of law.

Thin theories of rule of law

Before turning to the differences between thin and thick theories of rule of law, it is important to reiterate that there is general agreement in China and elsewhere that rule of law requires at minimum that the law impose meaningful limits on state actors, as reflected in the notions of a government of laws, the supremacy of the law, and the equality of all before the law.[37] There is also general agreement that a rule-of-law system must meet the standards of a thin theory, though there are some differences in the way scholars define a thin theory.[38]

For present purposes, the constitutive elements of a thin theory can be defined as including, in addition to meaningful restraints on state actors, the following:

- There must be procedural rules for law-making and to be valid, laws must be made by an entity with the authority to make laws in accordance with such rules;
- Transparency: laws must be made public and readily accessible;
- Law must be generally applicable: that is, law must not be aimed at a particular person and must treat similarly situated people equally;[39]
- Laws must be relatively clear;
- Laws must generally be prospective rather than retroactive;
- Laws must be consistent on the whole;
- Laws must be relatively stable;
- Laws must be fairly applied;
- Laws must be enforced: the gap between the law on the books and law in practice should be narrow;
- Laws must be reasonably acceptable to a majority of the populace or people affected (or at least the key groups affected) by the laws.

The requirement that laws must be reasonably acceptable to the majority of those affected by the law (and hence followed) is on this view an element of *rule of law*, not of *law per se*. Thin theories generally take as their starting point a positivist account of law. Following Hart, we can draw a distinction between validity and efficacy of a rule or law. A law is valid when it is passed in accordance with the system's rule of recognition even if it is not obeyed in practice and not enforced. However, a law is more efficacious the more it is obeyed. The existence of too many valid but routinely ignored laws undermines the legal system and rule of law, running afoul of the requirement that the gap between law on the books and law in practice be reasonably narrow.

For Hart, citizens need not like the laws or find them normatively justified. As long as people obey the laws (and officials accept the rule of recognition), the legal system could exist and function. However, as a practical matter, relying on compulsory enforcement for every law is costly and impractical.[40] For this reason, Geoffrey Walker includes general congruence of law with social values as one of the requirements of a thin theory of rule of law, although he notes: "In a sense we may be cheating a little by making this . . . point an element or part of the definition. Strictly speaking, it is a limit on the model, not an ingredient of it. The rule of law could theoretically exist without this requirement being satisfied. But it would not last long."[41]

That laws be reasonably acceptable to the majority of those affected by them does not mean that the laws are necessarily "good laws" in the sense of normatively justified. The majority might support immoral laws. Historically, immoral laws have all too often been buttressed by prevailing social practices and widely held norms and values. Furthermore, many laws serve an amoral purpose. For example, whether cars drive on the right or left is not a moral issue. Laws that solve such collective-action problems, facilitate commercial transactions, or otherwise make it easier for people to get on with their lives will be acceptable to most people simply because they work.[42]

Needless to say, a thin theory requires more than just these elements. A fully articulated thin theory would also specify the goals and purposes of the system as well as its institutions, rules, practices, and outcomes. Typical candidates for the more limited normative purposes served by thin theories of rule of law include:[43]

- stability, and preventing anarchy, and Hobbesian war of all against all;[44]
- securing government in accordance with law – rule of law as opposed to rule of man – by limiting arbitrariness on the part of the government;[45]

- enhancing predictability, which allows people to plan their affairs and hence promotes both individual freedom and economic development;[46]
- providing a fair mechanism for the resolution of disputes;[47] and
- bolstering the legitimacy of the government.[48]

A variety of institutions and processes are also required. The promulgation of law assumes a legislature and the government machinery necessary to make the laws publicly available. It also assumes rules for making laws. Congruence of laws on the books and actual practice assumes institutions for implementing and enforcing laws. While informal means of enforcing laws may be possible in some contexts, modern societies must also rely on formal means such as courts and administrative bodies. Furthermore, if the law is to guide behavior and provide certainty and predictability, laws must be applied and enforced in a reasonable way that does not completely defeat people's expectations. This implies normative and practical limits on the decision-makers who interpret and apply the laws and principles of due process or natural justice such as access to impartial tribunals, a chance to present evidence, and rules of evidence.

Advantages of thin theories

Depending on one's purposes, thin theories of rule of law may offer several advantages over thick theories. One potential advantage is that thick theories require a complete moral and political philosophy. As Raz observes, "If rule of law is the rule of the good law then to explain its nature is to propound a complete social philosophy. But if so the term lacks any useful function. We have no need to be converted to the rule of law just in order to believe that good should triumph. A nondemocratic legal system, based on the denial of human rights, of extensive poverty, on racial segregation, sexual inequalities, and religious persecution may, in principle, conform to the requirements of the rule of law better than any of the legal systems of the more enlightened Western democracies."[49]

Even the more limited thin concept of rule of law has many important virtues.[50] At minimum, it promises some degree of predictability and at least some limitation on arbitrariness, and hence some protection of individual rights and freedoms. By narrowing the focus, a thin theory highlights the importance of the virtues of rule of law.

Further, a thin theory allows for focused and productive discussion of rule of law among persons of different political persuasions. As Robert Summers notes, "A substantive theory necessarily ranges over highly diverse subject matter, and thus sprawls in its application. On a full-fledged substantive theory, arguments and criticisms purportedly in the name of the 'rule of law' tend to be arguments and criticisms in the name of too many different things at once."[51] Being able to narrow the focus of discussion and avoid getting bogged down in larger issues of political morality is particularly important in cross-cultural dialogue between, for example, American liberals and Chinese socialists or Muslim fundamentalists.

Moreover, as a practical matter, much of the moral force behind rule of law and its enduring importance as a political ideal today is predicated on the ability to use rule of law as a benchmark to condemn or praise particular rules, decisions, practices, and legal systems.[52] To the extent that there is common ground and agreement on at least some features of a thin theory of rule of law, many of the theoretical and practical problems associated with normative valuations in a pluralist society and world are avoided. Criticisms are more likely to be taken seriously and result in actual change given a shared understanding of rule of law. Conversely, criticisms of China's legal system that point out the many ways in which the system falls short of a liberal interpretation of rule of law are likely to fall on deaf ears and may indeed produce a backlash that undermines support for rule of law, and thus, ironically, impede reforms favored by liberals.

Some PRC scholars have suggested an additional reason for emphasizing a thin or procedural rule of law over a substantive rule of law for China at this time.[53] China has historically favored substantive justice over procedural justice.[54] In the clash between morals and law, morals have often won out. The tendency has been to favor particular justice at the expense of generality and rationality.[55] As one commentator observes, "Whereas Western legal procedure tends to depersonalize all claims in order to bring out more sharply the question at issue, Chinese tradition personalizes all claims, seeing them in the context of human relations."[56] While strong normative arguments may be made in favor of a particularized substantive justice, in practice this emphasis gives decision-makers considerable discretion and makes the process more subjective. To correct for the tendency toward substantive justice, the

legal system arguably should now stress the more rule-oriented procedural aspects of a thin rule of law.

Normative concerns about thin theories and the relation
between thin and thick theories

The primary objections to thin theories are based on normative
concerns.[57] First, many critics fear that a thin rule of law could be used in-
strumentally by an authoritarian government to strengthen the regime
and deprive individuals of their rights. In the absence of democracy
and opportunities for public participation in the law-making processes,
the ruling regime can pass illiberal laws that limit individuals' rights,
such as broad state-secrets laws, rules against endangering the state, or
regulations requiring that all social groups register with government
authorities.[58] By grounding rights in a thick conception of rule of law,
some scholars hope to offset the socialist tendency to view law in instrumental terms and to consider rights as positivist grants from the state
that may be revoked and limited by the state as it sees fit.[59]

Second, and related, many people simply find thin theories lacking in
sufficient substantive normative content. Given the traditional emphasis
on substantive justice, the virtues of a largely procedural thin theory
appear too insubstantial. For many, both in China and abroad, a rule of
law that is compatible with morally reprehensible evil empires like Nazi
Germany is simply not worth pursuing.[60]

To remedy the lack of adequate normative content to thin conceptions,
scholars both in the PRC and elsewhere have suggested that rule of law
requires "good laws."[61] Harold Berman, for instance, claims that rule of
law requires laws that are grounded in some normative foundation that
transcends the legal system itself. In the past, divine law or natural law
provided the foundation; today, a more secular notion of democracy
and human rights provides the foundation.[62] Similarly, Liu Junning has
distinguished rule of law (*fazhi*) from *fazhiguo*, which he interprets as a
rule-of-law state or *Rechtsstaat*.[63] Liu argues that the rule-of-law tradition is based more on a natural law tradition whereas the *Rechtsstaat*
is based on legal positivism. Rule of law takes rights more seriously in
that they are grounded in natural law; whereas rights in a *Rechtsstaat* are
granted by the state and may be limited by a simple majority of the legislature. A *Rechtsstaat* emphasizes following laws rather than the purpose

or values of the law and the need to protect individual freedom. It places more importance on the origin of laws rather than whether the laws are good or not.

In the absence of a deeply rooted natural law tradition, those who do not support democracy but believe that rule of law entails good laws must look elsewhere for a normative basis for laws. Pan Wei, for instance, contends that laws should be derived from "generally-accepted moral principles of the time," and therefore accepted as just by the public.

Like Pan, PRC scholars often go beyond claiming that rule of law requires good laws to asserting that rule of law entails justice for all.[64] Dong Yuyu, for instance, argues that ruling the country in accordance with law (*yifa zhiguo*) is not the same as rule of law (*fazhi*), even allowing that the former entails the supremacy of the law. He believes that rule of law requires more – specifically, rule of law entails peace, order, freedom, and justice.[65]

Although justice is a popular requirement for rule of law, there is little agreement over what justice is. Liberals, Socialists, Communitarians, Neoauthoritarians, Soft Authoritarians, New Conservatives, Old Conservatives, Buddhists, Daoists, Neo-Confucians, and New Confucians all differ on what is considered just, and hence what rule of law requires. By incorporating particular conceptions of the economy, political order, or human rights into rule of law, thick conceptions decrease the likelihood that a consensus will emerge as to its meaning. Indeed, one of the reasons for limiting the concept of rule of law to the requirements of a thin theory is to avoid getting mired in never-ending debates about the superiority of the various political theories all contending for the throne of justice.

While thin and thick versions of rule of law are analytically distinct, in the real world there are no freestanding thin rule-of-law legal systems that exist independently of a particular political, economic, social, and cultural context. Put differently, any legal system that meets the standards of a thin rule of law is inevitably embedded in a particular institutional, cultural, and values complex, whether that be Liberal Democratic, Statist Socialist, Neoauthoritarian, Communitarian, some combination of them, or some other alternative.

Theoretically, one way of conceiving of the relationship between a thin rule of law, particular thick conceptions of rule of law, and the broader context is in terms of concentric circles. The smallest circle consists of the core elements of a thin rule of law, which is embedded within a thick rule-of-law conception or framework. The thick conception is in turn part of a broader social and political philosophy that addresses a range of issues beyond those relating to the legal system and rule of law. This broader social and political philosophy would be one aspect of a more comprehensive general philosophy or worldview that might include metaphysics, religious beliefs, aesthetics, and so on.

Thus, relying on a thin rule of law as a benchmark to assess China's legal system does not allow one to completely avoid all substantive issues of the type that must be addressed by advocates of a thick theory of rule of law. It merely reduces the range of issues where such substantive values will be relevant and hence the scope of possible conflict. Although the features of a thin rule of law are common to all rule-of-law systems, they will vary to some extent in the way they are interpreted and implemented depending on one's substantive political views and values. For instance, socialists and liberals may agree that one of the purposes of a thin rule of law is to protect individual rights and interests but disagree about what those rights and interests are. Or they may agree that rule of law requires that laws be made by an entity with the authority to make laws but disagree as to whether members of that entity must be democratically elected. Accordingly, legal systems that meet the standards of a thin rule of law will still diverge to some extent with respect to purposes, institutions, rules, and outcomes due to the different contexts in which they are embedded.

Four ideal types: Liberal Democratic, Communitarian, Neoauthoritarian, Statist Socialist

Given the wide variety of political beliefs and conceptions of a just socio-political order, it is in theory possible to categorize thick rule-of-law theories in any number of ways. In order to facilitate discussion, however, PRC views can be divided into four schools: Liberal Democratic, Communitarian, Neoauthoritarian, and Statist Socialist. These four ideal types were constructed with the present realities of China in mind. For instance, I attribute to Statist Socialists a belief in a market economy. This is not to rule out the possibility of a Statist Socialist rule of law that adopts a centrally planned economy. However, China can no longer be described in such terms. My purpose is not to create an exhaustive set of categories that can be applied to all countries and legal systems, or even all Asian countries.[66] The categories may not be applicable at all to other countries, or even if applicable in a general sense, they may need to be redefined in light of the particular circumstances and issues.

Nor are these categories exhaustive with respect to China. For instance, given the wide regional differences and the importance of religion and non-Han values in some areas such as Tibet and Xinjiang, a form of semi-religious rule of law might be more appropriate.[67] Moreover, the ideal types could be further subdivided. Communitarian rule of law could come in a more statist Asian values version,[68] a pragmatic New Confucian version or a Deweyean civic republicanism version that assumes much of the value structure and institutional framework of a liberal democratic order.[69] Indeed, one could create an ever expanding taxonomy by making finer specifications of any of the variables or introducing new ones. However, at some point, one begins to lose the forest for the trees.[70] For present purposes, these four types are sufficient to capture the main differences in the dominant prevailing political and legal views.

The four variants are ideal types in the sense that they are representative models. As such, they are intended to reflect real positions. It is therefore possible to identify schools of thought and individuals that fall into each of the categories.[71] At the same time, they are a distillation of the views of many different individuals, drawn from not only written sources but thousands of conversations with scholars, legal academics, judges, lawyers, and citizens over the years.[72] As such, no one type may fit exactly the position of any one person or group. For instance, while most New Conservatives would support Neoauthoritarianism, some might favor Statist Socialism or Communitarianism.[73] Others might not fit easily into any category, but rather endorse elements from different schools. Moreover, although certain individuals may have expressed general support for some of the central tenets of the various ideal types, they will not have addressed all of the specific issues that I address. At times, therefore, the positions attributed to them are an extension of their ideas based on inferences from their general principles.

These models are not ideal types in the sense that they necessarily represent the most normatively attractive or defensible interpretation of these positions. For example, some form of deliberative democracy that rejects the state neutrality principle might be a more attractive conception of democracy. Rather, the models were developed for their explanatory value. They represent common interpretations of the various positions, with features selected in part to bring out the differences between the various positions. Choosing a common interpretation or a middle-of-the-road position that the greatest number of people of that persuasion prefer or could agree to (these two are not necessarily the same) rather than the most normatively defensible version has the advantage that the model will then have greater explanatory power as a descriptive tool and also as a predictor of how the legal system might develop and actual cases be decided. Conversely, a normatively superior but very narrowly supported version of some view (say a version supported only by elite intellectuals and philosophers with no political power) might be interesting as philosophy but relatively useless in predicting realpolitik issues such as how the legal system is likely to develop and how controversial cases will be decided in practice. Once the basic differences between the various positions are clear, philosophers and others can debate the relative merits of each position and try to persuade others as to their own normative favorites.

Further, each of the various types is compatible with a variety of institutions, practices, rules, and to some extent outcomes. Within Western Liberal Democratic legal orders, for example, there is considerable variation along each of these dimensions. Take such a basic issue as separation of powers. In the USA, separation of powers refers to a system in which the legislature, executive, and judiciary are constitutionally independent and equal branches. In contrast, the UK and Belgium, among others, are parliamentary supreme states. On the other hand, despite these structural differences, no country – not even the USA – adheres to the simplistic separation of powers where the legislature passes laws, the executive implements them, and the courts interpret and enforce them by adjudicating disputes. For better or worse, administrative agencies everywhere make, implement, and adjudicate laws.[74]

More generally, some liberal states have written constitutions, others, such as the UK, do not. Some are common law systems, others are civil. Civil law countries tend to prefer broadly drafted laws; common law countries more narrowly drafted laws.[75] In some liberal states, judges are elected; in others, judges are appointed; in still others, some judges are elected and some are appointed. In some, the legal profession is self-regulating. In others, the legal profession is subject to supervision by a government body such as the ministry of justice.

Conversely, different regimes may share similar purposes, institutions, practices, and rules. Given a general consensus on the purposes and elements of a thin theory, one would expect of course a certain amount of convergence with respect to institutions, practices, and rules. For instance, in order to enhance predictability and limit government arbitrariness, China has established many of the same mechanisms for controlling administrative discretion as have other regimes, as will be discussed in Chapter 9. It has also enacted a number of administrative laws modeled on comparable laws in the USA and Europe.

Notwithstanding the wide variation within particular regime types on the one hand and the overlap among different regime types on the other, the ideological differences that underlie different thick conceptions of rule of law tend to be reflected in variations in institutional arrangements, practices, rules, and, most importantly, in outcomes. Indeed, even were China to import wholesale the institutions and legal doctrines of the USA, the outcomes in particular cases would still differ as a result of fundamental differences in values, political beliefs, and philosophies. The four ideal types, therefore, serve a heuristic purpose in capturing some of the basic differences between alternative thick conceptions of rule of law in the PRC.

In addition, I refer to a rule-by-law regime where relevant for comparison purposes. Of course, rule-by-law systems come in different varieties as well. There are more moderate and more extreme versions. The legal system during the Mao era, particularly during the Cultural Revolution, was a good example of an extreme version, to the point where at times it could hardly be described as even a rule-by-law legal system, which, after all, implies some form of law-based order.[76] Notwithstanding variation within the category of rule by law, rule by law is distinguishable from rule-of-law systems in that the former rejects the central premise of rule of law that law is to impose meaningful limits on even the highest government officials, as discussed previously.[77] Nevertheless, a rule-by-law system, especially a more moderate form than that of the Mao era, may share some features with some versions of rule of law, particularly the Statist Socialist and Neoauthoritarian ones: for example, the rejection of elections in favor of single party rule. This is hardly surprising given that institutions, rules, or practices may serve more than one purpose or end. On the other hand, in some cases, certain features appear to be the same but differ in degree or the role they play in rule-of-law and rule-by-law regimes. For instance, while Communitarians accept some limits on civil society, the limits are much more restrictive in a rule-by-law system, even a moderate rule-by-law regime. Similarly, a rule-by-law system aims at a much higher degree of thought control than the others.

The economic regime

Although all four rule-of-law variants favor a market economy, they differ with respect to the degree, nature, and manner of government intervention. Notwithstanding the significant differences in the economies of Western liberal democracies that have led neoinstitutionalists and political economists to posit varieties of capitalism even within Europe,[78] economies in liberal democratic states tend to be characterized by minimal government regulation intended primarily to correct market failures, a clear distinction between the public sphere and private commercial sphere, and limited administration discretion to interfere in private business. In contrast, economic growth in many Asian countries, including China, has been attributed to a form of managed capitalism in which the state actively intervenes in the market, government officials blur the line between public and private spheres by establishing clientelist or corporatist relationships with private businesses, and universal laws are complemented, and sometimes supplanted, by administrative guidance, vertical and horizontal relationships, and informal mechanisms for resolving disputes.[79] In these Asian development states, the government relies on its licensing power and control over access to loans, technology, and other information and inputs to steer companies in the direction determined by the state. In some cases, the government will champion particular companies or sectors of the economy. The government may also have a direct or indirect economic interest in certain companies. Of course there is considerable variation in the amount, nature, and form of government intervention in Asian countries. Surely Hong Kong's economy has been as laissez-faire as any in the West. On the whole, however, Asian governments have taken a more interventionist approach to managing the economy.

China's economy is currently heavily regulated and characterized by clientelism and corporatism. Moreover, governments at all levels have both direct and indirect economic interests in companies. As will be discussed in Chapter 10, there is considerable debate about the merits of such heavy government intervention and close government–business relations in China and more generally, particularly since the Asian financial crisis.[80] While a more laissez-faire economy has its supporters, there is ample support, however, for the view that China's transition from a centrally planned economy to a market economy requires a strong (Neoauthoritarian) government able to make tough decisions without fear of having to appease the electorate.[81] Although Statist Socialists and Neoauthoritarians (and rule-by-law proponents) are most likely to adopt such views, many if not most Communitarians also support them. The difference between them is that Statist Socialists arguably favor a higher degree of government regulation than Neoauthoritarians and Communitarians.

Statist Socialists and Neoauthoritarians are also somewhat more likely to favor corporatist or clientelist relationships between government and businesses than Communitarians on the grounds that it increases the state's control over economic activities. However, all are concerned about the negative effects of corporatism and clientelism, both in terms of economic efficiency and increased corruption. Thus some shift away from such relationships as they currently exist toward a more open, transparent process based on generally applicable laws is likely (especially now that China has entered the WTO), even if in the end there remains a higher degree of interaction between government and business than in some Western countries.

Finally, public ownership is one pillar, albeit a shaky one, of Jiang Zemin's socialist rule-of-law state. To be sure, all states allow some public ownership. Nonetheless, in comparison to the others, Statist Socialists can be expected to favor somewhat higher levels of public ownership, more limitations on the kinds of shares that can be held by private and foreign investors, and more restrictions on the industries in which private and foreign companies may hold majority shares.

The political order

Liberal democratic states are characterized by genuine democratic elections for even the highest level of government office, a neutral state in which the normative agenda for society is determined by the people through elections, and a limited state with an expansive private sphere and robust civil society independent of the state.[82] In contrast, Statist Socialism is defined by single party rule, elections at only the lowest level of government, and at present a nomenklatura system of appointments whereby the highest-level personnel in all government organs including the courts are chosen or approved by the Party. Rather than a neutral state, the Party in its role as vanguard sets the normative agenda for society, which currently consists of the four cardinal principles: the leading role of the Party, adherence to socialism, the dictatorship of the proletariat, and Marxism–Leninism–Mao Zedong thought. In addition, there is a smaller private sphere and a correspondingly larger role for the state in supervising and guiding social activities. If Statist Socialists had their way, there would be at most a limited civil society characterized by a high level of corporatist and clientelist relationships with government. In these respects, there is little to distinguish Statist Socialists from rule-by-law advocates, although the latter might favor an even more totalitarian form of government.

Neoauthoritarians prefer single party rule to genuine democracy. They would either do away with elections, or were that not politically feasible, limit elections to lower levels of government. If forced to hold national-level elections, they would attempt to control the outcome of the elections by imposing limits on the opposition party or through their monopoly on major media channels. Like the Statist Socialists, they reject the neutral state and favor a large role for the government in controlling social activities. Nevertheless, they would tolerate a somewhat smaller role for the government and a correspondingly larger civil society, albeit one still subject to restrictions and characterized by clientelism and corporatism.

In contrast, Communitarians favor genuine multiparty democratic elections at all levels of government, though not necessarily right away. Given their fear of chaos, distrust of the allegedly ignorant masses, and the lack of requisite institutions, they are willing to postpone elections for the moment and to accept a gradual step-by-step process where elections are permitted at successively higher levels of government.[83] Like the Statist Socialists and Neoauthoritarians, they believe state leaders should determine the normative agenda for society, and hence allow a larger role for the state in managing social activities than in a liberal democratic state. However, they prefer a somewhat more expansive civil society. Although some groups, particularly commercial associations, might find close relationships with the government helpful, other more social or spiritual groups might not. The latter would be permitted to go their own way, subject to concerns about social order, public morality, and specific harms to members of the group or society at large. Rather than hard or statist corporatism, Communitarians favor a soft or societal version.[84]

Perspective on rights

Liberal Democrats favor a liberal understanding of rights that gives priority to civil and political rights over economic, social, cultural, and collective or group rights. Rights are conceived of in deontological terms as distinct from and normatively superior to interests. Rights are considered to be prior to the good (and interests) both in the sense that rights "trump" the good/interests and in that rights are based not on utility, interests, or consequences but on moral principles whose justification is derived independently of the good.[85] To protect individuals and minorities against the tyranny of the majority, rights impose limits on the interests of others, the good of society, and the will of the majority. Substantively, freedom is privileged over order, individual autonomy takes precedence over social solidarity and harmony, and freedom of thought and the right to think win out over the need for common ground and right thinking on important social issues. In addition, rights are emphasized rather than duties or virtues.

    In contrast, Communitarians endorse a communitarian or "Asian values" interpretation of human rights that emphasizes the indivisibility of rights. Greater emphasis is placed on collective rights and the need for economic growth, even if at the expense of individual civil and political rights.[86] Rather than a deontological conception of rights as antimajoritarian trumps on the social good, rights are conceived of in utilitarian or pragmatic terms as another type of interest to be weighed against other interests, including the interests of groups and society as a whole. Accordingly, stability is privileged over freedom, social solidarity and harmony are as important if not more so than autonomy, and freedom of thought and the right to think are limited by the need for common ground and consensus on important social issues.[87] Communitarians, Neoauthoritarians, Statist Socialists, and rule-by-law advocates also pay more attention than Liberal Democrats to the development of moral character, virtues, and the need to be aware of one's duties to other individuals, one's family, members of the community, and the nation.

Like Communitarians, Neoauthoritarians and Statist Socialists conceive of rights in utilitarian or pragmatic terms. However, they have a more state-centered view than Communitarians. Statist Socialists in particular are likely to conceive of rights as positivist grants of the state and useful tools for strengthening the nation and the ruling regime.[88] They are also more likely than Neoauthoritarians to invoke state sovereignty, Asian values, and the threat of cultural imperialism to prevent other countries from interfering in their internal affairs while overseeing the destruction of the communities, traditional cultures, and value systems that they are allegedly defending.[89] Nevertheless, Communitarians and Neoauthoritarians in China are also likely to object to strong-arm politics and the use of rights to impose culture-specific values on China or to extract trade concessions in the form of greater access to Chinese markets.[90] Moreover, like Communitarians, Neoauthoritarians and Statist Socialists privilege order over freedom. They go even farther than Communitarians, however, in tilting the scales toward social solidarity and harmony rather than autonomy, and are willing to impose more limits on freedom of thought and the right to think. While Neoauthoritarians would restrict the right of citizens to criticize the government, Statist Socialists would impose such broad restrictions that criticism of the government would be for all practical purposes prohibited. Indeed, Statist Socialists much prefer unity of thought to freedom of thought and right thinking to the right to think. Were it possible (without undermining their other goals such as economic growth), they would return to the strict thought control rule-by-law regime of the Mao era. At minimum, they draw the line at public attacks on the ruling party or challenges to single party socialism. Despite the changes in society over the last twenty years that have greatly reduced the effectiveness of "thought work," they continue to emphasize its importance to ensure common ground and consensus on important social issues defined by the Party line.[91]

The rule-by-law regime of the Mao era differed from any of the rule-of-law regimes in considering the concept of rights as a bourgeois liberal device to induce false consciousness in the proletariat. Although it did include some rights in its constitutions, such rights were considered programmatic goals to be realized at some future date. In addition, duties were privileged over rights, especially duties to the state, civil society was extremely limited, and efforts at thought control were pervasive.

Purposes of rule of law

Proponents of the various conceptions see rule of law serving certain similar purposes: enhancing predictability and certainty, which promotes economic growth and allows individuals to plan their affairs; preventing government arbitrariness; increasing government efficiency and rationality; providing a mechanism for dispute resolution; protecting individual rights; and bolstering regime legitimacy. They differ, however, with respect to the priorities of the various purposes, their degree of support or enthusiasm for any given purpose, and the details of how the goals are interpreted. Broadly stated, Liberal Democrats emphasize the role of rule of law in limiting the state and protecting the individual against government arbitrariness, whereas Communitarians favor a more balanced role for rule of law as a means of both limiting and strengthening the state. In contrast, Neoauthoritarians place somewhat greater emphasis on the state-strengthening aspect, which is assigned an even higher priority by Statist Socialists.

Indeed, although Statist Socialists accept – at least in theory – the primary requirement of rule of law that government officials and citizens alike are subject to law and must act in accordance with it, they accept such limits grudgingly. Not surprisingly, to date the reach of the law has been limited, with high-level government officials subject to a separate system of Party discipline rather than to the formal legal process. Moreover, while Statist Socialists appreciate the benefits of limiting government arbitrariness, they also prefer a system that allows them sufficient flexibility to pursue their legitimate (and sometimes illegitimate) ends. And while they regularly declare that rule of law is necessary to protect individual rights, it is not a high priority. In any case, the ability of the legal system to protect individual rights is severely hampered by their statist conception of rights and their extreme emphasis on stability and order over freedom.

Differences in the purposes of rule of law are evident in the weights attached to stability. All – even Liberal Democrats – agree that stability is important. Clearly one purpose of law in Western traditions has been to prevent anarchy and a Hobbesian war of all against all, as noted previously. China, for its part, has suffered tremendous upheaval in the last 150 years, from the uprisings against and eventual collapse of the Qing to the chaos and internal struggles of the Republican period to the turbulence of the antirightist movement, Great Leap Forward, and Cultural Revolution of the Mao era. With a quarter of the world's population, many of them below or near the poverty level, China (or the rest of the world) can hardly afford political chaos or anarchy. The current economic reforms have already resulted in massive unemployment and rising unrest. As the reforms continue and the number of unemployed shoots up, the potential for traumatic disruptions of the social order increases accordingly.[92]

Rule of law could serve the goal of stability in a variety of ways. First, it could limit the arbitrary acts of government.[93] One of the biggest sources of instability in the last fifty years has been the Party itself and the arbitrariness of senior leaders. One of the main reasons for promoting rule of law after the death of Mao was to avoid the chaos of the Cultural Revolution where the whims of Party leaders were substituted for laws. Rule of law is meant to make governance more regular and predictable. It is also needed to address the perennial problem confronting socialist regimes of political succession.[94] Whereas the death of Mao set off a struggle for power, rule of law is supposed to ensure a more seemly and seamless transition of power.[95]

In addition, rule of law serves stability by regularizing central–local relations. Conflicts between the central and local governments have increased dramatically as a result of economic reforms that have given local governments both more authority and responsibility. In their desire to promote local economic development, local governments regularly ignore central laws and policies, issue regulations that are inconsistent with national-level laws, or engage in local protectionism.[96] While there seems little chance of the central government losing control over local governments to the point where local governments emerge as Republican era-type warlords, as some alarmists have suggested, authority has become fragmented to such an extent that China arguably now has a de facto federalist form of government.[97] Not surprisingly, Jiang Zemin and other Statist Socialists emphasize the value of rule of law as a means of disciplining local governments and recentralizing power.

On the other hand, some scholars have noted that stability is often a code word in Chinese politics for greater centralization of power, an emphasis on collective over individual rights, and the continued dominance of the Party.[98] In this view, the government's emphasis on stability is overstated and is really just an attempt to limit challenges to Party rule. Former Vice Director of the Chinese Academy of Social Sciences, Li Shenzhi, for instance, argues that subsistence is no longer such a major problem. Accordingly, more emphasis should be placed on political reform and citizens' civil and political rights.[99] Similarly, another PRC scholar has argued that political reform need not lead to instability.[100] To some extent, the differences turn on empirical issues. How unstable is China? How likely is it that the activities of any one dissident or even a group of dissidents could endanger national security? But they also reflect fundamental differences in values. Although all appreciate the need for stability, liberals would place greater importance on freedom whereas Statist Socialists, Neoauthoritarians, and Communitarians would privilege, to varying degrees, order over freedom.

Broad agreement over other purposes also gives way to subtle differences upon further probing. All agree, for instance, that predictability and certainty are crucial for economic growth. But predictability and certainty may serve other purposes as well. Liberal Democrats value predictability because it enhances freedom by allowing people to plan their affairs and realize their ends in life, and thus promotes human dignity.[101] Underlying this view is a liberal view of the self as moral agent that emphasizes autonomy and the importance of making moral choices. But not all ethical traditions share this view of the self or place such importance on choice making. The dominant Chinese view of the self as social and the Confucian emphasis on doing what is right rather than the right to choose, call into question justifications of rule of law that appeal to this interpretation of human dignity.[102] Of course, the ability to plan one's affairs is valuable to some degree in China.[103] However, the weight attached to the ability to plan one's affairs and the reasons given in support are likely to differ between Liberal Democrats and the others, with Statist Socialists assigning it the least weight.

Similarly, all hope that rule of law will enhance the legitimacy of the ruling regime. However, by allowing elections and ample opportunities for public participation in law-making, legitimacy for Liberal Democrats and Communitarians is based on consent. In contrast, in the absence of elections and with only limited opportunities for public participation, legitimacy for Statist Socialists and Neoauthoritarians is primarily performance-based: that is, legitimacy depends on whether the laws, the legal system, and the regime as a whole produce good results.[104]

In contrast to rule-of-law regimes, in a rule-by-law regime, law is merely a tool to serve the interests of the state, and is not meant to impose limits on the rulers. Law serves the state by enhancing government efficiency, although that goal is often compromised by the heavily politicized nature of law and the dominance of policy. Law is not meant to protect the rights of individuals. Whereas rule-of-law regimes rely on the courts to resolve disputes, in the Mao era, for instance, the formal legal system was used primarily to suppress enemies. Disputes among the people were settled through mediation, and economic conflicts between state-owned entities were resolved administratively or by Party organs.

Institutions and practices

According to Weber, the defining feature of a modern legal system that merits the label rule of law is autonomy. Law is distinct from politics, and independent judges decide cases impartially in accordance with generally applicable laws using a distinct type of legal reasoning. To be sure, the line between politics and law is not always a clear one, as Critical Legal Scholars repeatedly remind us.[105] Nevertheless, as one commentator observes, "The difference between law and decree, between government proclamation and administrative power on the one hand and the genuine rule of law on the other, is perfectly well understood in all those countries where the rule of law is seriously threatened or has been abolished."[106]

While the outer extremes between a system dominated by politics – such as the legal system in the Mao era, particularly during the Cultural Revolution – and a rule-of-law system in which legal institutions and actors enjoy a high degree of autonomy are reasonably clear, there is considerable room for variation in the middle. Advocates of alternative conceptions of rule of law are likely to disagree over where to draw the line between law and politics, due in part to their divergent views about the economy, the political order, the nature and limits of rights, and the purposes that law is meant to serve.

Liberal Democrats favor a high degree of independence and autonomy. The legislature that makes laws is freely elected rather than appointed by the ruling party. The judiciary as a whole and individual judges are independent. Judges enjoy lifetime tenure and can be removed only for limited reasons and in accordance with strict procedures. The appointment process is relatively nonpoliticized. There are a variety of mechanisms for reining in administrative discretion, and the legal system is capable of holding even top-level government officials accountable. The legal profession is independent and often self-governing.

At the other end of the spectrum, Statist Socialists favor only a moderate to low level of separation between law and politics. In keeping with the minimal requirements of rule of law, whereas in the Mao era CCP policies were substituted for or trumped laws, CCP policy is now to be transformed into laws and regulations by entities authorized to make law in accordance with the stipulated procedures for law-making. Nevertheless, the legislature is not freely elected. As will be discussed in Chapter 5, Party influence on the law-making processes has diminished radically since the beginning of reforms. However, like ruling parties in parliamentary systems in other countries, the Party is able to ensure that major policy initiatives become law when it is united and willing to spend the political capital to do so.[107]

Statist Socialists also favor a more limited judicial independence. Courts have a functional independence in the sense that other branches of government are not to interfere in the way courts handle specific cases. Unlike in the Mao era, courts may decide cases without Party approval of the judgment. However, the courts may still be subject to macrosupervision by the NPC, the procuracy, and even Party organs. While the courts as a whole enjoy limited functional independence, the autonomy and independence of individual judges is even more restricted.[108] Accordingly, most cases are decided by a panel of judges, and a special adjudicative supervision committee within the court has the right to review particular decisions in case of manifest error.

The legal profession is granted a similar partial independence. Although not the "workers of the state" of the Mao era, lawyers still must meet political correctness standards to practice law and pass the annual inspection test. While the MOJ shares responsibility for supervising the legal profession with lawyers' associations, the MOJ retains most of the authority, including the power to punish lawyers. In part because of such political reasons, but mainly due to corruption and rent-seeking by the MOJ and its local affiliates, lawyers try to forge close clientelist relations with the MOJ.

In the administrative law area, government officials are granted considerable discretion, in part so that they may be more responsive to shifts in Party policy, but mainly for other reasons, including the need to respond quickly and flexibly to a rapidly changing economic environment. Limits on civil society, freedom of the press, and public participation in the law-making, interpretation and implementation processes make it difficult for the public to monitor government officials. The lack of elections eliminates whatever leverage the public might have over officials resulting from the possibility of voting the current government out of office.

Neoauthoritarians prefer a moderate separation between law and politics. As with Statist Socialists, the legislature is not elected. However, Neoauthoritarians favor greater judicial independence than Statist Socialists, although many would still limit the independence of the courts and individual judges in various ways. For instance, they may prefer China's unitary system in which the NPC is supreme and exercises supervision over the courts, to a US style separation of powers system. On the other hand, they support the development of a more professional and honest civil service, and an administrative law system capable of reining in wayward government officials and combating corruption.[109] They also advocate greater public participation and more expansive, though still limited, freedom of association, speech, and the press so that the public can play a greater role in the monitoring of government officials. The main purpose of administrative law, however, remains rational and efficient governance rather than the protection of individual rights. The elite corps of civil servants are to be given considerable flexibility in formulating and implementing administrative rules, which are the main form of legislation in day-to-day governance. The legal profession would be granted limited independence and subject to supervision by the MOJ, albeit a cleaner and more professional one. Nevertheless, lawyers would still seek to establish clientelist ties to the MOJ due to its control over licensing for special forms of business and other commercial reasons.[110]

Communitarians prefer a moderate to high degree of separation between law and politics. The legislature would be freely elected. There would be ample opportunities for public participation in rule-making, interpretation, and implementation. The public would also be able to throw out a government that is corrupt or performs poorly; as a whole, the administrative law system would be sufficiently strong to hold even top-level government officials accountable. Although Communitarians are sympathetic to the argument that a strong economy, particularly in times of transition, requires a strong executive, they balance the need for efficient government against the need to protect individual rights. Moreover, like Liberal Democrats, they support an autonomous judiciary, with life tenure for judges and relatively apolitical processes for appointing and removing judges. At the same time, Communitarians reject the liberal notion of a neutral state. Accordingly, they favor the practice whereby courts decide cases in light of a substantive moral agenda for society determined by the ruling elite. In that sense, they do not differ from Statist Socialists or Neoauthoritarians.[111] Rather what distinguishes them is the particular normative agenda. Communitarians believe that judges should emphasize harmony, stability, and the interests of the community over the interests of individuals as well as economic development. Neoauthoritarians and Statist Socialists agree in general but place more emphasis on economic development and upholding the authority of the state. In particular, Statist Socialists insist that the courts uphold the four cardinal principles – a position not supported by either Neoauthoritarians or Communitarians.

Rules

Liberal Democrats prefer liberal laws. Although there is room for disagreement among Liberal Democrats with respect to specific laws, liberal laws generally provide strong protection for broadly defined civil and political rights. Free speech may be subject to only narrow time, place, and manner restrictions. Social groups are free to organize without having to register with government authorities. Persons accused of crimes have the right to a lawyer, who may be present at all stages of formal interrogation; the accused may only be held for a very limited time without being charged; and the state may not rely on illegally obtained evidence in making its case. Euthanasia laws may allow individuals to choose to end their life or to ask others to assist them in doing so. Parents may keep their children out of school and educate them at home if they choose.

Communitarians, Neoauthoritarians, and Statist Socialists all endorse laws that limit individual freedom to one extent or another. For instance, all allow registration requirements for social groups to ensure public order. All accept substantive limits on speech as well as time, place and manner restrictions. No one is free to walk into a courtroom with a jacket that says "Fuck the Draft" on it.[112] Flag burning is outlawed.[113] The accused have a right to a lawyer but only after the police have had an initial opportunity to question them. The accused may be held for longer periods without being charged, and the period may be extended upon approval of the authorities. Illegally obtained evidence may be used in certain instances, though forced confessions and police torture are not allowed. Children are required to attend schools authorized by the state, and to study a curriculum approved by the Ministry of Education. More controversially, Statist Socialists and Neoauthoritarians, and perhaps even Communitarians, endorse broadly drafted laws to protect the state and social order, such as state-secrets laws and prohibitions against endangering the state.

Outcomes

Institutions in a broad sense include ideology, purposes, organizational structures and cultures, norms, practices, rules, and outcomes.[114] Although I have separated them for the sake of a clearer exposition, in reality they overlap and blend together, as is evident from the following examples concerning constitutional, administrative, and criminal law.[115]

In general, constitutions in socialist countries have played a very different role than constitutions in liberal democracies, in part because socialist states have made little pretense of abiding by basic rule-of-law requirements and accepting any constitutional limits on the ruling regime's power.[116] Reflecting their origins in Enlightenment theories of social contract, liberal constitutions emphasize a limited state and a separation between state and society. Rule of law plays a central role in imposing limits on the state and protecting the individual against an overreaching state by ensuring that the state does not encroach on the fundamental rights of individuals set out in the constitution. Liberal constitutions set out fundamental principles that are supposed to stand the test of time, including the basic rights of citizens.

In contrast, socialist constitutions are characterized by frequent change. The frequent change in socialist constitutions is consistent with socialist legal theory, which conceives of law as a superstructure that reflects the economic basis of society and in particular the ownership of the material modes of production. When the economic base changes, law – and the constitution – must change accordingly. Moreover, since Marxism posits an evolution toward an ideal state, with the economy passing through various stages, amendment of the constitution is to be expected. In the PRC, the 1978 constitution was replaced in 1982 by a more market-oriented constitution that reflected Deng Xiaoping's economic open-door and reform policies. The 1982 constitution has subsequently been amended three times as economic reforms have deepened and the economy has steadily moved away from a centrally planned economy toward a more market-oriented economy. Each time the amendments incorporated more market-oriented policies.

Although changes in PRC constitutions reflect transformations in the economic base of society, they also reflect fundamental shifts in political power. Again, this is entirely consistent with socialist legal theory, which conceives of law as a tool of the ruling class. Whereas in a capitalist society, law serves the bourgeoisie, in a socialist state law allegedly serves the people. However, in a Leninist socialist state, the Party acts as the vanguard of the people. Thus law becomes a tool of the Party. The constitution changes when there are major changes in Party leadership or Party policy. The 1954 constitution therefore reflected the victory of the CCP and the Party's consolidation of power. The 1975 Cultural Revolution constitution codified Mao's victory over his opponents and embodied his radical vision for a society that must engage in permanent revolution and ceaseless class struggle to defend socialism against the enemy within and abroad. The short-lived 1978 constitution signaled Deng's victory over Mao loyalists, the turn toward a more law-based order, and the need to concentrate on economic development rather than class struggle. However, Deng had yet to consolidate his power. By 1982, he was firmly in control. Thus the 1982 constitution confirmed the new emphasis on economic development. It also continued the trend, begun in the 1978 constitution, to downplay the dominance of the CCP, separate the Party from government, and turn over the functions of day-to-day governance to state organs.[117] Although the 1982 constitution incorporated Deng's four cardinal principles, they were placed in the preamble.

In contrast, the principles of the supremacy of the law and that no individual or party is beyond the law were incorporated into the body of the constitution. Nevertheless, the constitution did not explicitly endorse rule of law, even a socialist rule of law, until the amendment in 1999.

What role the constitution will play in the future depends in part on which version of rule of law prevails. Should Statist Socialism win out, given the relatively low level of separation between law and politics, the constitution is likely to continue to be subject to frequent change to reflect major changes in policies as determined by state leaders. Because Statist Socialists see rule of law as a means to strengthen the state, the role of the constitution in protecting rights will remain limited. As is the case today, the constitution might not be directly justiciable; individuals may avail themselves of the rights provided in the constitution only if such rights are implemented by specific legislation. On the other hand, even if Statist Socialism prevails, the constitution is likely to play a more important role as a baseline for measuring the legitimacy of state actions. To maintain credibility, the ruling regime will have to take the constitution more seriously.[118] As a result, the ruling regime will appeal to the constitution more often to justify its acts. Indicative of the transition toward rule of law, Beijing has already begun to appeal to the constitution at critical times, including when the government imposed martial law in 1989 and banned Falungong in 1999.

The constitution will play an even more important role if a Neoauthoritarian or Communitarian form of rule of law is adopted. Although the tension between strengthening and limiting the state would still be manifest in constitutional law, at minimum there would be greater emphasis on individual rights. As a result, the constitution would probably become directly justiciable.[119] It might also be subject to less change. The process for amending the constitution would differ, at least for Communitarians. Whereas nonelected state leaders would make the decision to amend the constitution for Statist Socialists and Neoauthoritarians, democratically elected representatives would make the decision in a Communitarian state.

Like constitutional law, the administrative law regime will vary depending on which version of rule of law wins out. Until recently in China, the main purpose of administrative law was considered to be to facilitate efficient administration. This view has now largely given way to the belief that administrative law must strike a balance between

protecting the rights of individuals and promoting government efficiency.[120] Although the tension between the two goals is evident in every
system, how China balances the two will depend on which of the various
alternatives of rule of law is adopted. To date, there is very limited public participation in the administrative law process. An Administrative
Procedure Law is being drafted, however, that will increase opportunities for public participation. Should the Communitarian or even the
Neoauthoritarian conception prevail, one should expect the law to allow
for greater public participation than if the Statist Socialist conception
prevailed.

Differences in conceptions of rule of law are also evident in the outcomes of administrative litigation cases. PRC courts have been reluctant to review aggressively administrative decisions. On the whole, they
have shown considerable deference to administrative agencies, for example, by interpreting very narrowly the abuse of authority standard
for quashing administrative decisions. In particular, they have been reluctant to interpret abuse of authority to include a concept of fundamental rights, as have courts in some Western liberal democracies.[121]
There are many reasons for the courts' deference other than ideology,
including institutional limits on the power of the courts, as discussed
in Chapter 9. But even setting aside the various institutional obstacles,
given the weak support for liberalism in China, PRC courts are less likely
than their counterparts in liberal democratic states to take full advantage of the abuse-of-authority standard as a means to protect individual
rights and rein in government officials at the expense of government
efficiency.

Criminal law is another area where outcomes are especially sensitive to differences in ideology and in the conceptions of rule of law.[122] In
light of the importance of stability to most Chinese,[123] civil and political
rights are likely to be subject to more limits than in liberal democracies.
Statist Socialists in particular will object to criticisms of the government
that challenge single party socialism. Accordingly, the continued persecution of dissidents is likely to continue if Statist Socialists (and perhaps
if Neoauthoritarians) prevail. At present, the authorities often rely on
reeducation through labor, an administrative sanction whereby dissidents may be detained for one to three years, with a possible extension
for another year, without many of the procedural rights afforded criminal suspects under the Criminal Procedure Law.[124] Although Liberal

Democrats object to reeducation through labor, others are likely to support it as necessary for social stability. Hence the complete elimination of reeducation through labor may not be politically feasible at this point. Arguably the best that Liberal Democrats can hope for at this point is that the process is changed to incorporate more procedural protections of the kind incorporated in the Criminal Procedure Law.

On the other hand, rule of law is not infinitely elastic. Any supporter of rule of law will question the manner in which the government has suppressed dissidents. Even in criminal cases, dissidents are often denied their rights under the Criminal Procedure Law, including a right to an open trial, to communicate with their lawyers and families, and so on.[125]

Falungong: a case study

The plight of Falungong demonstrates both the strength and limits of rule of law, and how differences in values and ideology affect outcomes. Falungong is a sect that combines Buddhist and Daoist ideas with traditional Chinese martial arts and health practices.[126] Falungong has been very popular among the elderly and those forced into early retirement or laid off as a result of economic reforms because it provides both spiritual sustenance to fill the moral emptiness that many people are feeling and also a social outlet – practitioners meet in the park every morning to do breathing and movement exercises, discuss Falungong texts, and just chat. By some estimates, there are 100 million believers in China, 40 million more than the number of Party members, though other estimates are as low as 10 million.[127] Indeed, many Party members are (or were) believers, as are (or were) members of the People's Liberation Army and government.[128] When a Beijing television station criticized the movement in June 1998, hundreds of believers turned out to protest.[129] In April 1999, 10,000 members surrounded the gates of Zhongnanhai where China's senior leaders reside to carry out a peaceful protest against government harassment.[130]

Party and government leaders were apparently taken by surprise at the size of the protest.[131] Worried by not only the number of believers but also by the ability of the sect to organize mass demonstrations without detection by the authorities, the government sought to infiltrate, discredit, and destroy the sect. The officially controlled media shifted into high gear. Stories of Falungong disciples cutting open their stomachs to look for the spinning dharma wheel or preventing loved ones from obtaining medical help were repeatedly broadcast on the television and radio and carried in all major newspapers.[132] Scientists were rounded up to denounce the sect's practices as superstition. The leader of the movement, Li Hongzhi, was accused of tax evasion, fraud, illegally organizing the May demonstration, and violating PRC laws regarding registration of religious and social organizations. China sought the assistance of Interpol and other nations in extraditing Li.[133] The police seized and destroyed more than 1.5 million books, videotapes, and compact discs containing Falungong teachings.[134] The sect was banned, and a number of regulations were passed limiting the activities of Falungong and other "cults."[135]

The Ministry of Civil Affairs issued a decision to ban the "Research Society of Falun Dafa and the Falungong organization under its control" as illegal organizations on July 22, 1999. On the same day, the Ministry of Public Security issued a notice that prohibited: displaying in any public place scrolls, pictures, or other marks or symbols promoting Falungong; distributing in any public place books, cassettes, or other materials promoting Falungong; gathering a crowd to perform group exercises and other activities promoting Falungong; sit-ins, petitions, and other means to hold assemblies, marches, or demonstrations in defence and promotion of Falungong; and fabricating or distorting facts, spreading rumors, or using other means to incite people and disturb the social order; organizing or taking part in activities to oppose the government's decisions. The Ministry of Personnel and the State Council also issued notices prohibiting civil servants from practicing Falungong. On October 30, 1999, the Standing Committee of the NPC passed the "Decision on Banning Heretical Organizations and Preventing and Punishing Heretical Activities." Casting a wider net, the Ministry of Public Security issued in November 1999 the "Regulations on Managing Mass Cultural and Sports Activities," banning gatherings by Qigong and other groups that threaten national security and public order.

Authorities moved quickly to carry out the crackdown, arresting publishers and sellers of Falungong books.[136] Falungong instruction centers and practice spots were closed down.[137] Police rounded up practitioners during their morning exercises, forced them into buses, and carted them off to stadiums on the outskirts of town, where they were detained, sometimes without water or food, for hours at a time.[138] Those that did not sign statements denouncing the campaign were detained for even longer periods and had their houses searched and possessions seized.[139] A number of people reportedly died as a result of torture while under detention.[140] Apparently in protest at the government's crackdown, five people reported to be Falungong adherents set themselves on fire in Tiananmen Square, leaving one dead and her twelve-year-old daughter, who subsequently died, badly burned.[141] Later, another Falungong practitioner died after pouring gasoline over himself and igniting it.[142]

A number of laws have been invoked against the organization and individual members. The "Falungong organization" and individual practitioners allegedly violated,[143] *inter alia*: (i) Articles 20 and 24 of the Constitution, which promote science and technology, by spreading nonsense that modern science is not a science; (ii) Article 296 of the Criminal Law and Articles 7 and 27 of the Law on Assembly, Processions and Demonstrations, which impose various restrictions on demonstrations, including prior approval; (iii) Article 300 of the Criminal Law, which prohibits the creation or use of heterodox organizations to undermine laws and regulations, cause death, defraud, or entice someone into illicit sexual relations,[144] and Article 24 of the Public Security and Punishments Management Regulations, which prohibits spreading superstition, causing death, rape, fraud, and disrupting the public order; (iv) publication laws that require approval for the publications of books; and (v) social organization registration regulations. PRC laws require all social organizations, including religious groups, to register with the government and impose a number of restrictions on religious practice and assembly in the name of social order and stability.[145] Falungong had been registered as a Qigong organization but withdrew from that organization in 1996. It then sought unsuccessfully to associate with various other organizations for registration purposes.

After the initial crackdown and the continued protests and suicides in Tiananmen, the list of violations was expanded to include: inciting and organizing Falungong practitioners to besiege state organs and news agencies; inciting people to commit self-immolation and suicide by urging them not to accept medical treatment; violating laws regarding the protection of minors; repeated violations of regulations regarding demonstrations and assembly as well as violations of the recently passed regulations banning Falungong by demonstrating in Tiananmen, distributing Falungong materials, defaming the government, and disturbing the social order.[146]

Assuming that the laws were passed in accordance with proper procedures by entities with the authority to do so under the constitution and organic laws, and that they are consistent with China's obligations under applicable international law, then the crackdown on an organization that did not register in accordance with PRC laws or violated the Criminal Law or other laws or regulations would *potentially* be consistent with rule of law. Of course, one could debate whether the laws themselves are "good laws," whether the crackdown on the sect was justified, and what the standard should be for determining whether the crackdown was justified.[147] But this involves one in the type of substantive moral issues that differentiate the various thick conceptions of rule of law. Representing the Statist Socialist position, Beijing argues that Falungong threatens social order by spreading superstitions; that it has deceived many people and resulted in more than 1,660 deaths;[148] and that in the past, religious sects have been the source of numerous uprisings that have led to the downfall of the reigning dynasty and social chaos.[149] As Perry and Selden note, historically kinship, village, and religious communities have played an important role in structuring patterns of resistance. Moreover, today, new sects such as the Heavenly Soldiers Fraternal Army (led by someone claiming to be the reincarnation of the Daoist deity the Jade Emperor) are tapping into both ancient styles of protest and Maoist principles and practices to challenge government policies.[150] Falungong members counter that it is a nonpolitical group whose teachings emphasize health practices that reduce stress. Liberal Democrats assert that Beijing should be more tolerant of religious and social groups and encourage the development of civil society by relaxing registration requirements, permitting a wider range of religious practices, allowing demonstrations without the prior approval of the public security bureau, and so on.[151] Although Communitarians and Neoauthoritarians are likely to be somewhat sympathetic to Beijing's complaints and the need for stability, and not likely to go so far as Liberal Democrats in relaxing restrictions on social groups, many would agree that the government's reaction was excessive.

It is not my purpose here to reach a final determination on the legal or moral merits of the ban on Falungong or the substantive merits of specific cases involving Falungong practitioners. Nor is it my purpose to reach a final determination on whether the ban and the various restrictions and sanctions comply with international law. Any such general conclusion would be premature given the conflicting factual accounts of the group's activities. Trying the case based on media reports, whether of the Western press or PRC press, strikes me as irresponsible.[152] Nevertheless, a few observations are in order, based on the information available, which at minimum demonstrates numerous violations of certain procedural rights.

First, it should be noted that China is not the only country that has banned sects or imposes criminal sanctions for organizing sects or proselytizing. France, for instance, passed a law in 2000 whereby (i) a civil court may order the dissolution of an organization convicted more than once of various enumerated offenses; (ii) a religious organization's criminal liability is increased when individual freedoms are jeopardized; (iii) any attempt to reincorporate or recreate a religious entity that had been dissolved is punishable by up to five years in jail; (iv) the establishment and proselytism of new religious movements is restricted so that minors, the elderly, and the ill are protected from such groups; and (v) the act of mental manipulation is punishable by up to five years in jail.[153]

Hong Kong, which has refused entry to Falungong members, apparently is considering passing a law similar to the French law in order to deal with Falungong.[154] Other countries, including Japan and Germany, impose various limitations on cults and their activities. All countries, including the USA, restrict certain religious practices that violate criminal laws.[155] Singapore, for instance, arrested and jailed or fined fifteen Falungong members for illegal assembly and obstruction to police duty.[156]

The UN and its human rights bodies have yet to address the issue of new religious movements and sects. As Abdelfattah Amor stated in his January 1998 report on the *Implementation of the Declaration on the Elimination of All Forms of Intolerance and of Discrimination Based on Religion or Belief*:

> As the Special Rapporteur's reports, including mission reports, have shown, the issue of "sects" or "new religious movements" is complicated by the fact that international human rights instruments provide no definition of the concept of religion and do not mention the concepts of sect and new religious movement . . . The Committee also points out that restrictions on the freedom to manifest religion or belief are permitted only if limitations are prescribed by law and are necessary to protect public safety, order, health or morals, or the fundamental

rights and freedoms of others and are not applied in a manner that vitiates the rights of freedom of thought, conscience and religion. The Committee also states that "limitations may be applied only for those purposes for which they were prescribed and must be directly related and proportionate to the specific need on which they are predicated. Restrictions may not be imposed for discriminatory purposes or applied in a discriminatory manner".

Added to this legal dimension is the general confusion regarding the term "sect" in particular. Although the idea of a sect was originally a neutral one and meant a community of individuals constituting a minority within a religion and having split from it, it often now has a pejorative connotation so that it is frequently regarded as synonymous with danger, and sometimes a non religious dimension when it is identified as a commercial enterprise. The term "sect" is therefore in need of further clarification, as are the terms "religions", "new religious movements" and "commercial enterprise".

It is crucial to look at this phenomenon objectively so as to avoid the two pitfalls of either infringing the freedom of religion and belief or exploiting freedom of religion and belief for purposes other than those for which it has been recognized and protected. Any action on this phenomenon presupposes understanding it by, first and foremost, determining its place in society and culture. The Special Rapporteur therefore recommends that the necessary resources be made available to enable him to initiate studies of the problem "of sects and new religious movements."

Analysis of whether the ban and other restrictions are consistent with international law would require at minimum an examination of whether the ban and each of the restrictions in question were (i) prescribed by law, (ii) for a legitimate purpose, specifically to protect public safety, order, health, or morals, or the fundamental rights and freedoms of others, and (iii) necessary or at least proportional for the purposes prescribed.

The first requirement would appear to be met, at least with respect to the ban of the Falungong and certain specific activities. (Arguably, subsequent legislation expanded the range of restricted activities and may have been applied retroactively, raising questions in such cases about the legality of retroactive sanctions.) As for the second requirement, there is a colorable claim that the ban on the sect was for the legitimate state purposes of protecting public safety, order, health, or morals, or the fundamental rights and freedoms of others.

As for the third requirement, reasonable people can disagree as to whether the ban was necessary and/or proportional.[157] Indeed, Zhu Rongji and Jiang Zemin reportedly disagreed over whether Falungong should be banned, with Jiang favoring a ban and Zhu favoring a more nuanced approach. It should be noted, however, that the doctrine of "margin of appreciation" allows states a certain latitude in determining what restrictions are necessary based on the particular circumstances of that state. The latitude varies according to the area of concern, with states tending to have more leeway regarding determinations of what is necessary to ensure national security and stability. In support of the crackdown, Beijing can point to the long history of religious groups destabilizing and overturning governments in China; the ruling regime's tenuous control on society as evidenced by the 1989 demonstrations and repeated demonstrations by laid-off workers and farmers; and the ability of Falungong to organize and mobilize large numbers of people in protest as indicated by their actions in surrounding Zhongnanhai and other public places such as television stations. Whether Falungong was initially politically oriented and/or Li Hongzhi had or has political motivations is relevant but not determinative as the movement could still be destabilizing even if it was not political in nature. Further, even if not originally political in nature, the movement could have become so. In fact, Falungong has become more of a threat to the regime recently, in part as a result of the government's crackdown. Li Hongzhi has increasingly called for resistance against the ruling regime and characterized the struggle in apocalyptic terms.[158]

At this point, the ruling regime appears to have painted itself into a corner. Having so publicly announced its intent to ban the sect, the regime must now carry out its threat or risk appearing weak, thereby emboldening other groups with a more overt political agenda. This is not to suggest of course that a government may bootstrap the legal basis for a crackdown by deliberately raising the stakes and threatening a crackdown. Clearly such an argument would only work in certain circumstances, where other organizations stand poised to challenge the regime and a sign of weakness could realistically lead to social disorder.

Even assuming the ban was legal, however, that would not mean that the government handled the situation in the most effective way. Rather than banning the sect, I believe the government should have allowed advocates and opponents of Falungong to debate publicly the pros and cons, and then brought charges against particular members allegedly guilty of fraud or manslaughter/negligent homicide or tax evasion or whatever the specific charge was. To be sure, the regime did mobilize religious leaders, scientists, legal scholars, and others to condemn the sect. The SPC and SPP also emphasized the importance of using court cases for propanganda purposes, to deter would-be practitioners and to convince nonpractitioners of the dangers of Falungong. However, the government's control of the official media, religious organizations, and academic institutions undermined to a considerable extent its efforts at convincing people that a harsh crackdown was necessary. The self-immolation of the six purported Falungong practitioners together with the graphic televised pictures of the young girl writhing in pain no doubt did more to turn public opinion against Falungong than all of the government's staged denouncements combined. Similarly, the lack of judicial independence and the limited reasoning in most judicial decisions undermines the effectiveness of court cases as a propaganda tool.

The government has declared that it would distinguish between leaders and followers, and reserve harsher criminal sanctions for the leaders while relying on persuasion to deal with the followers. Notwithstanding the announced policy to treat followers leniently, however, a number of persistent believers have been subject to administrative detention for up to fifteen days, subject to three years' detention pursuant to the administrative procedure of reeducation through labor or forcibly hospitalized in mental institutions.[159]

Although it might strike some as naive to expect that the ruling regime would have responded to 10,000 people surrounding Zhongnanhai in a measured way, Zhu Rongji and other leaders did apparently favor a more measured response. Unfortunately, the regime appears to have missed a good chance to gain legitimacy and strengthen the role of law, and to begin to articulate a sustainable long-term policy on just what kind of social activity will be tolerated. One of the advantages of taking on Falungong in public fora such as the media and the courts, particularly if the trials were conducted in an open and fair way, is that the government could establish some guidelines regarding the limits of free speech, freedom of assembly, and social activity that would be legally defensible and hence more likely to be accepted and considered legitimate by the public. If the government had wanted to be proactive rather than reactive, this would have been a good test case given that there is considerable public support for the government's decision to ban the sect, particularly after the self-immolations.

Setting aside the issue of whether Falungong should have been banned, the actions of the Supreme People's Court and some justice bureaus raise challenging questions about the minimal degree of judicial independence and separation between law and politics required to sustain even a Statist Socialist rule of law. SPC Vice President Liu Jiachen, after remarking that Jiang Zemin described the struggle to control Falungong as a political battle in which either the Party or the sect would survive, reported that the SPC had sent a notice to all courts calling on them to maintain stability.[160] The SPC instructed lower-level courts to uphold the correct political line and to apply the law to maintain the interests of the vast majority of the populace, social stability, and the authority of the state.[161] Liu then emphasized that the courts were to take great care in ensuring that cases were decided based on the facts and evidence and in accordance with law. The SPC even provided specific instructions regarding certain types of cases. Lower courts were ordered not to accept, without permission from the SPC, cases involving Falungong adherents or their family members who sue Li Hongzhi for civil damages. The SPC argued that such cases were primarily political in nature. Treating them as civil cases would politicize the judicial process and lead to adverse political consequences. Forcing the courts to decide whether the plaintiffs suffered direct loss from the activities would put the courts in a difficult position, presumably because a finding by the courts that there was no direct harm would undercut the Party's message regarding the danger of Falungong. Liu further observed that it would be difficult and time-consuming to provide notice to Li and to enforce any judgment against him, which could lead to discontent among the plaintiffs and the citizenry at large. The SPC also ordered lower courts not to accept administrative litigation cases brought by citizens whose "illegal" property – such as publications regarding Falungong – was confiscated. In addition, the SPC warned judges to strictly monitor the way in which cases were conducted to prevent Falungong members from using the courtroom as a public platform for spreading their views.

In response, at least in Beijing, the Bureau of Justice issued a notice requiring that all lawyers obtain the approval of the Bureau before agreeing to represent Falungong practitioners.[162] The notice also required lawyers to interpret the law consistently with the spirit of the central policies.

As is discussed in Chapter 8, there is considerable variation in the nature, degree, and institutional arrangements for achieving judicial independence even among Liberal Democratic rule-of-law states. For the SPC, in its capacity as supervisor of the judiciary, to call on lower courts to bear in mind the need for stability in deciding cases according to law is arguably acceptable under a Statist Socialist rule of law. Indeed, even the instruction to bear in mind the authority of the state is arguably acceptable under a Statist Socialist, Neoauthoritarian, and perhaps even a Communitarian rule of law.

Whether the SPC should instruct the courts not to accept certain cases because of their political nature is more debatable. In the USA and other countries known for rule of law, courts are able to rely on various legal doctrines such as the "political question" doctrine to avoid becoming embroiled in certain types of politically sensitive cases, particularly those that would put the judiciary at odds with other branches of governments or for which the judiciary is not competent to resolve the dispute because it does not yield judicially enforceable rights. US courts may also rely on the requirement that there be a case in controversy, a prohibition against collusive suits where there are no genuine adversary issues between the parties, and standing rules that require parties to show an injury in fact to be able to bring a claim. I do not mean to claim that US courts would necessarily bar suits by Falungong disciples based on the political question doctrine or these other doctrines. Nor do I intend to imply that a Statist Socialist rule of law or any other rule-of-law country must follow exactly US jurisprudence and case law. Rather, the point is that every legal system has some mechanisms for avoiding certain political issues that would excessively politicize the courts or put the judiciary on a collision course with other branches of government.

What does seem problematic is that the court would deprive citizens of their right to seek compensation for harms suffered and the paternalistic rationale provided by the SPC. If parties were injured by Li Hongzhi's teachings, why should they be deprived of their right to seek compensation? Surely they should be aware, or could be made aware by their lawyers or the judge handling the case, of the legal and practical difficulties in winning a civil case and in enforcing the judgment should they prevail. Similarly, if citizens are detained or their property is confiscated, they should have the right to challenge the legality of the decision to detain them or to confiscate the property. Of course, they might lose. Nevertheless, for the SPC to determine that they were in the possession of "illegal" property without a trial seems premature. Neither should parties have to wait for lower courts to obtain permission from the SPC to bring a suit, nor should lawyers have to wait for permission from the Beijing Bureau of Justice to agree to represent Falungong adherents. Even if citizens are able to challenge government acts in court as part of a criminal proceeding or administrative litigation, the government's overt interference in the judicial process runs counter to the principle of fair and impartial hearings.

Whatever the outcome on the substantive merits of whether the sect should be banned and whether the actions of the SPC and Beijing Bureau of Justice were consistent with judicial independence and rule of law, the way in which the crackdown was conducted undoubtedly violates any credible interpretation of rule of law. At minimum, rule of law requires that the detention and punishment of practitioners be in accordance with the law, and provides a basis for citizens to challenge state decisions.[163] Clearly torture, illegal detention, and other procedural violations are at odds with any tenable form of rule of law.[164]

In short, rule of law imposes certain restrictions on governments. On the other hand, the outcome of many particular issues will turn on the specific substantive moral, political, and economic beliefs that define a particular thick conception of rule of law. How much criticism of government should be allowed and under what circumstances? Should one be able to use offensive language in public? Should beggars be allowed on the street? Under what circumstances can someone be stopped and searched? Do the police need a warrant to enter your house and, if so, how and when can they obtain one? Is the right to silence absolute? Must individuals carry an identification card? Is the "anger of the people" a legitimate basis for meting out capital punishment? Are gay and lesbian marriages consistent with family values, a way of strengthening a newly envisioned family, or a threat to the very notion of family? Liberal Democrats, Communitarians, Neoauthoritarians, and

Statist Socialists will disagree over these issues, and indeed there will be many disagreements within any given school, just as there are disagreements over such issues in countries known for a Liberal Democratic rule of law.[165] Yet despite such disagreements, there is also considerable common ground about the basic requirements of rule of law as captured in thin conceptions, and general acceptance that rule of law differs from rule by law in that the former entails meaningful legal limits on the government actors.

Conclusion

Rule of law obviously may be defined in different ways; there is no single correct theory or interpretation.[166] How one defines rule of law depends largely on one's purposes. Investors seeking a basis for assessing legal system risk may be better served by a rule-of-law index that closely approximates the standards of a thin theory. Similarly, as discussed in Chapter 12, governments wishing to promote legal reform in China may find their offers to assist China in implementing rule of law more readily accepted if they are couched in terms of a thin rule of law rather than as part of a larger package of political reforms that includes democracy and an expansive liberal interpretation of civil and political rights. Conversely, human rights NGOs might find that a broader conception of rule of law suits their purposes better.

Needless to say, scholars and others are free to compare different rule-of-law types, and to argue for the superiority of one over the others. Indeed, given that there is considerable agreement about the basic requirements of a thin theory, these more fundamental differences are precisely the ones that deserve more scholarly attention. To date, there have been few attempts to develop in a systematic way alternatives to a Liberal Democratic conception of rule of law.[167]

Whatever one's views on the relative merits of the various thick conceptions of rule of law, for China's legal system to measure up favorably against the criteria of a thin rule of law would be a remarkable achievement. Before turning to the obstacles to the realization of rule of law, however, I pause to consider in the next chapter a variety of critiques of rule of law.

Table 1. A comparison of the four ideal rule-of-law types plus rule by law

Type of legal system	Economic regime	Political regime	Rights	Purposes of rule of law	Institutions/ practices	Rules
Liberal Democratic rule of law	Free market Minimum government interference and regulation Clear distinction between public and private Administrative discretion limited	Democratic elections at all levels; Neutral state Limited state Civil society as independent of state	Liberal Emphasis on civil and political Deontological view of rights as antimajoritarian trump on social good Freedom privileged over order Autonomy over social solidarity and harmony Freedom of thought and right to think over need for common ground and right thinking on important social issues More attention to rights than character-building, virtues, and duties	Limited government Prevent government arbitrariness Protect individual rights Predictability and certainty: economic growth, allow individuals to plan affairs Dispute resolution; protect property rights largely through formal legal system Government efficiency and rationality Legitimacy	High degree of separation between law and politics Independent and elected legislature Autonomous and independent judiciary, with life tenure for judges, appointment and removal relatively non-politicized Administrative law: mechanisms for reining in discretion, capable of holding even top leaders accountable; public participation; public can hold government officials accountable by throwing government out of office Independent legal profession	Protection of civil and political rights; no registration requirements for social groups; strong rights to protect accused in criminal cases

Table 1 (*cont.*)

Type of legal system	Economic regime	Political regime	Rights	Purposes of rule of law	Institutions/ practices	Rules
Communitarian rule of law	Market economy Managed capitalism More government intervention Public/private division not as clear More administrative discretion	Democratic, multiparty elections at all levels (eventually) Reject neutral state Larger role for state Civil society, but limits; groups free to go own way subject to general limits, although some groups, particularly commercial associations, may still establish corporatist or clientelist relations with government, but soft or societal form of corporatism	Asian values or communitarian Emphasis on indivisibility of rights, collective rights; economic growth at expense of rights (liberty tradeoff) Utilitarian or pragmatic conception of rights Stability and order privileged over freedom Social solidarity and harmony as important if not more so than autonomy Freedom of thought and right to think limited by need for common ground and consensus on important social issues	Balance between law as means of strengthening state and limiting state Stability Prevent government arbitrariness Protect individual rights Predictability and certainty: economic growth; allow individuals to plan affairs Government efficiency and rationality Dispute resolution, property rights protected through formal and informal mechanisms; more reliance on corporatist and clientelist ties Legitimacy	Moderate to high degree of separation between law and politics Independent and elected legislature Autonomous and independent judiciary, with life tenure for judges, appointment and removal relatively non-politicized; arguably likely to decide cases based on substantive agenda Administrative law: mechanisms for reining in discretion, capable of holding even top leaders accountable; but more deference to agencies in policy-making, emphasis on efficient government balanced to some extent by need to protect individual rights;	Broad laws to protect state: state-secrets laws; prohibitions against endangering the state Illiberal laws: limit civil society, freedom of expression: registration of social groups; or privilege group – no exclusion of tainted evidence

Type of legal system	Economic regime	Political regime	Rights	Purposes of rule of law	Institutions/practices	Rules
		Attention to character-building, virtues, and duties as well as rights			opportunities for public participation in rule making and interpretation; public can hold accountable by throwing out of office Independent legal profession, though perhaps monitored by state agency such as MOJ	Broad laws to protect state and social order: state-secrets laws; prohibitions against endangering the state Illiberal laws: limit civil society, freedom of expression: registration of social groups; or
Neo-authoritarian rule of law	Market economy Managed capitalism More government intervention Public/private division not as clear More administrative discretion	Single party rule; no elections or only at low level or appearance of genuine elections but limits on opposition party Reject neutral state Even larger role for state	Asian values or communitarian Emphasis on indivisibility of rights, collective rights; economic growth at expense of rights (liberty tradeoff) Utilitarian or pragmatic conception of rights; even more state-centered view	Balance between law as means of strengthening state and limiting state; favors strengthening Strengthen: Emphasis on stability; Predictability and certainty: mainly for economic growth, less to allow individuals to plan affairs	Moderate separation between law and politics Legislature not elected Judicial independence may or may not be limited Administrative law system, capable of checking government officials, professional civil service; more emphasis on rational government than protecting	

Table 1 (*cont.*)

Type of legal system	Economic regime	Political regime	Rights	Purposes of rule of law	Institutions/ practices	Rules
		Civil society, but limits, perhaps corporatist or clientelist relations with government	Stability and order privileged over freedom Social solidarity and harmony strongly outweigh autonomy Freedom of thought and right to think even more limited by need for common ground and consensus on important social issues; limits on right to criticize government Attention to character-building, virtues, and duties as well as rights	Government efficiency and rationality Dispute resolution, property rights protected through formal and informal mechanisms, more reliance on corporatist and clientelist ties Legitimacy Limits: Government must act in accordance with law Law to prevent government arbitrariness Protect individual rights, but not priority and limited	individuals; more deference to government in policy-making; opportunities for public participation and monitoring Legal profession supervised by MOJ	privilege group – no exclusion of tainted evidence
Statist socialist rule of law	Market economy Much government regulation High level of public ownership; more restrictions on private ownership	Single party rule; no elections or only at lowest levels; instead, a nomenklatura system of appointments	Emphasis on subsistence, economic growth at expense of rights (liberty tradeoff) State sovereignty	Emphasis on strengthening state Stability Predictability and certainty: economic growth	Moderate to low separation between law and politics Legislature not elected; Party influence on law-making process	Broad laws to protect state: state-secrets laws; prohibitions against endangering state

Type of legal system	Economic regime	Political regime	Rights	Purposes of rule of law	Institutions/ practices	Rules
		Much larger role for state No or very limited civil society, high level of corporatist or clientelist relations with government, hard or statist form of corporatism	Utilitarian or pragmatic conception of rights Reject neutral state Rights as grant from state Stability and order privileged over freedom Social solidarity and harmony over autonomy State prefers unity of thought to freedom of thought, right thinking to right to think; tendency to exercise strict thought control if possible; at minimum, strict limits against attacks on ruling party; emphasis on thought work to ensure common ground and consensus on important social issues	Law as means of enhancing government efficiency and rationality Dispute resolution, property rights protected through formal and informal mechanisms, more reliance on corporatist and clientelist ties Legitimacy Some limits on state: Government must act in accordance with law, but accept limits begrudgingly Prevent government arbitrariness Protect individual rights, but not priority and limited view of rights	Functional independence of judiciary; no interference by other branches; courts independent as opposed to judges, so adjudicative supervision; arguably likely to decide cases based on substantive normative principles defined by state; regime wants courts to serve Party interests Legal profession: subject to political requirements, partial independence, mainly due to corporatist nature of relationship with MOJ Administrative law: more discretion; more responsive to Party policy; system	Illiberal laws: limit civil society, freedom of expression: registration of social groups; or privilege group – no exclusion of tainted evidence; administrative penalties such as reeducation through labor

Table 1 (*cont.*)

Type of legal system	Economic regime	Political regime	Rights	Purposes of rule of law	Institutions/ practices	Rules
			Attention to character-building, virtues, and duties as well as rights		imposes weak limits on top leaders, limited public participation in rule making, interpretation and implementation; limited ability for media and public to monitor	
Rule by law	Could be planned economy, free market, or managed capitalism Government intervention high Public/private distinction nonexistent or unimportant Control by administrative policy and fiat	Single party rule, no elections Reject neutral state Totalitarian or authoritarian state No or very limited civil society, state dominated corporatist arrangements	Emphasis on subsistence, economic growth at expense of rights (liberty tradeoff) Socialist conception of rights as bourgeois; emphasis on duties, particularly duties to state Rights as grant of state Rights exist as programmatic goals only, no real protection of rights	Law is tool to serve interests of the state; Party's role not defined in law; law not intended to limit Party Law enhances government efficiency Law not meant to protect individual rights Dispute resolution, but many disputes settled	No minimal separation between law and politics Party policies supplant and trump laws Legislature not elected, just rubber stamp Courts not independent; Party determines outcome of specific cases; adjudicative committee used to enforce Party line; courts serve Party interests	Law relatively unimportant; much of day-to-day governance by policies Absence of many major laws – criminal law, contract law, civil procedure law Laws ignored

Type of legal system	Economic regime	Political regime	Rights	Purposes of rule of law	Institutions/practices	Rules
			State sovereignty Social solidarity and harmony over autonomy State enforces strict thought control; unity of thought over freedom of thought Strict limits against attacks on ruling party	administratively or by Party leaders rather than in courts Heavy reliance on mediation to resolve disputes "among the people," formal legal system used to suppress enemies Party members not subject to courts	Legal profession: lawyers as workers of the state; no independence; work in state firms; limited rights to defend accused Administrative law: main purpose is government efficiency; officials wide discretion, govern by fiat; no administrative laws provide individuals right to challenge government; no or extremely limited public participation in administrative process	

Notes

1   For overviews of legal reform in the last twenty years, see Alford (1999); Lubman (1999); Cai Dingjian (1999); *Legal System Building Reviewed* (1998).
2   In March 1999 the Constitution was amended to provide that China would be in the primary stage of socialism for a long time.
3   Shen Zongling (1998).
4   Liu Hainian (1996: 27–28). See also Chapter 10.
5   Fan Mingxing (1980), for instance, argued that law is always a tool and proposed that the terms *renzhi, fazhi, yifa zhiguo* 以法治国 (note the different first character than in the current formulation of *yifazhiguo* 依法治国) be given up in favor of people's democracy and socialist democracy.
6   Li Buyun (1998b: 133, 134); Liao Jingye (1980: 63–64). For a useful summary in English of the early rule-of-law debates, see Keith (1994: 8–18).
7   Li Buyun (1998a).
8   See, for example, Yang Mansong (1980).
9   See Wang and Cheng (1989).
10 Cited in Chen Jianfu (1999a: 72).
11 Both regulations have since been amended and upgraded to laws. PRC Administrative Supervision Law, adopted May 9, 1997 by the NPCSC [hereinafter, ASL]; PRC Administrative Reconsideration Law, adopted April 29, 1999 by the NPCSC [hereinafter, ARL].
12 For a discussion of socialist views of law in the '80s and early '90s, see Chih-yu Shih (1999: 10). As Shih notes, the class nature of law has been diluted even among those scholars who still discuss law in such terms.
13 According to the State Statistical Bureau, contracted FDI jumped from US $12 billion in 1991 to $58.1 billion in 1992. In 1993, contracted FDI rose to $111 billion, almost doubling the amount from 1992. See Economist Intelligence Unit (1997). Statistics from the Ministry of Foreign Trade and Economic Co-operation (MOFTEC) indicate contracted FDI was $69 billion in 1992; $123 billion in 1993; $93 billion in 1994; $103 billion in 1995; $81 billion in 1996; $61 billion in 1997; and $63 billion in 1998. Between 1978 and 1991, only 42,027 projects were approved. Then, in 1992 alone, approvals reached 40,050. The number of projects approved since then has been 83,505 (1993); 47,646 (1994); 37,104 (1995); 24,646 (1996); 21,183 (1997); 19,897 (1998). See http://www.moftec.com/official/html/statistics_data/utilization_ of_ foreign_capital.html; *1996 China Statistical Yearbook* (1997: 597).
14 Peerenboom (1998b: 35).
15 In practice, many arbitration commissions remain dependent financially and otherwise on local governments. Cohen and Kearney (2000).
16 For instance, a Securities Law was not passed until 1998. There is still no generally applicable bankruptcy law, though the Civil Procedure Law contains some generally applicable principles. Nor is there a general antitrust law or property law. In the administrative law area, legislators are now working on an Administrative Procedure Law, Administrative Licensing Law, and Compulsory Administrative Enforcement Law.

17   Li Buyun (1998b: 133). However, as discussed shortly, the early references to
     yifa zhiguo generally used a different *yi*, changing the meaning from ruling
     the country according to law to ruling the country by law, the latter having a
     more instrumental flavor. See note 5 above.

18   Wang Jiafu (1998). The speech was reportedly cowritten by several scholars,
     including Liu Hianian, Li Buyun, Wang Baoshu, Xia Yong, Liang Huixin, and
     Xiao Xianfu. See Keith and Lin (2001: 33).

19   Whether Wang and the others genuinely believed there was no conflict or they
     were simply trying to placate those within the Party who would be threat-
     ened by reforms is unclear. In general, as a matter of strategy, legal reform-
     ers try to portray reforms in a manner as nonthreatening to the Party as
     possible.

20   *Jiang Zemin's Congress Report* (1997). PRC scholars who have delivered lectures
     on law to Jiang and other senior leaders have noted that Jiang understands
     the difference between rule of law in which the law is supreme and a more
     instrumental rule by law. See Keith and Lin (2001: 28). Nevertheless, one may
     question the extent to which Jiang is genuinely committed to a rule of law in
     which law imposes meaningful restraints on even his own power, given the way
     law is shunted aside when dealing with dissidents, for example. Of course, Jiang
     may hold conflicting views. He may appreciate the benefits of rule of law but
     not want law to impose limits on his own power, as discussed in Chapter V.
     But if Jiang only wants the benefits of rule of law without being willing to
     bear the costs, then his commitment to rule of law would be questionable.
     As noted below, however, endorsing rule of law and incorporating it into the
     Constitution has certain costs. The public endorsement of rule of law fosters
     new norms that provide the basis for challenging the Party and the government.
     It also provides reformers with an opportunity to push for broader and more
     rapid reforms than Jiang and other leaders may have wanted. The Party and
     government can no longer simply ignore law without suffering a blow to their
     legitimacy. As law takes hold, the Party's ability to intervene in daily governance
     has become more limited, as evidenced by the increasing independence of
     people's congresses and agencies in law-making and rule-making, as well as by
     the decrease in direct Party intervention in particular legal cases. At minimum,
     Jiang's commitment to rule of law must be deep enough to offset these costs.
     In any event, as noted in Chapter 5, it would be a mistake to place too much
     weight on the views of senior Party leaders. The fate of rule of law turns on
     many other factors besides the degree of commitment to rule of law on the
     part of Party leaders.

21   The Party propaganda machine has begun to paint Jiang as the patron saint
     of rule of law. One lengthy article extolling Jiang's longstanding commitment
     to rule of law suggests that Jiang supported government in accordance with
     law as early as 1989. The article reports that in the wake of the Tiananmen
     crackdown, Jiang told a foreign correspondent that the Party should never
     replace the government and override law, and that China must stick to the
     principle of governing in accordance with law. The article then goes on to
     detail Jiang's more recent efforts to support rule of law. Moreover, it expressly

refers to Mao Zedong as the core of the first generation, Deng Xiaoping as the core of the second generation, and Jiang as the "core of the third generation," and defines Jiang's contribution as the core leadership of the third generation in terms of rule of law. See *Magazine Reviews Jiang Zemin's Efforts on Governing by Law* (2000).

22 See, for example, Gordon Chang (1999).

23 For a discussion of the programmatic nature of PRC constitutions, see Jones (1985); Cohen (1978).

24 Ghai (1993b).

25 Tsung-fu Chen (2000); Joon-Hyung Hong (2000).

26 Wang Guixiu (1998), among others, has observed that Deng's trip south stimulated economic reform but that political reforms have not kept pace with economic reform. Accordingly, he has called for greater political reform, including less centralization of power, separation of Party from government, and rule of law.

27 US Embassy Report (2000).

28 See, for example, Jiang Lishan (1997: 36–37); Liu Junning (1998).

29 Two major conferences were held on the topic, the first organized by the Chinese Academy of Social Sciences in Beijing from April 13–15; the second organized by the China Jurisprudence Association in Shenzhen from November 4–8. See *1996 Retrospective of Legal Research in China* (1997).

30 It is not my purpose here to canvass all of the various issues, arguments, or points of contention. For a general overview, see Albert Chen (1999a). For a discussion of debates through the early to mid-'90s, see Keith (1994); Shih (1999).

31 Gu Anliang, for instance, has argued that rule of law differs from both legal system and *yifa zhiguo*. "Yifa Zhiguo Jianshe Shehuizhuyi Fazhi Guojia Xueshu Yantaohui Jiyao" (1996: 5). Wu Jialing (1996) observed that the first part of the phrase *youfa keyi, youfa bi yi; zhifa bi yan, weifa bijiu* – there must be laws to rely on; where there is law, the law must be relied on; laws must be strictly enforced; violations of law must be remedied – referred to the reconstruction of the legal system whereas the last parts implied the rule of law.

32 Jiang Mingan (1998: 1–24). See also Dong Yuyu (1998: 55). Similarly, Guo Daohui has argued that rule of law implies supremacy of law and a value orientation, specifically democracy and justice. "Yifa Zhiguo Jianshe Shehuizhuyi Fazhi Guojia Xueshu Yantaohui Jiyao" (1996: 5–6).

33 Li Buyun (1998b: 135).

34 Li Shenzhi (1998); Li Shuguang (1998: 74). See also the comments of Gu Anliang, in "Yifa Zhiguo Jianshe Shehuizhuyi Fazhi Guojia Xueshu Yantaohui Jiyao" (1996: 5).

35 "Yifa Zhiguo Jianshe Shehuizhuyi Fazhi Guojia Xueshu Yantaohui Jiyao" (1996: 7) (comments of Guo Daohui).

36 Liu Junning (1998: 233).

37 See, for example, Wang Jiafu (1998: 127) (discussing supremacy of law); "Yifa Zhiguo Jianshe Shehuizhuyi Fazhi Guojia Xueshu Yantaohui Jiyao" (1996) (summarizing views of Gao Hongjun that rule of law requires, *inter alia*,

supremacy and autonomy of law). Liu Hainian (1998) argues that rule of law requires, *inter alia*, the supremacy of law, equality before the law, and administration in accordance with law. Li Buyun (1998c: 10–11) claims that rule of law requires that (i) laws must be based on the constitution; (ii) everyone must act in accordance with the law; (iii) the constitution and law are made in accordance with democratic procedures; (iv) all are equal before the law; and (v) judicial independence.

38 A quick comparison of the lists of rule-of-law elements of Fuller (1976: 39), Walker (1988: 23–42), Raz (1979: 214–19), Summers (1993), Fallon (1997: 8–9), and Finnis (1980: 270–71) reveals both common ground and some differences. Fuller emphasized that laws must be general, public, prospective, clear, consistent, capable of being followed, stable, and enforced. Preferring thick to thin theories, several PRC scholars begin with a list similar to Fuller's and then add various elements, some of them substantive. Xia Yong (1999), for example, adds supremacy of the law, judicial authority, and judicial justice to a list similar to Fuller's. See also Xu Xianming (1996: 37); Liu Junning (1998: 254–56).

39 However, as Raz (1979: 215–16) notes, laws may be both general and discriminatory (by treating all members of a particular race in the same way, for example). Raz does not object to particular rules but requires that they be made in accordance with open, clear, and stable procedures. But the generality of law is also based on rule-of-law ideals of limited government and that laws should apply to both officials and citizens alike. The requirement that law guide behavior is unclear as to scope: whose behavior?

40 Similarly, Joseph Raz's (1979) notion that people should be ruled by law and obey it suggests that the acceptability of the law and respect for law would be advantageous if not absolutely necessary (since people could conceivably be coerced to obey the law).

41 Walker (1988: 28). Su Li (1998: 6–7) makes a similar point. He observes that rule of law advocates in China have emphasized legislation, enforcement of law, and the strengthening of legal institutions, particularly the judiciary. He cautions, however, that there is more to rule of law. Because the state cannot rely solely on compulsory enforcement to ensure laws are obeyed, the particular customs, mores, ethics, and habits of a society are important to the successful implementation of rule of law. If laws are too far out of step with the values of the populace, they will not be followed in practice.

42 Long before Hart, Max Weber noted the relation between rule of law and legitimacy. He maintained that citizens were more likely to find clear, predictable laws that are fairly applied by an autonomous judiciary legitimate, and that they would be more likely to comply – without the need for coercion – with laws they found legitimate. See Rheinstein (1954).

43 Perhaps the most formal and substantively minimal basis for rule of law is that suggested by Raz (1979), who takes as his departure point the "basic intuition" that law must be capable of guiding behavior.

44 Walker (1988: 28–29); Fallon (1997: 8). See also below.

45 Dicey (1959).

46 Hayek (1944); Rheinstein (1954).
47 Gaus (1994).
48 Rheinstein (1954).
49 Raz (1979: 211).
50 Summers (1988: 161; 1993: 135–38).
51 Summers (1993: 137).
52 Fallon (1997: 43). See also Bindman (1988).
53 Sun Xiaoxia (1996: 12–13). Shen Guoming has also argued that traditionally
    there was too much emphasis on *quan* 权 – context-specific reasoning – rather
    than *jing* 经 – regularity and generality – and that China should now emphasize
    the formal aspects of rule of law over the substantive. Yifa Zhiguo Jianshe
    Shehuizhuyi Fazhi Guojia Xueshu Yantaohui Jiyao (1996: 10–11).
54 As we have seen, there were procedural requirements. However, the procedu-
    ral requirements were more oriented toward ensuring that officials properly
    performed their duties than toward protecting individual rights or interests.
    See, for example, Alford (1984); William Jones (1994). As Bodde and Morris
    (1967: 4) note, imperial law was only secondarily interested in defending the
    interests of one individual or group against another and not at all interested
    in defending individual or group interests against the state.
55 See, for example, Schwartz (1957).
56 Tay (1987: 562).
57 I discuss a number of theoretical concerns in Chapter 4.
58 Of course, even democracies that allow public participation may pass illiberal
    laws.
59 On the conception of rights in positivist rather than natural law terms, as
    something that is granted by the state and may be revoked by the state, see
    R. Randle Edwards (1986: 44–45). See also Li and Zhang (1997: 25).
60 Four further points are worth noting. First, in the rare case of a rule-of-law-
    compliant authoritarian government misusing law for normatively reprehen-
    sible ends, there surely are more direct and telling criticisms of the regime
    than that it is violating rule of law. A dictator who commits racial or ethnic
    genocide, or a corrupt authoritarian leader who misuses the legal system to
    advance the economic interests of his family and cronies while turning a blind
    eye to widespread abject poverty and human suffering, surely deserves to be
    subject to moral censure. But to claim that they are violating rule of law some-
    how misses the point. To focus on rule-of-law violations in the case of Hitler,
    Pol Pot, or South Africa highlights the wrong normative issues. Expanding
    the concept of rule of law makes such criticisms possible but at the price of
    obscuring the primary virtues of rule of law, thus increasing the likelihood
    that discussions of rule of law will get bogged down in disagreements over
    such insoluble issues as positive versus natural law, the nature of justice, the
    merits of socialism versus liberal democracy, and so on. Second, whether as
    an empirical matter Nazi Germany or apartheid South Africa met the stan-
    dards of a thin rule of law is much debated. Third, today countries and their
    legal systems are embedded in an international legal order. Accordingly, any
    country whose legal system meets the requirements of a thin rule of law must

comply with its international legal obligations, including its obligations with respect to human rights set forth in international treaties to which it is a party and those derived from international customary law and *jus cogens* principles. Although there is considerable debate as to the content of such rights, their interpretation, and how they are to be implemented, at minimum they provide some normative constraints on evil empires. Fourth, insisting on more robust normative constraints beyond what is required by international law leads to a slippery slope problem and the risk of imposing one's own values on others. Liberals may consider some laws that limit individual freedom in the name of maintaining social order morally repugnant and thus not "good laws." Communitarians, Neoauthoritarians, and Statist Socialists may simply disagree.

61 Wang Jiafu (1998: 117); Liu Junning (1998: 254–55); Xu Xianming (1996). It is not always clear whether the author means "good" in an effective, efficient, prudential sense, or "good" in a moral sense. The emphasis on the utility of the laws is understandable given the low quality of much legislation.

62 Berman (1983: 294; 1992: 43–60). Similarly, Butler (1991) distinguishes between law – *lex* – and justice – *jus* – and suggests that rule of law requires more than law and must incorporate elements of justice.

63 Liu Junning (1988: 233). One can question whether Liu is making too much of the use of *fazhiguo* as opposed to *fazhi*, particularly given that the Law on Legislation (art. 1) claimed that one of the purposes for the new law was to establish a socialist rule of law (*jianshe shehui zhuyi fazhi*). On the other hand, the law was amended at the last minute to incorporate explicit reference to the four cardinal principles (art. 3).

64 Liu Junning (1988: 255); Pan (2001); Xu (1996).

65 Dong (1998: 57).

66 Jayasuriya's (1999a, b) commendable effort to develop an alternative to a liberal conception of rule of law is marred by his strong-arm attempt to force all Asian countries into his statist model. As several of the other contributors point out, his model fails to capture the diversity within Asia. The model is even less applicable to three countries conspicuously missing from the volume – Japan, South Korea, and the Philippines. Nor does it fit well with Thailand, which is also only dealt with in passing.

67 I am indebted for this point to Xia Yong, Dean of the Chinese Academy of Social Sciences (CASS) Law Institute.

68 The debate over "Asian values" has tended to produce more heat than light. Supporters of universal human rights dismiss the claims of Asian governments as the self-serving rhetoric of dictators and misrepresent their position as a morally reprehensible and philosophically absurd anything-goes cultural relativism. Defenders of Asian values respond by attacking Western governments for past and present violations of human rights, and accuse them of cultural imperialism and ethnocentricity. Clearly, authoritarian regimes have at times used the rhetoric of Asian values for self-serving ends, playing the cultural card to deny citizens their rights and then fend off foreign criticism. Just as clearly there are many different voices within Asia, and anyone professing to speak for all Asians or of Asian values runs the risk of discounting these voices. Yet

we need to be careful not to dismiss Asian values as merely a cynical strategy seized on by authoritarian regimes to deny Asian citizens their rights. More philosophical and nuanced accounts point out that whatever Asian governments' political motivations, there are legitimate differences in values at stake. See, for example, Chan (1995); Bell (2000); Peerenboom (2000d).

69   As Davis (1998: 128–29) notes, communitarianism in Asia is different than in the West in that Western communitarians assume a liberal democratic framework. In contrast, Asian communitarians tend to be more conservative and authoritarian. Asian neo-conservative communitarians emphasize hierarchy and order rather than pluralism and a vibrant social discourse. Western communitarians put more stress on equality and liberation of the members of the community. For an attempt to develop a Deweyean–Confucian alternative to liberalism, see Hall and Ames (1999). De Bary (1998) argues for a more liberal form of Confucian communitarianism. Neither account addresses in any detail rule of law, political or legal institutions, legal rules, or outcomes with respect to particular controversial issues. Bell (2000) presents a detailed argument for a communitarian system based on non-liberal democratic traditions and values.

70   If China's legal system does at some point reach a stable equilibrium state, for example coming to rest in some form of Communitarian rule of law, it would become necessary to draw increasingly fine distinctions between the various forms of Communitarian rule of law. Similarly, the category of Liberal Democratic rule of law, while useful for comparative purposes with respect to competing conceptions of rule of law in China, is of little use without further specification for capturing competing conceptions of rule of law in Western developed liberal democracies. With respect to the USA for instance, one would need to distinguish between libertarians, conservatives, communitarians, and liberals, and then between various schools of liberals, including traditional liberal, social liberals, postmodern liberals, and so on. Moreover, particular issues might be more important in one context than another. For example, in the USA, the fault lines for competing conceptions of rule of law tend to run along the lines of different theories of constitutional interpretation. See Fallon (1997).

71   Jiang Zemin's report at the 15th Party Congress is an excellent example of Statist Socialism. See Jiang Zemin's Congress Report (1997). Neoauthoritarianism is generally associated with Zhao Ziyang and members of his think tank, though I use it in a more inclusive way. See, for example, Sautman (1992). For instance, it has resurfaced in the form of new conservatism and elitist democracy. Gu (1997) notes that despite some differences many new conservatives and elitist democrats share the same basic views of Neoauthoritarians with respect to democracy and the role of the elite in bringing about social order and harmony. Pan Wei, a political scientist at Beijing University, has put forth a "consultative rule of law" that incorporates and builds on the basic principles of Neoauthoritarianism, including the rejection of democracy in favor of a strong state, albeit with a much-reduced role for the Party. See Pan (2001). Liberal Democratic rule of law is well represented by Liu Junning and many

living abroad in exile, such as Baogang He. No PRC scholar has articulated a comprehensive theory of a Communitarian rule of law. However, PRC scholars have criticized aspects of the current system, taken exception to various features of a Liberal Democratic order, and developed pieces of a Communitarian alternative. For instance, Xia Yong has attempted to construct a virtue-based (*de*-based) theory of rights. Similarly, scholars in China and abroad have defended communitarian positions against liberal democratic critics, but generally on highly abstract philosophical grounds and primarily with respect to alternatives to democracy and liberal human rights. Moreover, the Communitarian position seems to capture the views of the majority of Chinese citizens who may wish for democracy, but not right now. (See Chapter 11 for survey data). They value individual rights but fear even more disorder and chaos. Accordingly, they draw a different balance than liberals between individuals' rights and group interests. This position is evident in the long-running debates over collectivism and the relation between rights and duties. See, for example, Shih (1999), for a discussion of such debates. Based on a survey of political speech and writings in China, Peng (1998) identifies four categories of political discourse that correspond to a large extent to the four positions I have identified here, with "radical democracy" representing the liberal democratic view, "established conservativism" representing statist socialism, "concerned traditionalism" representing neoauthoritarianism, and "alienated populism" representing a jaded and somewhat cynical, escapist communitarian view in which people are weary of political struggles and want to retreat into their own pursuits. One of the striking results is that despite radically divergent views on democracy, all four groups strongly support rule of law. However, while the radical democracy faction supports diverse opinions and free speech, the others do not.

72   In some cases, I have drawn on current institutions as well as existing rules, practices, and outcomes to demonstrate features of the various positions, particularly Statist Socialism and Neoauthoritarianism but also to some extent Communitarianism and rule by law. Although the current system does not exhibit many features of a Liberal Democratic order, it is possible to appeal to Western countries for concrete "real life" examples. The Communitarian variant is the most hypothetical (in the sense of not being grounded in existing institutions and practices) of the positions as the current system remains more state-dominated than the communitarian view would allow. One advantage of defining a Communitarian rule of law in a rigorous way is that it becomes possible to design a survey instrument to gauge the degree of support for it among the populace.

73   Xiao Gongqin, one of the leading New Conservatives theorists, considers himself a Neoauthoritarian. However, his support for the Party also aligns him with Statist Socialists. On New Conservatives, see Goldman (2000); McCormick and Kelly (1994).

74   Kenneth Warren (1982: 310), for instance, points out that "administrative agencies, much to the dismay of those who endorse a clear separation of powers in government, have legislative, judicial and administrative powers."

75 Glendon, Gordon, and Osakwe (1994: 56).

76 Chinese commentators often describe the Mao era, or at least the Cultural Revolution period, as rule by man (*renzhi*). However, even during the Cultural Revolution, the legal system continued to exist and limp along. Claims that China fell into a state of legal anarchy and of legal nihilism are overstated. In any event, my concern here is not with the distinction between rule of man and Mao era rule by law. More relevant for present purposes is the opposite end of the rule-by-law spectrum, where rule by law arguably butts up against rule of law.

77 See Chapter 4 for a critique of the view that rule by law should be defined in terms of the actual performance of the legal system rather than in terms of the conceptual issue of whether law is meant to limit the state and state actors.

78 For an assessment of the variety of capitalism literature, see Hall (1999); Hollingsworth and Boyer (1999). On the importance of institutions to economic development, see generally North (1990).

79 Gillespie (1999: 118, 123). See also Chapter 5.

80 Several of the essays in Stiglitz and Yusuf (2001) debate the pros and cons of a technocratic bureaucracy deciding industrial policy. Most are critical. Surveying the challenges faced by regulatory bureaucracies throughout Asia and the response of governments after the Asian financial crisis, Yusuf (2001: 25–26), for instance, argues that the heyday of technocratic bureaucracies overseeing development may be past. Yet others are more positive (Jomo 2001) or at least agnostic (Stiglitz 2001).

Perkins (2001) argues that the state-led approach that seemingly worked for Korea and Japan is not suitable for China in that China is a much larger economy. Thus policy-makers would have to direct an industrial sector larger than that of France. Moreover, much of the industrial output now comes from private enterprises, TVEs and small and medium size companies. In addition, China's bureaucrats, far from being market-savvy technocrats, were trained as Soviet-style central planners. In any event, China's bureaucrats now confront a different world than did Japanese bureaucrats in the 1960s and 1970s. Globalization and the strengthening of the international trade regime have changed the rules of the game. Some of the techniques relied on by Japan and South Korea, such as tariffs and quotas to protect particular industries and limitations on foreign investment, are no longer tolerated. While Perkins (2001: 288) suggests that China should continue to reduce government intervention, he notes that old habits die hard, and there is likely to be more government intervention than in "the case of some ideal free-market economy."

81 Sautman (1992). Timmermans (1996) notes that former Western European dictatorial states all opted for a parliamentary system where parliament was strong and the president largely ceremonial or weak, whereas Central Asian republics favored a strong presidency in the belief that political and economic reforms are more easily achieved with a strong executive. For a critique of the alleged advantage of authoritarianism, see Maravall (1994).

82 For a defense of the neutral state, see, for example, Dworkin (1978: 127); *West Virginia Board of Education* v. *Barnette*, 319 US 624 (1943). For a critique of the claim that liberal democracy is neutral, see Perry (1988: 57–73). That democracy should be neutral is contested by both communitarians and conservatives. See, for example, Sandel (1996b).

83 See Chapter 11 for survey data in support of this position.

84 The difference between hard or statist corporatism and soft or societal corporatism is discussed in Chapter 7. See also Schmitter (1974); Wiarda (1997).

85 Rawls (1971); Dworkin (1978).

86 Donnelley (1989) refers to the perceived need to limit individual civil and political rights to ensure development as the liberty tradeoff.

87 It is not logically necessary that Communitarians prefer stability over freedom whereas Liberals prefer freedom over stability. Nevertheless, as an empirical matter it appears Liberal Democrats value freedom more while Communitarians place more emphasis on order and stability. As such, it is in the end a value preference.

88 Nathan (1986b); Edwards (1986).

89 Ghai (1994).

90 See "Students' Attitudes toward Human Rights Surveyed" (1999), the results of which are discussed in Chapter 11.

91 Lynch (1999a). "Thought work" refers to all attempts to transmit socialist ideology, the Party line, and Party policies, and to control or eliminate competing ideas, concepts, and ideologies.

92 For an analysis of the likelihood of China becoming unstable and the factors that might contribute to it, see Shambaugh (2000). The authors discuss conflicts among the ruling elite and government–military relations, the declining role of the Party at the grass-roots level, economic reforms, urban and rural unrest, and minority regions.

93 Many legal reformers, while emphasizing stability, see rule of law as limiting the power of the Party and the state. An article in the *People's Daily*, for instance, emphasizes that rule of law serves stability by reining in wayward Party and government officials, holding cadres and Party leaders accountable for their actions, and alleviating tensions between cadres and the masses at the grass-roots level. The article also stresses that rule of law serves public order and stability when the police, procuracy, and judiciary act in accordance with law, when disputes are handled fairly, impartially, and in a transparent manner, and when the legal regime provides certainty and predictability in economic matters. In short, linking rule of law to stability and public order does not necessarily entail support for Statist Socialism. See *Renmin Ribao on Stability, Law Enforcement* (1998).

94 Wang Jiafu (1998: 119).

95 In fact, the transition from Deng to Jiang was relatively smooth, as has been the recent shuffling of top leaders, including Li Peng's move from the State Council to the NPC when his term expired. To be sure, one could question what, if anything, rule of law had to do with it. (One could raise similar questions about the Bush–Gore presidential elections and the US Supreme Court's role

in the elections.) Nevertheless, the fact that there are term limits does provide the backdrop against which political maneuvering occurs. In any event, the hope is that in the future succession will proceed in accordance with legal rules and that when senior officials reach the end of their terms they will step down or move to another post as required by law.

96   See Chapter 6.

97   Yasheng Huang (1996).

98   Noting that the Party contends that stability entails the continued dominance of the Party, Stanley Lubman (1999) has pointed out that rule of law coexists in the Constitution with the thought of Mao Zedong and Deng Xiaoping. Shi Qinfeng has remarked that whereas the purpose of rule of law is to limit the state, in China the purpose of rule of law is stability to ensure that the current regime remains in power. This view is typical of the Statist Socialist variety but not of the others. "Yifa Zhiguo Jianshe Shehuizhuyi Fazhi Guojia Xueshu Yantaohui Jiyao" (1996: 13).

99   Li Shenzhi (1998: 21).

100   Yu Keping (1998: 49–53).

101   Raz (1979: 221); Finnis (1980: 272); Liu Hainian (1998).

102   Peerenboom (1998a).

103   See, for example, Liu Hainian (1998).

104   As discussed more fully in Chapter 4, Jiang Zemin seems to believe that rule of law can help shore up the regime's legitimacy in a more direct way by providing a normative basis for a market economy.

105   See, generally, Kairys (1998).

106   Tay (1990).

107   See Chapter 5. This is not to claim of course that the Party is on all fours with ruling parties in parliamentary liberal democracies.

108   Over time, individual judges might be given more authority. However, Neoauthoritarians worry that for the moment allowing poorly trained judges to decide cases by themselves could result in incorrectly decided cases and also more corruption as it is easier to bribe one judge than a panel of judges.

109   See, for example, Pan Wei (2001). Statist Socialists might also favor an honest and professional civil service, though they may put greater emphasis on ideology and political factors in appointing civil servants and prefer that Party discipline committees be responsible for dealing with corruption among senior officials.

110   Communitarians share the same basic view of the legal profession as the Neoauthoritarians, though they would allow the legal profession a higher degree of autonomy and view the legal profession's obligations as being more toward society than the state. See Chapter 8.

111   Jayasuriya (1999a: 19) argues that judicial independence in East Asia is influenced by a statist ideology that rejects the liberal notion of a neutral state in favor of a paternalistic state which grounds its legitimacy in its superior ability to fathom what constitutes "the good" for society. Thus, he claims, courts are more likely to serve as an instrument for the implementation of the policy objectives of the state and ruling elite.

112   In *Cohen* v. *California*, 403 US 15 (1971), the US Supreme Court held that an
      individual's right to free speech extends to wearing a jacket with "Fuck the
      Draft" written on it, even though others may find such language offensive.
113   In *Texas* v. *Johnson*, 491 US 397 (1989), the US Supreme Court held by a nar-
      row five-to-four margin that laws prohibiting flag-burning unconstitutionally
      restricted free speech. In contrast, the Hong Kong Court of Final Appeal held
      that such laws were consistent with the PRC Constitution, Basic Law, and the
      free-speech provisions of the ICCPR. [1999] 3 HKLRD 907 (Court of Final
      Appeal). Several countries that are signatories to the ICCPR, including some
      Western countries generally considered liberal democracies, impose restric-
      tions on flag-burning. Germany, Italy, Portugal, and Norway, as well as Japan,
      all impose such restrictions.
114   North (1990).
115   Indeed, focusing on each dimension separately is somewhat misleading. While
      different regime types tend to be correlated with different institutions and
      rules, in some cases advocates of alternative conceptions of rule of law might
      espouse seemingly similar purposes or adopt similar institutions or rules. Yet
      in practice the outcomes will still differ widely. Because there is generally
      some degree of indeterminacy to legal rules, this is to be expected. Thus, even
      in the USA for example, conservative judges are likely to come to different
      conclusions in some cases than liberal judges notwithstanding the fact that
      they share the same institutional context.
116   Ghai (1993b).
117   Nathan (1986b: 112).
118   Noting that the constitution is often not paid sufficient heed in practice, Jiang
      Zemin emphasized the importance of the constitution in the new legal order
      and called for all sectors to take the constitution seriously. See "Deng's Theory
      Incorporated" (1999).
119   Many PRC scholars maintain that the constitution should be justiciable. See,
      for example, Wang Chenguang (1998). Interestingly, the Supreme People's
      Court recently issued a potentially landmark interpretation in its reply to
      an inquiry from Shandong High People's Court. The Supreme Court stated
      that the plaintiff's basic right to an education as provided in the constitution
      should be protected even though there was no implementing law regarding
      the right to education. While a number of questions remain as to the Court's
      interpretation, it would appear that the decision opens the door to parties to
      directly invoke the constitution when at least their basic (*jiben*) constitutional
      rights have been violated, even in the absence of implementing legislation, thus
      making the constitution directly justiciable. See the Supreme Court's Reply,
      No. 25, issued on August 13, 2001.
120   See, for example, Luo Haocai (1997).
121   Compare Craig (1994: 17–18), claiming that the standard of ultra vires is being
      reinterpreted along lines consistent with respect for fundamental rights in the
      UK, with Minxin Pei (1997a: 832, 856 tbl.12), reporting that abuse of authority
      was invoked in only 16 of 219 cases where PRC courts quashed the illegal acts
      of agencies, in comparison to 60 times for exceeding legal authority, 48 for

insufficient principal evidence, 40 for incorrect application of law, and even 32 for violation of legal procedures.

122   Maslen (1998: 286–92) goes so far as to question whether Japan's criminal law system may be described in terms of rule of law given that actual practices by police, prosecutors, and judges often invalidate or at least limit the rights provided to the accused under law. Maslen appears, however, to assume that rule of law requires a liberal interpretation of the rights of the accused, and that any practice that deviates from such an interpretation is inconsistent with rule of law. Although it may very well be the case that some aspects of the criminal system are at odds with any reasonable interpretation of rule of law, it may also be the case that Japan's system meets the basic requirements of a thin rule of law, but not a thick liberal conception.

123   See the surveys cited in Chapter 11.

124   Hecht (1996: 65–67).

125   Hecht (1996: 65–67). See also, "Human Rights Watch World Report 1998: China" (1998).

126   See Kuhn (1999).

127   Chu and Kuhn (1999: A1). There are approximately 62 million Party members. *Elusive Falungong Leader Says Mass Following Rattles China* (1999).

128   Chu (1999c). One report claimed that the Party itself estimated the number of Party members who believed in Falungong to be 400,000. *'Three-Pronged Purge' of Falungong Cited* (1999).

129   Chu (1999b). The station eventually backed down and fired the reporter.

130   Chu (1999b).

131   Chu (1999b). However, other reports claim that as early as 1996 the State Press and Publications Administration issued a circular suggesting that Falungong books be confiscated and banned, and that the China Qigong Research Society had removed Falungong from its membership. *Article on Truth of Falungong Gatherings* (1999).

132   Chu (1999c) reports that the official media claimed 750 people died as a result of the sect's teachings.

133   "China Offers Reward in Sect Crackdown" (1999).

134   Chu (1999c).

135   See Amnesty International (2000).

136   Amnesty International (2000).

137   Beijing Claims Victory against Sect (1999).

138   "China Holds More Members of Banned Meditation Group" (1999); Chu (1999c).

139   Chu (1999a).

140   Amnesty International (2000) claims that "there are many reports that detained Falun Gong practitioners have been subjected to torture or ill-treatment, and at least ten people have died in police custody in circumstances which are unclear, some reportedly due to torture." See also Johnson (2000a); US State Department Country Reports on Human Rights Practices for 1999 (2000).

141   Although Falungong spokespersons claim that suicide is not permitted according to Falungong teachings and suggested that the deaths might have

been staged by the government, the Hong Kong-based Information Center for Human Rights and Democracy reported that all but the twelve-year-old girl had protested the government's crackdown in Tiananmen Square previously. Other human rights activists have also claimed that the self-immolations were in protest over the crackdown. See Philip Pan (2001). The government-controlled PRC press has linked the individuals to Falungong, quoting family members and acquaintances who claimed that they were Falungong practitioners and claiming to have seized from their homes books, videotapes, flyers, and other Falungong materials. See *Xinhua Reports on Self-Immolation, Blames Falungong* (2001); *Xinhua Reports Family Background of Tiananmen Suicides* (2001).

142 See *Another Self-Immolation* (2001).

143 *Official on Laws Violated by Falungong* (1999); see also *Shanghai Legal Scholars Criticize Falungong* (1999).

144 Article 300 of the Criminal Law punishment is three to seven years imprisonment, except in especially serious cases, where the punishment is not less than seven years. On October 30, 1999, the SPC and SPP jointly issued an interpretation that clarified Article 300, the Interpretation on Questions Concerning the Concrete Application of Laws in Handling Criminal Cases of Organizing and Making Use of Heretical Organizations. The Interpretation noted that the following activities were prohibited under Article 300: besieging government institutions, holding illegal assemblies or demonstrations, and instigating civil disobedience. The Interpretation also noted that using illegal organizations to scheme, carry out, or instigate activities to endanger national unity, split the country, or undermine the socialist system would be punished in accordance with the provisions in the Criminal Law regarding state security. In addition, the Interpretation explained that "causing death" includes deceiving people into fasting, inflicting wounds on themselves, or foregoing medical treatment, resulting in their death. "Serious" cases punishable by at least seven years included establishing such illegal organizations or recruiting members across provinces or collaborating with overseas groups or else inciting members to violate laws resulting in serious consequences. Causing at least three deaths or injury to many people was also deemed serious.

145 Social Organization Registration and Management Regulations, promulgated by the State Council on Oct. 25, 1998; PRC Religious Activities Site Management Regulations, promulgated by the State Council on Jan. 31, 1994; PRC Assembly, March and Demonstration Law, adopted by the NPCSC, Oct. 31, 1989.

146 See *RMRB Article Lists Laws Violated by Falungong* (2001).

147 Should the standard be clear and present danger? If so, how clear must the danger be? How immediate? Should there be a formula that calculates an expected value by multiplying the magnitude of the possible harm (e.g., civil war, chaos) versus the likelihood of its occurrence? Or should there be some other formula? The history of US First Amendment jurisprudence provides an interesting comparison. Over time the standards have changed. As noted, before the 1940s, US courts regularly found against those seeking to claim protection under the First Amendment. See Rabban (1981).

148 Jin (2001).

149   See the remarks of Yu Shuning, spokesperson for the PRC Embassy, on Talk of the Nation, transcribed in *Why Falun Gong Has The Chinese Government So Nervous* (1999). The Chinese Ambassador in London asserted that the ban was aimed at protecting people's human rights and maintaining social stability. See *PRC Envoy: Falungong Ban Aimed at Defending Human Rights* (1999).

150   Perry and Selden (2000).

151   See, for example, Kolender (1994).

152   For a critical account of how both the Western press and PRC press have covered Falungong, see Rahn (2000). Rahn notes that the Western press has emphasized, with certain exceptions, variations on the theme of a repressive government abusing human rights, ignoring or downplaying controversial aspects of Li's teachings, and arguments about the potential dangers of Falungong. The PRC press, for its part, has waged an all-out war against Falungong reminiscent of earlier political campaigns waged during the Mao era. She also notes that the information from the Falungong organization itself has been self-serving and in some cases deceptive and misleading, particularly with respect to the receipt of "awards" from local governments in the USA. Such awards, which are routinely given out by local governments at the request of organizations without any investigation of the organization whatsoever (and in many cases simply repeat language drafted by the organization itself), have been used by Falungong to create the mistaken impression that US officials support Li Hongzhi's teachings. Rahn catalogues a number of Li's teachings that many are likely to find offensive or absurd, including the emphasis on Li's absolute authority and the need to accept his beliefs in total without questioning if one is to be a "true practitioner"; the need for Falungong practitioners to avoid contact with, and therefore contamination by, degenerate nonpractitioners; the belief that if one follows his teachings and practices Falungong, one will not get sick and therefore not need medicine; conversely, the notion that relying on medicine demonstrates a lack of faith and commitment; and the belief that there are creatures living in the ocean who are half-human, half-fish. Others have criticized Li and his organization for their apocalyptic teachings and homophobia. Rahn concludes by calling for independent verification of the various claims and a more well-balanced, comprehensive coverage of the issues.

153   See Smith (2000).

154   See Cheung (2001).

155   The USA, however, does not prohibit cults based on the content of their beliefs alone.

156   See *Singapore Court Imprisons Seven, Fines Eight Falungong Activists* (2001).

157   With respect to the proportionality of particular restrictions adopted by the regime in this case, whether each of the restricted activities was justified and their punishments proportional for the intended purpose would require a detailed analysis of each activity that is beyond the present scope.

158   See Pomfret (2001).

159   See Amnesty International (2000); Munro (2000).

160   Liu (1999).

161 Liu (1999). See also Notice Concerning the Implementation of the "Decision of the NPC Standing Committee on Banning Heretical Organizations and Preventing and Punishing Heretical Activities' and the SPC/SPP Explanation, issued November 5, 1999.

162 Beijing Bureau of Justice (1999). Lawyers in Shanghai and Nanjing that I contacted stated that they did not receive a similar notice.

163 Authorities reportedly banned family members from visiting arrested Falungong members and disconnected the telephone lines of those arrested to prevent family members from contacting overseas media. See *Key Falungong Members Face Trial in September* (1999).

164 Amnesty International (2000).

165 Berger (2000), for instance, discusses the impact of legislation limiting the right to silence in Great Britain, and also notes that the academic debate over the merits of the right to silence continues. Notwithstanding a variety of perspectives in the USA, the US position on many issues is often extreme even among other Western liberal democracies.

166 In Chapter 4, I respond to the suggestion of some commentators that the term rule of law should be reserved only for Liberal Democratic versions and that it should not be stretched to include alternative conceptions.

167 For a welcome exception, see the essays in Jayasuriya (1999c).

4

Rule of law and its critics

Rule of law is not without its critics. Skeptics claim that the efforts to promote rule of law in China are likely to fail, just as the earlier attempts of the law and development movement in the 1960s and '70s to export rule of law to developing states failed. Some PRC scholars caution that the rule-of-law movement has been largely a top-down effort and thus is not likely to be supported when legal reforms begin seriously to restrict the authority of the ruling regime. They also worry that as a product of modern Western states, rule of law cannot be transplanted to China, or that implementing rule of law will disrupt the existing social order and hence may be too costly. Critiques of rule of law from leftists in China emphasize the class nature of law, while Critical Legal Studies scholars (CRITS) abroad contend that law is a mask for oppression and serves the interests of the ruling elite. Even liberal reformers worry that in the absence of democracy and pluralistic forms of political participation, implementing rule of law will serve authoritarian ends and bolster the legitimacy of the Party. Others, as will be discussed in Chapter 10, question whether China needs rule of law and in particular whether rule of law is necessary for economic development.

In this chapter, I examine the critics' arguments and suggest that while implementing rule of law is not an answer to all of China's social, political, economic, or even legal problems, on balance it represents a major step forward relative to the status quo. First, however, I take up a number of theoretical issues that have led some legal philosophers to question the utility of rule of law as an analytical concept and some commentators to dismiss rule of law as a meaningless slogan. For instance, can the minimal conditions for rule of law be sufficiently specified to be useful? Should China's legal system at this point be described as rule by law, as in transition to rule of law, or as an imperfect rule of law? How do we know that the goal of legal reforms in China is rule of law as opposed to a more efficient rule by law or some third alternative? Given the many different interpretations of rule of law, should we just stop referring to rule of law altogether?

Theoretical issues

Notwithstanding considerable consensus about the general requirements of a thin conception of rule of law, there are still several areas of controversy that affect both thin and thick versions. Most fundamentally, there are a number of jurisprudential issues that go to the heart of rule of law by problematizing law itself. Simply put, rule-of-law theories must grapple with the perennial issue of what is law? Two sets of controversies are particularly relevant. First, the debate over positive versus natural law resurfaces in the distinction between thin and thick theories. To sum up a complex debate, generally speaking, thin theories are based on positive law, whereas natural law leads to thick theories for reasons discussed in the previous chapter (though not all thick theories need be predicated on natural law).

The second debate centers on whether law should be defined in terms of formal (state) law or more broadly in terms of binding norms and actual behavior.[1] The legal anthropologist Bronislaw Malinowski, for instance, defined law as a "class of binding rules which control most aspects of tribal life, which regulate personal relations, the exercise of power and of magic, the status of husband and wife and of their respective families."[2] In this way, social scientists were able to claim that all societies had law, avoiding the appearance of cultural chauvinism. The problem, however, is that unless "legal norms" are distinguished from other types of norms, the term *law* becomes virtually meaningless as an analytical tool. More recently, some legal pluralists have encountered the same problem by collapsing the distinction between formal law and "informal law." One way to avoid the difficulty, adopted by Weber, is to define law in terms of rules subject to coercive enforcement by authorized (state) actors.[3] Critics point out, however, that not all laws on the books are enforced and in many cases there is not even a credible threat of enforcement. This observation leads in two directions. The first path, taken here, emphasizes the pedigree of laws, that they are rules made in accordance with particular legal procedures, à la Hart, or the recognition of certain norms as laws by those within legal institutions, à la Paul

Bohannan.[4] The other path focuses on actual behavior, and thus denies that such norms are actually laws in the relevant sense. The approach may, but need not, result in a turn away from legal institutions and the state back toward a broad definition of law in terms of social norms.

There is no single correct definition of law. How one defines law will depend on one's purposes. The narrower formal (state) conception of law is better suited to present purposes than a broad social definition of law for several reasons. First, rule of law implies the ability to distinguish at least roughly between what is legal and what is not. Second, the primary focus of this book is institutional development and obstacles to rule of law resulting from shortcomings in China's legal institutions. These institutions are central to the formal state conception of law. Third, as discussed shortly, while China's customary norms and informal mechanisms for resolving disputes in some ways may complement rule of law, they are in other ways at odds with the implementation of a thin rule of law.

The issue of what is law arises in another context as well. I have emphasized the role of rule of law in imposing meaningful restraints on government actors and in limiting arbitrary state action. Historically, the emphasis on law's role in limiting the state is based on the liberal Lockean tradition that emphasizes the supremacy of the law and the equality of all before the law (though even Locke allows that government authorities have considerable discretion and thus may act outside the law, even against it, provided they do so for the public good). In contrast, Hobbes and Austin favored the view that whatever the sovereign says is the law is the law. Thus for Hobbes, the sovereign authority had to be above the law.[5] Similarly, the emperor in the Imperial Chinese legal system had the power to make law; and, at least in the view of some commentators, the Party's leading role means that it must to some extent be above the law in that the Party plays an important role in determining what the laws will be.

In all systems, the entities with the power to make or change laws are in some sense beyond the law. However, there may still be laws that limit their authority to make or change laws. The view that the sovereign is above the law and determines the law was modified slightly but significantly by positivists such as H.L.A. Hart for whom the touchstone for what constitutes a valid law is whether the rule was promulgated in accordance with proper procedures. Such procedures, and thus the authority for law, can be traced back to a basic legal norm or a "rule of recognition."[6] A dictatorial regime therefore could exercise legal authority and make law, as long as it complied with the procedural requirements for making law. Moreover, the rulers could be required to follow laws once made. Such a system is compatible with rule of law. On the other hand, a system in which the ruling regime's pronouncements simply have the force of law and the regime is not itself bound by such laws is better characterized as a rule by law or *Rechtsstaat*.

In any event, whether or not a legal system based on the rule of recognition that "whatever the sovereign (or the CCP) says is the law is the law" is consistent in theory with a thin rule of law, in practice any such system is likely to fall short of the other requirements of a thin theory. In most cases, concentration of power in the hands of a single person or party would result in arbitrary and conflicting laws, rapid change in the laws, and difficulty implementing such laws, and thus a large gap between law and practice.

A second objection to the (Lockean) emphasis on limiting state actors is that it reflects the concerns and biases of the liberal tradition, invoking images of atomistic individuals opposed to the state. In contrast, Chinese political traditions have emphasized a more harmonious relation between the state and the people, with persons viewed as socially situated selves defined in terms of their social roles and relationships to others. Whatever the merits of these generalizations, Chinese citizens today appreciate the importance of limiting arbitrary state action. With the pluralization of interests that has resulted from economic reforms, harmony among the divergent social groups, and between such groups and the state, is even less likely than in the past. Thus, the differences are likely to be more a matter of degree than kind. As noted below, Statist Socialists, Neoauthoritarians, Communitarians, and Liberal Democrats all accept that law must bind the state, though they differ on the degree. A related concern, discussed shortly, is that it is not clear how meaningful the limits on state actors must be to qualify as "rule of law."

Still another concern is that the emphasis on limiting the state may obscure the important role of law in limiting threats to personal freedom by others in society and preventing anarchy. Those living in a lawless society dominated by the Mafia appreciate that the state is not the only threat to liberty.[7] While one should not lose sight of this function of rule of law (or any other function for that matter), particularly given the rapid increase in violent crime in China and the growing power of triads, to date the main threat to personal liberties has been and remains an overreaching arbitrary state. Similarly, one should not lose sight of the concern of Habermas and the Frankfurt School that the legitimacy of law is undermined and rule of law threatened by an economic system dominated by large corporations and a bureaucratic system whose currency is power. Nor should one ignore the insights of systems theorists such as Nicolas Luhmann who view the political system (and the state), the economy, the administration, and the legal system as largely independent autopoetic systems. Nevertheless, in China, these institutions have yet to develop the degree of specialization and autonomy of their counterparts in more economically advanced Western states. At present, the state plays a greater role in China, and politics continues to encroach on the autonomy of other systems. Just as rule of law first served the purpose of restraining the monarchy and government actors in the West, so too in China the main problematic for rule of law remains how to hold those in authority accountable. The problems of late-stage modernity confronted in some Western states are less pressing in China, which is still in the process of establishing the institutions that define modernity such as a market economy, professionalized bureaucracy, and autonomous legal and political systems.

Specifying the minimal conditions for rule of law: do we always know rule of law when we see it?

One common objection to theories of rule of law in China and abroad is that they are inadequately theorized.[8] Even acknowledging considerable agreement about the basic elements of a thin theory, there is still considerable room for disagreement about the details. Some of the elements are vague, a matter of degree, and subject to exceptions. What precisely is meant by consistent? Some laws may not be directly contradictory, but may have inconsistent purposes. Some laws are clearer than others. Sometimes laws are changed and even made effective retroactively.[9] The notion of equality before the law raises the question of equal in what respect: what are the morally and legally relevant factors in deciding whether two people are similarly situated?[10] The general principle of supremacy of the law may in some cases need to give way to higher moral principles and considerations of equity or justified civil disobedience.[11]

Further, at times the various elements and goals conflict. Replacing a number of vague rules with clearer ones would result in greater clarity and perhaps predictability in the long run but would lead to instability and greater unpredictability in the short run. A more fundamental objection is that the notion that rule of law requires "meaningful restraints" on the state and state actors is too vague. Legal systems differ both in the degree and in the nature or manner of restraints on the state and state actors.

Put differently, if we accept, as we must, that implementation of the rule-of-law ideal is always a matter of degree, then the question arises when a system merits the label rule of law. There are several possible approaches to this problem. The first approach tries to provide an account of deviations from the ideal that individually or collectively are so serious as to be incompatible with rule of law.[12] It seeks to answer the questions, at what point do (relatively minor) shortcomings and deviations from some rule-of-law ideal, taken collectively, tip the scales such that the system no longer merits the label rule of law? Alternatively, are there some types of shortcomings that are so serious that they alone are sufficient to show the absence of rule of law (and the presence of rule by law)? For instance, if the president and other senior-most officials are not likely to be impeached or held accountable for illegal acts but all other officials are held accountable, is that an imperfect, even a deeply flawed, rule of law, or simply not rule of law at all? Is a legal system that routinely deprives dissidents and opposition political figures of a fair trial but handles all other cases in a fair way a flawed rule *of* law or an efficient rule *by* law?

There are considerable theoretical and practical difficulties to this minimal conditions approach. As documented in the following chapters, China's legal system suffers from a number of shortcomings, many of them institutional in nature. As a result, the system falls considerably short of the ideal in terms of such basic requirements as consistency and stability of laws, a reasonably narrow gap between law on the books and law in practice, and the fair application of laws. On the other hand, there has been marked improvement along all of these dimensions. There seems no nonarbitrary way of deciding whether the system should be described as an imperfect rule of law or simply not rule of law at all. Take the requirement of "consistency" as an example. Let us assume that we could show that 20 percent of all local regulations were inconsistent with central laws. Would that be sufficient to disqualify the system from being considered as a rule of law, albeit an imperfect one? What if 40% or 60% or 80% of such regulations were inconsistent? Would it matter whether the trend was toward less inconsistency, say if in the past 80% of regulations were inconsistent but now "only" 50% were? Would it matter if steps were being taken to reduce the level of inconsistency, as is indeed the case in China? Would the reasons for the high level of inconsistencies matter? During times of economic transition, higher levels are to be expected. Does that somehow make the high level of inconsistencies less objectionable than turf-fighting between administrative agencies or the lack of effective institutions for overturning inconsistent local regulations?

Perhaps of even greater concern is the still limited, albeit increasing, ability of the legal system to impose meaningful limits on government actors. As is discussed in Chapter 9, administrative officials enjoy considerable discretion. To be sure, administrative officials everywhere enjoy considerable discretion, and there are good reasons why administrative officials in China should have somewhat greater discretion than officials in countries where the legislature is more developed and the economy is more stable. But even assuming PRC officials should be granted a high degree of discretion, such discretion must be subject to legal limits to comply with the requirements of rule of law. Unfortunately, the main mechanisms for checking administrative discretion – the letter and petition system, supervision by the media and the Party, administrative reconsideration, administrative supervision, and administrative litigation – remain weak. Nevertheless, the very fact that such mechanisms have been established represents a major step toward realization of rule of law and away from rule by law. Moreover, although the mechanisms are weak, they are not completely ineffectual. As noted, plaintiffs do prevail in administrative litigation cases in some 40% of the cases, a rate higher than in the USA, Taiwan, or Japan.[13]

Despite the relatively high success rate, the PRC judiciary at present clearly lacks sufficient independence and authority to hold senior government officials accountable, at least without the support of the Party.[14] Is the limited accountability of senior officials in practice sufficient to deny China's legal system the label of rule of law? After all, even in the USA, senior government officials are frequently not held accountable for their actions. Despite the rhetoric of equality of all before the law, in reality senior government officials often receive special treatment in many countries. One need only consider Gerald Ford's pardoning of Richard Nixon or Bill Clinton's pardoning of former Housing Secretary Henry Cisneros and congressman Daniel Rostenkowski. Indeed, the light slap on the wrist Clinton received for lying under oath – suspension of his license to practice law for two years and a fine of $25,000 – smacks of special privilege.

Hilary Josephs concluded in her comparison of legal accountability for corruption in China and the USA that they "are quite alike in their general reluctance to prosecute high officials. Despite fundamental differences in political systems, and a common commitment to equality before the law, those in power are rarely called to task in either country for criminal misconduct associated with discharge of their official duties."[15] She also points out that in both countries, prosecutors' decisions are influenced by political factors, including party affiliations, with a greater readiness to target someone from the opposing political party or faction. Needless to say, China and the USA are not on all fours in this regard. In some ways, China takes corruption more seriously in that corrupt government officials are more likely to be prosecuted based on the core offense rather than ancillary crimes such as fraud or tax evasion, and serious offenses carry the death penalty, whereas in the USA the worst punishment is a definite term of imprisonment.[16]

To be sure, it is hard to imagine Jiang Zemin being asked to testify under oath in regard to alleged sexual harassment, as in the case of President Clinton.[17] Nor is it likely that Jiang could be impeached, or convicted of crimes and sentenced to jail once he leaves office, as with former South Korean Presidents Chun and Roh.[18] But should that be the minimum standard?[19] Given that China has implemented laws and established legal institutions capable of imposing limits on some governments officials, the inability to hold a small core of senior-most leaders accountable in all instances arguably demonstrates that rule of law is weak in China, not completely absent.

Similarly, all legal systems are politicized to some extent. Moreover, the degree and nature of politicization may differ depending on the type of rule of law that prevails. Nevertheless, the PRC legal system is undeniably unusually politicized, and clearly differs both in the degree and manner of politicization from other legal systems, particularly liberal democracies, known for rule of law. As is discussed in Chapter 5, although the Party and individual Party members are legally obligated to follow the law, the Party's role is not clearly defined in law. Implementation of even a Statist Socialist rule of law would require that the Party's role be spelled out more clearly in law. For instance, while political parties in other countries may play a role in appointing judges, that role is prescribed by law, whereas the role of the Party in appointing judges is not set forth in any publicly promulgated state law. Nor is the role of Party organs within the court or the role of the Political–Legal Committee prescribed by law. Even assuming the role of Party organs was spelled out in law, the degree and manner of influence of such organs over the work of the judiciary that would be consistent with rule of law would still be an issue. There have been some efforts to separate Party and state with respect to judicial matters. As is discussed in Chapter 7, Party organs rarely interfere directly in the courts' handling of specific cases. Yet dissidents are regularly denied a procedurally fair trial.

Whether politically sensitive cases are handled according to law, and even dissidents are afforded a fair trial, would seem to be one useful barometer of whether a legal system meets the requirements of rule of law. Because politically sensitive cases challenge the ruling regime most directly, a legal system capable of handling such cases fairly and in a manner consistent with the requirements of a thin rule of law will most likely handle commercial, criminal, and other less controversial cases in a similar way. Yet it is possible that a legal system could be rule-of-law compliant in some respects (say with respect to commercial law) and not compliant in other ways (say with respect to political cases), and indeed this arguably has been the case at some points in Taiwan, South Korea, Singapore, and other Asian countries.[20] Granted, in the long run, such a system is not likely to be sustainable because for a system to comply with the standards of a thin rule of law in the commercial area requires significant institutional development and autonomy. As is discussed in Chapter 5, once institutions gain a certain degree of autonomy and authority and those within the institution achieve a level of professionalism, the institutional actors are likely to pursue further changes to increase their autonomy and authority. As a result, there are likely to be spillover effects from one area of law to another as institutions develop. Again, Taiwan, South Korea, and more recently Indonesia, are examples of this trend. During the transition period, some will choose to describe the legal system as a developing albeit flawed rule of law.

Others, particularly liberal democrats who privilege civil and political rights over other rights, will be more likely to deny the system the label rule of law.

It should be noted, however, that a "fair" trial in politically sensitive cases need not mean that dissidents or political activists will win. In fact, even in the USA political activists regularly lost free speech cases well into this century under a variety of restrictive laws from the Alien and Sedition Acts of 1798 to the Espionage Act of 1917 to state laws criminalizing "subversive advocacy."[21] Likewise, slaves challenging slavery laws and people of color protesting various forms of racial discrimination have all too often met with defeat in US courts. Yet despite such outcomes, many would describe the US legal system at such times as rule of law. As noted, a thin rule of law does not ensure just outcomes. Thus, while the struggle to obtain a procedurally fair trial consistent with a thin rule of law may represent a significant achievement in some respects, at times it may seem a hollow victory to those sent to jail under repressive laws.

To sum up the discussion so far, the problem of defining precisely when a legal system meets the minimum threshold of (a thin) rule of law, despite its shortcomings, and when the shortcomings are so extensive or objectionable to deny the system the title of rule of law, is a generic jurisprudential problem not unique to China. Clearly, reasonable people can, do, and will disagree over the degree and type of shortcomings that will be sufficient to deprive a legal system of the exalted status of rule of law. Given the wide variation in legal systems and the many ways in which all legal systems fall short of the ideal of rule of law, attempting to articulate more precisely the standards of a thin theory or trying to state in a formal way the degree or kind of deviance from the ideal sufficient to deprive a legal system of the label rule of law is not likely to result in sufficient consensus to put an end to the general debate. The best that can be hoped for is a rather rough consensus based on the facts in a particular case. As US Supreme Court Justice Potter Stewart said about pornography, "I know it when I see it."[22] To be sure, one person's pornography is another person's art. As the ongoing debates over what is and what is not pornography demonstrate, the eyeball test allows for considerable personal bias. Inevitably, liberal democrats will weight more heavily certain deficiencies in China's legal system, such as the unfair treatment of dissidents and the system of reeducation through labor. Thus, the eyeball approach will not always lead to agreement. Nevertheless, in some cases, there will be a general consensus. For instance, few if any would challenge the claim that China's legal system during the Mao period was not rule of law.[23]

Given the difficulties associated with the first approach, an alternative approach would be to describe any system as rule of law in which there is a credible normative commitment to the principle that law is to bind the state and state actors, as evidenced by efforts to establish a legal system that meets the standard of a thin theory. Although in some cases there might still be disagreement about whether even such a minimal standard has been met, lowering the standard would shift the debate in most cases from whether a legal system ought to be described in terms of rule of law to how well rule of law is implemented in practice. Having cleared the initial hurdle of a credible commitment to the principle that law ought to bind the state and state actors, the focus then turns to the extent to which the ideal of rule of law is actually realized, with legal systems ranked on a sliding scale based on the criteria of thin theory, including the extent to which law does limit the state and state actors. Such an approach is arguably more consistent with the reality that all legal systems deviate from the ideal in various ways and to various degrees. Taking this tack, China's legal system, for instance, could be considered as a rule of law, albeit an imperfect one. Whereas the legal systems of Japan and Germany, for example, might merit a ranking of nine on a ten-point scale, China's legal system might only be assigned a score of two.[24]

This sliding scale approach is not without problems, however. An initial difficulty, though not an insurmountable one in my view, is in establishing the minimum requirements to show a "credible normative commitment" to the principle that law binds the state and state actors. For instance, in China's case, the principle that the Party, individual Party members, state organs, and government officials must comply with the law was set forth in Article 5 of the 1982 constitution. By itself, however, that would not be sufficient, particularly given the previous role of law and constitutions during the Mao era. At the time, few observers would have believed solely on the basis of a change in the constitution that the Party had accepted any meaningful limits on its power. Observers could reasonably have expected the ruling regime to produce more evidence of its change in policy, and in particular to back up its rhetoric with actions. Since then, however, the ruling regime has taken concrete steps to create a legal basis for challenging the state by passing a wide range of administrative laws and carrying out a host of reforms to strengthen legal institutions. The dominant understanding of the purpose of administrative law has also shifted from simply a focus on government efficiency and the use of administrative law to ensure that government officials serve the interest of the state to the now widely accepted "balance theory" whereby administrative law both protects individual rights and enhances government efficiency. As noted, the ruling regime reconfirmed its commitment to rule of law by amending the constitution in 1999. In addition, the state has expended considerable resources building up all of the legal institutions. The legislature is more assertive; courts enjoy greater albeit still limited independence; the legal profession is more autonomous and professional; and the procuracy and police forces have also been strengthened. As is discussed in Chapter 5, the Party has turned over much of the responsibility for daily governance to the usual state organs. The Party no longer rules primarily based on Party policy and Party dictates. With the greater reliance on law to govern, law has begun to gain normative authority and is becoming an independent source of legitimation independent of tradition or the charisma of revolutionary Party leaders whose views in the past provided the authority for policies and laws.

To be sure, many skeptics still question whether the ruling regime accepts the principle that law binds the state and state actors. Some argue that many of the reforms are actually consistent with a more efficient rule by law, especially a softer authoritarian version than that of the Mao era.[25] When vital interests of the Party are at stake, as in politically sensitive cases involving democracy dissidents or Falungong adherents, the interests of the Party prevail over legal niceties such as the procedural rights of the accused.

Yet there are good reasons to be skeptical about the skeptics' view. Undeniably, *some* of the recent reforms and developments, such as a certain amount of institution-building, greater reliance on law rather than policy, and even some devolution of power, are consistent with the view that the purpose of legal reforms is a more efficient rule by law. However, they are also consistent with a transition to rule of law. As is often the case, much turns on which side bears the burden of proof. The rule-by-law camp insists that those who see a transition toward rule of law provide conclusive proof. Turning the tables, however, why assume the skeptics' view is correct? The rule-by-law camp cannot show conclusively that reforms consistent with both a transition to rule of law and a more efficient rule by law are actually meant to support a new and improved rule by law any more than their counterparts can show conclusively they are meant to support rule of law.

That said, while some of the reforms are consistent with a ruling regime bent on creating a more efficient rule by law, they are not necessary for such a system. For instance, it is not clear why the ruling regime would have had to allow private law firms to create a more efficient rule by law. Moreover, the nature and extent of institution-building and the degree of devolution of authority call into question the view that the purpose of such reforms is simply to create a more efficient rule by law. As discussed shortly, in some cases reforms have been driven not by central authorities but by other actors within the system, who have pushed reforms in directions not anticipated by the central authorities. Indeed, different groups and individuals are likely to support reforms for different reasons. The skeptical view tends to emphasize the purpose of central Party leaders in supporting or tolerating legal reforms, rather than the motives of other segments of the polity in backing reforms. Yet many government officials, academics, and citizens no doubt support legal reforms because they believe such reforms will limit government arbitrariness and lead to better protection of individuals' rights and interests.

Moreover, while skeptics can explain away some reforms as consistent with a more efficient rule by law, other reforms cannot be dismissed so readily. The express commitment to rule of law and the efforts to establish a viable administrative law system that aims to both protect individual rights and enhance government efficiency, for instance, are at odds with the establishment of a more efficient rule by law.

Furthermore, setting a high standard for showing a credible commitment to the principle that law ought to bind the state and state actors (and hence is not rule by law) runs into the kinds of problems confronted earlier. Are such failures evidence of lack of normative commitment to rule-of-law principles or simply evidence of a weak rule of law? Taken to the extreme, diehard skeptics will be satisfied with nothing less than the full realization of the rule-of-law ideal, or at least a legal system that substantially complies with their own values and biases as to what is important. Thus, some skeptics may not be satisfied until current or former leaders are held accountable and political dissidents win free speech cases. Only then will they be convinced that there is a credible commitment to the principle that the law binds the state and state actors. Yet requiring such actions as conclusive proof of a credible commitment to rule of law demonstrates the shortcomings of this approach. The establishment of rule of law is a long-term process. No legal system can transform itself from rule by law into a fully implemented rule of law overnight. All countries now known for rule of law initially went through a period, in some cases lasting for centuries, in which legal institutions were weak and rule of law only imperfectly implemented at best. Although it may be impossible to pinpoint the exact moment the tide turned toward rule of law, at some point preceding the actual implementation of some reasonable approximation of the ideal of rule of law, there was inevitably a credible commitment to it. Similarly, in China, there will necessarily have been a credible commitment to rule of law long before the day when senior state leaders are held accountable and the courts decide dissident cases impartially, at which point even the most cynical skeptic will finally be willing to acknowledge that China is committed to (and indeed enjoys) rule of law. If and when that day arrives, it will be clear in retrospect that the skeptics' view during the transition period that the purpose of reforms was to create a more efficient rule by law will have been incorrect.

Alternatively, rule-by-law skeptics might define rule by law in terms of a much higher standard of actual performance of the legal system rather than the minimal standard of whether a credible commitment has been made to the principle that law binds the state and state actors. Yet anyone who defines rule by law in terms of a higher performance standard must define the point at which the system no longer counts as rule by law. As we have seen, it is difficult if not impossible to define the minimal conditions for achieving rule of law with any precision.

More importantly, the distinction between rule by law and rule of law seems to be a conceptual one rather than an empirical one. A system in which law is only meant to serve as a tool of the ruling regime without binding government officials is rule by law. It seems counterintuitive to argue that a system in which law is meant to be supreme but which falls short of that ideal in practice is for that reason rule by law.

Pragmatically, focusing on the conceptual distinction in the purpose of law rather than the extent to which law actually imposes meaningful limits on state actors provides a fairly bright line test for distinguishing between rule of law and rule by law. The legal systems of Imperial and Mao China, where law was conceived of as just a tool to achieve the interests of the state and was not meant to limit the ruler or Party, are best described as rule by law. In contrast, the change in the official rhetoric to a conception of law where law is to be supreme represents a major departure from the Imperial and Mao eras. Defining rule by law in terms of the extent to which the legal system actually imposes meaningful limits on state actors tends to lead to the current system being lumped together with the legal systems of the Imperial and Mao eras, despite their significant differences.

Of course, while it may no longer be accurate to describe China's legal system as rule by law, whether the system in its current form merits the label rule of law is another matter. Perhaps the biggest objection to the low-threshold, sliding-scale approach is that rule of law is an honorific term used to praise or criticize a legal system. Thus rule of law in ordinary usage implies a certain degree of achievement. Accordingly, many people would object to calling a legal system that scored a one or two on a ten-point thin-rule-of-law scale a rule of law, just as many commentators object to referring to China's legal system in terms of rule of law, even though it would seem to rank at least a two on such a scale.

In light of the many shortcomings of the legal system detailed throughout this work and the ordinary use of rule of law as an honorific term signaling a certain standard of achievement, I have described China's legal system as in transition toward rule of law but still falling short of the minimal standard of achievement required to be considered rule of law. Problems such as the treatment of political dissidents and the inability of the legal system to hold senior-most officials accountable would certainly give me pause in describing China's system as even an imperfect rule of law. But as troubling from a rule-of-law perspective are the many technical problems that arise in daily practice that have nothing to do with politically sensitive issues. The cumulative toll of these everyday deficiencies, in my view, is sufficient to deny China's current system the title of rule of law, even allowing that there is sufficient evidence of a credible normative commitment to the principle that law is to bind the state and state actors to render the characterization of the legal system as rule by law inapposite.

Suffice it to say that while what constitutes the minimal standard of achievement for rule of law as a general matter is subject to debate, just as in some cases most people of whatever political persuasion will be able to agree that a particular object is pornographic, most commentators both within China and abroad readily acknowledge that the legal system falls well short of the minimal standard of achievement implied by the honorific label rule of law.[26] Given the general consensus, there is no need at present to delve more deeply into the minimal conditions for rule of law (particularly since my principal purpose is to examine the progress and obstacles to rule of law in China rather than to attempt to resolve general jurisprudential issues relating to thin theories).

In the final analysis, little is to be gained by engaging in endless debates about which of the above approaches is more warranted. To some extent which approach one adopts will depend on one's purpose. Clearly, there is a rhetorical difference in claiming that China lacks rule of law or, conversely, that China's legal system is a weak rule of law or in transition toward rule of law. Government officials may prefer to argue that China has rule of law, albeit a weak one, to emphasize the difference between the current regime and previous regimes. Critics who wish to condemn China for the harsh treatment of dissidents will prefer to characterize China as lacking rule of law (or as implementing a more efficient rule by law). Yet substantively, those on all sides of these debates acknowledge both progress and problems. Many are also likely to share the same goal that China's legal system more fully approximate the ideal of rule of law. Accordingly, those who favor the sliding scale approach can simply take my comments that China currently lacks rule of law or is in transition toward rule of law to mean that China is in the process of more fully realizing the ideal of rule of law.

Imposition of a Western ideal? The lack of viable alternatives to rule of law

Still another approach would be to argue that because China is so different from other countries, it is likely to develop its own long-term, stable alternative to rule of law – a different kind of legal system that does not comply with the requirements of a thin theory. According to this view, my focus on rule of law is simply wrong-headed. Despite my efforts to escape imposing "Western" categories, I have still ended up doing just that by assuming that China must develop a legal system that meets the requirements of a thin theory.

Donald Clarke, for instance, raises a number of concerns about the "imperfect realization of an ideal" or "IRI" approach to comparative law, an approach that shares certain similarities with my approach, although there are also important differences.[27] According to Clarke, under this "essentially teleological approach," the Chinese legal system is identified and measured in terms of an ideal end state chosen by the analyst.[28] He notes that the IRI approach could work with any end state, but "in fact it is always invariably used in conjunction with an end state posited as the Western rule-of-law ideal. This rule-of-law ideal constitutes the paradigm, in the Kuhnian sense, that governs the entire enterprise of analyzing the Chinese legal system."[29]

Clarke argues that reliance on the paradigm of "the Western rule of law ideal" (or the Ideal Western Legal Order) has several theoretical and practical drawbacks. First, it "dictates" the questions one asks, what one considers to be relevant data, and how one interprets the phenomena observed. In the naïve version, China's legal system is simply compared to idealized portrayals of modern Western legal institutions, or even more narrowly to an idealized account of the US system, and found wanting. In the more sophisticated version, researchers overlook important aspects of the Chinese legal system, misinterpret phenomena, and either attach too much or too little importance to other phenomena. As a result, their predictions as to how the legal system will develop are likely to be wrong.

Clarke claims that practitioners of the IRI approach assume without argumentation or support "that China *has* legal institutions" and that the legal system is developing toward some form of rule of law:[30]

> In other words, the IRI approach assumes that we can talk meaningfully about Chinese law and legal institutions; that China has a set of institutions that can meaningfully be grouped together under a single rubric, and that it is meaningful (*i.e.*, it clarifies more than it obscures) to label this rubric "legal" – the same word we use to describe a set of institutions in our own society. Thus, even to embark on the study of something called "Chinese legal institutions" involves an *a priori* assumption that China has a set of institutions largely similar to the institutions we call "legal" in our society. If the institutions were not largely congruent – if, for example, we were discussing churches or the movie industry – we would not call the institutions "legal" in the first place. More specifically, the very act of naming certain institutions involves drawing conclusions about them before the investigation has

even begun. If we call a certain institution a "court," then we are claiming that this word conveys to the listener a more complete and accurate
picture of the institution in question than some other word. We could
equally well call the institution a "team," or an "office," or a "bureau";
the decision *not* to use those words represents an implicit assertion
about the nature of the institution in question. The problem is that
this assertion *precedes*, rather than follows, inquiry into the nature of
the institution.

The second assumption is that these institutions are "developing."
Academic articles adopting this approach are typically entitled "China's
Developing Law of Contract" or something similar. By "developing" is
meant moving from a more primitive and inferior stage to a more
sophisticated and better stage along a trajectory of linear progress
toward a well-understood end. The substantive content of this well-
understood end . . . is typically the Western rule of law ideal. In other
words, the sophisticated IRI approach understands a particular institution now by seeing it as a nascent version of an institution in the
Western rule of law ideal. We identify its imperfections in this way and
we predict its future changes (which we call "development" and not
simply "change").

Clarke is surely right to caution against an a priori assumption that
Chinese institutions are meant to serve the same purposes as those in
some Western liberal democracies. He is also surely correct to point out
that we are likely to misinterpret phenomena and go awry in our predictions as to how China will develop if we impose without questioning
our own modern Western (or worse yet, US-based) notion of how a legal system must function. However, while China is distinctive in some
respects, it increasingly confronts similar challenges to those faced by
other states with a market economy and a more pluralistic populace.
China has also already become more entwined in a global economy and
international legal order. Not surprisingly, there has been considerable
convergence in its legal system, including with respect to the legislature,
judiciary, and administrative agencies. No one would confuse these institutions with churches or the movie industry, to use Clarke's examples,
or even with the much more politicized entities of the Mao era.

The applicability of a thin theory of rule of law is not therefore simply
the unreflective *a priori* imposition of a Western ideal. First, it is not *an
imposition* of a Western ideal at all because there is widespread acceptance
of, and support for, a legal system that meets the requirements of a thin

rule of law in China. Second, at least in my case, the view that China is moving toward a thin rule of law is based on an empirical assessment of how institutions have changed since the Mao era and how they operate today rather than on an *a priori* assumption of the inevitable applicability of thin theories.

Given the convergence with respect to the purposes of the legal system, legal rules, and the functions and practices of the various institutions, one can reasonably describe China's institutions as *legal* institutions.[31] Indeed, it is difficult to imagine how else to describe them. To be sure, China's institutions are embedded in a very different context from that of economically advanced Western liberal democracies. Thus, there are likely to be significant differences in the institutions. But to deny that China's institutions are legal institutions simply because they differ in significant ways from institutions in some modern Western liberal democracies is to assume that institutions other than ours are not legal institutions in the proper sense.

As Clarke says, the ultimate standard for any definition, label, or paradigm is whether it is useful: does it serve the purpose it was intended to serve (and is that purpose itself useful)? In some cases, scholars may wish to stipulate a narrow definition of law or legal system in order to bring out more sharply the contrasts between different systems. This approach, however, may also lead the analyst to exaggerate the differences. For example, the current system differs dramatically from the Mao era. No longer can the NPC be described as a rubber stamp or the courts as just another bureaucracy with no more authority than the Post Office.[32]

At this point, it is unlikely that China will develop a legal system so radically different as to render a thin rule of law conceptually inapplicable. China's distinctiveness is likely to be reflected in variations in thick theories compatible with a thin theory, rather than in some sustainable, normatively acceptable and feasible alternative to a thin theory. Indeed, one of the problems in heeding Clarke's warning about relying on rule of law as a benchmark is that there is no other credible theory that better describes the current system. For years the alternative has been to describe China as an instrumental rule by law. But that is problematic for all of the reasons discussed previously. Whatever its descriptive inadequacies, rule by law is even less useful as a normative goal for future reforms.[33]

This is not to claim that Clarke or someone else could not come up with a new theory that better describes the system than "the Western rule of law ideal." In fact, if by the Western rule-of-law ideal one means Liberal Democratic rule of law, then I fully agree that any of the three alternatives (Statist Socialist, Neoauthoritarian, or Communitarian) and possibly others as well are likely to be more useful for understanding the future path of development in China (though all are still rule-of-law theories). Although Clarke claims that the main problem with the IRI approach, "is that its practitioners tend to leave unstated and unjustified its most crucial component: the ideal against which the Chinese legal system is identified and measured," Clarke himself never defines in any detail what he means by "the Western rule of law ideal."[34] As we have seen, rule of law is a contested concept, even in the West. In thinking about the role of law in China and the possible path of future development, it is necessary to distinguish between thin and thick theories and between different types of thick theories. By so doing, predictions about rule of law in China become more open-ended and *less* teleological (although obviously even the standards of a thin theory, while allowing some diversity in institutions and practices, are teleological in nature). In contrast to this more contextualized and open-ended approach, the original law and development movement, discussed below, assumed a much more rigidly uniform path of development ending in the implementation of a Liberal Democratic rule of law around the world.

Why we can't simply abandon rule-of-law talk or reserve rule of law for liberal democracies

In light of the many different interpretations of rule of law, might it not be best simply to abandon reference to rule of law altogether? Wouldn't it be more useful to adopt, for instance, a "microanalysis approach"?[35] Microanalysis tries to avoid or at least minimize generalizations, metaphors, and conceptualizations as explanatory mechanisms. Rather, microanalysts attempt to describe the way actions of independently motivated individuals create social systems by tracing the way individual actions aggregate to produce larger social structures and institutions.

While there is considerable merit in the suggestion that what matters most is not the label but the substance of particular legal reforms in China, abandoning reference to rule of law is neither possible nor desirable. As a practical matter, people both in China and abroad will continue to invoke rule of law. Given that fact, it is better to try to bring some clarity to the different uses of the term, by distinguishing between rule by law and rule of law and between thin and thick conceptions of rule of law and different types of thick conceptions, than to insist futilely that the term be avoided altogether.

Moreover, legal reformers have pragmatic reasons for referring to rule of law in that the normative appeal of rule of law may be used to support controversial legal and political reforms. Indeed, one of the reasons PRC scholars prefer thick conceptions to thin conceptions is that thick conceptions allow them to discuss topics that would otherwise be too sensitive to approach directly. For instance, bringing democracy and human rights under the umbrella of rule of law may open up discussion of sensitive topics such as multiparty elections, separation of powers,[36] and freedom of thought.[37]

In addition, rule of law provides a useful heuristic guide for legal reforms in that the elements of a thin (or even thick) theory may be used to clarify and prioritize areas in need of reform and to see the relationships between the various elements. It provides some structure to what otherwise could be a chaotic, piecemeal reform process.

Assuming then we cannot abandon rule-of-law talk altogether, perhaps we could limit rule of law to only the Liberal Democratic version. After all, given that "rule of law" has become associated with Liberal Democratic rule of law, one might argue that the term should not be stretched to include other variants. When talking about China, perhaps one should simply forgo the use of rule of law in favor of other terms.

Obviously, one is free to reserve the label "rule of law" for a particular version if one so chooses. However, one problem with this approach is that forcing PRC ideas about rule of law into our prevailing yet contingent categories smacks of cultural imperialism.

Second, the debate about legal reform in China has been couched in terms of rule of law, both in China and abroad. Of course, one could protest every time the term rule of law is used or at least point out that the term is being misused. But given that "rule of law" is a contested concept even in the West, any attempt to appropriate the term for a particular usage will fail: the debate will continue to be posed in terms of rule of law, both by those inside and outside of China. Rather than restricting the use of the term with respect to China, it is more useful to try to figure out what those who use the term mean by it and why they want to invoke it. As noted, how one defines rule of law will depend on what one's purpose is. Investors, governments and multilateral agencies, NGOs, moral philosophers, and political scientists all have different purposes for invoking rule of law, and may therefore find some ways of defining or measuring it more suitable to their particular purpose than others. That does not mean that they are free to define rule of law as they like. Enough people in the relevant discourse community must accept the usage for the speech act to be meaningful and for the definition to serve a useful purpose. There is, however, enough common ground to the various conceptions of rule of law, provided by the basic requirements of a thin rule of law, to render the invocation of rule of law in the Chinese context intelligible and useful.

Third, as just noted, many reformers in China want the debate couched in terms of rule of law for strategic reasons: rule of law entails at minimum some restraints on government leaders and opens up other possibilities for political reform.

Fourth, simply relying on either Liberal Democratic rule of law versus rule by law is no longer sufficient to capture what is happening in China. It is descriptively incorrect – the legal system is no longer a pure rule by law. Nor can we capture all of the nuances in the PRC debates about rule of law if we only have the overly simplistic categories of rule of law (i.e. our Liberal Democratic version) or else rule by law.[38] Without more refined categories, we simply will not be able to understand what is happening, either in terms of the evolution of PRC discourse or in practice with respect to the development of the legal system.

Fifth, the practical import of forcing PRC discourse and practice into our preconceived boxes of Liberal Democratic rule of law or authoritarian rule by law is that we are likely to come to the wrong conclusions about reforms. We are likely to be either too pessimistic or too optimistic. Either there is no fundamental change, or China is becoming "like us." But neither seems to be the case. Misreading what is happening is likely to lead to bad policy choices. Foreign governments and aid agencies could miss opportunities to support reforms that would improve the PRC system, for example, by failing to provide adequate resources for certain reforms because they do not believe such changes could possibly work in a rule-by-law system meant to serve the interests of the Party and nothing more. Alternatively, time and resources could be wasted on projects that are not consistent with the form of rule of law likely to emerge in China. Some rules or practices that work in the context of a Liberal Democratic rule of law might require liberal institutions and perhaps liberal values to succeed. They may fail to take hold in a different legal order, exacerbating the gap between law and practice.

Finally, and most important from a theoretical standpoint, objecting to the application of rule of law to China and other states that are not liberal democracies overstates the differences in the legal systems and fails to capture the considerable agreement with respect to the basic elements of a thin rule of law. Despite considerable variation, all four thick conceptions of rule of law endorse the basic principle that law must impose meaningful limits on the ruler, and all are compatible with a thin rule of law.

Déjà vu all over again? The old and new law and development movement

Clarke's warning about the uncritical application of the so-called Western rule-of-law ideal to China will sound eerily familiar to those who remember the original law and development movement; and indeed there is much to be learned from both the failures and the achievements of that early round of experimentation with legal transplants. In the 1960s, legal scholars in Western developed countries, working in conjunction with scholars from other disciplines, practicing lawyers, and international agencies, sought to export rule of law, liberal democracy, and capitalism to developing countries.[39] The movement was predicated on an evolutionary convergence theory: legal reform would lead to economic reform and ultimately political reform.[40] At the end of the rainbow lay capitalist liberal democracies. Law and development devotees emphasized legal education, strengthening of the courts, and the passage of legislation, particularly commercial laws, as the keys to success.[41] Within academia, the movement quickly got bogged down in the face of a variety of external critiques, internal self-doubts, and the empirical failure of some states to develop as expected.

Critics accused the movement of ethnocentrism and legal imperialism.[42] They pointed out that advisers rarely did field work and focused more on state-centered initiatives such as legislation and institution-building rather than the particular features of the target culture.[43] The critics saw the movement as trying to impose a historically contingent form of modernism, rule of law, and liberal democracy on others.[44]

Although at times it was not clear if the naysayers were objecting to modernism and economic development *per se* or to the means of achieving them, some seemed to want to turn back the tide of modernity and preserve traditional forms of society. Dependency theorists for their part challenged the motives of the movement, arguing that capitalist countries were exporting the ideology of modernism and development to create consumer markets and make the target countries dependent on the West.[45] They also noted that many Western countries wanted to take advantage of cheap labor costs, less stringent pollution controls, and to exploit natural resources. Some argued that in endorsing a laissez-faire philosophy and the free trade principles of a liberal trade regime, international trade law appears neutral on its face but actually favors stronger nations. Accordingly, they recommended that developing countries screen foreign direct investment (FDI) and protect their domestic markets by erecting trade barriers.[46]

Other critics called attention to the inherent difficulties in transplanting legal norms, doctrines, and institutions from one country to another. Oftentimes, the newly transplanted laws would go unenforced. The large gap between law and reality demonstrated how difficult it was to transplant a liberal democracy and a liberal legality based on a Lockean social contract between atomistic individuals and the state to a hierarchical society dominated by patron–client corporatist arrangements; it also raised more fundamental issues of whether other countries even wanted to be like the USA in the first place.[47]

Internally, many within the movement lost faith in the American way.[48] The turbulent '60s led many US scholars to question their government and the legal and political system that produced it. Scholars also developed a more critical view of law and the relation of law to society. The Weberian notions of an autonomous legal profession and formal rationality were subject to attack by Critical Legal Studies and Law and Society scholars.[49]

Internal and external critics pointed to the theoretical shortcomings of the movement. Some argued that legal reform was neither necessary nor sufficient for economic and political development. Others complained that the evolutionary theory could not be operationalized.[50] There were too many variables to specify. Exactly what was required to ensure development? How important are freedom of contract, private property rights, and free-markets, given the range of variation in each of these areas from country to country?[51] What institutions were required? An independent court? How independent must the courts be? What role do they play? Critics were, and are, fond of pointing out that many disputes are resolved without relying on courts. Moreover, the judiciary in developing countries rarely played the role of countermajoritarian protector of rights; rights were either protected by political bargaining or deliberately left unprotected.[52] Whereas traditional informal means of dispute resolution tended to disperse power, court-centered reforms aimed at strengthening the formal channels for dispute resolution tended to shift power toward the center.[53] In addition, critics challenged the importance of an independent legal profession. In some countries, the legal profession was co-opted and came to serve the interests of the ruling elite or pursued its own economic interests by protecting its monopoly over legal services.[54] Others pointed out that the emphasis on the instrumental and pragmatic aspects of law at the expense of larger normative issues played into the hands of authoritarian regimes.[55]

Perhaps the most important reason for the failure of the movement was that it promised too much. The evolutionary thesis that legal reform would inevitably lead to economic growth and liberal democracy was not borne out in practice. Many states failed to develop economically, or even if they did, some remained authoritarian. In fact, in the absence of political pluralism and opportunities for participation in government, a stronger legal system at times strengthened the hand of authoritarian regimes. In some cases, states were too weak in terms of both institutional infrastructure and authority to carry out the necessary reforms. They suffered from a weak court system and relatively undeveloped administrative and political structures. Caught between the internal demands from the have-nots for distributive justice and external calls for the "efficient" regulation of a market economy that implied fiscal belt-tightening, many governments veered from one extreme to the other, failing to satisfy anyone.[56]

The new law and development movement

Although the law and development movement was short-lived in US law schools, it had a life of its own outside the American academy. Scholars in other countries continued to research and write in the area.[57] Developing countries continued to pass laws and build institutions based on foreign models. Pressed by the need to resolve real problems and unable to afford the luxury of theoretical self-doubt and conceptual paralysis, practicing lawyers, often in the service of multinational companies, continued to preach the advantages of rule of law and to push for reforms, many of which have recently begun to bear fruit.[58] They were aided in their efforts by the United Nations, World Bank, IMF, Ford Foundation, and other organizations.

In the 1990s, the new law and development movement, now frequently couched in terms of rule of law and good governance, gained steam.[59] The enthusiasm for the revived movement is due to various factors.[60] First and most obvious is the dominance of market capitalism. With the fall of socialist governments in the Soviet Union and Eastern Europe and China's shift toward a market economy, capitalism appears to have prevailed. Earlier criticisms of modernity and calls for the preservation of traditional culture are muted.[61] Nowadays virtually everyone wants economic development, including most importantly government leaders who have staked their claims to legitimacy on growth and higher standards of living. While development theorists may have been correct that the failure of some countries to develop was due in part to their inferior initial starting position – which was often the historical legacy of colonialism – they were wrong about the benefits of a market economy and the means to achieve development.[62] A second and related factor is the rise of multinational corporations and increasing economic globalization.[63] Foreign investors demand a stable framework for investment.[64] Perceived failures to deliver such a framework may impede new investment or cause some companies to reconsider their investments and to withdraw funds. Another factor has been the international human rights movement, which has called attention to certain universal issues and put pressure on governments to bring their legal systems into compliance with international standards.[65]

Most important, the original law and development advocates may have abandoned ship too early.[66] Despite all of the criticisms, it now appears from the perspective of thirty years of additional experience that some minimal version of rule of law is a necessary if not sufficient condition for economic development in most cases, even though there is still considerable debate about just what is required and how important it is relative to other factors.[67]

Moreover, the new and old movements differ in several significant respects. Advocates today are much more circumspect in their claims about, and guarded in their aspirations for, the evolution from legal reform to economic and political reform. Leaders in many recipient countries are quite clear that they want economic development but not political change.[68] In the eyes of many, the success of the Asian tigers (and to a lesser extent Brazil) proves that liberal democracy is not a prerequisite for economic development. Asian governments in particular, buoyed by the success of Singapore, are increasingly insistent that they have their own Asian values on political and human rights issues.[69] Given this insistence, as noted in the last chapter, many foreign aid agencies have been careful to characterize their help as technical assistance on legal and economic issues independent of normative and political issues.[70] Thus the rule-of-law piece of the development puzzle has been separated from the democracy, liberalism, and human rights pieces, as I have done by distinguishing between thin and thick versions and different thick versions of rule of law.

Further, having learned from the failures of the original movement as well as scholarship by CRITs, feminists, critical race theorists, and comparative law specialists, contemporary advocates have a much more sophisticated view of law and its relation to development and politics.[71] They are more aware that legal change may serve the economic interests of the elite while exacerbating income inequalities and may bolster authoritarian governments by allowing them to claim greater legitimacy based on both economic growth and compliance with rule of law. Accordingly, whereas the focus of the earlier movement was on state-led reforms, the new law and development pays more attention to the various interests affected by institutional changes and reforms at the grass-roots level (as explained below, the bottom-up forces for change in China are more widespread and powerful than often suggested).[72]

Moreover, the role of the state has changed.[73] The original movement sought to export a liberal welfare state, which implied a big government. The new movement favors a more austere, market-oriented state with a more limited role for government in the economic area. The role of the state is now to carry out institutional reforms to create markets and ensure their smooth operation, and to provide rules to facilitate market transactions mainly by defining property rights, guaranteeing the enforcement of contracts, and maintaining law and order.[74] While not the big government of liberal welfare states, the state is also not the minimal one of classical liberal theory. It has a somewhat larger role to play in correcting market failures and stimulating and regulating the economy:

it is a "dynamic and economically aware entity" that complements the market.[75] In keeping with the revised view of the state, Statist Socialists, Neoauthoritarians and Communitarians all advocate a managed economy in which the government is more interventionist than in a Liberal Democratic order.

While the charges of ethnocentricism and imperialism were unjustified with respect to many members of the original movement,[76] on the whole, contemporary participants are arguably more sensitive to context,[77] though there are plenty of exceptions, particularly among practitioners and international agencies.[78] More people working in the area are aware of the diversity of legal systems around the world,[79] the problems of transplanting legal institutions and doctrines,[80] the variety of paths to economic development, and how approaches that may work in one country may not work in another context given the differences in traditions, culture, the current level of development, and other such contingent factors. It is precisely because of such diversity and path-dependency that we need to consider the possibility of alternatives to Liberal Democratic rule of law for China.

The top-down nature of reforms is less top-down than critics contend

Many of the general critiques of the law and development movement have their PRC-specific analogue. For instance, the top-down nature of reform is often cited as one of the major obstacles to rule of law in China.[81] Undeniably, the promotion of rule of law has been to a considerable extent, though by no means exclusively, a movement pushed along by state leaders.[82] The advantage of this approach is that without state support there would have been little if any progress. Particularly in the early years of reform, China lacked the institutional capacity, civil society, and means for democratic participation that could have propelled the movement forward in the face of state opposition.[83] Even today, the state has the resources to push for change and overcome inertia and challenges by those who stand to lose out if rule of law is implemented.

Whether state leaders will allow law to become sufficiently powerful to impose significant restraints on state power, and whether the CCP will ever allow legal and political reforms to threaten its own privileged position, remains to be seen. Nevertheless, as discussed in Chapter 5, there are grounds for optimism in that the implementation of rule of law turns on more than the views of Party leaders, and in any event, the Party may have little choice but to continue to promote rule of law to meet its goals, including economic growth, a more efficient and rational government, and legitimacy. Moreover, today the demand for rule of law comes from many different sectors. In fact, lower-level government entities, administrative agencies, courts, academics, interest groups, and individuals are responsible for most of the concrete proposals for reform.[84] For instance, much of the regulatory framework for business has been developed on an incremental basis in response to grass-roots initiatives. To meet the demands of investors, local governments regularly have forged ahead in carrying out commercial law reforms without central approval. Among countless examples, local governments approved the establishment of wholly foreign-owned enterprises and holding companies, and allowed investors to mortgage their assets, years before the central government passed laws sanctioning such activities. Similarly, by the time the Lawyers Law was passed in 1996, authorizing the establishment of partnership law firms, local justice bureaus had already approved hundreds of such firms.[85]

Administrative agencies are responsible for most legislation, with the number of regulations passed by lower-level entities greatly exceeding the number of central-level laws and regulations. While these lower-level agencies frequently pass regulations that are inconsistent with central-level laws and regulations to protect local interests or to further their own institutional interests, they nonetheless are a major source of bottom-up initiatives, and sometimes result in useful precedents that then are implemented nationwide. Of course, many of the regulations drafted by administrative agencies are simply a good faith effort to deal with everyday problems. The China Securities Regulatory Commission has passed hundreds of regulations in recent years in an effort to bring some order to the chaotic PRC securities markets. Similarly, the Supreme People's Court (SPC) has issued a number of notices and regulations to overcome difficulties in enforcing court judgments and arbitral awards.[86] In at least one instance, the SPC issued a notice establishing time limits for enforcing an award and clarifying the fees charged by courts for enforcement in direct response to the complaints of foreign lawyers at a conference held by the US Dept. of Commerce and the PRC Ministry of Foreign Trade and Economic Co-operation (MOFTEC).[87] In recent years, the MOJ established a network of hotlines in response to complaints from frustrated citizens about negligent lawyers and from equally frustrated lawyers that government officials were preventing them from carrying out their duties. Even national-level laws are frequently a response to operational concerns at lower levels. Many national laws are drafted based on the results of local experiments. In most cases, the drafting committee will do a tour around China to collect information during the early stages of the legislative process. The committee will also hold hearings and circulate drafts to the relevant local entities for comments.

Local courts have also been a source of numerous reforms. Many of the reforms included in the Supreme Court's five-year plan for reforms originally began as experiments by local courts to deal with concrete problems they were facing in practice.[88] More recently, facing a rise in the number of cases, some courts such as the Haidian Basic Court have begun experimenting with summary procedures. The experiments have caught the attention of central authorities. As a result, the National Judges College has now made summary procedures one of its focal points for further research.

Legal academics have proposed an endless series of reforms, often based on empirical research projects that highlight deficiencies in the actual operation of the law. To cite just a few examples, in the administrative area, Jiang Mingan's influential survey project provided a wealth of practical suggestions for reforms.[89] There have also been a number of studies of practical problems in the implementation of the criminal procedure law, leading to the issuance of clarifying regulations that sought to strengthen implementation of the law and reduce conflicting interpretations among the judiciary, procuracy, and public security.[90] Chen Guangzhong's criminal law research center has played a pivotal role in raising awareness of criminal law standards under international law. Academics have also been instrumental in preparing judicial training manuals and developing other methods to help raise the level of competence of the judiciary and legal profession, such as holding mock trials conducted by actual judges and lawyers from both a common law and civil system.[91] Moreover, many academics and legal actors working in institutions such as the NPC's Office of Legislative Affairs have taken a number of initiatives to strengthen the legal system, such as holding conferences attended by members from people's congresses from all around to discuss ways to improve the hearing system.[92] In one project aimed at strengthening the judiciary, a young law professor and several judges in Sichuan province conducted a study to examine the constraints preventing courts from fully and impartially exercising their judicial power. The project produced a book which included empirical results and proposals for reforms and recommendations to national and provincial authorities.[93]

In short, the central-level authorities clearly have played and will continue to play an important role in the reform process. Major reforms – such as institutional changes to create a more authoritative and independent judiciary – require central-level support. But on the whole the reform process is much less unidirectional than often suggested, with most of the concrete reform initiatives arising from below in response to the practical concerns of those on the front lines. Indeed, a number of academics working on legal reform and key members of state institutions such as the courts, procuracy, and people's congresses have complained about the seemingly haphazard nature of reforms. In a conference on judicial reform in August 2001, many participants called for the establishment of a central committee in charge of legal reforms to consolidate valuable experiences and share information gained from local experiments, minimize conflicting and inconsistent reform initiatives, mediate conflicts of interests between different interest groups and state entities, and, most importantly, provide an overall plan for future reforms.[94]

Overstating the costs of reform: broad social support rather than social alienation

Some PRC scholars worry not only about the nature of reform but about the pace. They argue that whereas in some Western countries rule of law evolved gradually, China has not had the luxury of slowly implementing legal reforms.[95] It has had to rebuild its legal system from scratch while simultaneously managing the transition from a centrally planned economy to a market-oriented economy. The allegedly state-centered nature of legal reform along with the speed of reform has resulted in a wide gap between law and practice.[96] Changing laws and attitudes has its costs. Rapid change may lead to chaos and confusion. The destruction of existing normative systems may give rise to feelings of resentment over the loss of traditional forms of life and alienation as people struggle to assimilate the new values. This is all the more the case in China given that its traditions do not provide fertile ground for rule of law. Establishment of rule of law will also challenge entrenched interests. Government and administrative officials used to ruling by fiat will need to mend their ways. Implementing rule of law therefore will require changing deeply held attitudes among government officials and the people alike.

At the same time, China has not faced the difficulties of some countries. Rule of law in the twentieth century has often been a product of war, revolution, or government coups rather than a gradual evolution.[97] In the case of Post-World War II countries, the victors imposed their values, including rule of law, on the loser. In East Germany and the Soviet Union, the velvet revolution resulted in the abrupt downfall of socialism and a negotiated settlement between the ruling socialist elite and emergent leaders representing society. In Africa, the retreat of colonial powers left a vacuum that has been filled imperfectly at best by rule of law.[98] In Latin America, the overthrow of corrupt authoritarian regimes made rule of law possible but also raised the issue of how best to deal with the leaders of the prior regime who were responsible for unknown numbers of killings and disappearances. In most of these cases, the central governments were weak. Moreover, the new rulers faced the daunting challenge of reforming the political and legal system and carrying out economic reform at the same time.

In contrast, China's march toward rule of law has been more gradual. While pressure from the outside has been a factor, China has pursued legal reform primarily for its own domestic reasons and largely at its own pace. Unlike the Soviet Union, China did not attempt radical economic and political reform at the same time. Rather, it has focused on economic reforms, and even in the economic area it has pursued a gradual approach rather than the big bang approach. Whereas political unrest has undermined the efforts to implement rule of law in many developing states, China has had the benefit of political stability.[99] The state, although not the all-powerful authoritarian force of the Mao era, is still relatively strong and capable of advancing the institutional reforms necessary to realize rule of law.[100]

Moreover, while there are costs to rule of law, there are also numerous benefits, particularly to the average citizen who might feel alienated by a more law-based order and the change in norms governing behavior. Significantly, concern about alienation seems to be more prevalent among contrarian intellectuals than the general public, who see law as a valuable tool in the fight against corruption and in the struggle to realize their rights.[101]

Transplanting rule of law: adapting reforms to China's circumstances

Earlier critics of the law and development movement attributed the large gap between law on the books and actual reality to the difficulty of transplanting laws from their place of origin in modern Western liberal democracies to the typically much different environs of the recipient country. Similarly, the wide gap between law and actual practice has led some commentators to question whether China can succeed in establishing rule of law by importing laws from other countries and relying on foreign legal institutions as the model for reforms.[102] Zhu Suli, a leading legal scholar at Beijing University, has cautioned against taking rule of law as an ideal and then trying to force society to fit a predetermined mold. Such an approach is likely to fail, he suggests, because it ignores the actual conditions and needs of society.[103] Rather than relying heavily on imported laws and models, China should make use of its own native resources (*bentu ziyuan*). Others echo his concern that importing laws without consideration of China's "national character" (*guoqing*),[104] including its moral traditions[105] or current circumstances[106] will increase the difficulties of implementation.

While most scholars appreciate the need to adapt foreign laws and institutions to China's particular circumstances, some are less worried about the difficulty of legal transplants taking root in Chinese soil – or at least they believe there is little alternative. Zhang Wenxian, one of China's leading legal philosophers, notes that China has little choice but to import foreign laws.[107] China does not have the time to develop a completely new set of laws. The pressing demands of China's domestic economic reforms and foreign investors require laws now.

As we have seen, rule of law is consistent with considerable variation. There is therefore ample room to adopt a form of rule of law that meets the requirements of a thin conception and fits China's own circumstances. Indeed, given the path-dependent nature of reforms, reformers will have to take China's current realities into consideration when making proposals if they are to design effective programs. Legislators obviously increase the chance that the transplant will be successful by

choosing suitable laws as their models and by adapting them according to actual circumstances.[108] For instance, importing the US securities
regulatory regime may not be particularly useful given China's immature securities markets and the current level of legal, professional, and
institutional development.[109] China may lack a sufficient number of
trained personnel to operate such a complicated regime.[110] Similarly,
asking the courts at this point in time to play the same role as courts
in the USA in reviewing administrative decisions and rule-making fails
to take into account the low level of professionalism of PRC judges, the
courts' lack of authority within the Chinese polity, and the problem of
judicial corruption.[111]

Inevitably, there will be a process of adaptation and assimilation in
implementing new laws, creating new institutions, and establishing new
practices. By taking advantage of input from the grassroots, reformers
will be better able to come up with more appropriate solutions in the
first place and then to modify existing laws, institutions, or practices
as needed. Allowing local experimentation and establishing feedback
mechanisms will also diminish the top-down nature of the reform process, narrow the gap between law on the books and actual practice, and
increase the likelihood that the transplant will be successful.[112]

On the other hand, the uniqueness of the Chinese situation should
not be overstated. China is increasingly a modern state, facing many of
the same challenges as other modern states – a market economy that requires clear rules and effective dispute resolution mechanisms, a growing
private sector and business community seeking protection of its rights
and fair opportunities to compete in the marketplace, and an increasingly pluralistic society able to take advantage of the latest technologies
to exchange information and ideas about such issues as corruption, environmental pollution, and the growing disparity between the rich and
poor. In designing a system that responds to the needs of a modern market economy and an increasingly pluralistic society, China's legal reformers should take advantage of the experiences of other countries. Moreover, even though portraying rule-of-law reforms as merely technical in
nature grossly understates the normative dimension, there is a significant
technical dimension to such reforms. Predictably, as economic reforms
have progressed and China has become part of the world community,
China's institutions and rules have increasingly come to resemble those
in other modern states.[113] With the escalating globalization that will

inevitably result from China's accession to the WTO, China's legal system will converge even more toward the best practices of other systems.

PRC scholars have also noted that law may in some cases play a role in leading society and bringing about social, political, and economic change. In many ways, the Administrative Litigation Law (ALL), for instance, was ahead of its time. Even today, it is underutilized for a variety of reasons to be discussed in Chapter 9. Nevertheless, the mere passage of the law, following as it did on the heels of Tiananmen, sent an important signal that China's leaders did not intend to give up on legal reforms and return to the old ways of the Mao era. Although perhaps more important for symbolic reasons in the early years,[114] the law has now come to have real teeth, and has altered the way in which government officials operate and the relationship between state and society. Critics who focus on the relatively small number of administrative litigation cases each year fail to appreciate the extent to which passage of the laws served a signaling function, alerting officials that the rules of the game had changed.[115] Similarly, the 1996 revisions to the Criminal Procedure Law announced a radical change in the relationship between the court, the legal profession, and the procuracy, which is now only beginning to be evidenced in practice. Meanwhile, by giving certain criminal defendants the right to a lawyer, the Lawyers Law presumed a legal aid system that did not exist at the time and is still only in the early stages of development. By incorporating the right, drafters may have accelerated the pace of development.

Undoubtedly, China's legal architects should make use of native resources in constructing the legal system. Unfortunately, however, when it comes to specifying exactly what these native resources are, PRC scholars have little to say.[116] Fu Zitang, for instance, claims that China's traditional culture contains ideas that support rule of law but he fails to tell us which ideas.[117] In any event, even if he were able to point to some features of the traditional legal system or morality that were conducive to rule of law, he would also have to explain how those ideas could be extracted from the conceptual and normative context in which they are embedded and pressed into the service of rule of law. In some cases that would be relatively straightforward, but in other cases it would be more difficult. For instance, there were various positive aspects to the Imperial legal system, including the distinction between intentional and negligent crimes, the careful attention paid to fact-finding, procedural safeguards to ensure that the truth prevailed, open trials, and punishments fixed in law.[118] Moreover, Legalists supported the principle of equality before the law (except for the ruler), though the system ultimately incorporated status distinctions out of deference to Confucian sensibilities. Yet because these features were embedded in a system whose purpose was to serve the interests of the ruler and the state, in practice they often were implemented in ways and led to outcomes in particular cases that are at odds with the requirements and purposes of any reasonable interpretation of rule of law and certainly conceptions of rule of law that emphasize the role of law in limiting the state and protecting individuals' rights and interests. Thus, the laudable importance attached to substantive justice contributed to the emphasis on confessions and the widespread use of torture. Similarly, although procedural laws limited the form and degree of torture, the state-centric nature of the legal system meant that in practice such laws could give way to the higher needs of the state. Indeed, when the evidence was sufficiently clear and yet the accused still dared to defy the state by refusing to confess even after being subject to torture, the magistrate could convict without a confession.

On their face, some of the provisions and practices of the Imperial legal system are appealing. But upon further exploration, they often reveal an ethical orientation at odds with rule of law. Accordingly, adopting such provisions or features requires that they be extracted from their native context before being transplanted to the radically different soils of rule of law.

By and large, however, PRC scholars agree that China's traditional "rule of man" culture not only has precious few features that support rule of law but that it constitutes one of the biggest obstacles to the realization of rule of law. Jiang Xianfu, for instance, speaks for many PRC legal scholars in concluding that despite a few positive features, native ethics are obsolete and an impediment to rule of law. He goes on to suggest that a new ethical system be created – one that is in keeping with rule of law and a market economy – which emphasizes freedom, equality, openness, and respect for others.[119]

Ironically, some scholars claim that the biggest native resource for the promotion of rule of law is the state and the Party.[120] The government and the CCP have the people, knowledge, power, economic resources, and organizational network to promote rule of law in the face of opposition by those who will lose out as a result of reforms.[121] More concretely,

Party institutions, such as the discipline committees, may play a role in curbing corruption or reining in abusive government and administrative officials.

On the other hand, the Party may also be an obstacle to the realization of rule of law. Indeed, as discussed in Chapter 5, many commentators see the Party as the biggest impediment to rule of law. At any rate, although there are benefits to relying on the Party in some cases to promote rule of law, in the long run excessive reliance is likely to impede the development of independent institutions necessary to realize rule of law. For instance, depending on Party discipline committees to curb corruption may actually be more effective than trying to hold Party members and high-level government officials accountable in the courts, given the weakness of the judiciary.[122] But removing cases involving Party members and top government officials from the courts further undermines the authority of the judiciary and the legitimacy of the legal system. In contrast, allowing the courts to handle such cases would have the long-term benefit of increasing the prestige, authority, and legitimacy of the courts.[123] Similarly, foreign investors who boisterously call for rule of law and yet run to the Party secretary when they are unable to enforce court judgments or arbitral awards are likely not only to appear hypocritical but to shoot themselves in the foot by impeding the long-term development of the judicial system.[124]

One possible native resource that might be useful is the traditional preference for informal means of resolving disputes.[125] Courts need not be the only means of resolving disputes, and the preference to settle disputes through mediation rather than litigation is regularly cited as one of China's contributions to a modern legal order. Of course, alternatives to litigation are also common in other countries, even the allegedly litigious USA.[126] Moreover, the preference for mediation and informal dispute settlement in China should not be exaggerated. The preference may be due in part to the lack of attractive alternatives. The Imperial legal system hardly encouraged litigation, with its use of torture and reliance on rapacious underlings who extracted fees from litigants.[127] In fact, as the legal system has improved in the last two decades, litigation has increased while mediation has decreased.[128] The growing preference for litigation as opposed to mediation is partially explained by economic development. Commercial transactions are increasingly complex. Because many mediators only have a rudimentary understanding of the law in

China, parties prefer to rely on more formal channels. The amount at stake has also risen steadily. Parties may not want to have poorly trained mediators deciding cases that involve such large sums of money. Moreover, the parties themselves are different. Many contracts are between companies, sometimes even foreign companies, that have no connection with each other beyond the arms-length transaction that forms the subject of the dispute. Thus they are unable to turn for mediation to a common superior or a third party to which both are connected.

Traditional means of resolving disputes may in some circumstances serve as valuable supplements to the formal court system, and thus may be incorporated into a rule of law with Chinese characteristics.[129] However, the informal means of dispute resolution in China, particularly mediation, also raises concerns from the rule-of-law perspective. Some PRC scholars have suggested that an emphasis on mediation supports the feudalistic attitude to avoid litigation. Moreover, stressing mediation may give people the impression that the courts are unreliable or lack authority. Others have pointed out that mediation is often much more coercive than is suggested in the more idealistic accounts that portray mediation as a means of saving face and restoring social harmony.[130] They also note that judicial mediation hinders the development of the judiciary and legal profession as judges and lawyers need not rely on professional legal training to resolve disputes.[131] With respect to mediation outside the courtroom, mediators generally lack legal training, although they are supposed to know the law.[132] The formal legal process's emphasis on procedural safeguards and strict scrutiny of evidence is absent, and in many cases, the final result will not comply with the law.

At any rate, even under the best of circumstances, informal dispute mechanisms are no substitute for a functioning court system that meets the basic requirements of a thin rule of law. Mediation and arbitration alone are insufficient. Mediation and arbitration occur against the backdrop of a court system. Without the credible threat of suing in court, the parties would have less reason to reach agreement through mediation.[133] Even when there is a credible threat of litigation, the parties will not always be able to reach an agreement through mediation and will have to resolve the conflict in court. In some cases, one of the parties to a mediation agreement might renege, or the party that loses at arbitration might refuse to comply with the award. The other party must then turn to the court to settle the dispute or enforce the agreement or award.

The irrelevance of Critical Legal Studies and Marxist critiques

Building on the broad-based political critiques of capitalism and liberalism by Marxist philosophers and more recently on the deconstructionist
techniques of postmodern literary theorists, CRITs have objected to rule
of law on a number of grounds. Most fundamentally, some CRITs see it
as a mask for oppression and injustice.[134] Others argue that law is much
more indeterminate than rule-of-law advocates presume, and that such
indeterminacy undermines rule of law's promise of predictability and
blurs the line between law and politics.[135] Conversely, some scholars (not
all of them CRITs), argue that law is too determinate, and that rule of
law amounts to a perverse kind of fetish for clear rules and bright lines
when life is far too complex and filled with nuances and fine shades of
gray to be reduced to any simple set of black and white rules.[136]

Primarily professors in US law schools, CRITs developed their critique of rule of law in the context of a modern wealthy liberal democracy with a highly professional, basically functional legal system that on
the whole protects individual rights reasonably well. In doing so, CRITs
expanded on the insights of the Legal Realists, who took as their main
target legal formalism. Formalism assumed a mechanical model of law.
The legal system is based on clear rules that can be applied in a mechanical, syllogistic way to a set of facts to produce a legal conclusion
or judgment. The CRITs demonstrated that any such formalistic understanding of the legal system or rule of law is misguided at best and
pernicious at worst in that it reifies the existing legal order, masking the
contingency of the law and the way in which rule of law serves as an
ideology. According to CRITs, rule of law overstates the predictability of
law and draws too sharp a line between law and politics. The legal system
consists of a maze of contradictory legal doctrines, with numerous laws
reflecting a conflict in fundamental values.[137] The result of such contradictions in doctrines and values is that in any case (or most or some
cases depending on the skepticism of the person making the claim) the
outcome is radically indeterminate and will turn on the ethical views,
political beliefs, or personal prejudices of the judge rather than legal
arguments.[138]

The CRITs' attack on rule of law should serve as a warning to those
who think that it is the answer to all of China's problems. Clearly it
is not. However, the main thrust of the CRITs' critique, taking as its

target a well-developed legal system that by and large complies with the requirements of rule of law, is largely irrelevant in the case of a country such as China that is struggling to establish a functional legal system. The problem in China has not been that anyone draws too sharp a line between law and politics but that the line has been obliterated for much of China's history; the pressing concern has been too much politics, not too little. The task nowadays is to establish at least some degree of separation between law and politics in the face of a Leninist ideology that assigns a leading role to the Party and senior Party leaders who may still to a greater or lesser extent see law as a tool of the Party-state.

Similarly, given the ruling regime's abuse of the legal system to punish enemies of the state and achieve overtly political ends during the Mao period, Chinese citizens hardly need to be warned not to expect too much from the legal system by way of certainty and predictability. Even if we set aside the misuse of law during the Mao era and look back at law during the Imperial period, the main worry was not legal formalism but rather that judges exercised too much discretion. While Max Weber's characterization of the Imperial legal system in terms of Kadi justice may have overstated the degree to which magistrates made decisions based on general moral principles rather than legal codes, the legal system did place a premium on particularized justice and did emphasize substantive justice at the expense of procedural justice.[139] Today, the legal system continues to struggle with the tendency to slight procedures and generally applicable laws in favor of context-specific decisions, often based on personal relations (*guanxi*). Put differently, having been Legal Realists rather than formalists all along, Chinese find the quip of an American legal scholar that "we are all Legal Realists now" a mildly amusing restatement of the obvious.[140]

The CRITs' concern that the rhetoric of rule of law masks oppression makes sense as a corrective to those who think the rights of minorities are secure just because they are written into the constitution or that rule of law entails the end of class politics and contentious issues of distributive justice. But Chinese citizens are well aware of class politics and that law can be used to oppress as well as liberate. The CRITs' assertion of the oppressive nature of law builds on a standard Marxist critique of law, a critique with which those who have grown up in socialist China are all too familiar. Although there are fewer articles written from the perspective of class conflict today and leftist critics of rule of law have been largely marginalized – as leftists have been marginalized in general within Chinese politics – even liberal reformers appreciate that law can serve the interests of the ruling elite rather than the general public. Nevertheless – or perhaps for that very reason – they have emphasized the role of law in limiting the ruling elite and protecting the rights and interests of the ruled.[141]

As a formal matter, a thin conception of rule of law is content neutral: the laws may either favor the interests of the ruling class or the interests of the proletariat. That will depend on a number of other issues, including the form of government, the channels for participation in the law-making process, and so forth. While it would be naïve to assume that law will not serve the interests of the wealthy and powerful in society, what is abundantly clear from reflecting on the rise and fall of socialist states is that the oppressed may be just as oppressed if not more so in the absence of rule of law. Not surprisingly, dissidents rotting away in Chinese jails see rule of law as a valuable weapon for challenging state acts rather than as a mask of oppression.[142]

Will rule of law support an authoritarian regime?

Skeptics who deny any fundamental change in the nature of the legal system fear that the purpose of the Party in carrying out legal reforms is simply to create a more effective tool to serve the Party-state.[143] As discussed above, there are good reasons to doubt that the intent or end result of legal reforms will be a more efficient rule by law. The more likely result is some form of rule of law. But even if the system is in transition from rule by law to rule of law, the Statist Socialist variety in particular still offers little opportunity for meaningful public participation. Arguably, the Party is simply acting strategically in accepting some limits on its power implicit in the notion of rule of law in order to strengthen its position. Zhu Suli, for instance, has suggested that rule of law will promote economic development, which in turn will strengthen the Party-state both fiscally and in terms of legitimacy. A stronger Party may be better positioned to resist meaningful political reforms.[144]

There is no gainsaying the fact that the instrumental aspects of legal reforms may enhance the efficiency of authoritarian governments. In the absence of democracy and pluralist institutions for public participation in the law-making, interpretation and implementation processes, law may come to serve the interests of the state and the ruling elite.

It is possible therefore that rule of law will serve authoritarian ends in China. Of course, many within China reject democracy and believe that at present China needs an authoritarian government (whether socialist or not) to oversee economic reforms and maintain stability, though they disagree about just how hard or soft the authoritarian regime should be. Clearly, both Statist Socialists and Neoauthoritarians, and even to some extent Communitarians, see the potential of legal reforms to strengthen the state as a positive aspect. In the long run, however, Communitarians view rule of law as a means of limiting the state and a stepping stone toward democracy. Moreover, all expect law to impose some limits on the state and thus to mitigate to one degree or another the harshness of the rule-by-law authoritarian regime of the Mao era.

While legal reforms could help Statist Socialists solidify their power and support a relatively hard authoritarianism, the dangers of the ruling regime misusing rule of law for its own authoritarian ends should not be overstated. As noted, even a Statist Socialist rule of law differs from instrumental rule by law in that law is not just a tool to be used by the ruling regime to control the people or promote the interests of the privileged few. Rule of law entails limits on the state and the ruling elite (who are also bound by the law), provides a basis for challenges by citizens of government arbitrariness, and serves to protect the rights and interests of the nonelite.[145] It is striking that while critics in many developed countries have the luxury of belittling the concept of rule of law, those who have had the misfortune to suffer its absence appreciate its virtues and count among its biggest supporters. Looking back on the alleged failure of the original law and development movement from the vantage point of over three decades of additional experience, one commentator has pointed out that the self-proclaimed death of the law and development movement in the 1970s did not prevent people living under authoritarian rule from continuing to press for rule of law as a constraint on the purely instrumental use of law by authoritarian rulers.[146]

Moreover, the choice facing Chinese reformers is not authoritarianism or democracy, but authoritarianism with rule of law or without it. Authoritarianism in China is not the result of legal reforms to implement rule of law. On the contrary, the ruling regime would be even more authoritarian in the absence of legal reforms. Where legal rules are applied with principled consistency to both the state and its citizens, as required by rule of law, they generally restrain rather than expand the arbitrary exercise of state power.[147] Further, as some PRC scholars have observed, while historically the development of rule of law has depended on pro-motion by the authorities, it also results in a change in the conception of authority. In the past, the Party's authority to rule was based to a con-siderable extent on the charisma of revolutionary leaders who fought off the Guomingdang and foreign oppressors and allowed China to regain its dignity and stand on its own two feet. However, with the death of the old guard, new leaders have had to base their authority on other grounds. To use Weber's terminology, implementation of rule of law entails greater reliance on formal rules by trained professionals rather than decision-making by charismatic individuals, and thus results in a transformation from charismatic to a more formal rational authority.[148]

Perhaps most important, in the long run, implementing rule of law will usually alter the balance of power between the state, society, and individuals, while at the same time alterations in the balance of power resulting from economic reforms and factors beyond the legal system will create further pressure to implement rule of law. The establishment of a legal system with some degree of autonomy acts as a counterweight to political power and provides a basis for challenging state power. While a strong civil society is not inevitable, it is more likely in a state that im-plements rule of law than in one that does not.[149] A strong civil society is arguably more likely to seek and more likely to obtain political re-forms aimed at further limiting the power of authoritarian states and increasing the power of society. Thus, even if the goal is democracy and protection of human rights, it makes sense to ensure at minimum that a thin rule of law is realized. A more likely result in China than a stronger authoritarian regime is that rule of law will be a force for liberalization and come to impose restraints on the rulers, as in Taiwan, South Korea, and even Indonesia, where former President Suharto was brought up on corruption charges.[150]

This is not to claim that rule of law will inevitably lead to political re-forms and the realization of democracy and human rights; that a strong civil society will necessarily emerge in China; or that even if a strong civil society does emerge, that it will be a force for democracy and individual rights, particularly a liberal version of individual rights. Although pro-ponents of political reforms in China frequently see an emerging civil society as a force of change, scholars writing about political reform in other countries in the 1960s and '70s documented the more negative aspects of civil society. All too often, civil society fostered the formation of interest groups that then pushed their own agenda, resulting in bad policies. Bad policies in turn produced more dissatisfaction and social unrest, leading ultimately to the collapse of democratic governments, which were then replaced by military dictatorships or other authoritarian governments. Simply put, more civil society does not necessarily mean more civic behavior or better government. Civil society is consistent with authoritarianism and fascism.[151]

Although realization of a thin rule of law increases the likelihood that political reform will be possible, whether Chinese citizens will want to take advantage of that possibility to push for liberal democracy and greater civil and political rights depends on their own political values. It is quite possible, indeed probable, that China could realize some version of rule of law without a marked increase in support for democracy and liberal versions of human rights. As I argue in Chapter 11, support for democracy and a liberal version of individual rights is weak in China. At present, while reforms in China have already dramatically increased personal freedom, civil society remains limited.[152] Furthermore, even when social groups do emerge, they are not always predisposed toward democracy.[153]

Will rule of law bolster the legitimacy of the Party?

Whether legal reforms will fortify the ruling regime and allow it to resist political reforms and democratization depends in part on whether implementing rule of law, particularly a Statist Socialist version, is sufficient to bolster the legitimacy of the Party. After the disastrous Cultural Revolution, the Party desperately needed to shore up its legitimacy both at home and abroad. Rule of law is intended to serve this purpose in several ways.[154] First, implementation of rule of law will result in better decisions and increase the likelihood of avoiding the kind of mistaken policy choices that plagued the Mao era.[155] Rule of law involves a change in the decision-making process both with respect to the making of laws and the resolution of particular cases. Policies are now to be translated into laws in accordance with proper procedures for law-making.[156] The law-making process provides for more discussion and more participation by a wider segment of the public, which should result in better laws. People's congress delegates are more highly educated, and aided in technical matters by professionally staffed subcommittees. Likewise, the creation of a more professional judiciary, better-trained lawyers, along with improvements in the procedural laws that give parties more rights at trial, allow parties greater opportunity to consult with a lawyer and this leads to better decisions in particular cases than during the heavily politicized Mao era.

Apart from producing better decisions, rule of law enhances the legitimacy of the regime by diffusing responsibility. The Party has based its claim to legitimacy and right to lead on its ability to know the truth, to determine the scientifically correct path that would best serve the people's interests.[157] Because the Party monopolized power, the Party was blamed for every mistake – the antirightist movement, the Great Leap Forward, the Cultural Revolution, China's failure to develop as rapidly as other countries, and so on. By shifting responsibility for some decisions to the NPC, administrative agencies, and courts, the Party arguably can no longer be held accountable for every problem. Further, emphasizing the process of law-making and fair procedures serves to de-emphasize to some degree the substantive results: compliance with proper procedures need not always produce substantively correct results.[158] By stressing process values typical of rule of law, the Party may hope that it can escape the burden of the Leninist assertion that the Party knows the scientifically correct solution to every social problem.

Perhaps most important, rule of law reinforces the legitimacy of the current regime by contributing to economic development. The current regime's ability to withstand the Tiananmen crisis and continue in power despite widespread corruption, environmental degradation, increasing unemployment, and the many other maladies plaguing contemporary society is due in no small measure to its ability to sustain high growth rates and ensure that the material standard of living for most people continues to rise.

In addition to these indirect ways in which rule of law supports the legitimacy of the current regime, Jiang Zemin and others seem to be counting on rule of law to shore up legitimacy in a more direct way. They appear to be hoping the ideology of rule of law will be able to fill the normative vacuum that currently exists in China.[159] Few today believe in socialism as a normative ideology. Under attack for the last fifty years, traditional normative systems such as Confucianism and Daoism have withered. Confronting an ethical crisis, the Party has attempted to revitalize Confucianism and has taken steps to create a socialist spiritual civilization in hopes of combating the widespread deterioration in moral standards. A 1996 CCP Resolution acknowledged that the standard of moral conduct had fallen, ethical and cultural progress had not kept pace with economic progress, and that many people had lost faith in socialism.[160] The Resolution traced the crisis to economic reforms, pressure from the superiority of developed capitalist countries, the infiltration of Western ideology, and the remnants of feudalism. It warned that liberalism will lead to capitalism and undermine political stability and unity. The Resolution advocated renewed emphasis on Marxism and that right be clearly distinguished from wrong on such issues as Marxism versus non-Marxism, the mutual development of various economic sectors with public ownership as the mainstay as opposed to privatization, and socialist democracy versus democracy as practiced in Western countries.

Unfortunately, the Resolution was not entirely clear as to what a socialist spiritual civilization is. It seems to be a hodgepodge consisting of attacks on wholesale Westernization and bourgeois liberalism combined with blatant appeals to nationalism, celebration of the importance of culture and art, praise for the indigenous and illustrious tradition of Confucianism, and exhortation of the masses to emulate such modern day Lei Fengs as Kong Fansen.[161] Whatever it is supposed to be, Party efforts to bring about this new socialist spiritual civilization have been largely ineffectual.[162] While many Chinese respond to the nationalist component of Jiang's spiritual civilization plank, few take seriously the emphasis on socialism.[163]

The chances of rule of law filling the normative vacuum are slim. At best, rule of law may serve as an ideology in only a limited way. In Weber's view, an autonomous and rational rule-of-law system engenders respect for the law. Accordingly, people are more willing to follow particular laws and obey judicial decisions even when it is not in their immediate interests to do so.[164] PRC citizens would perhaps be more likely to view the current regime favorably if it complied with rule-of-law norms. Surely they prefer a government that acts in accordance with law to the arbitrariness of the Mao regime, just as they no doubt prefer a regime that takes their rights seriously. Today, Chinese citizens enjoy more rights and freedoms than in the past. Of course China's human rights record still leaves much to be desired. Thus, the current regime could gain more legitimacy both at home and abroad if it complemented its economic record by taking rights more seriously.

Rule of law may also serve to some extent as an ideological basis for a market economy. According to Weber, the Protestant work ethic was one factor in economic development in Europe. However, Judeo-Christian values more generally have played a role in defining the nature of capitalism in Western countries by imposing some basic normative limits on economic behavior. Fundamental moral principles such as the need to respect the inherent dignity of each individual established minimal standards for treating even strangers, thus tempering to some extent the harshness of capitalism and making reliance on legal sanctions and the coercive force of the state somewhat less necessary. In contrast, in China the breakdown of the traditional normative order and the collapse of socialism as a viable alternative have resulted in a disorderly marketplace plagued by corruption, fraud, and deceptive practices. Unscrupulous entrepreneurs out to make a quick profit not only produce fake and shoddy goods but use poisonous substitutes rather than harmless placebos in their imitation alcohol or medicines which then end up killing people. Respect for laws and a rule-of-law ideology may be able to serve to some extent as a normative constraint on such unscrupulous behavior.

However, the likely legitimacy benefits of rule of law are easily overstated. With respect to the quality of law-making and the law-making process, greater reliance on people's congresses, governments, and administrative agencies may produce better laws than under the more centralized, Party-dominated regime of the Mao era. But opportunities for public participation are still extremely limited, and Chinese citizens do not directly elect legislatures except at the village level. If Statist Socialists or Neoauthoritarians prevail, as seems likely in the short term, the opportunities for public participation will remain limited. Thus any legitimacy derived from better quality laws will be primarily performance-based rather than consent-based: that is, based on whether the laws produce good results rather than any sense of having actually chosen the laws or at least the lawmakers.[165] One of the dangers of performance-based legitimacy is that the government must continually produce good results or suffer a loss of legitimacy. Unfortunately, many laws continue to be poorly drafted and ill-conceived. Similarly, the current regime's heavy reliance on economic development as a source of legitimacy makes it particularly vulnerable to downturns in the economy. And while the current regime might hope to diffuse some of the responsibility for such problems by invoking the process values of rule of law, it will succeed only to a limited degree given that the Party (as the ruling party) continues to control key policy decisions and to set the general parameters for political and economic reform.

The attempt to rely more directly on the ideology of rule of law to provide a normative basis for a market economy and to fill the moral vacuum that exists in contemporary China is also likely to be only partially successful at best. Rule of law alone will not be sufficient to produce a more humane capitalism or bring order to what at times appears to be the Far East equivalent of the Wild Wild West. Ultimately, a more robust moral code is also required.[166]

More generally, a thin rule of law does not itself provide much of a substantive normative basis on which to build a new moral order. Rule of law could serve a variety of ends, but those ends must be determined separately. As discussed in the previous chapter, Jiang Zemin and other Statist Socialists see rule of law as serving national and collective interests such as stability. To the extent that rule of law is meant to protect rights, Jiang favors a version of rights that is nationalistic. Rights are to serve the nation and the cause of development. Rights are not to threaten state sovereignty, and Beijing strenuously and repeatedly objects to any attempt by foreign governments to use rights issues to meddle in China's affairs. Further, the official PRC policy emphasizes collective rights over individual rights, and economic rights (in particular the right to subsistence) over civil and political rights. In contrast, other rule-of-law advocates see rule of law as protecting a much wider range of individual freedom. Disagreement about the fundamental normative issues that distinguish the various thick conceptions of rule of law undermine the attempt to rely on any particular conception to provide a robust common moral ground.

Ironically, in the end, the wishes of Jiang and other government leaders notwithstanding, reliance on rule of law to augment regime legitimacy could backfire and produce just the opposite result.[167] Repeated appeals to rule of law raise expectations among the people that the government will act accordingly. As a result, the large gap between the ideal of rule of law and actual practice could undermine the authority of the government. More directly, rule of law is also a potential threat to the current regime in that the law may be used to challenge state acts. Citizens increasingly are taking advantage of administrative law reforms that allow them to contest government decisions. Reforms have also produced a limited but growing civil society, and created or strengthened alternative bases of power such as the NPC, judiciary, administrative agencies, and local governments that could some day challenge the Party.

Conclusion

Although legal reforms could conceivably strengthen the ruling regime and allow it to resist political reforms, the more likely result is that implementation of rule of law will produce a more limited government and lead to a shift in power from the Party to state organs and society. Nevertheless, the possibility that legal reforms could serve the interests of the ruling elite and the various other critiques of rule of law serve to remind us that rule of law is no magic potion. A healthy dose of rule of law will not miraculously cause all of China's problems to disappear. By itself, it will not even provide a cure for all of the legal system's ills. Rule of law is an ideal at best imperfectly realized in any society. That rule of law is an aspirational ideal imperfectly realized in any society is, however, hardly reason to reject the concept. One does not generally abandon aspirational ideals such as justice, truth, or equality simply because they cannot be fully realized in practice. Rather one tries to approximate the ideal as closely as possible. The better lesson to be drawn from the failure of all legal systems to measure up to the ideal is that they all should be improved.

There will always be disagreement about the fundamental moral issues that distinguish the various forms of rule of law and provide the normative framework in which the legal system operates. As a result, there will always be debates about what rule of law requires and when rule of law's virtues of predictability and limits on the abuse of discretion should give way to other important social values and the demands of a more context-specific justice. While the meaning, purposes, and value of rule of law continue to be debated in China, everyone agrees that there are many theoretical and practical issues to be overcome as China strives to implement rule of law. Although many of the obstacles are institutional in nature, critics often portray the CCP as the major impediment to the realization of rule of law. As demonstrated in the next chapter, however, the Party plays a much smaller role than in the past in the day-to-day operation of the government as a whole and the legal system in particular.

Notes

1   See Tamanaha (1997).
2   Malinowski (1926: 66).
3   See Rheinstein (1954: 13).
4   Bohannan (1967: 47). Hart also maintains that officials must effectively accept the rule of recognition and its rules of change and adjudication as common public standards of official behavior for the legal system to function, though the test of a valid law is its pedigree. Hart (1961: 113).
5   See Goldstein (2001).
6   For the concept of rule of recognition, see Hart (1961).
7   See Goldstein (2001).
8   Of course, given the wide diversity of legal systems and that even a thin theory implicates numerous normative and culture-specific issues, the incompletely theorized nature of rule-of-law theories is both an advantage and disadvantage. On the positive side, it may allow people who disagree about certain theoretical issues to agree on more specific issues that arise in practice. For instance, one may disagree about what structural arrangements best ensure judicial independence and yet still agree that the current lack of judicial independence is a problem. For a discussion of the virtues of incompletely theorized arguments, see Sunstein (1996: 3–7).
9   Munzer (1982).
10 Westen (1982).
11 When particular laws may be set aside to secure other values is a difficult theoretical issue. As noted below, one of the criticisms of rule of law is that it tends to degenerate into rule fetishism. Rule of law promotes obedience to laws, whether such laws are good or bad, appropriate in the particular context or not. While most people would allow that in some cases laws should give way to higher values – see David (1984) for a discussion of the way different legal systems attempt to incorporate or appeal to higher values – they may disagree about the particular instances when laws should give way, who has the right to decide, the standards for making the decision, whether the discretion ceded the decision-maker to follow the rules is subject to review and if so by whom, and so forth.

Just as individuals may differ over such issues, so may societies given their different ethical traditions. Many of the most dominant Western ethical traditions have tended to focus on establishing the proper rules to guide interpersonal interactions, whether the Ten Commandments, the Kantian Categorical Imperative, the utilitarian principle of maximization of the good, or Rawls' two principles of justice (though there are exceptions of course, including Aristotelian ethics, pragmatism, and situational ethics). Moreover, such rules tend to be abstract and universally applicable to all contexts. Accordingly, those who have been influenced by such traditions may be more willing than those influenced by other traditions to accept a narrowly circumscribed rule of law that sacrifices equity and particularized justice for the virtues of generality, equality, impartiality, and certainty that result from limiting the discretion of the decision-maker. In contrast, Chinese ethical traditions, whether Confucian, Daoist, or Maoist, have rejected rule ethics and universal principles in favor of context-specific, pragmatic, situational ethics. See Peerenboom (1993a); Hall and Ames (1987). In the past, Confucian and Daoist sages were responsible for determining what was best in a given situation based on their own judgment rather than by appeal to fixed laws or universal ethical principles. More recently, socialist leaders and government officials have claimed the same right. Indeed, one of the most striking features of the legal system in China today is the wide discretion ceded government officials to interpret and implement the law. See Chapter 9.

China may well differ from other countries with respect to the ease with which law may be shoved aside to accommodate other values. (As noted in Chapter 9, a strict interpretation of rule of law that does not allow for any deviations from the rules will simply result in rule of law giving way to other values more often.) Nevertheless, theoretical disagreement over this issue does not call into question the basic premise that law is to be supreme or that law is meant to constrain the arbitrary acts of the government. To be sure, the effectiveness of law as a restraint on the government will depend in practice on how easily law may be shunted aside. Further, at some point, routine disregard of the law will raise questions as to a society's commitment to rule of law, though it is important to bear in mind that there may be other explanations why laws are not followed in practice including that the laws are poorly drafted, unworkable in practice, or the product of a bygone era, and out of step with present-day realities.

12 If this approach is adopted, then arguably one would also need to address similar issues with respect to the other end of the spectrum – that is, one would need to specify the optimal degree (and, where applicable, the form or type) of transparency, clarity, stability, consistency, etc. for realization of the rule-of-law ideal, and set out priority rules for dealing with conflicts where improvements with respect to one element – for example, clarity – will have an adverse affect on one or more other elements – such as stability. Given the difficulty of considering all of the conceivable context-specific factors that could influence such choices, whether it would be possible, and if possible of much practical use, to construct such a detailed formal theory is highly doubtful. Indeed, the notion of a single rule-of-law ideal is itself problematic.

Consider, for example, Howard Wiarda's (1997: 161) response to criticisms that corporatist theory is underdeveloped: "We think of the corporatist approach as a set of suggestions, a way of thinking and looking, an heuristic (teaching and learning) device, and not a formal model. It tells us what to look for, what patterns to observe and test, what questions to ask. It gives us suggestions as to important societal relationships and public policy processes; to most of us, this is utility enough – without the added requirement of a formal model." My approach is similarly pragmatic: to the extent that a thin rule of law is a useful way to understand some of the obstacles faced by citizens, investors, or legal reformers in China or can be used as a metric for cross-cultural comparisons or for analyzing political or economic phenomena, then use it. There is no need to wait for a fully developed thin or thick theory of the rule of law.

In my view, the elements of a thin theory are sufficiently specified for the present purpose of determining the direction of China's legal reforms and providing a workable standard for measuring the progress of such reforms. More generally, rather than attempting to further hone the elements into a fully developed ideal thin theory, a more useful approach would be to consider specific cases as they arise in the context of a particular legal system to determine whether more clarity or consistency is desirable or the gap between law and practice should be narrowed.

For the criticism that the rule-of-law paradigm may hinder more than assist in understanding legal reforms in China, see Clarke (1998–99; 2001), and the discussion below.

13 See Chapter 9.

14 See Chapter 5.

15 Josephs (2000: 271).

16 Josephs (2000: 271).

17 Clinton was forced to testify as part of Paula Jones' civil damages case when the US Supreme Court rejected his arguments that the civil case would be unduly disruptive and should be stayed until he left office.

18 Chun and Roh were sentenced to death and twenty-two years' imprisonment, respectively, on charges of corruption, treason, and mutiny during the military era. President Kim Young Sam reduced both sentences, and as president-elect, Kim Dae Jung pardoned both men as a goodwill gesture toward political conservatives.

19 The principle of equality for all, the public's demand for justice, and the legitimacy of the government all support holding senior officials accountable. Holding even former heads of state responsible for their prior actions may also signal a successor regime's commitment to rule of law and its intent to distance itself from the previous regime. On the other hand, there are good reasons in some cases for not prosecuting senior officials or for pardoning them for criminal acts. Impeachment of the president, for example, might lead to a constitutional crisis or destabilize a shaky government. Furthermore, the decision to prosecute may itself be politicized, and result in prolonged social confrontation. The citizenry's sense of national pride may be injured when senior leaders are publicly paraded before the eyes of the world. Pardons may also be justified on the grounds that the public humiliation of being removed from office or having your transgressions broadcast on the nightly news is sufficient punishment for wayward officials. Nevertheless, the question remains, setting aside such worries and assuming that in some cases the current or former head of state should be held accountable, is the inability of the legal system to hold such heads of state accountable sufficient to deny the legal system rule-of-law status (and to describe it as rule by law)?

20 See the discussion and citations in Chapters 5 and 10.

21 See Rabban (1981).

22 "Criminal laws in this area are constitutionally limited to hard-core pornography. I shall not today attempt further to define the kinds of material I

understand to be embraced with that shorthand description . . . But I know it when I see it." Justice Potter Stewart (concurring), *Jacobellis* v. *Ohio*, 378 US 184, 198 (1964).

23   As Goldstein (2001) concludes, the answer to the question "do we know the rule of law when we see it?" is "sometimes."

24   To rank a legal system there must be rules for assigning points to positive and negative features. There is likely to be some disagreement about how to interpret a statistic such as a 50 percent inconsistency rate in China, particularly given other factors such as the reasons for such a high level of inconsistency. Similarly, how much weight should be assigned to the inability of the legal system to hold senior officials accountable? Again, whether there is much point in trying to work out a detailed metric is highly doubtful. The best that can be expected are some rough rules of thumb. A more practical approach, employed for example by the International Country Risk Guide to measure business risk arising from shortcomings in the legal system, is to create a rule-of-law index by selecting a limited number of variables and then have observers familiar with the legal system assign a rank within a relatively narrow range, in the case of ICRG from 0 to 6. See Chapter 10. Adapting this approach to present purposes, countries could be ranked on a scale of one to ten based on how well they comply with the requirements of a thin theory.

25   Several reviewers and commentators raised this concern in response to earlier drafts of this book or oral presentations at conferences.

26   As noted, many people conflate rule of law with Liberal Democratic rule of law. Moreover, foreign commentators in particular often fail to appreciate the significant progress China has made in improving the legal system in a short time. Nevertheless, even when measured against the more technical standards of a thin theory, China's legal system still falls far short of not just some unobtainable ideal but reasonable expectations for how a system can and should operate.

27   Clarke (1998–99).

28   Clarke (1998–99: 51).

29   Clarke (1998–99: 51). In a longer revised version of the article, Clarke (2001) refers to the Ideal Western Legal Order rather than "the Western rule of law ideal."

30   Clarke (1998–99: 52–53).

31   See also Chapter 12 for a discussion of this issue.

32   On the comparison of the courts to the Post Office, see Clarke (1996: 56).

33   Clarke does not endorse rule by law as an alternative description; nor does he in the works cited attempt to present a systematic alternative interpretation or theory to the rule-of-law paradigm. Rather, he illustrates what he takes to be the shortcomings of the IRI approach by reference to three examples, the first relating to contract law, the second to the role of the constitution, and the third (in the 2001 version) to administrative law. In addition, he briefly alludes to Stephens' (1992) model of a disciplinarian order, which he points out was itself not fully developed and in any event was designed with the Imperial legal system in mind, not the present system.

34   Clarke (1998–99: 53).

35 See Rubin (2001), arguing for the need to move beyond the rhetoric of democracy to focus on how institutions actually work in the USA.
36 See, for example, Li Buyun (1998c: 8). Xie Pengcheng (1996) has suggested that rule of law requires judicial independence, which requires some degree of separation of powers, which requires a change in the balance of power between state and society and the development of civil society.
37 Hu (1998: 120–23).
38 Nor is it possible to simply rely on Jayasuriya's (1999a) statist rule of law as an alternative. The statist version fails to capture the differences between the Statist Socialist and Neoauthoritarian versions, and is at odds in significant respects with the Communitarian variant.
39 For overviews of the law and development movement, see Trubek (1974, 1972b); Burg (1977); Merryman (1977); Franck (1972); Gardner (1980); Tamanaha (1995).
40 The basic premises of the original law and development movement were derived from modernization theory: "development was an inevitable, evolutionary process of increasing societal differentiation that would ultimately produce economic, political, and social institutions similar to those of the West." Tamanaha (1995: 471).
41 Gardner (1980); Franck (1972). Ghai (1987) questions whether the original law and development movement had sufficient unity to be considered a movement given that there was no common set of questions, theory, or methodology: "It lacked the coherence that one associates with such a label. It looked at how custom affected development; the role of foreign investment protection legislation in promoting economic growth; the role and operation of local courts; legal transplants; constitutional law and development; public corporations and other state institutions for the regulation of the economy; family relations; commerce; and the potential and methods of legislation."
42 Trubek (1972b); Gardner (1980); Dhavan (1994).
43 Burg (1977: 496).
44 Chibundu (1997).
45 Greenberg (1980).
46 Kamuwanga (1987).
47 Wiarda (1971).
48 Trubek (1974; 1972b).
49 Hutchinson (1989); Kelman (1987).
50 Trubek (1972b); Friedman (1969); Burg (1977). Ann and Robert Seidman (1994) have sketched the requirements for a theory of law and development.
51 Upham (1994).
52 Franck (1972: 784–86); Seidman and Seidman (1994: 160) suggest that courts will have a limited role in the economic development process for a variety of reasons.
53 Rose (1998).
54 Trubek (1974).
55 Trubek (1974); Gardner (1980).
56 Chibundu (1997: 10).

57 Among forty papers presented by participants at a 1992 conference, only one was authored by a US scholar. Vyas (1994).

58 Tamanaha (1995).

59 Faundez (1997).

60 Trubek (1996).

61 Muted, but hardly silent. Kothari (1988), for instance, lists a number of negative effects of modernity and development including widening income gaps, increased unemployment resulting from the introduction of high technology, and the destruction of traditional culture. However, in the end, he acknowledges that simply criticizing or rejecting modernity is insufficient. Addis (1992) takes issue with theories of development that would destroy the lifestyles of existing ethnic groups.

62 Tamanaha (1995).

63 The economic implications of globalization are discussed in Chapter 10. For a discussion of the impact of economic, political, cultural, and legal globalization on legal reforms in China, particularly administrative law reforms, see Peerenboom (2001b).

64 According to the so-called Washington or Bretton Woods consensus, economic development requires the legal foundations of capitalism and a regulatory framework sufficient to attract FDI. See Trubek (1996).

65 Trubek (1996) observes that the human rights movements of the 1970s and '80s highlighted the need for rule of law if rights were to be taken seriously.

66 Lan Cao (1997: 547) points out the irony in the demise of the old law and development movement. The movement floundered in part due to the perceived ethnocentrism of US participants and their loss of faith in their own government. Yet the critique, founded on the myopia of US participants, was itself too myopic.

67 See Chapter 9 and the studies cited therein.

68 Rose (1998).

69 See, for example, Kausikan (1995–96). For critical accounts of Asian values, see Ghai (1994); Davis (1998). See also Chan (1995); Bauer and Bell (1999); Peerenboom (2000d).

70 See, for example, The World Bank Legal Department (1995). As Faundez (1997: 1) cautions, however, the line between technical assistance and policy-making is not clear. He also correctly observes that much of the technical assistance program of new law and development is actually not new: drafting constitutions and legislation, advising on institutional reform, providing technical support for the development of parliamentary procedures and practices, advising on judicial reform, offering short training courses on specific legal topics, and providing advice and guidance on legal education were all features of the original movement.

71 Trubek (1996); Rose (1998: 95).

72 Trubek (1996: 225) has noted the need to focus on the microfoundations of law. See also Blake (2000).

73 Faundez (1997: 13–14). However, as Leila Frischtak (1997) points out, the failure of structural adjustment programs to produce development together with the equity issue of rising income disparity even when there has been growth

has resulted in an expansive interpretation of good governance. The more holistic approach to reform emphasizes the full set of operating principles of a Western liberal democracy, including transparency, a free press, channels for participation and interest representation. Apart from assuming support for controversial liberal values and institutions, the holistic approach overlooks the limited capacity of governments in some cases. By attempting to change too much at once, this approach runs the risk of undermining the long term possibilities for reform. Accordingly, a more incremental, context-specific approach may be preferable in some instances.

74 Faundez (1997: 13).

75 Faundez (1997: 13).

76 Claiming the fears of imperialism to be overstated, Franck (1972) observes that most countries were eager to participate in legal reforms. He also points out that reformers were not as naive and ethnocentric as portrayed. They realized that context was important and that there was a limited role to what outsiders could do without counterpart institutions and adequate resources. He does admit, however, that few projects included country specialists on the team. Burg (1977: 514) agrees that law and development scholars were not as naive as Trubek and others made them out to be.

77 Black (1996), for instance, notes how advisers tried to take into consideration local conditions when helping draft Russia's company law, including the weakness and low level of competence of the courts, the attitudes of managers not used to paying attention to shareholders, and the need to protect minority shareholders.

78 The World Bank Legal Department (1995) concedes that while Bank staff recognize the need to understand local conditions, in some cases they fail to do the necessary homework due to time constraints. One example of the serious consequences that can result from the failure to adequately consider local conditions is the attempt to liberalize the financial sector in Africa in the absence of a proper regulatory framework. A single banking scandal wiped out 12.5 percent of Kenya's GDP. See Annibale (1997).

79 Whereas the earlier movement was largely led by Americans, the new movement is much more international. In addition to multilateral organizations such as the World Bank, many countries, including Canada, Great Britain, Australia, and the Scandinavian countries have participated in bilateral legal reform projects in China. See deLisle (1999).

80 The issue of transplantability of legal institutions has been much discussed. The most optimistic view is perhaps that of Alan Watson (1993: 96; 1976). Others, while somewhat more cautious, have reported success stories. See, for example, Nichols (1997).

81 Many PRC scholars have noted the tension between a government-led top-down initiative and rule of law. Jiang Lishan (1998a, 1998b); Su Li (1995); Li Shuguang (1998). See also Berkman (1996: 42), who claims that reliance on the CCP to implement law is incompatible with rule of law.

82 Jiang Lishan (1998a: 22–23; 1998b: 29); Su Li (1995); Keith (1994).

83 Guo Daohui (1996b: 3–4). For a sectoral analysis of the demand for rule of law, see Chapter 10.

84   Ocko (2000) argues that the top-down nature of reforms has been exaggerated and that legal scholars have played a greater role in initiating and shaping reforms than often suggested. See also Dowdle (2001a; 2001b).

85   Peerenboom (1998b).

86   Peerenboom (2000a).

87   The conference was the Ninth Sino–US Commercial Seminar, which was held in April, 1998. Peerenboom (2000a).

88   For a discussion of the Court's five-year plan, see Chapter 7.

89   See also Fang Ning *et al.* (2001).

90   Chen Weidong (2001) and his team of researchers completed an empirical study of the problems implementing the criminal procedure law that resulted in two volumes, the first describing the results of the survey and the second suggesting ways to address the problems, including amendments to existing legislation.

91   To develop the training manuals on criminal and civil law trial procedures, PRC law professors first conducted field studies of current judicial practices. They also observed trials in Hong Kong and held conferences with PRC and foreign scholars. This project is described in the Ford Foundation's summary of major judicial reform projects.

92   Cai Dingjian's center at Peking University held one such conference in which foreign advisors provided technical advice regarding hearings in their own system. Cai's center has also held conferences to discuss proposals to deal with legislative inconsistency, in addition to engaging in a survey project on individual case supervision by people's congresses, the procuracy, and adjudicative supervision committees within courts.

93   This project was funded by the Ford Foundation and is described in their summary of major judicial reform grants.

94   The conference was sponsored by CASS and held in Huairou. The need for a coordinating entity – whether an official committee established under perhaps the NPC or a civil organization of academics, government officials, and judges participating in their personal capacity – was a constant theme during a series of interviews with academics, judges, prosecutors, and officials at the National Judges Institute. The interviews were conducted as part of a Ford-sponsored project on the future of judicial reform in August 2001.

95   Jiang Lishan (1998b: 22); Su Li (1995: 1–2).

96   Jiang Lishan (1998b); Su Li (1995: 7–9); Corne (1996).

97   Teitel (1997).

98   Ghai (1993b).

99   Jiang Lishan (1998a: 21–22).

100 See Baum and Shevchenko (1999). For a contrary view, see Su Li (1998: 8), who claims that China does not have a strong state and in fact the demand for rule of law was a response to a weak government, weak financial system, and inefficient administration.

101 Poll results show strong support for rule of law. See Yali Peng (1998).

102 On the difficulties of transplanting foreign legal systems to China, see Corne (1996).

103   Su Li (1998: 10).

104   Sun Guohua (1996).

105   Ma Xiaohong, for instance, suggests that rule of law in China must take into account the traditional emphasis on morality and substantive justice. "Yifa Zhiguo Jianshe Shehuizhuyi Fazhi Guojia Xueshu Yantaohui Jiyao" (1996: 17).

106   Both Zhu Suli, see Su Li (1998), and Jiang Lishan (1998b: 22) note that China is still predominantly an agrarian society. In the villages, custom and traditional informal means of resolving disputes remain strong. However, as Zhu notes, society is changing and reliance on custom and traditional informal means of resolving disputes is no longer sufficient. See also Chapter 10.

107   Zhang Wenxian (1996).

108   Zhang Wenxian (1996) compares law to technology – China should import the most advanced and useable laws available. The analogy with technology is illuminating, however, in that in some cases, a low-tech approach may suit China's level of development better than a high-tech approach.

109   For a similar complaint that foreign advisors failed to take into consideration Russia's national characteristics, see Hendley (1996).

110   Gao Xiqing, Vice-chairman of China Securities Regulatory Commission (CSRC), has lamented the CSRC's inability to recruit and retain qualified personnel. See Crest (2000).

111   See Lubman (1999); see also Chapter 9. As reforms continue, however, the courts may be able to assume a greater role in reviewing administrative regulations. China's accession to the WTO may provide further impetus for further reform of the legal system. See Chapter 10.

112   For a discussion of the pros and cons of a state-centered command-and-control regulatory approach versus more bottom-up approaches, see Chapter 9.

113   Chen Jianfu (1999a) notes that ideological resistance to importing Western bourgeois laws gave way, after Deng's trip south in 1992, to the more pragmatic concern that China's market economy urgently requires laws reflecting and assimilating international practices.

114   Dubious, like many of the early commentators, about the likely impact of the ALL, Potter (1994a: 288) suggested that the "significance in the ALL lies mainly in the fact that it was even enacted."

115   See Alford (2001) and Chapter 9.

116   Zhu Suli suggests that China should take advantage of native resources from both the formal and informal legal systems but then does not state what these resources are or how they are to function alongside rule of law. In fact, he notes that reliance on local customs may conflict with the general applicability of laws, one of the typical features of rule of law. See Su Li (1995).

117   "Yifa Zhiguo Jianshe Shehuizhuyi Fazhi Guojia Xueshu Yantaohui Jiyao" (1996: 11–12).

118   For a discussion of some of the positive aspects, see Ocko (2000).

119   Jiang Xianfu (1997: 3–9).

120   Liu Cuixiao and Xie Pengcheng (1998).

121   Liu Cuixiao and Xie Pengcheng (1998). See also Xie Hui (1998), who claims that the CCP still has a certain amount of moral authority, particularly in rural areas.

122   Dowdle (1999). The same argument is made with respect to internal review of the administration. See Chapter 9.

123   This assumes that the courts would be able to reach fair verdicts. If not, the legitimacy of the courts would be impaired. But presumably the CCP would not turn such cases over to the courts unless they were prepared to back up the courts. In fact, the act of assigning the cases to the courts would itself be a sign that the CCP intends to support the courts and would (ironically) serve to bolster the independence and authority of the courts.

124   Peerenboom (2001a).

125   Jiang Lishan (1998a: 22).

126   Macaulay (1963).

127   Van der Sprenkel (1962).

128   The percentage of cases subject to mediation decreased from 56.8% in 1995 to 54.2% in 1996 to 50.9% in 1997, while litigation increased from 24.2% to 26.4% to 29.4% during the same period. See 1996 *China Law Yearbook*, p. 126; 1997 *China Law Yearbook*, p. 163; 1998 *China Law Yearbook*, p. 130.

129   In a study of the impact of legal systems in Asia on economic development, Pistor and Wellons (1999) found that on the whole legal systems in Asia tended to converge toward legal systems in Western countries, even with respect to dispute resolution. Nevertheless, there were still signs of divergence, particularly in regard to dispute resolution, even within Asian countries. Pistor and Wellons (1999).

130   Fu Hualing (1992). See also Clarke (1991b) for the coercive quality of much mediation in China.

131   Zhang Xingzhong (1989).

132   Fu Hualing (1992: 224, 229).

133   Finding that mediation in the Qing was influenced by the formal legal system in various ways, Philip Huang (1996) has suggested a third realm between the formal and informal systems.

134   Unger (1976: 181), for instance, asserts that "the very assumptions of the rule of law appear to be falsified by the reality of life in liberal society." In more recent works, however, Unger has acknowledged that rule of law may play a positive role, and that when rule of law prevails, "people enjoy security in a regime of rights." Unger (1996: 64).

135   Kennedy (1976; 1979).

136   Cass Sunstein (1995), hardly a CRIT, has noted that there are advantages and disadvantages to rules, and argued against the "extravagant enthusiasm for rules and an extravagantly rule-bound conception of the rule of law," advocating instead the position that "legal systems sometimes do and should abandon rules in favor of a form of casuistry."

137   One version of the indeterminacy thesis claims that no rule can determine its own outcomes. Those who make this claim often appeal to Wittgenstein for

support. The argument is that Wittgenstein's view of rules as social practices deprives rules of much of their rule-like character: we cannot know what the rule is until we see how people put it into practice. However, as Margaret Jane Radin (1989) notes, it is not clear that pointing out this philosophical characteristic of rules or noting that the interpretation and meaning of rules is embedded in a social context really changes anything. How one interprets and applies a rule will depend on contingent factors beyond the rule itself, such as conventional language practices, assumptions by the interpreter about the aims and purpose of the rule (and perhaps of the rule-makers in making the rules), interpretative practices within the society and institution, the values and biases of the interpreter, and so forth. But the fact that interpretation of a rule will depend on social conventions and personal values does not entail that a rule cannot lead to determinate outcomes in a given context. There will be many easy cases where everyone or almost everyone agrees on the proper outcome and the rules will be effective in guiding conduct in practice. Even in cases where there is disagreement, there may be broad agreement about the correct outcome. While there still may be radical disagreement from time to time, infrequent incidence of such disagreement need not undermine the general validity of rule of law predicated on reasonably determinate outcomes in most cases.

138 See, for example, Segal and Spaeth (1993).

139 By Kadi justice Weber meant the practice of deciding cases in an ad hoc manner, based on general moral principles and discretion as to what is appropriate in the particular circumstances. See Rheinstein (1954).

140 Singer (1988: 467).

141 Shih (1999: 8–9). Guo Daohui (1996b) observes that debates about the class nature of law have given way to discussions about private law and human rights.

142 Shen Yuanyuan (2000: 21) puts it nicely. While recognizing the limitations of rule of law, she still sees the concept as useful for China today: "By way of analogy, one might say that we should not delay the introduction of nutritious and high-protein food to people of a starving land because Americans have come to disregard such items for fear that they contain cholesterol."

143 See, for example, Chen Jianfu (1999a: 72).

144 Su Li (1998: 3).

145 Even the critics of the law and development movement found value in rule of law as a weapon against authoritarianism. Gardner (1980: 363), for instance, objected to the original law and development movement on the ground that its "legal instrumentalism proved vulnerable because it lacked, indeed rejected, any carefully developed philosophical or ethical perspective and because it offered a vision of law inadequately differentiated from state and power, and thus was unable to discriminate between 'ends' externally defined." Yet he also noted that the ideology of rule of law was useful in limiting the arbitrary acts of the government. Similarly, Yash Ghai (1993b) has remarked, based on the experiences of African countries, that although the neutral façades of

liberal constitutions that portray law as autonomous and impartial often masks social and economic inequities, the ideology of rule of law nevertheless acts to restrain rulers and protect individuals' rights and freedoms.

146   Tamanaha (1995).

147   Lan Cao (1997: 553).

148   Xie Hui (1998).

149   Guo Daohui (1996a: 3–4) has pointed out the need for a stronger civil society to balance the power of the state, and in particular the need for a rule of law society – i.e. a society that supports rule-of-law values. Fan Zhongxin argues that separation of government and enterprises and more freedom of association is needed to ensure civil society, which is a precondition for rule of law. See "Yifa Zhiguo Jianshe Shehuizhuyi Fazhi Guojia Xueshu Yantaohui Jiyao" (1996).

150   For changes in Taiwan, see Winn and Yeh (1995); Cooney (1999); for Korea, see K. Yang (1993); for Indonesia, see Bourchier (1999).

151   Nancy Bermeo (1997: 85) argues, for instance, that while civil society was densely organized in the Weimar Republic and Franco Spain, many of the strongest associational units were themselves anti-democratic.

152   Edward Gu (1998) discusses the limited space for civil society. Ma Shu-yun (1994) has pointed out that the discussion about civil society in China has been mainly among Westerners or Chinese in exile and that to the extent Chinese discussed the issue, they focused on modern citizenry "consisting of law-abiding and civil members of society." The relation between civil society and the state was thus seen as an intimate and harmonious one. See also White, Howell, and Shang (1996); Saich (2000).

153   White, Howell, and Shang (1996: 216–17) report that while organizations have different ideas about political reform most seem to prefer stability and a gradual approach to political reforms. See also Wank (1999: 70); Pearson (1997: 71); Chamberlain (1998).

154   On the legitimacy crisis, see Goodman (1987: 305–06). For the relation between law and legitimacy, see Potter (1994b); Epstein (1994).

155   See, for example, Wang Jiafu (1998: 119).

156   Tanner (1999). See also Chapter 5.

157   He Baogang (1996); Womack (1989).

158   McCormick and Kelly (1994) have pointed out that after the Cultural Revolution, the CCP tried to move away from substance towards procedures, as evidenced by Peng Zhen's attempt to build up the NPC and promote rule of law.

159   Jiang Zemin suggested in his speech to the 15th Party Congress that rule of law could support the creation of socialist spiritualization. *Jiang Zemin's Congress Report* (1997).

160   The Resolution of the Communist Party of China Central Committee Regarding Important Questions on Promoting Socialist Ethical and Cultural Progress, adopted at the Sixth Plenum of the 14th CCP Central Committee on Oct. 10, 1996. For a full text translation of the Resolution, see "Party Stresses Ethical, Cultural Progress" (1996).

161 See *Integration of Confucian Ethics, Socialism* (1998); *Academics Discuss Spiritual Civilization* (1998). Lei Feng was a model worker who dedicated himself to being a screw in the socialist machine.

162 Having reviewed the attempts to control the pluralization of culture and build a socialist spiritual civilization, Lynch (1999b) concludes that the government's efforts are failing.

163 Forney (1996).

164 Habermas (1975: 101) expresses a typical view of the meaning of legitimacy: "If binding decisions are legitimate, that is, if they can be made independently of the concrete exercise of force and of the manifest threat of sanctions, and can be regularly implemented even against the interests of those affected, then they must be considered as the fulfilment of recognized norms." Habermas grounds legitimacy in the nature of the political system as a whole, and in particular whether the "basic institutions of society and the basic political decisions would meet with **unforced agreement** of all those involved, if they could participate, as free and equal, in discursive will-formation." Habermas (1975: 186).

    Alan Hyde (1983) has challenged the notion that people follow laws because of the perceived legitimacy of the laws or legal system rather than because of habit or rational calculation. However, empirical studies have shown that legitimacy is a significant factor in why people comply with law. Tyler, for instance, found that legitimacy enhances effectiveness of legal authorities by increasing public compliance. Tyler (1990: 3–4) distinguishes between following rules for instrumental as opposed to normative reasons. An instrumental reason for following a law is that the outcome is favorable and thus it is in one's short term interest to follow the rule. Normative reasons for following laws may be based on personal morality or legitimacy: i.e. one follows the law because one feels the law is just; or one obeys the law because one feels the authority or institutions responsible for creating and enforcing the law have the right to dictate behavior.

165 Tyler (1990: 162–63) has argued, based on an empirical study in Chicago, that procedural justice, including a sense of having participated in the decision-making process, is more important to determining perceptions of legitimacy than outcomes. Thus, the CCP's attempt to base legitimacy on the quality of the laws rather than increased participation may be of limited use even assuming it is able to produce good results.

166 Some PRC scholars have suggested that Confucianism could serve as the moral basis for a market economy. See "1996 Zhongguo Faxue Yanjiu Huigu" (1997).

167 Alford (1993) has noted that the ruling regime's emphasis on legal reform is a double-edged sword in that it provides citizens with the weapons to challenge state acts. Epstein (1994) has also observed that the ruling regime's need to predicate legitimacy on rule of law puts pressure on the regime to move from a more instrumental rule by law to a rule of law that imposes meaningful constraints on government.

5

Retreat of the Party and the state

This chapter examines the theoretical relationship between single party socialism and rule of law as well as the actual role of the Party in legal reforms and the daily operation of the legal system. I argue that although single party socialism is not compatible with a Liberal Democratic or Communitarian rule of law, it is theoretically compatible with a Statist Socialist or Neoauthoritarian rule of law.[1] In practice, however, the Party, Party organs, and individual Party members often act in ways that are inconsistent with any form of rule of law. Nevertheless, the Party is only one of the obstacles to rule of law. In terms of the daily operation of the legal system, the most significant obstacles are systemic or institutional in nature. The Party plays only a limited role in the day-to-day operation of the legal system. Its role in law-making and administrative rule-making is increasingly indirect and limited to macro policy guidance and review; moreover, only rarely does the Party directly intervene in the adjudication of specific cases. Rather, the Party's main relevance to rule of law lies in its ability to promote or obstruct further institutional reforms required to implement rule of law.

The Party's role in the legal system must be understood against the backdrop of the changing role of the Party in the Chinese polity as a whole. Despite theoretical opposition from within the Party, the last twenty years have witnessed a growing separation of the Party and state in practice, to the point where references to the Party-state are often misleading and obscure as much as they reveal.[2] Notwithstanding the post-Tiananmen retreat from the official policy of separating the Party from the state and various attempts to claw back power,[3] the Party has in fact turned over – or, perhaps more accurately, been forced to turn over – much of daily governance to the usual state actors: the legislature, executive, and judiciary. The retreat of the Party has resulted in the transfer of power from the Party both to the state and to society.

Furthermore, just as there has been a retreat of the Party, so has there been a retreat of the state. Power has devolved from the central government to local governments, and from the government at all levels to society. Neither the Party nor the state is monolithic, of course. Both are composed of diverse organizations, factions, and ultimately individuals at various levels from the national on down to the lowest level of local government. These different entities have different interests and incentive structures. Reforms have resulted in the fragmentation of authority, with different level entities pursuing their own interests, often at the expense of central-level directives. The "Party-state" – to the extent that it is meant to refer to central Party and state organizations and the small coterie of senior leaders who decide important policy issues – has lost much of its ability to control lower-level entities.

To be sure, the retreat of the Party and state is not complete. Neither the Party nor the state is in danger of withering away any time soon. The Party undeniably is still a major force, capable of getting its way on key issues when the Party leadership is unified. Nor is the transition process a zero sum game. The retreat of the Party is compatible with a strong Party, albeit with a redefined role. In some ways, the Party may be becoming stronger.[4] Although the Party has a reduced role in daily governance, it may govern more effectively by governing less, and thus gain in legitimacy and stature. As discussed in the last chapter, the legitimacy of the Party is based primarily on performance, and in particular its ability to sustain economic growth.[5] Socialist ideology – out of step with the realities of a market economy and increasingly incoherent and vacuous – has little appeal for the citizenry or even Party members and is incapable of providing substantive policy guidance.

At the same time, having unleashed the forces of reform, the Party is no longer able to control completely the path of reforms. In some cases, the Party's goals are inconsistent. It may want economic growth and yet want to control the private sector, civil society, and the flow of ideas. But these goals are in tension with each other, and thus the Party has been forced to accept a larger private sector, a more robust civil society, and a freer and more chaotic marketplace of ideas as the price of sustainable economic growth. Even when its goals are clear and consistent, the Party is not always able to control the economic, social, cultural, and legal forces pushing for change. Institutions, once given power, will seek more. If there is anything that Chinese bureaucrats are adept at, it is political maneuvering to enhance their authority. Today, the struggles for power occur increasingly outside the Party as the various government agencies battle among themselves and with the legislature, judiciary, and procuracy. Much of the initiative for reform now comes from these state organs. As a result, the Party is becoming more reactive than proactive: oftentimes faced with a *fait accompli*, the Party acknowledges reality and sanctions reforms initiated by local governments that at the time of initiation were at odds with central laws and policies but which have proved successful or at least popular among certain constituencies.

Although the reduced influence of the Party on the state bodes well for the prospects of implementing rule of law, the reach of the law remains limited. There would need to be major institutional reforms and changes in the legal and political culture for law to impose effective limits on the Party with respect to life-or-death issues that affect the survivability of the Party or its ability to remain the dominant political authority in China. However, most issues do not involve the survivability of the Party. Similarly, the transfer of power from the Party and the state to society opens the possibility of a larger role for Chinese citizens in the lawmaking, interpretation, and implementation processes, and ultimately in the political process.

Behind the façade: the hollowing out of the Party and state

During the Cultural Revolution, the dangers of overcentralizing power were evident to all. Accordingly, in a 1980 speech, Deng emphasized the need to separate the Party and government:

> It is time for us to distinguish between the responsibilities of the Party and those of the government and to stop substituting the former for the latter ... This will help strengthen and improve the unified leadership of the Central Committee, facilitate the establishment of an effective work system at the various levels of government from top to bottom, and promote a better exercise of government functions and powers.[6]

Despite Deng's plea, few steps were taken to separate the Party and government. Party secretaries at the provincial level were forced to resign their posts as governor, mayor, or country magistrate, but other institutional ties between the Party and state remained in place. Thus, in 1987 Premier Zhao Ziyang was forced to champion once again separation

of the Party and the state. Appreciating that his proposals would encounter considerable political resistance, Zhao based his case largely
on economic grounds. He argued that the Party-dominated political
structure was suited to the early years of socialist transformation when
the Party was consolidating its power and the economy was centrally
planned. However, the system was not appropriate for "economic, political and cultural modernization under peacetime conditions or the
development of a socialist commodity economy."[7] Zhao proposed bold
reforms, including the elimination of Party groups within administrative agencies, reduction in Party work departments, and changes in the
nomenklatura system of appointments, all meant to increase the power
of local authorities relative to the center.[8]

    After Tiananmen, Zhao was ousted from power and his ambitious re-
forms were rolled back. Officially, the ruling regime backed off the policy
of separating Party and government. In light of the aborted attempts at
reforms and the continuing opposition to genuine democracy, it may
appear from a cursory glance that despite a myriad of minor reforms,
the Party remains firmly in control and there has been little fundamental
change from the Mao era. On the ideological front, the Party remains
committed to the four cardinal principles, and most importantly to the
leadership of the Party. Structurally, the dual system of government remains in place whereby people's congresses, local governments, administrative agencies, and the courts are responsible horizontally to Party
Committees and vertically to their superiors in the relevant hierarchy.[9]
Notwithstanding Zhao's efforts, Party groups continue to exist within
government entities, the courts, and other non-Party organizations.[10]
The nomenklatura system, recentralized after Tiananmen, continues to
operate. Thus key appointments are subject to Party approval, including
central-level approval of the chairman, vice-chairman, and members of
the Standing Committee of the NPC; the secretary-general and deputy
secretaries-general of the NPC; the chair and vice-chair of the Legislative
Affairs Commission; the president and vice-president of the Supreme
People's Court (SPC), and members of the Adjudicative Committee;
the secretary, deputy secretary, and members of the Party Group within
the SPC; and the presidents of provincial-level High People's Courts
(HPC) as well as their counterparts in the High People's Procuracy.[11]
Lower-level appointments are subject to approval by correspondingly
lower-level Party organizations.

But behind the seemingly enduring façade lies real change. There has been a quiet revolution from within that has resulted in a hollowing out of the Party and the state.[12] For instance, even though the CCP moved to impose tighter controls over the nomenklatura system after 1989, such measures have been largely ineffective.[13] Appointments of key personnel are increasingly a matter of negotiation between the central level and the provinces, in part because of elite conflict at the central level but also because economic reforms have made the provinces increasingly independent and aggressive.[14] The Party's diminished role and influence is most evident in the economic, legal, social, and cultural sectors. But even in the political arena, there have been subtle but significant changes.

The economy

In rural areas, where economic reforms first began in the late 1970s and early 1980s, the vast majority of farmers no longer work in communes or state-owned farms but now till their own plot of contracted land. The private sector of peasant households is now responsible for more than 95% of primary sector GDP, which includes agriculture, forestry, animal husbandry, and aquaculture.[15] Given that half of China's 700 million workers are employed in the primary sector, the privatization of agriculture alone has resulted in half of China's working population working in private employment. As a result of reforms, villagers are now less dependent on Party cadres, who no longer have a monopoly on economic resources.[16]

The rapid expansion of township village enterprises (TVEs) has further transformed life in the countryside. By 1995, TVEs employed more than 140 million people.[17] To be sure, the ownership status of many TVEs is unclear. Many private companies have chosen to establish an alliance with local governments, thus incorporating as a TVE or a collective, to avoid restrictions on private enterprises or to gain access to the benefits provided by the local government, such as readier access to financing, technology, or other inputs.[18] On the other hand, some TVEs and collectives are analogous to state-owned enterprises in the sense that they are owned by local governments and have been established using state-owned assets. In recent years, however, TVEs have encountered hard times as markets have matured and competition intensified. The number of people employed by TVEs fell by 5% in 1997, 19% in 1998, and even more in 1999.[19] In response, local governments have sought to cut their ties to many TVEs, abandoning them to the marketplace.[20] Given the more mature market for inputs and fewer disincentives to being classified as a private enterprise, entrepreneurs have sought to re-organize as a private company or to exit and start up their own private company. Accordingly, the long-term trend is for greater privatization of TVEs.

Economic reforms have also resulted in the relaxation of the rigid *hukou* or household registration system that prevented people in the countryside from moving to cities. Today, the floating population of migrant workers who have left their farms to come to the cities exceeds 100 million. Recognizing that economic reforms had undermined the capacity of the state to enforce the registration system and keep rural residents on the farm, the authorities began to issue regulations in the mid-1980s to manage the rising flow of migrant workers into the cities. Although the Party and state have sought to exercise control over the floating population, they have been at best only partially successful. Denied the full benefits of urban residents and thus of citizenship, migrant workers have organized their own communities that exist largely outside of state control.[21] Many of these migrant workers find employment in the rapidly growing private sector.

The Party has been compelled in the name of economic development to accept and indeed to encourage the growth of the private sector. As of year end 1998, there were 1.2 million private enterprises employing 17 million people, and 31 million small businesses (*getihu*) employing an additional 61 million employees.[22] In 1998, private enterprises had $122 billion in registered capital, did $64 billion worth of business, and paid over $8.4 billion in taxes, or 8.5% of total industrial and commercial taxes in China.[23] Private businesses created 40% of all new jobs and almost 60% of all new urban jobs between 1990 and 1997.[24] Foreign investment enterprises are another major component of the private sector.[25] By 1999, over 350,000 foreign investment enterprises (FIEs) had been established.[26] FIEs employed some 20 million local workers, accounting for 10% of the country's total nonagricultural labor force.[27] In 1999, FIEs alone generated 21% of total national industrial output,[28] and accounted for over 48% of the total external trade, including 46% of exports and 52% of imports.[29]

The exact size of the private sector is difficult to determine because it is not clear how many TVEs and collectives are actually private companies that have chosen to incorporate as a TVE or collective rather than a private enterprise in order to avoid the discriminatory policies against private enterprises.[30] If the private sector is defined broadly to include all TVEs and collectives, the private sector is responsible for over 70% of the industrial GDP.[31] But even excluding all TVEs and collectives, the private sector is still responsible for some 36% of industrial GDP. The true figure no doubt lies somewhere in between, perhaps around 51%.[32]

Whatever the exact size, the private sector's impact on the economy is clearly significant. Moreover, the private sector is significant not only for its present size but because it is the fastest growing sector of the economy, and likely to stay that way.[33] Indeed, the private sector has achieved its rapid growth despite a restrictive regulatory environment that puts it at a competitive advantage. The private sector has been subject to high registered capital requirements, a burdensome approval process, predatory local governments, restricted import and approval rights, and lack of access to capital. In 1997, 63% of bank loans went to state-owned enterprises (SOEs) that accounted for only 30% of industrial output.[34] Small businesses, which account for nearly 20% of industrial value-added, received only 3% of the banks' fixed-asset loans. And of the 900 listed companies in China, only a handful are private.

Although private enterprises continue to operate under a restrictive regulatory regime and are subject to discriminatory policies, the government has had little choice given the stagnant state-owned sector but to remove some of the barriers and promote the development of the private sector. The 1982 constitution has been amended three times, each time in ways that supported the development of the private economy. In 1988, the constitution was amended to allow for the transfer of land use rights. In 1993, the constitution was amended to replace references to rural people's communes and agricultural producers' cooperatives with a household contract responsibility system, and to replace references to a planned economy with a socialist market economy.[35] In 1997, Jiang Zemin set the stage for the third amendment by announcing at the 15th Party Congress new policies to encourage the private sector. Jiang declared the private sector to be an important component in the socialist market economy and promised to facilitate its development. While public ownership was to remain dominant in the economy as a whole,

Jiang defined public ownership broadly to include both SOEs and collectives. Further, public ownership could take various corporate forms. Thus SOEs were encouraged to reorganize as shareholding companies. Although the dominance of public ownership meant that the state would control certain key industries and maintain a controlling share in large SOEs, poorly performing medium-sized and smaller SOEs were to be reorganized, merged, leased, contracted out, sold off, or liquidated.[36] The constitution was subsequently amended in 1999 to provide for the development of diverse forms of ownership side by side with the dominant public ownership.[37] The status of the private sector was upgraded from a complement to the public economy to an important component of the economy.[38] Backing up the rhetoric, a number of concrete regulatory changes made private enterprises more competitive.[39] For instance, private enterprises have been given import–export rights and have been promised greater access to capital and land.[40] To that end, a number of new private banks targeting TVEs and small private companies have been established.[41] In addition, the creation of a second stock-market board for high-tech companies will increase opportunities for private firms to raise capital.

Party and state control has even diminished over SOEs.[42] A series of reforms since 1978, aimed at making SOEs more competitive and stopping the flood of red ink, has resulted in greater autonomy for SOE managers.[43] In 1979, the state sought to change the incentive structure for SOE managers by permitting SOEs to retain a percentage of their profits, to be used for employee bonuses or reinvestment. However, the lack of hard budget constraints and price distortions continued to result in an inefficient allocation of resources. In the mid-1980s, a second phase of reforms began in which SOEs entered into long-term contracts that set the amount of profits and taxes SOEs paid to the state. As a result, managers were given greater autonomy, provided they met their targets. In 1993, a third wave of reform emphasized modern corporate governance. Companies were to be incorporated under the new Company Law. Some were converted to stock companies. However, by itself, incorporation did not change the fundamental nature of ownership or the relation between the state and SOEs. The state remained the majority shareholder in most cases. SOEs were still not subject to hard budget constraints. Nor did incorporation resolve the various agency problems that had plagued SOEs: managers continued to siphon off state assets and to use whatever gains were produced from more efficient production to pay out higher employee salaries and bonuses. SOEs also continued to labor under the burden of heavy welfare obligations. The 15th Party Congress advocated greater privatization as a way of breaking the impasse. More recently, a fifth round of reforms have focused on debt for equity swaps in the hopes that alleviating the debt repayment burdens of SOEs will improve their balance sheets and allow them to invest in more productive activities. SOEs are likely to experience a sixth round of reform as a result of increased competition from foreign companies once China enters the WTO.

Clearly the Party and state are still a force to be reckoned with. Despite the transition to a household responsibility system in the countryside, local cadres continue to exercise considerable influence over farmers' lives. Local officials are responsible for allocating land. Even when farmers have contracted with the government for land for a fixed period, government officials will often ignore the contract and redistribute land according to their own objectives.[44] Yet the shift from a collective to household responsibility system has undeniably altered the dynamics of local governance, strengthening the hand of farmers and reducing the power of local cadres, who are more dependent on farmers for their incomes. As the sociologist Yan Yunxiang remarks, in many areas "reforms have eroded cadres' previous power and privilege by breaking their monopoly over resources and by creating new income opportunities that make the accumulations of personal wealth more attractive than the political rewards offered by the party state. Their political role in village society has also changed from that of tyrannical 'local emperor' ruling the village as the agent of the party state to prudent middlemen who negotiate between the state and village society."[45]

As for the private sector, while private businesses enjoy considerably more freedom than in the past, entrepreneurs still find it advantageous to establish corporatist and clientelist relations with government officials.[46] Officials continue to exercise wide discretionary power over licensing and to control access to scarce resources, particularly financing. Establishing close relations with key officials also allows private entrepreneurs to proactively ward off predatory bureaucrats seeking to impose random fees. In the absence of rule of law and a legal system that provides private business with the legal means to effectively challenge government officials, entrepreneurs have little choice but to maintain good relations with the authorities. Nevertheless, legal reforms, including the establishment of administrative reconsideration and litigation procedures for challenging government officials, combined with economic reforms resulting in greater availability of resources on the market and the elimination of many of the discriminatory policies against private enterprises, have reduced the dependence of the private sector on government. Over time, the private sector will grow. Although the Party still has the ability to set macroeconomic policies, it must take into consideration the interests of an increasingly robust and independent private sector. More business owners are becoming members of the people's congresses and the Chinese Political Consultative Committee.[47] The business community has also formed a large number of chambers of commerce and other business associations to press their cause in the political arena. Even though the Party has been reluctant to allow private enterprise owners to join the Party for ideological reasons, over 15% of private enterprise owners are Party members.[48] In addition, the Party has actively recruited private business owners from small business and shareholding cooperatives.

Similarly, the Party and state continue to exert significant albeit diminishing control over SOEs. Of course, that the state would have a say in the running of SOEs is to be expected given that the state (whether central or local) remains the majority shareholder in most SOEs. What is more worrisome is that Party and government officials exert influence through channels other than the normal corporate channels. For instance, Party or government officials may directly intervene in the operation of the companies or attempt to manage the business and make business decisions. Furthermore, they may make decisions based on political rather than economic factors. Indeed, some studies have found that SOE managers tend to have less autonomy when it comes to labor and major investment decisions.[49] On the other hand, the degree of dependence should not be overstated.[50] The studies also found that SOE managers did enjoy autonomy with respect to remuneration, production, pricing, technical innovation, choice of inputs and raw materials, marketing, and foreign trade. Moreover, about one-third of SOE managers reported that Party secretaries had little power to influence their business decisions, though one-half said Party secretaries had some power, while about one-fifth said the secretaries had a great deal of power.[51]

Most important, Party and government officials are not free to reach any decision they want. They must face up to the realities of the market. Thus, they must balance their desire to keep unemployment down with the need to achieve economic growth. While it remains true that the economy is influenced by the "Communist organizational framework," and that the dual system of leadership forces government officials to attend to political incentives and the directives of the Party,[52] officials increasingly find their choices constrained by the market. While the state relaxed its control over medium and small SOEs, it retained its grip on the largest enterprises that account for the vast majority of GDP and employment. But those enterprises are proving to be an albatross around the Party's neck. Despite the years of reforms, SOEs remain a major burden, absorbing a disproportionate share of available financing and thus depriving the more efficient private sector of much-needed funds.[53] Many continue to produce goods that nobody wants. Indeed, many are value subtracting, with the cost of production exceeding the value of goods produced. About half of all SOEs are insolvent or on the brink of insolvency. Moreover, the proportion of loss-making SOEs is rising, as is the level of aggregate SOE losses. Alarmingly, the inability of SOEs to repay loans is threatening the financial stability of China's banks – by some accounts more than 20% of the loans of China's four major banks may be nonperforming.

As one would expect, economists are divided as to what is needed to turn SOEs around. Some advocate more privatization,[54] others suggest there may be other ways.[55] Even without privatization, however, the trend is toward less Party and state involvement in the management of businesses.[56] China's accession to the WTO will further promote the process of separating government, and the Party, from enterprises. With the entrance of more foreign companies into the marketplace and the establishment of more FIEs, SOEs will face increased competition. As a result, Party and government officials will find it increasingly costly to operate SOEs based on noneconomic factors. Given the weak state of SOEs and the need to sustain economic growth to maintain legitimacy, the Party is no longer able to dictate the path of reforms. By joining the WTO, China has become subject to an international legal regime, which further diminishes the Party's ability to call all of the shots. As one economist observes: "The overall direction of economic change is largely independent of the identity of China's political leaders ... The levers of power are increasingly remote from the forces that determine the path of the economy."[57]

The social and cultural sphere

Chinese citizens enjoy much more freedom today than during the Mao era. Economic reforms have had the salutary effect of significantly reducing the dependence of Chinese citizens on their work units (danwei).[58] In the past, one's work unit was the center of one's life, controlling momentous decisions from where one would live to when one could have a child. Today, workers, especially skilled workers, have more job opportunities and thus are no longer wed to a specific work unit. Even those with limited alternatives are less reliant on their work units than previously. Nowadays, they are able to purchase goods on the market without relying on rationing coupons supplied by their work unit and to obtain medical care or even housing on their own. As a result, the ability of the Party to control workers' lives through the work unit has diminished.

Chinese workers also enjoy more leisure time than in the past, due to the shift from a six- to a five-day work week and other changes that have made daily life easier. No longer do people need to wash their clothes by hand or to queue up to buy vegetables. Moreover, many now have more disposable income, which allows them to pursue their own diverse interests. They are free to purchase the latest fashions, go to discos, and increasingly to travel both in China and abroad.

They are also able to take advantage of a much wider range of cultural products. During the height of the Cultural Revolution, Chinese citizens had to content themselves with a handful of politicized dramas and state-run television shows. Nowadays, the cultural marketplace is filled with foreign as well as domestic offerings. There is something for everyone, whether one is interested in Nietzsche or *The Dream of the Red Chamber*, pornography, or Italian opera. Satellite dishes, cable television channels, radio broadcasts, underground newspapers, smuggled books, the Internet, and pirated DVDs have exposed Chinese citizens to a wide range of diverse political and cultural messages. Economic reforms have forced the state-owned media to compete for audience attention. Consequently, even state-owned media must now cater to the taste of the public. Moreover, the decentralization and fragmentation of authority that has accompanied economic reforms have made it difficult for central authorities to rein in local governments. Even when central authorities are able to exert pressure on local governments to toe the Party line, the diffusion of technologies allows the public to make its own choices. Central Party leaders are no longer able to assume a captive audience for their propaganda: citizens just change the channel or pop in a DVD. Thus the Party finds it increasingly difficult to structure the symbolic environment to ensure that citizens will accept the legitimacy of Party policies and ultimately of the regime itself.[59]

Economic reforms have undoubtedly resulted in a more pluralistic society. Farmers, workers in rural TVEs, private businessmen, the emerging middle class, SOE employees whose wages have been frozen, and retired people living on fixed incomes have different interests. The conflicting interests have produced social cleavages. Inevitably, the widening income gap between rich and poor individuals, rural and urban areas, and coastal and hinterland regions leads to social differentiation and the formation of interest groups. An increasingly wealthy populace with more free time on its hands can be expected to form social groups based on common interests. Predictably, Chinese citizens are forming a wide range of economic and noneconomic social organizations. As of 1996, there were more than 186,000 social organizations registered with the Ministry of Civil Affairs and up to one million other citizen-run organizations and economic associations.[60] These groups – the vast majority of them local – run the gamut from chambers of commerce to women's groups, stamp collection societies, environmental organizations, literary salons, religious groups, and even overtly political groups.

The proliferation of pluralistic social groups has resulted in an increasingly complex relation between the state and society. The Party is loath, given its Leninist nature, to tolerate diverse ideological messages or the formation of competing political parties or social groups whose interests may conflict with the interests of the Party. Party leaders are clearly aware of the capacity of social organizations to topple governments, as evidenced by Poland's solidarity movement. The collapse of the Soviet Union, the fall of Suharto in Indonesia and Milosevic in Bosnia, the Guomingdang's defeat at the polls in Taiwan, and the 1989 demonstrations at home further reinforce the Party's determination to maintain tight control over any element that could challenge the ruling regime's authority. The Party's intolerance of even the most remote threat to its authority is abundantly evident in the harsh crackdown on Falungong. Predictably, the Party has sought to restrict the growth of social organizations and to manage and regulate their operations. For instance, in an effort to control the proliferation of social groups, the Regulations on the Registration and Management of Social Organizations were amended in 1998 to impose further restrictions on social organizations. In addition, the Party has sought to co-opt social organizations and bind them to the state through various forms of state patronage. In exchange for serving as a bridge between the state and society, organizations are granted a representational monopoly in a given sphere and a limited degree of autonomy. As a consequence, many – though not all – of the social organizations that have emerged as a result of reforms in the last two decades have been closely aligned with the ruling regime.

In light of such differences, some analysts have questioned the applicability of the concept of civil society to China, preferring instead to describe the relation between the state and social groups in terms of corporatism and clientelism.[61] Clearly there are differences between the emerging social groups in China and the more robust and mature civil societies in Western liberal democracies. Western social organizations tend to be characterized by their voluntary formation and independence from the state.[62] Embedded in social contract theory where individuals precede the state and exchange certain rights for the security provided by the state while retaining others, civil society is seen as a check on the powers of the state. In China, the relation between the state and society has traditionally been assumed to be harmonious rather than adversarial.[63] In the absence of a pre-existing sphere of autonomy, the state has enjoyed greater authority to intervene in what in the West would be considered the private sphere. Given the difference in traditions, one would arguably expect social organizations in China to be somewhat less independent and more likely to serve the interests of the state – or of society as a whole as determined by the state – than in the West, even setting aside the current regime's Leninist orientation and its desire to ensure ideological unity.

On the other hand, some commentators argue that civil society need not come in only one variety – a liberal democratic variety.[64] Accordingly, the concept may be adapted to the Chinese context. In this more functionalist or structuralist view, there is an emergent civil society in China, albeit one with Chinese characteristics; that is, there is an intermediate associational realm between the state and the basic building blocks of society, which is populated by pluralistic social groups. Just as I have distinguished between various versions of rule of law, one could distinguish between various forms of civil society, ranging from the liberal democratic to the more top-down, corporatist model favored by Statist Socialists and Neoauthoritarians.[65]

Whatever the labels, it is important to acknowledge the profound changes in state-society relations in the last two decades. As Tony Saich, former head of Ford Foundation's Beijing office, observes, the emphasis on state-dominated corporatism risks obscuring the dynamics of change and the capacity of social groups to pursue their own interests and to influence policy.[66] In some cases, social organizations choose to form alliances with the state because by doing so they exercise more power. By embedding themselves in the state, they increase their capacity to affect policy-making.[67] Furthermore, organizations have developed ways to avoid central control. The process is therefore less unidirectional and more symbiotic than suggested by traditional top-down corporatist accounts.

Most important of all, although the Party may wish to tightly control social organizations, it increasingly lacks the capacity to do so. Economic reforms will require further lay-offs of SOE workers, and government agencies will be further downsized as the separation between state and enterprises continues and state agencies focus on regulatory rather than economic activities. Accordingly, individuals will increasingly be responsible for finding employment and housing and bearing the costs of medical expenses, retirement, and other welfare benefits formerly borne by the state. As a consequence, Saich argues, the Party must tolerate the expansion of social organizations that will take on these additional functions shed by the government or else run the risk of social unrest. Once again, just as the Party's desire for economic growth contributed to its diminished capacity to control migrant workers, the private economy, and thought work, so it has created a dilemma for the Party with respect to social organizations. The Party would like to limit social organizations to prevent any challenges to its authority, and yet it must tolerate a rise in social organizations to provide the necessary social net.[68]

The political sector

Despite Jiang's promise to accelerate political reform at the 15th Party Congress in 1997, the pace and scope of political reform has not been as impressive as the changes in other areas. Nevertheless, even in the political arena, there have been significant developments.[69] On the positive side, reforms include the establishment and entrenchment of village elections; changes to the people's congress system that have produced a more aggressive, professional, and independent legislature such that the NPC and local people's congresses are no longer merely rubber stamps; the downsizing and restructuring of the government and reform of the civil service system; greater albeit still limited freedom of speech and the press; increased avenues for public participation in the political process; and a rising willingness on the part of rural and urban residents to challenge the authorities through a variety of channels, including formal legal proceedings.[70]

Various rationales have been advanced to explain the experiment with village elections. Clearly village elections were seen as a means of rectifying the deteriorating village–cadre relations and facilitating the implementation of tax collection and other central policies. Village elections would prevent civil unrest in the Chinese countryside by making cadres more accountable to villagers and would relieve provincial and central officials from the micro-management of village government and village economy. In addition, they would increase economic prosperity at the village level by allowing for the election of skilled entrepreneurs. On the ideological front, elections arguably appealed to the origins of Chinese socialism, fulfilling the tenet that government should heed the will of the masses.[71] More cynical commentators note that foreigners love elections, and that holding elections at even the low level of villages improves the ruling regime's image abroad.[72]

The breakdown of the Party system in the countryside no doubt explains much of the initial impetus for village elections. A 1984 survey found that only 60% of Party cells were functioning normally, while a 1992 State Council report found that 30% of Party cells had collapsed and another 60% were extremely weak and disorganized.[73] One study of 1,500 cadres found that 15% had abandoned their responsibilities and did nothing, 46% asked to be relieved from their duties, and 30% stayed in their posts but ignored their duties while concentrating on enriching their families.[74]

Party organizations have lost much of their authority in the country-side. The Party is often unable to attract new recruits and Party cadres are unable to persuade or pressure farmers to follow state policies.[75] In an effort to compel compliance with state directives, cadres have resorted to illegal means, leading to resistance among farmers, heightened resentment of the Party, and even less enforcement of state policies. Elections are intended to make it easier for cadres to enforce unpopular policies such as grain procurements, taxes, or birth control by allowing villagers a voice in the process. There is some evidence that the strategy is working, and that villagers are more likely to comply with unpopular policies where they have been able to elect their leaders.[76]

Yet how successful village elections have been remains the subject of much debate, in part due to wide differences from place to place that caution against sweeping generalizations. Even statistics on the number of villages that have held elections vary widely, with figures ranging from 10 to 60 percent or more.[77] Some studies report considerable Party interference in elections, including limitations on candidates, nullification of results, and vote buying;[78] others praise the elections as fair, or increasingly so in any event.[79]

Equally as important as the fairness of the elections is what happens after the elections. To what extent are the elected village committees able to decide matters without interference from the Party? In terms of the formal legal relationships, village committees are subject to the "leadership" of the CCP (*lingdao*) and "guidance" (*zhidao*) of township governments. Some analysts have claimed that there is an inherent contradiction between Party leadership and majority rule by elections, though that will depend largely on the form "leadership" takes.[80] Preliminary empirical studies reveal mixed results. In some villages, the elected village committee is the primary decision-maker and in other villages the Party secretary continues to call the shots.[81] What is clear, however, is that local cadres are now more dependent on support from the villagers than in the past, and as a result they are more likely to heed the complaints of villagers and be responsive to their concerns.[82]

Arguably more far-reaching than the impact of elections, civil services reforms have changed the nature of the state itself. Zhu Rongji has masterminded a major downsizing of the government, reducing the number of ministries from forty to twenty-nine, with the number of government officials to be slashed by 50%.[83] In light of the downsizing, many functions formerly handled by the government will need to be assumed by intermediary social organizations. The restructuring is in keeping not only with the retreat of the state but its redefined role in a market economy. In light of the policy of separating government and enterprises, government agencies are to become regulators rather than market participants.[84] The separation is needed to address the existing conflict of interest where administrative entities are both regulators of the market and competitors in the marketplace, leading to administrative monopolies and discrimination on the part of agencies against their competitors.

One of the goals of civil service reforms has been to establish a more professional and less ideological civil service. To be sure, key government officials are still subject to the nomenklatura system and most officials are Party members. Moreover, all officials must work within the constraints of a single party system. In that sense, the civil service is far from the politically neutral civil service of other states.[85] Nevertheless, the emphasis nowadays is increasingly on professional qualifications and less on ideology. Universities offer programs in administrative science. There are national and local training centers for government officials.[86] Since 1993, there have been competitive examinations for entering government service.[87] The recruitment, promotion, and appraisal processes are now less politicized and more transparent. Much of the impetus behind the new regulations came from the urgent need to root out rampant corruption. To that end, civil servants are rotated every five years. Senior officials are not allowed to hold posts in their native place. Conflict of interest rules prohibit government officials from handling matters that affect their relatives. There are rules against nepotism. More recently, government officials at the county level and above have become subject to disclosure rules that require them to declare their assets and business interests.[88]

Notwithstanding the absence of genuine elections at all but the lowest levels, Chinese citizens are freer to discuss political issues and have more avenues for public participation in politics than in the past. The breakdown of the propaganda system and enhanced access to diverse political messages have opened up the space for political speech. Chinese citizens are no longer subject to regular political meetings in their work units where leaders from the Party group disseminate the Party line by read-ing passages from the *People's Daily*. Studies have shown that the average person is less afraid to discuss sensitive political issues with his or her family, friends, neighbors, or colleagues.[89] College professors regularly criticize the government and discuss such sensitive issues as democracy, human rights, and rule of law.

Moreover, citizens have discovered a number of channels to partici-pate in daily governance. One survey found that people in Beijing are po-litically engaged.[90] Urban residents are able to participate in the election of lower-level people's congress delegates and in the election of work-unit leaders. People's congress elections are limited-choice elections and have little impact on high politics. Nevertheless, citizens actively partici-pate in the election of local people's congress delegates and in work-unit elections as a means of punishing unpopular work-unit leaders. Citizens also punish unpopular leaders by boycotting elections. Apart from the electoral process, urban residents can challenge policies or particular decisions by raising appeals either in person or in writing through the bureaucratic hierarchy, trade unions, political organizations, or people's congresses. Citizens also increasingly challenge government decisions in court through administrative litigation.[91] In addition, they can take their case to the media. Muckraking investigative reporting is now a staple of television and print news. In comparison to the eternally optimistic re-porting of state media during earlier years, viewers and readers can now regularly look forward to the details of some of the latest corruption scandals. But when all of these methods fail, workers have taken mat-ters into their own hands and engaged in strikes or slowdowns. Despite the imposition of tight restrictions on demonstrations in the wake of Tiananmen, some groups have used demonstrations as a way of protest-ing government policies.

Urban residents are not the only politically active constituency. Political participation in rural areas is also more frequent and varied than in the past.[92] Villagers often clash with the government over taxes, low grain prices, birth control measures, corruption, excessive fees, under-developed social welfare policies, land issues, and growing inequality.[93] In so doing, villagers rely on both traditional and new means to influ-ence policies. Increasingly, they are turning to **policy-based resistance** to defend their legitimate rights and interests, and citing laws, government policies, and other official communications.[94] Many villagers regularly attend village meetings and contact their people's congress delegates or members of the village council to raise complaints. When all else fails, they increasingly resort to demonstrations.[95]

Although it may be true that regime-challenging actions are rare and that protest activities are usually individualized and directed against work-unit leaders or local officials rather than the state itself,[96] there have been a number of protests and administrative litigation cases that are overtly political in nature. Among the more notable, Falungong disciples have boldly challenged the government's ban by demanding that criminal charges be brought against President Jiang and two other government officials.[97] Falungong adherents have also continued to demonstrate in Tiananmen, in open defiance of the government's ban. Similarly, over 100 victims and family members of those killed in the 1989 demonstrations submitted a petition to the procuracy demanding a criminal investigation and that those responsible for giving the orders be tried for intentional killing in accordance with China's Criminal Law.[98] Meanwhile, political dissidents have defied the Party by trying to register the China Democratic Party as a social organization.

There is then considerable evidence of changes in the Chinese polity. To be sure, such developments have not altered the fundamental reality of single party socialism. The Party remains hostile to genuine democracy. Moreover, despite the breakdown of thought control and the development of a freer marketplace of ideas, Party ideologues continue to struggle against the tide to stop the flow of ideas, as evidenced in the dismissal of liberal intellectuals such as Fan Gang, Liu Junning, and Li Shenzhi from their academic posts. The state also continues to impose limits on the press, bans books, shuts down newspapers, harasses foreign reporters, and searches for ways to control the Internet. It also continues to arrest dissidents, including the organizers of the China Democratic Party. Nor has it relaxed its control on unions.

Yet even when the Party seeks to assert control, it increasingly lacks the capacity to achieve its goals. Indicative of its weakness, the authorities have responded to rural demonstrations by trying to buy off the protesters. Even the dismissal of liberal scholars such as Liu Junning shows the diminished capacity of the state to instill fear in the citizenry. Whereas in the past, scholars who fell out of favor with senior Party leaders would most likely have been subject to administrative sanctions such as reeducation through labor or put under house arrest, now they just take up other posts, and continue to find venues to publish their work. Similarly, after Tiananmen, when the government demanded that participants report on their activities and the participation of others, most refused to accuse others. The Party continues to carry out campaigns: against spiritual pollution in 1983–84; bourgeois liberalization in 1987; wholesale Westernization; and peaceful evolution in the early 1990s; the three stresses in the late 1990s (*sanjiang* – stress politics, stress study, stress justice); and ongoing attempts to create a socialist spiritual civilization. But few citizens pay them any heed. Chinese citizens sense the change, and are less afraid to challenge the ruling regime than before. Liberal intellectuals continue to publish their views; dissidents protest for democracy; Falungong adherents, many of them elderly retired citizens, defy the authorities by regularly demonstrating in Tiananmen; urban and rural residents alike increasingly seek vindication of their rights by using the legal weapons created by twenty years of reforms.

The forces of change

A variety of forces have contributed to the Party's diminished capacity and stake in daily governance. Technological advancement has made it more difficult to control thought. Globalization and China's increasing involvement with the international economy and legal order have also been factors. China has signed a number of international treaties covering a wide range of issues from human rights to nuclear proliferation, pollution and the environment, and judicial assistance. As a result, China is now more accountable to international organizations and to other countries.[99] Accession to the WTO will further the process of integration into the world economy. China's concern with its international reputation is clearly evident in its vigorous opposition to motions in Geneva to censure China for human rights abuses. As noted, village elections gained support from the Party's desire to demonstrate to the international community that political reforms are ongoing. More subtly, but no less significantly, China's lawmakers regularly canvass other legal systems for models on which to base Chinese laws. The amendments to the Criminal Procedure Law were motivated in part by the desire to bring Chinese laws into compliance with international standards.

But the main forces for change have been domestic. The Party's need to shore up its legitimacy contributed to the process of the devolution of authority. When the Party controls all major decisions, it naturally is blamed for everything that goes wrong. As early as 1941, Deng Xiaoping pointed out the danger to the Party of such an approach:

> These comrades misunderstand Party leadership, believing that "Party leadership is above everything else." They interfere in government work, change at will decrees promulgated by the government at a higher level, and transfer cadres who work in organs of political power without going through the proper procedures . . . This has given the masses the impression that the Communist Party has the final say in everything . . . and is responsible for all mistakes made by the government. Hence the government is not respected by the masses and the Party has alienated itself from them. What stupidity![100]

The shifting base of Party legitimacy has led to not only an alteration in the relations between the Party and the state and society but a transformation in the nature of the Party itself. Because the Party's legitimacy is now based primarily on economic performance rather than the charisma of revolutionary leaders, the emphasis for membership and promotion within the Party has shifted from ideology to economics. In the mid-1950s, recruitment emphasized class struggle, egalitarianism, public ownership, and central planning. Thus, peasants constituted 60% of Party membership.[101] As economic development assumed more importance during the 1980s and 1990s, the Party needed more educated technocrats, and the membership profile changed accordingly. Today, 90% of the fourth generation leaders that will succeed Jiang Zemin and his generation have at least a college education.[102]

The younger leaders are more diverse than their predecessors in terms of formative experiences, political solidarity, ideological conviction, and career paths. Many fourth generation leaders grew up during the Cultural Revolution, and are disillusioned with politics and socialism, and less likely to put much faith in ideology. The fifth generation of leaders, having matured during the reform era and witnessed the fall of socialist states around the globe, tend to be pragmatic in their outlook. Among future leaders, there are more lawyers (5.5%), economists (10%), MBAs and financial experts, and even private entrepreneurs (15–20%).[103] There are also more non-Party members in senior leadership positions, though still less than 10%.[104] These future generations of Party leaders have had greater exposure to the West than their predecessors. Several fourth-generation leaders and an even larger number of fifth-generation leaders have been educated abroad and many more have traveled overseas.[105]

Such diversity explains in part why the Party finds it increasingly difficult to unify thought and ensure that its members toe the Party line. The Party's difficulties in controlling its membership are exacerbated by its size. There were 62 million members in 1998, amounting to 5% of the population. As some analysts have noted, there are too many members for Party leaders to control effectively but too few for the Party to be a separate political force.[106] Moreover, the Party is weaker and less unified than other political parties because many individuals join the Party not out of ideological commitment but as a means of social advancement. Party members come in a wide variety of stripes and hold sharply divergent views on fundamental issues. The Party tries to rein in its members through a combination of incentives and coercion. But the incentive structure is changing, with economic growth becoming more important than ideological issues in evaluating cadre performance.[107] Party discipline has been further weakened by corruption and the prevailing ethos of self-interested materialism.

Even were the Party able to impose internal discipline on its members, its ability to impact society at large has been dramatically curtailed as a result of economic reforms. Party groups in private sector companies and collectives tend to be weak or nonexistent. The floating population exists largely outside Party control. Meanwhile, the breakdown of the Party system in the countryside has led to a revival of family lineages, religion, and local warlords. Even in SOEs, Party groups have been largely pushed out of the decision-making loop and are increasingly irrelevant.[108]

The major force behind the changes, however, has been economic reforms, which have resulted in undeniable decentralization and fragmentation of authority. Whereas in the past, decentralization empowered provincial Party committees, in the reform era, decentralization has strengthened provincial and local governments.[109] Some analysts view decentralization as a calculated political bargain: Deng Xiaoping bought off provincial leaders by allowing more autonomy.[110] Whether intended or not, economic reforms and the devolution of authority to lower-level governments has made it increasingly difficult for the Party to ensure that central policies are implemented. Under the pressure to promote local economic development, lower-level government officials regularly circumvent, ignore, and undermine central regulations and policies.

To be sure, local governments still operate within a political framework defined largely by the Party, and the center still plays a large role in setting policy, allocating resources, and creating the conditions for bargaining.[111] Moreover, when the Party center really means business and the top leadership is united in its policy preferences, the center can prevail over the provinces, as evidenced by the recentralization of taxation that led to the center collecting 49% of consolidated tax revenue in 1997 as opposed to just 22% in 1993 or the imposition of macro policies to restrict the money supply and rein in inflation.[112] As Baum and Shevchenko observe, "post-reform Chinese leaders have deliberately exchanged some of the unified command power of a strong (but clumsy and insensitive) thumb for the heightened responsiveness of sensitive (but relatively fragile and delicate) fingers."[113] Nevertheless, the balance of power has shifted toward local governments.

In any event, that the center retains a certain amount of authority and institutional capacity is a plus rather than a negative for rule-of-law reforms. The experiences of the earlier law and development movement demonstrated that an excessively weak central state may lead to anarchy and chaos and undermine efforts to establish rule of law. PRC legal scholars have cited as one of the native resources for implementing rule of law in China the Party's ability to push through institutional reforms that will inevitably alter the balance of power among state organs. At the same time, others have argued that the Party itself is an obstacle to the realization of rule of law. Whether the Party will ultimately play a positive or negative role remains to be seen. The results to date are mixed: the Party has both promoted and obstructed the establishment of rule of law.

The Party's role in the legal system

Much of the skepticism about rule of law in China is based on the belief that single party socialism in which the Party plays a leading role is incompatible with rule of law.[114] But whether single party socialism is consistent with rule of law and in particular the supremacy of the law will depend on what one means by rule of law and the leading role of the

Party. One of the virtues of a thin conception of rule of law is that it is compatible with various forms of government, including in theory single party socialism. To be sure, single party socialism is not compatible with a Liberal Democratic rule of law or even Communitarian rule of law, as both advocate genuine democracy defined by multiparty elections at all levels of government. Nevertheless, a leadership role for the Party is potentially consistent with a Statist Socialist and Neoauthoritarian rule of law.

At the center of the theoretical debate about the applicability of rule of law to China is the tension between the leading role of the CCP and the supremacy of law. PRC legal scholars have struggled to reconcile the CCP's role with a rule of law in which law is supreme since the 1950s. When Mao encouraged critics to speak out during the One Hundred Flowers movement of 1956, legal scholars raised questions as to who was responsible for making laws, the Party or the NPC, and which was superior, Party policy or law? They argued for a separation between Party and government, with the NPC to be responsible for promulgating laws, which would trump Party policies. They also called for more independent courts to enforce state laws in an impartial way. Mao responded with the antirightist campaign, and by removing objectionable NPC delegates, reducing the role of the NPC, emphasizing Party policy and ideology over laws and expertise, shutting down the MOJ and Ministry of Supervision, and decreasing judicial independence. During this period, courts became subject to the system of dual leadership, the Political–Legal Committee assumed a more prominent role, and the Party began to review individual cases' decisions as a matter of course.[115]

The same issues have risen again in the post-Mao era.[116] Party leaders have acknowledged the need for law and to rebuild the legal system. As we have seen, the authorities have expended considerable efforts to create a comprehensive regulatory framework and to rebuild legal institutions. Yet the status of law, the relation of Party policy to law, the independence of the court, and the Party's role remain contested. It is important to stress, however, that few today advocate a return to a rule-by-man (*ren zhi*) system in which the dictates of CCP leaders supersede laws. Nor do most deny the need to rule the country in accordance with law or challenge the core idea that law is necessary to limit the arbitrary acts of the state. Further, those who argue for a leading role of the CCP generally do so on the basis that there is no contradiction between the CCP exercising leadership and the supremacy of the law.[117] Others simply accept that the two cannot be reconciled and advocate that law should be supreme.[118]

In every legal system, some authority – be it the Party, legislators, administrative officials, judges, or the people – is ultimately responsible for creating rules, interpreting them, and implementing them.[119] In a very general and simplified sense, one difference between a Statist Socialist rule of law and a Liberal Democratic rule of law is that in the former the Party reserves the right to make fundamental policy decisions whereas in a democracy such decisions are left to the people. Thus, the official interpretation of the role of the Party, set forth in the state and Party constitutions and endorsed by Jiang Zemin, is that the Party is to set the general policy direction for society. An article in the *People's Daily* presents the standard view:[120]

> As pointed out by Comrade Jiang Zemin, our Party's leadership is mainly political, ideological, and organizational, whereas the key form of political leadership is: To transform the Party's ideas into the state's will after going through a statutory procedure; and to bring into effect the Party's line, principle, and policy through activities organized by the Party and Party members' exemplary role set for the broad masses. The Party has to exercise leadership over the formulation of the Constitution and law, and also to act consciously within the bounds of the Constitution and law, work strictly according to law, and rule the country according to law.

Significantly, whereas in the Mao era, CCP policies substituted for or trumped laws,[121] CCP policy is now to be transformed into laws and regulations by entities authorized to make law in accordance with the stipulated procedures for law-making.[122] Although rule of law requires that laws be passed by entities with the authority to make law in accordance with proper procedures, it does not dictate where the ideas for laws must come from. The source could be the Party, the legislature, citizens, or private interest groups.

Nevertheless, for the Party's leading role to be compatible with rule of law, its role in society would have to be defined by law, Party organs and members would then have to act in accordance with law, and individual Party members would have to be subject to law. According to both the State and Party constitutions, the Party must conduct its activities within the limit permitted by the constitution and law.[123] Individual Party members must also conscientiously observe the law.[124]

Although Party organs and individual Party members officially are supposed to abide by the law, reality differs considerably. The actual role of the Party is not clearly defined in the state constitution or laws.[125] The Party's importance is more a matter of political reality than law. The power of Deng Xiaoping in the last years before his death was entirely extraconstitutional; he held no official government position, though he did retain his Party post as head of the Central Military Commission. Nor is there any mention in the constitution of the dual system of control that creates a parallel structure of party organizations at each level of government. Similarly, there is no formal legal basis for the nomenklatura system. Neither the constitution nor any other law provides for such powers. On the contrary, the involvement of the CCP in the appointment of judges, for instance, is at odds with the appointment process set forth in the Judges Law.[126]

Moreover, although in theory CCP policy must be transformed into laws and regulations by the entities with law-making authority to be legally binding, Party organs continue to issue joint regulations with government entities, albeit infrequently, even though they have no legal authority to do so. In practice, there are also still instances where CCP policy trumps the available laws and regulations.[127] In addition, senior Party members are often insulated from judicial sanctions because the Party generally handles violations of the law by Party members internally according to CCP disciplinary rules.[128] Conversely, the Party continues to use the legal system as well as administrative punishments such as reeducation through labor to attack dissidents, who in a mockery of justice are denied a fair trial.

While one could imagine a constitution that would spell out the CCP's role, including its right to make appointments and so forth, it is not the current constitution. Alternatively, while one could imagine the CCP acting only within the limits of its constitutionally prescribed role, that is not currently the case. Although ruling the country in accordance with law is the official policy, even CCP leaders admit that there are problems.[129] Party organs and members continue to interfere in day-to-day governance in ways that have no legal basis and go beyond the Party's leading role as general policy setter. The reality is that sometimes decisions that should be made by legislators, government officials, and courts are made by Party organs.

On the other hand, Party involvement in daily governance is undeniably less prevalent than in the past. The Party's role in the law-making process is considerably diminished, even though the Party still maintains various mechanisms for influencing the legislative process.[130] In 1991, the Party issued a document defining its leadership role with respect to law-making.[131] The document confirmed that the CCP's role should be limited to "leadership over the political line, direction and policies" and review and confirmation of draft laws. Not all draft laws need be submitted to the CCP for approval.[132] Moreover, in practice the review process usually consists of general comments on the law as a whole or major aspects rather than detailed calls for revision of specific provisions.[133]

Long regarded as a rubber stamp, the NPC has grown increasingly assertive. NPC and NPCSC delegates have voted down drafts of the Enterprise Bankruptcy Law, Public Demonstrations Law, the urban neighborhood committee law, and an amendment to the Highway Law, and demanded significant amendments to other laws.[134] The law-making process now involves considerable bargaining between various constituencies.[135] There is more opportunity for participation by different interest groups, particularly with respect to national laws.[136] Even local people's congresses are becoming more assertive.[137] In short, the outcome of the legislative process is increasingly determined by factors other than the dictates of the CCP.

In any event, the mere fact that a ruling party is effective at having its policies become law is not inconsistent with rule of law. The role of the Party in sponsoring and reviewing laws and appointing key personnel is similar in many respects to the role of the ruling party in many parliamentary systems. In such systems, the ruling party controls the legislative process and is generally able to push through the legislation it desires. As one British administrative law scholar points out, "the government can always ensure that its policies become law in much the way that it desires."[138] Sir William Wade concurs that there is no strict separation of powers in Britain and that acts of Parliament are drafted by the executive and "pushed through Parliament by the government's majority vote, sometimes with virtually no alteration and sometimes with only perfunctory discussion."[139] In light of such developments, some European legal scholars contend that the center of gravity has shifted away from the Parliament to the Executive such that Parliament's main function is now less legislative and more to keep the government in check.[140]

Obviously there are important differences between the CCP and ruling parties elsewhere – most notably, the CCP is not elected. Further, although the ruling party in other countries may make key government and in some cases judicial appointments, the CCP appoints a much larger number of people than the ruling party in most systems. Nor is the CCP subject to a vote of no-confidence. But while the nonelected character of the CCP and the nomenklatura system are incompatible with democracy, they are not necessarily incompatible with a thin rule of law or a Socialist Statist or Neoauthoritarian thick rule of law.

In the administrative area, CCP influence has also diminished and is mainly indirect. The CCP continues to influence rule-making by setting general policies and through the nomenklatura system. As in the legislative realm, however, CCP influence on administrative rule-making is breaking down and agencies are increasingly assertive in pursuing their own agendas.[141] If anything, administrative agencies are more determined than ever to fight for turf in order to stave off further cutbacks. At the same time, the efforts to create a more professional civil service have encouraged agencies to pay greater attention to technical issues and less to ideology when drafting regulations. Decentralization and the move toward a market economy have also contributed to the CCP's decreased importance in the administrative area.[142]

Furthermore, administrative entities pass thousands of regulations every year, many of them highly technical in nature.[143] Even were it so inclined, the CCP would lack the capacity to play a significant role in the rule-making process. Similarly, administrative agencies make countless specific decisions every day. Direct interference by the CCP is necessarily limited.

The Party's influence on the judiciary is discussed in detail in Chapter 7. Suffice it to say at this point that although the Party exerts influence on the judiciary by overseeing the appointment of judges and through the policy and law-making processes, the Party rarely becomes involved in determining the outcomes of specific cases.

The Party in perspective: will retreat of the Party and state lead to rule of law?

In summary, the Party's role in the daily operation of the legal system is greatly diminished. The Party's impact on the legal system is felt mainly in three ways. The first is ideological. China remains a socialist state committed to the four cardinal principles, including the leading role of the Party. Yet the importance of socialist ideology as such is easily overstated in this pragmatic era where what matters is not the color of the cat but whether it catches mice, as Deng Xiaoping quipped. It is difficult, for example, to reconcile socialist ideology with today's market economy replete with capital markets and a new "exploiting" private class. It is also difficult to see ideology as an insurmountable barrier to some credible form of rule of law given the Party's endorsement of rule of law and acceptance of the basic principle that the Party and state actors must act in accordance with law; the Party's support for the impressive array of institutional reforms that have been carried out over the last twenty years; and the Party's acceptance of human rights as a legitimate topic rather than simply a bourgeois concept designed to induce false consciousness in the downtrodden proletariat. In short, Party ideology has evolved considerably over the last twenty years, and it will continue to evolve in the future. Someday, the Party may even transform itself into a social labor or social democratic party. As Party ideology has evolved and continues to evolve, so has and will the Party's leading role in society. With the Party having officially endorsed rule of law and accepted limits on its power in theory, the main challenge for implementing rule of law in China is to strengthen the legal institutions so that they are capable of limiting the Party and state in practice.

The second way in which the Party's influence is felt is symbolic. When Party organs or members act beyond the law, it sends a signal to the rest of society that law need not be taken seriously. Clearly, the reach of the law remains limited; higher-level Party and government officials are still above the law in many ways.[144] On the other hand, Party cadres and government officials are increasingly taking law seriously, both paying verbal homage to the sanctity of law and, more importantly, adapting their behavior accordingly. Today, when the ruling regime declares martial law, bans Falungong, or arrests dissidents, it takes pains to cloak its actions in law. Although at present this practice of appealing to law to justify actions often appears to be nothing more than a political expediency, over time it could lead to genuine debates about the legality of Party actions and give rise to the expectation that the Party will comply with the law.

The third and most important way in which the Party continues to exert influence on the legal system is through its ability to promote or impede further reforms. The reluctance of senior leaders to unleash political and legal reforms that could threaten the Party has impeded the implementation of rule of law. No doubt some senior leaders are to some extent ambivalent about legal reforms: they may want the benefits that flow from a modern legal system and yet not want law to impose meaningful limits on them. They may want, for example, better enforcement of court judgments and arbitral awards so as not to scare off investors, and yet they are afraid to attack the basic institutional problem that lies at the heart of local protectionism by creating more independent courts. They are also wary of a more robust civil society and freer media that would be useful in attacking corruption and reining in wayward government officials, yet could also turn against the Party. The question is will they be able to resist the tide forever?

Ultimately, the key to the future realization of rule of law in China is not ideology but power.[145] How is power to be controlled and allocated in a single party socialist state? To the extent that law is to limit the Party, how does the legal system obtain sufficient authority to control a party that has been above the law? In a democracy, the final check on government power is the ability of the people to throw the government out and elect a new one. In the absence of multiparty democracy, an authoritarian government must either voluntarily relinquish some of its power or else have it taken away by force. Naturally, some Party leaders will resist giving up power so readily. They may therefore be disinclined to support reforms that would strengthen rule of law but also allow institutions to become so powerful that they could then provide the basis for challenging Party rule. The result may be that, at least on those issues that threaten the survivability of the Party, the needs of the Party continue to trump rule of law for some time.

Nevertheless, there is some reason to believe that the issue of power can be resolved in favor of rule of law and that law will come to impose meaningful restraints on Party and government leaders. First, although the views of senior leaders have been vital to legal reforms in China and will continue to influence the future development of the legal system to some extent, whether opposition on the part of certain leaders will be sufficient to block further reforms is doubtful. It is likely that different leaders hold different views, that many of them have not thought through their positions in a systematic way, and that their views are therefore likely to be inconsistent in some respects, and, at least for some of them, soft and subject to change. There are also generational differences, with younger people, particularly those trained in law or exposed to the West, tending to see law as more autonomous and less instrumental.[146] Differences among Party elite both in the substance of their views and the firmness with which they hold them make it difficult to predict how their views will be translated into action. Reform factions within the Party itself may push for deeper legal and political reforms, perhaps even someday genuine democracy. As Jiang Jingguo's deathbed support for greater democracy in Taiwan and the experiences of Korea and the Soviet Union show, authoritarian leaders are capable of relinquishing power given the right circumstances. Jiang Zemin and Party leaders' endorsement of the principle of ruling the country according to law and a socialist rule-of-law state, and their support of its subsequent incorporation into the constitution suggest that the Party is willing to accept limitations on its power.

Moreover, Party leaders may support further reforms to implement rule of law even if they are ambivalent simply for pragmatic reasons, including the desire to strengthen their own base of power. In his study of the NPC, Tanner suggests that the impetus behind the reforms that have enhanced significantly the authority of the NPC was not so much the desire for better law-making and rule of law. Although the Party leadership's commitment to legal reforms set the process in motion, rule of law and socialist democracy are in his view "weak reeds in Chinese politics."[147] Rather, he asserts, the "NPC's growth in power can be better understood in organizational–bureaucratic terms than as a result of a liberalizing preference for the rule of law." It was primarily the result of two forces: competition among top leaders, and their interest in fortifying their power base. When Peng Zhen and other senior leaders were "retired" to the NPC, they refused to go quietly. As former leading cadres, they employed their finely honed skills at bureaucratic in-fighting to expand their turf.[148]

But even allowing that the personal factors played a role, there were – as Tanner notes – other compelling reasons for rebuilding people's congresses, including the senior leaders' desire after the Cultural Revolution for regularity; the need for a more scientific decision-making process; the demands of economic reform that placed a premium on the kind of technical expertise that the Party was ill-suited to provide; and the Party's desire to share some of the burden for decision-making so that it could not be held accountable for everything that went wrong.[149]

Although Party leaders may be wary about rule of law, they are sufficiently pragmatic to appreciate its many advantages. In his speech at the 15th Party Congress, Jiang Zemin portrayed rule of law as central to economic development, national stability, and Party legitimacy.[150] Jiang has sung the praises of rule of law as a way of reining in increasingly unruly local governments. In their pursuit of economic growth, local officials have thumbed their noses at Beijing. Since lower-level officials are more likely than Party leaders to feel the bite of rule of law on a daily basis, perhaps their resistance is to be expected. But the interest of local officials in avoiding the law does not further the policy interests of CCP leaders and the central government. Jiang Zemin and other central leaders advocate rule of law in no small measure because they believe it will strengthen the hand of central authorities in controlling rebellious local officials and help rationalize governance. Simply put, if the Party is to achieve its goals of stability, implementation of central policies, economic development, and legitimacy, further legal reforms, including a stronger administrative law regime and a more independent judiciary, are required. Currently, widespread discontent over judicial corruption, bias, and incompetence is deterring investors, undermining the legitimacy and effectiveness of the legal system, and ultimately hurting the Party. Granted, from the Party's perspective, a stronger legal system with a more independent judiciary has both advantages and disadvantages. While the Party has for years acknowledged that local protectionism is undermining the independence of the judiciary, it has refused to address the institutional causes of the problem, presumably because it fears that an authoritative and independent judiciary able to decide commercial and administrative cases on their merits would also be able to decide politically sensitive cases on their merits. Thus the dilemma facing the Party is how to strengthen the judiciary without

allowing it to become too strong. In deciding whether to support further reforms the Party must determine whether the benefits outweigh the
costs. That calculus, however, is influenced by factors beyond the Party's
control.

The need to sustain economic growth will continue to put pressure on
China's leaders to carry out reforms, even if that means further erosion
of the Party's power. China's leaders realized early on that a market
economy required a legal system capable of providing the necessary
certainty and predictability demanded by investors. The slogan that a
market economy is a rule-of-law economy has been repeatedly invoked
in a mantra-like fashion. As we have seen, however, economic reforms
have resulted in a devolution of authority to lower-level governments
and also shifted the base of power in some measure from the Party and
state to society. As reforms continue, the balance of power will continue
to shift.

Rule of law is a function of institution-building and the creation
of a culture of legality. Progress has been made and continues to be
made on both fronts. Now that the genie is out of the bottle, legal reformers will continue to push for more independent and authoritative
courts, as will members of the judiciary, if for no other reason than path-
dependent institutional self-interest.[151] Political and legal reforms tend
to take on a life of their own, with institutions bursting out of the cages
meant to confine them.[152] Taiwan is a good example. Twenty years ago,
Taiwan's legal system evidenced many of the characteristics of the current PRC system. The ruling regime was authoritarian in nature; politics
trumped laws; the ruling party controlled the legislature; the judiciary
lacked independence and stature; martial law and broad state-security
laws led to the infringement of individual rights in the name of public security; Taiwan's citizens enjoyed few civil and political freedoms.
However, during the last two decades, the Council of Grand Justices has
assumed a much greater role in curbing administrative discretion and
limiting government as legal and political reforms progressed, thereby
contributing to further reforms.[153] In 1999, the Council challenged the
legislature, holding that amendments to the constitution were themselves unconstitutional.[154] The Council has also become more aggressive
in protecting human rights by relying on broad constitutional clauses
such as due process to promote freedom of speech and the press, and to
strike down criminal law statutes and practices similar in many respects

to current PRC statutes and practices.[155] South Korean courts have also become more aggressive as legal and political reforms have progressed, thus supporting and promoting further reforms.[156] In Indonesia, the Suharto government's desire to obtain legitimacy abroad and to deal with corruption and patrimonial practices that were adversely affecting business confidence led to the establishment of administrative courts. But then the courts turned on Suharto, pursuing key allies on corruption charges and defiantly striking down the government's decision to ban a popular weekly news magazine. In response to a groundswell of public support, the judiciary became increasingly aggressive in challenging the government, to the point where Suharto himself was brought up on charges of corruption.[157]

At this stage, it is highly unlikely that the Party could prevent further institutional change altogether, much less return to past practices. The judiciary, legal profession, and civil service are continually becoming more competent and professional. As they develop institutionally, they are better positioned to push for further reforms, creating a virtuous cycle. As noted in the previous chapter, the demand for rule of law has increasingly come from members of the judiciary, legal reformers in state organs such as the NPC, and administrative agencies.

Even local governments have begun to appreciate the advantages of a law-based order. Notwithstanding Guangdong's reputation for flexibility and finding creative ways to circumvent the rules, Guangdong officials were among the first to jump on the rule-of-law bandwagon because they felt that a flexible approach left them vulnerable to a predatory central government and that implementing rule of law would help them maintain their competitive edge over other provinces.[158] Although a leader in attracting FDI for years, Guangdong has found it more difficult to attract foreign investors as labor and land costs have risen. With preferential tax and economic policies expected to be phased out now that China has entered the WTO, Guangdong will face even more difficulties in the future. Accordingly, Guangdong officials have focused on implementing a number of legal reforms as a way of improving the investment environment and attracting investors, particularly multinationals, including strengthening enforcement of intellectual property rules, increasing the transparency of the approval process and other interactions between administrative agencies and businesses, and punishing corrupt officials who levy illegal fees.[159]

The demand for rule of law is also strong among academics, citizens, and domestic and foreign businesses. As economic reforms progressed, private citizens and domestic businesses accumulated more property and business interests to protect, and they are increasingly willing to take to the courts to protect them.[160] They are also increasingly vested in the ideology of rule of law.[161] Rights-consciousness and legal awareness has increased among the citizenry, and with it, litigation.[162] Resistance by the public, whether farmers or dissidents, is increasingly law-based.[163] Having appealed to rule of law as a means of bolstering its legitimacy, the ruling regime must now make good on its promises or suffer a backlash.

In short, the development of the legal system hinges on more than the ideas of the top leadership. Legal reforms will continue to be driven to a considerable extent by objective forces, including the needs of a market economy; the demands of foreign investors and domestic businesses; the Chinese citizenry's desire for justice; international pressure, as evidenced in the amendment of the Criminal Law and Criminal Procedure Law and China's accession to various human rights treaties;[164] GATT requirements, now that China has become a member of the WTO; and the ruling regime's desire for legitimacy, both at home and abroad. All of these forces, taken collectively, are likely to exert a much stronger force on the pace and trajectory of legal reforms than the wishes of some senior leaders who may be lukewarm or even opposed to rapid reforms.

Conclusion

China's legal system will most likely continue to converge toward a system that meets the standards of a thin rule of law, though the pace and the path of reforms will be determined primarily by domestic factors, one of which is the Party. Given its still considerable power within the Chinese polity and its leadership role as the vanguard of society, the Party undoubtedly will be able to influence the direction of legal reforms to some extent. Although the Party has lost the ability to control unilaterally ideological discourse and *a fortiori* to make socialism attractive and persuasive to the vast majority of Chinese citizens, it could shore up its legitimacy to some extent and still exert some influence on the ideological agenda by promoting and implementing rule of law. Rather than passively reacting to events, and being seen as an obstacle to meaningful reforms, it could take a proactive stance by championing a credible version of rule of law and carrying out the necessary institutional reforms to bring it about. At present, the Party's reluctance to sanction deeper institutional reforms undermines its attempt to bolster its legitimacy by appealing to rule of law and its record with respect to legal reforms.

Judging from the current proposals for judicial reform for the next five years and the Party's limited efforts at political reform since the 15th Party Congress,[165] it does not appear likely that the present generation of leaders will be willing to sanction the kinds of major institutional reforms needed to implement a system of rule of law in which even life-or-death issues for the Party are handled according to law and the legal system is able to hold even the most senior leaders accountable. Assuming that the next generation of leaders are willing to support the necessary institutional reforms to implement more fully rule of law, presumably it will be the Statist Socialist version outlined by Jiang Zemin, which has only been imperfectly realized thus far. Although a Statist Socialist rule of law would require meaningful limits on even senior Party leaders, it would offer the Party a more solid base for claiming legitimacy than the present system. With Mao remembered for his contributions to the establishment of the modern Chinese state and Deng Xiaoping heralded as the patron of economic reform, Jiang Zemin is desperately searching for a coherent vision to solidify his legacy. Bold political reforms are out of the question, and earlier attempts to articulate a Chinese socialist spiritual civilization and the more recent experiments with the "three representatives" and "rule of virtue" have proved uninspiring at best.[166] As one of the cornerstones of modernity along with a market economy, democracy, and human rights, rule of law is the most likely candidate available.[167]

A Statist Socialist rule of law would allow the Party to maintain its privileged political position and avoid genuine elections. Indeed, it is consistent with Jiang's three representatives policy in that the establishment of rule of law would further economic development, and thus be consistent with the "development of advanced productive forces"; require a change in the political and legal culture and in particular the development of a rule-of-law culture, which is consistent with the development of a modern and advanced culture; and it would further the fundamental interests of the broad majority of Chinese citizens. In essence, by accepting certain limitations on its power and allowing state organs – including the people's congresses, courts, and administrative agencies – to become more authoritative, the Party could conceivably enhance its legitimacy and effectiveness, and in so doing increase its chances of surviving and perhaps even of thriving in the long run.[168] Although implementing rule of law fully requires a transformation in the actual role of the Party, by proactively promoting a Statist Socialist rule of law, the Party may be able to ensure, at least for a period, the establishment of the form of rule of law most favorable to the Party. Under a Statist Socialist rule of law, the Party would remain a potent political force, capable of influencing if not unilaterally determining the agenda for further economic, legal, and political reforms. By sanctioning reforms and promoting laws and policies that strengthen the state, it might be able to remain in power long enough to reposition itself as a more populist party – perhaps even someday as a social labor or social democratic party – capable of winning future democratic elections.[169]

On the other hand, the establishment of a Statist Socialist rule of law may not gain for the Party the legitimacy it so desperately desires. Chinese citizens may not be satisfied with a Statist Socialist rule of law. Given the limited nature of reforms under such a system, including continued limitations on the press and civil society as well as the absence of genuine elections, a Statist Socialist rule-of-law system may be incapable of holding political leaders sufficiently accountable and addressing fundamental issues such as corruption. Deeper institutional reforms of the type contemplated by supporters of Neoauthoritarian or Communitarian forms of rule of law will most likely be required. Alternatively, Chinese citizens may not be content with a Statist Socialist rule of law simply on ideological grounds: they may, at least over time, prefer a more robust civil society, a freer press, and ultimately democracy. By sanctioning the deeper (albeit what it hopes will be limited) institutional reforms required to implement a Statist Socialist rule of law, the Party may be sliding farther down an irreversible slippery slope that will ultimately end in its loss of power. Senior leaders no doubt appreciate the risks, which are evident in Suharto's fall and the Guomindang's electoral defeat in Taiwan.[170] While such a strategy may be risky, so is attempting to maintain the status quo and obstructing further political and legal reforms – a lesson apparent from the collapse of the Soviet Union and other authoritarian regimes around the world.

Fortunately for Party leaders, the choices confronting them are not all or nothing. Most legal reforms do not involve life-or-death issues that implicate the survivability of the Party. At present, further reforms are possible. The legal system could be strengthened in a number of ways that do not directly threaten the Party but rather further its self-professed goals to rationalize governance, increase government efficiency, rein in local officials, and root out corruption. A number of systemic and institutional obstacles must be overcome before China will be able to implement fully any form of rule of law, including – as discussed in the next chapter – the legislative system.

Notes

1   Although Neoauthoritarians could support single party socialism, they might not. Neoauthoritarians see rule of law as strengthening the state but not necessarily the CCP.
2   Zheng Shiping (1997: 16) points out that because "the Party and state are two sets of political institutions with different organizational logic and tasks, attempts at building state institutions while strengthening the Party control over the state inevitably cause contradictions and tensions."
3   Party leaders and organs continue to emphasize the vital leadership role of the Party and to back policies and institutional changes that would strengthen the Party's grip over key sectors, particularly personnel. For instance, the Party has attempted to strengthen its control over provincial people's congresses by appointing provincial Party Committee Secretaries as heads of the people's congresses. See Kwang (2000). See also the 1995 Interim Regulations on Selection and Appointment of Party and Government Cadres. Yet the ineffectiveness of such measures is evidenced by the need to repeatedly issue policy statements trumpeting the importance of upholding the Party line and Party discipline and the need to call local Party leaders back to Beijing for additional ideological work.
4   Baum and Shevchenko (1999).
5   The Party has also appealed to nationalism and rule of law to bolster its legitimacy. See Chapter 4.
6   See Deng Xiaoping (1984: 303).
7   Zhao Ziyang (1987).
8   In all government entities, including the courts, there is a Party group, consisting of Party members, which is responsible for Party affairs and ensuring that the government entities adhere to the Party line.
9   See Lieberthal (1995).
10 Zheng Shiping (1997: 84).
11 Burns (1994). In addition, other appointments must be reported to Party central, including the heads and vice-heads of the divisions within the SPC,

vice-presidents of provincial-level courts, and the secretary-generals, deputy secretary-generals, commission heads, commission deputy heads, bureau heads and vice-heads at the provincial levels.

12 Walder (1995). See also the essays in Goldman and MacFarquhar (1999).

13 Burns (1994: 473).

14 Ultimately, the CCP usually approves of the person appointed, though that person may not be its first choice. Burns (1994: 459).

15 Studwell and Zhong (1999: 22).

16 See Yunxiang Yan (1995).

17 Pomfret (2000).

18 Thus, in one study of the textile industry in Xiqiao, Guandong, 38% of 210 TVEs were actually private enterprises, though they tended to be smaller ones. Unger and Chan (1999: 51). The director of the Bureau of Township Enterprises claimed that more than half of the capital of TVEs came from private sources, and that 60% of the added value of TVEs was from private individuals and enterprises. See "China's Townships Enterprises Face Changes" (2001).

19 Pomfret (2000).

20 Oi (1999); Oi and Walder (1999).

21 Solinger (1999).

22 Private enterprises or *siying qiye* refer to private wholly owned PRC companies that employ more than eight employees. In addition, there are *getihu* or small individual or household businesses that employ less than eight employees. *China Statistical Yearbook* (1999: 5–15, 155).

23 The private enterprises tend to be relatively small. Only 17,000 of them had registered capital (i.e., initial subscribed equity) of more than five million yuan ($600,000). See the *China Economics Yearbook* (1999: 735–37).

24 Parris (1999: 267); International Finance Corporation (2000: 14).

25 For a general discussion of FDI and its impact on China's GDP and trade, see Wu (1999).

26 Not all of the FIEs are legitimate foreign enterprises. In some cases, Chinese entities will establish branches or subsidiaries abroad. The branch or subsidiary will then enter into a joint venture with the PRC entity or establish a wholly foreign-owned enterprise. As a result, the PRC entity is able to take advantage of the preferential tax policies offered foreign investors.

27 Hong Kong Trade Development Council (2000).

28 *PRC Development Commission Reports on 5-Yr Growth in Foreign-Funded Firms* (2000).

29 Hong Kong Trade Development Council (2000). Other sources claim that FIEs produced over 20% of the total national industrial output, and paid in 16% of all industrial and commercial taxes. See *Background of Foreign Investment in China's Economy* (2000).

30 Many shareholding cooperatives are also private or involve significant private holdings.

31 Studwell and Zhong (1999: 24).

32 Studwell and Zhong (1999: 24).

33 International Finance Corporation (2000: 14–19).

34 Studwell and Zhong (1999: 35).

35 The amendments also increased the autonomy of SOEs and collectives by emphasizing their independent management. See Xin Chunying (1999: 394–405).

36 *Jiang Zemin's Congress Report* (1997).

37 Constitution, art. 6.

38 Constitution, art. 11.

39 See, for example, the Encouraging and Promoting the Development of Medium and Small Enterprises Several Policy Opinions, issued by the State Economic and Trade Commission on July 6, 2000.

40 The share of bank loans for the private sector reportedly rose from 37% in 1997 to 42% in 1998. Studwell and Zhong (1999: 24).

41 See "New Private Banks to Enhance Competition in Financial Industry" (2000).

42 See Guthrie (1999: 37–39).

43 Lardy (1999); The World Bank (1999).

44 Liu, Carter, and Yang (1998) note that while different regions have developed differently, the trend is toward clearer property rights with respect to rural land.

45 Yan Yunxiang (1995: 238).

46 Wank (1999); Oi (1999).

47 Parris (1999: 272–74).

48 Parris (1999: 275). Dickson (2000: 44) found that in a 1997 survey of three counties, 40% of large- and medium-scale private entrepreneurs were Party members.

49 Aimin Chen (1999: 484). See also Xia Li Lollar (1997), reporting the results of a 1994 survey, based on thirty-nine SOEs in Hebei.

50 In 2000, the State Economic and Trade Commission announced a new code of conduct for SOEs, which included *inter alia* a renewed commitment that government officials will not interfere in daily management issues. See "SOEs to Work under 'Code' to Improve" (2000).

51 Xia Li Lollar (1997: 55). Lollar found that smaller enterprises tended to have more autonomy than bigger ones. Xia Li Lollar (1997: 58).

52 Gore (1999) argues that the Party-state's influence on the economy remains significant. He notes that the size of the private sector is often exaggerated by including collectives and TVEs, that the dual leadership and *tiaokuai* systems (systems of vertical and horizontal lines of responsibility) of government are still in place, and that investment decisions are often distorted by political factors. The result is investment hunger and competition by local governments for projects that are not always efficient or rational, the miniaturization of projects that are smaller than economies of scale would dictate, and regional imbalances. Yet the political incentives to which local governments are responding derive not from the Party but from the governments' desire to generate economic development or their struggle to expand their own turf by seizing a larger share of resources. As Gore admits, economic reforms have led to decentralization and the fragmentation of authority. The ability of the central Party and state to control lower-level Party and government officials has diminished. Moreover, Gore (1999: 7) concludes that "China's high-powered growth

contains major structural weaknesses and is fundamentally unsustainable without a complete overhaul of its institutions." Thus, the remedy is further separation of the Party and the state from day-to-day economic operations.

53 The following discussion is drawn from Lardy (1999: 33–58). Lardy paints a grim picture of SOE reform. In contrast, others paint a somewhat rosier picture. Nolan and Wang (1999), for instance, argue that only forty-two of the top 500 SOEs reported losses, and the money-losers were concentrated in industries such as machinery and textiles. Moreover, part of the reason SOEs perform poorly is that they are forced to bear substantial welfare burdens, providing their employees with housing, medical treatment, day-care, and so on. In addition, many of the profit-making components of SOEs have been spun off into other companies. Further, they also note that economic growth slowed in recent years, resulting in decreased demand downstream. Indeed, 40-50% of FIEs reportedly lost money in 1993, even though they enjoy a 20% lower tax rate than SOEs and do not suffer from the same welfare burdens.

54 See, for example, Lardy (1999).

55 See, for example, Nolan and Wang (1999).

56 You Ji (1998).

57 Rawski (1999: 150).

58 Walder (1986).

59 See Lynch (1999a: 2, 7–8), who attributes the Party's loss of control over thought work (*sixiang gongzuo*) to property-rights reforms that have forced media units to assume responsibility for their own profits and losses, administrative fragmentation that has diminished the control of central authorities over local authorities, and the introduction of new technologies.

60 Saich (2000).

61 See, for example, Unger and Chan (1999).

62 White, Howell, and Shang (1996: 3). As White *et al.* note, the degree of independence of social groups from the states in Western liberal democracies is often overstated.

63 Ma Shu-yun (1994: 191) argues that, at least initially, PRC intellectuals who discussed civil society tended to focus on the notion of a modern citizen, "consisting of law-abiding and civil members of society . . . The relation between civil society and the state was thus seen as an intimate and harmonious one."

64 White, Howell, and Shang (1996) distinguish between a sociological definition of civil society and a political one that incorporates specific liberal democratic principles with respect to rule of law, civil rights, and the conception of the relation between the state and individuals.

65 I address the issue of civil society more systematically and develop four variants corresponding to the four ideal types of rule of law in a forthcoming conference volume to be edited by Daniel Bell. It should be noted that many Asian countries, for example, impose restrictions on social organizations, such as registration requirements.

66 Saich (2000).

67 O'Brien (1994b) makes a similar point with respect to local people's congresses. Bar associations are another example. By maintaining close relations with the

Ministry of Justice and its local branches, bar associations are better able to push for changes in the regulatory framework and thus to serve the interests of their members.

68   White, Howell, and Shang (1996: 213–14) note that although the state has influenced the development of a civil society it has not always been able to control it, in part because the state has not had a plan for how to handle newly emergent social organizations, and in part because it subscribes to different, and at times competing, rationales for promoting or allowing social organizations to proliferate in the first place. These rationales include the desire to co-opt rising social forces that could threaten the status quo; a "managerial rationale" that sees the need for new institutions to regulate an increasingly complex economy and society; a development rationale that seeks to use new organizations to facilitate economic growth; and a bureaucratic rationale that reflects the institutional responses of specific agencies to change.

69   Noting the wide variety of forms of resistance from tax riots, labor strikes, and inter-ethnic riots, to prodemocracy demonstrations, environmental, anticorruption, and gender protests, local electoral challenges, and even mass suicides, Perry and Seldon (2000) conclude that the "cumulative weight of these challenges has forced significant changes in law and social praxis in contemporary China, developments that have been largely missed by analysts whose vision is limited to the search for American-style democracy." Similarly, after providing a lengthy list of reform initiatives, Oksenberg (2001: 24–25) concludes that the conventional wisdom in the West that China has had economic reform without political reform is inaccurate, though he acknowledges that political reforms have proceeded slowly and that China at its core remains a Soviet–Leninist state.

70   Internal Party politics may have also become more institutionalized and democratic, though the lack of transparency makes it difficult to reach any firm conclusions. Whereas Teiwes (2001) sees evidence of a trend toward normal politics, including institutionalization of even elite politics within the Party, Fewsmith (2001: 90) questions whether norms of compromise have been internalized and the means for distributing power institutionalized. Hamrin (2001) acknowledges that there has been a regularization and institutionalization of politics, but suggests that politics are not normal in the sense of having reached a stable equilibrium. In her view, scientific socialism may not be sustainable given the accelerating pace of economic, social, cultural, and legal change in China.

71   Epstein (1997: 404).

72   O'Brien and Li (2000) note that international agencies such as the Ford Foundation have been eager to fund village elections and that Presidents Carter and Clinton have praised China's village elections. As Kelliher (1997: 70) points out, the rationales for village elections are largely instrumental in nature. Village elections would serve the interests of the state. Proponents rarely defended village elections by appealing to democracy as an intrinsic good or to notions such as the right to choose or popular sovereignty. Of course, as he notes, proponents would be inclined for pragmatic reasons to tailor their arguments

to the audience, and instrumental rationales were more likely to appeal to the authorities. For a discussion of the strategic considerations involved in promoting village elections, see Tianjian Shi (1999) and O'Brien and Li (2000). Both articles discuss the significant opposition to village elections within the Party and state bureaucracy.

73 Minxin Pei (1995: 73); see also Minxin Pei (1997b).

74 Kelliher (1997: 68).

75 If the person elected is not a Party member, he is often pressured to become one. Some argue that elections are therefore good for the Party because if a Party member is elected, the cadre will enjoy greater legitimacy and if a non-Party member is elected and then becomes a member of the Party, the Party is rejuvenated. Dickson (2000: 46).

76 Kelliher (1997: 73–74) cites as examples better fulfillment of grain quotas, fewer under-age marriages, reduced backlog of uncollected fees, more taxes paid, and more women sterilized. Similarly, Melanie Manion (1996) claims that villages that hold competitive elections experienced greater congruence between local cadres and villagers on a variety of policy issues than villages that did not hold competitive elections. Oi and Rozelle (2000: 539) found comparable results.

77 O'Brien and Li (2000: 485).

78 Kelliher (1997) claims that the CCP often fixes elections by making sure approved candidates win, sometimes appointing committees, and sometimes controlling the nomination process. In other cases, the Party requires that the committee head be the secretary or vice-secretary of the village party branch. As he notes, villagers often accept this arrangement because they think it will give them more influence over the local Party organizations. Pastor and Tan (2000) report that in the early 1990s village Party secretaries usually chaired or served on the village election committee, though the 1998 amendments to the village election law now provide that members of the village election committee shall be selected by the village assembly or village small groups, not the Party branch.

79 For a summary, see Pastor and Tan (2000).

80 Kelliher (1997: 82). O'Brien and Li (2000: 488) claim that "as long as [village committees] do not have final say over village political life, it must be recognized that however much [village committee] election procedures are improved and put into practice, a rethinking of the Party's role must occur before there is real democracy in China's villages." At present, they claim, grass-roots democracy is meant to serve the interests of and strengthen the state.

81 Oi and Rozelle (2000). O'Brien (1999a) has noted that some places are now experimenting with subjecting Party members to a vote of confidence, which he suggests will greatly enhance the prospects for real village democracy if the practice spreads.

82 Baum and Shevchenko (1999: 343).

83 See "Bureaucratic Mergers and Acquisitions" (1998); "Chinese Premier's Government Work Promises Reduction of Ministries" (1998). Burns (1993)

notes that there have been at least nine attempts to carry out government organization reform, including downsizing of the bureaucracy, in the past.

84   You Ji (1998); see also Chapter 9.
85   Tsao and Worthley (1995).
86   Huang Daqiang (1993).
87   For an overview of the Provisional Regulations Concerning Government Officials, see Guobin Zhu (1995).
88   Burns (2000: 589).
89   Tianjian Shi (2000: 546).
90   Tianjian Shi (1997).
91   See Chapter 9.
92   Jennings (1997: 370) notes that although there is some pursuit of collective goods, participation is generally characterized by the atomistic pursuit of selected self-interests based on one's personal economic situation.
93   Li and O'Brien (1996); Bernstein (2000: 96–97).
94   Li and O'Brien (1996: 29).
95   Bernstein (2000: 97–98) cites reports that there were more than 6,230 cases of turmoil in 1993, of which more than 800 involved 500 people or more, and 21 involved 5,000 people or more. As Bernstein points out, rural protests tend to be focused on local issues and to lack horizontal ties to other locations. Moreover, tensions and class differences between farmers and urban residents are unlikely to produce rural–urban alliances.
96   O'Brien (1999b: 153).
97   See "Falun Gong Practitioners Arrested for Suing Beijing Leaders" (2001).
98   An English translation of the petition is available from Human Rights in China, www.hrichina.org/.
99   Pearson (2000) argues that the PRC takes its treaty obligations seriously. Yahuda (1999) is somewhat more cautious, suggesting that China's depth of commitment to various international treaties remains unclear.
100 Deng Xiaoping (1941: 17–18). Deng added: "Some Party members have gone a step further, taking 'Party leadership is above everything else' to mean 'Party members are above everything else' and believing that the Party members can do evil and that the ones who violate the law can be forgiven. As a result, non-Party cadres regard the Party as 'the supreme authority.' (This is a bitter irony. Yet, unfortunately, some of our Party members take pride in it.)"
101 Burns (2000: 587).
102 Li Cheng (2000: 18).
103 Li Cheng (2000: 20).
104 Li Cheng (2000: 26).
105 Li Cheng (2000: 18–19).
106 Zheng Shiping (1997: 207).
107 Indicative of the seriousness of the problems the central Party is having controlling local-level Party cadres, the Party required more than 2,000 county Party secretaries to attend a six-month training session at the Central Party School normally reserved for the training of high-level cadres. See "Beijing's Anxiety" (2000).

108 Dickson (2000: 41).
109 Zheng Shiping (1997: 219).
110 Shirk (1993).
111 Yasheng Huang (1996); Baum and Shevchenko (1999: 338).
112 Yasheng Huang (1996: xix).
113 Baum and Shevchenko (1999: 351).
114 See Chapter 1 and the citations therein.
115 Zheng Shiping (1997: 74).
116 Jiang Lishan (1997: 38) notes that the Party has struggled with the issue of how to reconcile the Party's leadership role and the supremacy of law for twenty years and continues to do so. For a summary of the views of various contemporary PRC scholars, see Keith (1994); Hintzen (1999); Zhang Qi (1998).
117 For example, Wang Jiafu (1998: 121, 131) asserts that rule of law is compatible with centralization of power but the CCP must act within the limits of the law. See also Liu Hainian (1998).
118 Compare Li Buyun (1998a), arguing in an essay first published in 1982 that rule of law is compatible with the four cardinal principles, with his later essay (1998c: 18), in which he argues that if Party policy conflicts with law then law should prevail. See also Sun Xiaoxia (1998: 24), who argues that Party and government must be willing to pay the price to rule in accordance with law; in particular, party policies cannot override law.
119 See Shapiro (1993: 45).
120 Li Zhongjie (1998).
121 See Oksenberg (1971); Lieberthal and Oksenberg (1988). As Keller (1994: 724) and others have pointed out, the use of administrative regulations, party policies and other normative documents "were not produced by designated law making bodies or through fixed procedures and were otherwise indistinguishable from the administrative process itself" and thus "the use of normative documents during the Cultural Revolution ... only amounted to an informal system of law in the broadest sense."
122 The greater reliance on laws, rather than CCP policy, is widely acknowledged to be one of the hallmarks of the post-Mao era. See, for example, Jones and Finder (1999–2000: 54). In forcefully asserting that the Party must accept a new role in a rule-of-law system, Zhu Liyu, a law professor at People's University, and Wan Qigang, an administrator with the NPC, provide one of the clearest statements regarding the relationship between laws and Party policies. They note that laws and policies differ in terms of subject (i.e., who promulgated them), scope of effectiveness, method of implementation, form, and stability. Policies are the statements of the Party; laws are the statements of the state that reflect the will of the Party and the people; laws are applicable to all and backed up by the coercive power of the state; policies are applicable to Party members and enforced by the Party; and laws are enforced through a system of rules and legal institutions. Even Zhu and Wan, however, do not challenge the Party's control over the nomenklatura system of appointments. See Zhu and Wan (2000).
123 Constitution, art. 5; CCP constitution, preamble (1992).

124   Constitution, art. 5; CCP constitution, art. 3(4).
125   The difference between the formal structure of government set forth in the constitution and the reality of political power in China is often noted. See, for example, Cohen (1978); Jones (1985).
126   According to the Judges Law, judges are to be appointed by the people's congresses. See PRC Judges Law, art. 11 (1995) (adopted by the NPCSC).
127   See Dicks (1995).
128   Most CCP members who are disciplined internally or punished by the courts tend to be low-level officials. For instance, in 1998, courts handled 18,468 cases of economic crime and convicted 15,670 offenders. However, there were only 3 officials at the ministerial level, 54 officials at the prefecture or department level, and 434 at the county or division level. See the *1999 Supreme Court Work Report* (1999). The procuracy in 1998 investigated 40,162 persons for corruption, prosecuting 26,834 of them. Of those investigated, only 3 were provincial-level officials, 103 department- or bureau-level officials, and 1,714 country- or division-level officials. See the *1999 Supreme People's Procuratorate Work Report* (1999). In the rare case of punishment of high-level officials, Party leaders must first decide whether to turn the violator over to the courts or to handle the matter internally. If the matter is handled by the courts, the decision as to guilt and punishment is effectively determined by the Party.
129   See *Jiang Zemin's Congress Report* (1997).
130   Party control over the legislature is exercised in a variety of ways, some more direct than others, some more effective than others. These means include preapproval of the legislative agenda, pressure on legislative leaders to push bills forward, and the review of draft laws. The Party also makes its views known through Party cells within the legislature and through other channels of communication. The most important means of CCP control, however, remains the nomenklatura system of appointments. See Tanner (1994; 1999).
131   Tanner (1994: 397–401).
132   Tanner (1994: 396).
133   See Dowdle (1997). For a discussion of the Party's limited role in the drafting of the Lawyers Law, see Peerenboom (1998b: 43–45). In some cases, the Party plays a more prominent role, deciding key issues particularly when there is a conflict among the various government organs or departments. For instance, according to a PRC criminal law scholar who participated in the drafting process, the Party had to decide several issues in the amendment of the Criminal Procedure Law. In October 1995, the Legal Affairs Committee (*Fagongwei*) of the NPC completed a draft of the amendment and sent it out to relevant entities for comment. In November 1995, the Legal Affairs Committee held a meeting to hear comments from the Ministry of Public Security, SPC, SPP, MOJ, and legal experts. The Working Committee revised the amendment bill accordingly and reported to the Party Group of the NPCSC. After discussion, the Party Group submitted the bill to the CCP Politburo Standing Committee. The Standing Committee had to decide several controversial issues, including whether to eliminate the procuracy's right to grant immunity from prosecution (*mianyu qisu*); whether lawyers could

attend the investigative stages of a criminal prosecution; whether the accused should be acquitted if there was insufficient evidence (rather than the case being returned to the procuracy for further investigation, during which time the accused might continue to be detained); whether to provide for a summary procedure; whether the accused should have the right to legal aid; and whether shelter and investigation should be abolished. Taking into consideration the views of legal experts, academics, members of the MOJ, and the All China Lawyers Association and legislators, the Standing Committee decided each of these issues in the affirmative.

The Standing Committee then forwarded the bill with its decisions on the specific issues and the comment that it approved the bill in principle to the President's Committee of the NPCSC. In January 1996, Wang Hanbin, Ren Jianxin, and Luo Gan convened a meeting to work out the specific language for the various issues decided by the Party and to hear comments. The meeting was attended by the head of the Central Political–Legal Committee, SPC, SPP, Ministry of Public Security, Ministry of State Security, MOJ, and various internal NPC committees. On March 17, the amendment bill was approved by the NPC, with the final amendment reflecting the Party's views on all of the issues.

134   Tanner (1999: 90); Yang Xu (1999).

135   See Lieberthal and Oksenberg (1988); Tanner (1999).

136   For instance, the draft of the Unified Contract Law was widely circulated, including to foreign law firms and the American Chamber of Commerce.

137   Roderick MacFarquhar (1998) has found that provincial people's congresses are developing an institutional life of their own. Similarly, Minxin Pei (1995) has reported that some provincial and municipal people's congresses elected their own candidate rather than electing the candidate favored by the Party. In 2001, the Shenyang People's Congress broke new ground by voting down a work report submitted by the municipal intermediate people's court. PRC legal scholars praised the move as a sign of constitutional development and a more authoritative role for people's congresses. See *PRC People's Congress' Rejection of Report Said "Landmark Event"* (2001).

138   Craig (1994: 74).

139   Wade (1991: 5–6).

140   Craenen (1996b: 77) observes that the Parliament is able to "push its initiatives to the foreground and to obtain from Parliament what it considers necessary."

141   See, for example, Lieberthal and Oksenberg's (1998) case study of energy policy. They comment that the role of the Party was less than is usually assumed, and that policy formation was a protracted, disjointed, and incremental process of consensus-building.

142   See Moon and Ingraham (1998).

143   Some commentators have suggested that the CCP may play a more prominent role in the drafting of administrative regulations, particularly central-level regulations, that relate to personnel matters, public security, culture, and the media. It is reasonable to assume that the Party would have a greater role in personnel matters, given the importance of controlling personnel decisions,

and may be called on to resolve political conflicts within the bureaucracy or between the executive branch and other branches. However, the exact role of the Party is likely to vary from case to case. For a study of the Party's role in promulgation of the Provisional Regulations on State Civil Servants, see Cabestan (2000).

144   As noted in Chapter 3, China is not the only country that fails to hold senior officials accountable.

145   Zhang Pufan (1996) has pointed out that the main problem for rule of law in China today is the relation between power and law. See also Hu Yuhong (1996).

146   See Hintzen (1999); see also Li Cheng (2000).

147   Tanner (1999: 238). In his view, the legal system is best characterized as rule by law. Indeed, he (1999: 9) suggests that senior leaders' commitment to even rule by law is "uneven at best."

148   Tanner (1999: 38). Tanner adds: "Perhaps the greatest irony of this story is that the principal builders of China's organ of 'socialist democracy' have not been the so-called 'bourgeois liberal' intellectuals within the Party, but rather a group of men from precisely that sector of the Communist Party which is the very essence of classical totalitarianism: the 'Political–Legal System.' "

149   Tanner (1999: 52–53).

150   See *Jiang Zemin's Congress Report* (1997); see also Goodman (1987).

151   For a similar argument, see Minxin Pei (1995).

152   For the metaphor of China's legal reforms as a bird in a cage, see Lubman (1999).

153   See Sean Cooney (1999); Tsung-fu Chen (2000).

154   Tsung-fu Chen (2000).

155   Tsung-fu Chen (2000).

156   See K. Yang (1993); Joon-Hyung Hong (2000). Hong notes that the rising demand for rule of law among the citizenry who had come to believe in the ideology of rule of law put pressure on the government to continue reforms.

157   See David Bourchier (1999).

158   See Linda Chelan Li (2000: 208–14).

159   Lan (1999).

160   Liu Junning (1998: 41) argues that while rule of law and limited government are necessary to protect people's increasing property interests that have grown as a result of economic reforms, there still is not a large enough middle class demanding protection of its political rights to support political reforms and democracy.

161   For several polls showing strong support for rule of law, see Chapter 11.

162   See Xia Yong (1995).

163   See Chapter 10. For a discussion of law-based protests by farmers and rural residents, see Li and O'Brien (1996); Zweig (2000). Minxin Pei (2000) has pointed out that dissidents have changed their tactics from reliance on street resistance and illegal protests to greater reliance on legal channels. Even though dissidents regularly lose such cases, the legal challenges do put pressure on the

regime in that dissidents are able to publicize their claims. The regime also stands to suffer a loss in legitimacy when it acts inconsistently with its much-touted endorsement of rule of law.

164 Hecht (1996) describes the influence of international pressure and international legal norms in the Criminal Procedure Law amendment process.

165 See Chapters 7 and 10.

166 According to the three representatives policy, the CCP is supposed to become a faithful representative of the development of advanced productive forces, of advanced culture, and of the fundamental interests of the broadest mass of people in China. Although some commentators have wondered whether Jiang's endorsement of rule of virtue (*dezhi*) signifies a retreat from rule of law and a return to rule of man (*renzhi*), official statements are unequivocal that the emphasis on virtuous officials is meant to supplement rule of law rather than to replace it. With its Confucian overtones, the rule-of-virtue policy is another in a long string of campaigns to change the moral character of citizens and officials. Addressed to citizens, it is an attempt to fill the moral and spiritual vacuum that exists with something other than materialism and money-worshipping. Addressed to officials, it is an attempt to reduce corruption and create an honest corps of public servants. See *Renmin Ribao Views Jiang Zemin's Exposition of Rule by Law, Virtue* (2001).

167 For a discussion of recent attempts to paint Jiang as the patron saint of rule of law, see Chapter 3.

168 For possible alternative paths, see Oksenberg (2001); see also Chapter 12.

169 According to some reports, moderate and liberal Party leaders have shown an interest in European social democratic parties and have considered the possibility that the CCP could follow in the footsteps of some former members of the Soviet Union that repositioned themselves as social democratic parties. Apparently, a study group on social democratic parties has been set up within the State Council's Development Research Center, Party members have been sent abroad to study how the transition was accomplished in other countries, and scholars have been asked to produce reports on the transition process. See Willy Wo-Lap Lam (2000).

170 Stephenson's (2001) suggestion that foreign governments and NGOs are pulling something over on PRC officials by pursuing a "Trojan Horse" strategy that ostensibly focuses on technical legal issues but ultimately will lead to political reforms and greater demand for democracy and human rights is implausible at best. As discussed in Chapter 12, the Chinese side rejected "rule of law" in favor of "legal cooperation" to describe the joint PRC–US legal reform project because they were aware of the obvious differences between a Liberal Democratic conception of rule of law and their own Statist Socialist version. Surely PRC officials appreciate the risk of legal reforms and implementing rule of law, as evidenced by their caution in sanctioning deep institutional reforms required to create a more authoritative and independent judiciary.

Stephenson supports his argument that authoritarian regimes may be able to control the trajectory of legal reforms by appealing to the single case of

Franco Spain, ignoring the more recent and relevant experiences of China's Asian neighbors in Taiwan, South Korea, and Indonesia (and even the ultimate outcome in Spain). While Taiwan, South Korea, and Indonesia attempted to build firewalls between commercial law and others areas of law, over time such walls fell under the pressure of institution-building and political reform. Unlike Stephenson, PRC leaders are likely to pay close attention to these countries, and thus to appreciate the risks involved in legal reform.

Furthermore, Stephenson overstates the case for separation between commercial law for foreign investors and the rest of the legal system in China. While it is true that China was quick to pass laws for foreign investors, as economic reforms continued and the differences between domestic and foreign companies diminished, many of the special rules for foreign investors have been replaced with generally applicable laws. China's accession to the WTO will accelerate the process of merging the foreign and domestic legal regimes. Moreover, although Stephenson implies that China's leaders wanted to limit legal reforms to only the foreign commercial area, China's decision to develop the legal regime for foreign investors first was reasonable given the need to attract foreign capital and technology required for economic growth and the differences between the predominantly state-owned enterprises that existed at the time and foreign-invested enterprises. As an empirical matter, there have been significant improvements in all areas of law, including administrative law, criminal law, environmental law, and consumer protection law.

It should also be noted, as Stephenson himself acknowledges, that many of those working on projects for the USA would object to the pejorative connotation of "Trojan Horse," and deny that they are duplicitously trying to sneak liberal democracy into China under the cloak of rule of law. As I argue in Chapters 11 and 12, rule of law may stimulate political reform without leading to liberal democracy. Others are quite explicit that liberal democracy is their goal.

6

The legislative system: battling chaos

There are a number of excellent works describing the development of the National People's Congress (NPC).[1] There are also excellent studies of the law-making and administrative rule-making processes, though the procedures have changed to some extent as a result of recent developments in these areas.[2] My purpose here is to examine the legislative system from the perspective of the requirements of rule of law, and in particular a thin rule of law;[3] to illustrate current shortcomings in the system with concrete examples and discuss the reasons for the deficiencies;[4] and to consider various solutions.

As pointed out in previous chapters, China's efforts to create a market economy and rebuild the legal system have resulted in a legislative explosion. More than 350 laws and 6,000 lower-level regulations have been passed since 1978. The Party's diminished role in the law-making process and even more minimal role in the process of creating lower-level regulations has shifted the responsibility for the making of laws and regulations to the NPC, local people's congresses, governments, and administrative agencies. In response, these entities have gained in institutional capacity, professionalism, and stature. With respect to the NPC, the NPCSC has been streamlined and strengthened; the establishment of subcommittees, including the Legislative Affairs Commission, has brought more focus and expertise to the process; there are more and better-qualified staff members to call on for research and the drafting of laws; and NPC delegates are younger, more educated, and more qualified than in the past. Rule-making by local governments and administrative agencies has also improved as a result of institutional reforms. Civil service reforms have produced a more professional and less ideological civil service. Bureaucrats are more educated and better trained. The members of the State Council's Legislative Affairs Office responsible for drafting administrative regulations have received more legal training than in the past. China has also passed a number of laws and regulations setting out the procedures for law-making, including the Law on Legislation,[5] and for promulgating lower-level regulations. An Administrative Procedure Law, currently being drafted though not expected to be passed for several years, will bring greater regularity and transparency to the administrative rule-making process.

Yet despite these improvements, the legislative system continues to fall short of the minimal standards of a thin rule of law.[6] Rule of law requires a way of verifying whether laws are valid and legally binding, i.e. (i) they are made by an entity with authority to make laws; (ii) the entity was acting within its scope of authority; (iii) the entity followed proper procedures (if any); and (iv) laws and regulations are reasonably clear, stable, and consistent internally and with other legislation, particularly superior legislation. Legislative authority in China, however, is widely dispersed. The law-making and rule-making processes still lack transparency; opportunities for public participation are limited, notwithstanding some improvements over the last twenty years. The quality of much legislation remains low, in part due to the lack of practical experience and competence of drafters. Laws and regulations are subject to frequent change. Even more worrisome, there is a shockingly high incidence of inconsistency between lower and superior legislation.

These problems have not gone unnoticed and steps have been taken and are being taken to address them. Some of the problems are common to all legal systems, though the degree may differ, while others are specific to China. The reasons for them are varied and typically multiple and overlapping. In some cases, the Party is a factor. In most cases, it is not. Some deficiencies are due to the historical legacy of the Cultural Revolution. Sometimes the problems are attributable to conflicts among the bureaucracies. Some are the unavoidable by-product of being in the midst of a period of profound change. Some are amenable to immediate resolution, including technological solutions or a change in the regulatory framework. Others require deep institutional reforms to resolve, including an amendment of the Constitution and an alteration of the current balance of power between the Party and state and among state organs. Still others can only be addressed over time, as China's reforms reach a more stable equilibrium state.

Dispersion of law-making authority

One of the problems is the sheer complexity of the system. A number of entities have been afforded the right to legislate, which has resulted in a bewildering and inconsistent array of laws, regulations, provisions, measures, directives, notices, decisions, explanations, and so forth, all claiming to be normatively binding and treated so by the creating entity.[7] The NPC and local people's congresses, the State Council and its ministries and commissions, and local governments may all issue legislation.[8] In most areas, administrative agencies are mainly responsible for legislation with the total number of administrative regulations (including Rules and Normative Documents) greatly exceeding the number of NPC Laws.[9]

Not only is power dispersed, but the lines of authority for law-making are not clear. In many instances it is difficult if not impossible to state with certainty whether an entity was acting within its authority. The Constitution, the Law on Legislation, and organic laws give the State Council and administrative agencies, local people's congresses, and local governments vaguely delineated inherent authority to legislate. According to the traditional understanding of separation of powers, the legislative branch has exclusive authority to pass laws. The executive branch lacks the power to pass legislation unless the legislature delegates its law-making powers to the executive. In China, the State Council has the inherent authority to "adopt administrative measures, to enact administrative rules and regulations and to issue decisions and orders in accordance with the Constitution and the law."[10] Similarly, ministries and commissions subordinate to the State Council, local governments, and people's congresses also enjoy the inherent authority to pass legislation.[11] In addition to their inherent authority, all of these entities may be delegated authority to issue legislation. As in many countries, delegation is often broad. In 1984 and 1985, for instance, the NPC authorized the State Council to enact regulations relating to economic reform and foreign investment.[12]

The lack of clear lines of legislative authority has resulted in quality and consistency problems. Many regulations are poorly drafted, ill-advised or unworkable in practice. They also regularly conflict with superior legislation. According to a study in the mid-1980s in Hebei,

Beijing, and Tianjin, about two-thirds of local regulations were inconsistent with the Constitution.[13]

The NPC has attempted to impose order on the legislative system. The Law on Legislation clarifies the authority of the various entities, limits delegation and establishes a mechanism for reviewing lower-level legislation. However, for reasons to be explained shortly, such measures alone are not likely to suffice. The NPC has also sought to bring order to particular areas of law, including the contract regime. During the last two decades, the NPC passed the Technology Contract Law, Economic Contract Law, and Foreign Economic Contract Law, in addition to the General Principles of Civil Law, which also contained provisions relating to contracts. Meanwhile, the State Council and administrative departments passed scores of contract-related regulations, and the Supreme People's Court issued numerous interpretations. In response to the complicated and inconsistent contract regime that had developed as a result of numerous entities passing laws and regulations, the NPC passed the Contract Law to unify all contract legislation under a single law in 1999.[14] Unfortunately, it remains unclear whether the State Council and its ministries will, as in the past, be delegated the right or claim the inherent right to interpret and implement the Contract Law by passing regulations. Similarly, whether local people's congresses and governments will pass regulations that are ostensibly meant to adapt the Contract Law to local circumstances but in practice are often inconsistent with both the letter and spirit of the superior legislation remains to be seen. Unless the right to interpret the law and pass implementing regulations is strictly controlled or the means for quashing inconsistent lower-level legislation strengthened, the problems with inconsistency that led to the desire to pass a unified contract law in the first place will continue.

Law-making and rule-making procedures and transparency

The NPC's law-making process has become more open and transparent over the years. NPC delegates, specialized committees, and outside experts have been given more opportunities to review and comment on proposed legislation. According to the Law on Legislation, the Legislative

Affairs Commission and other NPC committees responsible for drafting should consider opinions on all laws on the NPCSC's agenda from various sources by holding conferences, discussion meetings, evidentiary hearings, and so on.[15] A draft should be distributed to relevant entities, organizations, and experts. Moreover, the draft of an important law may be made public for comment by government entities, interest groups, and citizens upon approval of the committee Chair.[16]

In some cases, academics have played a key role in the legislative process. Professor Chen Guangzhong was instrumental in pushing the amendment the Criminal Procedure Law, onto the NPC's legislative agenda. He then headed a team to draft the amendments.[17] The small group for drafting the Contract Law, formed under the auspices of the NPC's Legislative Affairs Committee, consisted of: Liang Huixing (CASS Law Institute); Jiang Ping (China University of Politics and Law); Wang Liming (People's University); Cui Jianyuan (Jilin University); Guo Mingrui (Yantai University); Li Fan (Supreme People's Court); He Xi (Beijing High Court); and Zhang Guangxing (editorial department of the CASS Law Institute Journal *Faxue Yanjiu*).[18]

Although the NPC now seeks input from a variety of sources at different stages, often including foreign legal systems and experts, on the whole, transparency and public participation remain limited.[19] Individual citizens and interest groups have few channels for influencing the law-making process. The NPC is just beginning the process of formulating rules for public hearings.[20] In the absence of elections, delegates are only loosely accountable to their constituency. Moreover, controls on civil society inhibit the formation and development of interest groups, thus diminishing the effectiveness of hearings and procedures aimed at increasing public participation.

Transparency and lack of public participation are even more problematic in administrative rule-making. Although China does not yet have a comprehensive administrative procedure law, there are various regulations that contain provisions regarding procedures for administrative rule-making. The 1987 Provisional Measures for the Formulation of Administrative Regulations set out certain procedural requirements for State Council Administrative Regulations.[21] The 1987 State Council Measures apply to Rules only by reference. Apparently, most agencies do not follow the State Council procedures. In Shandong, only

20 percent of Rules were passed in accordance with the State Council procedures.[22] While some local government have issued their own procedures for administrative rule-making, they are often not implemented in practice.[23]

Even where there are procedural rules, they do not require public input in the rule-making process. Most Rules and Normative Documents are made without the benefit of public participation or hearings attended by interested parties.

The opaqueness of the legislative process and the limited opportunity for public participation, particularly with respect to the passage of regulations by local congresses, governments, and administrative entities, often results in poorly drafted legislation that frustrates the rational expectations of investors, undermines China's own professed policy objectives, causes problems in implementation, and defeats the basic rule-of-law values of predictability and certainty.

By way of example, a multinational seed company had heard rumors that the Ministry of Agriculture was going to issue regulations limiting foreign companies to a minority share in joint venture seed companies. Unable to obtain any details about the restrictions or the expected date of publication, the company decided to push ahead with its plans to establish a joint venture in which it would have a majority stake. After more than two years of negotiation, the company was finally ready to sign a letter of intent with its Chinese partner. The Vice-President of the company flew in from India, the main negotiator from the USA, and in-house counsel from Brussels. When they met with their Chinese partner the next day to sign the letter of intent, they were told that the long-awaited regulation had been issued that very morning, and thus it would no longer be possible for the foreign side to own a majority interest. Naturally, the foreign negotiators wanted to see a copy of the regulation. However, when the head of the Chinese side, a member of the NPCSC, called the Ministry of Agriculture to obtain a copy of the regulation, he was told it was not yet available. The foreign party's counsel then tried the Ministry of Foreign Trade and Economic Co-operation (MOFTEC), one of the copromulgators of the regulation, only to be told that they knew nothing about its promulgation. Finally, upon returning to Beijing, the chief negotiator of the foreign side, a PRC national with longstanding family connections to leading figures in the Ministry of Agriculture, was able to obtain a copy of the new regulation, on the condition that she did not show it to foreigners (including her boss). All this for a regulation effective from the date of publication, which when the regulation was subsequently published turned out to be backdated to a date several weeks earlier than the meetings.[24]

One would expect foreign law firms to be particularly well situated to keep track of pending legislation, especially legislation that directly affects their interests. But even they have difficulty. In late 1996, foreign lawyers were almost caught unawares when the Ministry of Justice (MOJ) was set to issue rules that would have made it all but impossible for most firms to continue to operate in China. Toward the end of the year, just before most foreigners head home for extended Christmas holidays, rumors began to circulate about draconian rules that would, among other restrictions, prohibit foreign law firms from hiring PRC nationals with legal qualifications (even if the PRC national was qualified in a foreign jurisdiction).[25] Although the rumors were difficult to confirm until just before the regulations were to be issued, law firms and the foreign business community immediately banded together to stop the regulations. Embassies and business associations wrote letters to MOFTEC and the MOJ, US negotiators raised the issue in the context of WTO talks, and so on. All parties emphasized that as many foreign investors would not invest in China without legal advice from foreign lawyers, the rules would undermine China's efforts to attract foreign capital. Finally, the MOJ relented, declaring that no regulations would be passed, at least for the time being.[26]

Publication and accessibility of laws

People cannot follow the laws if they do not know what they are. There have been a number of campaigns to publicize major laws through various channels, including newspapers, television, and radio. Despite tremendous improvements, it is often difficult to find out what the laws are for a variety of reasons. Publication remains a problem. Although increasingly administrative agencies are publishing rules, as required under the Law on Legislation, there are still unpublished internal regulations (*neibu guiding*).[27]

As noted in the last chapter, during the Mao era, China relied heavily on Party policy and internal directives to govern. When China opened its doors to foreign investment in the late 1970s, early investors discovered that old habits died hard. Throughout the 1980s, foreign companies repeatedly decried the unfairness of being subject to inaccessible internal regulations that thwarted their efforts at rational decision-making. While internal regulations are much less of a problem today, they continue to exist and to frustrate investors.

At times, the absurdity of the situation would be comical if not for the potentially grave consequences. At the request of a client contemplating an investment of upwards of a hundred million dollars in a power plant, a colleague and I once met with the now defunct Ministry of Electric Power Industry to obtain details about the approval process. The official was helpful, running through the process in considerable detail, while we furiously scribbled notes, trying to keep up. At one point I happened to notice that he was reading from an official-looking document. When I requested a copy of the document, I was told it was *neibu* (i.e. internal). We pointed out that making the details of the approval process available to foreign investors would greatly enhance China's prospects for attracting the huge sums of capital required to meet China's surging electrical needs. While the official was sympathetic to our arguments, he claimed that his hands were tied. Indicative of the trend toward more transparency, however, the powers that be have since seen the light and issued regulations describing the approval process.[28]

In many cases, even regulations that are not internal are hard to track down. The Law on Legislation requires that regulations by local people's congresses, governments, and administrative agencies be published in the issuing entity's gazettes and newspapers with a corresponding geographic circulation. Thus, State Council Administrative Regulations must be published in the State Council Gazette and then circulated in a national newspaper, while local regulations must be published in local gazettes and circulated in local newspapers.[29] The Law on Legislation does not address Normative Documents, which are often made public, if at all, simply by posting a notice in the government or administrative office.

The lack of centralized records makes it difficult to know exactly what rules apply at any given time in any given place.[30] While there are currently a number of electronic databases available in China, all are far from comprehensive, particularly with respect to local regulations. Although the technology would now seem to be available to address

the problem, a regulation requiring all entities to transmit all new regulations, including Normative Documents, to a central agency would
make the process easier. Of course, a change in practice such that local
governments and agencies actually complied with the publication requirements would also be necessary. Interestingly, China has agreed as
one of the conditions of joining the WTO to publish all WTO-related
trade regulations in a single journal.

Quality of the legislation

While the quality of legislation has improved remarkably over the last
twenty years, much legislation remains poorly drafted and characterized by excessive generality and vagueness, omissions, undefined terms,
inconsistencies, and a lack of practical experience and appreciation for
law-making hierarchies on the part of the drafters.[31] Little surprise then
that PRC scholars regularly cite the need for better laws if rule of law is
to be realized in China.

Poor drafting

Poor drafting continues to undermine the ruling regime's use of law as
a means of achieving order and the ability of the regulated to rely on
law to protect their interests.[32] Of course one can point to examples
of poor drafting in the laws of any country. Moreover, what appears
to be poor drafting is often a reflection of hard negotiations, political
compromise, and the need on the part of the drafters to mediate the
conflicting interests of different constituencies.[33] That said, all too often
the only possible explanation for the many omissions, inconsistencies,
contradictions, and related maladies that plague much PRC legislation
is simply poor drafting.

   For instance, in 1996, the People's Bank of China issued regulations
concerning the provision of security to foreign entities by PRC entities, including foreign-invested enterprises (FIEs) such as joint ventures
(JVs) or wholly foreign-owned enterprises (WFOEs).[34] However, the
regulations failed to distinguish between first and third party security:
i.e. where a PRC entity uses its assets as security for its *own* borrowing
versus where it uses its assets to secure borrowing by another PRC entity.
Apparently, all were subject to approval by the State Administration of

Foreign Exchange (SAFE). However, as a loan from a foreign entity to an FIE only requires registration with SAFE rather than approval, the 1996 regulations seemed to produce the anomalous result that while the underlying loan was not subject to SAFE approval, the security to obtain the loan was.

SAFE and MOFTEC then sought to rectify the situation in January 1997 by issuing a clarifying notice providing that while third party security required SAFE approval, first party security from FIEs need only be registered.[35] Yet the notice inexplicably also stated that in addition to registration, FIEs must obtain the approval of MOFTEC or its authorized agents. Until then, MOFTEC approval had not been required for JVs to mortgage their assets, although such approval was required, for reasons that are far from clear, in the case of WFOEs.[36] In response to inquiries as to whether MOFTEC really intended to make such a fundamental change on the basis of one line in this notice, MOFTEC officials conceded that in fact the apparent change was really just a typo – the approval requirement should have applied to *waishang duzi qiye* (WFOEs) but not to *waishang touzi qiye* (FIEs, including WFOEs *and* JVs). Nevertheless, despite acknowledging the mistake, MOFTEC declared that it would go ahead anyway and require approval for JVs as well as WFOEs. When pressed, MOFTEC admitted that in practice few JVs had applied for approval. Indeed, many local approval authorities were not even aware of the typo-inspired requirement. To complete the saga on a more positive note, in early 1998 SAFE issued implementing regulations to the 1996 regulations that did away with the short-lived MOFTEC approval requirement for JVs securing first party loans.[37]

Poor drafting frequently results in confusion and uncertainty in implementation. The Administration of Project Financing Conducted outside China Tentative Procedures were intended to apply to large infrastructure projects, although the definition of "project finance" was so broad as to include non-recourse financing by your run-of-the-mill manufacturing JV.[38] When asked about this, the State Planning Commission stated that the regulations only applied to projects over US$30 million, although nothing in the regulations themselves suggested such a cut-off.[39] The Procedures also contained a rather large loophole: if project finance projects are those in which the creditors have no recourse against any assets or revenues other than those of the project, then it would seem easy enough to circumvent the regulations just by including some relatively insignificant third party guarantee.

Lack of practical experience on the part of drafters

One of the main reasons for poor drafting seems to be the lack of experience on the part of the drafters. Although that is perhaps to be expected in light of the historical legacy of the Cultural Revolution and the recentness of the transition to a market economy, the limited opportunities for public participation compound the problems. Greater reliance on outside experts and increased opportunities for interested groups and individuals to present their views would provide inexperienced drafters with the valuable information needed to avoid some of the more obvious mistakes that have resulted in some regulations being dead on arrival and incapable of implementation.

For instance, in 1997 MOFTEC issued regulations authorizing parties to pledge their equity interests in FIEs.[40] Setting aside a number of legal restrictions and approval requirements that may render such pledges commercially unattractive, the regulations raise several issues that call into question the competence of the drafters. First, the authority of MOFTEC to create a new type of security interest is unclear. Although the regulations state that investors may pledge their equity interests in accordance with the provisions of the *Security Law of the PRC*, in fact the rights of investors to pledge equity interests in FIEs were never clear under that law.[41]

Even assuming that MOFTEC had the authority to create a new type of security, whether the drafters really understood what they were doing remains debatable. One typical scenario for a pledge of an equity interest is where a bank lends to the joint venture or a party thereto and takes as security the party's interest in the joint venture. However, for the bank to be able to exercise its right and step into the shoes of the original investor it must be considered a "qualified investor."[42] When asked whether banks would qualify, three different MOFTEC officials expressed three different and conflicting views. Worried that a bank would not have the industry expertise to assume the responsibilities of the original investor, one official stated that banks would not be considered qualified investors. Another expressed exactly the opposite view, that a bank would qualify regardless of the circumstances. A third took a more nuanced position that a bank would be able to take over in certain circumstances, such as where at least one of the remaining parties has the necessary industry expertise to run the company.

Perhaps even more worrisome, even the main drafter of the regulation seemed unsure about how it was to be implemented. The regulation requires that when a pledgee exercises its pledge rights, the company shall submit valid documentary evidence of the pledgee's acquisition of the equity interest.[43] Presumably, however, the valid documentary evidence would be the yet-to-be-issued approval document of MOFTEC. When asked precisely what document MOFTEC wanted, the drafter was stumped, and asked the lawyer who raised the question what documents she thought should be submitted!

At times, lack of experience combines with a nationalist desire to protect the interest of Chinese companies to result in hastily issued regulations that are unworkable in practice. MOFTEC and the State Administration for Industry and Commerce issued regulations that require all parties to a joint venture to contribute equity at the same time unless special approval is obtained.[44] As in most cases the Chinese party to a joint venture will contribute land and buildings and thus have paid in its registered capital in full immediately upon establishment of the joint venture, the foreign investor would also be obligated to contribute its registered capital in full at the same time. This makes no commercial sense in that the foreign party will often contribute cash and equipment, which may not be needed by the joint venture for some time. Making such capital available before it is necessary is an extra cost that ultimately must be borne by the joint venture.

Even more bizarrely, the regulation provides that an investor with a controlling share of the company may not exercise decision-making authority until it pays its capital in full.[45] But if the majority partner cannot make decisions, who is to run the company? The minority shareholder? But why should a minority partner, with only say a 5% stake in the company, be given the right to run the company simply because the partner with a 95% share has yet to contribute perhaps as little as 1% of the outstanding registered capital? Moreover, how would it be legally possible for the minority party to run the company? If the majority shareholder cannot vote, would its presence at a board meeting count for quorum purposes? When contacted, MOFTEC officials had no idea how such issues were to be resolved. In practice, the regulations appear to have turned out to be a dead letter. Although not implemented, the regulation remains on the books and could potentially be hauled out in particular cases to the detriment of the majority investor.

Excessive generality and vagueness

PRC laws tend to be extremely general and vague, for a variety of reasons. Many of China's laws are modeled on the laws of civil law countries, which typically are more general and broadly drafted than statutes in common law countries.[46] Moreover, China is a huge country currently undergoing profound social and economic changes. Conditions in the poor inland and western regions differ dramatically from those in the coastal cities in the east. As a result, laws and regulations are broadly drafted to allow sufficient flexibility in implementation to meet local conditions. A traditional emphasis on particularized justice characteristic of the Confucian tradition, socialism's emphasis on uniting practice and theory,[47] and the pragmatic orientation of current leaders also favor laws that are often statements of general principles that must then be interpreted and applied to the particular situation by local officials and administrators.[48]

Regardless of the reasons, the excessive generality and vagueness of PRC laws gives local authorities great leeway in interpreting and implementing them, often undermining the predictability and certainty of law.[49] At minimum, it typically increases transaction costs by making it more difficult, time-consuming, and expensive to figure out just what the rules are at any time in a given place.[50] At worst, it breeds corruption and a reliance on connections that erodes the normative force of law.

Virtually any PRC law may be cited as an example. The equity joint venture has been the most popular vehicle for foreign investment over the last twenty years, and yet the Sino-Foreign Equity Joint Venture Law is only fifteen articles long. While the implementing regulations that were issued four years later filled in many of the gaps in the Equity Joint Venture Law, the Co-operative Joint Venture Law, consisting of a mere twenty-eight articles, was left to stand on its own for seven years until implementing regulations were finally issued. So lacking in detail was the 1979 Criminal Law that when amended in 1997, the number of articles increased from 192 to 452. Similarly, in an attempt to clarify the many issues raised or left unaddressed by the General Principles of Civil Law, the Supreme People's Court issued a 200 article interpretation, even though the Civil Law itself consisted of only 156 articles.

While PRC laws treat many issues in a general way, they often fail to address some issues at all. Presumably, sometimes such omissions are intended to afford greater flexibility in implementation or indicate a lack of consensus at the time of implementation. At other times the omission seems to be a mere oversight. Prior to the recent amendments of the Criminal Law, individuals guilty of "speculation" could be sentenced to death if exorbitant profits were made, notwithstanding the absence of a statutory definition of "speculation." In practice, courts interpreted "speculation" to include advertising, publishing pornographic materials, manipulating prices, violating State monopolies, and ticket scalping.[51]

Reference to nonexistent regulations

Another notable feature of PRC laws and regulations is the reference to other laws and regulations that have yet to be promulgated. Reference to nonexistent legislation causes uncertainty and worries among the regulated who fear that the future regulations will impose excessively burdensome obligations. The Lawyers Law, for instance, calls on lawyers to assume responsibility for legal aid in accordance with State regulations even though at the time there were no such regulations.[52] The Labor Law also contemplates the creation of a new social insurance system that will address such issues as workmen's compensation, unemployment, and retirement benefits.[53]

The main reasons for this practice are twofold: the preference for general laws that then must be filled in by subsequent legislation based on particular circumstances, and the fact that in many cases, the government is simply not in a position to address certain issues at the time a law is promulgated. The creation of a new social insurance system is an excellent example of the latter. The transition from a centrally planned economy to a more market-oriented economy and the government's inability to continue to subsidize money-losing state-owned enterprises has resulted in rapidly increasing rates of unemployment and the possibility of major social unrest unless steps are taken to shore up the social security net. Yet the enormity of the task has caused the government to proceed cautiously, allowing local governments to experiment with different approaches.

The stability of laws

Rapid change in laws or the ways laws are interpreted and implemented defeats the expectations of the parties. Given the speed with which laws change in China, investors have found it difficult to prepare feasibility studies and adhere to financial predictions.[54] The saga of duty exemptions for equipment imported by FIEs is indicative of the volatile regulatory environment and illustrates the dangers of such policy-driven oscillations. FIEs were allowed to import equipment duty free until 1996, when the government, flush with foreign investment, decided to do away with the exemptions. The State Council first announced that exemptions would no longer be available for enterprises established after January 1, 1996. This set off a mad rush among investors to set up companies before the year-end deadline. At the last minute, the State Council issued a notice extending the deadline to April 1, 1996, setting off another round of frenzied activity.[55]

The new rules phased out exemptions over a period of time for companies established prior to the deadline. As a result, the rules in essence retroactively deprived companies that had been approved before the notice went into effect of the right to import equipment whenever needed, even though in many cases the investors had submitted and obtained approval of feasibility studies that set forth the time schedule in detail.

Like so many regulations, the new rules proved to be unrealistic and unworkable in practice. Many companies simply were not able to import equipment on such short notice. In response to investors' complaints, Customs issued a notice extending the grace period another six months for certain companies. As the new deadline drew near and many companies had yet to complete import of equipment, the State Council again issued a notice extending the grace period another six months.[56]

Nevertheless, foreign investors were still not happy. After years of rapidly escalating investment, the number of new projects dropped precipitously. At first, confident MOFTEC officials declared such decreases to be temporary dips resulting from the large number of projects pushed through to meet the deadlines for exemption. They assured skeptics that the investment environment in China was sound and that foreign companies could not afford to pass up the opportunity to tap China's huge market. However, by late 1997, with foreign direct investment down more than 30 percent, anxious officials blinked. Duty exemptions were reinstated for projects that fell within certain categories under the newly revised investment guidelines.[57]

Investors are equally concerned about changes in the application of laws. In a 1992 survey, foreign investors ranked problems in the regulatory environment, including lack of uniformity and consistency in interpreting and implementing rules, as the number one obstacle.[58] Given the wide discretion of administrative authorities and local governments to interpret and implement laws and the fluidity of China's economic policies, oftentimes the law does not change but the application does. For some unknown reason, applications for holding companies were put on hold in 1997, although no new regulations were issued preventing their establishment.[59] On the other hand, despite no formal liberalization in the tight controls on retail stores, local governments approved a variety of retail arrangements. Thus the flexibility can cut both ways: sometimes restricting opportunities, other times expanding opportunities.

Conversely, at times new laws are issued that fail to produce any change in practice. Examples include technology regulations ostensibly replacing the approval process with a registration system but in practice not affecting any substantial change, at least initially;[60] the Company Law raising the hopes of investors by sanctioning the establishment of branches, only for such hopes to be dashed when MOFTEC subsequently announced, more than six years ago, that no branches would be allowed "for the time being"; the 1995 holding company regulations seeming to authorize balancing of foreign exchange of underlying subsidiaries, subject to approval by SAFE, even though in practice SAFE rarely if ever grants such approval;[61] and the much-disparaged regulations issued by Xinhua subjecting all foreign news agencies to Xinhua supervision and authorizing Xinhua to extort a percentage of all revenues under the guise of a management fee, which after intense lobbying by Western news agencies were never implemented, at least with respect to the management fee.[62]

Of course, regulations change everywhere, particularly in the economic area. And sometimes interpretation and implementation of existing laws will change or new laws will be issued that meet with resistance in practice or do not produce the degree or type of change expected by the drafters of the laws. Nevertheless, China is extreme both with respect to the rapidity with which large numbers of laws change and the changes in implementation or the lack of any such change even though the laws themselves have changed. While a higher degree of instability of the law is to be expected given the transition from a centrally planned economy to a market economy, such instability creates uncertainty and undermines investor confidence.

Another feature of PRC regulations that contributes to uncertainty is the reliance on **provisional regulations**. Given the pragmatic orientation of China's leaders, the socialist emphasis on informing theory with practice, and the current realities of China, in particular the wide diversity between regions and the need to carry out massive reforms in uncharted territories, the government has opted to issue a number of regulations on an experimental basis.[63] Should the experiment prove successful, the regulations are then made permanent. However, there is also the fear that the results will be poor and the experiment will come to an end or that the rules will be modified in some way. Again, examples abound, including provisional regulations on joint-venture trade companies, foreign-invested asset appraisal companies, foreign law firms, domestic and foreign insurance companies, and numerous provisional regulations in the areas of foreign exchange, banking, and finance.

Moreover, in **practice experimentation** often occurs first on an unauthorized basis and then, if successful, legislation is drafted and the law catches up.[64] Thus almost fifty foreign-invested holding companies had already been approved by the time MOFTEC finally issued regulations authorizing such companies in 1995.[65] Similarly, in 1988, the MOJ began to permit non-state-owned cooperative law firms on a trial basis, sanctioning a process that had begun a year earlier.[66] Taking advantage of the spirit of openness expressed in the MOJ's 1993 program to deepen legal reform, some entrepreneurial lawyers began to set up sole individual law firms, even though regulations at the time required firms to have at least three lawyers. Although the issue of sole proprietorships was hotly debated by the drafters of the 1996 Lawyers Law and a provision allowing such firms was deleted at the last minute in part because the results of the experiment were not yet clear, a number of sole individual firms still exist and some commentators remain hopeful that the experiment will continue.[67]

Inconsistency

One of the biggest obstacles to rule of law in China is the high degree of inconsistency between inferior and superior laws. However, in some cases, the inconsistency is not between a lower-level regulation and higher legislation. Rather, the inconsistency is at the level of policy. Regulations are passed that seem to be at odds with the government's own professed goals. Investors, both domestic and foreign, are often confused by the mixed signals emanating from China. On the one hand, the government trumpets China's open-door policy and warmly encourages foreign investment and calls for the expansion of the private sector; on the other, laws and regulations are issued that run counter to the government's policy objectives.

For instance, the 1985 Technology Import Contract Regulations and their implementing rules undermined the professed objective of China to attract advanced technology by imposing a number of hostile conditions on foreign technology providers, including limiting the term of a license "in general" to ten years, requiring that the licensor provide performance guarantees and assume liability for third party infringement and product liability claims, and, unless special approval was obtained, providing for retention of ownership of the technology by the licensee upon expiration of the license.[68] Needless to say, the result was that foreign investors either stayed home, transferred outdated technology, or pressed the Chinese side and approval authorities to accept contractual provisions that relieved the licensor of such burdensome obligations.

Examples of inferior legislation that is at odds with superior legislation are not hard to find.[69] In 1985, the State Council, MOFTEC's administrative superior, passed regulations that required the approval of MOFTEC or its local counterpart for all technology import contracts.[70] MOFTEC's 1996 regulations appeared to replace the approval requirement with an effective-upon-registration system for most technology import contracts, "except where otherwise specifically provided by current laws and regulations of the State."[71] Given that the 1985 regulations required approval of all technology import contracts, the exception, if taken seriously, would have swallowed the rule and defeated the alleged purpose of the 1996 regulation to replace the approval process with a registration system. Yet the authority of MOFTEC to create a new system that at least in theory does away with the previous approval system established by the State Council is far from clear. Although the State Council expressly authorized MOFTEC to interpret the 1985 regulations and formulate detailed implementing rules,[72] whether such delegation extends to the creation of an entirely new system that replaces the system established by the State Council would seem unlikely.

A particularly glaring example of lower-level legislation violating superior legislation is a 1997 State Council bankruptcy notice[73] that deprives creditors of rights provided under the Security Law, Civil Procedure Law, and the Bankruptcy Law, all passed by the Standing Committee of the NPC.[74] The notice calls for the proceeds of the sale of land use rights to be used first to pay the costs to resettle employees left unemployed as a result of the bankruptcy or merger of state-owned enterprises, even if a creditor has taken a security interest over such land use rights.[75] However, under the Bankruptcy Law, secured assets are not to be included as part of the bankruptcy assets.[76] Bankruptcy assets – that is, all assets of the company other than those encumbered with a security interest – are then to be sold off and the proceeds used to pay unsecured creditor claims in a specific order of priority.[77] The Civil Procedure Law similarly provides that secured creditors are paid before other claims, which are then paid out in a specific order of priority.[78] Likewise, under the Security Law, creditors with a security interest in land use rights have priority over rights to proceeds from the sale of such rights.[79]

The high level of inconsistency is due to various factors beyond the dispersion of law-making authority. As noted, superior legislation is often general and vague. Accordingly, it is sometimes not clear what the drafters intended. Lower-level entities must then pass regulations that are later determined to be inconsistent with superior legislation.[80] The problem is exacerbated by the failure of the NPC and State Council to issue interpretations of the laws and regulations.[81]

Often the conflict results from power grabs among China's various bureaucracies.[82] The transition to a market economy has exacerbated interagency conflicts. The recent downsizing of the executive branch has intensified the desire among the survivors to make themselves seem needed. The struggle for turf among administrative departments leads to a variety of departments claiming jurisdictional authority over the same area and issuing conflicting rules to protect their institutional interests.[83]

Administrative agencies are not the only ones who knowingly pass inconsistent legislation to promote their own interests. Local governments regularly do so as well. Economic reform has resulted in greater autonomy and fiscal responsibility for local governments. As a consequence, local governments often pass regulations that conflict with national legislation in an effort to attract investors and promote the growth of the local economy.[84] For instance, although for a number of years PRC laws only permitted the establishment of twenty-two retail joint ventures, all of which were required to obtain central-level approval, local authorities approved more than 340.[85] Similarly, local governments have routinely issued tax breaks to investors, ignoring repeated warnings from the central government that they do not have the authority to do so.[86]

Ideological struggles also play a role in legislative inconsistency. Two of the areas most rife with inconsistencies and conflicts between lower- and higher-level legislation are land [87] and labor,[88] in part because they are undergoing rapid reform as part of the transition from a centrally planned economy, but also due to their ideological importance. Mao rose to power on the promise of land reform. Allowing private ownership of land, even in the form of leaseholds, was a major step toward redefining socialism with Chinese characteristics. Similarly, laborers are supposedly the backbone of socialism. Breaking the iron rice bowl, whereby workers were guaranteed employment, housing, and other benefits, by giving employers the right to freely hire and fire employees and to pay them according to their performance, suddenly made China appear less like the workers' paradise and more like the much-maligned capitalist enemy.

China's rush to the market has further exacerbated the inconsistency problem. Predictably, the pace of economic reforms has contributed to a greater degree of inconsistency, instability, and lack of clarity in laws and administrative regulations as drafters grapple with new issues and rush to keep up with the rapidly changing environment.[89] In the absence of superior laws, lower-level entities are forced to issue regulations in response to market demands. When superior legislation is eventually passed, they often do not go back and annul or amend the existing inconsistent legislation.[90] Conversely, sometimes a law is passed incorporating certain concepts or provisions that turn out to be inconsistent with the trend of reform or unworkable in practice. Rather than amend the superior legislation itself, which can be time-consuming, particularly at the national level, local governments or agencies then pass legislation (often in the form of experimental implementing rules) that meets the needs of reform but is at odds with the superior legislation. If the implementing rules prove effective, the superior legislation will be amended in time.

Whatever the reasons, inconsistencies and conflicts in rules undermine the effectiveness of the legal system and investors' confidence in it. Conflicting rules create uncertainty for the regulated, who are not sure which laws to follow. For instance, even if investors would prefer to take advantage of more flexible, lower-level laws, they then live in fear that the central authorities will one day crack down on rogue local legislators and officials who have exceeded their authority. And with good reason – the central government, for instance, has forced many locally approved retail joint ventures to reorganize, with the Chinese party taking a majority interest; or in some cases the central government has forced these entities to dissolve altogether.[91]

The lack of effective means of sorting out conflicts

The lack of a practical way to sort out conflicts is as damaging to rule of law as the existence of conflicting rules. While in theory there are ways to reconcile inconsistencies,[92] in practice there is often no effective means for doing so in China. The power of constitutional supervision resides in the NPC and its Standing Committee.[93] Because the CCP rejects separation of powers, there is no independent constitutional review body.[94] Thus the NPC polices itself. Not only has the NPC yet to strike down any of the laws of its Standing Committee as unconstitutional, the Standing Committee has rarely annulled any lower-level rules on grounds of unconstitutionality.[95]

The NPCSC is also responsible for reviewing the consistency of lower-level legislation with NPC and NPCSC Laws.[96] However, only recently has the NPCSC established procedures and designated a body within the NPC for reviewing the consistency of lower-level legislation.[97] Whether the review mechanism stipulated in the Law on Legislation will be effective remains to be seen, though it is doubtful for reasons explained below.

As in the case of conflicts with Laws, it is difficult if not impossible to resolve conflicts between Administrative Regulations and lower-level legislation and among lower-level legislation.[98] The State Council,[99] lower-level people's congresses, and governments have all been reluctant to intervene.[100] Furthermore, although in many instances local governments and agencies are required to file Rules and Normative Documents with the local people's congress or government, the requirement is often ignored.[101] In Heilongjiang, for instance, the provincial government repeatedly sent out notices that all departments were required to submit for the record all Normative Documents within a stipulated time period. But the departments ignored the government order. Undeterred, the provincial government then issued a regulation ordering each department to assign a person to file all Normative Documents and providing that the Legislative Affairs Department would be responsible for reviewing all of the submitted documents. Unfortunately, the departments continued to ignore the regulation.[102]

In most legal systems, courts or similar bodies (whether special constitutional review bodies or administrative tribunals) would have the authority to strike down laws or regulations inconsistent with the constitution or superior legislation. However, courts in the PRC do not have the authority to overturn any type of legislation on grounds of unconstitutionality or even to overturn lower-level legislation that is inconsistent with superior legislation other than the constitution. Thus, under the ALL, PRC courts may not invalidate administrative regulations (abstract acts) that are inconsistent with the constitution or superior legislation, although the court need not follow the lower-level regulation in the specific case.[103] This ability to refuse to follow the inconsistent regulation in the specific case allows for a kind of indirect review of consistency. However, the inconsistent regulation remains in effect, and the issuing entity may continue to apply it in the future.

There are ways of tackling the problem of inconsistent regulations other than through the courts or the system of recording and oversight, including through administrative reconsideration or supervision.[104] Under the Administrative Reconsideration Law, it is now possible to challenge certain administrative regulations (i.e. abstract acts) provided that one does so in the context of a challenge to a specific act.[105] The reconsideration body may invalidate or amend the inconsistent regulation within its authority.[106]

Inconsistent regulations may also be challenged under the Administration Supervision Law. Administration supervision bodies are somewhat similar to ombudsmen elsewhere in that they are responsible for ensuring good governance. In China, as in some other countries such as the United States, administrative supervision bodies are part of the executive branch.[107] Supervisory organs have the power to recommend the correction of government regulations that are inconsistent with laws, regulations, or state policies.[108] For reasons explained more fully in Chapter 9, however, neither administrative reconsideration nor supervision has been an effective way of dealing with the problem of inconsistency thus far.

China is not unique in providing inherent authority to the executive branch or local governments or in denying the courts the authority to review only specific administrative acts.[109] France and Belgium, for example, provide for inherent executive authority.[110] In Belgium, courts also have limited powers to review abstract acts.[111] Regular courts and administrative tribunals may refuse to follow an administrative regulation inconsistent with superior legislation but the regulation is not struck down. Only the Council of State, Belgium's highest administrative tribunal, may annul a regulation and then only within sixty days of publication.[112] Additionally, in the Netherlands, administrative courts are not allowed to annul administrative regulations or a law passed by parliament.[113] However, the court may refuse to follow a regulation or law in a particular case, as in China.[114]

Although China is not alone in precluding the review of abstract acts, such systems are the minority. Moreover, whereas other countries have alternative mechanisms to deal with inconsistencies, the alternatives in China, such as the file and review system, administrative supervision, and administrative reconsideration, do not work in practice. The current system whereby PRC courts need not follow an administrative regulation that is inconsistent with superior legislation but the inconsistent lower regulation remains in effect, is both inefficient and unjust. It forces multiple parties to litigate the same issue over and over and may result in similarly situated parties being subject to different results depending on whether they decide to challenge an administrative decision or not. In other systems, agencies might be expected as part of the legal culture to annul a regulation deemed by a court to be inconsistent with superior legislation. However, given the problems of local and agency protectionism, the lowly stature of the courts, and a different legal culture, agencies in China are not likely to voluntarily repeal the regulation. Predictably, many voices have called for an expansion of the court's jurisdiction to encompass abstract acts.[115]

Tackling legislative inconsistency: the need for deeper institutional reforms

The main proposals for dealing with the inconsistency between lower and higher legislation and legislative disarray more generally have been to: (i) limit delegation and require the delegating body to state more specifically the purpose of delegation and standards for compliance; (ii) eliminate or limit the inherent authority of agencies and local governments to pass regulations; (iii) pass an administrative procedure law that would impose procedural requirements on administrative rule-making; (iv) improve the current mechanisms for handling inconsistency, including establishing a constitutional review body and special review bodies under the NPC, State Council, and people's congresses and governments; and (v) expand the scope of judicial review to include abstract acts and allow the courts to annul lower-level legislation that is inconsistent with superior legislation. While all of these suggestions may be pursued simultaneously, inconsistency will remain a problem unless the courts are given the power to review at least some abstract acts.

The recently enacted Law on Legislation limits the authority of the NPC to delegate power to the State Council and executive agencies, and to people's congresses and governments, by prohibiting delegation with respect to, *inter alia*, criminal law matters and issues that affect the basic rights of citizens.[116] It also stipulates that the delegating act must indicate the scope and purpose of delegation, and that the authorized entity must act in accordance with the purpose and scope of delegation and may not subdelegate the matter to another entity.[117] But attempting to rein in administrative discretion by limiting delegation or imposing specificity requirements has not proved effective in other countries where broad delegations of authority to administrative agencies have become the norm.[118] There is little reason to suspect that limitations on delegation will be any more effective in China.

While other countries also provide the executive with inherent rule-making authority, in China too many entities have been given expansive and vaguely defined rule-making authority. Although the Law on

Legislation clarifies the lines of authority to some extent, it does not deprive the various law-making entities of their inherent authority to pass legislation. People's congresses and governments may still issue regulations to implement superior legislation in accordance with local legislation, and ministries and commissions may still issue implementing regulations.[119]

To be sure, many PRC scholars argue that inherent authority may not be used to create new rights and obligations not recognized by superior law. In practice, however, entities have regularly done so, in part because there has often been no superior law on point. Presumably the need to exceed the scope of inherent authority will diminish as more laws are passed. There seems to be some acknowledgment of this principle. For instance, 1987 regulations in Shanghai permitted the government to issue regulations in the absence of relevant regulations by the local people's congresses. However, 1994 regulations eliminated this clause on the grounds that it led to abuse by local government and to inconsistency in regulations.[120]

While laudable, the Law on Legislation's attempt to limit delegation and the inherent authority of lower-level entities will not resolve the inconsistency problems. The Law on Legislation does not apply to Normative Documents at all and thus will not address the most problematic types of legislation. But even bringing Normative Documents under the Law on Legislation would not be sufficient, because simply clarifying the lines of authority will not do the trick. Agencies will still have considerable rule-making discretion, since superior legislation is often vague. Moreover, administrative agencies arguably *should* have considerable discretion at this stage given the need to adapt national laws to local conditions and novel situations created by economic and political reforms. In periods of reform, there is bound to be more inconsistency. Accordingly, there must be external checks on law-making. External checks are particularly crucial given the lack of a procedural law that would ensure public input and monitoring, the existence of widespread corruption, and the skewed incentive structure resulting from continued involvement of administrative agencies as participants in the economy.

An administrative procedure law would impose some limits on administrative rule-making. It would also allow for more public participation and monitoring. However, the benefits of rules providing for more participation should not be overstated. First, agencies in many legal systems are given a great deal of leeway in setting their own rule-making procedures. This is inevitable given the diversity of agencies and the wide range of rule-making, from formal rules of very general applicability to informal rules affecting only a narrow range of interests of a small number of people. In fact, many countries do not have a general procedure law that applies to rule-making. Even when they do, the requirements are fairly minimal. Thus in the United States, for example, most federal agency rule-making is characterized as informal and is only subject to notice and comment requirements.[121] Second, the effectiveness of a PRC administrative procedure law that relies on public participation will be hampered by the limited state of development of civil society and interest groups. Third, even more formal procedural requirements can restrain administrative rule-making outcomes only to a degree, and only then with the assistance of external – usually judicial – review. But courts in China have not been willing to hold agencies to the existing procedural requirements.[122]

The need to expand the scope of judicial review and enhance the independence and authority of the courts

Clarifying the lines of authority and imposing procedural requirements will not be sufficient to address the inconsistency problem. External review of laws and regulations is essential. The Law on Legislation strengthened the existing system of review by clarifying the procedures for challenging lower-level legislation that is inconsistent with the Constitution or Laws. Under the new law, citizens, social groups, enterprises, or government entities may petition the NPCSC for review of lower-level legislation they believe to be at odds with the Constitution or Laws.[123] The NPCSC's specialized subcommittees are responsible for reviewing the legislation for consistency. If a subcommittee believes there is an inconsistency, it can inform the entity that passed the legislation of its opinion or have the issuing entity attend a meeting to explain the legislation in question.[124] If the subcommittee decides the legislation is inconsistent, the issuing entity has two months to determine whether to annul or revise the legislation and to report back to the NPCSC. If the issuing entity does not revise the legislation, the subcommittee may turn the matter over to the Chairman's Committee. The Chairman's Committee may then request that the NPCSC annul the inconsistent legislation.

The Law on Legislation breaks new ground in establishing more detailed procedures for challenging inconsistent legislation and in providing interested individuals with the right to raise a complaint. But by itself the Law on Legislation will not be able to address fully the problem of inconsistent legislation. The process established in the Law on Legislation is itself flawed. First, the law creates a two-tier track.[125] Complaints from the State Council, Central Military Committee, Supreme People's Court and Procuracy, NPC subcommittees, and standing committees of provincial, major city, and autonomous zone people's congresses must be reviewed by the relevant NPC subcommittee. In contrast, complaints from individuals, social groups, and enterprises are first screened by the "work unit" (*gongzuo jigou*) of the NPCSC. The work unit will pass on to the specialized subcommittees for review only those petitions that it believes pass muster.

The Law on Legislation also fails to set time limits for several crucial steps in the process. How long the work unit has to forward a complaint to the relevant subcommittee is not stipulated. Nor is there a stipulated deadline for the subcommittee to make a decision once it receives the petition, for the subcommittee to turn the matter over to the Chairman's Committee if the entity that passed the legislation refuses to abide by the subcommittee's decision, for the Chairman's Committee to forward the matter to the NPCSC, or for the NPCSC to annul the legislation.

Equally if not more worrisome, interested parties are allowed to submit written petitions but are then not given an opportunity to make their case at the subcommittee's hearing or to the Chairman's Committee. The legislature is in effect performing a function performed by courts or tribunals in other jurisdictions without affording affected parties the kinds of procedural rights they would enjoy in a judicial proceeding.

The Law on Legislation is also limited in scope in that the review procedure applies only to inconsistencies with the Constitution or Laws.[126] Inconsistencies between and among Administrative Regulations, Local People's Congress Regulations, Government Rules, and Administrative Rules are to be dealt with by a file and review system that remains largely unchanged. Unfortunately, the Law on Legislation leaves it up to the lower-level review entities to formulate their own review procedures. The Law on Legislation does not require that the reviewing entity accept individual petitions. It does not even expressly require that local governments establish a designated body to receive and review the submitted legislation.

As noted previously, in the past, many lower-level congresses, governments, and administrative agencies failed to submit legislation for review as required. Compliance with filing requirements may improve with the passage of the Law on Legislation. But whether better compliance with recording requirements will solve the problem is doubtful. Many people's congresses and governments have yet to establish a special review organ to review subordinate legislation. Even if they do, it is unlikely that any such body could keep up with the large number of Local People's Congress Regulations, Rules, and Normative Documents.[127] In many cases, the review body will lack the technical competence to pass judgment on certain administrative regulations and in the absence of a case in controversy may not be able to identify inconsistencies with superior legislation.[128] The review body will also be subject to local protectionism because the review body typically will have the same incentive as the issuing entity to promote local interests.

In light of these shortcomings, there are obvious advantages to assigning primary responsibility for invalidating inconsistent legislation to the courts. Courts deal with particular cases and therefore could rely on the initiative of the parties to point out inconsistencies. Moreover, courts do not have the conflict of interest that administrative agencies have. Further, the current system is complicated. Different entities have different powers and jurisdiction, and no single entity is responsible for invalidating all types of inconsistent legislation. Allowing the courts to invalidate all inconsistent legislation would simplify matters as the courts have the authority to issue judgments that cut across bureaucratic and territorial lines. Judicial review may also be faster than the current methods. Finally, increasing the power of the courts would be beneficial to the larger project of realization of rule of law in China.[129] Providing PRC courts with greater authority would show that the government is committed to rule of law.[130]

To be sure, there are certain disadvantages and problems associated with assigning the task of review to the courts. Some are generic to judicial review everywhere. Judges are not necessarily qualified to decide issues of policy or technical issues. Courts typically lack the resources to research all of the policy and technical issues, and even if they had the resources, it would be a waste to duplicate all of the agency's work. Moreover, courts must proceed case by case and are not in a position to monitor the effect of their decisions, which may not be the ideal way to make policy.[131] But these criticisms are less apposite with respect to judicial review of the consistency of administrative regulations. Although the court will need to address some technical issues and cannot escape policy issues entirely, the question of the consistency of an administrative regulation is often a narrower issue.

A more significant obstacle is the PRC Constitution. For the courts to be given the power to invalidate abstract acts would require a change in the Constitution and a fundamental realigning of power. Simply amending the Constitution to provide for judicial review would not produce the desired result unless the lack of independence and weak stature of the courts were addressed at the same time. This would require structural reforms. Specifically, the current system where courts are funded by the same level of government and judges appointed and removed by the same level of people's congresses would need to be changed to ensure more independence and autonomy. Funding responsibility should be shifted to the provincial or central level. Personnel decisions could be handled in a number of ways. The decision-making authority could be shifted to the provincial-level people's congresses. Alternatively, responsibility could be turned over to or shared with a committee of judges, perhaps under the Ministry of Justice but preferably under the bar association.[132]

Even if courts were given the authority to invalidate administrative regulations, they would need time to build their stature. A newly empowered court could force a constitutional crisis were it to challenge directly an NPC Law, State Council Administrative Regulation or even a ministry level Rule.[133] Given the current political realities, it may be unwise (even assuming it were politically possible) to permit the court to invalidate State Council Administrative Regulations. It would be more prudent to limit the court's authority to the review of everything below the level of State Council Administrative Regulations or perhaps even lower. Most of the problems are with regulations below the level of the State Council anyway. Moreover, the courts could expect support from the central authorities because conflicts between lower-level regulations and Laws or State Council Administrative Regulations do not benefit the nation.

For the courts to have sufficient authority to challenge central-level ministries directly responsible to the State Council would represent a major realignment of power. It may not be politically feasible at this point. Similarly, the courts might have difficulty invalidating Local

People's Congress Regulations by provincial-level people's congresses and Rules by provincial governments, particularly if personnel decisions were left in the hands of provincial-level people's congresses and funding decisions in the hands of provincial-level governments. Even if changes were made with respect to funding and appointments, the judiciary at present suffers from problems of competence. Thus one possibility would be to limit the ability of the courts to invalidate abstract acts to all Normative Documents.[134] Over time, as the courts gained in confidence and stature, their scope of review could be expanded, first to Rules, then to Local People's Congress Regulations and Administrative Regulations.

Conclusion

China's legislative system falls short of the basic requirements of a thin theory of rule of law, as is readily acknowledged in China. Despite considerable progress, many problems remain. Some shortcomings are traceable to the historical legacy of the Cultural Revolution, which weakened or destroyed key institutions. The NPC and local people's congresses, civil service and administrative law regime, and the judiciary are all still in the process of being rebuilt and strengthened. An effective constitutional review mechanism has yet to be created. The file and record system leaves much to be desired. Training of personnel in all institutions continues.

The regulatory framework requires further development. There are no national regulations regarding Normative Documents. An Administrative Procedure Law is still being drafted. Existing regulations could also be improved. For instance, the Law on Legislation's provisions on public participation and hearings could be clarified and strengthened. Even when there are adequate regulations, they are often not followed. While there are many reasons why laws and regulations are not followed, one is that China lacks a rule-of-law culture in which law is respected.

The transition to a market economy is another factor. Inevitably, rules change more often during periods of transition, leading to instability and inconsistency. Economic reforms have also altered the incentive structure for local governments, leading to the passage of local rules that conflict with central laws and regulations. As is often the case, the problems are interrelated. Thus, weak institutions and mechanisms for dealing with legislative inconsistency exacerbate the problems brought about by economic reforms.

It bears noting that most problems have little if anything to do with the Party, at least not directly. The Party has no interest in MOFTEC officials inadvertently imposing new registration requirements for security based on a typo, or in passing incoherent regulations that are unworkable in practice, or in the drafters not knowing what documents the regulations they themselves drafted require to create a pledge. These are technical issues for which there is no Party line. Nor does the Party support local governments passing regulations at odds with central laws, or administrative agencies, struggling to protect their turf, delaying the passage of key laws, or passing regulations that conflict with regulations from other agencies. Not surprisingly, the Party has backed reforms to strengthen the relevant institutions and the regulatory framework; it has supported the Law on Legislation and the drafting of an Administrative Procedure Law; and it has even sought assistance from foreign organizations to improve the legislative process.[135]

But it is simply not within the power of the Party to remedy some of the existing deficiencies. It takes time to train people and to build institutions. It will also take time to develop a culture of legality. And it will take time for economic reforms to reach a more equilibrium state, which will result in more stability and fewer inconsistencies in laws.

To be sure, some major institutional reforms will require Party approval. Clearly the creation of a constitutional review body will need to be sanctioned by the Party. There have also been various proposals to strengthen the NPC that have not been implemented, due in part to Party opposition. For instance, proposals to increase electoral freedom, such as the suggestions to permit direct elections for delegates above the county level or to decrease Party control of the selection process of the NPC, have run into Party opposition. Other important reforms have also stalled. Currently, the NPC, with some 3,000 delegates, is too large to function effectively, yet proposals to decrease the size of the NPC or to create a bicameral NPC have gone nowhere. Similarly, the NPC now only meets once a year. Proposals to increase the number and length of meetings have been rejected so far. Most NPC delegates, even members of the NPCSC, hold other posts. As a consequence, many delegates are preoccupied with other matters. Requiring delegates to devote themselves full-time to their legislative duties would improve the quality and stature of the NPC, though there are no signs that such a change is forthcoming anytime soon.

Moreover, as discussed in the next chapter, the Party will have to overcome qualms about a more authoritative and independent court and permit deeper reforms of the judiciary than currently planned for the legal system to satisfy fully the minimal requirements of a thin rule of law.

Notes

1   See the works of Tanner (1994; 1999); O'Brien (1990); Dowdle (1997).
2   See Keller (1989; 1994); Corne (1996); Otto *et al.* (2000).
3   In this chapter, I focus on law-making and rule-making, reserving a discussion of the interpretation and implementation processes for Chapter 9.
4   By providing examples of concrete cases, I hope to put some flesh on what has been a rather abstract discussion of rule of law. To be sure, relying on a few cases to illustrate general principles is always subject to a number of methodological concerns. Are the cases representative? Couldn't one find similar examples in other systems? Don't all systems fall short of the rule-of-law ideal to some extent? While such concerns are important, they do not obviate the value of, or need for, concrete cases to illustrate the particular types of problems that China's legal system faces. All systems fall short of the rule-of-law ideal to some degree, but that degree is greater in China than in many countries. Similarly, while a few cases are no substitute for a more rigorous empirical comparison, there is little point in describing in exhaustive detail countless examples of problems that those familiar with the legal system can confirm are indeed all too typical. The value of a few illustrative cases lies in making real what otherwise can be a rather lifeless and abstract analysis. Just as sometimes a picture is worth more than a thousand words, a few stories can be more telling about the actual status of law in China and convey a more vivid sense of how law actually operates than pages of analysis alone.

    Many, though by no means all, of the examples are drawn from the foreign investment area. China has assigned a high priority to foreign investment law in the hopes of attracting foreign investment. Focusing attention on the segment of the legal system that is most likely to meet the standards of a thin rule of law sheds light on the upper limits of China's efforts to improve the legal system over the last twenty years and just how far it has to go.
5   Lifa Fa [Law on Legislation] (2000) (passed by the NPC).
6   See, generally, Li Buyun (1997).
7   Peter Corne (1997: 1) has observed that: "At first glance the PRC legal system appears almost unintelligible. It consists of multiple levels of laws, regulations, sub-legal documents and explanations, each with, up until now, ill-defined legal status and effect."

8 For present purposes, the legislative hierarchy may be classified as follows:
   (i) Constitution;
   (ii) Laws (*falu*) passed by the NPC and NPCSC;
   (iii) Administrative Regulations (*xingzheng fagui*) passed by the State Council;
   (iv) Local People's Congress Regulations (*difangxing fagui*) passed by the people's congresses and the standing committees of provinces, autonomous regions, cities directly under the central government and major cities, and special economic zones;
   (v) Rules (*guizhang*), including Government Rules (*zhengfu guizhang*) passed by people's governments of provinces, autonomous regions, cities directly under the central government and major cities, and Ministry Rules (*bumen guizhang*) passed by central-level ministries, commissions, agencies, or entities (such as the People's Bank of China) directly under the State Council; and
   (vi) Normative Documents (*guifanxing wenjian*), including all legislation passed by people's congresses and governments other than those mentioned above.
   See Law on Legislation, arts. 78–86. Legislation passed by the State Council, governments, and administrative departments with the authority to issue legislation may be Rules or merely Normative Documents depending on the nature of the legislation, the procedures for making the legislation, and whether the legislation was published or not. Accordingly, it is often difficult to determine whether legislation should be treated as a Rule or merely as a Normative Document.
   I distinguish between laws, regulations, administrative regulations, and rules in a generic sense, and as technical terms of art referring to particular types of PRC legislation as defined in the Law on Legislation by capitalizing the latter.
9 China is by no means unique in this regard. In many countries including the US the number of administrative regulations passed every year exceeds the number of laws passed by the legislature.
10 Constitution, art. 89.
11 Constitution, arts. 90, 99–100, 107.
12 See Resolution on the Government Work Report (1984) (adopted by the NPC); see also Decision Concerning the Delegation of Authority to the State Council to Enact Temporary Regulations Regarding the Economic Reform and Opening to Foreign Countries (1985) (issued by the NPC).
13 See Corne (1996: 152).
14 See Peerenboom (1999b).
15 Law on Legislation, art. 34.
16 Law on Legislation, art. 35.
17 Hecht (1996: 15).
18 Potter (2000).
19 Between 1982 and 1998, nine draft laws were made available for public discussion. The NPC received over 300 comments from citizens on the Administrative Litigation Law, 611 comments on the Law on Land Management, and

529 comments on the 1998 amendment to the Organic Law of the Village's Committee. See Zhu Jingwen (2000). In contrast, the NPC was flooded with more than 3,800 comments from the public on the draft amendments to the Marriage Law. See Meng Yan (2001a).

20 Interview in August 2000 with NPC staff member.

21 Provisional Measures for the Formulation of Administrative Regulations (1987) (adopted by the State Council) [hereinafter, 1987 State Council Measures].

22 Jiang Mingan, ed. (1998: 20).

23 For instance, in Hohot, Inner Mongolia between 1900 and 1995, only 34 of 242 Rules and Normative Documents were passed in accordance with local procedural regulations. Jiang Mingan, ed. (1998: 27).

24 See the Administration of the Examination, Approval and Registration of Foreign-Invested Crop Seed Enterprises Provisions (promulgated by the Ministry of Agriculture, State Planning Commission, MOFTEC and State Administration of Industry and Commerce, effective Sept. 8, 1997).

25 Forney (1996–97).

26 Klein (1997).

27 Law on Legislation, art. 77. Presumably, the legal effect of failing to publish a regulation in accordance with the Law on Legislation or other laws and regulations is that the regulation is deemed a Normative Document rather than a Rule. Normative Documents are not binding on the courts, though in practice courts may refer to them for guidance. See Chapter 9.

28 Several Provisions Regarding Foreign Investment in Electric Power Projects (Ministry of Power Industry, May 5, 1997).

29 Law on Legislation, articles 62, 70, 76, 77.

30 Lack of accessibility of laws and regulations is not a problem unique to China. Many countries experience similar problems, though perhaps to a lesser degree. For instance, a 1993 report in England concluded: "At present the accessibility of statute law to users and the wide public is slow, inconvenient, complicated and subject to several impediments. To put it bluntly, it is often very difficult to find out what the text of the law is – let alone what it means. Something must be done." Hansard Society Commission (1993: 108). Accordingly, the authors of the report recommended a Statute Law Database and financial assistance to agencies so that they can explain laws to people.

31 Corne (1996).

32 Nicholas Howson (1997: 11–12), for instance, described the PRC Company Law as "replete with inconsistencies and drafting absurdities" and concluded that such serious drafting problems "indicate a certain amount of unfamiliarity with legislation drawn up only a few years previous, and serve not only to cause basic confusion but also to discredit 'law' itself as a stable and consistent vehicle for governing commercial and investment activity."

33 Gao Xiqing (1996: 239), vice-director of China's Security Regulatory Commission, claims that the Security Law does not address or fails to resolve the overlapping and conflicting system of approvals and enforcement because of, *inter alia*, turf struggles among agencies and between local governments and the

central government. Although he acknowledges that there are serious problems in the Security Law, he argues that "the necessary consensus for the opening of the stock market would never have been achieved without compromises made among certain historically powerful government agencies."

34 Measures for the Control of the Provision of Security to Foreign Parties by Organizations within the People's Republic of China (promulgated and effective October 1, 1996).

35 Notice on Relevant Issues of Provision of Securities to Foreign Parties by Foreign Investment Enterprises, (96) Hui Zi Han Zi No. 320 (1996).

36 Detailed Rules for the Implementation of the People's Republic of China Concerning Wholly Foreign-Owned Enterprises Law, art. 24 (approved Oct. 28, 1990 by the State Council and issued Dec. 12, 1990 by MOFTEC).

37 Administration of the Provision of Security to Foreign Entities by Domestic Institutions inside China Procedures Implementing Regulations (1998) (effective Jan. 1, 1998).

38 The Administration of Project Financing Conducted outside China Tentative Procedures, art. 1 (promulgated by State Planning Commission and State Administration of Foreign Exchange on Apr. 16, 1997).

"For the purposes of these Procedures, 'project financing' shall refer to the financing method pursuant to which foreign exchange funds are raised outside China in the name of a construction project in China and where the debt payment liability to the foreign entity is limited to the expected revenue from and the assets of the project itself. Such financing method shall have the following characteristics:

(1) the creditors have no recourse against assets or revenue other than those of the construction project;

(2) no institutions in China effect any mortgage, pledge or debt payment with assets, rights, interests or revenue other than those of or in the construction project; or

(3) no institutions in China provide financing guarantees in any form."

39 Moreover, when the foreign investor, a major multilateral lending entity, sought the assurance of a written confirmation from the State Planning Commission (since renamed the State Planning and Development Commission) on the issue, the State Planning Commission initially refused. Finally, after a considerable delay, the State Planning Commission issued a vaguely worded statement that left open the possibility that the regulation could apply to some projects less than $30 million.

40 Several Provisions regarding Changes in Equity Interest of Investors in Foreign Investment Enterprises (promulgated by MOFTEC and SAIC, effective May 28, 1997).

41 While legally transferable shares (*gufen*) and share certificates (*gupiao*) could be transferred under the Security Law, investors in most FIEs do not have shares or share certificates. Security Law of the People's Republic of China [Security Law], art. 75(2) (adopted June 30, 1995). Under the MOFTEC regulations, investors are allowed to pledge their equity interest (*guquan*). Several Provisions regarding Changes in Equity Interest of Investors in Foreign Invested Enterprises, art. 2(4). The Security Law does contain a catch-phrase that permits

pledge of other rights in accordance with law (*yifa*). Security Law, art. 75(4). However, "in accordance with law" arguably is to be construed as pursuant to laws (*falu*), which technically refers to legislation passed by the NPC and its Standing Committee but not to regulations by lower-level administrative entities.

42   Several Provisions regarding Changes in Equity Interest of Investors in Foreign-Invested Enterprises, art. 4.

43   Several Provisions Regarding Changes in Equity Interest of Investors in Foreign-Invested Enterprises, art. 13.

44   Supplementary Provisions to the Several Provisions Regarding Capital Contributions by the Parties to Sino-Foreign Equity Joint Venture, art. 2 (promulgated by MOFTEC and SAIC, Sept. 29, 1997), herein after Supplementary Provisions.

45   Supplementary Provisions, art 2.

46   Portalis, one of the drafters of the French Civil Code, explained: "We have avoided the dangerous ambition to regulate and foresee everything. The function of law is to fix in broad outline the general maxims of justice, to establish principles rich in implications, and not to descend into the details of the questions that can arise in each subject." See Von Mehren and Gordonly (1977: 54). The German Civil Code is often praised for its technical precision. See Glendon, Gordon, and Osakwe (1994: 56). However, as with the French Civil Code, the BGB's general provisions and lack of definition of key concepts has ensured flexibility. Thus, argues Rheinhard Zimmermann (1996: 14–15): "The fathers of BGB refrained from defining and regulating purely doctrinal questions, central as they might be. Thus, we find neither definition nor explanation of basic concepts like legal capacity, contract, declaration of intention, damage, causation or unlawfulness; freedom of contract is not even mentioned. Moreover, as has repeatedly been observed, the BGB is characterized by a considerable degree of abstraction, both as far as style and content are concerned. All of this contributes to a considerable built-in flexibility which has, by and large, made the Civil Code stand the test of time."

47   For a discussion of the socialist emphasis on praxis and the emergence of pragmatism during the Deng era, particularly as it relates to criminal law, see Lo (1995).

48   Corne (1996) suggests that as the de facto ultimate authority in many cases, the core leadership of the Party may favor general laws since it can more readily effect change when policy changes by ensuring that laws are implemented in accordance with the new policy.

49   As noted, laws in other systems are often vague as well, and as a result, administrative agencies have considerable discretion in implementing the law. However, China lacks some of the institutional mechanisms that other countries have developed for limiting interpretation and controlling administrative discretion, such as a developed system of authoritative commentary as in some civil law countries or the common law precedential case method whereby judges narrow the range of possible interpretations through a series of cases. Even when China does have similar institutions, they do not always function

as well as in other systems. As will be discussed in Chapter 9, China has established many of the same mechanisms and institutions for controlling administrative discretion as in other countries. Yet the administrative law regime remains a major area of concern.

50 For an argument that vaguely defined rules may be more efficient in certain circumstances, see Dowdle (1999: 302–07). Clearly, in some cases, vaguely defined rules will be more efficient. For instance, vaguely defined rules are better than bad rules that are not able to be implemented in practice.

51 Finder and Fu (1997: 35–38). Noting the "elastic language" of the 1979 Criminal Law, Donald Clarke (1998: 14, 39–40) has pointed out that while the 1997 revised Criminal Law attempted to tighten up several of the vague provisions of the 1979 Criminal Law, many clauses remain vague.

52 Lawyers Law, art. 42.

53 Labor Law, Chapter 9.

54 Many investors were particularly frustrated by reductions in VAT export refunds from a full 17% rebate to 14% and then to 9%. Not only were the rule changes applied in a complex and seemingly irrational way based on date of establishment, they also penalized export-oriented companies most, even though China has continually encouraged companies to export and indeed in many instances made export a condition of approval. Recently, in light of the Asian financial crisis that reduced export competitiveness and resulted in less direct investment in China, the government reversed tack, and has now increased the VAT rebates to exporters.

55 Yeung and Chen (1997).

56 Wei Ke (1997).

57 "New Duty Exemptions Conceal Tighter Investment Control" (1998).

58 Potter (1995b: 176). A 1997 survey of 1,000 foreign business executives in Shanghai found their biggest complaint to be red tape, including government interference, complex procedures, inconsistent policies, and poor communications. Suggestions for improvement included increasing policy transparency, reducing bureaucracy, maintaining stable and consistent government policies, and strengthening the legal system. See Wu Zheng (1997).

59 Rapp (1999).

60 Markel and Peerenboom (1997).

61 Rapp (1999).

62 "USTR Says China Agrees Not to Restrict Financial News Wires" (1997).

63 In the early years of reform, Deng Xiaoping (1984: 158) called for the fast promulgation of laws, even if they would be imperfect and require subsequent amendment. He also advocated trying out laws on an experimental basis in particular locations before passing national regulations.

64 Gao Xiqing (1996: 230) has observed that local government experiments with shareholding companies in the early 1980s were carried out without legislative support. Amy Epstein (1997) likewise notes that experiments with village democracy in the early 1980s were later sanctified by the NPC's passage of the 1987 Organic Law of Villagers' Committees of the People's Republic of China (Experimental).

65 Howson (1997: 9).
66 Peerenboom (1998b: 34).
67 Peerenboom (1998b: 35–36).
68 Regulations on Administration of Technology Import Contracts of the Peo-
    ple's Republic of China (promulgated May 24, 1985 by the State Council);
    Detailed Rules for the Implementation of the Regulations on Administration
    of Technology Import Contracts of the People's Republic of China (approved
    December 30, 1987 by the State Council and promulgated January 20, 1988 by
    MOFTEC). The technology import and export regime has undergone a major
    overload now that China has entered the WTO.
69 Shenyang government recently passed regulations prohibiting pedestrians from
    seeking compensation arising out of accidents with automobiles where the
    pedestrian has violated jaywalking and other traffic rules. Liang Huixiang, a
    leading expert on civil law, has claimed that such regulations are inconsistent
    with Article 123 of the General Principles of Civil Law, which imposes liabil-
    ity on those who engage in hazardous activities such as high-speed means of
    transport, unless they can show the victim deliberately caused the injury. See
    Meng Yan (2001b).
70 Regulations on Administration of Technology Import Contracts of the People's
    Republic of China, art. 4.
71 Administration of Trade in Importation of Technology and Equipment Ten-
    tative Procedures, art. 15 (issued by MOFTEC in and effective as of March 22,
    1996).
72 Regulations on Administration of Technology Import Contracts of the People's
    Republic of China, art. 12.
73 Supplementary Notice on Issues Concerning the Trial Implementation in Sev-
    eral Cities of State-Owned Enterprise Bankruptcy and Merger and Reemploy-
    ment of Staff and Workers (promulgated by the State Council on March 2,
    1997).
74 Security Law; People's Republic of China Civil Procedure Law (adopted April 9,
    1991 by the NPC Standing Committee); People's Republic of China Enterprise
    Bankruptcy Law (for Trial Implementation) (enacted Dec. 2, 1986 by the NPC
    Standing Committee and effective Nov. 1, 1988). See also Clarke (1997: 9–15).
75 The notice also allows for the sale of allocated land use rights and the use
    of the proceeds first for the payment of resettlement costs, even though allo-
    cated land use rights may not be transferred without payment first of a grant
    fee. Provisional Measures on Administration of Allocated Land Use Rights
    (promulgated March 8, 1992 by State Land Administration Bureau).
76 Bankruptcy Law, art. 28.
77 Bankruptcy Law, art. 37.
78 Civil Procedure Law, art. 204.
79 Security Law, arts. 33, 56.
80 Conita Leung (1998: 1) has noted that "lawyers and even local officials are
    often confronted with difficulties in applying the laws and regulations that
    conflict with each other or are simply too vague to make any sense."
81 Given the reluctance of the NPC to interpret its own laws, the Supreme People's
    Court (SPC) has stepped into the gap and issued a number of interpretations.

However, the legal authority of the SPC to do so is unclear. Moreover, the SPC often goes beyond the original law in its interpretation, thus creating new law, in clear violation of its constitutional powers. See Chapter 7.

82 Keller (1994: 733) has observed that "the expansion of legislative powers to so many central and regional state bodies has in effect brought the rivalries and disorder of Chinese bureaucracy directly into the legislative structure."

83 See "Dispute Slows Passage of Securities Law" (1997), describing how the State Development and Planning Commission, People's Bank of China, Finance Ministry, State Commission for Restructuring the Economy, and State Council all refused to withdraw from "the profitable securities industry." Alford and Shen (1997) argue that environmental problems are attributable in part to conflicts among agencies.

84 Feinerman (1998: 21).

85 Shi and Stevenson-Yang (1998: 44).

86 "State Will Strengthen Supervision of Taxation" (1998).

87 Jonas Alsen (1996) cites ideological obstacles to marketization of land as one of the factors causing inconsistencies. Corne and Godwin (1997: 19) also attribute inconsistencies in land regulations to the socialist emphasis on state ownership of property.

88 Corne (1996).

89 As Seidman and Seidman (1994) observe, such problems are typical of transition states.

90 The passage of the 1992 State-Owned Industrial Enterprise Law resulted in the need to clean up 200,000 Rules and Normative Documents, including the repeal of 7,600 and amendment of 100,000 more. Jiang Mingan, ed. (1998: 191).

91 "Overhaul of Foreign Investment in China's Retail Sector" (1998–99).

92 See Law on Legislation, Chapter 5.

93 Constitution, art. 62(2), 62(11); art. 89(1), 89(13), 89(14).

94 Cai Dingjian (1995).

95 See Li Buyun, (1997: 19). According to one report, from 1993 to June 1999, there were 3,692 local regulations filed with the NPC, 2,045 of which were reviewed by NPC committees, which found that 93, or 4.5 percent, were inconsistent with the Constitution or current laws. See *China: 20 Years of Legal System Developments* (1999). In response to poor performance by the NPCSC, scholars have proposed a variety of possible reforms, including the creation of a constitutional review body, perhaps under theNPC or the NPCSC, the creation of a constitutional court, or expanding the authority of existing courts to include constitutional review. All suggestions have been met with resistance on a number of theoretical and practical grounds. See Cai Dingjian (1995).

96 Constitution, art. 89(13)–(14).

97 Law on Legislation, arts. 90–91.

98 Ma Huaide (1998: 40–41).

99 The 1990 Provisions on the Recording of Rules and Regulations require the filing of Rules with the State Council within thirty days of formulation. The Legislative Affairs Office is supposed to review them for consistency with

superior legislation. But the large number of Rules makes it practically im-possible for the Legislative Affairs Office to carry out a comprehensive review of every Rule. From 1987 to 1996, there were 28,000 Rules filed with the State Council, of which 1,500 were problematic. The State Council decided that 400 needed to be revised or abolished. The State Council and its related de-partments revised 214 and abolished 33. See *China: 20 Years of Legal System Developments* (1999).

100 According to statistics from 29 provinces, municipalities, and autonomous regions, 1,572 Government Rules were revised and 1,198 abolished between 1987 and 1996. See *China: 20 Years of Legal System Developments* (1999); see also Jiang Mingan, ed. (1998: 22), calling for changes in filing requirements and review processes.

101 Jiang Mingan, ed. (1998: 190), noting that although the Sichuan regulation requires the filing of all Rules and Normative Documents with the people's congress, agencies often do not file.

102 Jiang Mingan, ed. (1998 : 234).

103 ALL, arts. 2, 53.

104 Long-term partial solutions include improving the quality and legal pro-fessionalism of drafters and reducing the reliance on Rules and Normative Documents by passing more and clearer superior legislation. Jiang Mingan, ed. (1998: 30).

105 ARL, art. 7. For a discussion of the ARL, see Chapter 9.

106 ARL, arts. 26–28.

107 In contrast, in some countries ombudsmen are part of the legislative branch, as in the case of England's Parliamentary Commission for Arbitration. Craig (1994: 127).

108 ASL, art. 23.

109 Before the recent reforms, Eastern European socialist countries typically did not allow courts to review abstract acts. Hiroshi Oda (1984: 125–26) states that Soviet Union courts were required to apply inconsistent rules while in Romania, Bulgaria, and Poland courts could not invalidate the abstract rule but also did not need to apply it in the particular case.

110 Neville-Brown and Bell (1993: 10); Craenen (1996b: 11, 21).

111 Until recently, no court could annul or refuse to apply a law passed by the na-tional parliament. The legislature itself was responsible for review. See Craenen (1996b: 26); Alan (1992: 8, 109–10). Now ordinary courts may review the con-stitutionality of laws in limited circumstances. Although they do not have the power to annul the law, they can refuse to follow it in the specific case. In addition, a special constitutional body – the Court of Arbitration – may strike down all legislation on certain limited grounds. Alan (1992: 8).

112 Craenen (1996b: 26, 36–37); Alan (1992: 46, 231).

113 Koekkoek (1987: 67). Parliament considered whether to allow courts to review and annul abstract acts in 1998 but rejected the idea.

114 Koekkoek (1987: 67).

115 See for example, Jiang Mingan, ed. (1998: 17), arguing that judicial review should include abstract acts. Ying Songnian, ed. (1993: 755–59). Qian Cuihua

et al. (1997) also claim that abstract acts should be justiciable because they affect the rights and interests of many individuals and depriving the courts of the authority to review them weakens the judiciary. On the other hand, Zhang Jiansheng (1998) argues for a limited scope of judicial review that reflects the need to ensure administrative efficiency and the relative competence of administrative agencies.

116 Law on Legislation, art. 8.

117 Law on Legislation, art. 8.

118 As Fox (1997: 50) observes: "It is too soon to bury the non-delegation doctrine, although it clearly has had at least one and one-half feet in the grave for the past forty or fifty years." Craig (1994: 16) also notes that broad delegation in England gives agencies wide discretion. Klap (1994: 247–48) concurs that the dominance of the executive over parliament with respect to legislation is exemplified by vague standards of delegation such as it being "necessary for the sake of good environmental planning" or "in the interest of public housing."

119 Law on Legislation, arts. 40, 48, 55.

120 Jiang Mingan, ed. (1998: 3).

121 Strauss (1991: 673).

122 See Chapter 9.

123 Law on Legislation, art. 90.

124 Law on Legislation, art. 91.

125 Law on Legislation, art. 90.

126 The likelihood that the NPCSC would find its own law, or a law passed by the NPC, unconstitutional is slim.

127 Jiang Mingan, ed. (1998: 190).

128 Ma Huaide (1998: 41) has pointed out that the lack of a party to bring suit renders the review process passive and ineffective.

129 It is not surprising that one of the first reforms in many Central and Eastern European countries was to establish independent courts. See Rein Mullerson *et al.*, eds. (1998).

130 Ruti Teitel (1997) has noted the self-transformative aspect of judicial review and how it may demonstrate differences between a prior regime and a new regime with respect to rule of law and constitutionalism.

131 Warren (1982: 373). For a particularly negative view of judicial review of administrative rule-making in the United States, see Cross (1999).

132 Hu Yunteng of CASS has recommended that personnel decisions be handled by the MOJ. Editorial Office (1998: 10).

133 In Malaysia, for instance, the Mahathir government reacted to a string of judicial decisions against it in 1986 and 1987 by impeaching the Supreme Court judges that dared to defy the government. See Khoo Boo Teik (1995: 219–21).

134 This is essentially the approach taken in the ARL. See Chapter 9.

135 Seidman and Seidman (1994).

7

The judiciary: in search of independence, authority, and competence

Rule of law requires a judiciary that is independent, competent, and enjoys sufficient powers to resolve disputes fairly and impartially. China's judiciary falls short on each of these three dimensions.

As a matter of law, the PRC Constitution provides that the courts shall "in accordance with law, exercise judicial power independently and are not subject to interference by administrative organs, public organizations or individuals."[1] The Judges Law sought to strengthen the independence of the judiciary by providing that judges have the right to be free from external interference in their work.[2] In addition, judges were given the right to raise a complaint if a state organ or official committed an act infringing on their rights, and administrative entities, public organizations, and individuals may be held liable for interfering in particular cases.[3]

Under the PRC's unitary system, however, the courts are administratively and institutionally accountable to the corresponding level of people's congresses that created them, as stated in Article 128 of the Constitution. In addition, courts are subject to the dual leadership system, like any other entity. Thus, courts are subject to the Party Committee and other Party organizations at the same level, as well as to supervision by higher-level courts. The procuracy also exercises supervision over the judiciary, leading to the curious situation where procuratorates are subject to the authority of the court when they appear before the court as a prosecutor and yet they have the authority to challenge the "final" decisions of the court. The independence of the courts is further undermined by the way in which courts are funded. Courts in China are financed by governments at the same level. Thus, local courts are dependent on local governments for such basic necessities as the cost of court buildings, computers, and other equipment, as well as the housing, salaries, bonuses, medical insurance, and other welfare benefits of judges and staff.

Moreover, while the court as a whole is supposed to enjoy functional independence in handling cases, individual judges generally do not have the right to decide cases on their own. Most cases are heard by a collegiate panel of three judges. Further, until recently, the collegiate panel often was required by internal court rules or practice to obtain the approval of the division head, vice-president, president, or the court's adjudicative committee before issuing the judgment. Thus, the administrative rank of judges has been important in determining the final outcome, even though a higher administrative rank is not necessarily correlated with more legal knowledge.[4]

There are, in short, too many *popo* (mothers-in-law), as the popular saying goes. The lack of independence, however, is by no means the only challenge confronting the judiciary. The judiciary also suffers from various technical shortcomings and lacks adequate power and authority within China's current constitutional structure.

Many of the most typical complaints about the legal system by PRC citizens and foreign investors are technical in nature. For instance, litigants often complain that the courts charge too much and that they impose unauthorized fees. They also object to long delays in completing cases, and criticize the courts for being slow and inefficient. Although there are some 300,000 judicial personnel, including 180,000 judges,[5] cases can drag on for years.[6] Parties also regularly complain about the lack of transparency, the low level of competence of judges, and judicial corruption.

In defense of the courts, given the judiciary's limited powers under the current constitutional structure and its low stature within the polity, judges often are in the unenviable position of fighting battles with one hand tied behind their back. As in some civil law countries, the courts are supposed to apply the law rather than make it or even interpret it. Nor are they allowed to conduct judicial review or strike down government regulations inconsistent with higher legislation. Although to suggest, as some commentators have, that the courts are simply another administrative entity and no more authoritative than the post office does a disservice to the courts, it is undeniable that the courts are institutionally weak, particularly relative to the historically stronger State Council.[7]

Party leaders, government officials, senior members of the judiciary, academics, and citizens have all emphasized the need to strengthen the judiciary, and a number of steps have been taken to address some of the problems.[8] Recent reforms include the implementation of an open trial system; the transition from an inquisitorial to a more adversarial trial method; the separation of the functions of accepting, hearing, supervising, and enforcing cases; changes in the way judges are appointed; the issuance of new rules to distinguish judges from administrative personnel within the court, with higher qualification standards for both, including a unified judicial examination for incoming judges; the implementation of a system where presiding judges are selected based on merit and given more power, and a rotation system for senior judges, who are to be selected from the best judges in lower-level courts, lawyers, and academics; the campaign to require judges to include legal analysis and reasoning in their judgments, with at least some opinions to be published; and a variety of reforms to overcome the serious problems of judicial corruption and the inability of courts to enforce their judgments. Other initiatives have focused on budgetary issues and the need to improve the material facilities of courts.

Whether such reforms alone will be sufficient to produce the type of judiciary necessary for rule of law is doubtful, however. To set the background, I begin with an overview of the judiciary and its competence and then turn to the complicated issue of judicial independence, before discussing judicial authority and ending with an assessment of current reforms and a discussion of the need for deeper institutional reforms. I argue that comprehensive judicial reform is required. There must be improvements in judicial competence and efficiency, authority, and independence. However, judicial reforms must be sequenced and implemented in accordance with the judiciary's institutional capacity to change. Suddenly providing more authority and independence to incompetent and corrupt judges could result in more rather than fewer wrongly decided cases, which would then further undermine the legitimacy of the legal system.[9] On the other hand, it will be difficult to attract and retain qualified personnel to the judiciary without increasing the authority and independence of the courts. Accordingly, a series of incremental reforms is required whereby the authority and independence of the courts is increased over time as the judiciary becomes more competent and capable of handling the additional responsibility.

The judiciary at a glance

Although there are a number of studies of the structure, internal organization, and basic operations of people's courts, a brief overview is in order because the breadth and pace of reform has rendered many of the available accounts out-of-date in significant respects.[10] The system is still in a state of flux, with considerable variation from place to place and court to court. Accordingly, one can only provide a snapshot. At the same time, judicial reform will be a long process. Many of the issues are incapable of immediate resolution. Moreover, the manner in which different conceptions of rule of law become manifest in particular institutions such as the judiciary is likely to endure for some time. Thus many of the issues and topics are of more than transient concern.

The structure of the courts

There are four levels of courts in China: the Supreme People's Court (SPC), High People's Courts (HPC), Intermediate People's Courts (IPC), and Basic People's Courts (BPC). The SPC is responsible for interpretation of laws, administration of the judiciary, and adjudication, and also participates in certain legislative activities.[11] In practice, the SPC handles a limited number of cases, and recently has further reduced its caseload. HPCs are provincial-level courts established in the capital of provinces, directly administered centers such as Beijing or Shanghai, and autonomous regions such as Xinjiang. There are almost 400 IPCs, established in municipalities and prefectures. There are over 3,000 BPCs established in urban districts and rural counties. Some 80 percent of judicial personnel work in BPCs.[12] There are also some 17,000 People's Tribunals (*renmin fating*).[13] BPCs may establish people's tribunals as needed, without reference to geographical administrative jurisdictions.[14] A judgment of a People's Tribunal has the same legal effect as a BPC judgment. In addition, there are specialized courts that handle specific types of cases such as maritime, military, railroad, and forestry.

Internally, PRC courts are divided into substantive and administrative divisions. The substantive divisions include criminal, civil, administrative, case filing, judicial supervision, petitions and appeals, intellectual property, juvenile, and enforcement divisions. The SPC has recently reorganized the substantive divisions. In the past, there was an economic division in addition to the civil division.[15] The economic division has now been folded into the civil division, which has four sections: Section One for marriage, family, and real property; Section Two for contract and torts; Section Three for Intellectual Property; Section Four for maritime and foreign investment disputes. The SPC has also ordered the reorganization and downsizing of administrative divisions.[16] Administrative divisions include, among others, a research office, a supervision office, planning and finance section, an administration and equipment department, and a political department, which is involved in ideological work, policy, and personnel matters. With SPC approval, courts may establish additional divisions. For example, some courts have established bankruptcy and real estate divisions.

As discussed below, there are also various Party organs within the court, including the Party Group (*dangzu*), the Party Institutional Unit (*jiguan danwei*), and Party cells (*dangzhibu*). In addition, there is an adjudicative committee (*shenpan weiyuanhui*), consisting of the president of the court, vice-presidents, department chiefs, and senior judges. Its main task is to ensure quality control by deciding major or complicated cases and supervising the collegiate panels that decide other cases.

Every court is headed by a president. There are also several vice-presidents, some in charge of substantive matters and some in charge of administrative matters. In addition, each division has a division chief and may have one or more deputy chiefs. Judicial personnel are divided into judges (*faguan* or *shenpanyuan*) who hear cases and carry out adjudication work and administrative personnel, including secretaries and court police. Judges are divided into presiding judges (*shenpanzhang*), regular judges, and assistant judges. In addition, judges have an administrative rank based on their seniority.

The president of the court exercises considerable power within the court. He decides whether to submit cases to the adjudicative committee, though that power has been limited recently by SPC regulations to be discussed shortly. He may also play a role in assigning cases, and has an important voice, though not necessarily a decisive one, in recruitment, promotions, transfers, and removals. In addition, the president is responsible for interacting with other organs, including the local government and Party organs. As the president of the court is subject to the nomenklatura system, and generally acts as the intermediary between the

Political–Legal Committee and the court, the president may be expected to be sensitive to the Party's position on important cases. Because the president spends much of his time outside the court attending meetings, the vice-presidents handle much of the work of supervising daily operations. There are advantages to this arrangement, as the president often has a political rather than a legal background, whereas vice-presidents generally have legal training. Nowadays, in big cities such as Beijing, presidents usually have undergone legal training, and some have worked their way up through the ranks as judges.[17] Nevertheless, nationwide, the majority of presidents have little or no formal legal training. However, according to the 2001 amendments to the Judges Law, court presidents and vice-presidents must now be chosen from judges or others who have the qualification of judges.[18]

The courts in operation

A series of reforms designed to enhance efficiency and justice has altered every phase of the judicial process from the acceptance of the case to the trial, issuance of the opinion, and subsequent appeals. A basic requirement of rule of law is that people have reasonable access to the court system. Yet many citizens complain about the cost of litigation. Although court fees are relatively low, courts often impose unauthorized additional fees, usually because they are inadequately funded. The SPC has attempted to respond to the charges of excessive and irregular fees by clarifying the fee schedules and allowing courts to reduce litigation fees to as low as 30 percent for indigent parties.[19]

In the past, the same judge frequently was in charge of accepting a case, carrying out pretrial investigations, and then trying it. To reduce *ex parte* contacts between the judges hearing the case and the parties, different judges are now responsible for deciding whether to accept the case and trying the case. The new system is also supposed to enhance efficiency. One typical complaint has been that cases take too long to complete, although whether they take any longer than in the USA or other countries with a mature legal system is doubtful. In any event, the SPC has tried to impose deadlines for completing cases, subject to extensions for valid reasons. Judges who fail to complete cases on time are subject to sanctions. Judges are also encouraged to make greater use of summary procedures to dispose of simple cases more quickly.[20]

Whereas in the past judges took the lead in investigating the facts of the case and in questioning the parties and witnesses, the responsibility for preparing the case, presenting arguments, and examining witnesses has now been transferred primarily to lawyers, particularly in criminal cases but also increasingly in civil cases. The court's job is to apply the law to the specific factual situation, not to create new law. Technically, cases do not have precedential value, although in practice courts may rely on the decisions of superior courts as guidelines.

As noted, judicial independence in China does not mean that individual judges decide cases on their own. Except for minor cases, all cases are decided by a collegiate panel (*heyi ting*) consisting usually of three judges or in some cases two judges and a lay assessor. One of the judges is the presiding judge (*shenpanzhang*). In addition, there is always a responsible judge (*chengban faguan*), although in some cases the presiding judge will also be the responsible judge. The presiding judge oversees the trial. However, the responsible judge's examination of the primary evidence often determines the outcome of the case, and the responsible judge is usually the one that writes the final opinion.

Until recently, the collegiate panel often had to obtain the approval of the division chief, division committee, court president, or adjudicative committee before issuing the final judgment. The cumbersome approval process often led to long delays. Furthermore, because the judges on the panel who nominally decided the case had no real power, the approval process undermined their sense of professional responsibility and their social status. New rules issued in 1999, however, give more power to the presiding judge of the collegiate panel and sole judge in summary proceeding cases.[21] The collegiate panel or single judge now has the right to decide most cases, and the president is not allowed to interfere.[22] However, approval is still needed in major or difficult cases, or where there are major differences of opinion among the collegiate panel.[23]

So-called major (*zhongda*) or difficult (*yinan*) cases typically include certain criminal cases such as death penalty cases or economic crime cases involving corruption, bribery, or smuggling; cases involving large sums of money or that have a significant impact on the local or national economy, such as where an adverse judgment would cause a company to go bankrupt; cases in which the higher-level court will overturn a "precedent" or the decision of a lower-level court; significant cases involving foreign investors; and politically sensitive cases.[24] Cases may be politically sensitive because they involve a prominent political figure, dissidents, or social organizations such as Falungong. Or they may involve potential conflicts between the judiciary and other state organs, for example administrative litigation suits against government entities or criminal cases in which the court acquits the defendant and the procuracy petitions for reconsideration (*kangsu*).

The adjudicative committee decides cases by a majority vote, usually on the basis of an oral or written report by the responsible judge of the collegiate panel that heard the case. Thus, the president cannot necessarily determine the outcome. All votes and comments are recorded. The collegiate panel must follow the adjudicative committee's decision. The adjudicative committee handles most cases on its own without the involvement of Party organizations.

As in some civil law countries, written decisions in China have usually been fairly brief and generally did not contain dissents nor extensive discussion of the reasoning of the court. However, judges are now expected to include legal analysis and reasoning in their opinions. In some cases, judicial opinions have swelled to twenty or thirty pages.[25] There is also a move to publish more judgments.[26] The SPC has vowed to publish some SPC rulings and judgments in the *People's Daily*, *Legal Daily*, and other newspapers as well as in the SPC Gazette and on the SPC webpage. Judgments are to be published within one month of issuance. Some commentators have suggested that judgments be announced immediately after the trial is completed in order to cut down on corruption. However, the suggestion is not practical in complicated cases, which require time to research all of the legal issues and write a reasoned opinion.

All decisions may be appealed once, with the appeal being a *de novo* review of both facts and law, as is the case in some civil law countries. Consistent with China's traditional emphasis on substantive over procedural justice, the PRC legal system allows disgruntled parties to challenge a "final" decision after appeal by petitioning for adjudication supervision. This procedure may be initiated by the court, interested parties, or the procuratorate in criminal, civil, or administrative cases.[27]

In contrast to other countries that assign the task of enforcing court judgments and orders to a marshal or the police, PRC courts are responsible for enforcing their own judgments. Enforcement of civil judgments and arbitral awards is notoriously difficult in China, with as many as 50 percent of judgments and awards going unenforced.[28] Being assigned to the enforcement division is not enviable, and judges in the enforcement division are often among the least legally trained. Scholars are divided as to whether courts should be involved in enforcement work. Some believe that enforcement is not a judicial function, but should be left to the public security as in other countries. Others counter that turning enforcement over to the public security would exacerbate local protectionism and increase the cost to the parties. Some commentators suggest that even if the courts are going to continue to handle enforcement, a distinction should be drawn between judges and enforcement personnel.[29]

A somewhat unique feature of litigation in China is the emphasis on formal mediation by the courts.[30] The responsible judge in charge of the case typically will attempt to mediate the dispute and encourage the parties to settle. Although a traditional *cum* Confucian preference for harmony and face-saving may explain in part the emphasis on mediation, other factors are arguably more important. Mediation generally decreases the workload of the judges, who are able to dispose of the case without the need for a formal trial. Moreover, judges who are unsure of their grasp of the law and afraid of being overturned on appeal – and hence running the risk of having their salaries reduced – clearly have an incentive to resolve the dispute without the need for a final determination by the court. The difficulty of enforcing judgments is also a factor. Parties may be more likely to comply with the terms of their own settlement agreement than with the judgment of the court. As a result, there may be no need for compulsory enforcement, which saves judicial resources and allows the court to avoid the embarrassment of appearing impotent should they be unable to enforce their own judgments due to local protectionism or interference from political or party organs.

To be sure, there are a number of serious objections to formal mediation by the courts. Just how voluntary the process is remains open to debate. Most parties will find it difficult to resist the pressure to settle when the judge handling the case advises them that it would be in their best interest to do so. Judicial mediation also results in *ex parte* communications between the judge and the parties, increasing the likelihood of corruption. At minimum, the judge may be exposed to information that would otherwise not be admissible or would be challenged by the other side if presented in court. Despite scholarly criticism of judge-mediated settlements, the practice is likely to continue, though perhaps subject to various reforms that would introduce certain procedural safeguards to reduce the adverse affects of *ex parte* communications.

One of the more dramatic reforms in the last few years has been to open trials to the public. In March 1999, the SPC issued a regulation requiring open trials as a general rule.[31] If the court fails to hold an open trial, either the parties or the procuracy may challenge the court's judgment in a higher court, and the higher court should vacate the judgment and remand for a new trial. Many localities have also passed regulations calling for an open trial, including Beijing and Shanghai. By 1999, Shanghai's First Intermediate People's Court reportedly had open trials for all civil and economic cases of the first and second instance, and 40 percent of all second instance criminal cases and 37 percent of administrative cases.[32] Trials are now also regularly broadcast on television.

Nevertheless, a number of problems remain in the open trial system. Some courts lack courtrooms able to accommodate viewers. The open trial principle is also subject to limits, including an exception for cases that involve state secrets, personal privacy issues, divorce, trade secrets, and juveniles. In practice, access to politically sensitive cases is not easy. Foreigners, and especially foreign reporters, are still subject to restrictions. Although foreigners are supposed to be able to attend trials, they may need to obtain special permission.[33] Domestic reporters may also need prior approval in some cases, particularly administrative cases.

Technical competence

Decimated by the antirightist movement and the Cultural Revolution, the PRC judiciary suffers from a shortage of qualified judges. For many litigants seeking a just verdict and for reformers promoting rule of law, the low level of technical competence is a more serious problem than limitations on judicial independence. Even if the courts are independent, litigants will be thwarted in their efforts to obtain a just outcome in accordance with law if the judge or judges handling the case do not know the law. Meanwhile, legal reformers are hard-pressed to argue that poorly trained judges should be given more power and independence. Such arguments are all the more likely to fall on deaf ears when the judiciary is plagued by widespread corruption. Creating a qualified, professional, and honest judiciary is therefore a necessary prerequisite for rule of law.

A profile of judges: judicial competence and professionalism

Prior to the 1995 Judges Law, there were no requirements to be a judge except that one be a cadre. Until recently, there have been four main paths to becoming a judge. A minority of judges were law school graduates who entered the judiciary directly upon graduation, or law professors and legal researchers. In practice, many of those entering the judiciary directly from law school relied on their connections while more qualified graduates from top law schools found it difficult to enter.[34] Second, particularly during the 1970s and 1980s, judges were often drawn from the ranks of military officers. Government institutions, usually the procuracy and public security, or Party organs, such as the Political–Legal Committee, have been a third source for judges. Finally, lower-level personnel within courts were sometimes promoted to judges, based on their experience and connections. Thus, someone might start off as a court police officer equivalent to a bailiff, or a secretary who records the proceedings during trial. After several years, that person might be promoted to the enforcement division or be put in charge of accepting cases.

At the end of 1995, 80% of judges had at least *dazhuan* qualifications, which require a minimum of two years of legal training at college level.[35] However, only 5% had the equivalent of a four-year bachelor degree in law, and only 0.25% had graduate degrees.[36] As of 2000, a mere 19% of BPC presidents and vice-presidents, and 15% of judges and assistant judges, had four-year bachelor degrees, though not necessarily in law.[37]

The overall low level of competence of the judiciary has resulted in many incorrectly decided cases. In 1999, people's courts supervised and reviewed 96,739 cases, and corrected the judgment in 21,862 cases.[38] The alarmingly high level of wrongly decided cases has generated intense criticism by the citizenry, and threatens to undermine the legitimacy of the legal system.

In response, the authorities have passed a series of regulations and have taken a number of steps to reform the appointment system and to improve the quality of the judiciary, including requiring all judges to pass a national examination, raising the standards to qualify as a judge, requiring training for new judges before they assume their post and continuing legal education for sitting judges, making the promotion system more merit-based, and imposing sanctions if judges fail to perform their duties adequately.[39] Although the Judges Law required a national examination for new judges, the requirement has not been strictly enforced. By 2000, all new judges were required to take an examination, but each court prepared its own.[40] Moreover, some commentators complained that these examinations were much easier than the national examination for lawyers. As a consequence, lawyers tend to look down on judges as ill-trained government officials with a bureaucratic attitude.[41] In a development that caught many academics by surprise, the Judges Law was amended in 2001 to require judges to take a unified national judicial examination.[42]

Would-be judges must now also meet higher standards to qualify as a judge. Under the 1995 Judges Law, all judges were required to have a college education. However, the higher academic standards were somewhat deceptive. Candidates need not have studied law,[43] nor were they required to have a four-year degree (*benke*); a two-year degree (*dazhuan*) was sufficient. Indeed, many if not most judges obtained their *dazhuan* through part-time adult schools, where the education is more technical, less theoretical, and less rigorous.[44] In response to criticisms that the standards were still too low, the Judges Law was amended to provide that new judges must have a bachelor's degree in law or a bachelor's degree in some other subject combined with knowledge of law, plus two years of experience in legal work to become a judge in a lower court, or three years of work experience to be appointed to an HPC or the SPC. If one has a master's or Ph.D. in law or in another subject combined with equivalent legal knowledge, then only one year of experience is needed to become a judge in a lower court or two years of experience to be appointed to an HPC or the SPC.[45] Once they pass the examination, new judges are required to undergo three months' training before assuming their post.[46]

The Judges Law also addressed the issue of existing judges who lacked sufficient legal training, requiring that they either meet the standards for incoming judges or be removed. According to the SPC's five-year plan announced in 1998, unqualified judges are to be dismissed or transferred to non-adjudication posts. High and intermediate courts are supposed to work with the Party Organization Department (*zuzhi bu*) to investigate presidents and vice-presidents of basic courts. The SPC is then supposed to review their report.[47] Division chiefs are also supposed to be examined by the end of 2000.[48]

Reforms to make promotion more merit-based will also reward more qualified judges and encourage others to raise their level of competence. New graduates must generally start in lower courts, and work their way up. Supreme and high court judges are now to be selected from lower-level judges with at least five years' experience, and from academics and elite lawyers.[49] In the lower courts, BPC presidents who in the past were often appointed based on their political background rather than their legal skill are now supposed to meet the qualification requirements for judges.[50] As of the end of 2001, BPC presidents are to be selected from among the best judges in the court, and should be around thirty-five years old, with at least five years of trial experience.[51] Upon promotion to president or vice-president, all judges must undergo three months' training.[52]

Presiding judges are to be chosen by means of competitive selection.[53] Presiding judges in the SPC and HPCs must have at least a four-year college degree in law and five years' trial experience. In general, IPC presiding judges should have a four-year college degree in law and four years of trial experience, whereas BPC judges need at least a two-year *dazhuan* and three years' trial experience. Presiding judges must also possess superior verbal and written communication skills. If courts in remote areas are not able to meet these standards, they must obtain the approval of the next higher-level court to appoint presiding judges with lower qualifications. In 1999, the SPC selected forty-seven presiding judges based on competition and open assessment, and more than half were under forty-five years old.[54] By the end of 2001, all presiding judges are supposed to be selected through an open competition.[55]

In an effort to produce a smaller but more professional corps of administrative personnel, the SPC has called for an end to the practice of promoting administrative personnel to judges, and taken steps to distinguish between judges and other personnel.[56] SPC President Xiao Yang has announced plans to reduce the overall number of staff members by 10% and increase the percentage of judges among the total judicial staff from 59% to 72%.[57] He has also promised new regulations regarding the responsibilities, qualifications, and administration of clerks.[58]

In 1999 alone, 540 judicial staff members were dismissed or resigned while 1000 judges were transferred to posts that did not involve trial work.[59] It is true that the number dismissed or transferred only amounts to a small percentage of China's judges and judicial administrative personnel. However, the SPC has promised to accelerate the pace of removing unqualified judges and administrative personnel. Notably, given the higher requirements for qualifying as a judge and the campaign to get rid of unqualified judges, there will be fewer appointments of former military officers, a practice widely criticized in the foreign and domestic press and academic journals.[60] Indeed, the number of former military officers acting in a judicial capacity is already decreasing. Many have retired or will retire in the near future, while others have been switched to administrative positions within the court or been assigned to the corps of court police. In the SPC, for the most part only those former military officers who have gone on to obtain legal education are still serving as judges. The practice in lower-level courts appears to vary from place to place and court to court, though many still have military officers serving as judges.[61]

The SPC has also intensified efforts to provide judicial training.[62] For years, the SPC has trained HPC judges at the National Judges Institute (or its predecessor). HPCs in turn are responsible for training other judges. The SPC is currently in the process of training on a rotating basis all HPC and IPC presidents, vice-presidents, and division chiefs. The training of presidents, who spent twenty days at the National Judges Institute, was completed in 2000. The SPC then began to train vice-presidents. At the lower levels, all BPC judges are supposed to undergo training by the end of 2002.[63] Further, all judges are to undergo at least one month of training every three years.[64] In addition, intellectual property courts have been established in a number of cities, with judges in these courts receiving specialized training in intellectual property matters.

Reforms to the trial process have put pressure on judges to improve their performance. After twenty years of legal development, there is a much more substantial and technical body of law for judges to master. The move away from an inquisitorial to an adversarial system requires judges to rule on evidentiary issues in response to the objections of legal counsel. Judges must also deal with increasingly well-trained lawyers, who make increasingly sophisticated and complex legal arguments. As noted, they are now required to write more extensive judgments that set forth their reasoning and legal analysis rather than just reciting the facts of the case and stating the conclusion. With trials open to the public, judges are subject to scrutiny by the media and the citizenry. Judges must also bear in mind that they may be sanctioned for their mistakes under new rules that hold judges accountable for incorrect decisions.

In contrast to many countries, PRC judges do not enjoy life tenure. Rather, they are appointed for an open term, and continue to serve until they are removed. The Judges Law sets out various sanctions for judges, including dismissal.[65] Judges may be dismissed for lack of competence, poor health, or for engaging in various forms of misconduct such as embezzling money, extorting confessions by torture, or falsifying evidence. Some of the grounds for dismissal involve political considerations, such as divulging state secrets, spreading statements that damage the prestige of the State, joining illegal organizations, participating in assemblies, processions, demonstrations, or strikes against the State and the catch-all "failing to perform a judge's duty." However, judges may challenge a decision to impose sanctions or dismiss through an internal appeals process, appealing first to the organ that made the decision and then to the next highest level.[66] People's congresses at the same level are responsible for removing judges, while their standing committees may remove vice-presidents and division chiefs.[67] Despite the potential for abuse, the problem to date has not been that too many judges are being removed for political reasons but rather that too few judges are being dismissed for incompetence or corruption.

While in office, judges are guaranteed economic security in the sense that their salaries are to be increased regularly if they perform adequately. However, judicial salaries are quite low, and subject to wide regional variation.[68] In some poor jurisdictions, judges occasionally have not been paid their salaries.[69] Further, judges may have their salaries docked if they perform poorly. Some courts reduce a judge's salary, for example, when the percentage of cases overturned on appeal or remanded for further consideration exceeds a certain amount. Moreover, funding for the court as a whole is often inadequate. Many courtrooms in poor rural areas consist of nothing more than a desk and a few chairs. Needless to say, courts often lack computers and other modern equipment, making legal research and dissemination of information, including the publication of judgments and rulings, difficult.

The lack of funding has led to a number of problems in the operation of the courts. Courts, for instance, sometimes knowingly exceed their jurisdiction in accepting a case in order to obtain the case acceptance fees. Courts have also been known to impose quotas on judges to collect fees, to illegally confiscate property or freeze bank accounts, or to arbitrarily increase the amount of bail. Some even set up separate bank accounts and go into business to raise funds, though the practice is now prohibited, and all courts have been ordered to cut their ties to commercial businesses.[70] Even when funding is adequate, the reliance of the courts on local governments for their expenses undermines their independence.

Corruption

Any discussion of the technical competence of judges, the operation of the courts, or judicial independence must take into account the serious problem of judicial corruption. Rampant corruption within the courts has badly tarnished the image and stature of the judiciary. Stories abound of various forms of judicial malpractice such as judges demanding bribes, meeting *ex parte* with parties in restaurants or Karaoke bars, and demanding that parties fund lavish "investigation trips."[71] Lawyers have recounted instances where they received calls late at night to go to settle a bill run up by judges and their friends at restaurants and saunas or to pay for the shopping expedition of a judge who "forgot" her purse. In one case, a judge told a lawyer that the judgment the lawyer's client had been eagerly awaiting was about to be issued but that the process was taking longer than expected because the judge's old computer was too slow. He also mentioned in passing that if he only had one of the latest X brand laptops the process would no doubt be expedited considerably. Interestingly, some cities have reputations for being more corrupt than others. Judicial corruption is considered more serious in Beijing and Guangdong than in Shanghai, for instance.[72]

Reliable statistics on the scope of corruption are not available for obvious reasons. However, even official accounts acknowledge that the corruption is becoming more serious and widespread.[73] The SPC reported that in 1995 more than 1,000 court personnel were found guilty of violating their professional responsibilities, of which 47 (including 34 judges) were guilty of crimes.[74] The 1996 Supreme People's Procuratorate Work Report stated that 3,792 members of the judiciary were investigated for crimes, an increase of almost 40 percent over the previous year, including 1,055 cases of illegal personal enrichment, an increase of 100 percent over the previous year.[75] In response to protests by the public and NPC over judicial corruption, incompetence, and inefficiency, the SPC began an "educational rectification campaign" in the spring of 1998. The six-month campaign resulted in 12,000 citizen reports of illegal activities by courts and prosecutors, the disciplining of nearly 5,000 judges and prosecutors, and the correction of 8,110 mishandled cases.[76]

To what extent judicial corruption affects the outcome in particular cases is not clear. In some cases, judges extort bribes from both the plaintiff and the defendant, suggesting that the final result may be a wash. In other cases, the facts and law may be so clear that no judge would be willing to risk being charged with intentionally deciding a case incorrectly due to corruption. At most, a corrupt judge may be able to delay the day of reckoning or reduce the amount of damages owed. Whatever the outcome in specific cases, judicial corruption has a serious negative impact on the legal system as a whole. Corruption impedes the development of the legal profession, and adversely affects the relationship between lawyers and judges. Lawyers are forced to rely on their connections rather than legal arguments to win cases and earn a living.[77] As a result, they do not develop a respect for law or hone their legal skills. Many capable lawyers resent having to rely on connections or to take care of judges on the take, and look down on such judges as sleazy, incompetent bureaucrats. Judicial corruption is also one of the reasons why parties continue to rely so heavily on mediation and arbitration rather than litigation in court to settle disputes. Indeed, the China International Economic and Trade Arbitration Commission has long marketed itself by arguing that the courts are corrupt and incompetent. Perhaps most worrisome, scholars and senior leaders alike fear that corruption is threatening to erode further the authority of the courts and to undermine confidence in the Party and rule of law.[78]

Not surprisingly, therefore, the ruling regime has rushed to implement a variety of anticorruption measures. As an initial foray, the authorities ordered courts to divest themselves of their interests in money-making enterprises.[79] The SPC has also passed rules tightening up the recusal system.[80] The rules, which give parties the right to demand that judges be recused if they fail to withdraw voluntarily, clarify the circumstances for withdrawal, including when the judges have recommended lawyers to one of the parties, borrowed money or accepted gifts, dinner invitations, or other compensation such as repairs and furnishing of the judge's house from one of the parties or their lawyers or met *ex parte* with a party. The rules also prohibit the spouse, children, or parents of a judge or staff member of the court from appearing before the court as a lawyer. The rules apply to all judges, including the president of the court, vice-presidents, division heads, and members of the adjudicative committee.

The rules, however, only require judges to recuse themselves when their spouse or relative is a party or representing a party. Yet in many cases, the judges who handle the case do not make the final decision. As noted, the division chief, vice-president, president, and members of the adjudicative committee may play a pivotal role. Accordingly, litigants often have retained the spouses of senior judges to gain an advantage. The client then pays a very large fee to the spouse for his or her "legal services." To address this loophole, the SPC issued another regulation that goes one step further, prohibiting any immediate relative of a judge at the division level or above from undertaking legal services of any kind for compensation.[81]

The SPC's five-year reform plan would further attack corruption among the senior judges of the court by requiring that court presidents serve outside their home area. In addition, vice-presidents and division chiefs are to be rotated within the court.[82] Likewise, the shift to a presiding judge system where most cases are decided by the collegiate panel is intended to reduce the influence of senior judges over the outcome of particular cases. In addition, the SPC has passed a code of professional responsibility for judges. Some scholars and commentators have suggested that greater reliance on lay assessors would reduce corruption. Some have even suggested that China should adopt a jury system.[83]

Another approach to the problem of corruption has been to impose personal liability on judges for wrongly decided cases.[84] In keeping with the hierarchical administrative nature of the judiciary, HPC presidents must report to the SPC, provincial people's congress, and provincial Party committees if there are two or more major cases of judicial corruption within their province. In 1999, apparently ten of the thirty HPC presidents made reports to the SPC. In addition, the SPC appointed ten prestigious sitting and retired judges to serve as superintendents.[85] The SPC also promoted heightened scrutiny by the public and the media by backing open trials. Nevertheless, when the amendments to the

Judges Law were submitted to the NPC, delegates expressed concern that the focus was on internal supervision and not external supervision.[86] Accordingly, some delegates called for more intensive supervision by people's congresses and procuratorates.

The impulse to subject judges to additional supervision is understandable in light of the seriousness of judicial corruption. On the other hand, penalizing individual judges for allegedly mistaken decisions could lead to abuse and be used to undermine the independence of judges who decide controversial cases in a way not favored by the government or other interested parties. Similarly, excessive interference by people's congresses and the procuratorate could undermine the independence of the court, while simply creating new channels for corruption. Ultimately, a balance must be drawn between judicial independence and judicial accountability. Given China's current circumstances where corruption is endemic, a drastic cure is required, at least until the situation is brought under control. Thus, for the time being, it may be necessary to hold judges to unusually strict standards. However, every effort should be made to ensure that judges accused of wrongdoing are prosecuted fairly and impartially. The case for enhanced individual case supervision by procuracy and people's congresses is more doubtful, however, for the reasons to be discussed shortly.

Judicial independence

Judicial independence is a multifaceted concept.[87] The most basic form of judicial independence, *substantive* or *decisional independence*, refers to the ability of judges to decide cases independently in accordance with law and without interference from other parties or entities. One of the prerequisites for decisional independence is that judges enjoy *personal independence*, which requires that their terms of office be secure: appointments and promotions should be relatively depoliticized; judges should be provided with an adequate salary, and should not be dismissed or have their salaries reduced as long as they are performing adequately; transfers and promotions should be fair and according to preestablished rules; and judges should be assigned cases in an impartial manner.

Interference may come from either external sources, such as the CCP, people's congresses, the government, administrative agencies, the procuracy, the military, or members of society, or from internal sources.

Internal independence therefore refers to the ability of judges to decide cases without regard to administrative hierarchies within the court and in particular without interference from senior judges. While the principle of external independence is accepted in China, the principle of internal independence is not. *External independence* includes both the decisional independence of judges in deciding cases without interference from external sources and the *collective independence* of the judiciary, that is, the ability of the judiciary as a whole and any individual court as a collective entity to function free from undue influence by other entities. Collective independence requires that the courts be adequately funded and that they have sufficient powers vis-à-vis other political organs for the legal system to function as a system of laws. Courts must not only be strong enough to resist pressure from outside forces in deciding cases; they must also have the authority and power to ensure that their judgments are enforced and that other political actors comply with their orders. At present, the PRC judiciary suffers from shortcomings with respect to decisional independence, external independence, internal independence, collective independence, and personal independence.

To be sure, the extent and nature of judicial independence and the institutional arrangements for realizing it vary from country to country, even among Liberal Democratic rule-of-law states. In the United States, courts are an independent branch with broad powers to hear all types of cases and strike down congressional laws or executive branch regulations. In parliamentary supreme states such as England or Belgium the courts are answerable to parliament, and have limited powers to overturn laws or government regulations.[88] In common law systems, courts play an active role in policy-making; in civil law countries, courts have limited powers to make or interpret law. While all agree that rule of law requires some separation between law and politics, the degree of separation and the forms it takes vary from place to place.[89] There is, for example, surprisingly wide variation with respect to the crucial issue of appointment of judges.[90] In some systems, judges are career civil servants who must pass an examination to enter the judiciary. In other countries, academics or political figures without any prior practice as a lawyer or judge may be appointed to the bench, with the executive, legislature, judiciary, and/or the ministry of justice responsible for appointments or involved in the appointment process. Alternatively, judges may be elected. Some countries allow judges to be members of political parties, and even to hold simultaneous posts in the executive branch or the legislature. While political affiliation is an important factor in appointments and elections in some countries, other systems strive to depoliticize the selection process.[91] Liberal democracies endorse freedom of thought and speech, yet many require judges to take an oath promising to uphold the constitution and to commit to regime norms such as rule of law and the promotion of human rights; and while some systems allow judges to speak out on political issues, others impose a duty of reserve.

With respect to the personal independence of judges, some systems grant judges life tenure, others only provide for a fixed term. As for collective independence, some courts are funded locally while others are funded centrally. In some countries, the judiciary prepares the budget, in others the executive and/or the legislature is involved in preparing or approving the budget. Moreover, while judges must enjoy a certain degree of independence, they must also be held accountable. Different systems employ various means to keep judges in line. Some rely on supervision by the legislature or the executive; some are self-regulating, with judges responsible for policing and disciplining themselves; others rely on media scrutiny and elections. Legal systems also differ with respect to the degree of internal independence. Courts tend to be more hierarchical in civil law countries than in common law countries. Accordingly, the views of senior judges may carry more weight in practice if not according to law. Senior judges in civil law systems may also exercise greater control over important administrative matters such as assignment of cases and personnel issues.

In light of such wide variation among Liberal Democratic rule-of-law states, significant divergence between countries with different conceptions of rule of law is to be expected. As discussed in Chapter 3, the very purpose of rule of law in a Statist Socialist system differs from that of a Liberal Democratic rule of law, with more emphasis placed on law's role in serving the interests of the state and ensuring social stability and somewhat less emphasis on law's role in protecting individual rights, which are also interpreted differently in a liberal democracy. Were Statist Socialists, Neoauthoritarians, and perhaps even Communitarians to have their way, judges would decide cases in accordance with the substantive normative principles set by state leaders. In the case of Statist Socialists, that would mean upholding the four cardinal principles and ensuring economic growth and social stability. Neoauthoritarians would downplay the importance of socialism and the Party's interests but would still require or at least encourage judges to take into consideration state policies when deciding cases. Indeed, one of the unusual features of the SPC from the perspective of a Liberal Democratic rule of law is the SPC's role in transmitting general policy guidelines to lower-level courts, as in the recent campaign that emphasized the need for lower courts to consider macroeconomic policies when deciding cases in accordance with law. Differences in ideology may also be reflected in a myriad of specific institutional choices and practices, such as the appointment process, the standards for promoting judges, and the manner in which judges are held accountable.

On the other hand, considerable convergence between countries with different conceptions of rule of law is also to be expected. Notwithstanding significant variation with respect to judicial independence among both similar and competing conceptions of rule of law, excessive dependence of the courts on political entities or interference by political organs in specific cases obliterates the distinction between law and politics, undermines the ability of the courts to impose meaningful restraints on political actors, runs afoul of both general rule-of-law principles such as the supremacy of the law and equality of all before the law, and specific thin rule-of-law requirements such as the need for impartial and fair outcomes based on law. Confronting such common problems, different forms of rule of law may opt for similar institutional arrangements and practices.

Ironically, China's long history of weak courts with little independence may facilitate convergence. While some countries may be able to adopt certain practices and still maintain sufficient judicial independence because of their historical traditions and a longstanding culture of legality and rule of law, given its history, China may need to err on the side of caution, and adopt international best practices that are most likely to ensure sufficient independence. Judicial independence will require changes in the way courts are funded and judges appointed. Moreover, as judicial independence in China is threatened by undue interference from the Party, people's congresses, procuracy, senior judges within the court, and members of society, the creation of an independent court will have wide-ranging consequences for the balance of power among state organs and require changes in the legal culture of China.

The Party's influence on the judiciary

For the near future at least, PRC courts will have to work within the current structure in which the Party exercises a leadership role. According to Xiao Yang, judicial reform must observe certain basic principles: in addition to promoting judicial independence in trying cases in accordance with law and reflecting China's current circumstances while taking into consideration the experiences of other countries, reforms must uphold the leadership of the Party, enhance the unity of the state, and be consistent with the present government structure based on the democratic dictatorship of the people and the supremacy of the people's congress.[92] In a single party socialist state, the Party will inevitably exercise some degree of influence over the courts. However, that does not mean that courts are simply Party organs, or that the Party controls every action of the courts or determines the outcome of all or even most cases. In practice, the Party influences the courts in various ways and through various channels. The Party primarily exerts influence in the areas of ideology, policy, and personnel matters, though it sometimes is involved directly in deciding the outcome of particular cases. The Party influences the courts externally through the Party Committee (*dang weiyuanhui*), the Political–Legal Committee (*zhengfa weiyuanhui*), and the Organization Department, and internally through the Party Group, Party Institutional Organ, Party cells, Political Department (*zhengzhi bu*), and perhaps in some cases the adjudicative committee within the courts. The Party Institutional Organ and Party cells have little power. They generally take instructions from the Party Group and are in charge of such day-to-day issues as developing Party members, handling applications to become a Party member, organizing political study sessions, and transmitting Party policies to Party members within the court.[93]

The Political–Legal Committee (PLC) usually includes the deputy Party secretary in charge of political–legal matters, the president of the court and procuracy, and the heads of various ministries or bureaus including public security, state security, justice, civil affairs, and supervision.[94] The PLC is one department within the Party organization; thus there is a PLC at each level, with the PLC answering to the Party Committee at the same level and the PLC at the next highest level. Relatively little is known about the actual workings of the PLC or the inner workings of PRC courts more generally, and what is known is based largely on anecdotal evidence rather than systematic empirical work. Variations from place to place and over time complicate the task of obtaining an accurate picture. Nonetheless, it is clear that the PLC is primarily responsible for ideological work through setting and disseminating policy, though it is also involved in the decision-making process for certain important or difficult cases and on occasion in personnel decisions. There are no formal requirements to be a member of the PLC. One need not have studied law; one need not even be a Party member. Most PLC members have little formal legal training, having risen up through the Party ranks.

The Party Group within the courts is generally headed by the highest- or second highest-ranking Party official and includes all or most of the vice-presidents, the head of the discipline inspection committee, and the head of the Political Department. It is responsible for ideological work, policy dissemination and implementation, and supervision and punishment of Party personnel for violations of Party discipline.[95] It is the most authoritative entity within the court. Although it rarely becomes involved in particular cases, when the adjudicative committee is deeply divided or there is an extremely sensitive case that has attracted the attention of Party organizations, the Party Group may intervene. When it does, its decision is final. The Party Group tends to consider the wider implications of a case in addition to more narrowly legal factors. By their nature, the cases are complicated, and may involve national or cross-regional interests or the interests of large groups of people such as farmers or laid-off SOE workers.

On the ideological front, the central PLC plays a key role in transmitting Party policies and in some cases initiating national policies for the courts. For instance, the PLC was instrumental in promoting the anti-crime Strike Hard campaign aimed at ensuring law and order. The PLC also took the lead in implementing the Jiang Zemin-backed *sanjiang* or "three stresses" campaign that focused on the need to emphasize politics, study, and virtue, and in spreading the more recent "three representatives" discussed in Chapter 5. In addition, the PLC has worked to strengthen the courts by attacking corruption or by trying to address enforcement issues. Such campaigns are not necessarily inconsistent with the rule of law. Governments everywhere rail against crime, and surely efforts to reduce judicial corruption or enhance enforcement deserve to be applauded. However, if Party organs get carried away in their zeal to crack down on crime or root out corruption and pressure the courts to meet certain quotas, judges may feel that they are being asked to deny the accused their rights or at least that their professional judgment is being sacrificed to satisfy political objectives.

From time to time, the SPC will promote state policies by issuing policy statements or guidelines to lower courts to consider when handling certain types of cases. For instance, the SPC issued the "Opinions on Playing Fully the Role of Adjudication to Provide Judicial Protection and Legal Services for Economic Development."[96] Such measures almost always are in response to policies first announced by the Party, the government, or people's congresses. Some commentators have argued that these broad policy statements are inconsistent with rule of law and an independent judiciary.[97] To be sure, such an active role for the judiciary in promoting state policies may be at odds with the liberal democratic notion of a neutral state. Moreover, one would expect in a Liberal Democratic rule-of-law system a greater degree of separation than in a Statist Socialist or Neoauthoritarian system in which the legal system serves the Party and state. However, the SPC is not asking lower courts to violate or set aside the law when deciding cases. Rather, lower courts are exhorted to make sure the cases are handled in accordance with law. To the extent that the laws are not clear, judges should bear in mind the basic principles that underlie the laws as well as the social and economic consequences of their decisions.[98]

Apart from making policy statements, the SPC sometimes submits draft legislation to the NPC and its Standing Committee or participates in the drafting process, as with the Judges Law and Lawyers Law. The SPC also issues numerous judicial interpretations, including interpretations of laws such as the Civil Procedure Law, Contract Law, and so on, as well as interpretations on specific provisions or issues. In addition, the Court promulgates regulations regarding the work of the courts. For instance, in early 2000, the SPC issued the Regulations of the Supreme Court Concerning Several Issues Related to the Unified Administration of Enforcement Work by the High People's Courts, and Certain Regulations for Strengthening and Improving Entrustment Enforcement Work. These regulations are considered to be interpretations of law.[99] Despite the Party's interest in policy-setting, Party organs appear to play little or no role in these quasi-legislative activities of the SPC. In some cases, the adjudicative committee might report to the Party Group that it will issue regulations, but it generally does not submit the regulations to the Party Group for review or approval.

In contrast, the Party is actively involved in judicial appointments and promotions. According to the Judges Law, people's congresses at the same level elect the president of the court. The president then nominates the vice-presidents, members of the adjudicative committee, division chiefs, and vice-chiefs. In reality, however, all appointments must be approved or vetoed by the Party Organization Department. The rank of the judge determines the level of the Party Organization Department and the degree of scrutiny. In some cases the approval (*pizhun*) of the Party organ at a higher level is required; in some cases the approval of the Party organ at the same level is sufficient; while for lower-level judges simply submitting the appointment to the Organization Department for the record (*beian*) is sufficient, although even in that case the Organization Department can still veto the appointments, though it rarely does. To illustrate, the president of a provincial-level HPC has a bureau chief rank (*juji*). Thus, the appointment must be approved by the Central Party Organization Department. The vice-president of an HPC has a vice-bureau chief rank (*fujuji*), and thus is approved by the Organization Department at the provincial level, with the appointment filed for the record with the Central Organization Department. An HPC division head (*tingzhang*) has a department-level rank (*chuji*), and must be approved by the provincial Organization Department.

The process of selecting candidates varies depending on the level of the judge. Recommendations for president or vice-president may come from higher-level courts, the Party Group, the Party Committee, Organization Department, or PLC. Other senior judges, including the division chiefs and vice-chiefs, are typically nominated by the vice-president in charge of that area, and approved by the Party Group.[100] The promotion of lower-level judges usually begins with a discussion among the division chief and vice-chief, who then recommend candidates to the Political Department. After review, the approval of the Party Group is sought. Various factors are considered when deciding whether to promote judges, including the judge's legal ability and technical skills, seniority, and age in comparison to other judges at a similar level. Whether the candidate is a Party member or other political considerations are increasingly less important. After the candidate has been selected, the Organization

Department then collects information on the recommendees and prepares the file where approval is necessary. Once the Party vetoing hurdle
is cleared, the people's congress at the same level formally appoints the
president, and the people's congress standing committee formally appoints the vice-presidents, division chief, and vice-chiefs. Although the
NPC apparently has yet to reject a candidate, provincial and lower-level
people's congresses have rejected candidates from time to time.

To what extent the Party's ability to appoint judges influences outcomes is difficult to determine. Because many Party members have
joined the Party to take advantage of opportunities for personal advancement rather than out of ideological commitment to socialism or
the Party, being a Party member tells us little about a judge's political or
legal views: one could be a reformer or conservative, in favor of rule of
law or against it. It is possible that Party members may be more likely
to follow the Party line more readily than non-Party members simply
to avoid jeopardizing their career. But most cases turn on legal issues
for which there is no Party line, or no clear Party line. In any event, advocates of Statist Socialist, Neoauthoritarian, and even Communitarian
rule of law may find it less objectionable than supporters of a Liberal
Democratic rule of law that judges are subject to an ideological litmus
test as part of the appointment process, or that they be expected to
decide certain cases in terms of a substantive normative agenda determined by state leaders.[101] Of course, even in liberal democracies, judges
are appointed based on their political views – the appointment of US
Supreme Court judges is only one of many examples.

Most worrisome from the perspective of any credible version of rule
of law is direct interference by the Party or political organs in the courts'
handling of specific cases. Although the Party no longer requires that
every case be approved by the Party, and has vowed not to interfere in
specific cases, in practice Party organs or individual Party members do
sometimes become involved in specific cases. Usually, the Party intervenes through the PLC. However, Party influence may also be brought
to bear through the Party Committee, individual Party members, the
adjudicative committee, or the president of the court.

The PLC might become involved in politically sensitive cases, cases
that could have a significant impact on the local economy, and cases
involving conflicts between the courts and the procuracy or government.
Even when the PLC becomes involved, it generally does not dictate the

outcome. Rather, it typically just makes a recommendation to the court. Alternatively, it may express an opinion on certain aspects of the case, such as the guilt of the accused, but leave it to the court to determine the punishment.

While Party interference in the handling of specific cases is objectionable from a rule-of-law perspective, the extent of direct Party intervention should not be overstated. The Party's only interest in the outcome of most cases, whether commercial, criminal, or administrative, is that the result be perceived as fair by the parties and the general populace. Accordingly, the CCP only rarely interferes in the handling of specific cases, and when it does, at least in commercial cases, it may do so to ensure that the result accords with law. Interference by local government officials is much more prevalent than Party interference.

According to a survey of 280 judges published in 1993, while almost 70% of the judges claimed that as a rule they were subject to outside interference, they cited the CCP as the source in only 8% of the cases. In contrast, government organs were the source of interference in 26% of the cases and social contacts in 29%.[102] Another survey of a hundred intermediate and basic-level court judges in Chongqing asked the question: "When you handle compulsory enforcement, what kind of interference do you regularly experience?" Forty-five percent responded no interference, while 12% cited interference from the CCP, in comparison to 32% from government departments, 15% from people's congresses, 12% internal pressures from within the court, and 11% outside interference.[103] Although 88% of judges in a survey of administrative law in Jiangsu cited the lack of judicial independence as an obstacle to effective implementation of the ALL, only 14% cited interference from the Party as a factor.[104] Still another survey of eighty-nine arbitral award enforcement cases in China found that while interference from local government officials was common, CCP interference was rare and usually only occurred when there was a personal connection between an individual Party member and the respondent against which enforcement was being sought.[105]

It is true, government officials generally wear two hats. Thus, it is not always easy or possible to distinguish between Party and government interference. In some cases, particularly cases of local protectionism, local Party cadres may share the interests of government officials in ensuring economic growth in the region. However, the interests and incentives of government officials *qua* government official will not always be identical to their interests and incentives *qua* Party member. Given the separation between the Party and state, the breakdown in Party discipline, the diminished importance of socialism as an ideology, the jaded motivations of many Party members for joining the Party in the first place, the professionalization of the civil service, and the changing incentive structure in the market economy, government officials may be expected to identify more with their government position than their Party affiliation. In his study of the Party and state, Shiping Zheng points out that a provincial governor who is also a deputy secretary of the provincial Party committee will be assessed mainly in terms of his performance as a governor – for which he is responsible.[106] In contrast, he has a more minor role on the Party committee, as he is only one member of a decision-making committee. Accordingly, Zheng argues that most government officials' primary allegiance is to their government post rather than to the Party. Because membership in the Party has less bearing on one's political preferences and actions than institutional affiliation and one's current position, legislators, judges, procurators, ministers, and provincial governors should arguably be treated as members of their particular institution rather than Party officials.

In any event, Party involvement in specific cases does not necessarily mean that justice is sacrificed. In some instances, Party interference may serve to ensure that the case is handled in accordance with law. In the aforementioned arbitration survey, most lawyers felt that the CCP on balance played a positive role. The explanation for why this would be so is straightforward: the ruling regime has invested considerable resources in attracting foreign investment and does not want China's reputation sullied by negative publicity. Thus, local counsel is often able to turn to the Party to attack local protectionism. And indeed there were three cases where the involvement of the secretary or other senior member of the CCP Committee or PLC appeared to be decisive or at least instrumental in securing enforcement.[107]

In the long run, reliance on the CCP to enforce the law is detrimental to the development of the legal system and realization of rule of law, even if it does produce short-term benefits in particular cases. The dominance of the Party and its concern with maintaining a tight grip on power have prevented the judiciary, and to some extent the legal profession, from achieving greater autonomy and independence. By turning to the Party whenever it suits their immediate interests, PRC lawyers undermine the efforts to build a system in which the Party must act in accordance with law and the law is supreme. In so doing, they undermine their own stature as an autonomous profession not beholden to the Party-state. Similarly, foreign investors in particular run the risk of appearing hypocritical when they turn to the Party for assistance after having vociferously demanded rule of law and the establishment of an independent judiciary.

People's congresses and the judiciary

As in some other countries where the parliament is supreme, China rejects US-style separation of powers. In China, the NPC is the highest organ of state power. Thus, although the judiciary enjoys a functional independence, the NPC has the right to supervise the judiciary. The NPC exercises influence over the judiciary through its role in the appointment and approval process, though real power lies with the Party. It also exercises various forms of supervision. Every year, the SPC must submit a work report to the NPC for review. In 1997, 31 percent of NPC delegates refused to approve the SPC's report. As a result, the SPC initiated a number of measures to address issues of concern to the delegates such as growing crime, enforcement difficulties, and corruption.[108] Since the appointment of Xiao Yang as the president of the SPC, the SPC's annual report has been more substantive and forthcoming about the problems confronting the judiciary than in the past.

People's congresses also conduct studies of the implementation of major laws.[109] The NPC has generally inspected implementation of three to five laws a year.[110] Sometimes the same law will be investigated repeatedly for several years running, as in the case of the Agriculture Law, Environmental Protection Law, and Law on Product Quality. The results have been mixed. The inspection of the Environmental Protection Law led to the promulgation of additional laws and regulations, heightened awareness of the importance of the Law, and injunctions against particular egregious acts of pollution. On the other hand, inspection of the Agriculture Law revealed continued imposition of heavy burdens on farmers but provided no solutions.[111]

People's congresses may also address inquiries to the courts regarding general issues, though they seldom do.[112] Much more common, and controversial, is their role in supervising individual cases. Concerns with judicial corruption have given rise in recent years to calls for a more active role for people's congresses in supervising the outcome of specific cases. Yet the current proposals to increase legislative supervision are fraught with danger. The NPC tried to pass a law in 1999 and 2000, but backed off in the face of serious opposition, especially from leading PRC legal scholars.[113] Undeterred, local people's congresses have jumped into the fray and issued their own regulations. In an attempt to regain some control over the process, the SPC issued regulations in 1998 laying out some ground rules for legislative supervision.[114]

Representatives will naturally want to protect the interests of their constituencies by challenging adverse decisions. Thus, the SPC has stressed the need for some procedure to decide which cases to investigate. Such a procedure should require more than just the support of a single member of the local people's congress or even the support of a small number in order to avoid local protectionist pressures. On the other hand, any procedure that would require the vote of a large number of representatives would be impractical and add to the already heavy burden of people's congresses. One possibility might be to establish a special subcommittee to make the final decision.

Given the risk to judicial independence, supervision should be subject to limits. For instance, the scope of investigation should be restricted to the legality of the decision (as opposed to its appropriateness) or perhaps even the narrow issue of whether the court's decision was negligent or due to corruption. Further, people's congresses should not have the power to impose their own will and dictate the outcome of the case. Rather, the case should be sent back for retrial by a new collegiate panel.

While one can appreciate the need to take steps to curtail the serious problem of corruption in the courts, whether emphasizing supervision is the best way is debatable. Creating new channels for supervision simply creates new channels for corruption, particularly in the absence of procedural safeguards. As such, it raises the issue of who will supervise the supervisors?

Local governments and the judiciary

In the modern era of the regulatory state, administrative agencies play a large role in making, interpreting, and implementing regulations. As will be discussed in Chapter 9, some commentators view the wide powers ceded to administrative agencies as inconsistent with or at least a threat to rule of law. Others, accepting reality, reconcile the role of agencies with rule of law by noting that except in rare circumstances, the powers of government agencies are subject to various restraints, including review by a court or special administrative tribunal. In China, however, the courts are often unable to hold the government in check. Indeed, as we have seen, interference from government officials is one of the most common forms of external interference and a much more serious threat to the independence of the courts in the vast majority of cases, particularly administrative and commercial cases, than the Party. Government officials are able to pressure judges to find in favor of the administrative agency in administrative litigation cases or of local companies in commercial disputes because of the institutional arrangement whereby the local people's congresses appoint and remove judges and the local government funds the courts.

Of course, a number of other factors besides the way courts are funded and judges appointed contribute to local protectionism, including economic reforms.[115] Economic reforms have led to a devolution of authority, and fiscal responsibility, to local governments. Cut off from central government subsidies, local governments must rely on tax revenues generated from local companies to meet their budgetary needs. State-owned enterprise reforms have also led to increased unemployment, adding social welfare and retraining costs to the already strained budgets of local governments. Local governments worry that enforcement of an adverse judgment or award could result in the loss of key equipment or the closing of a factory. Increased unemployment not only causes budgetary problems but may lead to social unrest. To further complicate matters, in some cases, local governments may be a shareholder of the defendant and thus have a direct economic interest in the outcome.

Local protectionism may take many forms, some more serious than others. Local government officials may put pressure on a court to decide a case in favor of the local party, deny an outsider's application for enforcement, or just drag out the enforcement process, usually by requesting additional documents or leaving a case pending. Local protectionism is therefore a matter of degree: it may impede, or be an absolute bar to, recovery.[116]

Local governments are not free to engage in protectionism as they wish. Concerned that local governments are undermining central policies and impairing healthy economic development, the central authorities have attempted to rein in local protectionism, even going so far as to declare 1999 the Year of Enforcement. Similarly, local courts cannot simply take their orders from the government, even were they so inclined; they must also answer to higher courts. However, as discussed in Chapter 5, the central government's leverage over local governments has decreased as a result of reforms. Reliance on hortatory campaigns to rein in local officials is not sufficient, and indeed that is one reason why central leaders have backed legal reforms and efforts to strengthen rule of law. Yet the effectiveness of the courts in combating local protectionism is limited by the current funding and appointment system. Thus, without deeper institutional reforms to the judiciary that would decrease the dependence of the courts on local governments and people's congresses, local protectionism will remain a problem.

The procuracy, public security, and police

During the Mao era, the courts, procuracy, and public security, including the police, were supposed to work together to serve the interests of the state; they were to join together in a tightly clenched fist to smash crime. Legal reforms over the last two decades have increased the functional independence, professionalism, and specialization of each institution, leading to tensions among them. Rather than forming a tight fist, each finger is now used, often as not, to point blame at others for rising crime or to warn them that they are overreaching their authority.

That reforms would produce tensions among the formerly united institutions is to be expected. Historically, the public security was the strongest institution, especially during the Cultural Revolution when the procuracy was shut down and the judiciary weakened. Even now, the head of the PLC at times may be the chief of public security. Such an arrangement may lead to conflicts if the head of public security uses his position on the PLC to try to impose his way on the courts and the procuratorate.[117] Meanwhile, under the PRC constitution, the procuracy has the right to supervise the courts, and thus views itself as superior to the courts. On the other hand, although the courts generally have been considered the weakest of the troika, reforms have given them an increasingly important role, particularly with respect to commercial matters. For all of their faults, judges tend to be better educated than procuratorates, and to enjoy a higher social status. Moreover, procuratorates appear before the court as a party to a dispute and must observe the rules of the court and obey the court's orders.

As in other countries, there are also institution-based differences in the worldviews of judges, prosecutors, and police. The rank and file of the procuracy, public security, and police tend to be more supportive of statist ideology and the need for law and order than judges. Thus, the public security and procuracy strongly opposed certain amendments to the Criminal Procedure Law that would limit the use of deadly force in apprehending suspects, provide suspects with the right to counsel at an early stage, or bar illegally obtained evidence.[118]

Not surprisingly, the various institutions have often clashed over which is superior, with each battling mightily to protect its turf. The struggle for power has led to the judiciary and procuracy issuing inconsistent interpretations of key legislation,[119] the procuracy objecting during the drafting of the Law on Legislation to the SPC's practice of interpreting laws, and even the refusal by members of the procuracy to stand, as required by court rules, when the presiding judge enters the courtroom.[120] Similarly, the police and procuratorates have been accused of failing to cooperate with judges in trials by not appearing when they are supposed to or not turning over evidence or documents as requested. There are also numerous reports of police harassing and physically abusing lawyers who try to meet with their clients, as well as reports of lawyers who are arrested on trumped up charges of harboring criminals or conspiring in crimes. As the prevailing dominant authority, the Party is often forced to intervene to mediate such disputes between the various institutions.

In light of such hostilities, one area ripe for future reform is the procuracy's right to supervise the court. Procuracy supervision may be of a general nature, where for instance the procuracy investigates allegations of corruption within the courts. Alternatively, and more objectionable, the procuracy may supervise individual cases by challenging final court decisions even after the normal appeals process has been completed.[121] Procuratorates may petition to have both criminal and civil cases reconsidered. Until recently, procuratorate petitions were relatively uncommon, particularly in civil matters. In light of the new emphasis on supervision, however, the procuracy is apparently taking its responsibility more seriously and regularly challenging court decisions even in civil cases.[122] In 1999, procuratorates protested court judgments in 14,069 cases (out of a total of over 5.5 million). Courts ended up revising the judgment in 3,185 cases, while upholding the judgment in 3,751 cases. The procuracy withdrew the application in 951 cases; the court retried 1,429 cases, and resolved 4,752 cases through mediation.[123] Such zeal on the part of the procuracy threatens to further undermine the independence and the authority of the court, and again raises the issue of who will supervise the supervisors? Moreover, in the charged atmosphere where both the judiciary and procuracy are battling for power, the procuracy's right to challenge the final decisions of the courts exacerbates tensions between the two institutions.

The relation between higher- and lower-level courts

Normally one does not think of higher-level courts as a threat to judicial independence. However, judicial independence may be undermined when higher courts exert undue influence on lower courts outside the normal channels of appeal. In the PRC, higher-level courts are responsible for supervising lower-level courts, with supervision taking various forms. Like courts everywhere, PRC courts directly supervise the work of lower courts by reviewing their decisions on appeal. Further, the SPC provides guidance to lower courts by promulgating interpretations, issuing internal regulations, setting policies, and deciding cases that have quasi-precedential value. Higher courts may also play a role in the appointment, promotion, and disciplining processes of judges, particularly senior judges, in lower courts.

In addition, higher courts often engage in a longstanding practice of responding to inquiries from lower courts for advice regarding legal issues in particular cases currently before the lower court. Lower court judges may request advice formally in writing or sometimes less formally by telephone. The lower courts are not bound by the higher court's answer, though in most cases the higher court's advice will be followed or at least given great weight.[124] Scholars have criticized the practice for depriving the litigant of the right to appeal, since the higher court will already have decided key issues, albeit in the absence of a complete record and without the parties having had the opportunity to present their case. Despite scholarly opposition, the practice is likely to continue. Although Xiao Yang recommended that lower-level courts assume more responsibility in deciding cases on their own in order to speed up trials and to ensure that the rights of the parties are better protected, he accepted if not encouraged the practice of lower-level courts seeking instructions from higher courts where there are issues of interpretation or application of law in major or complicated cases.[125] Nevertheless, in practice, lower-level courts reportedly are seeking instruction from higher courts less and less, with the frequency varying from court to court and judge to judge.

In any event, the power of higher-level courts should not be overstated. Higher-level courts are often unable to control lower-level courts. Many courts openly defy the orders of their superiors, even if those orders emanate from the Supreme Court. For instance, few lower courts seem to take seriously the six-month time limit for completing enforcement of a court judgment or arbitral award imposed under the Enforcement Regulation. Many courts defeat the purpose of the SPC's 1995 notice to facilitate enforcement of arbitral awards by just sitting on enforcement cases.[126] Moreover, in several cases, when the SPC or members of the SPC have intervened and ordered the lower court to enforce the awards, the lower courts simply disregarded the court's order.[127]

In one widely publicized case involving a civil judgment, a Guangdong construction company sought enforcement of a $900,000 judgment against a Hainan company.[128] The Guangdong company applied for enforcement in May 1996 in Haikou. The Haikou court suspended enforcement without explanation. The SPC then instructed the Haikou basic-level court to execute the judgment immediately. However, the Hainan Audit Office intervened to dispute the amount. The plaintiff took the case to the media. In response to a June 1997 article in the *People's Daily* about the case, the SPC again ordered the local court to execute the judgment, once again to no avail. Despite further articles in the *People's Daily*, the local court continued to resist enforcement.

Social pressures

As indicated in the surveys cited previously, social pressures from relatives, friends, and acquaintances are a major source of outside interference. In a society that places a premium on *guanxi* (personal networks) and *renqing* (human feelings or empathy), judges often find themselves besieged by intermediaries seeking to intervene on behalf of a criminal suspect or one of the parties in a commercial dispute. After the arrest of one particular individual, police had to post a sign on the door of the station saying "those who come to appeal to our sympathy (*jiang renqing*), stop."[129] Yet judges who refuse to at least listen to the entreaties of their friends and family will be considered to lack human feeling and run the risk of being social outcasts.

Admittedly, personal connections come into play to some extent in every country, as do human feelings. Moreover, implementation of rule of law in China will inevitably reflect China's national characteristics, including the importance of *guanxi* and *renqing*. Accordingly, personal networks and social norms may play a somewhat greater role at the margins than in other systems. At the same time, however, rule of law requires impartial application of laws and a fair resolution of disputes. Confucius may have been right that a truly humane society requires humane individuals attuned to the needs of others, filled with a spirit of human empathy. But in the absence of a society of sagely *junzi* (moral exemplars), judges must be able to resist social pressures to render a fair verdict in accordance with law. PRC citizens must come to learn and accept and perhaps one day appreciate, as have citizens in Taiwan, Hong Kong, and other Asian countries, that there are limits to empathy and personal connections.

The authority of the courts

The authority of the judiciary is weakened not only by its institutional dependence on local government and the CCP and its vulnerability to other external and internal influences, but also by the limited powers granted courts within the PRC governmental structure. As in many civil law countries, courts in China do not have the power formally to make law. In practice, of course, courts everywhere "make law," to the extent that they are allowed to interpret law, and such interpretations are then taken as binding in the particular case and on lower courts in subsequent cases. In that limited sense, both lower and higher courts make law in the PRC. Indeed, the SPC makes law even more directly in a variety of ways, including the issuance of official opinions, explanations or other forms of interpretation of laws, and the publication of model cases, as well as through its participation in the law-making process for laws that relate to the legal system.[130] Nevertheless, the power of courts to make law is much more limited than in a common-law precedent-based system.

Perhaps most surprising to Westerners, particularly from common law countries, is the severely circumscribed interpretative authority of PRC courts. Although under the Constitution the NPC Standing Committee has the exclusive authority to interpret laws enacted by the NPC and the Standing Committee itself, it has delegated this authority to the SPC, Supreme People's Procuratorate, and State Council.[131] Despite this delegation of interpretative authority, numerous restrictions remain on the SPC's interpretative powers. Significantly, the NPC did not delegate to the SPC the right to interpret the Constitution. Thus, as discussed in Chapter 6, neither the SPC nor any other court has the authority to conduct judicial review and strike down laws or regulations on the ground of unconstitutionality. Indeed, neither the SPC nor any other court has the right to interpret or declare invalid administrative regulations or regulations passed by the people's governments or people's congresses, although courts may refuse to enforce a regulation contrary to national law. The State Council, the highest administrative entity in the PRC, and its subordinate ministries and agencies, are responsible for interpreting administrative and local government regulations.[132]

Further, the Court was only given the right to interpret laws where necessary for judicial work. That is, the Court is supposed to limit its interpretation to that necessary to decide issues that have arisen, or arguably are likely to arise, in specific cases. Moreover, the interpretative powers of the Court in theory are limited to clarifying laws without altering their original meaning or adding to their content. In practice, however, the SPC has pushed the limits of its delegated authority, issuing a number of general interpretations of key laws. The Court's opinion on the General Principles of Civil Law, for example, consisted of some 200 articles, while the General Principles of Civil Law itself only contained 156 articles. The SPC has had little choice but to issue such interpretations given the failure of the NPCSC to issue interpretations as contemplated in the Constitution. The NPCSC has interpreted laws only a few dozen times since 1955 and only four times since 1996.[133] The SPC may be excused for overstepping its authority in order to fill the vacuum left by the NPCSC. However, some of the interpretations have stretched the boundary of "interpretation," at times even creating legal rules that contradict the original legislation.[134] For instance, the SPC's Opinion of the Civil Law allowed for the formation of partnerships without a written agreement, even though a written agreement was required by the Civil Law.

The authority and stature of the courts is further weakened by turning matters over to other entities that are normally handled by the judiciary in other countries. Although many countries may allow the police to issue fines or impose minor administrative penalties, in the PRC, public security officers are able to detain people for fifteen days as an administrative penalty or even to sentence offenders to three years reeducation through labor, with the possibility of an extension for a fourth year. Such decisions are subject to review by the courts through administrative litigation, and thus the process is not wholly outside the reach of the judiciary. However, as these procedures are considered administrative rather than criminal, the accused do not enjoy the rights provided to those charged with a crime under the Criminal Procedure Law. Similarly, disputes involving Party members are usually handled by the Party Discipline Committee or other Party organs, with the Party deciding whether the Party member should be turned over to the court for criminal prosecution. Likewise, by steering parties toward mediation and arbitration, the Civil Procedure Law may have had the unintended side effect of further eroding the authority and stature of the courts. While the Civil Procedure Law has been amended to emphasize the voluntary nature of mediation, PRC authorities continue to sing the praises of mediation and arbitration, perhaps to the detriment of the long-term development of the courts.

Conclusion: whither judicial reform?

Throughout China's long history, there has been little if any separation between the administration and the judiciary. During the Mao era and even to a considerable extent today, the judiciary has answered to the local government and CCP organs. Thus, courts have been viewed as Party/state organs and judges as government administrators or bureaucrats. Within the bureaucracy, the stature of the judiciary and judges has been low. While the SPC and the State Council possess an equal status under the Constitution, the State Council is ranked one notch above the Court in the PRC administrative hierarchy. At the provincial level, therefore, the president of the HPC is equivalent in rank to the vice-governor of the province. Internally, courts are organized hierarchically and have functioned like administrative entities. The administrative rank of judges has been very important within the court, with senior judges exercising considerable influence over the outcome of cases and the promotion of junior judges. In short, judges have been inclined to see themselves as part of the government, their interests aligned with the CCP and the state.

As economic and legal reforms have progressed, however, the role of the courts has changed. Economic reforms have produced a more divided and pluralistic society, growing social cleavages, and a rapidly expanding middle class with significant economic interests to protect. As a consequence, citizens are increasingly looking to the courts to resolve disputes and to provide a neutral forum for reducing social tensions. The judiciary therefore is being asked to play a larger and more crucial role than in the past. Moreover, in today's modern market economy, companies are no longer able to tolerate long delays in concluding commercial cases or judges who lack the competence to decide complex legal issues. The inability of the courts to rise to the challenge and overcome technical shortcomings and respond to the demands of the citizenry for an efficient, authoritative, impartial, and just dispute resolution mechanism is undermining the legitimacy of the legal system and the ruling regime. As SPC President Xiao Yang forthrightly admitted, there is no choice but to reform.[135]

Judicial reform is clearly central to the successful implementation of rule of law in China. As such, it raises many of the issues discussed in Chapter 5 with respect to the role of the Party in future reforms. As we have seen, in keeping with the Party's reduced role in day-to-day governance, the Party rarely influences directly the outcome of particular cases. As the ultimate authority, however, the Party is able to promote or hinder the implementation of rule of law by supporting or opposing the deep institutional reforms required to establish a truly independent judiciary. Yet the Party is not free to do as it pleases; its choices are constrained by a number of factors, including the need to sustain economic growth. While wary about deep institutional reforms, Jiang Zemin and other senior Party leaders have acknowledged repeatedly the need for a more independent, competent, and authoritative judiciary.[136] More importantly, they have supported a number of proposals to that end. Indeed, the last few years have witnessed a flurry of reforms, many of them initiated by those in the judiciary in response to the suggestions of judges working on the front lines as well as to the suggestions and criticisms of academics and citizens, but which could not have been carried out without the express or tacit consent of the Party.

To date, however, reforms have not altered structurally the institutional relationships between the judiciary and the Party or state organs.[137] Any such change would require a constitutional amendment, and in the case of the Party, support from senior leaders. As with economic reforms, the ruling regime has adopted a gradual approach to legal reforms.[138] It has preferred to first try out reforms on a limited experimental basis, and to begin with the reforms that are easiest to achieve. The near future is likely to bring further piecemeal reforms. Ultimately, however, implementation of rule of law will require deeper institutional changes that will inevitably alter the balance of power between the judiciary and the Party as well as the legislature and executive branch, including local governments, the procuracy, public security, and the police.

Continued problems with judicial competence

Although many of the recent reforms are laudable, they are subject to various shortcomings and not likely to be sufficient to address the more fundamental problems plaguing the judiciary. For instance, the authorities have sought to increase the competence, professionalism, and independence of judges by reforming the appointment and promotion processes. Thus, new judges are to be chosen from lawyers and academics as well as recent law school graduates. Yet it is unlikely that many academics and lawyers will want to become judges. Law professors enjoy a higher social status than judges, and often are able to take advantage of their expertise to earn outside income several times higher than judicial salaries. As is true elsewhere, professors may also prefer the autonomy that comes with an academic position. Moreover, many fear that they would be frustrated by the hierarchical nature of the courts, and worry that they would end up butting heads with the president of the court and other senior judges who may resent the efforts of academics to change the way things are done. Similarly, elite lawyers, many of whom are in their prime money-making years, may be reluctant to trade their high income, autonomy, and authority as a partner in a major firm for a meager judge's salary and the headaches of having to deal with poorly trained senior judges. Recent graduates may be willing to enter the judiciary, but it will be years before they rise to positions of power within the court, especially if the current administrative ranking system remains in place.

Further, even though promotions are more merit-based with higher-level courts playing a greater role in choosing among the best judges of lower courts, a number of factors that have little to do with one's performance still come into play, especially given that the process remains subject to Party control. Even if better judges are promoted, it won't be easy to rid the courts of deadwood. Some judges may be ready for early retirement, but what will happen to the rest? Where will they go? Unqualified judges are likely to resist transfer to administrative positions, which they rightly perceive to be a demotion (and which would drastically diminish their ability to collect bribes). At any rate, there are a limited number of administrative positions, and likely to be fewer if the SPC is able to implement its plans for downsizing. Thus, transferring judges to administrative posts will mean that administrative personnel are left without a job, adding to the swelling ranks of unemployed.

Judicial training for judges once they have assumed their posts is at best a remedial measure and no substitute for a solid foundation in law. While the training of senior judges is a positive development, one must be realistic about the outcome. The training of court presidents at the National Judges Institute in 2000 lasted twenty days – a long time for presidents to be away from their posts but a short time to impart all that needs to be imparted, particularly given that many court presidents lack a foundation in law and one-third of the time was spent on Deng Xiaoping theory and other such ideological matters.[139] In some cases, higher-level courts will hold training sessions for specific new laws, such as the Contract Law.[140] However, with the rapid pace of new and amended legislation, higher courts can hardly be expected to hold training sessions for every new law and regulation.

As a result, the PRC courts are likely to suffer from poorly trained judges for at least another generation. Many judges will continue to handle cases in the old way, relying on their experience and gut reaction.[141] They will continue to exhibit a bureaucratic attitude, treating junior judges and lawyers with near equal disdain. While the long-term trend is toward a more competent judiciary, it will take years to raise the overall level of competence, and further reforms will be required. Raising the pay and eliminating the administrative ranking system of judges would help attract more qualified candidates. Ultimately, however, the judiciary will attract better candidates when judges enjoy a higher social status, which will not happen until judges have the authority to decide cases impartially and without undue interference, and actually do so.[142]

Corruption

As is discussed in Chapter 9, corruption is systemic; it is a pervasive social problem. One can hardly expect judges to be honest when government and Party officials from top to bottom are busily filling their pockets. Thus, measures aimed specifically at reducing judicial corruption are likely to be of limited effectiveness in the absence of more comprehensive approaches. That said, strengthening the recusal system and rotating senior judges may help curtail corruption to some extent. However, rules against *ex parte* communications and rules requiring judges to withdraw where there is a conflict of interest have been on the books for years, and been of little use. While the new rules do tighten some of the loopholes, there may still be ways to circumvent the rules. The new rules apply to the judge's children, but not to the children's spouses. Furthermore, spouses or children of senior judges may simply set up consulting companies or accept fees directly as individuals, and then refer the client to lawyers at their former firm who will appear in court. In any event, how the rules will be implemented remains to be seen.

Many commentators have advocated raising judges' salaries as a way of reducing corruption. Surely judges will be tempted to supplement their income in other ways if their salary and benefits are so low that they cannot enjoy a decent standard of living. But attacking corruption through economic means alone is not likely to be successful because the problem is not purely an economic one. No matter how high their salaries, judges who resent the much higher incomes of some lawyers and the wealth acquired by children of government officials as a result of their connections will always be tempted to accept bribes, which can easily exceed even the highest judicial salary by hundreds if not thousands of times.

Similarly, the attempts to increase external supervision over the judiciary may help reduce corruption to some extent but may give rise to new problems. For instance, opening trials to the media and public is a positive development, though it runs counter to the Party's desire for secrecy and control. Thus, the effectiveness of public scrutiny as a means of rooting out corruption is likely to continue to be impeded by the lack of a free press. Supervision by other entities is a double-edged sword. On balance, allowing the procuracy to challenge judicial decisions probably does more harm than good, whereas supervision by the people's congress is arguably less objectionable provided that it is subject to clear limits as discussed previously.

In the end, an honest judiciary depends more on the internal norms and sense of professional responsibility of judges than on external supervision or the salary of the judges. But instilling a sense of pride in the profession requires more than the promulgation of a code of judicial ethics. Judges will take the profession more seriously when others do. Most judges in any country make less than they would in private practice. But their sacrifice in income is offset by a higher social status. In the USA, for example, judges are respected and held in high regard while lawyers are the butt of countless jokes. In China, however, judges will not win that respect until they prove themselves worthy, which will not happen unless and until they and the judiciary as a whole are given more authority and power.

The authority of the judiciary and individual judges

The authority of individual judges is undermined by the system in which major or difficult cases are decided by the adjudicative committee. PRC legal scholars have debated the advantages and disadvantages of the system for more than a decade. Supporters argue that review by more senior judges is necessary in light of the low level of competence of many judges. They also suggest that the system reduces corruption. Some claim that the system enhances the independence of the judiciary in that the adjudicative committee, which generally includes the president and other high-ranking Party members within the court, may be better able to resist outside influences than more junior judges.[143]

On the other hand, the vast majority of PRC legal scholars oppose the system and advocate the abolition of the adjudicative committee. As many have noted, under the current system, the judges who decide the case are not the ones who hear it. Accordingly, the judges who do hear the case feel they have no power. Thus, they have little incentive to pay attention to the arguments during trial. Nor do they feel responsible for the judgment, even when it is issued in their names. Further, these scholars note, judges hearing the cases become timid, and are quick to hand over tough cases to the adjudicative committee rather than working through the issues themselves, even though doing so may result in delays. In addition, the system places considerable power in the hands of the president and vice-president of the court, who have in the past acted as gatekeepers for the adjudicative committee. It may also increase the opportunities for corruption in that disgruntled parties may persuade senior judges to intervene on their behalf. At minimum, these scholars conclude, it has not been an effective means of reducing judicial corruption. Some scholars have countered the assertion that the system increases independence by claiming that the adjudicative committee is susceptible to Party influence and likely to uphold the Party line.[144]

Objections of legal scholars notwithstanding, the likelihood of abolishing the adjudicative committee in the near future is low. Thus, some scholars argue that rather than tilting at windmills, reformers should focus their energies on reducing the role of the adjudicative committee and implementing procedural reforms to the way the committee operates. Consistent with this strategy, the SPC's reforms to the presiding judge system give individual judges and the collegiate panel more power to decide cases without the need to obtain the approval of the division chief, president, or the adjudicative committee. Presiding judges are also to receive a higher salary, which may earn them a somewhat higher status and improve their morale, though how much higher the salary will be is not yet clear. How effective the new rules will be remains to be seen. They fail to clarify *who* has the right to decide which cases are major or difficult. More importantly, given the hierarchical nature of the courts, it is doubtful that junior judges will be able to resist attempts to intervene by more senior judges, particularly given that senior judges are still influential in promotion decisions. As a result, the adjudicative committee is likely to still end up deciding many cases.

If so, the SPC may wish to consider further reforms. It should, for instance, clarify what kinds of cases are considered major or difficult, and leave it to the collegiate panel to decide when to seek the opinion of the adjudicative committee. The deliberations of the adjudicative committee should also be open to the public or at least a matter of public record, except in those cases that genuinely involve state secrets or other legitimate reasons for maintaining confidentiality. Moreover, the members of the adjudicative committee should be chosen based on legal qualifications rather than political considerations.[145]

Giving individual judges more authority within the court will be of little use if the authority of the judiciary as a whole is not enhanced vis-à-vis other government entities. One way to strengthen the authority of the courts would be to adjust the position of the courts relative to the procuracy to ensure that the court is able to command respect in the courtroom. Specifically, the procuracy's right to supervise the courts by challenging specific case decisions outside the normal appeal process should be eliminated. It has exacerbated the tension between the procuracy and the courts and undermined the independence and authority of the courts, while adding a new channel for corruption. Should judges prove impervious to social pressure or more overt forms of bribery, disgruntled parties can try their luck with the procuracy. To further strengthen the courts relative to the procuracy, the use of administrative penalties should also be restricted. Cases involving detention for more than a few days should be turned over to the courts. The likelihood of abolishing reeducation through labor, widely criticized abroad, at present is low. Even reform-minded legal scholars support it as necessary to ensure social order. Nevertheless, it should be subject to additional procedural requirements and safeguards. Suspects should enjoy the full complement of rights they would enjoy were the proceedings handled in accordance with the Criminal Procedure Law. Imposing higher procedural standards would provide a firmer basis for the courts to strictly scrutinize the public security organ's decision pursuant to administrative litigation.

China is unlikely to change its unitary system in which the NPC is the highest organ of state power. Nor does it need to. People's congresses are relatively weak, and so far have not been much of a threat to courts. However, that could change if people's congresses begin to intervene aggressively in specific cases under the guise of supervision, particularly in the absence of sufficient procedural safeguards. If so, the right of the people's congresses to intervene in specific cases may need to be eliminated or at least restricted.

The judiciary as an institution could also be strengthened by expanding the powers of the courts in other areas. As noted, courts have limited powers to interpret law and no right to strike down regulations passed by administrative agencies or local governments that are inconsistent with superior law. Giving the courts the power to strike down certain lower-level legislation that is inconsistent with higher-level legislation would greatly enhance their authority vis-à-vis local governments and administrative agencies. As discussed in the previous chapter, allowing all courts to conduct constitutional review or strike down all forms of legislation is not politically feasible at this point and in any event would be unwise given the level of competence of many judges. But it may be possible to begin with types of lower-level legislation, e.g. Normative Documents and Rules (*guizhang*), with the authority to strike down legislation varying depending on the level of the court. Were the courts to be given such powers, their job would be made easier if the legislature passed a law authorizing the courts to void laws and regulations for vagueness. At present, laws and regulations are often so vaguely drafted that the courts find it difficult to determine whether lower-level legislation is consistent. In addition, rather than requiring the courts to seek interpretation from the NPC or the government entity that passed the regulations, courts might also be given greater authority to interpret laws and regulations. At minimum, the SPC's practice of issuing general interpretations of laws should be recognized and given a basis in law.

The inability of courts to enforce their own judgments and rulings is a serious threat to the authority, prestige, and image of the judiciary. If courts appear to be nothing more than paper tigers, parties that lose the battle in court will simply refuse to comply with the judgment. Recognizing that the court's enforcement problems are due to the institutional arrangements that leave judges and the court beholden to local governments,[146] the SPC has responded by trying to shift some responsibility for appointments, funding, and decision-making to higher-level courts. In 1995, the SPC passed a notice whereby the SPC claimed the right to make the final decision whether to refuse enforcement of arbitral awards.[147] When lower-level courts, bowing to local pressure, undermined the notice by simply sitting on an award, the SPC became more aggressive, issuing regulations imposing time deadlines and addressing a number of other obstacles to enforcement.[148]

In an effort to impose further discipline on lower-level courts and combat local protectionism, the SPC issued more regulations in January 2000.[149] One regulation centralizes enforcement and strengthens the power of provincial-level HPCs. An HPC may instruct a lower court to change its decision or to rectify an action if the HPC believes that the lower court made a mistake.[150] The HPC may reassign a case from a BPC to an IPC or even decide the case itself. Further, the regulation addresses the lack of incentive for lower courts and individual judges to enforce awards by authorizing the HPC to criticize the lower court for failing to carry out its instructions, and where the circumstances are serious, to recommend disciplinary sanctions.

The regulation also attempts to overcome local protectionism by insulating enforcement personnel from certain personnel decisions by the local government. The consent of the next higher-level court is required to remove the main enforcement personnel of the execution chambers.[151] In response to the problem of local governments cutting off support for recalcitrant courts that insist on upholding the law, the regulation empowers the HPC to dispatch lower-level court enforcement personnel and judicial police to aid in enforcement. Furthermore, HPCs are supposed to prepare a budget for their enforcement expenses after consulting with the financial authorities, the planning authorities, and other relevant authorities.[152] The various level governments are then supposed to fund these expenses. Finally, if the HPC encounters obstacles from the public security bureau, procuracy, or other governmental entities, it is supposed to report the matter to the SPC.

In short, the SPC has sought to address a much larger institutional problem that affects the stature and operation of the courts generally by carving out a special niche for enforcement.[153] But it is doubtful that the changes will suffice. Even provincial-level governments are not immune from protectionist sentiments. HPCs are still likely to have a greater interest in local companies in the cities where the HPC is located and more generally in companies within their own province. Nor is it likely that provincial-level governments will provide enough funding to HPCs to adequately carry out enforcement without a mandatory requirement that they do so. Moreover, while the new regulation prohibits local people's congresses from removing judges without higher-level approval, it does not prevent them from blocking a judge's opportunity for advancement. All personnel decisions other than appointment and removal will still be determined by the local people's congress and senior members of the court who remain beholden to the local Party, people's congress, and government. In the end, more radical reforms than those contemplated in the SPC's recent regulation will be necessary to create a court with sufficient authority to enforce awards.

The need for deeper institutional reforms and more independent courts

Recognizing the need for deeper institutional reforms to address the systemic problems facing the judiciary, PRC legal scholars have explored a number of possibilities. To overcome the problem of local protectionism, some scholars have called for the creation of a federalist system of national and local courts or a system of regional courts.[154] Others recommend that the SPC set up "branches."[155] Still another suggestion is to have higher-level judges sit on cases being heard in lower-level courts that involve cross-regional disputes.[156] Others have proposed the establishment of a specialized administrative court with the power to annul local legislation inconsistent with superior legislation.[157]

Predictably, scholars are divided as to the merits of these proposals. For instance, some scholars have argued that a federalist or regional system of courts does not fit well with the unitary structure of the Chinese state. Such a system would lead to further decentralization and increased jurisdictional conflicts, thereby exacerbating tensions between the central government and local governments.[158] Moreover, a federalist system is by its nature complex. Whether PRC judges, prosecutors, and lawyers are up to the challenge of a more complicated system is questionable.

At minimum, however, the current way in which courts are funded and judges appointed needs to be reconsidered, with responsibility for funding and appointments shifted from local governments and people's congresses to more centralized entities.[159] The central government or provincial governments could be directly responsible for funding. Alternatively, the SPC or HPCs could prepare an annual budget to be submitted to and approved by the NPC or State Council, or in the case of HPCs, the provincial people's congress or government.

Appointments are a more sensitive area. Although there is little prospect of completely eliminating the Party's role in the appointment process, that role could be diminished by limiting the need for Party approval to only the president of the court. Such a move would be consistent with the long-term trend to emphasize the legal skills of the judges who actually decide cases. Moreover, the Party's role could be limited to a more minimal vetting of judges selected initially by others for their legal qualifications. Whatever the role of the Party, to overcome local protectionism, appointments and dismissal could become primarily the responsibility of higher-level people's congresses, the MOJ (and its local bureaus) and/or the bar association, or some combination thereof.[160] For instance, higher-level courts could nominate judges, subject to approval by the people's congresses.[161]

The Party's role could be further reduced by eliminating Party cells within the court and PLCs below the central level, as was contemplated during the Zhao Ziyang era. The central-level PLC would still be responsible for policy setting. Guo Daohui, one of China's most senior legal scholars, has suggested that the committee be renamed the Rule of Law Committee, and its agenda redefined to focus on the promotion and implementation of rule of law.[162] Unfortunately, few commentators hold out much hope for such reforms in the near future. With authority increasingly fragmented, and conflicts among regions and between the central authorities and wayward local governments growing, the Party is unlikely to reduce its presence on the local level. On the contrary, conservative Party leaders such as Li Peng regularly call for the strengthening of Party leadership over the courts rather than its reduction.[163] Even some liberal legal scholars worry that withdrawal of the Party could exacerbate conflicts and lead to social disorder.

Clearly any fundamental change to the legal system will entail amendment of the Constitution and organic laws. Just as clearly, any such change will alter the current balance of power and the nature of the relationships between the judiciary and the Party as well as other state organs. Will the Party approve major institutional changes? If so, what will the role of the Party be in the new political order? In fulfilling its leadership role as the vanguard of society, will the Party limit itself to being a general policy setter? Ultimately, where will real power rest, with the Party or with the law? No doubt it will be a long time before the legal system will be strong enough to bind the Party on life-or-death issues. In the meantime, however, the Party's role may be gradually reduced while legal institutions are strengthened. It bears reiterating that while a truly independent court might constitute a challenge to the authority of the Party, many of the proposed reforms do not directly threaten the Party. In fact, arguably they would serve the Party's ends by reining in local governments and addressing to some extent the problem of inconsistent regulations that thwart central laws and policies. Similarly, citizens will warmly welcome any reduction in corruption in the courts

and improvements in the quality of justice. As a result, the legitimacy of
the current regime will be strengthened.

Even were the Party willing to accept a new role, other political organs
can be expected to resist reforms that strengthen the judiciary at their
expense. The procuracy and people's congresses are likely to oppose any
attempt to limit their right to supervise the judiciary. The State Council
will object to proposals that give the courts the right to strike down
administrative regulations. The Ministry of Public Security will fight
efforts to do away with reeducation through labor or to impose further
restrictions on administrative penalties.[164]

Moreover, an independent and authoritative judiciary alone is not
enough to ensure rule of law. It will take years to produce a competent and honest corps of judges. There must also exist good laws for the
judges to apply. A culture of legality is equally important. Everyone must
do their part. The level of legal consciousness must be raised; citizens
must know the law to be able to follow it and to take advantage of the
rights provided to them. Police and procuratorates are the front line,
and exercise considerable discretion over which cases go to court. Much
of what they do is not visible to the outside world. They must exercise
their discretion reasonably, and abide by the law in carrying out their duties. The shockingly high incidence of torture in China calls into doubt
the willingness of the police to abide by the law and their commitment
to rule of law.[165] Similarly, as will be discussed in Chapter 9, although
government officials play a pivotal role in making, interpreting, and
implementing law, the administrative law regime is beset by problems,
including a judiciary too weak to hold local government officials accountable. And, as will be discussed in the next chapter, the nascent
legal profession must respond to the challenges of a market economy
and a new legal order if rule of law is to become a reality.

Notes

1 Constitution, art. 126.
2 PRC Judges Law, art. 8 (adopted by the NPC on Feb. 28, 1995).
3 Judges Law, art. 43.
4 Zhang Wusheng and Wu Zeyong (2000: 65). Wang Liming (2000) is one of
   many scholars who has called for an end to the system of administrative ranking
   of judges.
5 Xiao Yang (2000: 113); Li Hanchang (2000: 48). As Clarke (2001) notes, accurate numbers regarding the total number of judges are hard to come by.

Moreover, making sense of the numbers is even more difficult as in many cases some of those counted as judges in practice do not hear many or any cases, including senior judges such as the president and vice-presidents and those in charge of more administrative departments within the court.

6   One reason for the slow pace is that judges are often required to do nonadjudication work, such as cleaning the windows when high-ranking officials are coming to inspect the court or planting trees as part of a greenification campaign. Li Yuwen (2002).

7   Clarke (1996: 56) claims, only half tongue in cheek, that "the court is essentially just another bureaucracy, with no more power to tell banks what to do than the post office."

8   See, for example, The Central CCP's Decision on Further Strengthening Political and Legal Personnel Force. Xiao Yang (1999: 160) has observed that while most "comrades" are well aware of the need to reform the judiciary, some still underestimate the benefits of reform or overstate the difficulties.

9   Ratliff and Buscaglia's (1997) portrait of the judiciary in many Latin-American countries highlights similar problems with respect to limited access, long delays, corruption, limited authority, and the lack of independence. They also caution against attempts to give the judiciary too much independence until judges are more qualified and less corrupt.

10   For still useful accounts, see Clarke (1996); Finder (1993); Lubman (1999: 250–97); Brown (1997). For more recent accounts, see Finder (2001); Li Yuwen (2002).

11   The best study of the SPC continues to be that of Finder (1993).

12   Xiao Yang (2000: 113); Li Hanchang (2000: 48); Liu Jinghuai and Guo Chunyu (2000: 28).

13   Zhang Wusheng and Wu Zeyong (2000: 70).

14   See Regulations Concerning Several Issues with Respect to People's Tribunals (issued by the SPC on July 15, 1999).

15   The distinction between economic and civil cases goes back to Soviet legal theories and a centrally planned economy, with economic cases involving vertical disputes between state-owned enterprise legal persons within an administrative hierarchy and civil cases involving horizontal disputes between equal parties. This anachronistic distinction makes little sense in a market economy that treats legal persons and natural persons the same with respect to the capacity to contract.

16   The SPC reduced the number of overall staff by 10 percent but increased the number of judges by 11 percent. See *China's Supreme Court Concludes 4-Month Reorganization* (2000).

17   Senior judges, including the president, will soon be required to personally hear cases, which could present a challenge to those presidents who have little legal training. However, given how busy court presidents are, they are not likely to hear many cases. Moreover, they can choose relatively simple cases or rely on the other judges on the collegiate panel. See "Renmin Fayuan Wunian Gaige Gangyao" (1999)[hereafter the SPC Five Year Plan].

18   Article 12 of the Judges Law as amended June 30, 2001. As discussed below, new judges must pass a unified judicial examination and have a bachelor's

degree in law or in another subject provided they are knowledgeable about law.

19 See the Supplementary Regulations for the People's Courts Litigation Fees Measures, issued by the SPC on July 28, 1999, and the Regulations for the Provision of Judicial Assistance to Indigent Parties, issued by the SPC on July 27, 2000.

20 Some scholars have expressed concern that the summary procedure may not work as well as in other countries because PRC lawyers do not prepare the case as well as their counterparts elsewhere. As a result, the judge may not be able to figure out what the factual and legal issues are without a fuller hearing.

21 According to the 2001 SPC Work Report, all HPCs and IPCs and 50 percent of BPCs had implemented the new presiding-judge system as of the end of 2000.

22 Prior to the amendment of the Criminal Procedure Law in 1996, the president of the court could take what he considered to be major or difficult cases away from the collegiate panel and reassign them to the Adjudication Committee. Under the revised Criminal Procedure Law, the collegiate panel is given the right to refer difficult, complex, or major cases to the president who will then decide whether to assign the case to the Adjudication Committee. However, once the decision is made, if the president finds definite error in the determination of facts or the application of law on the part of the collegiate panel, he may submit the case to the Adjudication Committee that he nominates for decision. Criminal Procedure Law, art. 205; Civil Procedure Law, art. 177; Administrative Litigation Law, art. 63.

23 Trial Measures for the Selection and Appointment of Presiding Judges in People's Courts, art. 5 (passed by the SPC on July 11, 2000). See also SPC Five Year Plan, arts. 18, 20.

24 According to Article 115 of the SPC's 1996 Opinion Concerning Several Issues on Implementation of the PRC Criminal Procedure Law (Trial Implementation), the collegiate panel may request advice with respect to such major or difficult cases as: (i) possible death penalty cases; (ii) cases where the members of the collegiate panel seriously disagree; (iii) cases challenged by the procuratorate; (iv) cases that have significant social influence; and (v) other cases for which the collegiate bench thinks it is necessary. See also Finder (2001).

25 See *Xiao Yang Discusses Court Reforms* (1999).

26 Measures for Administration of Publishing Rulings and Judgments (issued by the SPC and effective June 15, 2000). The Measures prohibit publication in cases involving state secrets or where publication would harm national interests, where the ruling or judgment reveals concrete capital punishment figures, and where the reasoning of the opinion is not sufficiently incisive or persuasive.

27 When initiated by the procuracy, the process is called *kangsu*.

28 Clarke (1996); Peerenboom (2001a).

29 Wang Liming (2000: 186–89).

30 For an extensive and excellent discussion, see Lubman (1999).

31 The Regulation on Strict Application of the Open Trial System.

32 Cited in Li Yuwen (2002).

33 Li Yuwen (2002).

34 Members of the Research Office of the CCP Central Commission of Political Science and Law have complained that unqualified people are entering on the basis of connections while qualified people cannot enter, and that it is difficult to remove unqualified judges. See *Strengthening PRC's Legal, Judicial Work* (1999).

35 Peerenboom (1998b: 61–62). Zhao Junru puts the figure at 70 percent. See Clarke (2001).

36 Zhuang Huining (2000: 26). According to one report, fewer than 200 judges have master's degrees and less than 100 have a doctorate. See "China – Open Recruitment to Select Best Judges" (1999).

37 Liu Jinghuai and Guo Chunyu (2000: 29).

38 2000 SPC Work Report. According to one report, fifteen HPCs reported 10,340 mistaken cases in the first six months of 1998. Interestingly, 84 percent involved jurisdictional or procedural problems, while only 16 percent were incorrect on the substantive issues. See Xiao Yang (1998: 79). Historically, PRC judges have paid little attention to procedural issues. However, the high rate of procedural and jurisdictional problems also suggests that corruption may be involved rather than lack of competence. For example, as discussed in the text, courts often exceed their jurisdiction, in violation of procedure, in order to earn the fees for handling the case.

39 See, for example, Several Opinions of the SPC Concerning the Implementation of the Central Communist Party "Decision on Further Strengthening Political and Legal Personnel Force" to Establish a Highly Professional Force of Judges (1999), Provisional Rules on Judges' Rank (1998), Answers to Several Issues Concerning "Implementation Measures of Appraisal of Judges' Rank" (1998), 1996–2000 Training Plan for Court Cadres Throughout China (1996).

40 In Beijing, 4,080 judges and judicial staff, accounting for more than 98 percent of all judges and staff in Beijing's HPC, IPCs, and BPCs, took an examination administered by the HPC in 2000. Prior to the examination, judges and judicial personnel attended training sessions from April to September. Those who fail the first time are given a second chance. If they fail again, they must be transferred or resign. The examination will take place every five years. No statistics were given on the number who passed. See "Knowledge of Law Tested in Beijing" (2000).

41 Dong Hua (2000: 45).

42 See the amended Judges Law Article 12.

43 Judges Law, art. 9. To qualify as a judge, one must be at least twenty-three years old, healthy, willing to uphold the constitution, possess good political and moral character, and have not previously committed a crime or been deprived of an official position. In addition, graduates from law school must have at least one year of work experience. Graduates from college who did not study law must have at least two years' experience. There is no work experience requirement for postgraduates in law.

44 At least one report claims that most judges have credentials from part-time adult schools. See Li Hanchang (2000). For criticism of the low standards for

obtaining a *dazhuan* and a breakdown of the education level of judges in one court, see Zuo Weimin (2000: 192–93).

45 Judges Law, art. 9(6). Current judges who do not meet the standards are supposed to undergo remedial training. Upon approval by the SPC, some regions that have difficulty attracting judges that meet the standards may for a period of time accept people with only a *dazhuan*. Judges Law, art. 9(6). Indicative of the rapid pace and sometimes haphazard path of reforms, the SPC had just issued rules in 1999 providing that to sit for the national judges' examination, one must have at least a *dazhuan* in law plus two years' experience, or a four-year bachelor's degree in law and one year of experience, or a four-year bachelor's degree and a master's degree in some area other than law plus legal knowledge and one year of experience, or a graduate degree in law. Provisional Measures for the Examination of New Judges and Assistant Judges (SPC, 1999).

46 Regulations on Training of Judges 2000, art. 15.

47 Certain Opinions on Basic Level Construction of the People's Courts 1998, art. 10.

48 Certain Opinions on Basic Level Construction of the People's Courts, art. 12.

49 SPC Five Year Plan, art. 35. The SPC declared an open-recruitment policy and announced that in looking for ten senior judges, it would subject them to strict examination. But it also seemed to require that the judges have Beijing residence! See "China – Open Recruitment to Select Best Judges" (1999). It should be noted that the requirements in the Five Year Plan are higher than the qualifications set forth in the amended Judges Law.

50 Certain Opinions on Basic Level Construction of the People's Courts, art. 10. See also Judges Law, art. 12.

51 Certain Opinions on Basic Level Construction of the People's Courts, art. 10.

52 Regulations on Training of Judges, art. 15.

53 Trial Measures for the Selection and Appointment of Presiding Judges 2000, art. 4. Candidates may submit a written application or be recommended by the court president. After a preliminary screening, the names of candidates are made public, and the candidates undergo examination, including a test. The adjudicative committee then chooses the judges based on the results of the examination.

54 *China Selects SPC "Presiding Judges" Through Public Competition* (2000).

55 Certain Opinions on Basic Level Construction of the People's Courts, art. 14.

56 See the speech of SPC Vice-President Zhu Mingshan in *PRC to Reform Judge Selection System* (1999).

57 Studies have found no significant correlation between judicial efficiency and the size of the government budget allocated to the courts. Countries such as Norway, Japan, and Germany spend a lower percentage than Venezuela, Peru, and Argentina. See Buscaglia and Domingo (1997).

58 *PRC Supreme Court Restructuring Outlined* (2000).

59 *2000 SPC Report to NPC*.

60 He Weifang (1995) has been particularly critical of the judiciary, especially former military personnel turned judges. See also Clarke (1996); Lubman (1999).

61   There may be more former military officers serving as judges in remote locations where it is not easy to attract other candidates. In addition, if the
president of the court and other senior judges come from a military background, they may feel threatened by better-educated junior lawyers and thus
prefer to hire former military officers.

62   On October 20, 2000, the SPC issued the Regulations on Training for Judges.
See also the 2001–05 Plan for Nationwide Education and Training of Court
Cadres.

63   Certain Opinions on Basic Level Construction of the People's Courts 1998,
art. 30.

64   Five Year Plan, art. 36; Regulations on Training for Judges, art. 15.

65   Judges Law, arts. 13, 30, 38.

66   Judges Law, art. 42.

67   Judges Law, art. 11.

68   NPC delegates considered the issue of judicial salaries when considering
amendments to the Judges Law. However, they decided it was an administrative matter and not suitable for legislation. Zhuang Huining (2000: 26).
MOJ officials reportedly are considering raising judicial salaries as a way of
reducing corruption. See *Justice Official on China Mulling Higher Salary to
Improve Quality of Judges* (2000).

69   See *Official on Problems in Judicial Practice* (1999).

70   *NPC Deputies, CPPCC Members Inspect Supreme Court* (1998).

71   *Court President on Ranks of Judges, Police* (1998).

72   PRC lawyers and legal scholars have offered various explanations. Some note
the Shanghai judges are paid a higher salary than most judges. The salary
is sufficient to live comfortably. Also, Shanghai lawyers may make less than
in Beijing, so that there is more parity in the salaries of judges and lawyers.
Others suggest that Shanghai is better managed on the whole, with more focus
on efficiency and clean government, whereas the general environment is more
corrupt in Guangdong, and in Beijing, more corrupt and more bureaucratic.

73   *Court President on Ranks of Judges, Police* (1998).

74   *1996 SPC Work Report,* in *1996 Law Yearbook* (1997: 29).

75   *1997 Law Yearbook* (1998: 51). In 2000, the SPP investigated 4,626 judicial
personnel. See *Procurator General Delivers Supreme People's Procuratorate Work
Report* (2001).

76   *Court President on Ranks of Judges, Police* (1998).

77   The judiciary and legal profession regularly exchange accusations regarding
who is responsible for bribes. Lawyers claim that they are just responding to
demands from judges, while judges assert that lawyers seek them out to offer
enticements. To the extent judges admit that many of their colleagues take the
initiative in approaching lawyers, they suggest that lawyers are still to blame
for creating the vicious cycle in the first place.

78   Cai (1999); Xiao Yang (2000). Surprisingly, given all of the concerns about
judicial independence and the general level of grumbling one hears about
the courts, there is some evidence that people are satisfied that the courts
can and do render just verdicts in most cases. Jiang Ping (1995: 611) cites

three surveys that show general support for the court's ability to be just. In a survey of 1,041 people in Harbin, 60% of respondents thought the courts would handle administrative cases in a just way, 28% thought that courts could not necessarily handle them in a just way, 3% thought courts could not render a just verdict, and 9% did not know. A second survey of 180 plaintiffs in administrative suits revealed that 23% agreed with the result while 31% thought the results were fair and had no complaints, 15% thought the results were not too fair, and 10% thought the results were not fair. The remaining 20% concluded it was hard to say. These numbers are plausible given that plaintiffs generally prevail to some extent in 40% of cases nationwide. Here, about 53% of the people agreed with the results. Presumably, most of the 40% who prevail in whole or in part would agree with the result. Further, even if one accepts some bias in favor of agencies, presumably at least some of the cases decided in favor of the defendant are just. Accordingly, that a certain percentage of plaintiffs would come to realize that the court's decision in favor of the plaintiff was just is reasonable. A third survey also showed that 71% of plaintiffs thought that judges handled cases in accordance with law and that they could be trusted. The numbers are surprisingly high even assuming that a significant number of people may have provided what they thought were safe answers rather than their heartfelt views. See also "Judges – a Case of Misunderstanding" (1999), reporting that nearly half of respondents had a positive view of judges while 40% had a negative view.

79   See the comments of Feng Rui, in Editorial Office (1998); *Beijing's Political–Legal Organs Cut Business Ties* (1998).

80   Several Rules Concerning Strict Compliance by Adjudicative Personnel with the Recusal System (issued by the SPC, January 31, 2000).

81   Several Rules Concerning the Undertaking of Paid Legal Services and Commercial Activities by Spouses and Children of Leading Cadres at the Tribunal (Bureau) Level and above (2001).

82   SPC Five Year Plan, art. 35.

83   Li Yuwen (2002). Other scholars argue that jurors are apt to be prejudiced and swayed by human sympathy, and that a jury system would cost more. Wang Liming (2000: 386).

84   See the Procedures for Trial Implementation for Punishments of Violations of Discipline in People's Courts Trials 1998, Procedures for Trial Implementation for Holding People's Court Judges Responsible for Violations of Law in Court Trials 1998, and Work Regulations of Supreme People's Court Superintendents 1998.

85   See *Supreme Court Appoints 10 Judicial Superintendents* (1998); *"Unprecedented" Internal Shakeup of Judiciary Noted* (1998).

86   Zhuang Huining (2000: 27).

87   Shetreet and Deschenes (1985).

88   As Doris Marie Provine (1996: 177) observes: "In France, as in other countries that follow a civil law tradition, courts are not a coequal branch of government...The courts were on the losing side of the French Revolution, and they suffered a tremendous loss of power and prestige in its aftermath. Two

centuries later, the commitment to independence from the other branches is still in doubt. Courts in France are not known for standing up to government officials, and no one expects them to play an active role in government."

89 Kritzer (1996: 81) notes that whereas the relationship between law and politics is readily acknowledged in the United States, English legal scholars treat law and courts as distinct from politics, and in fact the appointment process is much less politicized, to cite one example.

90 Article 2.14 of the Universal Declaration of the Independence of Justice, unanimously adopted at the First World Conference on the Independence of Justice held in Montreal on June 10th, 1983, acknowledges that: "There is no single proper method of judicial selection provided it safeguards against judicial appointments for improper motives." Query whether the practice in the United States of Presidents nominating Supreme Court justices based on political affiliation constitutes an improper motive. Compare then the practice in the PRC, where the Party approves or vetoes all candidates, the vast majority of whom are Party members.

91 Between 1963 and 1992, 58 to 73 percent of federal appellate judges and 49 to 61 percent of federal district judges had a record of political activism before appointment. Goldman (1993: 282–97), cited in Jacob (1996: 19). Moreover, the majority of state judges are elected in the USA.

92 SPC Five Year Plan, art. 4.

93 As one former judge noted, the secretary of the Party cell might call a meeting to study the latest Party policy only to find that no one shows up.

94 Interviews with PRC law professors and judges. See also Shiping Zheng (1997: 172); Finder (2001).

95 The Party Group's approval is required to penalize a Party member for a breach of Party discipline. On the other hand, the Party Group does not usually get involved in penalizing judges for incompetence or other shortcomings that do not constitute violations of Party discipline.

96 Issued by the SPC on March 3, 2000.

97 Chen Jianfu (2002); Zuo Weimin (2000: 201–02).

98 In a speech published in the SPC Gazette, Xiao Yang (1999) repeatedly emphasized the need to follow laws and decide cases based on the fundamental principles set forth in the Constitution and in the laws and regulations. The SPC plays a much more controversial role when, under instructions from the PLC, it issues instructions to lower-level courts on how to handle particular controversies arising in conjunction with Falungong. See Chapter III.

99 Finder (2001).

100 In some cases, the Political Department may be involved in the process. However, the vice president in charge of the Political Department is generally lower in rank than the vice-president of substantive divisions. Thus, the latter's opinion is more important, and only the Party Group's approval is necessary.

101 As pointed out in Chapter 3, the various schools would likely disagree over the particular normative agenda. Moreover, Communitarians would insist that the leaders who set the agenda be elected.

102 See Gong Xiangrui, ed. (1993: 33).

103   See Jiang Mingan (1998: 63).
104   See Fang Ning *et al.* (2001: 305).
105   Peerenboom (2001a).
106   Shiping Zheng (1997: 19).
107   Usually, local counsel will try to overcome local protectionism through a variety of channels. Thus, it is not always possible to determine what exactly turned the tide. It bears reiterating that there were only four out of eighty-nine cases in which Party members became involved, either positively or negatively. To be sure, the Party may have played a role in additional cases. Although the survey included a question about the CCP and asked the respondent to identify the source of local protectionism, not all respondents were in a position to know whether the CCP was involved and not all responded to every question. See Peerenboom (2001a).
        To illustrate the potentially positive role of the party, in one case, CIETAC issued an award in favor of the foreign party. When the Chinese respondent failed to comply with the award, the foreign party sought enforcement. Unfortunately, the Chinese party had strong connections to senior judges in the court. The court was very passive, claiming that the Chinese party had no assets. It then just left the matter pending. The foreign party's lawyer enlisted the support of the head of the PLC, after which the court adopted a much more proactive stance. It turned out that the shareholders of the Chinese company had transferred company assets to a third party in their own names. The foreign party's lawyers were able to show that the shareholders of the respondent were also the shareholders of the third party. The court then carried out a surprise investigation of the third party and seized its assets.
108   See "Vote of Disapproval Prompts Campaign to Clean up China's Courts" (1997).
109   For a discussion of the Provisions on Strengthening the Inspection of Legal Implementation, adopted by the NPCSC in 1993, see Cai Dingjian (2002).
110   Between 1993 and 1997, it inspected a total of twenty-one laws. See Cai Dingjian (2002).
111   Cai Dingjian (2002).
112   Xiao Yang claims that the SPC responded to 123 suggestions, proposals, and motions from the NPC and CPPCC in 2000. See the *2001 SPC Work Report.*
113   *Opinions on Draft for Supervising Cases* (1998).
114   SPC Opinion Concerning the Acceptance by People's Courts of Supervision by People's Congresses and People's Congress Standing Committees, December 24, 1998; Decision of the Supreme People's Court Concerning Strengthening Liason Work with Members of People's Congresses, issued December 29, 2000; Provisional Regulations Concerning the Handling of Letters from Members of the NPC by People's Courts, issued by the SPC on December 29, 2000.
115   According to one official spokesperson, other factors include the way government agencies are funded, the poor quality of legislation, the lack of effective supervision mechanisms, and ideological factors. See *Liaowang Assails "Local Protectionism"* (1999).

116 Although local protectionism (*difang baohu zhuyi*) is widely assumed to be a major obstacle to enforcement, it surprisingly did not emerge as a statistically significant factor in one recent survey of enforcement of arbitral awards in China. Even though parties in the survey attributed difficulties in enforcement at least partly to local protectionism in almost 60% of the cases, the successful enforcement rate was only marginally higher (61%) in the absence of local protectionism than when local protectionism existed (54%). This counterintuitive result appears to be due to multicollinearity, which in turn may result from the difficulty of specifying and quantifying local protectionism given its many forms with different degrees of seriousness. See Peerenboom (2001a).
117 Liu Renwen (1999: 144).
118 Dowdle (1997).
119 See the Regulations Concerning Several Problems in Implementation of the Criminal Procedure Law (issued Jan. 19, 1998).
120 Interviews with a drafter of the Law on Legislation and a PRC professor of criminal law.
121 Constitution, art. 129; Criminal Procedure Law 1997, art. 185. See also Woo (1991).
122 Interview with PRC scholar working on judicial reform, Beijing, June, 1999. In 1998, procuratorates handled 131,859 petitions for adjudicative supervision in civil cases, examining 54,492 of them, and lodging protests against the court's decision in 11,925 cases, while offering suggestions in 8,082 cases. See *1999 Supreme People's Procuratorate Work Report* (1999).
123 *2000 SPC Report to NPC.*
124 Finder (2001).
125 *2000 SPC Report to NPC.*
126 See the SPC Notice Regarding Several Issues Relating to the People's Courts' Handling of Foreign-Related and Foreign Arbitration Matters (issued Aug. 28, 1995).
127 See Peerenboom (2001a).
128 Jianfu Chen (1999b: 7).
129 Fu Hualing (1994: 286).
130 As noted previously, the SPC will often participate in the drafting process or provide comments on draft legislation, although other bodies will be primarily responsible for drafting. Finder (1993: 167–90, 211, 216). See also Liu Nanping (1991).
131 See the Resolution Concerning the Strengthening of Legal Interpretative Work (adopted June 19, 1981). In 1997, the SPC finally published regulations regarding judicial interpretations. See the Several Regulations Regarding Judicial Interpretation Work.
132 Resolution Concerning the Strengthening of Legal Interpretative Work.
133 Cai Dingjian (2002). Cai argues that the NPCSC should not be charged with interpretation because it does not meet frequently enough and many delegates are not legal experts. He advocates that a special agency be established within the NPC to handle interpretation.

134 See Finder (1993: 168).
135 SPC Five Year Plan, art. 1; see also Xiao Yang (1998; 1999).
136 *Jiang Zemin's Congress Report* (1997); *1999 SPC Work Report* (1999).
137 The absence of structural change in institutional relationships between the judiciary and Party or state organs does not prove the skeptics point that there has been no fundamental change in the legal system as a whole. Such a conclusion conflates judicial reform with legal reform more generally. Judicial reform remains the weak link, and the area where deep institutional changes have been most resisted. As such, it is not representative of overall legal system reforms. Moreover, even in the judiciary, there have been significant changes. Finally, many of the problems that plague the judiciary are simply not amenable to immediate solution. The regime's inability to move rapidly forward in creating a more authoritative judiciary need not be attributed therefore to an enduring preference for rule by law among senior leaders.
138 *Judge Xiao: Legal Reform Should Proceed Gradually* (2000).
139 Interview with a judge from the National Judges Institute in December 2000. The judge noted that training for lower level judges focused more on legal issues and less on ideology.
140 *Supreme Court Training Staff on Contract Law* (1999).
141 Zuo Weimin (2000: 185–87) argues that many judges continue to decide cases based on policy and general ethical principles rather than law. He notes that at least one court president complained that one of the problems with recent graduates who become judges is that they tend to apply the law too rigidly without taking into consideration the overall context.
142 This is not to suggest that judges in the PRC will enjoy the same exalted status as judges in common law systems. The status of judges in civil law countries tends to be lower than that in common law countries, in part because judges have more restricted powers and the career path of a judge is more akin to that of a civil servant.
143 Wang Liming (2000: 193).
144 Woo (1991).
145 Wang Liming (2000: 200).
146 The court's lack of authority stands out among the various economic, social, cultural, and political obstacles to enforcement not only because it is so central but also because it is capable of being addressed in the relatively short term, whereas the other obstacles defy any short-term solutions.
147 Notice of the Supreme People's Court Regarding Several Issues Relating to the People's Courts' Handling of Foreign-Related and Foreign Arbitration Matters (Aug. 28, 1995). If an IPC intends to refuse to recognize or enforce a foreign or foreign-related award, it must first submit a report to the HPC. If the HPC agrees with the IPC that the award should not be enforced, the HPC must report the case to the SPC. Only after the SPC approves may the IPC refuse to recognize or enforce the award.
148 SPC Provisions on Certain Issues Relating to the People's Courts' Enforcement Work Regulation (Trial Implementation) (July 8, 1998); Regulation of the Supreme People's Court Regarding the Problems of Collecting Fees and Time

Limits for Review of Recognition and Enforcement of Foreign Arbitral Awards (Oct. 21, 1998). See also Peerenboom (2001a).

149 See Regulations of the Supreme People's Court Concerning Several Issues Related to the Unified Administration of Enforcement Work by the High People's Courts (Jan. 14, 2000) [the "Unified Administration Regulation"]. A month later, the SPC issued Certain Regulations for Strengthening and Improving Entrustment Enforcement Work (effective Mar. 11, 2000). The latter regulation attempts to address the problem of lack of enforcement by a local court asked to enforce a judgment or order of another PRC court against a local company. It also clarified jurisdictional issues and how enforcement cases are to be handled when the party has assets in more than one jurisdiction.

150 See Unified Administration Regulation, art. 5. If the SPC issues an order prescribing enforcement, then the HPC must issue an order calling for enforcement. Unified Administration Regulation, art. 8.

151 Unified Administration Regulation, art. 11. The legality of this requirement is questionable in that Article 11 of the Judges Law gives the right to appoint and remove senior judges to the people's congresses at the same level. Court presidents have the right to appoint or remove lower-level judges.

152 Unified Administration Regulation, art. 12.

153 The low stature of the courts affects several areas of law. For instance, the effectiveness of China's Administrative Litigation Law is compromised by the reluctance of courts to hold administrative agencies liable or to interpret standards for quashing administrative acts such as "abuse of authority" broadly. In the criminal area, judges are often unable to resist pressure from the procuracy and government officials to "strike hard" at anyone charged with a crime.

154 Cao Siyuan (1997) has proposed a system of regional courts. Cai Dingjian (1999: 161) has proposed a federal system.

155 Zhang Wusheng and Wu Zeyong (2000: 66).

156 Wang Liming (2000). One wonders about the feasibility of such a system. Having SPC judges travelling through the country and HPC judges circulating throughout the province would be expensive and a drain on the higher courts' human resources. One also wonders whether the higher court judge would not dominate the other judges on the panel and unilaterally decide the case. Presumably, the higher court judge who handled the case would not be involved if the case were appealed. However, higher courts may be more reluctant to overturn on appeal the decision of a lower court when one of their colleagues was involved in the decision.

157 Ma Huaide (1998).

158 Wang Liming (2000: 173).

159 For a contrary view, see Hu Yunteng (1999), who argues that centralized funding would impose too heavy a burden on the central government.

160 Such an approach is consistent with Xiao Yang's proposal that Party Groups in the IPC work with Party Committees at lower levels to choose BPC senior judges, including presidents, from among the ranks of the most qualified judges, academics, and lawyers. Xiao Yang (2000: 114).

161   Wang Liming (2000: 16). The president of one BPC in Beijing proposed that appointments be made by an HPC committee consisting of the HPC president, other senior judges, and members from the Party Organization Department and PLC. Dong Hua (2000: 46).

162   Guo Daohui (1999).

163   *Li Peng Speaks on PRC Judicial Reform* (2000).

164   Chinese officials dismissed the calls by Mary Robinson, the United Nations human rights commissioner, to do away with reeducation through labor. See Kynge (2001).

165   Human Rights in China (2000). Senior leaders from Li Peng to Luo Gan have condemned the high incidence of torture and a number of steps have been taken to address the problem, including the restructuring of police departments, requiring prison guards to sit for professional examinations every five years, appointing section-level officers based on open competition, and firing incompetent police. See *Beijing Restructures Police Department in Institutional Reform* (2000); *China to Test 300,000 Prison Guards for "Quality"* (2000); *Li Peng on Implementation of Criminal Procedure Law* (2000).

8

The legal profession: the quest
for independence and professionalism

A competent and independent legal profession is generally assumed to be necessary for rule of law.[1] Thus the original law and development movement in the 1960s made legal education reform and legal training a high priority.[2] Even today, the new law and development movement continues to take the establishment of a competent and independent legal profession as one of the cornerstones of rule of law and to devote considerable resources to the education and training of lawyers.[3]

Although most thin versions of rule of law do not include express reference to the legal profession among the listed elements,[4] most advocates of thin theories take care to point out that the stipulated elements are not meant to be exhaustive and that rule of law requires in addition various institutions, of which a legal profession is one. Indeed, the need for a legal profession follows from typical elements of a thin theory. The requirements that laws be published and that there be congruence between law on the books and law in practice assumes that there are legal professionals to interpret and apply rules. Impartial and fair trials require representation by someone who knows the law and is independent of the judges deciding the cases and the political authorities who made the laws.

Not surprisingly, an independent legal profession is a prominent feature of thick conceptions of rule of law that emphasize human rights. Thus the United Nation's Basic Principles on the Role of Lawyers proclaims that "adequate protection of human rights and fundamental freedoms to which all persons are entitled, be they economic, social, cultural, or civil and political, requires that all persons have effective access to legal services provided by an independent legal profession."[5]

The legal profession's relationship to rule of law may be characterized in terms of three general roles. The first focuses on the role of lawyers and others with legal training as the purveyors of technical legal skills needed to operate a modern legal system. The legal profession is pivotal in the drafting, dissemination, interpretation, and implementation of laws. Second, beyond their technical skills, lawyers may serve as a force for social change. They may do so by promoting the establishment of rule of law through the use of litigation, by participating in legislation, by advocating institution-building reforms, and by demonstrating, through their daily activities, the value and utility of law. More generally, the legal profession has an important role to play in changing the legal culture by fighting to uphold rule-of-law values and promoting a culture of legality, as in India when the legal profession rose up against government attempts to compromise the independence of the courts.[6] Third, in some countries the legal profession has also been a force for broader political reforms such as the establishment of democracy and an expansive view of human rights, both integral components of certain thick conceptions of rule of law. In South Africa, for example, some members of the bar attempted to use law to challenge the apartheid regime.[7]

China's legal profession has made great strides on the technical side. Although there are still major shortcomings, there has been a rapid increase in the number of lawyers and the overall level of expertise. More modest progress has been achieved in instilling a sense of professional responsibility among lawyers and ensuring that all citizens, even the indigent, have access to qualified legal counsel.

The legal profession has also become much more independent. Driven largely by economic reforms that have resulted in changes in the organizational structure of PRC firms and the rise of partnerships, Chinese lawyers can no longer be characterized as workers of the state. To be sure, the independence and autonomy of the legal profession is still subject to limits. As discussed in Chapter 5, the CCP is suspicious of independent social organizations, and has restricted their growth and development through a combination of regulations and enticements meant to bind them to the state. In fact, the independence of the legal profession is limited more by the desire of lawyers to establish corporatist and clientelist relations with the MOJ and its local organs in order to take advantage of economic opportunities than it is by political limitations on the profession's activities. Nevertheless, the legal profession is likely to become more independent over time as the market for legal services matures and the need to rely on the MOJ for business diminishes.

While some convergence is therefore to be expected, the PRC legal profession may, and probably will, differ in important respects from legal professions in liberal democratic states because of the differences in fundamental values that distinguish Statist Socialist, Neoauthoritarian, Communitarian, and Liberal Democratic versions of rule of law. Such differences are likely to be manifest in the degree of independence of the legal profession and in the balance drawn between a lawyer's duty to serve individual clients and the state (for the Statist Socialists and Neoauthoritarians) or society (for Communitarians).

Although the PRC legal profession will most likely be a positive force in establishing rule of law, whether it will emerge as a force in support of liberal democracy (and thus a Liberal Democratic rule of law) is doubtful. But to focus solely or primarily on the independence of the legal profession and its political orientation would be a mistake. Implementation of a thin rule of law depends as much on technical issues as on ideology. China's legal profession has come a long way, particularly when one considers the historical context.

Historical overview

Traditional China held neither law nor lawyers in high esteem. As discussed in Chapter 2, Confucius maintained that a humane and harmonious society required a morally cultivated populace, and that laws and lawyers would lead to a litigious society in which individuals pursued their own interests at the expense of others. Imperial rulers, for their part, used litigation brokers as scapegoats, unjustly blaming them for the high incidence of litigation that the understaffed Imperial judicial system was incapable of handling. Although the antipathy of Confucians and China's Imperial rulers prevented the development of a cohesive legal profession, litigation brokers actually played a positive role in assisting peasants in bringing legitimate claims and thus were popular among the lower classes.[8] As the role of legal counselors became more prominent and China turned to Japan and the West for inspiration during the Qing, the legal profession increasingly became the subject of legislation.[9]

China's first regulations expressly on lawyers and the legal profession were passed in 1912. The Provisional Regulations on Lawyers specified the responsibilities, training, and qualifications of lawyers.[10] After numerous amendments, the Provisional Regulations on Lawyers were replaced in 1927 by the Regulations on Lawyers. These regulations were followed by a draft Lawyers Law in 1935, which finally took effect in 1941.

During the period from the turn of the century to the establishment of the PRC in 1949, bar associations were formed, several law journals appeared, and the number of lawyers grew rapidly. Whereas in 1913 there were only 1,700 lawyers registered with the Ministry of Justice (MOJ), by 1935 there were more than 10,000.[11]

Although the legal profession was gaining ground in China, there were numerous problems. The number of lawyers was extremely limited relative to the size of the population, with only one lawyer per 45,000 people.[12] Moreover, most of the lawyers were concentrated in a handful of big cities. Also, the quality of many lawyers was low. One could qualify as a lawyer in a variety of ways, through public or private schools, either domestic or foreign, or through practical experience. The period of education or training could be as short as eighteen months, and one was not required to obtain a degree or certificate. Further, legal education was poor, with the instructors themselves often poorly trained. Attempts were made to address the quality problem by instituting a qualifying examination requirement, but the regulations were not enforced. Most lawyers continued to be admitted without passing the examination.[13] And despite regulations codifying the basic professional responsibilities of lawyers, many lawyers lacked a firm sense of professional ethics. In short, while the seeds of a legal profession had been sown and had begun to take root and sprout in China, the profession had a long way to go to maturity.[14]

The Mao era

Promptly upon taking power in 1949, the PRC government repealed the laws governing the legal profession promulgated by the Guomindang and set out to establish a new socialist legal system.[15] Accordingly, in 1956, the State Council approved the MOJ's notice regarding lawyers,[16] which addressed such issues as the nature, purpose, responsibilities, and permissible organizations of lawyers.

By early 1957, there were 19 bar associations, 820 legal advisory offices, 2,572 full-time lawyers, and 350 part-time lawyers.[17] Citizens were growing accustomed to turning to lawyers for assistance. The Beijing

Legal Advisory Office handled just 27 civil litigation cases in May of 1956 compared to 277 cases during the same period a year later.[18] Moreover, lawyers appeared to be having at least some success in representing their clients. Of the 1,204 criminal cases reported by 59 legal advisory offices as of June 1957, 63 resulted in innocent verdicts, and an additional 49 resulted in no punishment being imposed.[19] Amid all of this activity, drafting of the Provisional Regulations on Lawyers commenced.

During this early period, the role of lawyers was to serve the state and "the people" (renmin) by assisting in the building of a new China, one organized along socialist lines. Lawyers served the state and the people by contributing to the formation of a planned economy and drafting the relatively simple contracts and documents required by such an economy.[20] On the criminal side, the law was used largely as a tool of class struggle in the years immediately following the victory of the Communist Party.[21] Justice was often dispensed by administrative agencies or by ad hoc people's tribunals. To the extent lawyers were involved at all, their participation was limited to seeking leniency in punishment. However, by the mid-1950s, encouraged by policies aimed at judicial reform, some lawyers had begun to take a more aggressive approach to criminal defense.[22]

The development of a legal profession in China came to an abrupt halt in 1957 with the advent of the antirightist campaign, which hit lawyers particularly hard. As noted in Chapter 2, lawyers had seized the opportunity presented by Mao's policy of "letting a hundred flowers bloom" to demand changes in the legal system. Moreover, the nature of their work – defending criminals against the state and drafting contracts to promote and protect the economic interests of their clients – tended to bring them into conflict with socialist ideology. Labeled capitalists and rightists, many lawyers were persecuted. Law offices were shut down and the MOJ disbanded. Lawyers fared even worse during the Cultural Revolution, during which time all but a handful of law schools were shut down and even those that continued to operate focused on politics rather than law.

The early reform era: 1980–96

Deng Xiaoping realized early on that lawyers were essential to the success of economic reforms. Lawyers were needed to assist in drafting the massive amounts of legislation required to transform a centrally planned economy into a more open market-oriented economy and to advise and draft contracts and other legal documents on behalf of state-owned enterprises and other entities in the new economy. They were central to the creation of a legal structure that would prevent the excesses of the Cultural Revolution, allow China to become part of the international economy, and provide legitimacy both domestically and abroad to a ruling regime whose image and credibility had been badly tarnished.

Debilitated by the anti-rightist campaign and the Cultural Revolution, poorly trained, or aging, China's lawyers were no match for the task. The legal profession had to be rebuilt virtually from scratch. In 1980, Deng estimated that China would need between 100,000 and 200,000 lawyers to meet the demands of the new reform.[23] Law schools reopened, legal journals reappeared, law offices and bar associations sprang up as China rushed to meet the need.[24] With the newfound interest in law came the need to regulate lawyers and the legal profession. In 1980, the National People's Congress (NPC) passed the Provisional Regulations of the PRC on Lawyers, which took effect in 1982.

Consisting of a mere twenty-one articles, the Provisional Regulations covered three broad topics: the purpose, scope of activities, rights and responsibilities, and qualifications of lawyers; the organizational forms of lawyers' work units; and bar associations. Given the pressing need for lawyers, the Provisional Regulations were designed to promote the rapid expansion of the legal force. As a result, qualification requirements were minimal and flexible, with an emphasis on political criteria and practice. Lawyers were not required to pass a bar examination. Rather, one could apply for approval if one had received minimal formal education or on-the-job training. In addition, one had to love the PRC, support the socialist system, and be eligible to vote and stand for election.[25]

Lawyers were defined as workers of the state.[26] They labored in state-owned law advisory offices that relied on the state for financial support. Their mission was to provide legal assistance to government organs, work units, social groups, people's communes, and citizens in order to ensure the correct implementation of the law, protect the interests of the state and collective, and the legal rights and interests of citizens.[27] In carrying out their responsibilities, lawyers were supposed to promote the socialist legal order and be faithful to the cause of socialism and the interests of the people.[28]

The legal profession was not self-regulating but rather subject to government oversight. Although the Provisional Regulations called for the establishment of bar associations, the All China Lawyers' Association was not established until 1986. Moreover, national and local bar associations remained weak. Thus lawyers, law offices, and lawyers' associations reported to, and were governed by, the MOJ and its local branches.

In practice, the role of lawyers was relatively limited in the early to mid-1980s. They tended to act for state-owned enterprises or administrative units, preparing the rather simple contracts needed by a still largely centrally planned economy. In the event of disputes, they helped mediate, arbitrate, or in some cases litigate. They also served as defense counsel to the limited extent permitted under the PRC Criminal Law and Criminal Procedure Law, which allowed access to counsel just seven days prior to trial.[29] Moreover, given the common practice of deciding cases before trial,[30] lawyers frequently could do little more than persuade the defendant to confess in the hope of obtaining a lenient punishment.

In 1996, China passed the Lawyers Law, which superseded the Provisional Regulations. In the sixteen-year period between the passing of the Provisional Regulations and the Lawyers Law, China experienced dramatic changes as a result of the economic reforms initiated by Deng and the more limited political reforms that accompanied them. Along the way, a variety of problems in the legal profession emerged, resulting in the need for a new Lawyers Law.

The Lawyers Law is divided into eight chapters: general principles; requirements for lawyers to practice; law firms; business operations undertaken by practicing lawyers and rights and obligations of lawyers; lawyers' associations; legal aid; legal liability; and supplementary principles. Article 1 of the Lawyers Law states that its purpose is to perfect the system of lawyers, to ensure that the professional activities conducted by lawyers are carried out in accordance with the law, to standardize the professional conduct of lawyers, to protect the legal rights and interests of the parties concerned, to ensure the correct implementation of the law, and to realize fully the active role of lawyers in the development of a socialist legal system.

More broadly, the Lawyers Law has the following objectives. First, to bring China's regulatory framework more into compliance with reality by replacing the outdated Provisional Regulations with a legal structure that better accords with a socialist market economy, in particular by redefining the role of lawyer and codifying the changes in organizational forms of law firms. Second, to pacify the masses angered by the unethical behavior of lawyers by emphasizing the professional responsibilities of lawyers and strengthening the system for disciplining wayward lawyers. Third, to protect the rights of lawyers and ensure that lawyers are not interfered with or subjected to physical or other forms of abuse when carrying out their responsibilities in accordance with law. Fourth, to protect the rights and interests of clients of the legal profession through a variety of channels, including: (i) promoting a more independent legal profession; (ii) improving the quality of lawyers by setting higher standards for qualification, holding lawyers to a higher standard of professional responsibility, and improving management over lawyers; (iii) clarifying the rights of lawyers to represent clients and the obligations of lawyers to their clients; (iv) protecting lawyers from interference and abuse; and (v) laying the foundation for a legal aid system.

The Lawyers Law was only one of many measures taken to improve the legal profession. Considerable attention has also been paid to establishing and strengthening bar associations, improving legal education, and training lawyers, judges, government officials, procurators, public notaries, and others involved in the law-making, interpretation, and implementation processes. In addition to countless domestic initiatives, China has turned abroad to international organizations and to foreign governments, academics, lawyers, and bar associations for assistance. A number of programs have been established to bring PRC lawyers to foreign countries for study and training. The Ford Foundation, US–Asia Law Institute, Asia Foundation, and the American Bar Association have been active, among many others, in legal training, in efforts to improve the organization and management of China's bar associations and in advising how to improve the internal management of private law firms.[31]

The increasing independence of the legal profession

The Lawyers Law both reflected the reality of the increasing independence of the legal profession and promoted its further independence by redefining lawyers, codifying the change in the organizational structure of firms, encouraging the development of bar associations, downgrading the supervisory role of the MOJ and partially reallocating responsibility for overseeing the profession from the MOJ to the bar association, and clarifying the obligations of other arms of the justice system to cooperate with lawyers.

Redefining lawyers

The Provisional Regulations were heavily imbued with the spirit of socialism. In carrying out their duties, lawyers were to protect the interests of the state, promote the socialist legal order through all of their activities, and remain ever faithful to the cause of socialism.[32] In contrast, the Lawyers Law redefines lawyers in a much less politically charged way: a lawyer is a legal practitioner who holds a certificate to practice law and who provides legal services to society.[33] PRC commentators make much of the change, proudly pointing out that lawyers are no longer servants of the state.[34]

Despite the change, the Lawyers Law retains enough of the rhetoric of socialism to alarm skeptics. The drafters expressly rejected the definition of lawyers as "free professionals" or "free and independent professionals" (*ziyou zhiyezhe* or *ziyou duli zhiyezhe*) adopted in some countries to emphasize that lawyers are not servants of the state, but rather have a certain institutional autonomy in carrying out their responsibilities and a duty to their clients.[35] One of the goals of the Lawyers Law is to maximize the active role of lawyers in developing the socialist legal system.[36] Lawyers are still required to maintain the confidentiality of state secrets, which are broadly defined in the PRC.[37] They are also required to abide by the PRC Constitution, which requires all citizens to protect the public order, respect social ethics, and refrain from committing any acts detrimental to the security, honor, and interests of the motherland.[38] An MOJ notice issued subsequent to the passage of the Lawyers Law threw fuel on the fire by emphasizing the need to ensure correct political thinking among lawyers, who were required to "put the interests of society first."[39] Firms with three or more CCP members are also required to set up a Party group, while firms with less than three CCP members are supposed to form such groups in association with other firms, and CCP members are to take a leading role in the political training of other lawyers.[40]

Yet care should be taken not to overstate the importance of this socialist rhetoric. China since the late 1990s is no longer the China of 1950, or 1970, or even of the 1980s. For many people, including many lawyers, the rhetoric of socialism is simply irrelevant. Economic reforms have enabled many lawyers to develop lucrative practices, representing both domestic and foreign clients.

Lawyers working in other areas, such as administrative litigation or criminal law, are still subject to pressure and interference from administrative organs and other elements in the criminal justice apparatus such as the procuratorate, police, or even the courts.[41] However, one of the purposes of the Lawyers Law is to emphasize the right of lawyers to carry out their responsibilities in accordance with law, thus promoting their independence. Today, lawyers are increasingly willing to challenge the state by representing clients in administrative litigation suits and by serving as defense counsel. In 1998, criminal defendants were represented by lawyers over 50 percent of the time, 10 percent higher than in 1996.[42] While many lawyers are unwilling to take on criminal cases, the reason is often financial – criminal cases are generally not profitable – rather than political. Admittedly money is not the only issue. Frustration with the lack of cooperation from and interference by administrators and court officials, and a general sense that lawyers can do little to influence the outcome are also factors.[43] In addition, many lawyers are still reluctant to handle high-profile political cases. Political dissidents on occasion have been unable to find counsel willing to represent them, perhaps because in the past the authorities have revoked the licenses of lawyers representing such defendants.[44] As noted in Chapter 3, during the recent campaign to wipe out Falungong, the Beijing Bureau of Justice required all lawyers to obtain Bureau approval to represent Falungong practitioners.

Nevertheless, the degree of politicization of the legal profession and the legal process is lessening. The efforts to publicize and implement rule of law have begun to alter the legal culture. The change in the definition of lawyer and the toning down of the rhetoric of socialism, particularly when coupled with structural reforms to the organization of law firms, represent steps in the direction of greater independence of the legal profession.

More independent law firms

Arguably of much greater significance to the development of an independent legal profession than the change in the rhetorical tone of the Lawyers Law is the development of law firms not beholden financially to the state. The Lawyers Law ratified the structural reforms that began in the mid-1980s by expressly recognizing three forms of law firms: state-owned, cooperative,[45] and partnership.[46]

Although the confirmation of cooperative and partnership firms is significant, skeptics note that state-funded law firms account for the vast majority of PRC firms. As of year end 1998, there were 8,946 firms, of which 27% were partnerships, 11% were cooperatives, and 59% were state funded.[47] However, while state-funded law firms may be subject to somewhat more administrative direction and hence are less independent than cooperative or partnership firms, the pressure to make money and be profitable has caused even many state-funded firms to place a premium on service to paying clients. More importantly, while 76% of China's firms were originally established with state funds, 48.6 percent of those no longer rely on the state for financial support.[48] In any event, the long-term trend is clearly toward more partnership firms.[49]

During drafting of the Lawyers Law, some participants actually suggested doing away with state-funded law firms. However, the prevailing view was that this was not practical at present as in many places state-funded law firms account for virtually all of the firms. Were they to be closed down, many places would be left without legal services, especially in poor areas where people cannot afford even the minimal standard fees.[50]

The dual management system: MOJ and lawyers' associations

The Lawyers Law also promoted the independence of lawyers and law firms by downgrading the role of the MOJ in the day-to-day management of law firms. Under the Provisional Regulations, law offices were administratively responsible to the MOJ, their department-in-charge (*zhuguan bumen*). Early drafts of the Lawyers Law retained this relationship. However, many lawmakers felt that this characterization of the relationship did not reflect the reality of the market economy in which law firms are "intermediary organizations" (*zhongjie zuzhi*) with more decision-making autonomy than suggested by the hierarchical subordinate-entity-subject-to-its-department-in-charge concept. Thus drafters eliminated the concept of the department-in-charge and changed references to "management" (*guanli*) by the MOJ to supervision and guidance (*jiandu, zhidao*) of lawyers, law firms, and lawyers' associations.[51]

The Lawyers Law also created a dual management structure, with lawyers regulated and supervised not just by the MOJ but also by bar associations, which every lawyer must join. The Provisional Regulations had provided for the establishment of a bar association to "protect the lawful rights and interests of lawyers, exchange work experiences, further the progress of lawyers' work and promote contacts between legal workers both at home and abroad."[52] Although a national bar association was not established until 1986, a number of provincial-level bar associations were established in the 1980s. Beginning in 1993, the MOJ also approved the establishment of bar associations in several large and medium-sized cities.[53]

The responsibilities of bar associations nowadays include: protecting the rights and interests of lawyers; summarizing and exchanging information regarding the work experience of lawyers; organizing professional training; educating, examining, and supervising lawyers in professional ethics and disciplinary rules; and mediating disputes that arise during the course of legal practice. In addition, bar associations are expressly authorized to reward and punish lawyers pursuant to their articles of association.[54]

As early as 1993, the MOJ had announced its intention to make a transition to a system where bar associations are primarily responsible for managing the legal profession under the macro-level administrative oversight of the MOJ. During the drafting of the Lawyers Law, some argued that bar associations should be responsible for imposing discipline and sanctions and handling other administrative matters, much as in other countries. However, the prevailing view was that the MOJ should remain responsible for discipline because bar associations, particularly local bar associations, were still too weak to handle the responsibility.[55] Moreover, others felt that given the prevalence of violations of professional ethics and disciplinary rules and the vehemence of public opinion, most people would not trust lawyers to regulate lawyers.[56]

Limited independence: economics over politics in the growth of clientelism and corporatism

Despite the marked and dramatic increase in the independence and autonomy of the legal profession, there are still many ways in which Chinese lawyers are tied to and dependent upon the government, thus undermining their independence. To begin with, the national and local bar associations are institutionally linked to and dependent on the MOJ and its local counterparts. Many of the top leaders of the national bar are current or former MOJ officials and still on the government payroll.[57] In Guangdong, thirteen of the twenty-nine provincial-level bar associations were still sharing offices with justice bureaus as of 1995.[58] Moreover, the MOJ has economic reasons for continuing to control lawyers and law firms: the MOJ budget is funded by law firms, which must contribute 10 to 15 percent of their profits to the MOJ.[59]

Notwithstanding the change in language from "manage" to "supervise" and "guide," the MOJ retains considerable leverage over lawyers. The former head of the MOJ and now president of the Supreme Court, Xiao Yang, has dismissed the change in language, stating that "guidance and supervision *is* management."[60] He also told reporters: "The regulations of the Lawyers Law regarding the administrative supervision and guidance of lawyers, law firms and bar associations by the judicial agencies has in no way decreased or weakened the management function of the judicial agencies with respect to lawyers, but on the contrary imposed new and higher requirements."[61]

Under the current system, the MOJ is still responsible for administering the bar examination,[62] assessing lawyers' qualifications, issuing practicing certificates to lawyers and business certificates to law firms and conducting the annual renewal review,[63] supervising compliance with professional responsibilities and disciplinary rules, and ultimately disciplining lawyers. Concerns about adequate separation between the government and the bar are heightened by provisions in the Lawyers Law requiring judicial agencies to consider "good conduct" when deciding whether to issue a practicing certificate, and by MOJ regulations requiring new lawyers to undergo training by a supervisor with correct political thinking and requiring that supervisor to submit a report on the lawyer's political thinking and moral character once training is completed.[64] Moreover, lawyers must submit, as part of the annual renewal application, a summary of their work during the last year, a certificate of completion of training, a report regarding compliance with professional responsibilities and disciplinary rules, and a certificate evidencing fulfillment of obligations set forth in the articles of association of the bar association.[65]

On the other hand, the Lawyers Law expressly provides disgruntled lawyers with the right to challenge MOJ decisions. Lawyers may challenge both the denial of a practicing certificate and disciplinary sanctions by bringing suit directly in court or appealing to the next higher-level judicial department for review. If they disagree with the review, they can then file suit in court.[66] Moreover, there do not appear to be any reported cases of lawyers having their license revoked for political activities.[67] Furthermore, some justice bureaus have begun to delegate authority over approval of lawyers to bar associations.[68]

To be sure, in practice, lawyers continue to be subject to a variety of pressures from the MOJ and its local branches. But the pressure is often economic rather than political. The MOJ and its local judicial bureaus exercise some degree of control over firms by virtue of their ability to train and license particular lawyers and law firms to handle lucrative types of work and to recommend favored lawyers for training positions in foreign firms. For instance, in response to the 15th Party Congress call to accelerate economic reform in the state sector by promoting mergers and acquisitions and the conversion of state-owned enterprises into share-holding companies (many of which will be listed on domestic and foreign exchanges), the MOJ organized a training session for select lawyers and firms regarding state-owned asset appraisals. Only those lawyers and firms that undergo the necessary training and receive the authorization of the MOJ are able to undertake this extremely profitable line of business. Similarly, lawyers must receive special certificates issued by the MOJ and the China Securities Regulatory Commission to handle securities work.

The threat of losing one's license for political reasons is much less worrisome to most lawyers than the fear of losing business opportunities. This is because few lawyers have any interest in taking on sensitive political cases, while most are quite concerned about making money. As in other lines of business, the transition to a market economy has resulted in the establishment of clientelist relationships as lawyers seek the patronage of the MOJ.

A close relationship with the MOJ or its local affiliates is important for reasons other than additional business opportunities. In fact, the MOJ has only a limited capacity to hand out new opportunities, and many firms are able to generate their own business without its assistance. Nevertheless, lawyers must still maintain friendly relations with the MOJ or its local affiliates to avoid the pervasive problems of corruption and red tape. As in other agencies, justice officials often abuse their position by engaging in predatory rent-seeking behavior.

In one instance, Beijing Bureau of Justice officials demanded that an applicant who was applying for a license produce a number of documents before they would allow her to transfer her work file to the Bureau, a prerequisite for obtaining a license. They demanded that the applicant produce a document confirming her change in status from student to cadre upon leaving the university, even though she had graduated more than fifteen years earlier, had obtained a law degree from abroad and qualified as a lawyer in New York, and had spent several years working for foreign law firms. The officials also insisted that she present a certificate confirming that she did not have any children, ostensibly for the purpose of monitoring compliance with the one-child policy. Resentful that the lawyer was going to be earning a salary tens if not hundreds of times greater than their salary, the officials openly insinuated that many of the problems could be resolved if the lawyer provided a bribe. They even called another partner in the firm to complain that the applicant had apparently spent too much time abroad and in foreign firms and had forgotten how things worked in China. Although the lawyer could have challenged the Bureau's decision under the administration reconsideration or litigation procedures, she was advised not to by the others in her firm for fear that the Bureau would retaliate.

Retaliation is a real possibility. The Beijing Bureau of Justice, for instance, has pressured firms to register their webpages with an internet company established by the relative of one of the Bureau's officials. When some firms resisted, the official threatened not to renew their licenses at the next annual inspection. Some Beijing firms have also been forced to hire relatives of officials from the MOJ, Beijing Bureau of Justice, and other ministries and bureaus such as the State Administration of Foreign Exchange in order to maintain good relations. Even though many firms object to such predatory behavior, firms are compelled to acquiesce to the demands of the MOJ and other agencies and to establish clientelist ties for a variety of reasons. Sometimes firms want access to business opportunities provided by the MOJ or to information from other bureaus needed to serve their clients. Usually, however, the local justice bureau is able to extract rents from firms because of its control over the annual inspection and approval process. It is no secret that lawyers and law firms regularly engage in tax evasion, though recent changes in the way law firms are taxed may reduce the level of tax evasion. Moreover, many do not complete the mandatory forty hours of continued legal education every year, largely because the classes are too rudimentary and a waste of time.[69]

Local law firms are not the only ones subject to pressures from the MOJ and its local bureaus. Foreign law firms must also maintain good relations if they want to succeed. In 1997, the Beijing Bureau of Justice asked certain American firms to pony up to support a "study tour" of the USA. The tour included stops in Las Vegas and Disneyland. In addition, the Bureau suggested that foreign firms take PRC lawyers recommended by the Bureau for training, especially training abroad – a suggestion vigorously opposed by many of the foreign firms.

In another instance of abuse of power, an official from the MOJ tried to force a foreign law firm to steer work to her husband at a local firm. The official scheduled a dinner with the managing partner of the foreign firm, where she introduced her husband as her classmate. After extolling her husband's legal abilities, she suggested that the foreign firm direct some work to a local firm where he worked. As is common practice in most PRC firms, her husband would then receive a large commission on the revenues generated by that work. The same foreign firm was again victimized when a justice official demanded that the resident partner buy blankets and other bedding supplies that an out-of-town relative had been unable to sell at a sales convention.

Under PRC law, foreign firms are not allowed to interpret and advise on PRC law. But it is well known that foreign law firms regularly advise clients on a wide range of investment-related matters. In addition, foreign firms frequently run afoul of other restrictive PRC regulations, such as the prohibition against hiring PRC lawyers or the requirement that foreign lawyers have a minimum of three years' experience to practice in China. Given their vulnerable position, foreign firms are reluctant to incur the wrath of greedy officials.

Independence vis-à-vis other arms of the justice system and the Party

An even bigger threat to the independence of the legal profession lies not in the MOJ but in other areas of the legal and political system. Lawyers are only one arm of the socialist legal system, along with the courts, procuratorate, police, and CCP apparatus. In the past, all were viewed as complementary components of one integrated system that ultimately served the state and the cause of socialism. In theory, there

was no conflict between defending the interests of the state and defending the rights and interests of individuals because the state served the
interests of the people, and what was in the interest of the state was in
the interest of individuals. Although such reasoning has not been completely abandoned,[70] it is no longer dominant, as evidenced by the recent
changes in the Criminal Procedure Law. The 1996 amendments to the
Criminal Procedure Law provide for a more adversarial criminal process
with the burden of collecting information and making arguments falling
primarily on the shoulders of the procuratorate and defense counsel.[71]
As a result, all parties have had to learn and accept new roles. The court,
traditionally used to taking the lead in questioning witnesses and mar-
shaling evidence, has had to learn to accept a more impartial role as a
neutral adjudicator. The procuratorate and police have had to accept the
more expanded role of lawyers in the discovery process and to tolerate
the probing cross-examinations and challenges of defense counsel. And
the Party has had to refrain from influencing decisions. Unless old behavior patterns were broken, the efforts to create an independent legal
profession would be severely compromised.

   Such fundamental changes in the legal culture cannot be achieved
overnight, however. In practice, lawyers often continue to run into obstacles from recalcitrant police and procuratorates who by training,
habit, and temperament are not disposed to cooperate with legal counsel seeking to have those arrested by the police and prosecuted by the
procuratorates acquitted. In 1997, Guangdong Province Public Security
Bureau issued a report acknowledging problems in implementing the
revised Criminal Procedure Law and emphasizing the need to ensure
that lawyers are able to carry out their duties under the law.[72] The report noted that many local police officials were responding to lawyers'
requests to meet with clients by adopting the approach of "if possible to
avoid, avoid; if possible to delay, delay." The report also warned against
arbitrarily invoking the excuse that the case involves state secrets or is
currently under investigation to deny lawyers their right to visit with
clients. The report attributed problems in implementation to the failure
of local police to study adequately the revised law and to the fears of local
police that lawyers would interfere in the investigative process, resulting
in suspects withdrawing confessions and refusing to cooperate with the
authorities. In response to such problems, the Supreme People's Court,
Supreme People's Procuratorate, Ministry of Public Security, Ministry

of State Security, MOJ, and the NPC Standing Committee Legislative Affairs Commission issued new regulations in 1998 aimed at improving implementation of the Criminal Procedure Law.[73]

The relationship between lawyers and judges also continues to be a rocky one. Given their low state salaries, many judges are jealous and resentful of lawyers who can afford fancy suits, new cars, and villas in the suburbs. Lawyers, for their part, are often contemptuous of corrupt and incompetent judges. They resent having to simplify their arguments and to curry favor by obsequiously deferring to judges who think that their official status entitles them to be treated like the emperor's closest advisers. In some regions, the conflicts between judges and lawyers have been so bad that the local government has had to intervene to broker a peace settlement. Observing that disputes between lawyers and judges were hurting the reputation of the judiciary and legal profession and damaging the investment environment, the Dalian Economic and Development Zone drafted a Judges and Lawyers Pact aimed at reducing the tensions.[74]

Physical safety of lawyers in carrying out responsibilities

Although the authorities readily acknowledge that lawyers cannot protect their clients if lawyers' own personal safety and rights cannot be protected even in court, abuses of lawyers continue to occur.[75] Attacks on lawyers by distraught spouses and threats and intimidation by the opposing side happen to some extent everywhere. However, China stands out for the frequency of such attacks,[76] the lack of response by the courts to such invasions of lawyers' rights, and indeed the participation of the courts, procuracy, police, and other government organs in such cases.[77] In one case involving an economic dispute in Hebei province, for instance, three court personnel handcuffed the lawyer to a bench and proceeded to beat him for over an hour, causing a cerebral concussion and injuries to other parts of the body.[78] To add insult to injury, the court personnel further hindered his work by detaining him for fifteen days. In another case, a county court in Hunan province placed a lawyer in custody for 259 days and sentenced him to three years in prison for dereliction of duty.[79] The charge arose when a murder suspect the lawyer was defending, having colluded with guards, escaped during a visit with his lawyer – even though the lawyer himself had played no part in the escape.

A number of steps have been taken to rectify the situation. The MOJ has established hotlines to protect lawyers and to assist them in overcoming resistance by obstructionist judges, police, prosecutors, or government officials. Bar associations have become more aggressive in challenging procuratorates who arrest lawyers on trumped-up charges of falsifying evidence or concealing a crime. Frequently, bar associations enlist the support of the MOJ or the local bureau of justice, government entities that are likely to have more political clout in dealing with the courts and other government agencies.[80] Notwithstanding such positive measures, unless more is done to ensure that lawyers are afforded the protections guaranteed to them by law, such attacks will have a chilling effect on the willingness of lawyers to take on controversial cases and extend themselves on behalf of their clients. In the absence of lawyers willing to zealously pursue their client's interests, individuals may not be able to take full advantage of the rights granted them under the Criminal Procedural Law and other laws.

Access to competent and honest lawyers

The independence of the legal profession is only one factor in implementing rule of law. For the legal profession to adequately serve rule of law, there must be a sufficient number of qualified and honest lawyers accessible to those in need of legal services. Despite rapid growth and improvements in the quality, there are still relatively few lawyers, particularly in rural areas. The supply of legal aid falls far short of demand, and the legal profession as a whole suffers from a low level of competence and widespread professional responsibility violations.

A shortage of lawyers despite rapid growth

In 1978, there were only a few thousand lawyers in China. Responding not only to Deng's call to assist China in its modernization efforts but to the lure of hard, cold cash and profits beyond the wildest dreams of the average Chinese citizen, the number of lawyers shot up rapidly. In 1993 alone, spurred on by Deng's southern tour in which he reiterated his support for economic reforms, the number of lawyers increased by almost 40 percent.[81] As of 1998, there were 8,946 law firms and more than 110,000 lawyers.[82] Moreover, the numbers are likely to continue to rise, probably at an even higher rate, as more and more people seek the riches of a law career. In 2000, 215,000 people took the national lawyer's qualification examination, for which the pass rate was set at 10%.[83]

Notwithstanding the rapid increase in the number and quality of PRC lawyers, China still faces a serious shortage of qualified lawyers. In 1998, China's 110,000 lawyers accounted for a mere 0.008% of the population.[84] Moreover, of these 110,000, only about half were full-time.[85] In comparison, lawyers account for 0.32% of the population in the United States and 0.09% in West Germany.[86] Apart from sheer numbers, there are distribution problems. Most lawyers want to work in big cities on commercial matters, which are the most profitable. Citizens in the countryside must often rely on so-called barefoot lawyers, who are not lawyers at law in the sense that they have not qualified to practice in accordance with the standards set out in the Lawyers Law.[87]

Representation rates in civil, economic, criminal, and administrative cases give some sense of the pressing need for more lawyers. Between 1992 and 1998, representation rates in civil litigation cases hovered around 10 to 15% and around 26% in economic cases.[88] In contrast, criminal defendants have increasingly turned to lawyers, with the rate of representation rising to over 50% in 1998. Interestingly, representation rates for plaintiffs in administrative litigation cases decreased to just over 10% in 1996 before making a slight comeback to between 15 and 20% in 1997 and 1998.[89]

The limits of legal aid

A shortage of lawyers is only part of the story for the low representation rates. All too often, parties cannot afford lawyers, even given the low fees mandated for many types of cases under PRC regulations.[90] China is only beginning to establish a legal aid system. The Lawyers Law contains in principle a commitment to a legal aid system.[91] One may obtain legal aid "pursuant to State regulations" if one is unable to pay attorney's fees in cases involving family support, work-related injury, criminal actions, state compensation claims, or payment of pensions for deceased persons.[92] In addition, lawyers "must assume legal aid obligations pursuant to State regulations," with detailed measures to be formulated by the MOJ and approved by the State Council.[93]

In practice, however, legal aid remains more of a hope than a reality.[94] There are many obstacles to a comprehensive legal aid system, the biggest one being lack of resources. The lack of resources is itself a function of various factors.[95] The rhetoric of socialism led many to believe that the all-powerful and compassionate state would provide all that was needed to ensure the material and spiritual well-being of the people. Thus organizations have grown accustomed to looking to the state for all of their needs. In this new era of tightened government purses, legal aid centers have been forced to turn to society rather than to the state. China, however, lacks a tradition of charitable giving. This may be due in part to Confucianism, which conceives of ethical obligations as a series of ever-expanding concentric circles, much like the ripples in water caused by a falling stone. Thus one's ethical obligations become more attenuated as one moves out from the core of self and family to the community, the nation, and the cosmos.[96] The lack of a general altruistic sense tends to mean that giving stops at the family. Of course, China is still a developing society. Most people simply lack the economic means to contribute to charities. And those that do have lots of money may not want to call attention to that fact – particularly if they are princelings[97] or others who have become rich through connections or illegal channels. Moreover, there are currently few tax incentives to encourage the wealthy to donate, though regulations issued in 1997 did provide some tax relief. The lack of experience in fundraising on the part of NGOs and social organizations is another factor. Many bar associations, legal aid centers, and other organizations lack a long-term plan. The absence of public accountability and the lack of financial disclosure requirements further undermine fundraising efforts, as potential donors are reluctant to hand over large sums of money without some assurances that the funds will be used for their proper purpose rather than for the principals to purchase new cars.

Whatever the reasons, without the benefit of legal counsel, individuals often do not understand their rights or are unable to take advantage of them. In many cases, parties may enter into agreements that violate the law or fail to take steps to bring themselves into compliance simply because they are not aware of legal requirements or their obligations under the law. In criminal cases, innocent individuals may be convicted simply because they could not afford a lawyer to poke holes in the prosecutor's often weak case.

Qualifications and professionalism

Even when citizens are entitled to legal aid or are able to afford their own lawyer, they will only be able to take full advantage of their rights under law if their lawyer is competent. The quality of the legal profession is as important as the degree of independence and sheer size. The legal profession must meet minimal standards for even a thin rule of law to be implemented. Without a sufficient corps of qualified, honest lawyers to draft contracts, structure project finance deals and represent defendants in criminal cases, rule of law remains but a lifeless ideal incapable of realization.

The legal profession's rapid growth in the last twenty years could not have been achieved without certain compromises in quality. The 1981 Provisional Regulations set lax standards for qualification, emphasizing practice and political criteria over a college education in law. The response to the quality problems resulting from the low standards of the Provisional Regulations was threefold: implementation of a national bar examination; restrictions on who may apply to qualify by approval and who can issue the approval; and introduction of an apprentice requirement as a prerequisite to obtaining a license.

The 1996 Lawyers Law continued the efforts to improve the quality of China's lawyers. The Law increased the standards for qualification, narrowed the window for qualification through approval without passing the bar examination, reaffirmed the one-year apprentice requirement to obtain a practicing certificate, and made renewal of the certificate subject to continuing education and training. After passing the bar examination, lawyers must also undergo a one-year apprenticeship before obtaining their license and then undertake forty hours a year of continuing legal education and training. The Lawyers Law also reiterated the importance of professional ethics and disciplinary rules, and provided for punishment and legal liability of law firms and lawyers who do not meet their professional responsibilities.[98]

Despite the ongoing efforts to improve the quality of the legal profession, quality remains an issue. While there is an ever-increasing number of outstanding and dedicated PRC lawyers, many still fall far short of the standards expected of their counterparts elsewhere, even after several years of practice.[99] During negotiations or litigation, many lawyers express opinions without legal basis, fall back on general claims about PRC law unsupported by citations to specific clauses, or appeal to general notions of fairness and what should, at least in the eyes of the particular lawyer, be the case. When they do cite specific provisions, there is often no analysis of how the provisions apply to the particular factual situation or how they support their conclusions. One study of 130 civil disputes (mainly disputes over housing and commercial spaces, compensation for property damage or loss, debts, and divorce and custody) found that 27% of the lawyers remained silent, 43% made brief comments, 25% were very active, while only 4% made explicit reference to substantive or procedural law.[100] Ironically, the results were virtually the same for the control group of cases where nonlawyers represented themselves. Even the arguments tended to be the same, with lawyers often appealing to general moral principles rather than particular legal provisions.

Many lawyers seem to lack a sense of the gravity of their responsibility and are quick to jump to conclusions. This is most striking in the issuance of legal opinions. As foreign law firms are not allowed to issue an opinion on matters of PRC law, foreign investors need to engage a local law firm to do so. Eager to please the foreign investor in hopes of securing future business, many local lawyers, even some from top firms, will issue virtually any opinion the client wants, much to the amazement of the foreign investor's more cautious foreign lawyers who are wary of possible malpractice claims.[101] More generally, the work product of many local lawyers suffers from a lack of attention to detail, both in terms of the presentation of the material and the substantive analysis.

The low quality of many local lawyers may be attributed to a number of factors. Until the Lawyers Law was amended in 2001, PRC lawyers were not required to have a college degree in law or any other type of college degree to sit for the bar examination. As a result many lawyers qualified to take the bar examination through self-study, and as of the mid-1990s almost a third of China's lawyers had no formal education beyond high school.[102] Many lawyers qualified without taking the bar examination.[103] As in other countries with a civil law tradition, the emphasis on memorization of black letter law in law schools means that few of those who do graduate from law school have the necessary critical reasoning and analytical skills to practice law upon graduation.

While lawyers are now required to partake in continuing legal education, post-qualification training is still in its early stages and has yet to be strictly enforced. For the most part, the training tends to be in the form of lectures on black letter law, whereas the more pressing need would seem to be for greater emphasis on legal method and the ability to analyze and apply specific laws and fundamental legal concepts to particular and perhaps novel situations. Given the size of China, the wide variation in levels of expertise and the nature of the practice of law among PRC lawyers, designing and implementing worthwhile training programs is a major challenge.

Arguably one of the most important impediments to developing a highly professional legal force is the absence of good models. Unlike other countries, where young lawyers work side by side with experienced senior lawyers, China's lawyers to a considerable extent have had to figure out for themselves what it means to be a lawyer.

The internal organization and management of PRC law firms may also be a factor. Many firms invest little in their associates. One striking feature of local firms is the huge disparity between compensation of associates and partners. In some of the top foreign firms, the ratio between compensation of a senior partner and senior associate may range from 3:1 to, perhaps, 8:1. The ratio in elite PRC firms is more likely to be 10:1 to 25:1. The ratio of a senior partner to a first-year associate is likely to be even more striking. Moreover, in many firms, little time is spent training junior associates. Further, in making partnership and salary decisions, an associate's ability to generate new clients is often more important than the quality of service or the associate's legal skills. Given the pay structure, junior lawyers have an incentive to concentrate on rainmaking rather than developing their legal skills. Qualified associates, paid relatively little, are also likely to jump ship to start up their own firms, creating continuity and depth problems. As a consequence, most PRC firms tend to be small and thin in terms of experienced lawyers.

Perhaps the most important obstacle to professionalization, however, is that many lawyers find it easier and often more effective to rely on personal relations and connections rather than legal analysis and arguments to achieve their goals. When foreign firms seeking local counsel for litigation, advice on particular legal issues, or assistance in obtaining approvals ask PRC lawyers why they or their firm should be hired, all too often the response is in terms of connections to officials at certain ministries or relationships with judges, rather than descriptions of cases handled or the quality of their work product. To be sure, such connections *are* often necessary (if not sufficient) to obtain information and approvals from the various ministries or to prevail in litigation. While many lawyers would much prefer to rely on legal arguments rather than personal relationships to serve their clients, given the present realities, they have no choice but to rely on connections for fear that if they do not, their clients will be disadvantaged. Until matters are decided on the basis of law rather than connections, there will be little incentive for lawyers to hone their legal skills. Of course, raising the level of lawyers alone will not help – unless the quality of the judiciary is improved, lawyers who try to make sophisticated legal arguments will be wasting their breath.

Corruption and professional ethics

Rule of law assumes that lawyers will be acting in the best interests of their clients rather than their own interests. When lawyers pursue their own interests at the expense of the interests of their clients, the system fails to function as designed. Unfortunately, the legal profession has been tainted by a rampant disregard of professional ethics resulting from the low level of training and professionalism of lawyers as well as more general social trends. As noted previously, China is undergoing a period of soul-searching. To fill the normative void, many Chinese have turned to money-worshipping (*baijin zhuyi*). Such unbridled pursuit of riches has resulted in corruption, ethical improprieties, and increased crime rates. As lawyers are subject to the same pressures as everyone else, the lure of quick profits combined with the lack of a well-developed legal profession has led to significant professional responsibility problems.

Lawyers have been accused of offenses such as engaging in unfair competition to attract clients (including payment of introduction fees, consulting fees, royalties, or kickbacks to anyone who introduces clients); improper influence of procuratorate, court, and arbitration officials; improper charging practices, including accepting under-the-table payment in excess of the stipulated standards; engaging in corruption and bribery or causing others to do the same; falsifying evidence; and failure to pay taxes. Such violations, often reported in the popular press, have tarnished the image of lawyers among the general populace.

One of the main purposes of the Lawyers Law was to further the efforts of the MOJ to promote professional responsibility and compliance with disciplinary rules.[104] The Lawyers Law expressly provides that lawyers may not meet judges, prosecutors, or arbitrators in violation of regulations; entertain, give gifts, or offer bribes to judges, prosecutors, or arbitrators or induce others to do so; provide false evidence or conceal facts or threaten or induce others to provide false evidence or conceal facts; hinder the other party from obtaining evidence; exploit one's position to seek gains from the concerned parties or to accept money or goods from the other party; solicit business by defaming other lawyers, paying introduction fees, or other improper means; work in two or more law firms at once; or represent both sides to a dispute.[105] In addition, lawyers must maintain the confidentiality of state secrets and the trade and personal secrets of their clients.[106] And, indicative of how widespread the problem of tax evasion has been lawyers are expressly required to pay taxes.[107]

The Lawyers Law also prohibits former judges or prosecutors from acting as defense counsel or legal representatives for two years from the time they leave their posts and bans current government employees from moonlighting as lawyers.[108] These restrictions are potentially significant in that current and former members of the courts and procuratorate are often privy to confidential information and may use their connections to influence decisions. However, the impact of these restrictions may be undermined if such persons are able to circumvent the rules by calling themselves "legal consultants," as many do now.[109]

In terms of substantive content, the Lawyers Law broke little new ground, as most of the professional responsibilities set forth in the Lawyers Law occur in existing regulations that taken together are more comprehensive in scope and detail.[110] In any event, the main problem has not been so much the lack of regulations as the lack of compliance and enforcement. According to one source, from 1992 to 1996, only 105 lawyers were subject to disciplinary sanctions in all of China.[111] To date, China's lawyers have rarely been sued for malpractice. In the absence of private litigation and a strong bar capable of reining in wayward lawyers, consumers of legal services have turned to the MOJ and local bar associations for protection. Accordingly, the MOJ has now established hotlines to report cases of attorney malpractice. Meanwhile, in 2000, the Beijing

Lawyers Association received sixty-seven complaints from disgruntled clients, accepting forty for further investigation.[112]

The future of the legal profession in China

Increased technical capacity

As economic and legal reforms deepen, the technical capacity of the legal profession will be improved. Over time, the number of lawyers will rise to meet the growing demand. As the pressing need to generate lawyers diminishes, the focus will continue to shift toward improving the professional qualifications of lawyers.

Accordingly, the long-term trend is undoubtedly toward more qualified lawyers. Legal education is improving. There are now better instructors. Although law professors are paid relatively little and thus often seek opportunities to supplement their incomes by practicing, ironically they are often better instructors as their experience in practice gives them a better appreciation of law in operation. There have also been changes in the curriculum. Some schools are beginning to experiment with the case-oriented Socratic method and are focusing on legal analysis and developing the necessary analytical skills to function effectively in practice. Some have also begun to experiment with clinical education.

Improvements in the legal profession will continue to be driven largely by market forces. At least in the big cities, lawyers now face tough competition, as the number of law firms and lawyers has grown. Although firms now tend to compete on the basis of price, lowering their fees to undercut rivals and attract clients, discounting fees alone will not be sufficient to secure clients in the long run. Ultimately, law firms must deliver – they must win lawsuits and provide the kind of professional services that increasingly sophisticated clients are coming to expect or else lose their clients to more qualified firms that are able to produce results. As companies become more sophisticated consumers of legal services, China's legal corps will have to keep pace and raise their level of performance.

PRC lawyers will be under additional pressure to raise their standards now that China has entered the WTO, in part to take advantage of the additional business opportunities that will arise and in part to respond to increased competition from foreign firms. That said, the impact of WTO accession should not be overstated. In the short term, any increase in competition from foreign firms is likely to be limited. Foreign firms will continue to be subject to a number of onerous restrictions.[113] Moreover, foreign and local firms tend to service different segments of the market. The former have a competitive advantage when it comes to large projects that require a team of several lawyers or projects that involve offshore elements, foreign governing law, and international precedents. Conversely, PRC firms are increasingly able to handle the basic needs of most foreign investors in China, including trade contracts, technology licensing, corporate restructuring, and the establishment of joint ventures, wholly foreign-owned enterprises, or other types of companies. Local firms also have a monopoly over litigation and have a competitive advantage when it comes to language-intensive work such as merger and acquisition projects that require considerable due diligence.

Thus, at least for the immediate future, foreign and PRC firms are likely to develop different markets, particularly given the restriction on joint ventures, mergers, and other forms of significant collaborative relationships between foreign and local firms. Whereas foreign accounting firms are forced to joint venture with local accounting firms, such arrangements are off-limits to foreign law firms. Although post-WTO regulations that appear to allow for some form of joint law firm in the Western region may be a harbinger of change, it remains the case that PRC authorities view law as more intimately related to politics than accounting, which is considered a technical and neutral economic area. Indeed, one official from the MOJ acknowledged that foreign lawyers would not be allowed to sit for the bar examination and foreign firms would not be allowed to merge with PRC firms largely because of the possibility that foreign lawyers would then take an aggressive stance in political cases.[114]

Notwithstanding such limitations, PRC lawyers will have more opportunities to work with foreign lawyers on various projects as they begin to handle a greater share of the foreign investment pie. Such increased contacts, along with the demands of the market, will provide PRC commercial lawyers with incentives to professionalize.

Although the extent to which greater professionalization in the commercial area will spill over to other areas is unclear, some overall improvement is to be expected. Even in noncommercial areas, lawyers will be subject to increased competition. As the profession matures, better-managed firms will gain a competitive advantage by being able to attract the best and brightest law school graduates. Perhaps most important, the many efforts to improve the legal system and promote rule of law are changing the legal culture. By celebrating the legal profession's crucial role in ensuring justice through stories of lawyers fighting for others' rights and overcoming obstacles, such as physical abuse and harassment, the mass media as well as professional journals such as *China Lawyer* (*Zhongguo Lushi*) instill professional pride in lawyers. As the legal profession matures and becomes more independent, leading lawyers will play a more prominent role in defining the values of the profession. As the quality of the legal profession improves, lawyers will gain more stature in society.

To be sure, the road ahead is a long one. Most lawyers are still in the money-making phase of their career (a phase which many of them, like lawyers everywhere, will never outgrow). They have little sense of professional responsibility or obligations to the legal profession as such. Thus, violations of professional ethics will in all likelihood continue to occur. The legal profession is young and immature, and it takes time to develop a firm sense of professional ethics. The task is made all the more difficult by the fact that many of China's lawyers remain poorly educated and trained. Moreover, there are as of yet no signs of a burgeoning practice in legal malpractice suits. Further, lawyers will continue to be influenced by contemporary China's emphasis on money-making and the existence, if not tolerance, of widespread corruption. Perhaps most important, many lawyers realize that sometimes the quickest and perhaps only way to solve a problem – whether it be to gain an acquittal, obtain approval for a project, or secure enforcement of a judgment – is to rely on one's connections. Such encounters between lawyer and ministry official or court personnel all too easily lead to improper influence and in some cases bribery.

Independence within limits

The legal profession will continue to become more independent as economic and legal reforms progress. In the short term, however, the Party's desire to control autonomous social organizations will impede the profession's growing independence to some extent. An equal if not greater obstacle is the institutional weakness of bar associations. Even were it so inclined, the MOJ could not delegate all responsibility for monitoring, supervising, and disciplining lawyers to bar associations. Even Yang Jing-guo, former secretary general of the All China Lawyer's Association, has conceded that China's bar associations are not up to the task of adminis-tering the profession.[115] According to one survey, 52 percent of lawyers interviewed did not find the bar associations helpful while only 18 per-cent found them helpful.[116] Like other civil groups, bar associations need to be linked to government entities to survive and be effective.[117] For instance, the Shanghai bar association was quick to come to the aid of a Shanghai lawyer who had been arrested on trumped-up charges as a result of his zealous defense in a criminal case. However, ultimately the bar was forced to enlist the support of the Shanghai Bureau of Justice to resolve the case.[118]

On the positive side, bar associations are building up their institu-tional capacities. As the number of lawyers grows, bar associations collect more dues, and are therefore becoming more financially stable and less dependent on the government for funding. In terms of personnel, as lawyers in the private sector grow older, at least some are likely to look for new challenges and to want to play a more active role in building the legal profession. In some cities, senior lawyers at elite firms have already begun to assume leadership positions in bar associations.

Economic reforms have also altered the relationship between the MOJ and bar associations and the legal profession as a whole. The MOJ and its local counterparts have gained leverage over firms by being able to control appointments to state-run firms and to offer business opportu-nities to loyal firms and lawyers. The trend, however, is clearly toward the establishment of private firms in which the partners are free to make personnel and other management decisions with little or no input from justice organs. Moreover, as the marketplace for quality legal services expands, firms no longer need to rely on justice organs for business op-portunities. To remain relevant in the new environment, justice bureaus have sought to realign themselves to serve lawyers rather than the state. Thus, some justice bureaus have delegated appointment and renewal work to bar associations, requested the local bar association to be in-volved in the disciplining of lawyers, worked with bar associations to protect lawyers, and even opened websites to coordinate legal service exchanges and provide information on new regulations.[119] They have also demonstrated a sensitivity to the lobbying of lawyers by passing regulations that favor the interests of lawyers, particularly domestic lawyers.[120]

Firms have been vulnerable to extortion from justice bureaus because they are often not in compliance with legal requirements, many of which are impractical or unreasonable. As the regulatory framework becomes more rational and less restrictive, firms will find it increasingly easier to comply with the rules and hence will be less vulnerable. For example, many lawyers evade taxes, in part because they object to the unusual requirement whereby they are taxed both at the partnership level and individually. In 2000, however, the tax laws were changed so that law firms were no longer to be taxed at the partnership level.[121] Similarly, China's accession to the WTO will lead to fewer restrictions on foreign law firms, and thus less need to curry favor with the authorities. For instance, foreign firms will be allowed to have more than one office. Firms that have been circumventing the restriction in various creative ways will no longer need to worry that the MOJ will close them down unless they succumb to the MOJ's demands.[122]

Although the legal profession is likely to become more independent, the nature and degree of independence of the PRC bar is likely to differ from that in liberal democratic societies. The legal profession, like the legal system as a whole, is inevitably embedded in a larger socio-political context. Legal professions that meet the standards of a thin rule of law are likely to differ in ways that reflect the larger normative and ideological context in which they exist and operate. In emphasizing freedom of expression, belief, association, and assembly, the United Nations' Basic Principles on the Role of Lawyers presents a typical view of the legal profession in a liberal democracy.[123] Lawyers have the right to take part in public discussion of matters concerning the law, the administration of justice, and the promotion and protection of human rights. They also have the right to join or form local, national, or international organizations, including "self-governing professional associations."

In contrast, a Statist Socialist rule-of-law regime places more emphasis on lawyers' obligation to serve the interests of the state. Moreover, lawyers must work within certain ideological parameters, currently set by the four cardinal principles. In a Statist Socialist rule-of-law regime, the legal profession is subject to more regulation by the state than in a liberal democracy, in keeping with the general divergence in outlook toward civil society. Like other social organizations, bar associations must register with a government agency, which is responsible for monitoring and supervising them. Lawyers and law firms are also subject to the supervision of the MOJ and its local affiliates.

Neoauthoritarians and Communitarians would impose fewer restrictions on the legal profession than Statist Socialists, though the legal profession would still be subject to more regulation than in a liberal democracy. However, neither Neoauthoritarians nor Communitarians would impose such tight ideological strictures as under Statist Socialism. Significantly, neither would emphasize socialism or allegiance to the Party.

While both Statist Socialists and Neoauthoritarians favor state-led civil society, Communitarians support a less top-down approach that gives more autonomy to grass-roots organizations. Although Communitarians, like Liberal Democrats, view the legal profession and bar associations as intermediary organizations existing between the state and individual members of society, they differ in their conception of the nature of the relation of bar associations to the state. Liberal Democrats emphasize the independence and autonomy of the bar association and tend to highlight the adversarial role of the legal profession in limiting state power and protecting individuals against an overreaching state and majority. In contrast, Communitarians highlight the need to work with the state to realize social harmony and reconcile conflicting interests between individuals, social groups, and the state.[124]

The difference in rule-of-law regimes is also apparent in the conception of the lawyer's role vis-à-vis individual clients and society. Every system must confront the issue of how to balance a lawyer's duty to individual clients and to society as a whole. In keeping with their individualist orientation, Liberal Democratic rule-of-law regimes tend to emphasize the adversarial process and a lawyer's duty to zealously defend his or her client.[125] In contrast, Statist Socialists and Neoauthoritarians weight more heavily a lawyer's duty to serve the interests of the state and society. Communitarians attach more weight to the state's interests than Liberal Democrats but less than Neoauthoritarians and much less than Statist Socialists; they also attach more weight to society and less to individuals than Liberal Democrats, though more to individuals than Statist Socialists and Neoauthoritarians. Significantly, the Lawyers Law defines a lawyer as someone who provides legal services to society, as opposed to individual clients, although lawyers are required to protect the rights and interests of their clients.[126]

These ideological differences will color particular institutions, practices, and outcomes in specific cases. Take, for example, confidentiality requirements and disclosure rules. Communications between lawyers and clients are considered confidential in every system. On the other hand, every system limits the scope of confidentiality by requiring lawyers to disclose information obtained from their clients in certain circumstances. Even in the USA, lawyers who are told by their client that the client intends to go out and kill his spouse immediately after leaving the lawyer's office *may* inform the police, though they are not required to do so.[127] But what if the client insinuates that he will lie on the stand? Should the lawyer refuse to put him on the stand or reveal to the court what the client said?[128] If the client tells the lawyer where the murder weapon is located, should the lawyer tell the police? In the USA, lawyers are not allowed to reveal such information.[129] If an accused serial child rapist confesses to the lawyer that he is in fact guilty and if acquitted will go out and rape more children, and yet the lawyer has the opportunity to get the criminal off on a procedural technicality, is the lawyer required, as part of her professional obligation to zealously defend her client, to take advantage of the technicality?[130] In the USA, the lawyer is obligated to raise the procedural argument.

A legal profession is made up of individuals. Individuals are part of a society, and they reflect the traditions, values, and norms of that society. The willingness and ability of lawyers to defend suspected criminals zealously is inevitably influenced by the cultural and social context in which they operate. In China, one of the unintended side effects of economic reforms has been much higher levels of crime, particularly violent crime. As a result, the public has enthusiastically supported the government's harsh campaign to strike hard at criminals (*yanda*).[131] A traditional emphasis on stability and social order and a deeply rooted fear of chaos culminate in a public that is unsympathetic to the plight of criminal defendants. Notwithstanding objections from international human rights agencies to China's unprecedented use of capital punishment, the overwhelming majority of PRC citizens strongly support the death penalty.[132] In a 1995 survey of 5,006 citizens, less than 1 percent believed that the death penalty should be abolished, while more than 22 percent believed that there were too few death sentences.[133] Moreover,

there is little tolerance for lawyers who attempt to have the accused acquitted on a technicality. As has been true for the last two thousand
years, the Chinese criminal system favors substantive over procedural
justice. Any lawyer who manages against the odds to have the accused
acquitted on procedural grounds is not likely to be considered a hero or
held up as a model for other lawyers.

At a more fundamental level, differences in values with respect to the
relation of the individual to society support different intuitions about
criminal justice in China as compared to more liberal Western societies.
Consider the following hypothetical:[134] assume that one knew for a fact
that nine of ten suspects were guilty but one did not know and could
not discover which one of the ten was innocent; would it be better to let
all ten go and risk further harm to society or punish one innocent person? Westerners overwhelmingly respond that all should be released. In
the past, the overwhelming response among Chinese, even law students
at some of China's most prestigious universities, was that all should
be punished. In recent years, the principle of the presumption of innocence has begun to take hold, in part due to the publicity surrounding
the revisions to the Criminal Procedure Law. As a result, more Chinese
currently favor releasing them all. However, basic values change slowly,
and the vast majority still opt for punishing them all.[135]

One commentator once described the difference between the PRC
and US criminal law systems as a slow downhill slide versus a sudden
precipitous drop over a cliff.[136] In China, individuals are likely to be reprimanded by family, friends, neighbors, and colleagues at various stages
before their behavior crosses the line into criminal activity. In contrast,
in the USA, where individual privacy is assigned a higher premium, individuals are given freer rein to pursue their own ends right up until they
cross the line. Given the ample opportunities for most individuals to
rectify their behavior along the way, anyone who ran afoul of the formal
penal system in Imperial China was assumed to be guilty. Traditionally, crimes were considered a breach of social if not cosmic harmony.
Today, the criminal justice system continues to attach great weight to
the consequences of one's acts and, in particular, the harm to society
caused by one's actions. Although the Criminal Code defines crime in
terms of *mens rea* – intention and negligence – and prohibits punishment solely on the basis of harm, it nevertheless explicitly provides as
a guiding principle of sentencing that punishment is to be meted out

based on the amount of harm to society.[137] In meting out punishment, the courts often take into account the people's desire for vengeance, as indicated in the popular expression in capital sentencing cases that "if you don't execute, you won't satisfy the anger of the people" (*busha, bu zu yi ping minfen*). Moreover, both the traditional and contemporary legal systems emphasize the importance of confession, in part out of the belief that by confessing, criminals demonstrate their willingness to be rehabilitated and to restore social harmony.

To be sure, Chinese citizens increasingly appreciate that in some cases those accused of crimes are innocent, and they should have a lawyer able to defend them and bring the truth to light. PRC lawyers who believe their client is innocent are likely to mount a zealous defense. Given the general hostile environment, however, the lawyer may be forced to advise the client that as a tactical matter the best approach is to confess and appeal for leniency. In many cases, the client will already have confessed to the crime. Under the Criminal Procedure Law, public security officers are able to interrogate a suspect for up to twenty-four hours before the accused has the right to a lawyer. In practice, they often find other reasons to deny a suspect access to a lawyer, for instance, claiming that the case involves state secrets. If the accused has confessed, defense lawyers have little room to maneuver. But even when the accused has not confessed to the authorities, if the lawyer does not believe in the innocence of the accused, the likelihood of the lawyer mounting a zealous defense that attempts to exploit all minor procedural violations and loopholes in the law arguably would be lower than in some Western countries with a different worldview and a more adversarial legal profession.

Whose interests will the legal profession serve?
Lawyers as a force of social change

China's legal profession is still in the process of becoming a profession. Professions typically exhibit such features as the possession of esoteric but useful knowledge and skills, specialized training or education, formal organization of practitioners with a common identification and commitment, and adherence to ethical codes and norms of loyalty or service.[138] Others would add to the list the legal protection of the monopoly of skills.[139] There are more positive and negative views of professions. The functionalist approach views the development of a profession as a response to market demands that call for greater specialization and training.[140] Skeptics, including Critical Legal Scholars, are less sanguine about the social benefits of professions. They portray professions as serving the interests of those in the profession by monopolizing services; indeed, professions serve the interests of those already in the profession by erecting and maintaining barriers to entry.[141]

Will the PRC legal profession serve the interests of lawyers, society, or the state? The experiments with legal reform in South American countries in the 1960s and '70s demonstrated that rule of law can serve authoritarian ends, particularly where the legal profession lacks independence. They also demonstrated that the independence of the legal profession may be threatened in more subtle ways than direct government control over the issuance and renewal of licenses and the sanctioning of wayward lawyers. The state can use its discretionary power to distribute economic opportunities to co-opt lawyers. In many cases, the carrot may be more effective than the stick.

In China, bar associations, law firms, and lawyers derive economic advantages from being tied to the MOJ. Such clientelist ties are likely to continue as long as the benefits outweigh the costs. Thus, at least in the short term, the legal profession and certain lawyers and law firms may be inclined to serve the interests of the state in exchange for continued access to economic benefits. However, as already noted, market reforms are resulting in less regulation and hence fewer restrictions on firms as well as new business opportunities without the costs associated with relying on government entities for economic handouts. Accordingly, the value of clientelist ties to the MOJ or its local counterparts is decreasing. For many firms, particularly the elite firms, it simply is not worth the trouble to maintain close relations to the government. Rather, it is more profitable to serve the interests of their clients rather than the state, at least in commercial cases.

Of course, the calculus in certain politically sensitive cases may differ. Lawyers may shy away from such cases in order to avoid jeopardizing their lucrative commercial practices. Even lawyers without financially rewarding private practices may see little purpose in rocking the boat and putting themselves at risk, particularly given that no amount of effort on their part is likely to influence the outcome of such cases. On the other hand, the legal profession has managed to play an important role in political reforms and social change in other repressive regimes including Taiwan,[142] South Africa,[143] and Hungary.[144]

The role of the legal profession as a force for social change may be measured along two dimensions. The first focuses on the part lawyers play in defending and promoting rule of law. The second focuses on whether the legal profession will emerge as a force for broader political reforms, including the establishment of democracy and an expansive view of individual rights. As for the first, the legal profession has already emerged as an important advocate for rule of law, and will continue to be a positive force for further reform of the legal system. As for the second, the legal profession is not likely to be a major force for broader political reform.

Of course, not all lawyers will benefit from a transition to a rule-of-law system in which the outcome of cases turns on legal arguments rather than connections. Today, a lawyer's *guanxi* is often crucial in determining the outcome of a case or at least in expediting the case and ensuring that the client's arguments are heard. Although reliance on relationships may have a short-term beneficial effect in some cases, it defeats the long-term interests of those in the legal profession who support the development of rule of law in China and would prefer to have cases handled in accordance with the law. To realize rule of law and enhance the professionalism and stature of the legal profession, all of China's lawyers must learn to play by the rules and forego traditional reliance on personal connections with key decision-makers.

Currently, PRC lawyers can be divided into three categories: those that lack legal skills but are able to survive and indeed thrive in the contemporary environment due to their *guanxi* and clientelist ties to judges, the MOJ, and other officials; those who have legal skills but lack *guanxi* and would prefer a more law-based order; and those who have both legal skills and *guanxi* and thus can survive in the contemporary environment but generally prefer a more law-based order due to an aversion to the seedy nature of a *guanxi*-based practice. Over time, as new lawyers with better technical skills but fewer connections enter the field, the balance may very well tip in favor of a law-based order.[145]

The likelihood that the legal profession will support rule of law rises when we include not just practicing lawyers but legal academics and those working in universities, think tanks, legal aid offices, consumer rights organizations, bar associations, and other law-related social organizations. These individuals and organizations promote rule of law in a variety of ways. In the USA and other countries with a common law system, the legal profession and NGOs frequently use litigation as a way of shaping law and bringing about social change. PRC lawyers and legal organizations have also attempted to use this strategy. The Beijing University Law Department's Centre for Women's Law Studies and Legal Services has pursued a policy of litigating complicated, representative cases involving women's issues, such as sexual harassment suits, a suit on behalf of a single mother over the right to occupy the family apartment after divorce, a claim against an SOE for terminating a female employee in violation of labor regulations, a suit against the police for the false arrest of three women on allegedly trumped-up prostitution charges, and a case against township government officials for incorrectly implementing family planning policies.[146] Lawyers have also brought class action suits in environmental cases.

Reliance on litigation to effect social change in China is subject to various limitations, however. As in Taiwan and other civil law countries, lawyers in China are not as able to rely on litigation to bring about change because the system is not a precedential one: a court's decision in one case is not binding in other cases.[147] Moreover, as discussed in the preceding chapter, the power of the PRC judiciary to make law is limited. PRC judges, like their counterparts in civil law countries, are supposed to interpret and apply the law rather than to make it. PRC courts are also limited in their remedies. As discussed in Chapter 6, under the ALL, courts may quash specific acts by an administrative agency that are in violation of law but they cannot overturn the abstract act (i.e., the regulation) on which the act was based. Nor can they order the agency to amend or repeal the regulation.

Despite such limitations, litigation has proved a useful tactic in certain circumstances for certain purposes. High-profile cases often attract media attention. Indeed, the Beijing Women's Centre and lawyers in class action cases regularly seek the support of the media. Public outcry may influence the outcome of the case or lead to legislative change. At minimum, it results in dissemination of information and makes citizens more aware of their rights.

In civil law countries, the legal profession's main channels for legal reforms are through legislation and institution-building. Lawyers are often particularly well situated to draft or advise on the drafting of laws and regulations given their training and experience. Lawyers and legal aid organizations work on the front line, in the trenches as it were, and hence understand the shortcomings in the institutional and regulatory framework. As a result, they are often well situated to propose reforms and new legislation.[148] Not only are they likely to possess valuable practical information, they are likely to be sensitive to issues of interpretation and language as a result of their experiences in interpreting laws and advising clients. Legal academics, for their part, bring a scholarly depth and comparative perspective. Not surprisingly, the legal profession – including those who graduated from law school and served as members of the NPC's Legislative Affairs Commission, the State Council's Legislative Affairs Office, or in other ministries, administrative agencies, or government organs responsible for law-making, as well as academics and practicing lawyers – has been at the center of the legislative explosion during the last twenty years and borne much of the burden for the drafting of thousands of laws, regulations, and administrative decrees.

Admittedly the cramped opportunities for public participation in the law-making and administrative rule-making processes limit the ability of the legal profession and legal organizations to influence the legislative process. Moreover, the lobbying efforts of lawyers are impeded by their relatively low status. The social status of PRC lawyers is not as high as in common law states, where lawyers play a greater role in setting the social agenda through high-profile litigation. Chinese lawyers have also suffered reputational damage from much-publicized professional responsibility violations. Nevertheless, individual lawyers and academics, institutes such as the Chinese Academy of Social Sciences (CASS), and social organizations such as bar associations and the Beijing Women's Centre have been instrumental in the legislative process as advisers, consultants, and in some cases drafters.

Lawyers, academics, and legal organizations have also been strong advocates of institutional reforms. Closest to home, lawyers have called for a more autonomous legal profession or better protection of lawyers in carrying out their duties. The legal profession has also worked to improve the legislative system, the security regulatory framework, the arbitration system, the system for enforcing court judgments and arbitral awards, and other aspects of the legal system by suggesting ways in which these institutions could be improved based on their experiences in practice or, in the case of academics, their research of the domestic system and comparative research of other legal systems. The legal profession has also pushed for a more independent judiciary.

Apart from litigation, legislation, and institution-building, lawyers, academics, bar associations, and other legal organizations also promote rule of law by influencing the legal culture. The legal profession has been instrumental in working to implement rule of law by disseminating information and advising on laws, as well as monitoring enforcement and in some cases litigating to ensure enforcement. Lawyers and bar associations have taken part in campaigns to publicize new laws, and have been crucial, through writing newspaper articles, speaking on radio and television shows, and advising clients in daily practice, in helping PRC citizens better understand and take advantage of the new rights provided to them. Given the complexity of many regulations and of most modern legal systems, lawyers are needed to give effect to laws. Thus, PRC lawyers regularly draft contracts and advise businesspeople or citizens on how to establish a company, what the procedures are for registering a mortgage, or how to file for a divorce. In so doing, they demonstrate the importance and utility of law. Lawyers are also increasingly involved in litigation. As Chinese citizens' awareness of their legal rights has grown, so has the number of lawsuits, as PRC individuals have turned in greater numbers to the courts for redress when they have felt that their rights were violated.[149]

Through scholarly conferences, articles in academic journals and the popular press, and radio and television talk shows, the legal community is able to preach the virtues of rule of law while pushing for further legal reforms. Perhaps most important, through such efforts the legal profession can help shape public discourse as to the meaning of rule of law and serve as a counterpoint to the Party's Statist Socialist conception of rule of law. Indeed, academics, often from CASS, have given more than a dozen lectures to senior leaders on legal topics, including the meaning of rule of law. Granted, there is no way of knowing how many, if any, senior Party leaders and government officials have been persuaded by the competing conceptions of rule of law proposed by academics. Similarly, it is difficult to measure the impact of the efforts of the legal community to promote rule of law on the general populace. Presumably most citizens are more interested in concrete issues than theoretical debates. At the same time, the demand for rule of law among the citizenry is high and growing, indicating that legal consciousness-raising activities have not been for naught.[150]

While the legal profession will in all likelihood be a positive force for the establishment of rule of law, whether lawyers will become a significant force for further political reforms is more doubtful. As the elite of society, the legal profession may exhibit the same tendencies as other PRC elites to align themselves with the state and conceive of their role in terms of the loyal (Confucian) official who remonstrates but does not rebel.[151] Moreover, most lawyers appear to be more concerned about making money than politics. As is true of other segments of the upwardly mobile, lawyers are not likely to want to risk social instability, and their own privileged positions, to push for political reforms. Although economic reforms have given rise to a limited civil society, many of the new social groups are politically conservative, especially the many commercial and business associations that have sprung up to promote and protect the economic interests of their members.[152] It is also possible that the legal profession will seek to remain politically neutral as a reaction to the overpoliticization of the legal system in the past. Ironically, some may even perceive efforts to champion a particular political position as inconsistent with rule of law's commitment to separate law from politics. To be sure, by ignoring politics, the legal profession's efforts to promote rule of law could result in a Statist Socialist rule of law that lends legitimacy to the ruling regime without providing democracy and better protection for human rights. On the other hand, even if the legal profession were to emerge as a strong advocate of democracy and liberalism, the profession may find itself out of step with the more conservative and communitarian political beliefs of the majority of PRC citizens. If so, the profession might lose the support of society for its legal reform agenda to implement rule of law. Thus, the more likely path for the legal profession is as an advocate for a non-Liberal Democratic rule of law but not for more general political reforms.

Notes

1 To cite one among many possible examples, in an article on the role of judges and lawyers in defending rule of law, Adama Dieng (1997: 551) claims that the "experiences of many generations of jurists from highly diverse nationalities" demonstrate that rule of law requires an independent legal profession. For similar such claims, see the citations in Lee (2000: footnote 39).

2 See Chapter 4.

3 See deLisle (1999).

4 See Chapter 3. Geoffrey Walker (1988: 36–37) is an exception, as he explicitly includes a competent and independent legal profession among the requisites of a thin theory of rule of law.

5 Basic Principles on the Role of Lawyers, adopted by the Eighth United Nations Congress on the Prevention of Crime and Treatment of Offenders, held in Havana, Cuba, August–September 1990, and welcomed by the 45th General Assembly of the United Nations in resolution 45/121, adopted December 14, 1990. The Basic Principles cite several international rights documents that require access to counsel, particularly in criminal cases. China has signed two of them and ratified the second: the International Covenant on Civil and Political Rights, and the International Covenant on Economic, Social and Cultural Rights. The Universal Declaration of Human Rights (UDHR) contains similar provisions requiring a fair and impartial trial in which the accused "has had all of the guarantees necessary for his defence." Scholars are divided on whether the UDHR is legally binding in whole or in part or not at all on members of the United Nations.

6 Walker (1988: 36–37).

7 Abel (1995: 20–21) notes, however, that on the whole the South African legal profession failed to champion rule of law and that "the vast majority of practitioners and the organized profession actively or passively supported the government." More generally, while the legal profession in Ghana and Malaysia supported the judiciary against attacks by the authoritarian ruling regimes, the legal profession failed to oppose McCarthyism in the USA, the German occupation of France, or Fascism in Italy. Abel (1995: 10).

8 Macauley (1998). On the importance of law in practice, see generally Scogin (1990: 1325–1404); Bernhardt and Huang (1994).

9 While never promulgated, the 1906 draft Qing Criminal and Civil Litigation Law included a chapter on lawyers. This law was revised in 1911 as the Draft Criminal Litigation Law and Draft Civil Litigation Law. However, the Qing dynasty toppled before these laws took effect. Xiao Shengxi, ed. (1996: 30).

10 These regulations were supplemented by more detailed regulations on registration, disciplinary actions, and examinations of lawyers. Conner (1996: 216); Xiao Shengxi, ed. (1996: 30–32).

11 Growth then slowed over the next decade, so that by 1943, there were only 9,245 lawyers registered with the MOJ. Conner (1996: 230).

12 By way of comparison, Japan in 1935 had one lawyer for every 9,700 people. Conner (1996: 230).

13 Conner (1996: 219–22).

14 Alford (1995: 27).

15 Common Program of the Chinese People's Political Consultative Conference, art. 17 (adopted September 29, 1949).

16 See Report Regarding the Establishment of Lawyers' Work (approved July 10, 1956).

17 Xiao Shengxi, ed. (1996: 35).

18 Zhang Geng, ed. (1997: 4).

19 Zhang Geng, ed. (1997: 5).

20 Alford (1995: 29).

21 See generally Jerome Cohen (1968); Shao-chuan Leng and Hungdah Chiu (1985: 10–17).

22 Gelatt (1991: 753).

23 Zhang Geng and Hu Kangsheng, eds. (1996: 40).

24 By October 1980, there were 3 provincial bar associations and 17 provincial or municipal bar association preparation committees, 381 law offices, and 3,000 full-time lawyers. Zhang Geng, ed. (1997: 4).

25 Provisional Regulations of the PRC on Lawyers, art. 8 (adopted by the NPC, 1980) [hereinafter Provisional Regulations].

26 Provisional Regulations, art. 1.

27 Provisional Regulations, art. 1.

28 Provisional Regulations, arts. 2, 3.

29 See the 1979 Criminal Procedure Law, art. 110(3). Facing a surge in crime in the early 1980s, the NPC eliminated, as part of its "Strike Hard" campaign, the requirement that defendants be given seven days' prior notice of their trial in cases involving violent offenses such as murder, rape, or armed robbery. See the Decision of the Standing Committee of the National People's Congress Concerning the Procedure for the Rapid Adjudication of Criminal Elements Who Seriously Endanger Social Order, art. 1 (adopted September 2, 1983).

30 This practice was known as *xianding, houshen* – decide first, try later. See Li Shaoping (1990: 39).

31 See deLisle (1999: 219). In 1998, in response to the agreement between Presidents Jiang and Clinton to pursue legal cooperation, the ABA signed an agreement with the All China Lawyers Association to promote rule of law in various ways, including training of PRC lawyers in the USA and strengthening PRC bar associations.

32 Provisional Regulations, arts. 1–3.

33 Lawyers Law, art. 2 (adopted by the NPC, 1996).

34 See, for example, Shen Dailu (1996: 7); Tang Jinping (1996: 39).

35 Zhang Geng, ed. (1997: 9, 24–25); Xiao Shengxi, ed. (1996: 54).

36 Lawyers Law, art. 1. Article 5 of the 1993 Lawyers Professional Responsibility and Practice Discipline Standards requires every lawyer to resolutely serve in the construction of the socialist economy, reform, and opening to the outside world, in the construction of socialist democracy, and in the consolidation of the democratic dictatorship of the people and the long-term stability of China.

37 Lawyers Law, art. 33. Gelatt (1989: 255).
38 PRC Constitution, arts. 53, 54.
39 Decision Concerning the Strict Enforcement of the Lawyers Law and the Further Strengthening of the Establishment of the Lawyer Force, art. 3 (issued September 26, 1996).
40 Decision Concerning the Strict Enforcement of the Lawyers Law and the Further Strengthening of the Establishment of the Lawyer Force, art. 7.
41 See Chapters 5 and 9.
42 1999 *China Law Yearbook* (2000: 1039).
43 As explained below, the accused will often have confessed by the time the lawyer becomes involved.
44 US Department of State Country Reports on Human Rights Practices for 1996 (1997: 622); Lawyers Committee for Human Rights (1993: 47–51).
45 The idea of eliminating cooperative firms was debated during the legislative process. One side took the position that cooperative law firms were an experiment in response to the need for an alternative to state-owned law firms and the allocation system. Given that partnership firms were now allowed and that in fact cooperative firms were functionally indistinguishable from partnership firms, there is no need to preserve cooperative firms, particularly given their limited liability form. However, others argued that since there were a number of cooperative firms already, it would be better to maintain the status quo. Zhang Geng and Hu Kangsheng, eds. (1996: 98–99).
46 The Lawyers Law also recognizes the right of foreign law firms to set up offices in China subject to State Council regulations. Lawyers Law, art. 51. For a more detailed discussion, see Peerenboom (1998b).
47 Sun Guolian (1999).
48 Zhang Geng and Hu Kangsheng, eds. (1996: 95).
49 Between 1997 and 1998 alone, the number of partnerships grew by over 7 percent while the number of state-funded firms declined by 11 percent. Chen Yanni (1998: 1).
50 Chen Yanni (1998: 96–97).
51 Chen Yanni (1998: 19); see also Shen Bailu (1996: 4); Lawyers Law, art. 4.
52 Provisional Regulations, art. 19.
53 Zhang Geng and Hu Kangsheng, eds. (1996: 261).
54 Lawyers Law, art. 40.
55 Zhang Geng, ed. (1997: 30).
56 Shen Bailu (1996: 5).
57 Zhang Geng, ed. (1997: 30).
58 Luo Qizhi (1998: 21).
59 Luo Qizhi (1998: 20).
60 Zhang Geng, ed. (1997: 224).
61 "Zhongguo Minzhu yu Fazhi Jianshe de Kua Shiji Gongcheng" *China Lawyer* (1997: 7). As the head of the MOJ, Xiao Yang had an institutional incentive in insisting on an expansive role for the MOJ. Whether he would still support such a position now that he has become the head of the SPC is unclear.

62 An earlier draft of the Lawyers Law had provided that the bar association would organize and administer the national bar examination, but this provision was deleted by the NPC Law Committee. Zhang Geng and Hu Kangsheng, eds. (1996: 26).

63 An earlier draft of the Lawyers Law provided that law firms would need to be examined and approved by the MOJ and then submit a work report every year to the MOJ and bar association. The drafters decided to change the process from examination and approval (*shencha pizhun*) to examination and verification (*shenhe*) – ostensibly a more objective and less demanding process but in practice often the same – and to eliminate the annual report to emphasize the independence of law firms and the less intrusive role of the MOJ as supervisor rather than administrative superior in charge of approval. Zhang Geng and Hu Kangsheng, eds. (1996: 92). However, 1997 regulations reinstate the annual report and review requirement. See Law Firm Registration Administration Measures Law, art. 21 (issued by the NPC, October 25, 1996).

64 Lawyers Law, art. 8(3); Lawyers' Practicing Certificate Administration Measures, arts. 5, 7 (issued Nov. 25, 1996).

65 Lawyers' Practicing Certificate Administration Measures, art. 13.

66 Lawyers Law, art. 48.

67 MOJ officials and leaders of the All China Lawyers Association have noted in personal communications that in practice the correct political thinking requirement is not strictly enforced. No official from the MOJ, no PRC lawyer, nor any academic with whom I have spoken knew or had heard of any case where a lawyer's license was revoked for political activities. However, one lawyer who was a Party member but wanted to give up his Party membership claimed the Beijing Bureau of Justice threatened not to renew his license if he withdrew from the Party. July 1999 interview.

68 Lee (2000: 400).

69 By relying on *guanxi*, lawyers are frequently able to obtain the necessary certifications from one of their acquaintances at the justice bureau.

70 See the speech by Supreme Court President Xiao Yang, which appeared in the Party-dominated journal, *Qiushi*, translated and reprinted in *Building the Socialist Legal System* (1998).

71 See the revised Criminal Procedure Law, arts. 155–60 (adopted by the NPC, 1996). See also Chen Guangzhong and Yan Duan, eds. (1996). However, the court does retain certain powers to conduct investigations and question witnesses. See Criminal Procedure Law, arts. 155, 156, 158.

72 "Guangdongsheng Gong'anting Qiangdiao yao Baozhang Lushi Yifa Luxing Zhize" (1997).

73 Regulations Concerning Several Problems in Implementation of the Criminal Procedure Law (issued January 19, 1998).

74 Wang Zucai (1997: 3).

75 Peerenboom (1998b: 31–33).

76 One report cited seven cases of physical abuse in seven different provinces within a four-month period. Xiao Shengxi, ed. (1996: 203–04). The All China

Lawyers Association reportedly received fifty-nine complaints of lawyers being threatened or harassed by enforcement officials between 1996 and 1998. He Sheng (1998).

77   At least one source attributes the high incidence of abuse of lawyers to: the low level of legal consciousness by parties to disputes; the poor quality of court personnel and other members involved in the process; and prejudice toward lawyers among the general populace. Xiao Shengxi, ed. (1996: 205).

78   Peerenboom (1998b: 33).

79   Peerenboom (1998b: 33).

80   Lee (2000: 402).

81   Xiao Shengxi, ed. (1996: 41).

82   1999 Law Yearbook (2000: 1039).

83   See "Lawyers' Test Draws Increasing Numbers" (2000). In contrast, in 1998, 142,500 sat for the exam. *Lawyer Qualification Exam Draws 142,500 Applicants* (1998).

84   *Lawyer Qualification Exam Draws 142,500 Applicants* (1998).

85   1999 Law Yearbook (2000: 1039). Gu Peidong (1999) puts the number of full-time lawyers slightly higher, at 80,000.

86   Jacob (1996: 273). Comparison across countries is difficult as certain legal tasks may be handled by nonlawyers in some countries and by lawyers in other countries.

87   Fu Hualing (forthcoming 2002) describes the attempt of the MOJ to create a parallel legal profession, one for the cities and one for the rural areas. In the countryside, Township Legal Services Stations (TLSSs) provide various legal services including representation in civil and economic disputes (but not criminal suits). They also assist in mediation and dissemination of legal information. In the past, a TLSS would serve a single township. Now, TLSSs are being restructured so that one TLSS will serve several townships, in part to enhance the independence of TLSSs. TLSSs are staffed by rural legal workers approved by the justice bureau. According to the MOJ, there are some 120,000 such workers. To qualify, they must be politically reliable, impartial, honest, and healthy. In addition, they should have at least a high school equivalent education and some legal knowledge. The MOJ has sought to impose tighter quality controls by requiring rural TLSS workers to take an examination and register with the justice bureau. However, many do not bother to take the test or register as doing so is costly and provides no benefits. The MOJ has also established hotlines at the county level for those seeking legal advice and assistance.

88   These statistics are from *China Law Yearbooks* for the years 1993 to 1999, and reflect the combined representation rates for first and second instance cases.

89   The Yearbook does not specify how often lawyers represented the plaintiff as opposed to the agency defendant. To calculate the representation rates for plaintiffs, I divided the total representation rates in half. However, it is not clear that in fact plaintiffs and defendants engage counsel at similar rates.

90   Although the 1989 SPC Methods of Collecting Litigation Fees by People's Courts stipulate relatively low case acceptance fees, they also allow for other

fees which may quickly add to the bill, including fees for appraisal, announcing the case, translation of documents, enforcement measures, and "other fees." As courts are under financial pressure, they often impose additional charges and rarely waive fees.

91 The provisions in the Lawyers Law are not entirely consistent with the provisions in other regulations. See Peerenboom (1998b: 86–87).

92 Lawyers Law, art. 41. In July 2000, the SPC issued the Regulations for the Provision of Judicial Assistance to Indigent Parties.

93 Lawyers Law, arts. 42, 43. According to members of the MOJ's Legal Aid Center, the MOJ currently allows the provinces to determine the specific requirements for lawyers based on local conditions. Most require lawyers to handle one to three *pro bono* cases a year. Law firms may also buy their way out of legal aid obligations, with the amount being determined locally.

94 By June 1998, there were some 180 legal aid centers or offices. According to the MOJ, they handled more than 70,000 cases in 1997. By the end of 2000, there were reportedly 1,853 legal aid offices, with 6,109 full-time employees. These offices handled more than 170,000 cases on behalf of more than 228,000 people, in addition to providing legal advice to some 830,000 people. See *China Offers More Judicial Assistance to Citizens* (2001).

95 Lee (2000).

96 The image is most clearly stated in the *Daxue* (Great Learning). The Mohists were strongly opposed to the Confucian ethic of graded obligations, arguing for a more all-encompassing ethic of universal consideration (*jianai*).

97 *Gaogan zidi* – the children of high-level cadres or princelings.

98 Peerenboom (1998b: 60–67).

99 The following is based largely on personal experience from practicing in China for a number of years (including recently as Of Counsel for a PRC firm), fieldwork in connection with a survey of enforcement of arbitral awards, and discussions with other lawyers (foreign and PRC), MOJ officials, and academics.

100 Thireau and Hua (1997: 360–61).

101 The boldness of local attorneys is explicable in part by the absence to date of malpractice suits based on incorrect legal opinions. As of year-end 1997, MOJ officials in charge of lawyer discipline were unaware of any such suits.

102 Zhang Geng and Hu Kangsheng, eds. (1996: 42).

103 According to Shen Hongwei (2000: 81), as of 2000, only 60,000 of China's 110,000 lawyers had passed the bar.

104 Lawyers Law, arts. 1, 3. See also Peerenboom (1998b: 41–42), discussing other legislation aimed at raising the level of professional responsibility.

105 Lawyers Law, arts. 12, 14, 31, 35.

106 Lawyers Law, art. 33.

107 Lawyers Law, art. 23.

108 Lawyers Law, arts. 12, 36.

109 Yuen (1996: 9).

110 See, for example, the Lawyers Disciplinary Rules (issued October 22, 1992); Lawyers Professional Responsibility and Practice Discipline Standards (issued

December 26, 1993); Several Regulations to Oppose Unfair Competition in the Legal Profession (issued February 20, 1995).

111   Zhang Geng and Hu Kangsheng, eds. (1996: 56). However, one MOJ official stated in personal communication that approximately one hundred lawyers were disciplined in 1996 alone, mainly for providing poor quality service, accepting fees but then failing to provide services or other fee-related disputes, accepting compensation from the other side in exchange for selling out one's client, or committing crimes such as harboring a criminal.

112   "Summary of the 2000 Work Report of the Beijing Lawyers Association," 1 *Beijing Lawyer* (2001: 6).

113   Xiao Hongming (2000).

114   Xiao Hongming (2000).

115   So (1996: 8).

116   Luo Qizhi (1998: 16). The study was based on a survey of sixty-seven lawyers.

117   See generally O'Brien (1994b), discussing the willingness of people's congresses to pursue a strategy of entwinement and embeddedness whereby lower-level people's congresses voluntarily seek out links to higher-level congresses and organs of state power and thus sacrifice some of their autonomy in order to gain access to power and other benefits.

118   Lee (2000: 402).

119   *China: Justice Ministry Opens Website for China's Lawyers* (1998).

120   See Chapter 6 for a discussion of regulations drafted by the MOJ, at the request of local lawyers, that would have imposed severe limitations on foreign law firms practicing in China.

121   See the Regulations on Individual Tax Collection from Investors in Sole Proprietorship and Partnerships (issued by the Finance Ministry and State Tax Bureau on September 19, 2000 and effective January 1, 2001).

122   Unfortunately, foreign firms will still be subject to numerous restrictions, including the blanket prohibition against interpreting and advising on PRC law though they may now advise on the "legal environment." Were such a requirement strictly enforced, no foreign firm could practice in China. Thus, foreign firms may still be vulnerable to extortion.

123   See Articles 23 and 24 of the Basic Principles on the Role of Lawyers.

124   Social organizations, including bar associations, may now be forced to espouse such non-threatening communitarian values, because they need to enlist the support of the government to be effective. Direct challenges to the ruling regime are not likely to succeed and could result in a backlash against the legal profession, the bar association, and other social organizations working for rule of law. On the other hand, such positions are also likely to be the result of differences in traditions and fundamental values.

125   To be sure, there is also considerable variation among liberal democracies. See the volumes edited by Abel and Lewis (1988) on legal professions in common law and civil law countries.

126   Lawyers Law, arts. 2, 26, 27, 28.

127   Rule 1.6(b) of the ABA Model Rules of Professional Conduct provides that a "lawyer *may* reveal [confidential] information to the extent that the lawyer *reasonably believes necessary* to prevent the client from committing *a criminal*

act that the lawyer believes *is likely* to result in *imminent death or substantial bodily harm."* (Emphasis added.) Article 117a of the American Law Institute's Restatement of Law Governing Lawyers sets an even higher bar for disclosure: the lawyer is only permitted to reveal such information if the lawyer reasonably believes it is necessary to prevent *certain* death or serious bodily harm. Lawyers are not allowed to disclose communications in which the client stated that he or she intended to commit noncriminal tortious acts.

128   In the USA, the general rule in noncriminal cases is that a lawyer's duty of candor toward the court requires the lawyer to disclose false testimony by the client. The rule in criminal cases is less clear. One solution is to allow the accused to testify by a narrative without guidance through the lawyer's questioning. Two other solutions, diametrically opposed, are either to allow the lawyer not to reveal perjury or to require the lawyer to reveal the perjury. Morgan and Rotunda (2000: 64).

129   However, lawyers are not allowed to remove, alter, or take possession of evidence, at least in California. See *People* v. *Meredith* (1981) 29 Cal.3d 682, 695. Thus, if the client discloses the whereabouts of the weapon and the lawyer digs it up and examines it, the lawyer is now obligated to turn it over to the prosecution. Similarly, if the accused gives the weapon to the lawyer, the lawyer must turn it over.

130   This is not merely a hypothetical. A former public defender confided that he once found himself confronting precisely this issue. He chose not to pursue the technicality, and then resigned his post to become a social worker.

131   Polls in 1995, 1996, and 1997 found that social stability and crime topped the concerns of urban residents. In 2000, a poll of 3,000 urban residents in ten cities found that social stability and crime ranked fourth, behind environmental issues, unemployment, and children's education. See the US Embassy's Beijing Environment, Science and Technology Update for November 3, 2000.

132   Amnesty International (1997a) reported more than 6,100 death sentences and 4,367 confirmed executions in 1996 alone, and noted that these numbers are based on public reports and likely to fall far short of the actual numbers.

133   Hu Yunteng (forthcoming 2002).

134   Peerenboom (1995).

135   I asked a research assistant to conduct a survey of residents of Beijing and Tianjin in the summer of 2000. Almost two-thirds of the 106 respondents (63%) favored punishing them all. Interestingly, 83% of Tianjin residents favored punishment in contrast to only 56% of Beijing residents. The divergence appears to be explained by differences in educational levels. There were many more college-educated respondents in Beijing. Among respondents with a college education, 60% favored releasing all of the suspects versus only 10% among those without a college education.

136   Victor Li (1971).

137   Criminal Procedure Law, arts. 11–13. Of course, harm is also relevant in Western systems in some cases. I discuss this issue in greater detail in Peerenboom (1995).

138   Moore (1970).

139   Wilensky (1964: 142–46).
140   Moore (1970); Parsons (1968).
141   Larson (1977); Abel (1989).
142   Winn and Tang-chi (1995).
143   Abel (1995).
144   Sajo (1993) notes that although the legal profession neither took the lead in pushing for democracy in Hungary nor constituted the main force for social change, lawyers did become increasingly active once the transition to democracy began. The Independent Lawyers' Forum, established to promote legal reform, acted as a catalyst for the Opposition Round Table Talks that resulted in a unified opposition to the ruling communist regime.
145   To be sure, the legal profession's role in promoting rule of law is not simply a function of the number of lawyers that would benefit from a more law-based order. A minority of well-placed senior lawyers and judges bound together in mutually beneficial clientelist relationships could thwart or at least hinder the efforts of those interested in promoting rule of law and decision-making based on law rather than connections.
146   Lee (2000: 390).
147   See Winn and Tang-chi (1995).
148   One study of legal aid centers staffed by students concluded that such organiza- tions gave students a much better sense of how law operates in society. Despite some recent changes, legal education in China still tends to emphasize black letter law and the memorization of rules rather than how those laws are imple- mented in practice. By working in legal aid centers, students learn firsthand the importance of the institutional context and how the quality of legal per- sonnel may affect how law is implemented. As a result, they tend to come away with a more comprehensive approach toward legal reform. Legal aid work also promotes an image of lawyers as ethically obligated to serve society and instills a professional ethos that involves a commitment to public interest. Lee (2000: 398).
149   Between 1993 and 1997, the number of cases of first instance increased on av- erage by 11.5%. Interestingly, however, after years of rapid increase, the total number of cases increased by only 0.2% in 1997, with the total number of cases of first instance actually decreasing 0.5%. Criminal cases decreased by 26% and economic cases decreased by 2%, while civil cases increased 5.93% and administrative cases by 13%. In 1998, the total number of first instance cases rebounded slightly, increasing by 2.3%, due largely to a 10% increase in crim- inal cases. 1998 *China Law Yearbook* (1999: 128–32); 1999 *China Law Yearbook* (2000: 19, 112). In 1999, the number of cases increased by 5.2%, with criminal cases leading the way with a 12% increase. See the *SPC 2000 Work Report.*
150   One of the striking results of a recent survey was the widespread support for rule of law among those that held otherwise sharply divergent political views, particularly with respect to democracy. See Yali Peng (1998).
151   On the other hand, lawyers were actively involved in opposition politics in Taiwan. Several of the key members of the Democratic Progressive Party were

lawyers, and in comparison to Guomindang members, a higher percentage of DPP members in the Legislative Yuan had legal backgrounds. Winn and Yeh (1995) suggest that political activists with legal backgrounds might have turned to opposition politics rather than litigation as a strategy for achieving reform due to, *inter alia*, the limited ability of litigation in civil law systems to effect change by setting precedents and the weakness of the legal profession under authoritarian rule.

152 Pearson (1997); Wank (1999). See also the discussion of civil society and political reform in Chapter 11.

9

The administrative law regime: reining in an unruly bureaucracy

Because the essence of rule of law is the ability of law to impose meaning-ful limits on the state and individual members of the ruling elite, an effective administrative law regime that limits the arbitrary acts of government is essential to rule of law. Yet despite broad agreement as to the importance of administrative law, administrative law is one area where there is tremendous variation among legal systems around the world. Simply put, there is no single correct way to deal with common administrative problems, a fact often overlooked by China's critics.[1] Thus, while all states rely on generally applicable laws to one degree or another to provide predictability and certainty, and attempt to limit abuses of discretion, they may differ with respect to how much administrative discretion is desirable. East Asian development states tend to favor a larger, more flexible role for the executive in managing the economy than Western liberal states.[2] Administrative officials in China also enjoy considerable discretion, in part because the rapidly changing economic environment requires flexibility.

In light of the diversity among administrative law regimes, the lack of a single blueprint for success, and a distinctive set of institutional, cultural, economic, and political constraints, the development of China's administrative law regime inevitably will be determined primarily by its own contingent, context-specific conditions, including which version of rule of law prevails.[3] Legal reformers will choose from the various items on the administrative law reform menu the ones that most suit China's particular circumstances, including perhaps some homegrown options.

On the other hand, although the menu of options with respect to goals, institutions, mechanisms for controlling administrative discretion, and legal doctrines is expansive and potentially unlimited, modern states with well-developed legal systems and functioning administrative law regimes have tended to converge on a range of favored choices.[4] Not surprisingly, as administrative law reforms have progressed in China, there are signs of increasing convergence with respect to the purpose of administrative law, institutions, rules, and even outcomes. During the Imperial- and Mao-era rule-by-law regimes, the emphasis of administrative law was on government efficiency, top-down management, and ensuring that government officials and citizens obeyed central policies rather than the protection of individual rights. In contrast, administrative law is now understood to entail balancing government efficiency with the need to protect individual rights and interests.[5] As part of its efforts to implement rule of law, China has also established and strengthened institutions and mechanisms for reining in the bureaucracy that are similar to those in other countries, including legislative oversight committees, supervision committees that are the functional equivalent of ombudsmen, internal administration reconsideration procedures, and judicial review. It has also passed a number of laws that are similar to and indeed often modeled on laws from other jurisdictions. As a result of such changes, the administrative law system is greatly improved.

On the whole, however, China's administrative law regime remains weak due to various context-specific factors, many of which have little to do with the administrative law system as such, including shortcomings in the legislative system, weak courts, poorly trained judges and lawyers, corruption, a low level of legal consciousness among government officials and the citizenry, and the fragmentation and overlapping of authority that have resulted from the transition to a more market-oriented economy.[6] After a brief overview of the evolution of administrative law, I turn to these general systemic problems, which structure the internal dynamics of administrative law reform by highlighting the major areas in need of reform while simultaneously limiting the universe of feasible solutions.

I then discuss the weaknesses in the various mechanisms for reining in government officials, including legislative supervision, administrative supervision, Party discipline, administrative reconsideration, and judicial review. Each of these mechanisms is hampered by the institutional and systemic problems and reflects the limits of the current legal and political environment.

Next I consider the future for administrative law reform in China, and in particular whether China will be able to take advantage of recent trends in administrative law in other countries. The modern era has been the era of the regulatory state. Administrative agencies have increasingly shouldered the responsibilities of law-making, interpretation, implementation, and adjudication. Traditionally, administrative law scholars have been concerned with limiting administrative discretion to prevent abuse and to ensure rule of law, and with rendering officials accountable to overcome the so-called democracy deficit resulting from the tremendous power ceded to non-elected administrative officials.[7] In the last several decades, disenchantment with the modern regulatory state's top-down, command-and-control style of regulation has led to a reconception of the role of the state and new "post-modern" approaches,[8] including deregulation,[9] increased reliance on private actors to perform some of the tasks traditionally undertaken by administrative agencies,[10] more involvement of interest groups in negotiated rule-making processes, and experimentation with new ways of regulating and controlling agencies that are more decentralized and flexible and that involve greater participation at the local level by members of the general public and private interest groups.[11]

China may be able to take advantage of some of the recent innovations in administrative law. But it will not be able to leapfrog over the modernist stage of legal system development directly to the postmodern stage in the way it has bypassed VCRs and gone directly to DVDs. Although a new age may be dawning in the United States and in other modern democratic states with developed legal systems, China is still in the process of putting in place the basic building blocks of a modern legal system. The postmodern approaches to administrative law assume a functioning judiciary as a backstop, even if they downplay the role of judicial review in favor of greater public participation and other ways of avoiding and resolving disputes. Similarly, China lacks the market economy and liberal democratic political system assumed by advocates of deregulation and more bottom-up democratic experimentalism.[12] Deregulation and reliance on the market generally are not appropriate strategies in light of pervasive market failures, including market distortions due to administrative monopolies. Nor does China have the robust civil society and organized public interest groups from which bottom-up solutions are likely to emerge. Moreover, as a practical matter, greater reliance on local initiatives runs counter to the Party's emphasis on maintaining tight central control over the political sphere and over social organizations and interest groups.

What then can be done to improve China's administrative law regime? I conclude by considering future reforms that China might be able to adopt given its current state of development, while at the same time highlighting the limits of the law in bringing about a limited government in which the arbitrary acts of government officials are held in check. External mechanisms for reining in wayward bureaucrats can only go so far. The most difficult task of all will be to create a culture of legality where government officials and citizens alike show respect for the law through their voluntary compliance.

The evolution of administrative law

Although rule of law requires that laws impose meaningful restraints on government actors, historically, law in China has been conceived of in instrumental terms as a tool to ensure that the will of the rulers or the policies of the CCP are carried out. As pointed out in Chapter 2, the function of law has not been to impose meaningful constraints on the ruling elite or to protect individual rights and freedoms against arbitrary infringement by the government. While there were administrative laws, such laws were meant to ensure that government officials faithfully carried out the ruler's decisions.

Since 1949, the fate of administrative law has largely tracked the vicissitudes of law and the legal system more generally. The early years of the Mao era were a time of promise, with more than 870 pieces of administrative legislation passed from 1954–57.[13] Research on administrative law topics also flourished. However, the antirightist movement in 1957 put an end to law reform in administrative law as well as in other areas.

Administrative law reform began slowly in the post-Mao era. The emphasis in the early Deng years was on the use of law as an instrument of economic development. Economic reforms called for an expansive role for government rather than a limited one. Accordingly, relatively little attention was paid to administrative law and in particular to the use of administrative law as a means of restraining government actors, though some laws did provide for administrative suits against the government.[14]

The 1982 constitution was a step forward in that it contained provisions regarding administrative procedures, compensation, and the right to sue.[15] As the constitution is not directly justiciable, between 1982 and 1988 more than 130 implementing laws and regulations provided for administrative litigation in specific instances.[16] By the end of 1988, the Supreme People's Court had established an administrative law division and more than 1,400 local courts had created administrative panels to hear administrative cases. In 1987, drafting of an Administrative Litigation Law (ALL) commenced.[17]

Although the slogan of administration in accordance with the law (*yifa xingzheng*) dates back to the late 1970s, there was not much law for government officials to rely on in the early years. But by 1987, after nearly a decade of legal reform and intense legislative activity, the CCP Central Committee was ready to endorse administration according to law. The idea that law should restrain the administration and protect individuals against government arbitrariness started to gain acceptance. In 1989, the ALL was passed, providing a general basis for citizens to sue government officials.

The pace of administrative law legislation picked up in the 1990s. In 1990, the Administrative Supervision Regulations and the Administrative Reconsideration Regulations were passed. The 1993 State Civil Servant Provisional Regulations changed the way government officials were selected and promoted, requiring that they pass exams and yearly appraisals, and introduced a rotation system. In 1994, the State Compensation Law was passed, followed by the Administrative Penalties Law in 1996. The Administrative Supervision Regulations and Administrative Reconsideration Regulations were amended and upgraded to Laws in 1997 and 1999 respectively. Currently, an Administrative Procedures Law, Administrative Licensing Law, and a law on compulsory administrative enforcement are all in the works.

Administration in accordance with law has been justified on many of the same grounds as rule of law more generally. The dangers of unlimited government were apparent from the arbitrariness of the Cultural Revolution. Economic reforms required a more predictable and accountable administration. The leaders' desire for legitimacy both at home and abroad mandated that the government be held accountable for its actions. In particular, the problem of corruption within the government was eroding support for the CCP. Clearly, the ruling regime sees administrative law as a way to rationalize governance, enhance administrative efficiency, and rein in local governments. At the other end of the spectrum, administration according to law responded to people's demands for greater protection of their rights and interests. As economic reforms progressed, people began to have more property and business interests to protect. Legal reforms and the efforts at disseminating legal knowledge have made people more aware of their rights, and they have been increasingly willing to take to the courts to protect them.

Systemic problems: the path-dependency of reforms

Although many of the institutional or systemic problems that limit the effectiveness of the administrative law system have been discussed previously, the discussion here focuses on the specific ways in which some of these obstacles are relevant to administrative law.[18] So doing highlights the path-dependent nature of reforms, as well as their interdependence and complexity. Simply addressing one set of issues is not sufficient; multiple overlapping issues must be addressed, in some cases simultaneously.

Weak courts

Given the weak stature of the courts and their dependence on the local government for financial resources, courts naturally are reluctant at times to challenge administrative agencies. Judges sometimes refuse to accept cases for fear of insulting government officials or damaging relations with the local government.[19] To avoid problems, judges have been known to reject a case for minor deficiencies in the complaint or to duck a case by suggesting to the plaintiff that he or she is not likely to win and should drop the suit. Some have even gone so far as to knowingly decide incorrectly against the plaintiff but then to tell the plaintiff to appeal to a higher court less vulnerable to local protectionism.[20]

Judges may also not know much about administrative law. Few judges have an administrative background or specialized training in administrative law issues.[21] China's courts are divided into specialized divisions, and the administrative law division is not considered a choice assignment.[22] Many judges resist appointment to the administrative division because of the politically sensitive nature of the cases.

Nevertheless, the weakness of the courts and the low level of compe-tence of judges should not be overstated; to a considerable extent, they are able to perform their job. In fact, plaintiffs in China have a much higher chance of obtaining a satisfactory result than in the United States, Taiwan, and Japan. Plaintiffs prevail in whole or in part in almost 40% of the cases in China but only 12% in the United States and in Taiwan, and between 4–8% in Japan.[23] Of course, that does not mean that the courts are more effective in China than in the USA. One would need to examine the merits of the cases to make any such judgment. It could be that in the United States, administrative agencies generally comply with the law and thus should be expected to prevail more often, whereas in China admin-istrative agencies actually comply with the law even less than the 40% plaintiff victory rate would suggest. That said, clearly the courts are not just a rubber stamp; they do have some authority. But there are certain types of hard cases that would be difficult for a plaintiff to win, including major political cases against the government such as challenges brought by well-known dissidents to reeducation through labor.[24]

Legal culture and traditions

Institutions that are organizationally similar may function very differ-ently and produce very different results due to the different contexts in which they are embedded. China's pursuit of administrative rule of law inevitably is influenced by its general culture and traditions and the more specific culture and traditions of government administration and agencies. While the China of today differs from Imperial China in many ways, the attitudes of government officials and lay people still show signs of traditional views about the role of government.

As noted in Chapter 2, Imperial China rejected the notion of a neu-tral and limited government in favor of a strong, paternalistic state that determined the moral agenda for society. At the head of the state was the all-powerful ruler, whose personal vision of a good society provided the moral compass. Below him were administrators responsible for en-suring that the ruler's vision of a good society was realized. Although the ruler had a moral obligation to ensure the material and spiritual well-being of the people, there were no legal limits on the power of the ruler.[25] Government officials were considered parental authority figures and often referred to as *fumu guan* (father and mother officials).[26] The

Confucian emphasis on hierarchical social roles reinforced the idea that lay people were supposed to defer to the superior judgments of government officials who knew best what was in their interest and in the interest of society as a whole.

The CCP's victory did nothing to challenge these fundamental beliefs about the nature of governance or the relations between government officials and the people. The liberal democratic notion of a neutral state has been rejected in favor of a strong government that continues to set the moral agenda for society. It was assumed that because the Party had no other interest than what was in the best interest of the people (and knew what that interest was), there was little need for external restraints on the Party or the government that carried out Party policy.[27] If a mistake was made or people felt the need to point out that their interests had been overlooked, they could simply bring the issue to the attention of government officials. Thus the primary means of challenging an administrative decision was by complaining to the agency or to the procuratorate.[28] For the most part, however, people were expected to defer to the judgment of government officials. Backed up by the awesome power of the Party, government officials were used to giving orders and having them obeyed. Given the low status of formal law during much of the Mao period, officials often ignored the law when not convenient.

Socialism did bring about some changes. Bureaucrats became even more entrenched. The politicization of society in general also affected administrative agencies. Government officials became sensitive to subtle changes in the political winds. They learned that there was little incentive to stick out their necks. Bureaucrats everywhere may be risk averse, but in the politically charged environment of Maoist China, where the consequences for being on the wrong side of an issue were severe, bureaucrats had every reason to be even more cautious. Moreover, the general lack of material incentives and rewards for superior performance resulted in government officials who were disinclined to go out of their way to serve the people or the public interest.

Administrative officials today often display many of the same traits. They tend to expect that people should defer to their better judgment and are disinclined to view themselves as servants of the people. They are more likely to pay attention to the shifting political winds and the dictates of their superiors than to the needs of the public or the individuals who come into contact with the system. And they still frequently disregard or circumvent law when compliance would be inconvenient.

The tendency to disregard law is in part a function of the continued importance of *renqing* (human feelings)[29] and *guanxi* (personal connections and social networks). Personal connections and social networks are valuable everywhere but perhaps are of greater significance in China and Asian countries than in some parts of the world.[30] Their significance may be traced back to the Confucian emphasis on social roles, clan ethics, and *li* (ritual propriety).[31] They are also a reflection of more contemporary economic, social, and political realities. Connections were particularly important during the Mao period and in the early Deng years.[32] In the absence of a market economy, people had to rely on connections to avoid being sent down to the countryside, to obtain a good work assignment, to gain access to a good hospital, to have their radio fixed, and so on. The transition to the market economy has also provided ample opportunities to take advantage of one's connections. One result of the transition has been the emergence of clientelist relationships that rely heavily on connections. But while some scholars see the importance of *guanxi* as increasing,[33] others see it as decreasing due to the emergence of a formal legal structure and a market economy.[34] The market makes it unnecessary to rely on connections in many situations. Often it is simply easier and more convenient to obtain what one wants by paying for it. The strengthening of the legal system also makes it more difficult and risky to rely on connections to circumvent legal requirements.

Despite disagreements about just how important connections are in the different areas of contemporary Chinese society, and the reasons for their enduring significance, no one denies that connections continue to be important in China today. The salience of connections and the "economy of gift-giving" puts pressure on administrative officials to bend the rules. An official who treated a family member or a classmate like any other person would be thought of as lacking in human feeling. David Wank relates the story of an official asked to help out a friend seeking a license. Although the friend did not meet the legal requirements, the official granted the license anyway.

> If you don't give special consideration then your friend loses face (*mianzi*). Others will come to see you as someone who does not behave properly (*zuoren*). [But isn't special consideration illegal?] It may not be legal (*hefa*) by the center but it accords with local sentiment and

practice . . . You also have to think realistically. Xiamen is a small place and everybody knows each other. You must realize you will live here for your entire life. You must pay attention to your reputation. If you do not show sufficient spirit to help others, you will find it difficult to live here. Nobody will support you when you need it.[35]

Granted, there is a big difference between helping someone out by arranging an appointment without having to stand in line and approving an investment project even though it does not meet important substantive criteria for approval. Similarly, there is a difference between returning a favor for someone who has helped one with an appointment and a large bribe to obtain approval of a project that would not otherwise be approved. But while the extreme cases may be clear, there are many cases in the middle where it is difficult to draw lines.

Given the traditional views of the role and status of government officials vis-à-vis the citizenry, it is not surprising that many officials have been slow to accept the notion that one of the main purposes of administrative law is to protect individual rights and interests and that rule of law requires that government officials themselves act in accordance with and be subject to the law. According to one survey, almost half of the officials surveyed thought that at the time of the implementation of the ALL it would decrease administrative efficiency.[36] Many feared that it would decrease the authority of government officials.[37] The idea of officials being hauled into courts to account for their actions was both threatening and demeaning.

Officials have responded by developing various techniques to avoid litigation. Sometimes they issue decisions in the name of the CCP.[38] Other times they might change their decision to appease the plaintiff, negotiate a reduction in fines in exchange for dropping the suit, refuse to issue decisions in writing, neglect to tell the person of her right to challenge the decision through administrative reconsideration or litigation,[39] or pressure the plaintiff to withdraw the suit. Administrative agencies also pressure courts to reject the case or to find in favor of the defendant. On occasion, administrative officials will seek the assistance of government or CCP leaders. In other cases, they will threaten the court or particular judges.[40] Once the case is accepted, many officials refuse to cooperate with the courts. They refuse to accept the summons, appear in court, respond to the complaint, provide evidence, or comply with the court decision. Some even fabricate or destroy evidence.[41]

However, attitudes are changing. Although almost half of officials surveyed thought that at the time the ALL was implemented, it would decrease government efficiency, now only 5% admit to thinking so.[42] Moreover, although only 35% thought initially that the ALL would promote legal consciousness and the development of the legal system, now more than 75% think so.[43] A recent survey in Jiangsu found similar results, with 5% of officials believing that the ALL was too restrictive and reduced efficiency, while 73% claimed that the law caused them to be more attentive to their duties and strengthened their sense of rule of law. In addition, some 48% agreed that the ALL was helpful in improving the work of administrative agencies.[44]

The influence of culture and tradition is also apparent in the attitudes and behavior of Chinese citizens. The idea that an average person could challenge the decision of government officials represents a radical change in the Chinese worldview. Not surprisingly, it has taken some time to get used to. The number of administrative cases has been growing year by year. In 1995, there were 51,373 ALL suits, an increase of 48 percent over the previous year.[45] Although the number of suits in other areas has tapered off in recent years, the number of administrative litigation cases has risen steadily, falling just short of 100,000 cases in 1999.[46] Notwithstanding such increases in the numbers over the last decade, there are still many fewer cases than one might expect, particularly given how often plaintiffs are successful. In fact, there are amazingly few cases relative to the total number of specific administrative acts. In Harbin in 1991, the public security, administration of industry and commerce, tax, and traffic bureaus issued 88,329 fines and penalties, but only 211 (0.2%) were challenged through administrative reconsideration and only 81 (0.1%) under the ALL.[47] In 1996, there were 20,000 driver license confiscation cases in Guangxi but not one was challenged through either administrative reconsideration or litigation.[48] There are approximately 50,000 family planning decisions a year in Guangxi but only about 10 challenges under the ALL.[49] And there were 1,600 cases of reeducation through labor in 1996 but only 35 requests (2.2%) for administrative reconsideration.[50]

There are many reasons for the low numbers besides a traditional reluctance to challenge authority.[51] People may not understand their rights. They may fear retaliation or believe that challenging the decision is useless because officials protect each other.[52] Disgruntled citizens might believe that it is better to deal with the problem through other, more effective channels, perhaps relying on personal connections or making their case directly to the CCP. In addition, the costs may be too high. People may believe that it is not worth the time, effort, and expense to challenge the decision.

Nevertheless, the relatively low number of administrative cases should not cause one to dismiss the significance of administrative law cases. The mere threat of being sued has forced officials to change their attitudes and agencies to modify their behavior, and has a deterrent effect (although that effect would obviously be strengthened were more cases brought and the probability of being penalized increased). More importantly, the very fact that administrative officials are now subject to administrative suits serves a signaling function in putting officials on notice that the days when officials were the law are over. As such, administrative litigation cases are an important symbol of the regime's commitment to the rule-of-law principle that all must obey the law, and have been instrumental in slowly changing the legal culture both within agencies and in society at large.

Legal professionalism and consciousness

The general level of legal awareness remains low in China among citizens and government officials, though efforts to promote rule of law and heighten legal consciousness are beginning to have some effect. For instance, whereas a 1992 survey of over 1,000 citizens in Harbin found that 82% had not heard of administrative reconsideration and 65% had not heard of the ALL,[53] a more recent survey in Jiangsu found that 97% of the citizens polled had heard of citizens suing government officials.[54] Surprisingly, however, given the high rate of plaintiff success in ALL cases, almost 22% had not heard of citizens winning such suits. Indicative of how much more work needs to be done to raise legal consciousness, still another poll revealed that almost half of the people surveyed did not know the difference between judges and prosecutors.[55]

The role of lawyers in administrative litigation suits is particularly crucial. Representation by legal counsel in administrative law cases is more frequent than in economic or civil cases.[56] When asked about the key to success in administration litigation, 83% of the respondents thought having a good lawyer was important.[57] In contrast, only 27%

thought connections were important, while 18% thought money was important.[58] Lawyers may be particularly crucial in administrative cases because the cases tend to be "complicated" both legally and politically. People may be afraid to sue officials directly and may want the protection of a lawyer who not only knows the law (and thus might not be intimidated), but who also may serve as a buffer between the plaintiff and the government defendant.[59] While the ALL does not allow mediation in administrative litigation except with respect to the issue of damages, lawyers reportedly often end up mediating both before and during the court session.[60] Given the low level of legal consciousness on the part of officials, at times all that is required is a clear presentation of the law by a lawyer (or the court) to persuade an official that a mistake has been made. The official will then change the decision, which accounts in part for the extremely high percentage of cases that are withdrawn due to a change in the decision on the part of the agency.[61]

Despite the importance of lawyers to a just outcome in administrative law cases, there is good reason to be concerned that China's lawyers are not up to the task. As discussed in the preceding chapter, many of China's lawyers are poorly educated and trained in general. When it comes to administrative law, the situation is even more grim. A lawyer's training in administrative law may be limited to a course in preparation for the national examination. Few, if any, lawyers specialize in administrative law. Administrative law cases account for less than 2 percent of all lawsuits.[62] Moreover, administrative litigation is less profitable and more of a headache than economic or civil litigation or nonlitigation commercial work. Lawyers have complained of difficulties in conducting discovery on administrative agency defendants. In some cases, they may be afraid to challenge powerful administrative or government interests for fear of jeopardizing their profitable clientelist ties with the government and the justice bureau.

Corruption

Corruption is a serious and growing problem in China. Although the exact scope of corruption is difficult if not impossible to determine, there is more than enough evidence to conclude that the problem is serious.[63] Moreover, the nature of corruption is changing. In keeping with the trend of economic reform and Deng's view that to get rich is glorious, money is increasingly the means and end of corruption, whereas in the past power and privileged access were more important. Further, the stakes are rising. Corruption cases involve larger and larger amounts. Corruption is also becoming more democratic. Economic reforms have now provided more opportunities for those lower down the ladder to take advantage of their position to extort rents. As a result, corruption has spread to all aspects of society, including the Party, administration, public security, procuracy, and courts.

As one would expect, the causes of corruption are many. Economic reform has clearly been a major factor. Price reforms and the dual pricing system have created opportunities for profiteering. Decentralization has created more opportunities for local officials to use their new-found authority to approve projects and to make resource allocation decisions to extract bribes. The lack of separation between the state and enterprises has created incentives for local governments and ministries to steer resources and opportunities toward companies in which they hold an interest. The emergence of a private economy has created new sources of wealth to be exploited by government agencies needing to bolster their revenues in light of cut-backs in funding from the central government. Many businesses may find that paying bribes to expedite the frequently inefficient approval process of administrative agencies is well justified on economic grounds.

An ethical crisis resulting from the loss of faith in socialism exacerbates the problem. Plagued by corruption, the Party is seen by many today as nothing more than a vehicle for personal enrichment and power. Furthermore, the Party's efforts over the years to destroy traditional normative systems such as Confucianism, Daoism, and Buddhism have taken their toll. Although the Party has attempted to revitalize Confucianism and has taken steps to create a socialist spiritual civilization in hopes of combating the widespread deterioration in moral standards, such measures have been largely ineffectual, as noted in Chapter 4. To fill the void, many Chinese have turned to money-worshipping and a hard-edged capitalist materialism. Such unbridled pursuit of riches has resulted in widespread corruption.

The perception of unjust enrichment and a lack of distributive justice further contribute to corruption. The inevitable result of Deng's some-get-rich-first policy was that some people would get rich first, thus increasing the distance between the haves and have-nots. But perhaps more important than the difference between the rich and the poor is the sense that the rich got rich by unfair means. Government officials and their sons and daughters were able to exploit their privileged position to divert state resources to private use or take advantage of other opportunities not available to others. The absence of equal opportunity and fair competition encourages people to ignore the rules to get ahead. Cultural factors also come into play. While many transition countries experience high levels of corruption, China's problems have been traced back to deep-rooted patterns of paternalism and nepotism and the reliance on *guanxi* and personal connections.[64]

In other countries, the courts are usually one of the main ways to attack corruption. However, the low stature of the PRC courts, and their dependence on local governments for funding make them unlikely candidates to hold the line against corruption in the CCP or the more powerful government and administrative agencies. Indeed, as noted in Chapter 7, the judiciary itself is plagued by corruption. Similar problems of authority and funding impede administrative supervision organs.[65] In addition, the lack of democracy and limits on speech undermine the effectiveness of supervision by the public.

Widespread corruption undermines the authority and legitimacy of the state, whether the administration or the courts. In so doing, it further contributes to the crisis of values, thus leading to a vicious cycle of escalating corruption. Specific acts of corruption also distort administrative decision-making. Although in some cases corruption may have efficiency-enhancing effects, the overall result is likely to be less efficiency and surely a decrease in the quality of justice.[66]

Economic transition and the incomplete separation of government from enterprises

During the era of the centrally planned economy, administrative agencies were integrally involved in commercial activities. A ministry would be responsible for carrying out Party policies and regulating the industry; and, as the department in charge of a particular industry, it would be responsible for allocating resources, resolving disputes between companies under its charge, and ensuring that such companies met their quotas. In many cases, ministries had a virtual monopoly. It became clear early on in the reform period that the transition to a market economy required separating government from enterprises. State-owned enterprises were to be given greater autonomy in operating. And ministries were to be divided in two, with the ministry retaining responsibility for regulating but distancing itself from commercial activities. In the process, new companies were established or existing companies reorganized. Although the new or reorganized companies were meant to be independent of the ministry, in fact they frequently have retained close ties. A similar process occurred at lower levels of government. Despite the efforts to clearly separate government from enterprises, local governments and administrative entities still often maintain a commercial interest in particular companies or at least close ties to them. Moreover, under the pressure to raise revenues, many administrative agencies have set up subsidiaries.[67]

The widespread involvement of administrative agencies in commercial activities creates a number of problems, particularly given the ineffective means for challenging administrative decisions. Administrative agencies frequently use their regulatory power to benefit the companies in which they have an interest. They may pass regulations that limit competition, refuse to approve the establishment of competitors, or force companies to joint venture with their affiliates if they are to gain approval and access to the PRC market.

For instance, in 1997, the Ministry of Agriculture pushed through new regulations to protect domestic seed companies, including the Ministry's own affiliated entity, the National Seed Group Corporation (NSC).[68] The new regulations limited foreign investment to a minority share in seed crop joint ventures.[69] The Ministry sought to ensure that NSC would emerge as a global competitor in other ways as well. When one large multinational corporation sought to set up a joint venture with one of NSC's domestic competitors, the Ministry let it be known that the chances of obtaining approval to establish the joint venture were not good. As a result, the foreign company and local competitor decided to establish a company under the $30 million threshold for central approval. The Ministry moved to close that route in the 1997 regulation by requiring central approval for all projects, regardless of size.

The incomplete separation of government and enterprises has contributed to widespread predatory behavior by local governments and the growth of clientelism. As discussed more fully in the next chapter, in the absence of clearly defined property rights and a court system capable of enforcing them, private, collective, and state-owned firms have sought to cultivate relations with the government. The government controls key resources such as access to technology and loans, is responsible for a variety of approvals that are required to do business, and may at times be in a better position to broker a settlement or enforce contractual obligations than the court.

On the other hand, local governments may take advantage of their position to muscle their way into companies or interfere with their operations. Often, they will impose random and arbitrary fees on companies. Thus, although some companies may benefit from close relations with the local governments, increasingly companies prefer that government officials be kept at a safe distance.[70] But for companies to be able to go it alone, the administrative law regime must be capable of protecting them against overreaching government officials. Without further legal reforms, the efforts to achieve separation of government and enterprises will be slowed. More important, the most dynamic segment of the economy – those companies that can succeed without government assistance – will be hampered.

Administrative discretion and rule of law

One of the most frequent complaints about China's legal system is that administrative officials have too much discretion. But China is hardly alone in struggling to reconcile the requirements of rule of law with the wide-ranging authority afforded government agencies in modern bureaucratic states. Indeed, whether discretion is compatible with rule of law, and if so what kind and how much, are much debated issues. One extreme view portrays discretion as the antithesis of rule of law. Government agencies must always deduce their decision from generally applicable laws promulgated in advance.[71]

On the other hand, there are those who argue that discretion is not only compatible with rule of law but that no system could operate without discretion. As the well-known administrative law scholar Kenneth Culp Davis observes: "Every government and legal system in world history has involved both rules and discretion. No government has ever been a government of law and not of men in the sense of eliminating all discretionary power. *Every government has always been a government of laws and of men.*"[72]

Indeed, discretion is desirable: legal systems are better off for allowing a certain degree of discretion. As Davis points out: "Discretion is a tool, indispensable for individualization of justice . . . Rules alone, untempered by discretion, cannot cope with the complexities of modern government and modern justice. Discretion is our principal source of creativeness in government and in law."[73] Proponents of this view allow that administrative officials often make decisions in the absence of principles or rules known in advance (and in many instances are responsible for creating the rule by which the particular case is to be decided), but argue that a decision may be discretionary in the sense that it is not guided by legal principle or laws and yet not be irrational or unjust.[74] If rule of law actually required the elimination of all discretion and that all decisions be based on principles or laws known in advance, then no country would have rule of law. Accordingly, on this view, rule of law does not require the elimination of all discretion, just that discretion be limited by law.[75]

Although arguments can be made for or against the compatibility of discretion with rule of law, in the end not much hinges on whether discretion is incorporated into the concept of rule of law or left outside of it. Rule of law is only one of many social values. Defining rule of law to exclude discretion accentuates the virtues of predictability and certainty but makes it more likely that rule of law so defined will in certain circumstances give way to other important values, such as practicality, government efficiency, or equity in the particular circumstances.[76]

Thus whether or not one builds discretion into the concept of rule of law, as long as one accepts that some degree of bounded discretion is desirable, one will need to address a number of important issues. How much discretion is desirable? Too much discretion will undermine many of the most important virtues of rule of law: predictability, certainty, equal treatment of similarly situated people, and the ability of law to guide behavior and make planning possible.[77] But too little will unduly restrict agencies from governing effectively and achieving just results in particular cases. Under what circumstances then will agencies be given the discretion to make new laws or interpret existing ones or to deviate from the letter of the law at the point of application? Do we want administrative agencies to have the final authority? Or should the job of doing equity and interpreting laws be left to the courts? And perhaps most important, what kinds of constraints will there be on the agency's discretion? If the decision is subject to judicial review, how rigorous will the review be?

Although these questions can be debated in the abstract, different situations will call for different responses.[78] In China today, several factors weigh in favor of affording administrative officials considerable discretion at the point of application. In comparison to their counterparts in more stable economies, administrative officials in China need more discretionary authority to deviate from existing rules to meet the demands of a rapidly changing economy. Many laws, written with a centrally planned economy in mind, are at odds with today's more market-oriented economy. Further, in a country as large and diverse as China, general regulations that may make sense for most of the country may not make sense in a particular area. The lack of experience and low level of legal training of many of the drafters often result in poorly drafted or impractical laws and regulations, and inadequate publication of many rules may catch the regulated unaware. Hence officials may be justified in not applying the regulation in a particular case to avoid an unjust result.

Similarly, a number of factors support giving administrative officials greater discretion with respect to rule-making than in other countries. In any system, administrative agencies are given the authority to make and interpret regulations and to set standards because of the technical nature of the subject matter. Issues of competence may be even more pressing in China and support more rule-making by the administration as opposed to the legislature both because of the technical subject matter of much regulation and the low level of professionalism of the legislature relative to the administration. As we have seen, people's congresses are big and unwieldy. There is no way the legislature can meet all of the needs for regulations created by economic reforms. Administrative agencies need to share rule-making responsibility. In fact, in many instances, administrative agencies have been forced to issue rules because the NPC has not been able to pass legislation in the area.[79] The only available rules are administrative rules. Further, although the legislatures are often responsible for interpreting legislation, they are ill-equipped and too overburdened to do so. Thus much of the burden for interpretation has fallen to administrative agencies that are faced with the need to resolve concrete problems arising in practice.

China's legal reformers face a dilemma. They can either: (i) provide administrative officials with sufficient discretion to meet the demands of a fluid economic environment and accommodate widespread variations in local conditions, in which case they must accept certain abuses of discretion that are bound to occur in the absence of more effective means of limiting administrative discretion; or (ii) they can pass laws that give administrative officials less discretion than is optimal. The latter approach will produce suboptimal results in some cases where officials follow the law. It will also force or at least encourage officials to disregard the law where circumstances are compelling, thus exacerbating the gap between law and practice and contributing to an atmosphere in which law is not taken seriously.

The dilemma is nicely illustrated by the debates surrounding the scope of authority of local governments and administrative agencies to create licensing requirements. Fearing that local governments and administrative agencies would abuse any discretion given them, drafters of the Administrative Licensing Law sought to rein them in by imposing severe constraints on their authority to create licensing requirements.[80] However, as some of the foreign administrative law specialists asked to comment on an early draft observed, there are a number of circumstances where licensing by local governments and agencies is not only appropriate but necessary. The drafters were forced to choose between passing a law that unduly restricts local governments and agencies, which would produce suboptimal results, or passing a law that when considered by itself would be a more reasonable law but when considered in the overall context of China's current legal system would provide local governments and officials with too much discretion.

While the long-term solution is clearly to improve the various mechanisms for checking administrative discretion, in the meantime tough choices must be made. In the case of the Licensing Law, the drafters seemed to be leaning toward imposing excessively tight limits on local officials.[81]

In sum, the common complaint that administrative officials have too much discretion in China fails to address the crucial issue of how much and what kind of discretion officials should have. Although reasonable people may disagree on these issues, it is unrealistic to expect that all discretion could be eliminated and overly simplistic to think that it should be. On the other hand, at times the complaint is the very different one that agency officials are exceeding or abusing their discretion. This complaint goes to the failure of the various means for checking discretion to impose meaningful restraints on administrative officials.

Weak mechanisms for reining in the bureaucracy

China relies on many of the same types of mechanisms as other countries do to rein in the bureaucracy; yet the mechanisms fail to produce comparable results. In part, the difference can be attributed to the particular features of the PRC mechanisms. But to a considerable extent, the various means of controlling administrative officials suffer from the general institutional and systemic problems just discussed.

Legislative supervision

Legislative supervision of the administration takes a variety of forms, including hearing and reviewing or approving work reports, controlling the budget of administrative agencies, making appointment and removal decisions, investigating of hot topics, investigating of law enforcement, issuing interpretations of legislation, and legislative review of local government rules for consistency with higher-level legislation.[82] While all of these means are potentially useful, they all have inherent limitations, some of which are common to all legal systems and some of which are particular to the PRC context.

For instance, hearing and approving work reports allows the legislature to express dissatisfaction with administrative agencies. In some cases, criticism by the NPC has resulted in actual changes in practice.[83] However, the people's congresses only hear a relatively small number of work reports in a year,[84] and their power to effect change is limited largely to moral censure.[85] Similarly, the NPC has the authority to approve and supervise the budgets of administrative agencies, but more than half of administrative spending in China is off budget.[86] And while potentially useful, China has not made much use of oversight committees to date, though some provinces have been more aggressive than others.[87]

More generally, the ability of people's congresses to rein in the government and administrative agencies is undercut by their questionable legitimacy and low level of competence. Because of the nature of the election process, people's congresses do not enjoy the legitimacy and stature that legislatures in other countries enjoy. While people's congresses have begun to shed their rubber-stamp image, they are still relatively weak. Although they formally have the power to make certain appointments, for example, real appointment authority lies elsewhere. The Henan Provincial People's Congress approved all but 6 out of 548 nominees for government posts between 1986 and 1993.[88] Since 1993, only 1 of 684 has been rejected.[89] Moreover, many delegates are retired government officials and are poorly educated, although that is slowly changing.[90] Given the technical nature of much administrative decision-making, it is not clear that having a poorly educated and trained legislature second-guessing the administration would produce better results.

Taking a longer view, even if the people's congresses were to become more democratic, legitimate, and powerful, there are inherent problems in relying on legislatures to rein in administrative discretion. Legislatures are majoritarian institutions subject to majoritarian pressures. Accordingly, courts are generally more suited to protect the rights and freedoms of individuals against administrative overreaching. Furthermore, the experience of modern parliaments has been that the head of the ruling party and the executive branch have dominated the law-making process. The legislative branch has been reduced to a largely checking function. At best, people's congresses can be expected to play an important but minor role in reining in administrative agencies.

Administration supervision and Party discipline

The Ministry of Supervision was established in 1954, but was terminated in 1959. It was restored in 1986 and merged with the CCP Discipline Committee system in 1993. In 1990, the State Council passed the Administrative Supervision Regulations, which were subsequently amended and upgraded to a law in 1997.

The Ministry of Supervision and its subordinate bodies function somewhat like ombudsmen in other jurisdictions. Supervision organs are charged with supervising government and administrative officials and their appointed personnel.[91] Their goal is to promote good governance.[92] Whereas courts are generally limited to examining the legality of administrative acts as opposed to their appropriateness, supervision organs may look into the appropriateness of administrative decisions.[93] They have jurisdiction over both administrative rule-making and specific act decision-making.[94] Specifically, they are to ensure that government agencies follow and implement the law and that the decisions, orders, and directions of government departments are consistent with superior legislation and state policies. They may also examine personnel decisions and cases of administrative discipline and punishment.

In practice, supervision organs investigate a wide variety of matters, including breach of discipline by government officials, such as government officials living in better housing than they are entitled to, or using public funds to buy a house, the assessment of illegal fees and fines, and the taking of bribes and other acts of corruption by government officials.[95] They may initiate a case on their own or in response to a citizen's complaint. In 1996, CCP discipline committees and supervision organs received 63,401 letters, which was a 31 percent increase over the year before.[96]

Supervisory organs have several powers. They may conduct discovery on administrative departments and officials, issue injunctions to cease acts in violation of law or disciplinary rules, temporarily remove or seal evidence, order officials to provide explanations for their acts, and freeze bank accounts in cases of suspected corruption. If they decide that the government has acted illegally or inappropriately, they may recommend to the competent administrative body that a sanction be imposed.[97] The agency or official should follow the recommendation unless there is good reason, in which case the agency or official may appeal the recommendation to the next highest-level supervision organ.[98] The superior organ may also directly modify or annul inappropriate administrative punishments.[99]

Despite these powers, supervisory organs have played only a marginal role in limiting administrative misbehavior. The main reason is that they lack sufficient independence and authority to monitor government agencies. As part of the executive branch, they are answerable to the same-level people's government that created them as well as to higher-level supervisory organs. They must report investigations to the same-level government for the record and must obtain the approval of the government for any important decisions.[100] Critics also note that supervisory organs are understaffed, lack sufficient powers to impose sanctions, depend on local governments for funding, and are incapable of dealing with corruption or violations at high levels of government.[101]

The 1993 merger of CCP discipline committees with supervisory organs has caused additional problems. Different cities have implemented the merger differently, some completely merging both personnel and workload and others trying to maintain some degree of separation. But in practice, the CCP often dominates.[102] While there are a number of drawbacks to Party discipline, some observers have suggested that combining administrative supervision with Party discipline has strengthened the former.[103] Party supervision does have the advantage of being able to reach higher-level officials provided the CCP approves. However, the Party has not been aggressive in investigating and punishing its own members, notwithstanding its get-tough rhetoric produced for public consumption. Moreover, the investigations are often handled by Party members at the same level. In many instances, they will be subject to the same kind of social networking (*guanxi*) pressures that influence administrative decision-making. In addition, they may reasonably be expected to feel sympathy for the plight of their unfortunate comrades on the theory that there but for the grace of God go I.[104]

Administrative reconsideration

Administrative reconsideration is a common means for reining in administrative discretion and making administrative agencies act in accordance with law. Administrative reconsideration offers several advantages over judicial review. Administrative review bodies may have a better understanding of the issues than courts of general jurisdiction, particularly with regard to highly technical matters. They may also have a better sense of the realities of running the government and the difficulties of setting policies. Administrative reconsideration is also often faster and less expensive than litigation in court.

In China, administrative reconsideration offers a number of additional advantages over litigation under the ALL.[105] First, it is free.[106] Second, administrative reconsideration bodies may consider both the legality and appropriateness of administrative decisions.[107] Third, parties may challenge not only the specific act but in some cases the abstract act on which it is based.[108] If the reconsideration body finds the regulation inconsistent with higher legislation, it may annul the inconsistent regulation or, if it does not have the authority, it may refer the problem to the body that has such authority.[109]

Despite the potential value of administrative reconsideration, it has not been an effective means of reining in administrative discretion. Relative to the total number of specific acts, the number of administrative reconsideration cases is miniscule.[110] Moreover, the number has been decreasing year by year, whereas the number of ALL cases has been increasing.[111] Further, it appears based on partial statistics that plaintiffs are less likely to prevail in reconsideration than in litigation.[112]

Administrative reconsideration is ineffective for many of the same reasons that render administrative litigation ineffective: the low level of legal awareness on the part of citizens; their fear of retaliation; the preference of injured parties for relying on connections; the failure of agencies to comply with procedural requirements – including the requirement to inform parties of the right to reconsideration; and the fear of losing face causing agencies to settle disputes with disgruntled parties.[113] There are, however, obstacles specific to administrative reconsideration.[114] Some agencies have yet to establish reconsideration organs. Others have not dedicated full-time personnel to this job. Some departments give demerits to those whose decisions are quashed.[115] Originally, the Administrative Reconsideration Regulations provided for vertical jurisdiction (*tiao tiao*).[116] That is, a petitioner sought reconsideration at the next highest administrative entity. The advantage was that higher-level agencies often had more expertise and were likely to be more impartial and less subject to the pressures of local protectionism.[117] However, this was inconvenient and excessively expensive for many plaintiffs, because the superior agency may have been located in a distant city. The ARR was then amended in 1994 to provide jurisdiction at the same-level government (*kuai kuai*), as well as with the superior agency, unless the regulations specifically stated otherwise.[118]

But as feared, the restructuring has led to problems with lack of expertise and local protectionism. Like the courts, reconsideration bodies are subject to a wide range of external pressures, primarily from the local government. However, reconsideration bodies have the additional problem of being part of the agency that made the decision. Some legal systems attempt to obtain greater independence by staffing the reconsideration bodies with personnel who are provided similar tenure to judges and whose promotion and other personnel matters are handled by a different government body.[119] They also require that the person who investigated the complaint not be the same person who hears the case and impose strict limits on *ex parte* communications between the agency personnel and the reconsideration body personnel. China has no such restrictions.

There are also numerous doctrinal problems that limit the effectiveness of administrative reconsideration. As under the ALL, the CCP and procuracy are not included within the jurisdictional scope of administrative reconsideration. The deadline for challenging a decision is short – sixty days from the time the person becomes aware of the decision, except in unusual circumstances.[120] The ARL spells out very few procedural requirements. The decision to hold a hearing is left to the reconsideration body.[121] If a hearing is held, the parties are often passive and unclear as to their rights to participate at the hearing, although they may retain counsel.[122] The ARL provides that applicants may review the evidence supplied by the defendant agency except where state secrets are involved.[123] However, it does not expressly give the applicant a chance to respond to any of the evidence provided by the agency. The review body can carry out investigations or depose interested parties, but whether to do so is up to the review body.[124]

Letters and petition system

Most governments, people's congresses, and courts have a petition and appeals section to handle citizens' complaints.[125] Thus, every year hundreds of thousands of disgruntled citizens write letters to senior government leaders or make a pilgrimage to provincial capitals or even to Beijing to seek an audience with government officials. The effectiveness of filing petitions or beseeching the authorities for relief varies depending on the nature of the complaint, the status and connections of the party making the complaint, the persistence of the petitioner, and the petitioner's ability to catch the attention of the powers that be. Gaining the support of the media to champion one's cause increases the likelihood of receiving a prompt response. On the whole, however, the likelihood of letters and petitions producing the desired result is low.

The popularity of this traditional method of protest may be due in part to the persisting belief among citizens that father-and-mother government officials have a moral duty to rectify injustices. On the other hand, it may also be due to the cost of formal proceedings, the poor understanding on the part of many citizens as to the available formal mechanisms for obtaining relief, or the ineffectiveness of other more formal legal channels for seeking redress.

Administrative litigation

Although administrative litigation results in some relief for the applicant in approximately 40 percent of the cases, the overall effectiveness of administrative litigation has been limited, judging by the small number of suits relative to what are acknowledged to be widespread administrative problems. To some extent, the limited effectiveness of administrative litigation is due to doctrinal shortcomings in the ALL.[126] For instance, the CCP, the Procuracy, state-owned enterprises, and quasi-administrative units (*shiye danwei* – such as state universities and various departments of agencies that do not have independent accounting) are not considered administrative entities under the ALL and hence are not subject to administrative litigation. Another problem has been determining whether acts of the public security bureau constitute administrative acts or nonadministrative criminal investigations, though the SPC's recent interpretation of the ALL may help clarify this issue.[127]

Standing requirements also limit the effectiveness of judicial review in China. The ALL allows parties to bring suit when their "legitimate rights and interests" are infringed by a specific administrative act of an administrative organ or its personnel.[128] Article 11 then sets out certain acts that can be challenged. The listed acts all involve **personal or property rights**. Limiting the scope to infringement of personal or property rights excludes other important rights, most notably political rights such as the rights to march and to demonstrate, freedom of association and assembly, and rights of free speech and free publication.[129]

The requirement that one's legitimate rights and interests be infringed has also been construed narrowly to prevent those with only indirect or tangential interests in an act from bringing suit.[130] The narrow interpretation prevents interest groups or individuals acting as "private attorney generals" from using the law to challenge the administration. On the positive side, Article 11 contemplates the expansion of judicial review to include other types of cases as provided by laws or regulations. Thus, as some scholars predict, it is possible that political rights and freedoms may become subject to review over time.[131]

But the biggest constraints on effective judicial review are the institutional or systemic obstacles discussed previously, including the low level of legal consciousness and unwillingness of many citizens to bring suit, a culture of deference to authority, and a weak judiciary. The weakness of the courts is readily apparent in their handling of administrative litigation cases.

A difficult issue faced by all systems is how deferential judges should be to agency interpretations of statutes and their own regulations.[132] A 1981 NPCSC resolution gave the State Council and its departments the authority to interpret questions involving the application of laws and decrees in areas unrelated to judicial and procuratorial work.[133] Administrative departments are also responsible for interpreting regulations of a local character.[134] Further, the right to interpret a regulation may be delegated to an agency. For example, the State Council may pass an Administrative Regulation and then delegate authority to interpret the regulation and pass implementing regulations to a ministry such as MOFTEC. In many cases, an agency will draft a regulation and give itself the right to interpret the regulation.

In contrast to the broad interpretive powers granted administrative agencies, PRC courts have extremely limited interpretive powers. Inevitably, they must interpret a regulation on which a specific act is based to determine if the act was legal, which will in turn depend on whether the regulation is consistent with superior legislation.[135] In doing so, if the court is not sure about the interpretation of the regulation and thus whether it is inconsistent, it must seek clarification from the entity that issued it or from its superior.[136] If the court then finds that the regulation as interpreted by the agency is inconsistent with superior laws and regulations, the court need not follow the agency's interpretation.[137] In practice, however, courts may be inclined to defer to an agency's interpretation given the courts' weak stature and their dependence on local government.

Moreover, agencies may achieve the same result as an interpretation of a law or regulation by issuing Rules or Normative Documents. Under the ALL, courts are bound by Laws, Administrative Regulations, and Local People's Congress Rules, but need only refer to Rules.[138] The ALL simply ignores Normative Documents, which are not binding on the court.

Since the court is not bound by Rules or Normative Documents, agencies cannot force their regulations or interpretations on courts – at least as a legal matter – as is sometimes alleged.[139] In practice, however, PRC courts may end up giving considerable weight to Rules and Normative Documents because there is often no superior legislation on point and the court finds the Rules or Normative Documents reasonable.[140] This is, to some extent, a problem of the immaturity of the legal system, and this problem will be addressed over time as more law is produced. More troubling is where courts defer to Rules and Normative Documents even when they do not find them reasonable because of their weak stature relative to agencies.[141]

The courts' fear of upsetting administrative agencies is also evident in their reluctance to take advantage of the broad standards of review provided under the ALL. The ALL authorizes the court to annul or remand for reconsideration administrative decisions if the agency makes its decision without sufficient essential evidence, incorrectly applies laws or regulations, violates legal procedures, exceeds its authority, or abuses its authority.[142] These standards for review are quite broad and could, in the hands of an aggressive judiciary, be developed in a way that permits the courts in effect to review acts for their appropriateness. For instance, whereas courts in many legal systems are generally deferential in reviewing administrative findings of fact,[143] in China the insufficiency of essential evidence standard allows for stricter scrutiny of the factual basis for decisions. Judges could force officials to be more accountable and to establish a record by setting a high standard for the type, quality, and quantity of evidence required to justify an agency decision.

Similarly, "exceeding authority" or "abuse of authority" permit a wide range of interpretation, and have been interpreted in other countries to include principles of proper purpose, relevance, reasonableness, consistency with fundamental rights, and proportionality.[144] For example, was the decision made to further the public interest, as intended, or to enhance one's political future or increase one's personal riches? Did the agency consider all relevant factors in making the decision? Did it consider any irrelevant factors, such as race or the color of the applicant's hair? The principle of reasonableness may be interpreted narrowly as imposing a minimal rationality standard that would rule out arbitrary and capricious decisions or it may be interpreted more robustly. The more robust the interpretation, the closer the court gets to substituting its own judgment and replacing a review of legality with a review of appropriateness.[145]

The standards of exceeding authority and abuse of authority are still in a state of flux in China. Generally, PRC scholars and courts appear to take the view that excess of authority refers to the case where the agency does not have the authority for the act, whereas abuse of authority refers to the situation where the act is within the jurisdiction of the agency, but is not in keeping with the purpose of the law or is unreasonable.[146] Put differently, excess of authority is where an agency uses powers that do not belong to the agency, whereas abuse of authority is where an agency uses its powers but in the wrong way.[147] Hence, for the labor bureau to issue a business license would be to exceed its authority, because the act is not related to the function of the agency. Alternatively, an agency may act in a way that is generally in keeping with its mission, but which exceeds its jurisdiction in a particular case.[148] Thus, a local government may approve retail joint ventures even though approval at the central level is required.

PRC scholars are even more divided about the meaning of abuse of authority. Some would find an act that is not consistent with the legislative objective, spirit, or principle to be an abuse of discretion.[149] Others would subject acts within the discretionary authority of the agency to a reasonableness test. Some would apply an objective test of reasonableness while others would inject a subjective element by requiring that the agency had intended to abuse its authority. Each of the following has been put forth as an example of abuse of authority: improper motive and purpose, failure to consider relevant factors, consideration of irrelevant factors, arbitrariness or capriciousness, inconsistency in administrative decisions, inappropriate delay, failure to take action, procedural irregularities, and manifest unjustness.[150]

Courts have yet to take full advantage of the abuse-of-discretion standard to limit administrative discretion,[151] although judicial practice, like scholarly opinion, is unsettled, with cases reflecting the different understandings of abuse of authority.[152] Overall, however, courts have not been aggressive in their application of the available standards of review. They have been **particularly reluctant to hold agencies to procedural requirements**. Scholars generally draw a distinction between minor procedural violations that do not affect the outcome of the decision and major procedural violations.[153] But even allowing this concession, courts do not seem to take procedural requirements seriously. Traditionally, courts have emphasized substantive justice over procedural justice. Moreover, China has yet to pass an Administrative Procedure Law. Accordingly, procedural requirements are contained in piecemeal legislation and tend to lack detail.[154] Courts may also be willing to look the other way because of the low level of legal training of most government officials. Whatever the reasons, the failure to take procedures seriously has drawn the attention of both scholars and government officials, even, surprisingly, Li Peng.[155] Many hope, perhaps somewhat unrealistically, that the Administrative Procedure Law will go a long way toward addressing the problem.[156]

Although there is no theoretical reason why the courts could not develop broad standards of review, in practice their stature in the political hierarchy, combined with their dependence on local government for funding and personnel decisions, does not augur well for an aggressive court. The low level of professionalism of many judges and corruption within the court make it all the less likely that the courts will be able to rein in administrative discretion by relying on expansive interpretations of the standards of judicial review.

Walk before you run: postmodern administrative law reforms in the absence of the basic infrastructure of a modern legal system and liberal democracy

An expansive regulatory state has been one of the defining features of modernity. The modern regulatory state arose as a response to technological advances and increasingly complex economic issues. Overwhelmed by a growing number of technical scientific and economic issues, legislatures around the world have delegated much of their rulemaking responsibility to specialist agencies. Recently, however, disenchantment with the regulatory state has led to proposals for new postmodern approaches to regulating. Initially, agencies were viewed as neutral technocrats who served the public by deciding technical issues based on special expertise.[157] The initial view of administrative agencies as neutral problem-solvers who serve the public interest has proved too naïve and idealistic. Critical Legal Scholars challenged the neutrality and expertise of administrative agencies, arguing that politics pervaded agency decision.[158] Philosophers challenged the value-neutrality of science. Meanwhile, public choice proponents demonstrated that agencies at times put their own institutional interests ahead of the public interest and were susceptible to capture by special interests.[159] The traditional hierarchical, top-down, overly centralized command-and-control mode of regulation has been attacked for being undemocratic and failing to allow for sufficient public participation. Furthermore, the process often produces poor results. Critics argue that top-down solutions assume that one size fits all, whereas the particular circumstances of different localities require more nuanced solutions. Top-down solutions tend to be overinclusive or underinclusive and fail to respond to needs on the ground, in part because they fail to tap into local knowledge. Moreover, the process is often exceedingly slow. Meanwhile, technology and initial conditions are changing rapidly. As a result, the proposed solution is already out-of-date by the time it is ready to be implemented.

As people in Western rule-of-law countries lost faith in agencies as neutral truth seekers, they demanded greater transparency and public participation in order to hold government officials accountable. As they grew disenchanted with top-down command-and-control approaches to regulation and the legitimacy and utility of judicial review, they sought new ways of regulating. One of the proposed cures for the ills of the modern regulatory state has been deregulation. A second response to the agency-centered, top-down approach is to increase the role of private actors in rule-making, service provision, policy design, and implementation. If agencies are subject to capture, then let private actors take on some of their functions. If the command-and-control approach is too out of touch with what is happening on the ground, then decentralize. Presumably private actors on the ground are better positioned to know what the problems are and to identify possible solutions. Moreover, greater involvement of private actors reduces the democracy deficit by inviting more public participation, thus holding out the possibility of shared-governance or perhaps even self-governance.[160]

An even more radical approach would replace the hierarchical, agency-centered command-and-control system with a "directly deliberative polyarchy" based on democratic experimentalism.[161] This approach, derived from Japanese industrial management techniques, relies on a fundamentally different method of problem-solving. The first step is benchmarking, which entails surveying current or promising ways of solving problems that are superior to those currently used, yet within the existing (local) system's capacity to emulate and eventually surpass. Next comes simultaneous engineering, where interested parties propose changes to the provisional design or solution based on their own experiences and needs. The final component is error correction and learning by monitoring. Participants and independent actors monitor progress by pooling information from their own experiments with information from other localities about the results of their approach to similar problems.

This mode of regulating is *direct* because much of the input about goals, standards for assessment, and program design comes from below. Citizens define the problems, determine standards, weigh options, and choose solutions. It is *deliberative* because decisions are based on reasoned discussion rather than just voting.[162] It is a *polyarchy* in that the performance of each jurisdiction is taken into consideration in the deliberations of other jurisdictions like it. And it is *democratic* in that citizens hold government officials accountable through elections. With its emphasis on political participation, local governance, and individuals taking the lead in identifying and solving local problems, the system is rooted in civic republicanism and a pragmatic, Dewey-inspired participatory democracy.

Each of the branches has a somewhat different role in this system than they currently do in the United States. The legislature authorizes and finances experimental reforms, in exchange for a commitment by the funding recipients to pool information.[163] Government officials campaign and are elected on the basis of their proposals for solving problems that take into account current best practices, local conditions, and benchmarking for new solutions. Administrative agencies coordinate information and assist local, provincial, and national governments in benchmarking, simultaneous engineering, and error correction, and serve as a link between the national government and local governments. When agencies issue rules, they do so based on rolling best practices. The judiciary ensures that the experiments fall within the scope authorized by the legislature and the solutions do not violate individual rights. Courts also verify that the decision-makers engaged in a deliberative process, and review the records that set forth the agency's reasons for its decision. Plaintiffs who wish to challenge an agency's rule or decision do so by arguing that the decision-maker failed to engage in a deliberative process or adopted practices that were inferior to the best practices in other jurisdictions. The agency would then have to explain its reason for adopting the practice and why other practices would not work as well in light of the particular circumstances. Judges would become active problem-solvers rather than just passive referees.[164]

To what extent are these postmodern alternatives to overly central-ized command-and-control regimes suitable for China? Deregulation is generally not a viable option in China at present given the relatively undeveloped state of markets and the many market imperfections. But what of privatization and experimental democracy? Both seem to offer certain advantages.

China has yet to rely very much on private actors. However, greater reliance on private actors is consistent with the recent move to downsize the administration and the government's efforts to separate government and enterprises and turn various government functions over to non-state actors. For instance, local governments have begun to contract out for mediation services.[165] Private schools and universities are popping up, and private hospitals are providing medical care to those who can afford it.

The experimental, pragmatic nature of a directly deliberative poly-archy is consistent with a deep streak of pragmatism running through Chinese political philosophy,[166] socialism's commitment to uniting the-ory with practice, and modern leaders' emphasis on results – captured in Deng's famous quip that the color of the cat does not matter as long as it catches mice. Indeed, one of the defining features of PRC gov-ernance is the heavy reliance on experiments. As noted in Chapter 6, the central government regularly approves experiments on a regional basis or passes provisional regulations. Similarly, the emphasis on local solutions to local problems responds to the tremendous regional vari-ation in China and is consistent with the spirit of current practices. China has already developed various ways of dealing with local vari-ation, including the establishment of separate regulatory regimes for different areas (as with special economic zones) or drafting very general laws and then giving local governments the discretion to interpret or implement the laws in light of local circumstances. Finally, the more bottom-up, incremental approach suits well China's current transition state. All too often, China's legislatures and administrative agencies have been unable to keep up with the rapid pace of change. As a result, local governments have forged ahead with experimental reforms in response to market demands without any legal basis. Because laws and regulations are frequently out-of-date by the time they are issued, they are routinely ignored in practice.

On the other hand, there are many reasons to question the feasibility of greater reliance on private actors and democratic experimentalism given China's current circumstances. A bottom-up experimental approach is consistent with some aspects of socialist ideology but at odds with other aspects. Democratic centralism assumes that once the center has accumulated information from the various localities, the center will make the final decision. Furthermore, the pragmatic aspect of the process of uniting theory and practice coexists uneasily with the more dogmatic aspect of socialism that insists on a single scientifically correct solution and unification of thought around the Party line.

Moreover, both approaches assume organized interest groups and a vibrant civil society. Neither exists in China. Nor are there any signs that the ruling regime intends to loosen its grip. On the contrary, it appears committed to maintaining tight controls on China's fledgling civil society, as discussed in Chapter 5. Although the ruling regime has been forced to turn over some responsibilities to private actors, it remains deeply suspicious of the private sector.

Even assuming the political feasibility of the new approaches, their effectiveness would be compromised by many of the factors that undermine the effectiveness of the current administrative law regime. Both privatization and democratic experimentalism assume a citizenry capable of participating in the process of designing standards, weighing options, and correcting errors. Literacy rates and education levels are much lower in China than in developed Western liberal democracies. Even advocates of democracy in China worry about the ability of their fellow citizens to sort through technical issues.[167] To be sure, such concerns on the part of the urban elite often mask the real worry that China's rural population will understand all too well what is at stake and use their disproportionate numbers to reverse the preferential policies whereby rural areas have subsidized urban centers. As the experiment with village elections shows, uneducated peasants understand local issues and know what is in their immediate interest. But whether they will challenge local officials and demand a say in the decision-making process given longstanding patterns of deference to authority remains unclear.

The fierce turf struggles that have resulted from recent downsizing of the government suggest that administrative agencies, for their part, are likely to resist giving up control to private actors. Meanwhile, central agencies are likely to object to the greater role played by local governments and agencies. In addition, the experimental approach's heavy reliance on agencies sharing information across department lines runs counter to the vertically organized bureaucratic system (*xitong*) and the agencies' institutional interests in survival during this period of transition.[168]

Local government and administrative officials play a key role in the more decentralized experimental approach. China today suffers from excessive decentralization and fragmentation, however. Given that economic reforms have produced increasingly independent local governments hell-bent on achieving economic growth, even when the central government identifies rolling best practices, there is no guarantee that local governments will follow them. As we have seen, in their pursuit of growth, local governments regularly pass local regulations that are inconsistent with national laws and fail to implement central laws. For instance, they offer tax breaks to investors despite repeated warnings from the central government that they are not authorized to do so. As a result, the ratio of tax revenues relative to GDP is much lower in China than in other emerging economies, even Russia.[169]

Although some local variation is desirable, there are times when national standards are needed. The experimental approach assumes that central authorities will be able to pool information from various localities that face similar problems, coordinate and disseminate information, and establish rolling best practices. But local governments that routinely engage in local protectionism, erect barriers to interregional trade, and pressure courts to find in favor of local companies are unlikely to pool information. This is all the more true when the local governments have gone ahead with experiments without proper authorization and the results are bad. Not all local experiments are success stories.

While greater reliance on private actors and bottom-up experiments is partly a response to the problem of holding agency officials accountable, private actors create their own accountability problems.[170] Private actors are relatively insulated from legislative, executive, and judicial oversight under China's current laws. In most cases, they could not be challenged under the ARL or ALL, as is true under comparable laws in other countries.[171] Moreover, private actors have their own incentives, which may not coincide with the interests of the broader public. They generally are driven by profit. They may be part of an interest group with a particular narrow agenda. They may lack norms of professionalism or public service, especially given the moral vacuum that exists nowadays.

In a corrupt environment where much depends on closely knit clientelist relationships, outside monitoring is not likely to be effective and those on the inside are not likely to share either positive or negative results with others. Without the **flow of information**, learning by monitoring and error correction do not work. Moreover, democratic experimentalism also assumes an open, tolerant environment in which to engage in reasoned deliberation. But newly emerging groups are often neither liberal nor tolerant.[172] They frequently are more interested in jealously guarding their privileged access to power than in expanding the circle to include others in a deliberative process. More generally, monitoring by the public assumes a variety of organized public interest groups and freedom of information, press, and association, none of which exist in China.

An alternative would be to rely on agencies to oversee private actors or monitor the experimental process. However, that approach presupposes agencies that are basically competent and disinterested, whereas agencies in China are out to protect their own interests and are susceptible to corruption. In theory, democratic elections could provide a means of monitoring. But without elections, government and agency officials cannot be thrown out of office. As we have seen, reliance on legislative oversight, ombudsmen, or internal administrative review have not been effective means of monitoring administrative agencies to date.

Ultimately, then, the courts would have to remain the final backstop. They would have to ensure that agencies are not captured by special interests and that the relevant interest groups are not excluded from the process due to clientelist or corporatist relationships. They would also have to hold private actors to their contractual obligations when the government contracted out for services.[173] And they would have to be capable of assessing the relative technical merits of various alternative solutions. Unfortunately, PRC courts are not up to the job at present.

Beholden to the local government, they are not likely to challenge the local government's choice of one method over another, even assuming there are individuals who would be so bold as to bring suit. Judges also lack the authority and training to become active problem-solvers. To date judges have been given very little power even to interpret laws, and legal education in the PRC emphasizes black letter law rather than creative thinking and problem-solving skills.

Both greater reliance on private actors and more bottom-up experimentalism rely on the infrastructure of a modern state, including a legal system that meets basic rule-of-law requirements, democratic elections, and an active civil society. But that infrastructure is not yet in place in China. To note that these postmodern approaches assume, and are more effective given the existence of, the infrastructure of a modern state does not preclude the possibility that they could be adapted to the Chinese context and be of use in certain circumstances. Obviously there are advantages to involving those affected by a problem in the process of finding a solution. And pooling information and relying on benchmarking is only common sense. Similarly, there may be instances where contracting out government functions to private actors is a viable alternative. Moreover, in the future, China might become democratic and develop a more robust civil society, particularly if Communitarians prevail over Statist Socialists and Neoauthoritarians. In the meantime, however, the postmodern approaches should be seen as complements rather than alternatives to a more traditional administrative law regime and should not detract from efforts to establish the foundations of a modern regulatory state.

Conclusion: administrative law reforms, path-dependency, and the limits of law

China's administrative law regime shows clear signs of convergence with respect to a common set of goals, institutions, and rules shared by other well-developed legal systems. There is even evidence of convergence with respect to outcomes. Given that China is in the midst of creating a modern legal system, greater convergence in the future is likely, regardless of which particular thick conception of rule of law prevails. Nevertheless, the ways in which the PRC legal system continues to diverge from other systems are perhaps as important as the ways in which it converges.

Even where China has established similar institutions or adopted similar rules, outcomes often differ because the institutions do not work as designed and rules are not followed due to a host of context-specific, path-dependent factors.

Moreover, despite signs of convergence, the nature, pace, and effect of administrative reforms have been, and will continue to be, shaped mainly by China's particular circumstances. The slow pace of political reform, for instance, has impeded the development of the administrative law system. The refusal to permit elections above the village level prevents citizens from throwing corrupt officials out of office. Apart from elections, public participation in the legislative law-making and administrative rule-making and decision-making processes remains limited. The courts are weak, beholden institutionally to local governments, and limited under the Constitution in their powers to strike down or interpret administrative regulations.

Looking into the future, ideological struggles over the proper conception of rule of law will be one factor shaping administrative law reforms. The particular balance drawn between promoting government efficiency and protecting the rights of individuals will depend in part on which of the various alternatives of rule of law prevails. Given the low likelihood of a Liberal Democratic rule of law prevailing in the near future, PRC courts will be less likely than their counterparts in liberal democracies to take full advantage of a vague abuse-of-authority standard to protect individual rights and rein in government officials at the expense of government efficiency. Nor are PRC courts as likely to strike down government decisions on narrow procedural grounds.

On a concrete level, administrative law reformers in China face a number of challenges, whatever form of rule of law is adopted.[174] Many of the political, economic, cultural, historical, and institutional factors that have influenced reforms to date will continue to interact in sometimes expected, sometimes unexpected ways to determine the path of development of China's administrative law regime. Because China's administrative law woes are due in large part to general institutional or systemic problems, addressing them will require far-reaching changes that will alter the nature of Chinese society and the current balance of power between state and society, Party and government, the central governments and local governments, and among the three main branches of government.

Market reforms have already shifted the balance of power away from the state toward society. The balance will continue to shift with the further separation of government and enterprises, the elimination of administrative monopolies, and the creation of a professional civil service in which government officials serve the public as regulators rather than extracting rents or competing with private companies in the marketplace. At present, the government continues to subject most economic and social activities to licensing requirements. The decision as to what needs to be regulated is ultimately a political one. Statist Socialists and Neoauthoritarians would impose tighter restrictions on a wider range of economic and social activities than Communitarians or Liberal Democrats, though all tolerate more private activity, particularly in the economic area, than in the past. Laws such as the Administrative Licensing Law will help delineate the boundaries of individual autonomy and freedom. Holding government officials to clearly defined substantive and procedural standards will ensure that citizens are able to take full advantage of whatever freedoms they are granted.

Administrative law reforms have empowered society, albeit modestly in practice, by giving citizens the right to challenge state actors through administrative reconsideration, administrative litigation, or letters and petitions to legislative delegates and administrative supervision committees. The next step is to increase public participation in the rule-making and decision-making processes. The Law on Legislation opens the door slightly for greater public participation in the making of national laws. The Administrative Procedure Law may go even farther in providing the public with access to administrative rule-making and decision-making.

A more robust civil society, a freer media, and greater reliance on private actors would all benefit the cause of administrative law reform but would require a further shift in power toward society, and are not likely in the short term. A more robust civil society would provide the interest groups that play such a central role in bottom-up alternatives to command-and-control regulation. Along with a more independent media, interest groups could shoulder more of the responsibility for monitoring administrative behavior.

The degree and nature of public participation afforded by the Administrative Procedure Law and the extent to which civil society is allowed to develop will be determined in part by the political power of the various rule-of-law factions. Statist Socialists are likely to favor more limited public participation and a more restricted civil society than the others. However, the ultimate outcome will turn on factors other than ideology, including the particular beliefs of the drafters of the law and the various other forces underlying legal reforms discussed in Chapter 5.

The balance of power among the branches of government, particularly the judiciary and executive, must also change if administrative reforms are to be effective. The courts are simply too weak. The independence of the courts needs to be increased by changing the way courts are funded and judges are appointed, and the authority of the judiciary must be enhanced in various ways, including by giving judges the right to overturn certain abstract acts.

Because economic and legal reforms are ongoing and political reforms have barely begun, the balance of power between the central government and local governments remains in flux. Local government and administrative officials generally violate or bend central rules to promote local economic development. While it may be possible to alter the allocation of resources to some extent or to permit areas facing especially dire straits certain privileges, tensions are likely to continue as long as some regions remain poor and local governments are forced to bear much of the cost of economic reform. In the long run, effective administration will require some mix of command-and-control and bottom-up modes of regulation. The immediate task facing the central government, however, is to find some way to rein in local authorities and ensure that central policies are implemented while still allowing local government and administrative officials sufficient flexibility to respond to local circumstances. The obvious solution – to strengthen the various mechanisms for limiting administration discretion – will require time.

One possibility might be to explore ways to change the incentive structure for local officials. Currently, local officials are evaluated in accordance with a cadre responsibility system that emphasizes quantifiable targets over qualitative ones.[175] Officials who meet their targets are rewarded financially with bonuses and larger allocations of discretionary funds and in other ways such as promotions or honorary awards. Perhaps a quantifiable rule-of-law index could be created. Officials would be evaluated based on indices such as the percentage of local regulations that are inconsistent with superior legislation; court judgments and arbitral awards that are unenforced at the year's end; administrative cases in which the administrative agency decision is reversed in whole or in part; local court judgments that are reversed on appeal; and local judges subject to discipline for corruption.[176]

As for the more traditional means of controlling administrative behavior, legislative oversight would be enhanced by creating more oversight committees staffed by full-time employees with the proper legal and technical background. Committees to examine corruption in the administration or the effectiveness of particular agencies could play a positive role. Giving people's congresses greater powers to supervise administrative budgets and expenditures might help to some extent.

Administrative supervision would be improved by increasing the independence and authority of administrative supervision organs. This could be achieved by making them answerable only to the legislature and not the local governments and funding them at the provincial level. Separating supervision organs from CCP discipline committees might reduce their authority in the short term but would have long-term rule-of-law benefits.

Supervision by the public and media could also be improved. First, people need to be made aware of their rights. The apparent misperception that suing officials is fruitless should be corrected through greater publicity of the many cases in which citizens prevail. Tough rules against retaliation by government officials combined with strict implementation would also help alleviate the fears of many citizens. Realistically, however, it is unlikely that the public or media will emerge as a strong force for reining in the administration anytime soon. China is not likely to pass a freedom of information act in the foreseeable future. Nor is the government likely to relax its control on the media.

Citizens would be more likely to resort to administrative reconsideration if the review bodies were more independent. China might consider tough rules against *ex parte* communication and a system where reconsideration personnel are not members of the agency whose actions they are reviewing. Unfortunately, drafters of the revised ARL failed to take advantage of the opportunity presented by the upgrading of the ARR to improve the reconsideration process in any significant way. Accordingly, the popularity of administrative reconsideration will most likely continue to wane. Admittedly, administrative reconsideration by its nature is subject to inherent limitations due to the lack of, or at least the appearance of the lack of, independence. Nevertheless, it is disappointing that the legislators did not do more to give the reconsideration process teeth.

Administrative litigation could be strengthened in a variety of ways. In addition to allowing courts to review abstract acts and enhancing the independence of the courts, the scope of review could be expanded to include rights other than personal or property rights, such as political rights. While China need not adopt a private attorney-general theory of standing, a clearer and more liberal interpretation of standing would be useful. Enhancing the stature of the judiciary will help the courts overcome their reluctance to take full advantage of the ALL's rather broad review standards. For example, they may take a broader view of what counts as inconsistent and use the abuse-of-power standard to examine purpose, relevance, reasonableness, proportionality, and so on. A more expansive interpretation and aggressive application of the current standards would go a long way toward achieving a review of the appropriateness of agency decision-making without substituting the judgment of the court for that of the agency.

However, allowing the courts to review the appropriateness of agency decisions at present, untethered by the need to find agency abuse of discretion, would be unwise. During a period of transition, agencies will need more discretion than in more settled periods. Agencies are grappling with a number of novel issues, many of them technical in nature. The current level of legal education and technical training of most judges and the lack of judicial resources to examine many of the technical and policy issues would argue against giving the courts expansive authority to second-guess agencies. Further, court challenges of the appropriateness of agency decisions is likely to meet with much greater hostility and resistance than a decision that a regulation is inconsistent with higher-level legislation. The courts should marshal their political resources and choose their battles judiciously.

Although China is likely to continue to converge on the best practices of other administrative law systems, such convergence need not preclude the possibility of China developing its own unique institutions. For instance, it is possible that China could develop a censorate system along the lines proposed by Sun Yatsen or create an independent anticorruption agency à la Hong Kong.[177] Of course, China currently has ombudsmen-like administrative supervision bodies and a system of letters and petitions. As we have seen, supervision bodies are very weak, in part because they are subordinate to the State Council. But perhaps a stronger, more independent entity could be created. While it is unlikely that the censorate would be created as a constitutional equal to the NPC given the current constitutional structure, perhaps it could be established under the NPC. Nevertheless, the effectiveness of any such entity would still depend on various context-specific factors, including the lack of a culture of legality.

Although various external checks can reduce administrative abuse of discretion, there are limits to what the law can achieve. In the end, no legal system can rely primarily on compulsory enforcement to ensure compliance.[178] The core of any administrative law regime is government officials who respect the law. Citizens and officials alike must internalize norms of respect for law that render compulsory enforcement unnecessary in most cases. It is essential therefore that efforts to establish rule of law and internal norms of legality continue. As it has so far, the Party will need to take the lead in promoting rule of law. Party leaders must make good on their promise to separate the Party from government and on their own commitment to act in accordance with law.[179] Party organizations must make known their displeasure with interference in court affairs by Party members or government officials, take corruption seriously, and subject Party members to the courts. And they must encourage government officials to change their attitudes, provide them with more legal training, and subject them to stricter discipline.

Unfortunately, however, senior Party leaders and legal reformers cannot simply legislate a culture of legality. It will take time to overcome the lingering influence of culture and tradition, weak institutions, and the challenges presented by the still-incomplete economic transition. Ultimately Party leaders will need to sign off on deeper institutional reforms that could in the end come back to haunt the Party. While the Party may be forced to risk such reforms to stay in power, whether it will do so is a matter of realpolitik and exceeds the limited reach of the law. If the Party does decide to continue to retreat from day-to-day governance and to turn over certain functions to other state actors, these other actors can be expected to contest for power. Retreat of the Party-state does not create a power vacuum. Rather, the result is a semi-structured space in which the existing institutions seek to gain additional power. The State Council and administrative agencies have shown themselves to be effective gladiators in the struggle for power among the other branches. Although a stronger court would be less of an immediate threat to the legislative branch, people's congresses would also lose some power vis-à-vis the courts.

Inevitably, the path of development of a country's legal system reflects its contingent circumstances. Although China can draw on the experiences of other countries, it will need to solve its problems in light of its own particular circumstances. The creation of a modern administrative law system is a slow process. While considerable progress has been made in realizing rule of law generally and administrative rule of law more particularly, clearly much remains to be done.

Notes

1 See Chapter 3. Critics of China's administrative law regime often fail to acknowledge the diversity among administrative law systems everywhere and the common challenges and failures of such systems. Many of the features that draw heaviest criticism are by no means unique to China and in some cases are common to most administrative law systems. Examples include the unitary structure of government, the courts' lack of authority to strike down abstract acts that are inconsistent with superior legislation, the limiting of judicial review to the legality rather than the appropriateness of administrative acts, the preclusion of certain administrative decisions from judicial review, and the requirement in some cases that parties first exhaust their internal administrative remedies before seeking judicial review. It is true that institutions, mechanisms for controlling administrative discretion, and legal rules that work well in one context often do not function well in China for reasons discussed below.

2 Gillespie (1999).

3 As Edward Rubin (1997) has observed, administrative law is particularly difficult to transfer from one system to another because it is highly political in character, it primarily governs the state's relationships to its own citizens, and it is heavily dependent on the nation's underlying culture for its effectiveness. By way of illustration, Majone (1997) points out several ways that the development of administrative law in France and the UK was influenced by traditional modes of governance and existing institutions.

4 Jayasuriya (1999b: 174), for instance, acknowledges that even in East Asian countries with a statist ideology that conceives of law as a tool to pursue a substantive normative agenda determined by state leaders, the development of a market economy has led to greater rationalization within the state, a stronger and more independent judiciary, and a more symmetrical relationship between the judiciary and executive.

5 Luo Haocai (1997). To be sure, the balance drawn in China can be expected to differ from the balance drawn in liberal democracies.

6 For critical accounts, see generally, Corne (1997); Jiang Mingan, ed. (1998).

7 Freedman (1978); Davis (1969).

8 These approaches are postmodern in that they are a reaction to the modern regulatory state. In addition, they challenge the kind of top-down, one-size-fits-all

reasoning that typified modernism's quest for metanarratives and grand solutions to problems based on a belief in a single rational order. They are also postmodern in that they build on and take as their starting point the main pillars of modernity: a market economy, liberal democracy, a robust civil society, and rule of law.

PRC scholars have debated the meaning and value of postmodernism for legal reforms in China. See, for example, Li Weidong (1996); Su Li (1996); Zuo Weimin (2000). Li and Zuo question whether China can bypass the modernist stage of legal institution-building and move directly to some vaguely described postmodern stage. Li sees postmodernism as at best a complementary corrective to some of the excesses of modernism, and perhaps even a threat to legal reforms to the extent that it diverts scholarly attention away from concrete measures to strengthen institutions. He suggests that the arguments of some scholars who wish to develop an indigenous form of rule of law based on China's native resources (*bentu ziyuan*) share some similarities to postmodernism in that they challenge the teleological assumption that all legal systems are converging on the institutions that currently exist in economically advanced Western liberal democracies.

Su Li (the pen name of Zhu Suli, Dean of Peking University Law School), a pivotal figure in developing the argument for native resources, points out that while the line of reasoning for native resources shares certain similarities with postmodernism's critique of modernism, the argument for developing legal institutions that are compatible with and take advantage of China's native resources can stand on its own. Su agrees with Li that the impact of postmodernism on legal reforms is likely to be minimal but for different reasons. In Su's view, postmodern ideas are likely to be of interest to a small group of legal scholars, and useful in reminding them that the legal reform process is more open-ended and indeterminate than sometimes suggested. On the other hand, Su believes the path of legal reforms is determined primarily by those in the trenches – lawmakers, judges, lawyers, and litigants – rather than academics. Those working within the legal system or who need to rely on the legal system place a premium on predictability and certainty. Thus, the impact of the deconstructive, critical, and potentially revolutionary aspect of postmodernism is likely to be mitigated in practice.

In my view, discussions about "postmodernism" become most meaningful when brought down to a more concrete level. Accordingly, I have focused on particular institutional choices faced by legal reformers. In making such choices, legal reformers must take into consideration China's actual conditions, including the current state of development of its legal institutions. In that sense, legal reforms are path dependant.

9   See Edley (1990).
10 Freeman (2000).
11 Dorf and Sabel (1998).
12 Obviously I do not mean to attribute to proponents of deregulation or democratic experimentalism in the United States the view that these approaches would necessarily be suitable for China. Rather, the point is that even if China's reformers wanted to adopt such approaches, the feasibility and effectiveness

of such approaches is limited by the present context. Moreover, some commentators have raised similar critiques of top-down regulatory approaches in China and argued that China should explore possibilities of more bottom-up alternatives. See, for example, Dowdle (1999).

13 Lin Feng (1996).

14 Finder (1989).

15 PRC Constitution, art. 41.

16 Lin Feng (1996: 115).

17 Personal communication with one of the drafters.

18 Having discussed the Party's role vis-à-vis administrative law in Chapter 5 and the problems the legislative system causes with respect to administrative law, I return to the role of the Party and shortcomings in the legislative system in the conclusion, where I consider possible future reforms.

19 Jiang Ping (1995); Jiang Mingan, ed. (1998) reports that courts often try to avoid accepting administrative cases because the fees are low in comparison to civil and economic cases, and they also take a long time to complete, which could be a black mark on the judge's record.

20 Jiang Ping (1995: 615).

21 Jiang Ping (1995: 646–67) claims that 70% of judges have no administrative law training at all.

22 Fang Ning *et al.* (2001: 304) found in their survey of judges in Jiangsu that only 57% of judges were willing to serve as administrative law judges. Even among that group, almost one-third gave as their reason that they would have little choice but to work where assigned. It should be noted, however, that 38% did cite their desire to serve in the construction of rule of law in China.

23 In 1995, there were 51,370 administrative suits, with the decision of the administrative unit being modified or quashed 15% of the time. In addition, the plaintiff withdrew suit in approximately 23% of the cases when the administrative unit changed its decision prior to judgment. 1997 *China Law Yearbook*, p. 48. Despite the increase in the total number of administrative suits to over 90,000 in 1997, the success rate was virtually unchanged, with 15% of the decisions quashed or modified and 25% ending in withdrawal after the agency agreed to change its decision. 1998 *China Law Yearbook*, p. 134. For the US figure, see Schuck and Elliot (1990: 1061), citing figures for 1985. For Japan and Taiwan, see Pistor and Wellons (1999: 254, 257).

24 Amnesty International (1997b: 24) claims that few appeals of reeducation through labor and other administrative detention orders have been successful and that all appeals known to have been made by political detainees have been systematically rejected.

25 The concepts of *tianming* (the mandate of heaven) and *minben* (the people as the basis) defined the outer moral limits for rulers.

26 Lower-level government officials were subject to both legal and moral limits, as reflected in the concern that they act impartially and in the interests of the general good (*gong*) rather than in a biased way or in their own personal interest (*si*).

27 Other socialist countries also took this view. Wiersbowsk and C. McCaffrey (1984).

28 Jyh-Pin Fa and Shao-chan Leng (1991: 449–50).

29 Some authors prefer the term *ganqing* (emotions or feelings). See, for example, Kipnis (1997).

30 For studies of the importance of guanxi, see generally Kipnis (1997: 306); Yunxiang Yan (1996); Mayfair Yang (1994); Guthrie (1998).

31 Ambrose King (1991); Yang (1994). Others attribute the significance of *guanxi* to features of contemporary institutions and economic and political factors. See Oi (1989); Guthrie (1998: 255). Kipnis (1997) steers a middle path by drawing a distinction between culture and tradition. *Guanxi* is deeply embedded in culture but contemporary Chinese culture differs from traditional culture in significant ways.

32 Mayfair Yang (1994: 147); Walder (1986).

33 Mayfair Yang (1994); Lin (2001: 154) cites a number of studies highlighting the importance of guanxi in the reform era.

34 On the basis of a survey of general managers, Guthrie (1998) suggests that the reliance on *guanxi* practice is decreasing in the urban industrial sector due to the formation of formal legal structures and the emergence of a market economy. Company behavior and decision-making is increasingly determined by legal rules and procedures rather than personal connections. Market reforms have put increasing pressure on managers to show a profit. Therefore, price, quality, and reliability are more important than personal connections. However, Guthrie also notes that the importance of *guanxi* practice varies depending on one's place in the administrative hierarchy. Managers of smaller companies view *guanxi* practice as more important. As Guthrie (1999) notes, those who claim that the importance of *guanxi* practice is increasing often base their views on studies of rural areas or empirical work from the 1980s. In addition, in some cases they fail to distinguish between cultivating relationships and friendships for normal business purposes, as occurs in all societies, and the use of relationships as a way to circumvent the rules.

35 Wank (1999).

36 Jiang Mingan, ed. (1998: 348).

37 Fa and Leng (1991: 461) point out that one of the "major obstacles is the resistant and cynical attitude of the bureaucracy."

38 Jiang Ping (1995: 634). As discussed below, Party decisions are not reviewable under the ALL because the CCP is not an administrative entity.

39 Jiang Ping (1995: 635) reports that a survey of 1,741 administrative penalty cases revealed that the penalized party was not told of his or her right to challenge the decision in 69 percent of the cases.

40 Jiang Ping (1995: 635) reports two instances where the village government confiscated the court's cars.

41 Jiang Mingan, ed. (1998: 352).

42 Jiang Mingan, ed. (1998: 348, 352).

43 Jiang Mingan (1998: 348, 352).

44 See Fang Ning *et al.* (2001: 303).

442   CHINA'S LONG MARCH TOWARD RULE OF LAW

45 1997 *China Law Yearbook*, p. 48.
46 *2000 Supreme People's Court Report to NPC*.
47 Jiang Ping (1995: 598) notes that in 1992 in Hainan, less than 1 percent of administrative penalties were challenged under the ARR and ALL respectively.
48 Jiang Mingan, ed. (1998: 58).
49 Jiang Mingan, ed. (1998: 326).
50 Jiang Mingan, ed. (1998: 280). More generally, less than 0.4% of public security decisions were challenged in Anwei province between 1994–96.
51 In some instances people are challenging the decisions but the cases are not being accepted, perhaps because the agency changes its decision before the case is accepted or because the court or reconsideration body is under pressure not to accept the case.
52 Jiang Ping suggests that while there are not many cases of revenge – he estimates only 1 out of 1000 – their influence is greater than their numbers. Jiang Ping (1995: 628). Fang Ning *et al.* (2001: 307) found in their survey that in administrative litigation about 5% of plaintiffs complained of retaliation or some form of harassment. They also found that 32% of the people polled believed that the courts would be inclined toward the government.
53 Jiang Mingan, ed. (1998: 262). But see Minxin Pei (1997a: 862), citing a 1992 poll where 88 percent of respondents claimed to have heard of the ALL.
54 Fang Ning *et al.* (2001: 303). A 1997 survey of thirty-six market stall owners in Guangxi, however, found that 41 percent had not heard of the ALL. Jiang Mingan, ed. (1998: 324).
55 "Judges – a Case of Misunderstanding" (1999).
56 Plaintiffs engaged lawyers in administrative cases 38% of the time in 1992, 21% in 1995, and 19% in 1997. In contrast, lawyers participated in 10%, 11%, and 26% of civil cases in 1992, 1995, and 1998 respectively and in approximately 26–7% of economic cases in each of those years. Assuming that the plaintiff engaged counsel half the time in the civil and economic cases, the representation rates would be less than in administrative cases.
57 Jiang Mingan, ed. (1998: 430). Not surprisingly, respondents attributed a positive outcome to a just verdict (100%). They also cited legal knowledge (88%) and having a good case on the merits (81%) as important factors.
58 Jiang Mingan, ed. (1998). See also Minxin Pei (1997a: 853).
59 As noted, administrative litigationplaintiffs have been engaging counsel less often than in the past. Pei suggests that the decrease may be due to (i) the perceived impact of counsel; (ii) the feeling that lawyers are less needed given the rise in out-of-court settlement of administrative law cases; (iii) the rapid rise in the number of ALL cases, which has exceeded the growth in the legal profession; and (iv) a decrease in representation by the defendant agencies. Yet the survey results cited above suggest that plaintiffs continue to believe lawyers play a vital role. Nor would plaintiffs be likely to forego a lawyer simply because the agency defendant chooses to do so. On the other hand, the lack of competence of many lawyers to handle administrative law cases might explain the decline in representation rates. Few lawyers are trained in administrative law and many think such cases are too much trouble and not profitable. Whether the rise in out-of-court settlement would explain the

decrease is debatable. Arguably, having a lawyer who can present your case to the court and to an agency facilitates settlement. Alternatively, since parties may be reluctant to sue unless they feel they have a strong case, perhaps they feel they do not need a lawyer. If so, they might want to reconsider their choice in light of the 60 percent failure rate.

60 ALL, arts. 50, 67.

61 Pei (1997a: 842) discusses the "puzzle" of the rapidly increasing withdrawal rates that grew from 27 percent of the cases in 1988 to 51 percent in 1995.

62 1998 *China Law Yearbook*, p. 1238.

63 Hao and Johnson (1995); Josephs (2000).

64 See "Yifa Zhiguo Jianshe Shehuizhuyi Fazhi Guojia Xueshu Yantaohui Jiyao" (1996: 4).

65 As Liu Renwen points out, the internal means of control, such as administrative supervision, are not able to deal with corruption at the highest levels. "Yifa Zhiguo Jianshe Shehuizhuyi Fazhi Guojia Xueshu Yantaohui Jiyao" (1996: 4).

66 See Chapter 10 for discussion of empirical studies that find a statistically significant correlation between corruption and lower economic growth. See also Rose-Ackerman (1999: 3).

67 Lin and Zhang (1999: 203–25).

68 Peerenboom and Zhou (1997).

69 Administration of the Examination, Approval and Registration of Foreign-Invested Crop Seed Enterprises Procedures (issued jointly by the Ministry of Agriculture, State Planning Commission, MOFTEC, and the State Administration of Industry and Commerce, 1997).

70 See the discussion and studies cited in Chapter 10.

71 Hayek (1944: 72), for example, states: "Stripped of all technicalities, [rule of law] means that government in all its action is bound by rules fixed and announced beforehand – rules which make it possible to foresee with fair certainty how the authority will use its coercive power in given circumstances and to plan one's individual affairs on the basis of this knowledge."

72 Davis (1969: 17). Similarly, Galligan (1986: 1) points out that "a noticeable feature of every modern legal system is the extent to which officials, whether they be judicial or administrative, make decisions in the absence of previously fixed, relatively clear, and binding legal standards." Of course, one could argue that notwithstanding the fact that some degree of discretion is inevitable in practice, such discretion is still incompatible with the rule of law. A system falls short of the ideal of rule of law to the extent that discretion exists. Burton (1994), for instance, questions whether emphasis on particularized justice in the name of equity is consistent with rule of law.

73 See Davis (1969: 25). Waldron (1989: 82) notes that while consistent application of a rule may enhance predictability, such predictability may not be desirable if the rule is not a good one.

74 Davis (1969: 29).

75 Rakoff (2000) contrasts the views of many European scholars with those of American administrative law scholars who favor the less-rigid view of rule of law.

76   Summers (1993: 159).
77   Macedo (1994) notes that while discretion in the name of equity may promote justice in certain circumstances, following rules has advantages as well, and that allowing decision-maker discretion opens up the possibility of abuse of discretion and decision-making based on personal prejudice and bias.
78   Sunstein (1995) sets out some general guidelines but notes the need for context-specific determinations.
79   For instance, until the passage of the Securities Law in 1999, China's securities markets were regulated primarily by administrative regulations. Even with the passage of the Securities Law, administrative regulations will continue to be an important source of legislation.
80   Xinzheng Xukefa (Zhengqiu Yijiangao) [Administrative Licensing Law (Draft for Comments)].
81   The drafters were mainly members of the NPC's Legal Committee. Naturally, local governments may have a different opinion on the matter, so the outcome is by no means determined.
82   Dowdle (1997).
83   See "Vote of disapproval prompts campaign to clean up China's courts" (1997).
84   The NPC heard twelve work reports in 1992, fourteen in 1993, seven in 1994, ten in 1995, and eight in 1996. The Sichuan People's Congress heard eighteen in 1992, twenty-five in 1993, twenty in 1994, twenty-seven in 1995, and eighteen in 1996. Jiang Mingan, ed. (1998: 181).
85   NPC criticisms have the additional benefit of mobilizing and emboldening other political actors that might otherwise have remained passive, as pointed out by Michael Dowdle in personal communication.
86   Dowdle (1997: 94).
87   Linda Chelan Li (2000: 204) reports that people's congresses in Guangdong have conducted more than 800 appraisals of government officials since 1992, resulting in the removal of five elected officials and several hundred nonelected officials.
88   Jiang Mingan, ed. (1998: 169).
89   Jiang Mingan, ed. (1998: 169). Li Cheng (2000: 26) reports that in 1998 provincial people's congresses elected five vice-governors nominated by people's congress delegates over Party candidates.
90   The number of delegates with an undergraduate degree or higher increased from 69 percent in the 8th NPC to 81 percent in the 9th NPC. See *Name List of Deputies to 9th NPC Published* (1998).
91   Supervision Law, art. 2.
92   Supervision Law, art. 1.
93   However, they can only recommend that obviously inappropriate personnel decisions be changed. Supervision Law, art. 23(4).
94   Supervision Law, art. 23.
95   Jiang Mingan, ed. (1998: 223).
96   *Ibid.* at 217. They accepted 4,978 cases, up almost 29 percent from 1995, resulting in the sanctioning of 4,494 Party members, up almost 25 percent.
97   Supervision Law, art. 24.

98 Supervision Law, arts. 25, 39.

99 Supervision Law, art. 38.

100 Supervision Law, arts. 29, 34. They must also report to the next higher-level supervisory organ and obtain approval in such situations.

101 Jiang Mingan, ed. (1998: 220).

102 Jiang Mingan, ed. (1998: 225–26).

103 Jiang Mingan, ed. (1998: 228).

104 In any event, many PRC scholars have objected to the merger of the CCP discipline committees and supervision organs, notwithstanding certain short-term benefits, as incompatible with rule of law and not worth it in the long run. One of the linchpins for rule of law is restricting the CCP's involvement in government to its legally circumscribed role. Creating a separate system of justice for Party members overseen by the Party is not conducive to that long-term goal.

105 PRC scholars frequently argue that administrative reconsideration promotes closeness between the people and government and helps solve social contra-dictions.

106 In the past, many administrative agencies were charging for administrative reconsideration. The ARL makes clear that there is to be no charge for recon-sideration, and that the agencies are to bear the cost. ARL, art. 39.

107 ARL, art. 3(3).

108 ARL, art. 7, provides for review of regulations (*guiding*) of the (i) State Council ministries, (ii) people's governments at the county level and above and their work departments, and (iii) village and township people's governments, but *excluding* Administrative Rules and Government Rules. In short, reconsider-ation bodies may not review Laws, Administrative Regulations, or Rules but may review all government and administrative agency Normative Documents.

109 ARL, arts. 26–28.

110 There were only 220,000 administrative reconsideration cases from 1991 until 1997 nationwide. See *NPC Standing Committee to View Administrative Appeals Law* (1998).

111 In Beijing, the numbers have decreased from 314 in 1991 to just over 200 in 1995. In comparison, the number of ALL cases in Beijing increased from 142 in 1991 to 430 in 1996. Jiang Mingan, ed. (1998: 252).

112 ALL plaintiffs prevail in approximately 40% of the cases. In contrast, be-tween 1991 and 1996, administrative reconsideration review bodies in Beijing quashed or modified the decision in just over 30% of the cases. Moreover, over time, they quashed or modified fewer decisions. In 1991–92, the agencies lost more than a hundred times a year. In 1993–94, they lost less than a hundred cases a year while in 1995–96 they lost less than fifty times per year. Jiang Mingan, ed. (1998: 253). In Xinjiang, review bodies reportedly quashed or modified on average 43.7% of the cases per year. But the high levels of quash-ing or modifying of agency decisions in the early years distort the average. For instance, in 1990–91, review bodies quashed 67% of the shelter and investi-gation decisions. In 1992, they quashed 73% of such decisions. By 1996, they only quashed 20%. Jiang Mingan, ed. (1998: 275).

113   Cai Shangyi (1994).

114   Yang Jiejun (1997) notes problems with jurisdiction, scope of review, limits on standing, procedural shortcomings, and exclusion of certain normative documents from review.

115   Yang Cheng and Liu Jingzhu (1997).

116   1990 Administrative Reconsideration Regulations, art. 11. The exceptions were where there was no superior organization, where laws and regulations expressly conferred jurisdiction on the same-level government, and where the State Council would be the administrative superior.

117   On the other hand, in some cases, the lower-level department will already have sought instructions from the higher department before making its decision, rendering appeal to the higher-level department futile. See Yang Cheng and Liu Jingzhu (1997).

118   ARR, art. 11. The revised ARL continues the practice, allowing the plaintiff to choose whether to appeal to the same-level government or the administrative superior, unless laws or regulations expressly confer jurisdiction on the same-level government or the administrative superior is the State Council. ARL, arts. 12–15.

119   Warren (1982: 289–92).

120   ARL, art. 9. The ARR only provided for fifteen days.

121   ARL, art. 22.

122   ARL, art. 10. The ARL reflects the belief that administrative reconsideration should differ from judicial review and that reconsideration procedures should be simpler. NPC Standing Committee Examines Draft Review Law (1998).

123   ARL, art. 23.

124   ARL, art. 22.

125   See Finder (1993) for a discussion of how the SPC handles petitions. See also Finder (1989) for a discussion of letters and petitions as it relates to administrative agencies. The petitions and appeals office may turn the matter over to administrative supervision organs or send the complainant back to the agency to pursue administrative reconsideration.

126   Potter (1994a).

127   Fang Shirong (1996: 98–105). See also The SPC Interpretation Regarding Several Problems in the Implementation of the PRC Administrative Litigation Law, art. 1(2), (issued by the SPC on March 10, 2000) [hereinafter, SPC ALL Interpretation], noting that only those acts clearly authorized by the Criminal Procedure Law are outside the scope of jurisdiction of the ALL.

128   ALL, art. 2.

129   Lin Feng (1996: 137).

130   Zou Rong (1998) discusses a case where the foreign party to a joint venture whose approval certificate was revoked did not have standing to sue because the foreign party was not the object of the approval reply revoking the appropriate certificate. The SPC's recent interpretation of the ALL now clearly provides parties to joint ventures with the right to challenge an act that affects the joint venture. See SPC ALL Interpretation, art. 15

131   See, for example, Liu Zheng (1998: 58).

132 Consider the controversy caused by the deferential standard announced by the US Supreme Court in *Chevron U.S.A., Inc.* v. *NRDC*, 467 US. 837 (1984). See also Schuck and Elliot, 1990.

133 Resolution of the Standing Committee of the National People's Congress Providing an Improved Interpretation of Law, art. 2 (1981) (adopted by the NPCSC).

134 Resolution of the Standing Committee of the National People's Congress Providing an Improved Interpretation of Law, art. 4.

135 Luo Haocai, ed. (1997: 158–59).

136 ALL, art. 53; SPC ALL Interpretation, art. 51(5).

137 Luo Haocai, ed. (1997: 159).

138 ALL, arts. 52, 53.

139 Lubman (1999: 144), for instance, asserts that "Chinese administrative agencies have the power to issue and interpret their own rules and *to require the courts to enforce them*" (emphasis in original). Although Lubman did not specify whether he means that they have the power as a legal matter or simply as a practical matter, he has stated in personal communication that he meant as a practical matter. Courts may even refuse to follow State Council Administrative Regulations, which are in general binding on the courts, if they believe such regulations are inconsistent with Laws.

140 Luo Haocai (1996: 162). Article 68 of the revised SPC ALL Interpretation now authorizes courts to cite legal and effective Rules and Normative Documents in their judgments.

141 PRC administrative law professors, judges, and lawyers disagree over how often this occurs. At present, we simply lack the empirical basis to draw any firm conclusions.

142 ALL, art. 54.

143 Schwartz (1991: 632–34).

144 Hu Jiangmiao (1992) provides a useful comparative summary of interpretation in China, the United States, France, and Germany.

145 In general, PRC courts may review acts for their legality but not their appropriateness. See ALL, art. 5. That is, the court will not substitute its judgment for the administrator's provided that the agency has acted within its legal authority. Even if the court would have made a different decision or acted differently in the circumstances, the court will defer to the agency unless the act is illegal. The only exception to the general rule is that a court may alter the decision of an agency with regard to an administrative penalty if it thinks the penalty is manifestly unjust. Many commentators abroad and in China have argued that the courts should be able to review the appropriateness of administrative acts and decisions. See, for example, Potter (1994b. 102), Peng Quiaui (1999); Guo Songjie (1996). That courts review the legality rather than the appropriateness of administrative acts and do not substitute their judgment for that of the agencies is, however, a basic principle of most legal systems. Warren (1982: 374) presents the standard view: "The word illegal is underscored since the courts cannot provide relief for those who have been hurt by unethical, cruel, insensitive, or blundering administrative acts which are

otherwise legal." Admittedly, some systems do allow courts to review the appropriateness of at least some administrative decisions. Moreover, in many systems, the line between legality versus appropriateness becomes blurred as the courts apply ever-widening standards of review. Alan (1992: 226) notes, for instance, that while courts in Belgium generally may only review administrative acts for legality, they have incorporated a reasonableness test that blurs the line between legality and appropriateness. Reviewing decisions in terms of such vague standards as reasonableness and proportionality or on the basis of whether they violate fundamental rights allows courts to base their decisions on their views of the appropriateness of the administrative act.

146 Lin Feng (1996: 194–95). Xie Hui (1992) argues that exceeding authority refers to both internal and external substantive *ultra vires* and procedural *ultra vires*. Other scholars argue that art. 54(d) should not include procedural *ultra vires* because art. 54(c) addresses procedural violations.

147 Fang Shirong (1996: 153–62).

148 Zhu Xinli (1996: 117) argues that excess of authority does not include consideration of purpose, appropriateness, or proportionality as in other countries, but refers to decisions that exceed the jurisdiction of the agency with respect to subject matter, geographic limitations, level within the administrative hierarchy, or quantitative jurisdictional limits.

149 Lin Feng (1996: 214–16).

150 Hu Jiangmiao (1992: 12–13); Shi Yuping (1996).

151 For a statistical analysis, see Minxin Pei (1997a).

152 For a discussion of several cases, see Lin Feng (1996: 216–48).

153 Jiang Mingan, ed. (1993: 202).

154 The 1996 Administrative Penalty Law incorporated the most detailed procedural requirements to date.

155 Li noted the bias toward substantive rules and the need to take procedures more seriously. *Li Peng Speaks on PRC Judicial Reform* (2000).

156 See Chapter 6.

157 Landis (1938).

158 Kairys (1998).

159 Becker (1983); Macey (1986).

160 See Freeman (2000).

161 Dorf and Sabel (1998: 287–88).

162 When consensus is not possible, voting is used to break the deadlock. Dorf and Sabel (1998: 320).

163 Dorf and Sabel (1998: 288).

164 Dorf and Sabel (1998: 403).

165 Fu Hualing (1992).

166 Peerenboom (1993a); Hall and Ames (1999).

167 See Chapter 11.

168 Government entities are organized along vertical (*tiao*) and horizontal (*kuai*) lines as discussed in Chapter 5.

169 Lardy (2000).

170 Freeman (2000: 574).

171 Of course, the scope of jurisdiction could be expanded.

172 See Chapter 11.

173 Indeed, contracting out to private actors assumes the participation of agencies that can draft contracts, lawyers that can make legal arguments, citizens that will bring suit, and impartial courts that provide competent judicial review.

174 PRC scholars have made numerous suggestions for improving the system. See, for example, Pi Chunxie and Li Yuji (1998).

175 O'Brien and Li (1999).

176 The system would have to be structured to avoid creating perverse incentives for local government officials to pressure courts to cover up mistakes in order to obtain a high score – for example, by refusing to hold administrative agencies liable in administrative litigation cases or by refusing to overturn on appeal incorrect decisions of the lower courts. Thus, officials would receive points for voluntarily addressing certain issues. In addition, outside monitors could be used for audit purposes. If the monitors discovered that local governments were covering up problems to avoid losing points, they would be penalized by a loss of several times the amount of points at stake.

177 Sun advocated five branches of government, with the control and examination branches complementing the legislative, executive, and judicial branches. The examination branch would set the standards for memberships in the other branches and oversee appointments while the control branch or censorate would monitor the behavior of the members of the other branches. Sun Yatsen (1990). The idea of a separate agency to monitor other agencies has been revived recently. Pan Wei (2001), for instance, advocates a "consultative rule of law" built on, *inter alia*, a professional civil service of the type enjoyed in Hong Kong and Singapore, an anticorruption system that would be headed by an entity which is independent of the civil service and partially insulated from judicial review, and consultative committees comprised of retired civil servants, concerned citizen representatives, and entrepreneurs who would oversee the civil service. See also Rubin (1997), arguing for a separate agency, like an auditor or inspector general's office, that would monitor other agencies.

178 The comparative administrative law scholars Neville-Brown and Bell (1993) put it well: "The standard of behaviour of an administration depends in the last resort upon the quality and traditions of the public officials who compose it rather than upon such sanctions as may be exercised through judicial control."

179 According to one report, Beijing Political–Legal organs handed over to receiver units 212 enterprises worth RMB 2.7 billion by 1998. See *Beijing's Political–Legal Organs Cut Business Ties* (1998).

10

Rule of law and economic development

One of the main motivating forces behind China's turn toward rule of law has been the belief that legal reforms are necessary for economic development. In emphasizing the importance of law to economic development, Chinese legal scholars and leaders align themselves with a long tradition of Western legal scholars, economists, and development agencies from Weber to the World Bank who have argued that rule of law is conducive to economic growth. A 1997 World Bank report, for instance, claimed that "countries with stable government, predictable methods of changing laws, secure property rights, and a strong judiciary saw higher investment and growth than countries lacking these institutions."[1]

The assumption that rule of law is necessary to sustain economic development has not gone unchallenged, however. Critics come in two general kinds: generalist and China-specific. Generalist critics question both the theoretical basis and the empirical data for asserting that rule of law leads to economic growth. Even assuming rule of law is normally integral to economic development, China-specific critics question whether law has had much to do with China's remarkable growth in the last twenty years, and suggest that China may be an exception to the general rule.

If the critics are right and rule of law is not necessary for sustained economic growth, at least in China, then one of the ruling regime's main incentives for promoting legal reforms will be undercut, calling into question the future of rule of law in China. To be sure, as I have repeatedly emphasized, the regime supports rule of law for a number of reasons, including the desire to rationalize governance and rein in local government officials. Moreover, the demand for rule of law comes from a variety of sources, both domestic and international. Even if rule of law does not contribute to economic growth, it does promise fairer and more just outcomes. Accordingly, the citizenry will continue to pressure the ruling regime to implement rule of law regardless of its role in economic development. Nevertheless, the movement to push for rule of law would be weakened if it did not contribute to economic growth.

I first consider the theoretical arguments for and against the claim that rule of law contributes to economic development, as well as the empirical evidence. I then turn to the arguments that even if rule of law is generally required for sustained growth, China is an exception. I suggest that implementation of rule of law is necessary for sustained economic development in China. Finally, I consider the importance of rule of law for different sectors of the economy, and the likely impact of the WTO on foreign investment and legal reforms. I postpone discussion of the related issue of whether legal reforms and economic development will lead to political reforms until the next chapter.

Law and economic development: theory and practice

Several theories in support of law's role in sustained economic development

Weber was one of the first to draw a connection between law and economic development.[2] While not ignoring the influence of other elements, Weber attributed Europe's stunning economic development to two main factors: cultural values, in particular a Protestant work ethic; and its institutions, especially its legal system. Economic actors in a market economy require predictability and certainty to be able to plan their affairs and to ensure that they will reap the benefits of their efforts, inventions, and investments. According to Weber, Europe's legal system provided that certainty, whereas other systems did not, because it was a logically formal and rational system. A legal system that relies on generally applicable rules is rational, whereas a system is irrational when the judge or adjudicator decides cases in an ad hoc manner, relying on his or her discretion as to what is appropriate in the particular circumstances. A system is formal when autonomous legal professionals rely on a distinctive form of legal reasoning to apply laws, which are themselves distinguishable from general moral norms, religious doctrines, and political principles.[3] And a system is logical when laws are the product of a reasoned and purposeful law-making process rather than simply the codification of customary norms or sacred rules passed down through the ages.

In emphasizing the need for states to abandon traditional institutions in favor of a hierarchically organized state bureaucracy and autonomous legal profession, Weber presaged modernization theory, which emerged after World War II and inspired the original law and development movement. Leading modernization theorists such as W. W. Rostow attributed the lack of development in some countries to their traditional economic, social and political institutions and cultural practices, and values.[4] The remedy was for developing countries to replace their existing institutions, practices, and values with modern ones based on the West. On the assumption that one size fits all, developing countries were to adopt private markets, liberal political institutions, including multiparty democracy and a welfare state, and a modern administrative and legal system. An autonomous legal system of the type praised by Weber and found in Western developed states would not only promote economic growth by providing the requisite certainty, but would also foster political development by limiting arbitrary government actions and serving as the backbone of a liberal democratic system in which individuals and interest groups were able to vie for power.

Armed with modernization theory's teleological and evolutionary view that legal reforms would lead to economic development, which would in turn lead to political reforms and the creation of liberal democracies, members of the original law and development movement took their crusade to developing countries. Unfortunately, all did not work out as planned. As discussed in Chapter 4, many states failed to achieve economic growth. Even when they did, some remained authoritarian or corporatist in nature rather than democratic, with little political pluralism or opportunities for participation in government. Even among those states that did become democratic, not all became liberal democracies.

Despite the setbacks, economists continued to argue that institutions, particularly legal institutions, mattered. Neoclassical growth theories predicted that poor countries would grow faster than wealthy countries because of technological advances and diminishing returns to capital in developed countries.[5] When that did not happen, economists attributed the lack of growth to faulty institutions, including the lack of rule of law, secure property rights, and a political system that limited executive discretion. This line of thought built on the work of economic historian Douglass North, who argued that enforceable property rights and fair rules for competition allow individual entrepreneurs and the most efficient firms to secure the benefits of their labors, while reducing the state's capacity for expropriation.[6] Conversely, when property rights or the policy environment are characterized by frequent change and a high degree of administrative discretion, economic actors are less likely to make efficient adjustments to changes in technology or government policy.[7] Indeed, poor institutions may very well favor inefficient entrepreneurs who rely more on connections and personal ties than economically efficient skills. Lacking proper institutions and enforceable property rights, developing countries have not been able to take advantage of whatever opportunities for growth do exist.

Inspired by North as well as the apparent global triumph of market capitalism and thirty more years of experimentation and data regarding the role of legal institutions in fostering growth, the new law and development movement quickly gained ground in the 1990s. While differing in several significant ways from the earlier movement,[8] the new movement continues to assign a central role to law and legal institutions in promoting growth. Consistent with North's views, the new movement perceives law as restraining the state and empowering private actors. It also emphasizes the need for clear and enforceable property rights and sound commercial laws more generally, including corporate, securities, and banking laws to facilitate the raising and free flow of capital; bankruptcy laws to eliminate inefficient firms and ensure that their assets are put to more productive uses; and intellectual property laws to encourage investment in research and development of new products and technologies. At the same time, all are aware that good laws alone are not enough. Proper institutions are essential, including an independent and competent judiciary, an autonomous and qualified legal profession, and an administrative law regime capable of holding predatory government officials in check.[9]

Globalization theory has fortified the theoretical basis of the new movement. In the past thirty years many countries, including China, have experienced rapid growth in foreign trade, FDI, and inflows and outflows of foreign capital.[10] The penetration of domestic markets by multinational corporations and the increased cross-border flow of technology, information, capital, and management skills have altered the domestic production patterns in many states. Equally important, globalization arguably has put pressure on developing countries to reform their institutions and adopt international best practices to attract foreign investment and compete in international markets. Representative of the new law and development's globalization gospel, the World Bank claims that attracting FDI requires a commitment to a transparent regime of investors' rights and regulations, a legal system that offers equal treatment and protection to foreign and domestic investors, sound macroeconomic fundamentals, and investment in human capital.[11] Indeed, by acceding to various treaties and joining international organizations such as the WTO, China has agreed to reform its legal system to make it more rule-of-law compliant.

In short, convergence theory holds that as a result of globalization all nations are converging on market economies with common institutions, policies, and modes of production. In this view, imitation, the diffusion of best practices, and the mobility of trade and capital will lead to similar institutions and practices. Variations among countries are due to contingent circumstances – differences in political systems, natural and human resources, initial levels of development, and so on – but over time such distinctions fade unless obstructed by the government or powerful interest groups.[12]

Critical theory

Some critics of the various development theories question whether the focus should be economic development, and in particular higher growth rates.[13] They point out that economic growth is consistent with enduring if not growing inequalities in incomes, increased environmental degradation, and continued discrimination against women and minorities.[14] Accordingly, they suggest that the concept of development must be broadened beyond fixation with the growth rate and indeed beyond narrow economic concerns. Greater attention must be paid to the way in which any additional wealth is redistributed; the environmental costs of economic development must also be taken into account; and efforts must be made to address the inequalities experienced by women and ethnic minorities.[15]

Others accept the general goal of economic growth but question the importance of law in achieving it. Despite important differences, legal realists, CRITs, and postmodernists, by highlighting the indeterminacy of language and the role of power and politics in the legal system, challenge the central tenet of Weber's argument that law provides the necessary predictability and certainty to support capitalist markets.[16] Given the vagueness of language, legal rules are more open-ended and subject to interpretation than Weber's image of a formally rational legal system allows. As discussed in Chapter 4, some CRITs argue that the law is riddled by fundamental antinomies. Accordingly, rather than impartial judges applying generally applicable laws to the particular factual situation, judges allegedly pick and choose from the contradictory legal principles whatever principle justifies the outcome that fits with their political preferences, class and gender biases, and normative views. Postmodernists add that not only is language indeterminate but that all languages or systems of discourse, including legal language, reflect relations of power in society. Reality is a social construct, created in part by systems of discourse. Because those who have the power are able to create the dominant discourse, they are able to define what comes to be accepted as reality. What matters, then, is not the law, but who is in power and their values, beliefs, and preferences.[17]

Another line of criticism argues that the heavy emphasis on formal legal institutions ignores the particular circumstances of individual countries, the crucial role of culture, and the significant advantages of informal institutions.[18] Economic development depends on a whole host of factors: economic policies, indigenous political institutions, and traditional norms and cultural practices. Contrary to the views of modernization theorists such as Rostow who believed that all systems must pass through the same stages on their way to development, there is no single path. Whereas in Western countries the engine for growth has been individual private entrepreneurs, with the state playing a limited role, in Asian countries the state has been more active.[19] Rather than relying primarily on generally applicable laws, Asian states have relied on the discretionary administrative policies of a technocratic bureaucracy. The administrative system has been geared toward maximum flexibility and minimum transparency, and characterized by collusion between regulators and regulated. Thus, antitrust rules were ignored to facilitate cartelization; import rules were manipulated to maintain high informal barriers; shareholder rights were rarely invoked, and so on.[20]

Skeptics also observe that a formal legal system that meets the standards of even a thin rule of law is costly to establish and operate.

As they rightly point out, it would be prohibitively expensive to rely on the formal legal system to enforce all contracts. Thus, even in the litigious USA commercial disputes are regularly resolved without recourse to the court.[21] In this view, norms of generalized morality, social trust, self-enforcing market mechanisms, and informal substitutes for formal law may provide the necessary predictability and certainty required by economic actors for a fraction of the cost.[22] Reliance on such mechanisms promotes economic development by lowering the costs of doing business, both to the state and to the parties. The savings may then be put to more productive uses. Reliance on social relationships and family connections reduces parties' transaction costs because parties connected in tight social networks need not bear the informational costs of conducting due diligence on the other party. Nor need they invest in high-paid lawyers to draft lengthy contracts because they can rely on trust, loss of face, and the threat of reputational damage to ensure contracts are performed. If a breach does occur, the parties can turn to informal means of resolving disputes, including mediation, that are arguably less expensive than litigation in court. Informal methods of resolving disputes may also result in more context-specific solutions that allow the parties to continue their relationship and thus serve their interests better than the kind of winner-take-all solution that a formal court might find. Moreover, critics note that the high incidence of family businesses and the relational nature of much business in Asian countries appears to have helped cushion the shock of the Asian financial crisis by providing a social welfare network in countries where the social security system is typically weak, and by making it possible to raise capital to start over, thus contributing to a speedy economic recovery.

The role of foreign capital in the Asian financial crisis also raised doubts about globalization. While some critics question whether globalization is a positive development, others question whether globalization is really occurring, and whether countries are converging on particular economic institutions as opposed to developing their own distinct varieties of capitalism. Skeptics point out that the world economy arguably was more integrated prior to World War II, at the height of the gold standard.[23] Moreover, foreign trade still accounts for only a small part of the GDP of most countries, with the vast majority of domestic production being for local consumption.[24] FDI is highly concentrated among developed countries and a small number of developing countries, and in any event accounts for only a fraction of the GDP in even these select countries.[25] Nor is capital as mobile as it is often portrayed. For instance, most multinational corporations are still closely tied to a particular nation in terms of the location of most of their business, assets, employees, and key decision-making.[26]

Even assuming higher levels of economic integration, critics claim that it is doubtful that all nations are converging on market economies with common institutions, policies, and modes of production. Rather than convergence on a single model, there are different varieties of capitalism.[27] Neoinstitutionalists, for their part, claim that economic policy and performance are affected by the organization of the political economy,[28] but they are divided on the issue of convergence. Some believe that the embeddedness of institutions leads to divergent social systems (or modes) of production, while others see convergence as the more likely end result.[29] Inevitably, global trends are impacted by domestic politics. For instance, some developing countries may find that the domestic costs of strict enforcement of intellectual property laws outweigh the benefits, most of which accrue to foreign companies.[30] Accordingly, they may refuse to enforce rigorously intellectual property laws unless sufficient international pressure can be brought to bear.[31] In any event, to a considerable extent convergence or divergence is in the eye of the beholder, and depends on which countries and indices one examines. Clearly there is more convergence among developed states than less developed states.[32]

Assuming that national economies are becoming more integrated, whether such globalization is a positive development or an ominous threat to national identities and local ways of life is contested in China and abroad. Some argue that far from fostering international best practices, globalization creates a race to the bottom, particularly with respect to the rights of labor. More generally, debates continue over whether globalization will promote faster economic growth, whether it will foster or undermine macroeconomic stability (as seemed to be the case in the Asian financial crisis), and whether it will create new jobs or increase income inequality and unemployment among low-skilled workers.[33] Economic reformers in China have had to contend with a vociferous, if minority, conservative faction. The conservatives have vehemently opposed reforms on the grounds that China's open-door policies will lead to spiritual pollution in the form of decadent Western bourgeois

ideas while increased foreign capital will result in an overheated economy, higher rates of inflation, and social unrest as in the 1989 Tiananmen
demonstrations.[34] The Asian financial crisis caused even some market-
oriented reformers to wonder whether reliance on FDI and foreign capital would undermine national security and leave China vulnerable to
foreign interests. As a result, a number of restrictions were imposed
on foreign exchange transactions, and plans for making capital accounts
freely convertible were subsequently put on hold.

Many domestic critics of China's accession to the WTO worry that
domestic companies and financial institutions will be crushed by foreign competitors – a sharp rise in agricultural imports will lead to
massive rural unemployment and at the same time, state-owned enterprises will have to shed urban employees in an effort to become more
competitive. The result could be heightened social tensions and perhaps chaos as disgruntled urban workers and displaced farmers from
the countryside take to the streets to demand jobs. Should the two
groups unite, the government will be hard pressed to maintain order. In
the process, economic reforms might be put on hold, and growth may
slow.

Testing the theories: empirical evidence for rule of law as necessary for sustained economic development

Notwithstanding the oftentimes heated theoretical debates, there is considerable evidence that rule of law is necessary if not sufficient in most
cases for sustained economic development. A number of long-term,
multiple-country empirical studies have shown rule of law to be positively correlated with growth.[35] Robert Barro analyzed data from eighty-
five countries for the periods 1965–75, 1975–85, and 1985–90.[36] He
tested the impact of a number of independent variables, including rule
of law.[37] His rule-of-law index was based on International Country
Risk Guide (ICRG) survey data compiled from the subjective responses
of business persons regarding law and order. The law subcomponent
assesses the strength and impartiality of the legal system and the order
subcomponent assesses the popular observance of law. Higher scores indicate sound political institutions, a strong court system, and provisions
for an orderly succession of power. Lower scores indicate a tradition of
dependence on physical force or illegal means to settle claims. Barro's

regression analysis found that an improvement in one rank in the 0 to 6 rule-of-law index raised growth rates by 0.5 percent.[38]

Other studies have found that clear and enforceable property rights are positively correlated with growth.[39] Knack and Keefer relied on both the ICRG and the Business Environmental Risk Intelligence (BERI) surveys. The BERI survey does not directly ask about rule of law but includes questions about contract enforceability, the likelihood of nationalization, infrastructure, and bureaucratic delays. Knack and Keefer conclude that institutions that protect property rights are crucial to economic growth and investment and the effect of such institutions continues to exist even after controlling for investment.

In a somewhat broader study, Clague, Knack, Keefer, and Olson tested growth rates against the BERI standards; the contract-intensive money ratio (CIM), which is the ratio of non-currency money to total money supply;[40] and the aggregate ICRG index, which is a composite of the indices for the quality of the bureaucracy, corruption in government, rule of law, expropriation risk, and the risk of government repudiation of contracts. Higher ICRG, CIM, and BERI scores were associated with higher annual per capita growth rates, even in less developed countries.[41]

Another study based on the ICRG showed that rule of law is an important factor in determining the size of capital markets (both debt and equity) and that improvements in rule of law are associated with more domestically listed firms and initial public offerings per capita, a greater ratio of private sector debt to GNP, and a higher amount of outsider participation in a country's capital markets.[42] In a similar vein, Ross Levine found that countries that give a high priority to creditors receiving the full present value of their claims in bankruptcy or corporate reorganizations and in which the legal system effectively enforces contracts generally have more developed financial intermediaries and higher growth rates.[43] Moving a country from the lowest quartile of countries with respect to the legal protection of creditors to the next quartile translates into a 29 percent rise in financial development, which increases growth by almost one percentage point a year.

Still another study of seventy countries found that the "efficiency and integrity of the legal environment as it affects business, particularly foreign firms" was positively and significantly correlated with economic growth, even controlling for GDP per capita. It also found that, contrary to the speculations of some theoreticians that corruption might increase

economic growth, corruption lowers private investment, thereby reducing growth rates.[44]

Further, it now seems, based on the successes and failures of the Asian
countries and the attempt of Russia to create markets, that a legal system that meets the basic requirements of a thin theory of rule of law is
essential for sustainable development.[45] In Russia, privatization in the
absence of rule of law led to widespread looting and diversion of state
assets into private hands. In retrospect it is clear that Russian institutions
were insufficiently developed to carry out massive privatization and
ensure the smooth operation of capital markets. Economic reforms were
undermined not only by weak courts but by weak supporting institutions. Russia's credit rating services, securities regulators, accountants,
and legal profession were simply not up to the demands of a modern
economy.[46]

In Asia, the 1997 financial crisis exposed the underside of the Asian
miracle. The lack of transparency, inadequate regulatory systems, and
limits on political participation contributed to the crisis.[47] The close
cooperation between government and business that was once seen as
the key to growth in many Asian countries was subsequently attacked
for resulting in less transparency and accountability.[48]

Assessing the evidence: the need for caution

Despite such seemingly overwhelming and consistent evidence, there are
still ample grounds for caution. The problems operationalizing the relationship between law and development that plagued the original law and
development movement have yet to be resolved. Simply put, rule of law
is hard to define with sufficient specificity to test empirically. Several of
the empirical studies relied on subjective measures from two sources, the
ICRG and BERI surveys.[49] Both collect information by asking in-country
observers to rate countries numerically in terms of various criteria.
Consistency is an issue in that the surveys rely on subjective responses
to questionnaires by different people in different countries. Another,
and arguably more important issue, is whether the criteria that form
the subject matter of the survey adequately capture rule of law.[50] Even if
they do, the regression studies generally do not purport to show that rule
of law *causes* development, only that rule of law is positively correlated
with economic development.[51] The aggregate rule-of-law studies also

do not specify the particular institutional arrangements, laws, or legal practices that are necessary for growth. A cursory glance around the globe is sufficient to demonstrate that countries known for rule of law differ dramatically in each of these areas. As noted, however, exclusive reliance on growth rates to measure economic development is problematic as high growth rates are consistent with wide income disparities, environmental degradation, and other injustices.

Even those at the center of the new law and development movement acknowledge the persistent difficulty in operationalizing the relation between law and development, and the inability to specify with any reasonable degree of certainty precisely what is required for economic development.[52] Chastened by fifty years of failed predictions by leading development pundits and international organizations, the World Bank recently unveiled a Comprehensive Development Framework that declares that everything matters: economic policies; political and legal institutions, including rule of law, property rights regimes, and security market regulatory mechanisms; human resources; physical resources; geography; and culture. The Bank is also careful to point out that this holistic approach is difficult to operationalize and is meant as a pragmatic guideline rather than a detailed blueprint. Hedging its bets still further, the Bank takes pains to add that the "mixed record of development programs in the past suggests the need for both caution in application and realism about expected results."[53]

Nevertheless, the difficulties in operationalizing the relationship between economic development, rule of law, and other factors should not blind us to some important lessons that can be drawn from the experiments in stimulating economic growth during the last several decades. Not surprisingly, economic growth requires good economic policies, including sound macroeconomic policies that keep inflation down and avoid recessions, as well as policies that encourage high savings, provide strong returns to investment, reduce corruption, increase competition, promote education, and liberalize trade.[54] The free flow of information, capital, and technology are also important. Political processes that are open, participatory, and inclusive are beneficial, as demonstrated by the Asian financial crisis, the looting of state-owned assets in Russia, the problems with crony capitalism in Indonesia, and the difficulties in achieving equitable growth in South American countries.[55] Efficient markets depend on a variety of institutions and professions to disseminate information and reduce the costs of doing business and the likelihood of ending up in disputes. A professional corps of accountants, appraisers, credit-rating services, securities companies, and regulatory systems are all needed. As the empirical studies show, a legal system capable of enforcing contracts, maintaining competition, upholding property rights, and protecting investors against excessively predatory governments is also useful.[56] Social capital is also important. Informal mechanisms for resolving disputes as well as cultural norms that allow cooperation and encourage trust, and thus reduce transaction costs, are important complements to the formal legal system.

Is China an exception?

Even assuming that rule of law is in general necessary for sustained economic development, the rapid economic growth in China since 1978, despite the weak legal system, has led many to question whether China is an exception to the general principle.[57] How has China managed to attract so much foreign investment and achieve such high growth rates notwithstanding the apparent lack of rule of law and seemingly un-enforceable property rights?

There are several hypotheses that might explain this apparent anomaly.[58] First, there may be fewer problems with rule of law and enforceable property rights than generally perceived. Second, investors may not be rational or at least their investment decisions may not be rational. Rational investors will invest when the expected gains exceed the expected losses and the profit rate is greater than could be realized elsewhere. Expected gains and losses are a function of the size of the gain or loss and the probability of realizing them. Perhaps investors are simply not acting rationally and discounting or ignoring the risks.

A third possibility is that notwithstanding the empirical studies, rule of law and enforceable property rights may not be as important to foreign investment and economic growth as initially thought. Rule of law may not be all that important because there are substitutes or alternatives that provide the certainty and predictability needed by investors. Or rule of law and clear property rights may not be all that important because China is somehow unique. If so, it may be able to take advantage of certain idiosyncratic features not available to most countries to attract investment and achieve growth without rule of law. China is no doubt unusual in many ways, including the size of its markets and the almost mystical appeal it holds for foreigners. Perhaps its huge markets justify the investment despite rule-of-law risks.[59] Or perhaps the unusually high proportion of investment from overseas Chinese diminishes the need for rule of law and enforceable property rights.[60]

A fourth possibility, of course, is that despite the high growth rates, the lack of rule of law has impeded economic growth, and that China's growth rates could have been even higher.

Just how bad is the legal system?

The first hypothesis suggests that the high levels of foreign investment, coupled with the high growth rates, might be explained at least in part by improvements in the legal system. In this view, property rights are more enforceable and rule-of-law issues less pressing than the oftentimes scathingly critical accounts of China's legal system would suggest. There is some evidence for this view.[61] Clearly, the legal system is much more developed than it was twenty years ago. In 1978, China lacked the basic laws that define a market: there was no contract law, no company law, no intellectual property laws, no securities laws, no banking laws – or at least none appropriate for a market economy. To the extent commercial laws did exist, they reflected the needs of a centrally planned economy. As China moved toward a market economy, these earlier laws were repealed or amended.

In the early years of China's open-door policy, foreign investors were put off by the lack of a functioning legal system, vague and incomplete laws governing foreign investment, and the absence of a credible intellectual property regime. Between 1978 and 1992, the amount of foreign investment in China was quite small.[62] The vast majority of investment in China has been post 1992. Although the legal system was far from complete in 1992 and remains a source of investor concern today, there clearly has been considerable progress in providing investors with a framework with at least a somewhat higher degree of predictability.[63]

Furthermore, despite the widely publicized problems with enforcing court judgments and arbitral awards in China, property rights are more enforceable than often suggested. While foreign investors and the Western media regularly portray enforcement as all but impossible,[64] survey data demonstrates that courts do enforce both court judgments and arbitral awards. One recent survey found that applicants who turned to the courts for compulsory enforcement of arbitral awards were able to recover at least half of the award in 40 percent of the cases.[65] Moreover, in many cases, nonenforcement is for legitimate reasons set forth in international treaties and PRC law or due to the respondent's lack of assets. Put differently, the rate of nonenforcement for suspect or illegitimate reasons such as local protectionism, judicial incompetence, corruption, and the like was between 17 percent and 29 percent. While far from perfect, these results are much better than the exceedingly grim predictions in the popular press. Further, investors' contractual rights are even more secure than the enforcement rates suggest since presumably in most cases the losing party will comply voluntarily with the award.[66]

On the other hand, China's legal system undeniably still falls far short of any reasonable standards for rule of law. For instance, even when successful in recovering on their awards, companies often experience numerous obstacles and delays resulting from basic rule-of-law problems, and usually end up recovering only a percentage of the award. Moreover, the risk of nonenforcement of an arbitral award is only one of many rule-of-law risks. Depending on the nature of the investment or transaction, parties may be concerned about the rapidly changing regulatory framework, inconsistent application of rules, predatory local governments that impose arbitrary fees on deep-pocketed foreign companies, technology leakage resulting from shortcomings and nonimplementation of China's intellectual property laws, the lack of transparency, judicial corruption, and so on. Taken together, the various rule-of-law problems would appear to constitute a significant risk.

Are investors rational?

Have investors been irrationally ignoring or discounting such risks, as the second thesis suggests? Clearly some investors have made irrational decisions. For instance, one of the reasons so many arbitral awards go unenforced is that investors fail to investigate adequately the legal and financial status of the PRC companies they are doing business with. Even allowing that extensive due diligence at the time of contracting may have been cost prohibitive, surely investors should at least attempt to verify that the company has assets before seeking enforcement. They also should consider other ways of structuring the deal to reduce the risk of nonenforcement.[67]

More generally, the investment decisions of foreign businesses have not always been based on a rational assessment of the relative risks and gains.[68] Investors in China often lack sufficient information to make a fully informed choice. The absence of reliable information about arbitral award enforcement is only one example. Even such basic information as the profitability of foreign-invested enterprises is hard to come by, and what information is available is conflicting.[69] In any event, the fluid regulatory and economic environment resulting from ongoing legal and economic reforms make long-term predictions based on currently available information dubious at best.

But even in the absence of information problems, some investors appear to have acted irrationally. Eyes dazed by the (fictive) promise of a market of over a billion captive consumers, foreign investors have been willing to discount or ignore the considerable risks of doing business in China. Many multinational companies have eagerly invested in China, even though they expected to lose money, simply to test the market and to learn about the opportunities for (and obstacles to) doing business in the PRC. While perhaps rational from a long-term business perspective, such investments are not driven by a concern with the lack of rule of law or clear property rights.

Other decisions have been driven not by any long-term strategic plan but rather by organizational politics and dynamics. Even the senior management of major multinational companies at times appears to have been swept up in the hype over the Pac-Rim century, and rushed to enter China simply because others were doing so.[70] During the heady days of 1994–96, senior management often gave their negotiators marching orders to complete a certain number of projects by the end of the year.[71] Needless to say, that put the negotiators in a weak bargaining position. In some cases, the troop soldiers went ahead with a deal even though they knew it was going to be a loser rather than buck senior management. In other cases, lower-level management saw China as a good place to advance their careers and aggressively pursued projects. During the drawn-out negotiation process typical for joint ventures in China, they may have come to realize that the project was likely to end up losing money. However, having spent a couple of years working on it, they naturally were reluctant to inform their superiors that they had made a mistake, particularly when they were the main advocates for the project in the first place. Rather than risk the immediate fallout, some may have opted to postpone the day of reckoning in the hope that the company might miraculously turn out to make money or at least that intervening factors would prevent the blame from being placed on their shoulders.[72]

Presumably, however, most investors do attempt to make rational decisions, subject to information limitations. Although investors face many risks when doing business in China, the high rate of investment would suggest that many investors have not found either rule-of-law risks or the broader range of political and commercial risks sufficient to stop investment (though, as explained shortly, that may be changing). The third thesis would attribute this to the relative unimportance of rule of law or to the existence of substitutes for it.

Clientelism, corporatism, and Chinese capitalism as alternatives to rule of law

Some scholars have attributed China's phenomenal growth in the absence of rule of law to a distinct form of "Chinese capitalism," using clientelism and corporatism as alternatives or partial substitutes for rule of law. Carol Jones is most explicit in suggesting that rule of law may not be required for economic development and that "informal alternatives to legal regulation may be more efficient than competitive markets based on law."[73] In her view, the Four Dragons of Singapore, Taiwan, South Korea, and Hong Kong have been dominated by a "rule of relationships" rather than rule of law and yet have enjoyed remarkable economic growth, leading her to conclude "formal rational law may not be quite as crucial to capitalism as Weber imagined."

Chinese capitalism is characterized by a preference for family businesses, a tendency to resolve disputes through informal mechanisms rather than the courts, a common sinic cultural heritage, adherence to Confucian values, and an emphasis on relationships.[74] The key to Chinese capitalism is an emphasis on relationships and networks of familial, personal, and social connections. The first point to note is that reliance on relationships is not necessarily at odds with rule of law. In most instances, the two systems are complementary. Family businesses and networks of personal relationships exist in all legal systems. The cultural context may vary from one country to the next, leading to differences in the degree of importance or differences in particular practices, but there are general similarities in all societies. Nor need a formal rule-of-law legal system drive out all informal practices. Informal means of resolving disputes complement the formal system in all modern rule-of-law legal systems.

Nevertheless, while relationships and informal means of resolving disputes may complement the formal legal system, they are at best partial substitutes for rule of law and the formal legal system. In fact, many of the informal mechanisms often cited as alternatives to rule of law are themselves dependent on the formal legal system to function. For instance, informal dispute mechanisms such as mediation are more effective when they are backed up by a formal legal system that will enforce judgments because the threat of taking the matter to court stimulates settlements and creates an incentive for the parties to honor the agreement.

Moreover, as the economy grows, reliance on relationships rather than generally applicable laws and formal legal institutions becomes less effective. When the economy is small and the members of the business community closely related, it is easy to publicize a breach of contract and let others know that someone is not to be trusted. However, as the number of transactions increases, it becomes more difficult to convey information about a particular party to all those that might have an interest in such information. Further, the transactions become more complex, making it difficult to rely on informal means of resolving disputes. As the amount in controversy grows, parties become reluctant to trust in the capacity of third parties without legal training to resolve disputes. There are also more transactions between parties with no connections beyond the particular transaction. In many cases, the parties may be complete strangers to each other, and not share an institutional superior or a mutually trusted third party that could mediate a dispute.

Furthermore, rule of law is necessary to protect parties that are not repeat players or for whom the threat of withdrawing future business is not a sufficient deterrent to cause the other party to act in accordance with law. Consumer protection laws, for example, are needed to protect individual consumers against fraud because companies need not be concerned about one unhappy customer as long as there are many others. A "rule of relationships" also does nothing to prevent parties from imposing externalities on outsiders. Predictably, one of the costs of economic development in China has been widespread environmental pollution.[75]

Critics frequently argue that rule of law's alleged emphasis on formal dispute settlement through the courts destroys traditional normative systems and displaces informal mechanisms for resolving disputes.[76] While perhaps true to some extent, the real threat to the existence of many informal systems typically is not the encroachment of the formal legal system but changes in the economic, social, and cultural context.[77] Pistor and Wellons' study of the relationship between law and economic development in China, Taiwan, Japan, South Korea, Malaysia, and India found that between 1960 and 1995, in five of the six countries, the exception being Malaysia, the trend was to become more market-oriented (as opposed to state-allocative) and more rule-based (as opposed to discretionary).[78] Moreover, they note:

> Typically, the changes, rather than emerging from the legal system itself, were primarily top-down, induced by government policy. Economic policies played the key role in initiating the trend first toward and then away from state-allocative law. The greater scope of market-based transactions these policy changes created enhanced the relevance of formal law for economic transactions. While previously state policies and bureaucratic guidance provided business with a high-level of certainty, this function now had to be provided by the legal system. In this sense the demand for formal law may be said to have increased.[79]

Economic development and reforms exposed weaknesses in laws and legal institutions, leading to changes in the formal legal system. But changes in the economy also exposed weaknesses in the informal mechanisms for securing contracts and resolving disputes, thereby increasing reliance on the formal legal system and correspondingly increasing demand for changes in the formal legal system.

Their study looked at four specific areas: dispute settlement, business governance and capital formation, credit and security, and administrative litigation. In each area, there were signs of convergence, though to different degrees.[80] With the exception of Japan, all countries in East Asia, including China, witnessed a rise in litigation at the expense of mediation as the economy developed and became more market-oriented. Moreover, as the private sector grew, corporate form became more important. Significantly, family businesses tended to encounter greater difficulties in raising capital, putting them at a competitive disadvantage with other companies. Outside investors may be reluctant to buy into companies that are tightly controlled by family members, particularly in the absence of strong minority shareholder protection provisions. Although there was not enough data to draw firm conclusions about the relative importance of formal law versus reliance on social capital and trust in forming, securing, and implementing contracts, as markets became more important, so did the need for effective security mechanisms. Conversely, relational lending in which the creditor and borrower share a formal ownership relationship decreased over time. At any rate, substitutes for security interests themselves relied on formal law.[81] For instance, in Taiwan, businesses were able to use postdated checks to secure loans in the absence of other collateral because the criminal code subjected people who bounced checks to imprisonment. When the criminal law was amended to do away with imprisonment for bouncing checks, the practice became less popular.

The experiences of other Asian countries tend to confirm that exclusive or even predominant reliance on a rule of relationships in China will not be sufficient to sustain long-term growth. Those who attribute the success of Asian countries to relation-based capitalism often underestimate the role law has played in economic development in the region, in part because they tend to elide rule of law with democracy and a liberal version of rights that emphasizes civil and political rights.[82] Of the Asian countries that have experienced sustained growth, most have enjoyed legal systems that comply with the standards of a thin rule of law. Although the political regimes may not have been democratic and the legal system may not have provided much protection for civil and political rights in some cases, the Asian countries that experienced economic growth generally scored high with respect to the legal protection of economic interests. A survey of economic freedoms in 102 countries between 1993 and 1995 found that 7 of the top 20 countries were in Asia.[83] Of course, not all Asian countries have experienced rapid growth.[84] Only six – Japan, South Korea, Taiwan, Hong Kong, Singapore, and China – experienced sustained growth over 5 percent for the period from 1965 until 1995.[85] With the exception of China, the legal systems of the six countries that have achieved highest economic growth measure up favorably with the requirements of a thin rule of law, particularly with respect to commercial matters.[86] In contrast, the legal systems of the lowest performing countries are among the weakest in the region.

While some scholars have attributed China's growth in the absence of rule of law to a rule of relationships, others have pointed to clientelism and corporatism.[87] To the extent that clientelism refers to reliance on personal and social relationship networks (*guanxi*), it is another way of describing the rule of relationships and is subject to the same qualifications and limitations. Yet by distinguishing between various forms of clientelism, certain differences in tone or emphasis begin to emerge.[88] Horizontal clientelism refers to relationships between equal parties. The arguments discussed previously about the economic benefits of relationships mainly applied to transactions between equal parties – to horizontal clientelism – rather than to vertical clientelism. Vertical clientelism refers to patron–client relations between superiors and subordinates, of which relationships between the regulators and the regulated, government and business, are the most important in explaining China's growth. Vertical relationships may range from the informal seeking of advice or assistance from a former classmate who is now an official to the extensive ties between the central government and big business that typify Asian statist development models to the crony capitalism of Indonesia and the Philippines.

In emphasizing the relation between government and businesses, vertical clientelism is similar to corporatism as used by some scholars to explain economic growth in China despite the absence of clear property rights. The meaning of corporatism is difficult to state succinctly.[89] Like rule of law, corporatism has come to serve many masters, and has been used in the Chinese context in somewhat novel ways. Corporatism has been understood as an alternative political theory to liberalism and Marxism.[90] Whereas liberalism focuses on individual liberty, and Marxism on class struggle, corporatism focuses on state–society relations. More specifically, corporatism serves as a halfway point between liberalism and Marxism or Fascism. Liberalism is characterized by a weak state and strong autonomous interest groups. Marxism–Leninism and Fascism are characterized by a totalitarian or at least authoritarian state with weak or non-existent autonomous interest groups and little if any grass-roots participation from below in decision-making. In contrast, corporatism combines a strong state with interest groups that enjoy some degree of autonomy. Corporatism comes in two main varieties, a hard or statist (authoritarian) version and a soft or societal (neocorporatist) version, with the strength of the state and the degree of autonomy of the interest groups determining where the system falls on the hard–soft continuum.[91] The consensus has been that state corporatism better fits China and other Asian countries more generally, to the extent that the concepts are applicable.

As noted in the introductory chapter, corporatism has been used in three main ways in China.[92] Some have used it as a way of looking at state–society relations and a measure of civil society, which most closely fits with its usage outside the Chinese context.[93] Others have used it to describe East Asian statist models of economic development. Margaret Pearson, for example, draws the link between corporatism and an East Asian statist model of development where "business is subordinate to and depends heavily on ties with the technobureaucracy to accomplish its goals."[94] A third group of scholars has used it to explain local forms of government–business relations. Jean Oi, for instance, uses corporatism to capture the way in which local governments have treated the local economy as a single corporate entity. Particularly in the 1980s, "local governments ran firms as diversified corporations, redistributing profits and risks, and thereby allowing rapid growth with limited resources."[95] They were able to do this because they enjoyed extensive controls over local companies, many of which were state-owned enterprises, collectives, or township and village enterprises (TVEs) in which the local government was a shareholder and indeed often the main shareholder. Moreover, local governments wield considerable power over local companies even when they are not shareholders due to their control over approvals, licenses, financing, and access to technology and other scarce resources. Predictably, managers in local companies have sought to establish close relations with government officials, resulting in patron–client relationships.[96]

The statist and local state model of corporatism may be understood as forms of vertical clientelism in that both emphasize the relationship between government and business. Statist corporatism focuses on the relationship between the central government and big business. Local state corporatism emphasizes the relation between the local government and local businesses.

Vertical clientelism and corporatism are in some ways compatible and in other ways at odds with a thin rule of law. It is normal for business people to seek close relations with the government. That happens everywhere. But such relationships have their costs and may lead to results that are inconsistent with rule of law. In some instances, decision-making based on particularistic relations may violate the rule-of-law requirement that publicly promulgated, generally applicable laws be fairly and impartially applied. When parties can rely on their relations with government officials for approvals, they may need to worry less about whether they comply with the legal requirements.

Corporatist arrangements in which the local government is involved in running local businesses also often run afoul of rule-of-law requirements. The loser is typically the state. As we have seen, national laws regularly give way to local interests. Local governments offer unauthorized tax breaks to companies that deprive the center of revenue or reduce the profitability of companies by collecting fees that go into local off-budget coffers. Government officials siphon off state assets to set up spin-off companies, leaving the state holding unproductive assets and saddled with liabilities.

But the state is not the only one that suffers from the lack of generally applicable laws and rule of law. Nonstate actors also suffer. Local government involvement in business is one of the major causes of the widespread regionalism and local protectionism. Local governments seek to protect local companies from outside competition through the erection of trade barriers. Litigants from outside the region have a difficult time winning cases against powerful local companies. Even if they win, they often cannot get the local court to enforce the judgment. Clientelism also opens the door for corruption and rent-seeking. As discussed in the preceding chapter, administrative departments use their licensing power to create administrative monopolies or to extract rents from applicants.

Moreover, clientelism hurts companies that are more economically efficient but lack the proper connections. Government officials allocate inputs and financing to maximize the benefits they receive from the patronage. Analytically, companies can be divided into four types. The first type could not survive in a competitive market solely on the basis of the quality and price of its products or services. Its survival depends on *guanxi*. The second type has connections but does not need to rely on them to survive and do well in a competitive market. The third type could do well in a competitive market but lacks *guanxi*, so is driven out of business in the existing imperfect market that is dependent on connections. The fourth type is not well connected but nonetheless is able to survive and succeed in today's market. It might be able to do even better in a market less dependent on connections, but not necessarily.

From a social perspective, categories one and three represent social loss. All else being equal, more efficient companies produce more for society at cheaper prices. Society loses the benefit of efficient but *guanxi*-poor category three companies entirely because they are not able to survive without connections. The costs of relying on connections for category one companies are passed on to the consumer and society in the form of lower-quality and/or higher-priced products or services. The cost may not be entirely dead weight loss. There may be some benefits of relying on *guanxi*, some social grease as it were. For instance, low-paid but highly qualified and competent officials might leave government if they were not able to take advantage of free dinners and trips paid for by companies. But surely there are more efficient and equitable ways to compensate officials and allocate resources than through an indirect tax on consumers. Category four companies also represent a loss to society, at least to the extent that the companies would be able to do even better in a market less dependent on connections.

At a more fundamental level, corporatism and clientelism undermine rule of law by diminishing respect for the law and debasing the courts, legal professions, and other professions necessary to realize rule of law. There is little point in relying on the courts when local governments are the only ones able to compel performance or enforce contracts. Lawyers need not sharpen their legal skills when cases turn on connections rather than legal arguments. Accountants and appraisers need not hone their appraisal techniques when the value of the asset is to be determined by government officials colluding with others to ensure a low price in exchange for kickbacks, an equity share in the newly formed company, or other material benefits.

In sum, reliance on relationships, whether vertical or horizontal, has its disadvantages. The high costs associated with clientelism and corporatism suggest that China may not be able to continue to develop economically without rule of law, and even if it could, that it might not want to given the costs in terms of equity, fairness, and justice. Although rule of law also has its costs in that establishing and operating a formal legal system is expensive, as the number of transactions grows, the costs of rule of law become more bearable. Accordingly, one would expect an increase in the demand for rule of law as the economy continues to expand and the number and size of transactions grow.[97] Indeed, as will be discussed shortly, recent studies suggest that China may already be outgrowing relationship-based alternatives much as it has outgrown the plan.[98]

Has the lack of rule of law impeded growth?

One problem with the third thesis that posits reliance on relationships as a substitute for a formal legal system is that it is impossible to quantify the negative effects of the lack of rule of law and enforceable property rights on investment and economic growth rates. Investors may have assessed the risks and simply not invested. There is no way to calculate what the levels of investment and the growth rates would have been if China's legal system protected property rights adequately and measured up favorably against rule-of-law standards.

But there is some evidence that the lack of rule of law and clear property rights have already taken a toll and will increasingly become an impediment to investment and growth in the future. Anecdotal evidence confirms that some companies were scared away or chose to minimize their investment or to deliver second-grade technology rather than the most up-to-date technology.[99] More systematic empirical studies suggest that China has received less investment from the USA, Germany, France, and the UK relative to other countries (on a per capita basis) than the "average" host country.[100] As will be discussed shortly, many economic reforms, including state-owned enterprise reforms, have not been possible because of, or have been complicated by, problems in the legal system.[101] Most important, growth slowed in the mid to late 1990s,[102] and FDI fell into a tailspin.[103] As investors learn more about China, they may be gaining a better sense of the way the lack of rule of law impacts the bottom line, with problems such as the failure to implement laws or inconsistent and arbitrary implementation of laws regularly topping the list of investor complaints.[104] Admittedly, the downturn in foreign investment and growth rates cannot be attributed solely to shortcomings in the legal system. Surely the Asian financial crisis has also had a negative impact on investment, as evidenced by the recent upturn in FDI once Asian countries began to recover. Investment has also been spurred by the prospects of China entering the WTO, as foreign investors began to rev up in anticipation of new business opportunities. Nevertheless, despite the recent reversal of the decline, FDI remains far off the peak in the mid-1990s.

As for the high growth rates in the past, some economists have argued that China's growth resulted in large part from productivity improvements mainly from the reallocation of labor from low- to high-productivity sectors, in particular from agriculture to manufacturing and services, and in recent years from massive government expenditure in fixed assets.[105] However, long-term growth requires an increase in productivity within individual sectors.[106] According to World Bank studies, only one-fourth of China's growth resulted from improvements in each sector.[107] Thus, China's years of easy growth may be coming to an end. As it becomes more difficult to sustain growth, the lack of rule of law may become an even bigger constraint.

China may yet prove to be an exception to the general rule that rule of law and enforceable property rights are necessary to achieve sustained economic development, but it does not seem likely. In any event, the debate could be rendered moot as the development of China's legal system continues, given that China appears committed to legal reform and the establishment of a legal system that meets the requirements of a thin rule of law at least on economic matters.

Who benefits from rule of law? A sectoral analysis

Not all sectors of the economy benefit equally from rule of law. Some economic actors have more need for rule of law than others. Well-connected companies that can take advantage of clientelist relationships have less need for rule of law than companies without such connections. Companies that engage in repeated small transactions with other companies that are part of tightly knit networks need rule of law less than companies that enter into large one-off transactions with distant companies with which they have no relationship beyond the particular transaction. Different levels of government also differ in their demand for rule of law. Given that local corporatism often works to the disadvantage of the central government, the ruling regime has supported rule of law, with senior leaders emphasizing law's role in reining in local governments and ensuring that they abide by central laws and regulations. Thus simply looking at the aggregate number of transactions does not provide an accurate gauge of the demand for rule of law.

The demand for rule of law is a function of various factors, including the sector of the economy; prevailing practices and value systems; existing institutions, including legal, administrative, regulatory, and political institutions; the level of development and complexity of the market; and the availability of alternative ways of solving problems. A sector by sector analysis provides a more accurate picture of the demand for rule of law, the limits of rule of law, and the policy and institutional reforms needed to complement rule of law and make it more effective.

The private sector: foreign investors and domestic private enterprises

Foreign investors, particularly large multinational companies and investors from Western companies, have been among the most vocal in calling for rule of law. This is not surprising given that newly arrived foreign companies are least able to take advantage of thick relational networks as partial substitutes for rule of law. Especially in the early years of reform, foreign investors often opted for joint ventures rather than establishing wholly foreign-owned enterprises in the belief that having a well-connected Chinese partner was crucial for success. As foreign companies gained experience in China and established their own networks, they increasingly turned to wholly foreign-owned companies.[108] As outsiders, foreigners are short on social capital and less likely to rely on trust than parties who share the same cultural background. If anything, cultural differences tend to reinforce foreign investors' demands for rule of law in that most foreign investors, especially large multinational companies, are used to operating in environments with well-developed legal systems. Their teams of MBAs, accountants, and in-house lawyers find (job) security in relying on publicly promulgated laws that are faithfully implemented by administrative agencies and impartially applied by courts. A system in which the rules are not made public, administrative agencies interpret regulations inconsistently, and judges are corrupt is both foreign and frightening.

Foreign investors are also likely to be involved in high-value transactions, many of which may be one-off deals – for instance, technology transfers or sales of large pieces of equipment. For many foreign investors who establish foreign-invested enterprises in China, the biggest decisions are where to establish the company, whether to establish a joint venture and if so, which Chinese party to choose. At the time of initial investment the investor must decide where to commit a considerable amount of money often without the leverage that comes from being a repeat player. The investor is often banking on the local government and Chinese partner keeping their commitments. If they do not, the investor will have very little recourse but to turn to the legal system.[109] However, in the absence of a developed legal system, foreign investors have been forced to rely on political channels, including taking the matter up with MOFTEC and higher-level government officials or even the Party.

Some commentators have questioned the importance of foreign investment to China's economy.[110] However, as noted in Chapter 5, FIEs employ 10% of the non-agriculture work force, generate over 20% of total national industrial output, and account for over 48% of all trade. Moreover, China has huge capital demands. By some estimates, China needs 3.0 to 4.2% of GDP just to bail out banks, another 2 to 5% of GDP annually to clean up the environment, plus an additional US$744 billion, or about 8 to 9% of GDP annually, for electric power, telecommunications, transportation, water, and sanitation infrastructure projects.[111] Empirical studies have also demonstrated that FDI has had a statistically significant positive impact on China's provincial and bilateral trade flows and economic growth.[112]

Of course, not all foreign investors are similarly situated. China has had the good fortune of being able to tap into a large overseas Chinese community, which has been a major factor in spurring economic growth, providing necessary capital and technology.[113] The lack of a well-developed legal system is perhaps less of an obstacle to overseas Chinese investors than to Western multinational corporations. In many projects, the investment of overseas Chinese has been relatively small.[114] Overseas Chinese have also often invested in their home towns or gone into business with family members, thus reducing the need to rely on contracts and formal mechanisms of enforcement. For various reasons, some cultural, many Chinese businesspeople may be more willing than Western investors to rely on personal connections and informal means of resolving disputes.[115] Given the small size of projects, the family nature of the businesses, and a somewhat greater willingness to rely on connections more than enforceable contracts to do business, some overseas Chinese may not have perceived the lack of rule of law as such an obstacle.

However, not all overseas Chinese companies are well connected or small mom-and-pop operations. Moreover, overseas Chinese investors, like other investors, still suffer from the frequent changes in laws, the inconsistent application of laws, and predatory government officials who impose random fees on profitable companies.[116] While they may prefer to deal with such problems by courting government officials, there are costs to establishing and maintaining such relationships. Further, all of the work and expense can quickly go down the drain if a particular official is transferred to another post or arrested on corruption charges. In any event, there are inherent limits to reliance on relationships, as we have seen.

China's growing domestic private sector faces its own challenges. One might predict that rule of law would be less important to domestic private firms, given that most are small. In general, small companies have less direct need for a complex legal regime. Small companies rarely own intellectual property and generally do not issue shares, so they have no need for a complex property rights regime that creates and protects intangibles or various types of equities. Nor do they need capital markets since they generally don't raise money from the public.[117] Most of their transactions are likely to involve relatively small amounts, and be with repeat players that are part of their relationship network. As a result, they are more likely to rely on informal means for resolving disputes rather than engage in expensive litigation in court.

Yet private companies in China have a greater appetite for rule of law than might be expected. Private companies are among the most frequent litigants against the government in administrative law suits.[118] Although perhaps initially counterintuitive, the reason is straightforward. Private companies historically have been outside the state-owned enterprise system, and discriminated against for ideological reasons. As a result, they have been vulnerable to predatory local governments. Further, the outsider status of many private companies means that they cannot turn to the government to help them settle disputes or pressure recalcitrant parties to perform their contractual obligations. Left without many of the devices that other parties regularly rely on to settle disputes, private companies must turn to the courts.

The history of private businesses demonstrates both the importance and limits of rule of law. Private businesses need laws to exist and to define their rights and powers. As discussed in Chapter 5, the 1998 amendment of the Constitution and the subsequent passage of the State Council's Provisional Regulations Concerning Private Enterprises formally sanctioned the existence of private businesses, though they remained subject to numerous restrictions and periodic political campaigns.[119] Over time, because of the superior performance of the private sector, the government has been forced to lift the restrictions. The decisions to allow private companies to exist and then to give them additional rights were obviously political decisions, driven largely by economic concerns. But simply changing the rules and declaring central-level support for private enterprises has not meant that private companies in fact have enjoyed the rights provided in the rules. Private companies have been continually discriminated against and harassed by local government officials, police, and others who have treated them as a relatively powerless target for extortion. Although private sector litigants have turned to the courts, they have often lost. Many private businesspeople come from the lower social class and operate at the boundaries of law. Judges frequently are not sympathetic to their plight, in part because judges are resentful that persons from such backgrounds have obtained so much wealth, often in questionable ways.

In light of the discriminatory treatment – and in the belief that if you can't beat them, join them – private business owners have gone into business with government officials, forming township and village enterprises and collectives or even private shareholding companies. In so doing, private entrepreneurs gave up some of their independence and a share of their profits in exchange for political coverage and access to inputs, financing, technology, and all of the benefits of patronage that were subject to the discretionary authority of government officials. These marriages of convenience frequently have ended in divorce, for reasons explained shortly.

Another result of the tenuous legal and political status of private business has been that private entrepreneurs hide their revenue and spend more on consumption rather than reinvesting and growing their companies.[120] Entrepreneurs in China, like elsewhere, are by nature proactive, innovative, and risk-taking. However, in China, they tend to be less oriented toward long-term growth, mainly due to the lack of clear legal rules that protect private interests and provide secure property rights. As one economist notes:

> In the absence of adequate legal protection of private property rights, they are constantly concerned about possible hostility directed against

them in a future political campaign and about the possible appropria-
tion of their assets. Consequently, they are reluctant to make long-term
investments in the growth of their enterprises. Instead, they invest to
gain rapid returns on their capital, emphasize liquidity, and spend
their returns on their personal consumption rather than [reinvesting
in their businesses].[121]

The state loses potential tax revenues both because private companies
hide their revenues and because their tendency to buy fancy cars and
villas rather than reinvesting in and growing their businesses prevents
them from earning more profits, and thus lowers the potential tax base.

The demand for rule of law among the domestic private sector is
growing and will continue to grow. Private enterprises need protection
against predatory government officials. Moreover, as the discriminatory
policies fall by the wayside, private companies will want to expand. They
will begin to reinvest and grow their businesses if they are confident that
they will be able to reap the benefits of their investments. To grow, private companies will need to gain import and export rights and access
to capital markets by listing on securities exchanges. As they develop
their brand names and gain market share, they will also demand greater
protection of their intellectual property rights. Indeed, PRC nationals
already account for 85 percent of patent applications in China, with
the number of applications having increased from 10,000 in 1990 to
550,000 in 1995.[122] Indicative of how widespread counterfeiting hurts
PRC companies as well as foreign companies, in 1995, the Guangdong
Administration of Industry and Commerce handled 845 trademark infringement cases, 70 percent of which involved PRC companies as the
plaintiff.[123] PRC companies have even begun to form their own interest groups, such as the Software Industry Association of Guangzhou, to
help them protect their rights.

Private enterprises will still continue to invest in clientelist relationships as long as the benefits exceed the costs and so doing is the most
effective and efficient way to secure their interests. However, the cost–
benefit analysis is changing. As the market develops, companies become
less dependent on the government for capital, technology, and other
inputs; as reforms continue, fewer activities are subject to approvals
and licenses, and the process is more regularized; and as the legal system
improves, there is less need to rely on relationships to enforce contracts

and protect their property rights. With the benefits decreasing, the costs of maintaining relationships become harder to justify. As a consequence, private enterprises are likely to follow the path of TVEs, where the reforms have already changed the cost–benefit calculus for both the entrepreneur and the government.

The rural sector: rural households (farmers) and rural industries (TVEs)

The importance of law in the countryside is much contested. While some commentators portray the lack of an effective legal system as a source of instability in rural China and a threat to the regime,[124] others suggest that demand for rule of law is low in rural areas.[125] The latter point out that law and the formal legal system have not played a prominent role in the countryside, where villagers continue to live in small, closely knit communities, often dominated by a single clan, and where traditional norms that emphasize harmony, wise leaders, and informal mechanisms to resolve disputes remain strong. To the extent farmers enter into contracts at all, the amount is small. Deeply embedded in social networks, villagers are not likely to rely on the legal system to resolve disputes. In short, rule of law may be one of the pillars of modernity, but much of rural China continues to live in a largely premodern state.

On the other hand, land use rights are central to the livelihood of farmers. Accordingly, one might predict that rule of law would be particularly important to rural households in that farmers would want to clarify their rights to land and to secure them through enforceable contracts backed up by a reliable legal system. In fact, some economists have argued that the lack of secure land use rights has caused farmers to exploit the land for short-term gains and to invest insufficiently in the land to sustain long-term growth, suggesting that farmers are aware of their tenuous claim to land use rights.[126] Others have suggested that the slowdown in rural growth in the mid-'80s is attributable to the lack of clear and enforceable land use rights.[127] In response, the 1998 Land Management Law called for the execution of written contracts that provided for thirty-year land leases and restricted the right of the government to readjust land use.[128]

In general, the trend has been toward greater security of tenure and fewer restrictions on the use of rights, including the right to grow whatever one wants or even leave the land fallow and the right to lease or sell the land use rights.[129] At the same time, however, the government has an interest in ensuring that the land is put to good use, quotas are filled to ensure the food supply to the state, and sufficient grain is grown before farmers plant other more lucrative crops. In addition, local governments want to accommodate growth in families or the return of village members to farming. They may also want to maintain some measure of equality, which would be threatened if some families could purchase land use rights. Thus the general trend toward clearer and more freely alienable property rights is subject to regional variation. On the whole, local governments in areas where jobs are more readily available in rural industry or nearby cities may be less concerned with alienation of land use rights. Conversely, governments in areas where land is scarce and grain quotas are more difficult to meet may impose more restrictions on the use of land and be more willing to step in and reclaim land if it is not used properly.

Illustrating how the demand for rule of law depends on a variety of factors, including cultural norms, at least one study found that some farmers preferred less secure property rights that left local officials free to adjust land allocations to account for increases in the size of families.[130] The farmers' preference is arguably accountable to a normative system that values egalitarianism and full employment. It would also seem to indicate a trust in local government officials to make the right decisions and allocate land fairly. In this case, social capital in the form of relational networks of trust would seem to be at least a partial substitute for rule of law. Perhaps the ability of villagers to elect their own officials reinforces trust in that officials who wanted to remain in office would need to comply with community standards of fairness in reallocating land.

But social trust and substitutes for law only go so far. Land disputes have become a major source of unrest in rural China and indeed throughout China. The Land Bureau is the leading defendant in administrative litigation suits, accounting for some 15 percent of all such cases.[131] It is easy to understand why. Urbanization has increased the demand for and value of land.[132] Thus the stakes are high, often involving millions of dollars. When the government requisitions land, village and urban residents alike are frequently frustrated with the disruption of their lives and unhappy with the terms of resettlement. Tempers are all the more likely to flare when rural cadres illegally requisition and sell off collective land, and then pocket the proceeds. Moreover, despite the passage of the Land

Management Law, a survey of seventeen provinces conducted one year after the law was promulgated found that only half of the farmers had entered into thirty-year land use contracts, that less than 40 percent had been physically issued the contract, and that 25 percent of the contracts contained provisions for adjusting the land.[133] Predictably, only one-third of farmers were reasonably confident that there would be no adjustments and that their land use rights were secure, suggesting that they may lack the necessary confidence to make long-term investments in the land.

Apart from protecting their land use rights, a functional legal system would help villagers fend off predatory government officials. Rural governments regularly impose illegal taxes and random fees on villagers. Sometimes the funds are used to build roads or for other socially useful projects. However, local cadres frequently misappropriate the funds for personal use. The imposition of these excessive burdens on villagers has "resulted in a festering crisis between peasants and the state."[134] A viable administrative law regime would help rural residents deal with the abuse of power by government officials. Furthermore, as economic reforms have progressed, rural residents have become involved in a wider range of commercial disputes. Like others, they frequently find themselves the victims of fake products.[135] They are also likely to run into local protectionism and regional barriers which result from the inability of the central government to implement central policies. All are problems for which a more effective legal system would provide some relief.

In recent years, villagers have frequently engaged in widespread protests, which on numerous occasions have ended in violence.[136] Angry villagers have burned government buildings and beaten, even killed, government officials, including tax collectors. There are many reasons why villagers are pushed to such extremes, including that the illegal governmental acts often affect large numbers of people, and villagers may believe there is safety in numbers.[137] However, widespread protests are attributable, in no small measure, to the lack of other effective remedies, including legal remedies.

By promoting rule of law and educating villagers about their rights, the government has embarked on a dangerous path. The government's efforts to raise legal consciousness in the countryside is paying dividends in that villagers are increasingly resorting to litigation to protect their rights.[138] They also often make law-based arguments when protesting illegal acts by local cadres and when petitioning higher-level government

officials.[139] Unfortunately, legal institutions in rural areas are presently –
and likely to remain so for the foreseeable future – too weak to make
good on the government's promise to protect the rights and interests of
villagers. Courts are widely dispersed, inadequately funded, and staffed
by judges and clerks with little legal training. There is generally one
people's tribunal per four townships or 100,000 residents.[140] Most consist of one room, one table, one chair, and one person. Despite efforts
to increase the independence of the tribunal, the financial dependence
of the courts on the township government undermines the tribunal's
autonomy. As discussed previously, rural areas suffer from a shortage
of qualified judges and lawyers.[141] In response to the pressing need for
legal advice, the government has established Township Legal Services
Stations. However, the stations are staffed by clerks who generally lack
formal legal training and have not passed the bar examination, as noted
in Chapter 8.

When villagers have disputes, they frequently turn to Party leaders or
higher-level government officials for redress. Whether doing so reflects
traditional norms or the ineffectiveness of formal legal channels, or
both, is difficult to determine, as pointed out in the preceding chapter.
What is clear is that petitioning higher-level government officials is not
likely to result in a favorable resolution of most villagers' problems. One
study found that higher-level officials rejected or delayed responding
to nine out of twenty-five petitions. Moreover, in twelve other cases,
local officials refused to comply with the decisions of their superiors or
delayed performance. Some villagers have been able to put the media
to good use in pressing their cause. However, reliance on the media is
subject to limits. Reporters and news carriers have been subject to libel,
slander, and defamation suits, and irate local officials have pressured
news agencies to fire muckraking reporters. In any event, the media can
only cover a limited number of stories.

Political solutions have also failed to provide adequate relief. Village
elections were to provide an outlet for social tensions and to create a
mechanism for holding corrupt officials accountable. Yet officials at the
township level and above, who are beyond the reach of village elections,
are responsible for much of the corruption and illegal behavior. Nor
have village elections been terribly effective at holding village officials
in check, as village leaders have manipulated elections and engaged in
electoral fraud to ensure that they remain in power.[142]

Legal reforms aimed at implementing rule of law obviously will not be able to resolve all of the problems farmers face, many of which are economic and political in origin. The central government has put local officials in an untenable position. Local officials are forced to meet family planning quotas, shoulder the brunt of social welfare obligations, provide public schooling, improve the basic infrastructure, and achieve high growth rates, all without much assistance from the central government. They are also forced to reduce crime and control other socially and politically unwanted behavior, such as protests by Falungong disciples. When they don't succeed, they may lose their job or be fined.[143] Nevertheless, rule of law may alleviate some of the problems faced by farmers.

In any event, to limit discussion of rural demand for rule of law to farmers tilling the land would be a mistake. Increasingly, villagers have turned to rural industry for employment. Despite recent problems, TVEs still employ over 100 million people, accounting for 30 percent of rural residents.[144] TVEs were extremely successful in the 1980s, notwithstanding the lack of clear property rights. In many TVEs, ownership rights were held by vaguely defined collectives. In addition, local governments often had a direct stake in such companies. Whether an owner or not, local Party and government officials exerted considerable influence over the management of TVEs, frequently controlling such key decisions as the selection of the manager, investment and financing, and distribution of profits.[145] The success of TVEs led some commentators to suggest that there may be effective (transitional) substitutes for systems of civil law and independent, impartial courts and agencies.[146]

The initial success of TVEs was due to a variety of factors. During the early years of reform, TVEs were able to exploit wide-open markets. There was a demand for virtually everything, and little competition from other manufacturers or service providers. To the extent urban SOEs provided competition, TVEs were able to take advantage of abundant cheap labor in the countryside to charge lower prices. Some TVEs also benefited from (often illegal) tax breaks offered by local officials. The small scale of TVEs allowed them to respond quickly to China's fluid markets. Because TVEs were not part of the SOE system, they were subject to the demands of the market and to hard budget constraints.[147] Local governments, without the luxury of being able to fall back on deficit financing, depended on the revenue generated from local companies.[148]

To be sure, the rise of TVEs was never consistent. In some places, TVEs proliferated while elsewhere few were established. Whereas some local governments were closely involved in their operation, other local governments remained at an arm's-length distance. The path of development depended to a large extent on initial starting conditions. Corporatism was more prevalent where Party and government officials were able to take advantage of an existing commune and brigade industrial base, and their expertise in business, to raise capital and expand their business networks.[149] In other places such as Wenzhou, private entrepreneurs had access to nongovernmental sources of capital, including overseas Chinese. As a result, they were able to insist on more autonomy. Meanwhile, some poorer regions lacked the wherewithal to set up TVEs.

Despite their initial success, TVEs began to falter in the 1990s, with many going bankrupt or being sold off or reorganized as private firms.[150] Just as the success of TVEs was due to a variety of contingent circumstances, so too the fall of TVEs reflects a host of context-specific factors, including the deepening of market reforms.[151] As markets developed, TVEs faced increasing competition from SOEs, foreign-invested enterprises (FIEs), international companies, and even other TVEs. Most TVEs relied primarily on abundant unskilled labor to keep prices down and gain market share. Without more sophisticated technology, many were not able to survive in the face of intensified competition. The credit crunch during the late 1980s and 1990s exacerbated their problems by making it difficult for TVEs to acquire technology or to grow their business. The lack of clear property rights also hindered growth and development.[152] Outside investors were reluctant to buy into TVEs given the lack of clear ownership rights and the influence of local government on management decisions.[153] Seeking to minimize unemployment, village leaders would take from the rich to support the poor, forcing strong companies to purchase or subsidize weaker ones. In addition, many TVEs suffered from unsophisticated management, a problem exacerbated by cultural norms. High salaries for managers ran counter to egalitarian norms in the countryside. The low salaries decreased manager's incentives to increase profits, and caused them to seek other ways of augmenting their income. Some managers siphoned off assets or took payment in the form of in-kind benefits such as high-priced cars that remained on the company's books but were nonproductive assets.

The dramatic reversal of the fortunes of TVEs raises doubts about the benefits of clientelism, and supports the view that clientelism is to a large extent a short-term reaction to an undeveloped and immature market economy and weak legal system.[154] Similarly, the trend toward privatization supports the thesis that clear property rights and a legal system capable of enforcing them are critical for sustained growth. As markets have developed and the discriminatory policies against private enterprises have been relaxed, many entrepreneurs have decided that they are better off going it alone. Many TVEs have reached the size where they no longer need to rely on the government for financing or technology and do not want to put up with the considerable costs of clientelist arrangements such as government interference in management, pressure to merge with unsuccessful companies or to keep an excessive number of employees on the payroll, diversion of profits, and so on.[155]

Ironically, local governments are also rethinking the wisdom of corporatism.[156] From the perspective of local governments, corporatist arrangements have always been a mixed blessing. On the positive side, the government is able to allocate resources in a way that achieves its goals, including curbing unemployment. But there are also costs. Government officials in places where TVEs are prevalent found themselves stretched too thin. They were unable to monitor the daily operational decisions of management and to prevent managers from finding ways to augment their salaries at the company's expense. Most importantly, the poor performance of TVEs began to affect the bottom line. To keep unemployment down and minimize the likelihood of social unrest, governments were forced to support failing companies by paying workers' salaries. In some cases, management had even guaranteed investors a return on their investment. When the companies failed to strike it rich as expected, investors (and often employees who were encouraged or forced to invest in the company) looked to the local government.[157] Meanwhile, when TVEs went bankrupt, local banks were left with the bad debt. With private companies outperforming other types of companies, local governments have found it less beneficial to continue to prop up SOEs, collectives, and TVEs. Accordingly, governments have begun to divest from TVEs and collectives where possible, and then to collect taxes, land fees, and other fees from the newly formed private companies.[158]

To what extent will TVEs benefit from, and hence demand, further reforms to implement rule of law? As more TVEs are privatized, they face the same problems as urban private enterprises, including predatory local governments, and thus are likely to support further reforms for all of the reasons discussed previously. Furthermore, although many TVEs produce for local markets only, others have found it difficult to grow the business by expanding into new markets because of regional barriers. In an effort to protect their own companies and maintain their tax base, local governments have prohibited sales by companies from outside the region, imposed additional fees on nonlocal companies, and obstructed the enforcement of court judgments against local companies. Central government reports have warned that regionalism has spread from consumer goods to all products and into the investment field, and from counties and cities to provinces.[159]

Clarifying the property rights of TVEs by itself cannot solve the many problems facing TVEs.[160] At minimum, clearer property rights need to be enforced, which as we have seen in Chapter 7, would require major institutional changes to the judiciary. But even were property rights enforceable, market imperfections still make it beneficial to maintain relations with government officials to gain access to financing, technology, and other inputs. In that sense, legal reforms will be more effective if they are complemented by further market reforms. Managers should be paid more; regional barriers should be eliminated, allowing goods and capital to flow more freely; TVEs should be encouraged to open branches in other regions and hire qualified workers from outside the area.[161] Market mechanisms may also complement legal reforms aimed at curtailing rent-seeking by local governments in that collusion between regulators and regulated harms the general investment environment, causing investors to invest elsewhere. As the competition for investment intensifies, local governments may be forced to weigh the collusion rents against the benefits of increased investment.[162]

Granted, even assuming investors have sufficient information about the predatory habits of local governments, in some cases they will have little choice but to set up shop in certain regions where strategic partners or key inputs are located. Ultimately, political reforms to complement legal and market reforms may be necessary to deal with corrupt government officials out to fill their own pockets at the expense of local firms. It may be necessary to allow local residents to vote out officials above the village level who fail to produce economic results by ruining the investment environment and scaring away investors or who enrich themselves at the expense of the local populace.

Urban industry: state-owned enterprises

To date, the government's approach to SOE reform has relied on increased but still incomplete marketization without significant privatization. As noted in Chapter 5, the results have been mixed. Despite some improvement, SOE reform remains one of the government's priorities. To what extent has law played a role in SOE reforms? Has the lack of rule of law impeded SOE reforms? And do SOEs exist outside the legal domain, as one legal scholar has suggested?[163]

The initial attempts at SOE reforms failed in part because they were not sufficient to alter the behavior of government officials. Although regulations were passed to enhance the autonomy of SOE managers and to increase their incentive to earn profits by permitting SOEs to retain a portion of their profits, government officials regularly ignored the rules, and intervened in the daily operations of companies. Similarly, the experiment with long-term contracts that fixed the amount of profits and taxes SOEs were to pay to the state failed in part because the government refused to hold up its end of the bargain.[164] SOEs and their government superiors, whether central or local, continued to negotiate over prices, supplies, employee layoffs, social welfare obligations, taxes, and profits.[165]

The inability to control government officials is attributable in part to the legal system. The 1988 State Owned Enterprise Law suffered from a number of shortcomings. Like other laws, the SOE Law was vague and unclear on crucial issues, leaving it to the State Council to pass implementing regulations to flesh out and specify the rights provided to management. In 1992 the State Council passed the more detailed Autonomous Management Rights Regulations. However, the rights granted management continued to be subject to various restrictions, including the need to seek the approval of the "responsible government departments."[166] It is true that as the main shareholder, the state has a right to monitor the performance of the company and the management. Yet even when government officials exceed their rights and interfere directly in daily management decisions, management has not turned to the courts. The weakness of the courts and their dependence on the local government for funding may explain to some extent management's reluctance to seek protection from the courts. But presumably the main reason is that managers fear that the government owner will have them removed, as is its right as majority shareholder.[167] No amount of legal system reform will alter the fundamental principle that management serves at the behest of ownership. Of course, SOEs continued to perform poorly for many reasons that had nothing to do with the legal system, including distortions in the pricing system, outdated equipment and technology, the lack of hard budget constraints, and political restraints on the number of companies that could go bankrupt or workers that could be terminated.

The third round of reform focusing on corporatization of SOEs also failed for a combination of legal, economic, and political reasons. The lack of clear property rights contributed to the slow pace of corporatization by making it difficult to determine which level of government or which government department or agency owned what.[168] Nor did corporatization resolve fundamental principal–agency problems. Adopting a modern corporate form was supposed to clarify property rights and separate ownership from management, leading to less meddling by government officials. Yet in practice government officials have continued to intervene in daily operations.[169] Ironically, at other times managers have been given too much latitude. With ownership rights being held by multiple government entities or by remote state asset management companies, the task of monitoring often slips through the cracks, either because the owners fail to coordinate with each other or because the government owners, unlike private owners, lack the incentive to monitor performance. Since the compensation level of managers is only weakly related, if related at all, to profitability, managers have little incentive to distribute profits to the government rather than increasing bonuses and other benefits for employees or diverting funds to their own private use. The failure to adequately monitor firms has resulted in considerable self-dealing and asset stripping by management, though in some cases government officials have knowingly participated in the process.[170]

The fourth round of reform focusing on privatization has suffered from similar problems of unclear property rights, the inability to determine which government entities owned what, asset stripping, and a variety of other problems. Privatization has been impeded, for instance, by the lack of competent accountants and appraisers. According to China's Auditor General, more than two-thirds of the accounts of nearly 1,300 of China's biggest state companies are inaccurate.[171] Mergers, acquisitions, and reorganizations have also been hampered by the lack of adequate records and SOEs' frequently spotty compliance with laws and regulations. Many SOEs have restructured, transferred assets, changed names, and established subsidiaries without regard to legal requirements. As a result, many of the actions they have taken may be void as a matter of law. At minimum, it is frequently difficult if not impossible to establish clear title to assets.

When companies list on stock exchanges, there is usually a long list of legal risks set forth in the prospectus. Some arise from the failure of SOEs to comply with regulations prior to listing while others reflect more systemic legal risks such as unclear regulations, rapid change in the regulatory framework, and difficulty in enforcing contracts. For political and economic reasons, the government has refused to privatize the largest SOEs, and even when SOEs have listed, the government remains the controlling shareholder. Limitations on the sale of state and legal person shares have further reduced liquidity. In some instances, the rules seem ad hoc and arbitrary. For example, there are more restrictions on trading the legal person shares of listed companies than of nonlisted companies. In other cases, firms have used the funds raised by issuing shares for inappropriate purposes, as in Qingdao Beer's much-publicized use of IPO funds for illegal loans. A weak securities regulatory system has exacerbated problems.

Clearly the main forces driving and limiting SOE reforms are political and economic in nature. The ruling regime has been forced to embark on SOE reforms to sustain economic growth and retain whatever legitimacy it has. At the same time, it has had to proceed cautiously to avoid social unrest that could result from the massive unemployment that would also certainly follow if insolvent SOEs were allowed to go bankrupt or were sold off and reorganized without restrictions on the new owners. Ultimately, turning SOEs around will require changes in corporate governance, more marketization, reform of the banking and financial sectors, the imposition of hard budget constraints, a reduction in the welfare burdens of SOEs, and perhaps greater privatization. Nevertheless, while the lack of a developed legal system has been by no means the only factor limiting SOE reforms, it has been one important factor. Thus without further legal reforms, the government's efforts to reform SOEs will be impeded, and may fail.[172]

Whatever law's role in SOE reforms, to claim that the state sector exists outside the realm of legality is a gross overstatement.[173] SOEs are required to comply with generally applicable regulations, including labor, land, environmental, import–export, foreign exchange, tax, accounting, asset management, and intellectual property rules, as well as the requirements of such laws as the Company Law, Security Law, and other commercial laws. Notwithstanding the limited reach of the law in some instances, SOEs cannot ignore these laws with impunity. When they fail to meet environmental standards, they can be, and often are, fined. When they fail to honor their contracts or manufacture products that do not meet product quality standards, they can be, and often are, sued. Indeed, laid-off SOE workers or workers claiming retirement benefits, medical payment reimbursements, and other benefits have regularly taken SOEs to court.[174] As in the case of rural uprisings, when urban workers fail to obtain what they believe to be a just outcome through the legal system, they have taken their protests to the streets. Of 247 reported street protests in Henan Province in 1998, 199 cases involved property rights claims by workers.[175] Having committed to rule of law and having raised the expectations of people, the ruling regime must take responsibility for the failures of the legal system and be prepared to deal with increased social unrest.

The implications of China's accession to the WTO for rule of law and economic development

In acceding to the WTO, China has undertaken many obligations, both commercial and legal.[176] Besides lowering tariffs and allowing foreign companies greater market access, China will be required to make and apply laws in a "uniform, impartial and reasonable" manner.[177] It must also provide for review of certain administrative decisions by a judicial authority.[178] Proponents of China's accession have argued therefore that apart from the potential economic benefits for foreign investors,[179] China's accession to the WTO will promote rule of law.[180] Some have even suggested that it will lead to political reforms and better protection of human rights.[181]

There have already been significant changes in the legal system as China has prepared to enter into the WTO. The main foreign investment laws have been, or are in the process of being, amended, including laws that govern equity and cooperative joint ventures, wholly owned enterprises, patents, copyrights, trademarks, technology imports, taxation, and foreign exchange. China has also agreed to establish an official journal dedicated to the publication of all trade-related laws, regulations, and other measures, and to provide a reasonable period for comment before such laws, regulations, and measures are enforced. In addition, it will establish an enquiry point where any individual, company, or WTO member state may request information about trade-related rules. The established entity will be required to provide complete and authoritative responses to WTO member states, and accurate and reliable information to individuals and companies, generally within thirty days and in no event later than forty-five days.[182]

Investors can expect further beneficial changes. For instance, investors will gain from tariff reductions. However, tariffs are already relatively low, particularly for a developing country, as a result of a series of reductions over the last decade. Potentially of much greater significance, a number of restrictions on foreign investors have been or will be lifted. Foreign investors will gain access to markets that were off-limits or heavily restricted, including telecommunications, insurance, and banking. They will also be free from local content restrictions that forced them to use local inputs, and from mandatory export requirements. Perhaps the biggest breakthrough, however, is in the area of sales, distribution, and after-sales services, which could change dramatically the way foreign companies do business in China. Rather than setting up production companies in China, foreign companies will now be able to import their full product line. If they want a sales presence in China, they will be able to set up branches rather than representative offices. They will also be able to ship directly, without going through import–export companies, as domestic companies are granted import rights. In addition, they will be able to rationalize investments and implement vertical integration strategies by establishing downstream supply companies that provide inputs for several manufacturing plants and by setting up upstream sales, distribution, and after-sales service centers to service the plants.

Despite such positive developments, there is good reason to be cautious about the immediate impact of the WTO on rule of law in China and the economic benefits for foreign investors in the absence of further legal reforms. China's entry into the WTO will not have an immediate impact on many of the problems that make doing business in China difficult, such as the low level of competency among the judiciary and the legal profession, the confusing array of inconsistent legislation, the rapid change in laws, corruption, and the general disrespect for law. Indeed, in the short term, efforts to bring China's laws and regulations into compliance with WTO requirements is likely to increase confusion and uncertainty. The task of reviewing and revising line by line the hundreds, if not thousands, of relevant laws and regulations is monumental.[183]

Moreover, the WTO's rules are strongest with respect to prohibiting quantitative barriers to trade such as high tariffs or numerical quotas. They are less successful in dealing with nontariff barriers. But this is likely to be the area where investors encounter the most problems.[184] One of the biggest headaches for foreign investors has been the need to obtain approval for virtually every type of commercial activity, whether it be the establishment of a company, the import or export of technology, or the provision of security by PRC parties to foreign parties. Entry into the WTO will not lead to the immediate dismantling of the entire burdensome approval system. Many transactions will still be subject to approval (or several approvals) on a case-by-case basis.[185] As a result, the fate of foreign investors will remain in the hands of administrative officials who have considerable discretion over whether to approve the transaction.

China has amended a number of laws to provide for judicial review of administrative officials that previously were not subject to review, including its intellectual property laws. As we have seen, however, the various means of reining in the bureaucracy and controlling administration discretion are all of limited effectiveness in practice. Judicial review in particular remains weak. Unless steps are taken to address the weak stature of the courts and their dependence on the local government for financial resources, courts will be unable to play the role contemplated by the WTO. Foreign investors who are unable to obtain justice in PRC courts are likely to turn to the WTO for assistance. The vagueness of some of China's obligations under the Protocol of Accession and the difficulty it will have fully implementing such obligations given current realities increases the likelihood of suits arising. For instance, to ensure uniform and impartial application of trade-related rules, China has promised to establish a mechanism under which individuals and enterprises can bring to the attention of the national authorities cases of non-uniform application of the trade regime. The scope of "non-uniform application of the trade regime" could be interpreted by foreign investors and member states quite broadly to include inconsistencies in legislation, use of the approval process to deny foreign companies access to markets or licenses to engage in certain activities, and so forth. Nor is it clear whether China's current mechanisms for dealing with problems such as legislative inconsistency or challenging administrative decisions – including, for example, the review system established under the Law on Legislation and the administrative reconsideration and administrative litigation systems – are sufficient to fulfill China's obligation. It also bears noting that China is only obligated to create a mechanism. The Protocol says nothing about how effective that mechanism must be. Foreign investors, however, are not likely to be content with a mechanism that technically fulfills China's obligation but in practice does not meet their needs. Whether the WTO has the capacity to handle the potentially huge number of suits that could arise is unclear.[186] Nor is it clear what the effects of repeated confrontation with China would be on the WTO as an organization.[187]

There is then ample reason to be cautious about the immediate impact of entering the WTO on legal reform in China and the possible harm to the WTO that could result from China's inability to provide acceptable domestic remedies to commercial disputes. On the whole, however, China's accession most likely will have a positive effect on the development of the legal system in the longer term.[188] Reformers within China will be able to take advantage of the WTO to work for further reforms, including institutional reforms, whose effects will spread beyond the limited area of foreign investment. WTO accession will create additional pressure to push ahead with efforts to separate government and enterprises and to overhaul the administrative system. Party reservations notwithstanding, the need to comply with the WTO's requirements may provide reformers with the political capital necessary to push through some of the suggested reforms aimed at strengthening the judiciary.[189] However, creating a strong and competent judiciary is a long-term project.

WTO accession will also stimulate further economic reforms. Increased competition from foreign companies could accelerate SOE reform and lead to adjustments in the industrial structure. If they are to remain competitive, SOEs will need to be relieved of their social welfare burdens and have their tax rates reduced to the same level as other companies. Some industries will be forced to become more efficient, including auto, textiles, and small appliances. Increased opportunities in telecommunications could lead to an influx of capital and technology and stimulate growth and development among domestic telecom companies. Domestic insurance companies may benefit from joint ventures with foreign companies. Competition in the banking sector could accelerate financial sector reform. PRC banks will find it difficult to compete with foreign banks if they are forced to continue to prop up SOEs and make loans on the basis of policy considerations rather than market factors. Although many less efficient firms will be forced into bankruptcy, the need to deal with the rising number of insolvent companies may break the political impasse that has delayed promulgation of a new bankruptcy law.

Conclusion

The relationship between law and economic development raises a number of theoretical and empirical issues, which caution against hard and fast conclusions. With that caveat in mind, certain lessons can be drawn based on the literature and decades of practical experience. First, rule of law is clearly not sufficient to produce sustained economic development. However, a legal system that complies with the requirements of a thin rule of law is in all likelihood necessary if China is to sustain long-term economic growth.

Second, and a corollary of the first, it is highly unlikely that China will prove to be an exception to the general principle that rule of law is an important factor in long-term economic development. Relationships (*guanxi*), clientelism, corporatism, and informal mechanisms for resolving disputes, raising capital, and securing contracts are at best imperfect substitutes that themselves often depend on formal legal institutions that meet the standards of a thin rule of law. Moreover, although these mechanisms are to some extent compatible with rule of law, some are also incompatible in certain ways with rule of law. Thus, while there will always be some role for relationships, social trust, and informal mechanisms, and perhaps for clientelist arrangements, that role will have to change if rule of law is to prevail.

Third, rule of law is a function of demand. Economic reforms and development enhance the demand for rule of law, while legal reforms and rule of law contribute to economic development. There is both a push and a pull aspect to the process.

Fourth, rule of law affects different groups differently. Although most segments of society may benefit, some groups, companies, or individuals – particularly those that rely on government connections – will be worse off if rule of law is implemented. Foreign investors are among those who stand to gain the most. But the establishment of rule of law will have spillover effects in terms of institutions, rules, practices, and mores that will benefit domestic companies, private entrepreneurs, and individual citizens as well. While the government's initial strategy was to develop two regulatory regimes, one for foreign investors and the other for domestic companies, the two have merged over time. With China's entrance into the WTO, the two will merge further. Another component of the government's strategy has been to emphasize commercial law in order to provide a foundation for economic growth. However, the development of commercial law and the legal and political institutions to implement it have had, and will continue to have, important spillover effects into noncommercial areas. A more independent and competent judiciary, a more highly trained legal profession, and a more disciplined administration are of benefit to all. Further, institutional development is self-reinforcing. The successful resolution of cases, whether commercial or not, demonstrates the improvements in the legal system, resulting in increased trust in the judiciary and greater demand for the courts to resolve all manner of disputes.

Fifth, rule of law is not always the most effective solution. In some cases, reliance on market-based alternatives or political channels may be more effective ways to discipline parties or resolve disputes than reliance on formal law. Moreover, laws are most effective when they are consistent with cultural values, informal practices, and the general level of institutional and economic development. In fact, the legal system works best when there is no need to rely exclusively on the formal legal system, when the parties are able to take advantage of social capital and informal mechanisms that complement the formal legal system, and when legal remedies are reinforced by market and political solutions, including elections, to hold government officials accountable. Establishing a rule-of-law culture where the rule-makers make good laws, administrators faithfully implement them, and people willingly abide by them reduces the number of disputes and the costs of running the system. Thus, reforming the legal system alone without concomitant changes in other institutions, economic policies, and cultural practices will limit the effectiveness of reforms.

Finally, although rule of law may be necessary for economic development and implementing rule of law may give rise to pressure to reform other political institutions, the implementation of rule of law and sustained high economic growth will not necessarily lead to democracy, much less liberal democracy, for reasons discussed in the next chapter.

Notes

1 The World Bank (1999: 23), citing the *World Development Report 1997: The State in a Changing World.*
2 See Rheinstein (1954). Weber's views have attracted the attention of both generalists, such as Trubek (1972a), Ginsburg (2000), and those writing with reference to development in China in particular. See Ghai (1993a); Lan Cao (1997); Albert Chen (1999b); Carol Jones (1994).
3 See Chapter 2. Building on Weber, Unger (1976) distinguishes four ways in which a legal system may be autonomous. Substantive autonomy refers to law as a system of norms that differs from nonlegal norms including customary moralities, political and religious norms. Institutional autonomy requires specialized agencies (the courts, administrative tribunals, arbitration institutes) to apply law. Methodological autonomy refers to a distinctively legal way of reasoning. Occupational autonomy exists when judges and the legal profession form a distinct profession.
4 Rostow (1960). For a general discussion of modernization theory, see Tamanaha (1995); Davis and Trebilcock (1999).
5 Barro (1997: 1).
6 North (1981; 1990).
7 Knack and Keefer (1997: 591).
8 See Chapter 4.
9 As noted in Chapter 4, the movement is split between those who advocate a more narrow technical approach to reforms that focus on legal and economic institutions and those who support a more holistic approach that calls for the adoption of the full set of Western liberal democratic institutions, including a free press, civil society, multiparty elections, and channels for pluralist participation and interest representation.
10 Wade (1996: 60, 62–64).

11 The World Bank (1999: 7).

12 See Suzanne Berger (1996:1).

13 Taylor *et al.* (1997). However, as Jolly (1997: 15) notes, while it is possible to alleviate poverty even if there is no growth, it is not possible to sustain poverty alleviation without growth.

14 Blake (2000) notes that, according to micro law and development theory, "unless countries pay attention to civil society, especially the poorest of the poor, development policy is doomed to fail." Thus, development should help the poor become empowered, and allow them more say in defining the development agenda.

15 Some feminist critiques, for example, emphasize the need to facilitate the integration of women into the economic system and to remove gender-based discriminatory practices. See Davis and Trebilcock (1999: 26).

16 See Chapter 4. Chen (1999b: 100–01) provides a succinct summary of the critical perspective as it relates to economic development.

17 Tamanaha (1997) concludes on the basis of a review of the empirical literature that there is much less indeterminance than critical scholars suggest, especially below the Supreme Court.

18 See, for example, Upham (1994); Carol Jones (1994).

19 Gillespie (1999); Ginsburg (2000); Amsden (1989).

20 For a summary of this position, see Ginsburg (2000: 836–37).

21 Macaulay (1963).

22 Carol Jones (1994); Dowdle (1999). For a discussion of the role and limits of norms and social capital, see Platteau (1994).

23 Rodrick (1997); Hirst and Thompson (1996: 49).

24 Wade (1996: 66–67) points out that increased levels of trade are concentrated among northern countries but that even then 90 percent of production is for domestic consumption.

25 Wade (1996: 70); Hirst and Thompson (1996: 2).

26 Critics note the high correlation between domestic savings rates and investment rates even in OECD countries and the differences in the prices of borrowed funds in different national markets. See Wade (1996: 74, 79).

27 For an assessment of the variety of capitalism literature, see Peter Hall (1999). See below for a discussion of Chinese capitalism.

28 See Hall (1999: 139).

29 Hollingsworth and Boyer (1999) note that the authors contributing to the volume differ as to whether social systems of production will continue to have a strong national flavor or tend toward convergence.

30 In China, local governments benefit directly and indirectly from the production and sale of counterfeit goods. Local governments often have a direct economic stake in the manufacturers; and even when they do not, they benefit indirectly through higher taxes and lower unemployment rates. Moreover, consumers with limited resources may prefer cheaper counterfeit products. A concerted effort on the part of the central government to attack counterfeiting would exacerbate central and local tensions, anger many poorer consumers already adversely affected by reform, and perhaps lead to higher unemployment

and increased social unrest. Nor is it clear that counterfeiting is impeding economic growth, at least in the short term. It may even be fueling growth. Thus, given the high social and political cost and the uncertain impact on economic growth, it is unlikely that the central government will assign a high priority to curtailing counterfeiting. See Chow (2000).

31 Ginsburg (2000: 840).

32 See Boyer (1999).

33 See Sachs (1998).

34 Yong Wang (2000).

35 For a detailed review of the survey data, see Davis and Trebilcock (1999). See also Pistor and Wellons (1999).

36 Barro (1996).

37 Other variables included were GDP, the rate of male higher and secondary schooling, life expectancy, the fertility rate, the government consumption ratio, a democracy index, the inflation rate, and the growth rate in the ratio of export to import prices. The rule-of-law index was for data from the early 1980s.

38 Barro (1997: 28).

39 Knack and Keefer (1995).

40 The idea is that in societies where property rights are secure and contracts can be reliably enforced, parties have little reason to use cash for large transactions or to maintain large cash holdings. Clague *et al.* (1997a: 70).

41 Clague *et al.* (1997a: 76). The authors also argue that secure property rights and effective contract enforcement mechanisms are not in themselves inegalitarian institutions but rather have powerful equality-promoting effects. Clague *et al.* (1997a: 80).

42 La Porta *et al.* (1997). Demirguc-Kunt and Maksimovic (1998) also found that companies are more likely to fund growth through external financing in countries that score high on the ICRG index for Law and Order.

43 Levine (1999).

44 Mauro (1995). A World Bank Study of 4000 business persons in 69 countries supports the Mauro study's conclusion that corruption inhibits investment and thus leads to lower growth rates. Corruption was cited as one of the three most important obstacles to growth in less developed countries, though not in Asian countries, and one other region dominated by transition economies. See Brunetti *et al.* (1998).

45 Sachs and Pistor (1997); Schusselbauer (1999).

46 Gray and Hendley (1997). Black *et al.* (2000) note that the profit incentive to restructure private enterprises will be adversely affected by not only an ineffective legal system to prevent looting but also a punitive tax system, official corruption, organized crime, an unfriendly bureaucracy, and a business culture in which skirting the law is accepted as normal and perhaps necessary behavior. Hendley (1996) cautions that structural changes in the form of new laws and institutions are necessary but not sufficient for market democracy. She argues that legal reforms failed because they were too top-down and technocratic. They focused too much on passing new legislation and creating

stronger legal institutions and not enough on culture and engendering respect for law.

47 There are at least two general explanations for the crisis. One looks to fundamental structural weaknesses and shortcomings in institutions, including rule of law, in Asian states; the other focuses on the liquidity shortage and the role of international investors in withdrawing capital as a triggering event. Of course, both explanations could have merit. Seung Wha Chang (2000). See generally the essays in Stiglitz and Yusuf (2001).

48 Sarkar (1998). Even in Japan, the reputation of regulatory agencies has suffered in recent years, leading to efforts to downsize the bureaucracy and shift some of the decision-making power to elected political officials. See Magnier (2001).

49 The Gastil indices of economic freedoms, civil liberties, and political freedoms have also been used to test the factors that determine economic development, and in particular the relation between democracy and economic development. As is discussed in the next chapter, the Freedom's House's survey of "economic freedoms" provides another related measure.

50 Obviously, the surveys were not designed to track the elements of a thin theory of rule of law as I have defined it. Nor would it be easy to design a survey that would be able to capture in a straightforward way some of the elements. As the elements of a thin rule of law are compatible with considerable variation in institutions, collecting data on the types and operation of the legislature, judiciary, legal profession, and administrative law system would be useful.

51 But see Levine (1999).

52 McAuslan (1997: 25–44).

53 The World Bank (1999: 21).

54 The World Bank (1999: 17).

55 As Khan and Jomo (2000) point out, however, there is no simple correlation between rent-seeking and economic growth, or between the degree of rent-seeking and the degree of vulnerability to the Asian financial crisis. They conclude: "Rent-seeking was, and is, endemic in both developing and developed countries. The difference is that in developing countries the rent-seeking can be more extensive, can include illegal forms and is more damaging for growth. At the same time, many types of rents and rent-seeking played a key role in the process of development and are likely to do so again in the future."

56 Kahn and Jomo (2000) point out that it is not realistic or desirable to eliminate all rent-seeking, as some rent-seeking may be more efficient. Similarly, Rose-Ackerman (1999) observes that it would be too costly to eliminate all corruption.

57 As noted in Chapter 1, economists, political scientists, and legal scholars have all discussed this "puzzle."

58 See also Clarke (1996: 88–91).

59 One of the surprises for some investors is that China consists of many different markets. While some regions are relatively wealthy, others are extremely poor. Simply looking at per capita income is misleading.

60 Carol Jones (1994).

61 See Minxin Pei (2001a).

62 See the statistics provided by MOFTEC, available at http://www. moftec.gov.cn.

63 Clearly the increase in development is not due only or even primarily to improvements in the legal system. The sudden spike in investment after 1992 is attributable more to Deng's trip south than any specific changes in the legal regime or even investment policy. Deng's trip had significant psychological benefits, signalling that the open-door policy would continue. Local governments and approval authorities took note, as did foreign investors. Lardy (1995) attributes the increase in investment to (i) a general increase in FDI in developing countries; (ii) political stability in the years following Tiananmen; (iii) liberalization of the foreign investment regime; (iv) and a rise in recycled funds from PRC firms that transfer funds to offshore entities and then transfer the funds back in the form of investment in foreign-invested enterprises that qualify for preferential treatment, such as lower tax rates.

64 See the citation, in Chapter 12.

65 Peerenboom (2001a).

66 I argue elsewhere (2001a) that few if any rational investors are likely to forego investments in China on the basis of a relatively low enforcement rate alone.

67 For instance, in some cases it may be possible to require payment in advance, rely on a letter of credit, or obtain a third-party guarantee.

68 This is true not only of China. One study of foreign investment found that almost half of the foreign companies that invested in Sri Lanka did not investigate the effectiveness of the legal system before investing, and that another quarter conducted only a superficial investigation of the laws and regulations. See Perry (2000). Whether the failure to conduct more intensive studies was irrational would depend on a variety of factors, including the size of the investment, the nature of the company (large publicly listed multinational, small entrepreneur, etc.), the cost of a more extensive investigation, and the likelihood of coming into contact with the legal system and in particular the need to rely on the courts to settle disputes. Investors inevitably are affected by bounded rationality, and must make decisions based on less than perfect information. Given limits on the available information and uncertainty about the precise ways in which the legal system will affect their future business, investors typically will only be able to assign a rough value to legal system risk. Further, legal system risk will be only one of many risks.

69 Some surveys claim that FIEs in China are losing money. See, for example, "Path to Profit" (1998), which reports that one-third to more than one-half of FIEs are losing money and profits are thin for those in the black. In contrast, another report claims that most FIEs over $100,000 in registered capital are showing profit. "China Opens Sectors to Foreign Investment" (1998). Still another report claims that 72 percent of the 175 FIEs established by the top thirty multinational companies on *Fortune's* Global Top 500 list are profitable. "PRC Government Restructuring Continues" (1998). To focus exclusively on the reported profits, however, would be a mistake. Many foreign firms extract revenues from their companies in China through channels other than remittance of profit, including pretax technology royalties, supply contracts, and management contracts.

70   A number of studies have demonstrated herd behavior among corporate managers. See, for example, Bainbridge (1998); Kahan and Klausner (1996). There are various explanations for why managers tend to follow others blindly. Where information is limited, as in China, managers may be hoping to free ride on the information of others. A manager may also suffer less reputational damage if a decision turns out to be wrong when many others made the same decision. See Bainbridge (2000).

71   These observations are based on personal experience as a legal advisor on the projects.

72   Besides, given the rapid change in management today, the negotiators may not even be with the company when the losses start piling up.

73   Carol Jones (1994).

74   Carol Jones (1994); Redding (1990); Ghai (1993a).

75   There are many reasons for China's poor environmental record. See Alford and Shen (1997).

76   Gopal (1996).

77   In Taiwan, rotating credit associations and mutual aid societies arose in response to the conservative nature of the formal financing sector that made credit hard to obtain. Some attribute a decrease in the popularity of such associations to changes in Taiwanese society, including increased transactions between strangers, a weakening of traditional values that supported the associations such as the importance of relationships and face, a decline in moral standards, and an increase in greed. Although less popular, they still fill a niche in the economy because investors receive higher interest rates than banks and don't pay taxes on the earnings while borrowers have quick and easy access to funds without the need to go through complicated procedures or meet the requirements of the bank. See Lin Pao-an (1991); Winn (1994).

78   Pistor and Wellons (1999). Interestingly, several Asian states relied on discretionary state intervention to overcome the financial crisis. The government in Hong Kong, for instance, intervened to prop up the stock market and the value of the Hong Kong dollar. The Malaysian government imposed capital restrictions. In South Korea, a newly created government agency, the Financial Supervisory Commission, oversaw reforms of the financial sector, securities markets, and corporate governments, often drafting laws and regulations without input from lawyers in public or private practice, which were then passed by the National Assembly with only marginal modifications. The FSC also relied on a number of internal guidelines that probably are not subject to judicial review. Some commentators are critical of the long-term consequences of such government interventions. See Chung Wha Chang (2000)

79   Pistor and Wellons (1999: 8).

80   Pistor and Wellons' study ultimately supports the differentiation hypothesis rather than the convergence thesis. The differentiation hypothesis holds that different parts of the legal system respond differently to economic development, and that while some parts show signs of convergence, others develop along an idiosyncratic path. This finding is consistent with my argument that

the path-dependent nature of reforms and differences in values will ensure that China's legal system will exhibit signs of both convergence and divergence.

81 Pistor and Wellons (1999: 16).

82 For the argument that law played a greater role than normally suggested, see in addition to Pistor and Wellons (1999), Ravich (2000); Ramseyer and Nakazato (1999).

83 Rowen (1998: 7). Economic freedoms include protection of the value of money, free exchange of property, a fair judiciary, few trade restrictions, labor market freedoms, and freedom from economic coercion by political opponents.

84 Rowen (1998: 2) cautions that there is no single model of East Asian development. East Asian countries started in different places, grew at different rates, under different types of political regimes, and using a variety of policies.

85 Thailand, Malaysia, and Indonesia grew more slowly, at around 3.5 percent per year. Seven countries, including North Korea, Mongolia, Vietnam, Cambodia, Laos, Phillipines, and Mynamar, averaged less than 2 percent growth. Rowen (1998: 2).

86 Rowen (1998). Seung Wha Chang (2000: 272) makes a similar point with respect to South Korea, arguing that the courts were fairly independent when it came to politically insensitive cases.

87 Most of those who have argued for the continued importance of corporatism and clientelism have not expressly addressed the issue of their relationship to rule of law. (An exception is Dowdle (1999: 302–07), who explicitly argues that China ought to pursue a corporatist or neocorporatist regulatory strategy aimed at developing robust social networks rather than pursuing an allegedly "top-down" rule-of-law approach to regulation.) The focus of the debate has not been so much whether China needs rule of law for economic development but whether it needs clear, enforceable property rights, and whether clientelism and corporatism can provide alternatives. Rule of law only comes into play to the extent that clear property rights and courts capable of enforcing them are essential elements of rule of law.

The main targets of these authors have been the neoclassical economists who allegedly claim that free markets will sweep away corporatism and clientelism as economic reforms deepen or those who suggest that economic reforms will lead to the emergence of a civil society and ultimately democracy. Pearson (1997), for example, argues that economic development in China is more likely to lead to a state–society relationship based on clientelism and corporatism than democracy.

It is often unclear whether the authors are arguing that clientelism, corporatism, and vague property rights are useful in a transitional period characterized by large market imperfections and serious shortcomings in the legal system, or that they are advantageous even in a more developed market economy with a legal system that measures up favorably against the standards of a thin rule of law. Wank (1999), however, suggests that clientelism will survive economic and legal reforms, and that clientelist arrangements are at times both more efficient and more equitable. In contrast, the prevailing view among economists seems to be that clientelism, corporatism, and vague property

rights offer advantages during a transitional period but are nonetheless suboptimal. As market and legal reforms progress, they become less beneficial.
See, for example, David Li (1996); Kung (1999); Jiahua Che and Yingyi Qian
(1998); Wing Thye Woo (1999).

88 For a more extensive discussion of clientelism, see Wank (1999). See also
    Pearson (1997) who distinguishes between formal and informal, and vertical
    and horizontal clientelism. Scholars also distinguish between various kinds of
    guanxi, as discussed in Chapter 9.

89 Schmitter's (1974: 93–94) seminal definition of corporatism remains one of the
    most cited and influential: "Corporatism can be defined as a system of inter-
    est representation in which the constituent units are organized into a limited
    number of singular, compulsory, noncompetitive, hierarchically ordered and
    functionally differentiated categories, recognized or licensed (if not created)
    by the state and granted a deliberate representational monopoly within their
    respective categories in exchange for observing certain controls on their
    selection of leaders and articulation of demands and supports."

90 Wiarda (1997).

91 Although Schmitter draws the distinction between state and societal corpo-
    ratism, his definition leans toward the statist variety, emphasizing the role of
    the state in sanctioning interest groups that then enjoy a monopoly in exchange
    for accepting state control. His definition has been criticized for placing too
    much emphasis on the role of the state, for relying too heavily on economic
    and institutional factors as the motivating force behind corporatism as op-
    posed to cultural factors, and for focusing too much on labor unions and big
    business rather than social groups and religious institutions and indigenous
    movements. In contrast, soft corporatism is more participatory, pluralistic,
    and democratic. Wiarda, for instance, takes the defining elements of corpo-
    ratism to be a strong, directing state; a structured, limited pluralism with
    interest groups that are neither controlled by the state nor completely au-
    tonomous; and the incorporation of interest groups into the government –
    interest groups are not just consulted by the government but have a seat at
    the table in the policy-making process. He sees Scandinavian countries as
    incorporating elements of soft corporatism.

92 Dowdle uses corporatism in a fourth way. Dowdle (1999, 2001a) contrasts
    corporatism and the rule of law as alternative means of achieving social co-
    ordination. In his view, rule of law is characterized by centrally promulgated,
    generally applicable laws. Rule of law's top-down, centralist approach is ill-
    suited to China's wide regional variations and rapidly changing environment
    as a result of ongoing economic transitions. In contrast, corporatist arrange-
    ments promote the development of social networks that link all of the actors
    in a particular environment. In China's case, experimentation at the local level
    has produced a tremendous amount of important information. However, the
    channels for communicating such information to regulators is limited. In
    some cases, parties will simply ignore centrally promulgated legal rules and
    pursue local alternatives. In other cases, the alliance between local regulators
    and the regulated that typifies corporatism in China opens up channels for

communicating crucial information not available to central regulators, resulting in more context-specific and arguably better rules. Thus he suggests
that China ought to pursue a corporatist or neocorporatist regulatory strategy
aimed at developing robust social networks rather than pursuing rule of law.
Although Dowdle's purpose is not to explain China's past economic growth,
his emphasis on establishing social networks is similar in some respects to the
emphasis on relationships as an alternative to law. As such, it is subject to the
same limitations and qualifications: namely that this type of local corporatism
is not at odds with rule of law but may complement rule of law, but that rule
of law is also needed. Rule of law is compatible with this type of corporatism's
emphasis on local differences. Rule of law need not be construed as simply
a top-down imposition of rules. China's own laws are often drafted in a deliberately vague way or expressly delegate authority to local governments to
interpret the laws in light of local conditions in order to provide local governments with flexibility in implementation. Rule of law is also consistent with a
federalist system that divides responsibility between national and local governments, thus allowing for more experimentation. Although China has adopted
a unitary system, local governments are given considerable authority to legislate. Nor need one deny that laws that reflect norms will be easier to enforce.
Cooter (1997). Thus, there are clear advantages to "bottom-up" strategies in
some cases. Further, there are surely short-term and even long-term pragmatic
benefits to be derived from corporatist ties to government. As discussed previously, by embedding themselves within the bureaucracy, organizations trade
off autonomy for power. Of course, the downside of groups aligning themselves with government organizations is that the government may then attempt
to control their actions, thereby impeding their long-term development and
potential to effect change. Dowdle's arguments build on Sabel's directly deliberative polyarchy based on a pragmatic democratic experimentalism. As such,
his position is subject to many of the same qualifications and criticisms raised
in Chapter 9.

93   Unger and Chan (1995).
94   Pearson (1997) also uses it in the more standard way to capture the relation
     between state and private entrepreneurs as a potentially autonomous interest
     group.
95   Oi (1999: 12); Walder (1998).
96   This phenomenon is perhaps best described as "corporationism" rather than
     corporatism.
97   Pistor and Wellons (1999) observed that demand for rule of law grew as the
     economy developed. See also Levine (1999).
98   Guthrie (1998); Whiting (2001).
99   This is based on my experience representing foreign companies.
100 Wei Shangjin (1995). Wei controls for population size, literacy rates, level of
     human capital, and level of development as well as policies that limit exports
     to certain countries or provide preferential treatment to foreign investors.
101 Steinfeld (1998) argues that SOE reforms aimed at creating market incen-
     tives, defining property rights, corporatizing, or privatizing SOEs have failed

because of the lack of the necessary regulatory environment, including hard budget constraints, rule of law, and a legal system capable of enforcing legal obligations.

102   After exceeding 10 percent for a number of years, growth slowed to just over 7 percent in 1999. See http://www.tdctrade.com/main/china.htm (updated June 1, 2000).

103   Contracted investment has fallen dramatically from a high in 1993 of over $110 billion to just over $41 billion in 1999, a decrease of 21 percent from the year before. Actual investment also fell 11 percent in 1999 to $40 billion. The number of new foreign ventures has decreased from a high of 83,000 in 1993 to just 17,000 in 1999. See http://www.moftec.gov.cn (visited June 24, 2000).

104   Potter (1995b: 176); Wu Zheng (1997).

105   China Economic Quarterly (2000: 6). There is considerable debate over how to measure total factor productivity and its role in growth both in China and elsewhere in Asia. See Perkins (2001: 279–87); Stiglitz (2001: 510–12).

106   Lardy (1998: 10).

107   Lardy (1998).

108   There are many reasons why investors have turned increasingly toward wholly foreign-owned enterprises. See Peerenboom (1999c).

109   Most joint venture disputes are subject to arbitration, often abroad. However, even if the foreign party prevails at arbitration, it may have to rely on the PRC legal system to enforce the award if the Chinese party does not voluntarily comply with the award and it does not have assets abroad.

110   See, for example, Dowdle (1999).

111   Lardy (1998: 160, 188, 190).

112   Chen Chunlai (1999); Chen C. *et al.* (1995); Shan *et al.* (1999).

113   At the extreme end of the spectrum, Segal (1999) estimates that only 20 percent of FDI comes from nonethnic Chinese.

114   See Perry (2000), suggesting that small businesses may be better placed to avoid contact with the state, have less-complicated business affairs than large companies, or be better positioned to rely on informal mechanisms. Small investors may also be less likely to get caught if they break the law and have less at stake if they do get caught. In contrast to multinational companies, small investors do not have to consider their reputation.

115   Hamilton, ed. (1991); Redding (1990).

116   On the other hand, small investors may actually have more need of an effective legal system than large companies in that small companies have less lobbying clout and are more vulnerable to long delays in resolving disputes, the inability to enforce court judgments, and government rent seeking. See Perry (2000).

117   Rapacynski (1996).

118   Minxin Pei (2001a).

119   As Conner (1991) notes, private enterprises had sprung up even without a formal legal basis.

120   Che and Qian (1998).

121   Justin Tan (1996).

122 Zhang Naigen (1997: 17, n. 10).

123 Cheetham (1996: 27).

124 See Zweig (2000); Bernstein and Lu (2000).

125 See, for example, Su Li (1998). Even he acknowledges, however, that reliance on relationships and customary norms is not sufficient.

126 Summarizing evidence from multi-country empirical studies, Davis and Trebilcock (1999: 6) conclude that the relationship between rights and land and development is not straightforward. Formalizing the title to land and assigning to individuals land rights formerly held communally has produced mixed results. Removals of restrictions on alienability of rights does not seem to affect dramatically patterns of land dealing or land holdings. And while land redistribution programs were successful in Japan, Taiwan, and South Korea, they were less successful in other developing countries. Von Mehren and Sawers (1992: 93) conclude that while legalism, and in particular the conceptual innovation of title, had an important impact on the economic development of Thailand's agricultural sector by clarifying ownership rights and enabling the creation of security interests in land, law cannot be seen as an entirely independent variable. Rather "law plays a more modest, though important reinforcing role in the process of social change."

127 See Liu, Carter, and Yang (1998) for a review of the literature.

128 The Law prohibited so-called major land adjustments and limited small adjustments. See Article 14.

129 Liu, Carter, and Yang (1998).

130 Kung and Liu (1997).

131 1999 *China Law Yearbook*, p. 1023.

132 Zweig (2000).

133 Prosterman *et al.* (2000).

134 Bernstein and Lu (2000: 742).

135 Zweig (2000).

136 Bernstein and Lu (2000); Li and O'Brien (1996).

137 Zweig (2000).

138 Xia Yong (1995); Zweig (2000). Over 90 percent of farmers were aware of the Land Management Law's restrictions on adjusting land use rights one year after the law was passed. Prosterman *et al.* (2000). As Zweig notes, however, villagers regularly disregard contracts and often exhibit a poor understanding of the legal system.

139 Li and O'Brien (1996).

140 See Fu Hualing (2002).

141 In one survey, in thirteen of the forty disputes that made it to court, the plaintiffs hired a lawyer or some type of legal worker. However, the incompetence of the lawyer contributed to the client's defeat in several cases. See Zweig (2000).

142 Bernstein and Lu (2000); Zweig (2000).

143 According to one report, provincial government officials in Shandong fine mayors and heads of counties whenever Falungong disciples from their

jurisdiction conduct protests in Beijing. The mayors and county heads then fine the head of the Political–Legal Committee, who then fines the village head, who fines the police. Whether the practice exists outside of Shandong is not clear. See Johnson (2000a).

144 *PRC State Commission Says Township Enterprises Maintaining "Strong Growth"* (2000). A small percentage of TVEs are actually located in urban areas.

145 Che and Qian (1998).

146 Walder and Oi (1999: 2).

147 As Whiting (2001: 12) notes, however, not all TVEs were subject to hard budget constraints.

148 Gelb, Jefferson, and Singh (1993: 116). On the other hand, local government officials were encouraged to invest in TVEs because the number of TVEs established figured into the promotion of cadres. See Putterman (1997: 1650).

149 Whiting (1999); Walder and Oi (1999).

150 The director of the Bureau of Township Enterprises claims that 80 percent of TVEs have undergone restructuring in the last five years. See "China's Township Enterprises Face Changes" (2001).

151 Yatsko (1998); Che and Qian (1998).

152 Whiting (2001: 122) concludes in her study of TVEs that the lack of a credible commitment to property rights adversely affected the ability of companies to obtain long-term, large-scale private investment. Local officials responded by actively seeking to reduce the risks to industrial investors by supporting property rights to which the central state could credibly commit.

153 Woo (1999).

154 Sargeson and Zhang (1999).

155 Kung (1999: 95) argues: "As markets develop, the relational-specific *guanxi* input formerly supplied by local cadres has become less important as it is gradually replaced by arm's-length transactions undertaken by the enterprise manager. And as competition intensifies and the number of village enterprises multiplies and businesses expand, sound enterprise performance relies increasingly on the efforts of the manager."

156 Hubbard (1999) argues that local government entrepreneurship increases as market-oriented reforms begin, and wanes as market development proceeds, and that high returns to bureaucratic entrepreneurship in the transition are a symptom of low levels of market development. Gray and Hendley (1997: 164) observe that neoclassical economic theory would predict diminished importance of clientelist and corporatist arrangements and more demand for universally applicable laws as market reforms deepen.

157 Byrd (1990); Vermeer (1999). In addition, employees frequently blamed Party leaders and government officials for management decisions, and held the Party and the government responsible when managers favored their own relatives.

158 Kung (1999); Walder and Oi (1999); Walder (1998).

159 See *Xinhua Views Harm Done by "Local Protectionism"* (2000); Yan and Liu (1998).

160 In many TVEs, property rights are already reasonably clear.
161 Putterman (1997).
162 Kuo (1994); Hubbard (1999).
163 Lubman (1999: 106).
164 Shirley and Xu (2001) found that on average performance contracts did not improve performance and may have made it worse. However, performance contracts did improve productivity in slightly more than half of the participants. Successful performance contracts featured sensible targets, stronger incentives, longer terms, and managerial bonds. They also tended to be in more competitive industries, and where SOEs were under the oversight of local governments.
165 Although Lubman (1999: 107) suggests that "SOEs and their superiors are locked in an inextricable embrace in which they must bargain with each other, while in the bargaining process accountability fades away," ongoing reforms and the development of the market have decreased the importance of bargaining to some extent.
166 The World Bank (1997: 21).
167 For companies that have been corporatized, the government owner seeking to remove management must comply with the procedures set forth in the Company Law and the enterprise's articles of association.
168 As of 1996, only 5 percent of SOEs were corporatized. The World Bank (1997: 24).
169 The notion that the separation of ownership and management would reduce government meddling was based on the theories and experiences of Western countries. However, in Western countries, ownership is widely dispersed, resulting in passive owners. In contrast, in China the state continues to hold a vast majority of the shares, and thus it has more incentive to intervene as well as more authority to influence decision-making. See Dodds (1996: 732).
170 As Francis (1999) points out, using state-owned assets to establish spin-off enterprises may in some cases facilitate the transfer of human capital and technological resources from the state-owned sector to more dynamic business ventures, encourage entrepreneurship by reducing the levels of risk involved in initiating new businesses and reducing start-up costs, and increase the level of competition in the economy. Of course, in other cases, asset stripping merely benefits particular individuals.
171 The report also noted that 15 percent of the funds allocated for major road projects were unaccounted for. See O'Neil (2001).
172 Although too early to assess fully, debt-for-equity swaps are not likely to save SOEs. Debt-for-equity swaps have been impeded by many of the shortcomings in the legal system that have plagued the first four rounds of SOE reforms.
173 SOE reforms have themselves required the passage of numerous laws and amendments of existing laws.
174 Tao (1999: 165).
175 Tao (1999: 165).

176   See Summary of US–China Bilateral WTO Agreement (1999).
177   General Agreement on Tariffs and Trade. Article 10 (1947).
178   See, for example, Agreement on Trade-Related Aspects of Intellectual Property
       Rights, Including Trade in Counterfeit Goods, art. 41.
179   Some commentators argue that even the likely economic benefits will be lim-
       ited. See "Life after the WTO Honeymoon: Theory and Practice" (2000).
180   "WTO Will Promote Rule of Law in China."
181   See Clinton (2000). See also Asia Watch, http://www.hrw.org/press/1999/nov/
       chann1115.htm. Of course, Burma, Pakistan, Congo, and Cuba have been
       GATT/WTO members for years. Clearly WTO membership is not a magic
       formula for converting governments to human rights and rule of law. See
       "Clinton Administration's Deal with China on WTO" (2000).
182   The information in this paragraph is based on the July 10, 2001 version of the
       Draft Protocol of the Accession of China. How realistic these commitments
       are is debatable. Given the huge number of trade-related rules promulgated by
       different-level governments and administrative agencies, for China to publish
       all regulations in a single journal does not seem feasible, even if that journal
       consists of several volumes for different topics or regions. Even the USA does
       not publish all trade-related rules in a single place. Similarly, under PRC law,
       only the NPCSC may issue authoritative interpretations of law. In practice,
       it rarely does so, in part because it is already burdened with other matters.
       It is highly unlikely that the entity established to handle WTO requests for
       information and interpretations will be able to turn to the NPCSC for assis-
       tance. Accordingly, it is questionable whether that entity will be able to provide
       "authoritative" interpretations. Under PRC law, any interpretation by such an
       entity would be at best a *guizhang*. As discussed in Chapter 9, courts may refer
       to, but are not bound by, *guizhang*. A more general issue is whether WTO rules,
       including the Protocol of Accession, will become directly justiciable in China.
       PRC scholars are divided on this point.
183   Government officials appeared to first appreciate the sheer size and difficulty of
       the task as late as the end of 2000. See *PRC to Amend Laws for WTO Entry* (2000).
       Revising local regulations will be even more difficult due to the lack of sufficient
       legally trained personnel and local protectionism. Shanghai officials stated
       that more than 530 regulations must be amended or repealed. See "Shanghai
       Revises 534 Business Regulations" (2000).
184   See "Life after the WTO Honeymoon" (2000).
185   However, some types of transactions, such as import–export trade agreements,
       may no longer require approval. And in some cases, the nature of the approval
       process will change from one of substantive review to registration.
186   Because only states may raise suits, investors will first have to persuade their
       governments to raise a complaint. Governments may be reluctant to challenge
       China repeatedly for a number of political and economic reasons. Further, the
       WTO dispute resolution mechanism includes a consultation stage that may
       allow the parties to work out a compromise solution.
187   Steinberg (1998).

188   Foreign investors warmly welcomed as a sign of China's commitment to meet
      its WTO obligations a decision by the MOFTEC and the State Economic and
      Trade Commission to find in favor of two Russian steel companies against
      a PRC state-owned enterprise in an anti-dumping case. See Slobodzian
      (2000).

189   See *PRC to Establish "Modern" Trial System in Preparation for WTO Membership*
      (2000).

11

Rule of law, democracy, and human rights

The preceding chapters have focused on rule of law in China: its evolution, competing conceptions of it, institutional obstacles to its realization, and its role in economic development. Yet many who invoke rule of law (particularly in the West) do so not in the name of providing the necessary predictability required in a market economy but rather in relation to two of the other hallmarks of modernity discussed in the Introduction: democracy and human rights.[1] In this chapter, therefore, I discuss the relationship between rule of law, democracy, and human rights.

After a brief summary of various conceptions of democracy and the main arguments for and against implementing democracy in China at this time, I turn to the debate surrounding the relationship between democracy and economic development. Though the empirical evidence is mixed on the general issue of their relationship, there is ample evidence that authoritarian regimes may achieve sustained economic growth, and that economic development and rule of law need not lead to liberal democracy, at least for a long time. I argue that, for a variety of reasons, the short-term prospects for democracy in China are not promising. In the long run, however, China is likely to become democratic, though probably not a *liberal* democracy. Rather, the more likely outcome will be a nonliberal soft authoritarian or communitarian form of democracy. Rule of law may serve as an intermediate step along that route.

Political reform

Early theorists such as Lipset argued that economic development would lead to political development.[2] Indeed, some liberals think that China is becoming like us, that it is moving toward genuine multiparty democracy and greater protection of individual rights.[3] Most are more dubious, although they firmly believe China *should* be becoming more like us.

Admittedly, liberals come in different stripes. One type is the evolutionary liberal who believes that economic reforms will lead to political
reform and a transition to liberal democracy.[4] As the economy develops,
a middle class (or civil society) emerges, demanding that its property
rights be protected, thus reinforcing legal reforms and the transition
to rule of law and democracy. Moreover, once their materialistic needs
are met, citizens will demand more say over political issues.[5] As part of
the ongoing legal reforms, the ruling regime will already have receded
from day-to-day governance and devolved power to other state organs,
including the legislature and the courts. Eventually, unable or unwilling
to resist the tide of reform, the ruling regime will bow to the demands of
the citizenry and carry out political reforms, including genuine multiparty democracy. The citizenry, for its part, will opt for a liberal regime
that favors liberal values, including extensive individual autonomy and
strong civil and political rights.

The ranks of evolutionary liberals who openly endorse such a rigid
mechanistic view of development are smaller than in the past, due in part
to the mixed results of the law and development movement in the 1960s
and 1970s and the failure of the third wave of democracy to produce
sustainable liberal democracies.[6]

Like the evolutionary liberal, the end-of-history liberal sees democracy and human rights (and rule of law) in teleological terms, as the
final resting place for all modern political systems.[7] However, the end-
of-history liberal's claim is more of a normative claim about what should
be than a how-to primer setting out the necessary steps to the promised
land. Chastened by the failure of countries to achieve sustained economic
growth and modernization, but buoyed by the downfall of the Soviet
Union, the third wave of democratization,[8] and the turn to market-
based economies, the end-of-history liberal is sure as to direction but
unclear as to means. While rejecting the claim that a mechanical series of
legal and/or economic reforms will inevitably lead to liberal democracy,
the end-of-history liberal nonetheless sees liberal democracy complete
with extensive civil and political liberties as the only viable alternative
in the post-socialist era.[9]

In assessing the likelihood of political convergence in China, it is
helpful to clarify certain key terms. A genuine democracy requires at
minimum open, competitive elections, under universal franchise, of
those in posts where actual policy decisions are made (the electoral

dimension). It also requires sufficient freedom of association, assembly, speech, and press to ensure that candidates are able to make their views known and compete effectively in the elections, and so that citizens are able to participate with reasonable effectiveness in the electoral process (the participatory process dimension).[10] In addition, it requires the legal institutions to ensure that these freedoms are in fact realized and the election is carried out fairly (the rule-of-law dimension).[11] Democracy therefore implies rule of law, but not vice versa.[12]

It is also helpful to distinguish between *majoritarian democracy*, as a form of government in which the people exercise their right of self-determination and decide political issues through the majoritarian decision-making process and elections; *rights-based democracy* as a particular form of democracy that emphasizes individual rights as a check on the majoritarian decision-making process;[13] and *liberal rights-based democracy*, which is a particular type of democracy that emphasizes individual rights and autonomy to a greater extent than communitarianism, for example. Rights-based democrats worry that the majoritarian decision-making process may subject individuals and minorities to the tyranny of the majority. To protect the rights and interests of individuals and minorities, rights-based democrats place limits on the majoritarian voting process by removing certain issues from the legislative arena.[14]

China could become democratic without becoming a liberal rights-based democracy. Although the third wave of democratization has brought majoritarian democracy to many nations, it has not necessarily made them more liberal. As an empirical matter, democracy is consistent with "regular and extensive violations of human rights, suppression of minority groups, flagrant abuses of state power, hidden domination by the military or other centres of power not accountable to the public, and serious constraints on the ability of various interests to organize and be heard."[15] But even as a normative matter, well-functioning states that take rights seriously and protect an extensive range of rights need not adopt a liberal view of rights. Accordingly, even if China becomes more democratic, there is no guarantee that Chinese citizens will endorse a liberal view of human rights that gives priority to civil and political rights over economic rights and collective interests, or that they will interpret civil and political rights in the same way as liberals, or that they will strike a similar balance between concern for the individual and concern for the interests of families, communities, and the nation. A thin rule of law is consistent with various conceptions of rights, from liberal to communitarian to more statist variants.[16] Regardless of how rights are conceived, however, rule of law is necessary for their adequate protection.[17]

Democracy

Democracy has been defended on various grounds. One line of argument holds that democracy is a good in itself – that it is intrinsically valuable – regardless of its consequences. This view highlights two fundamental values: autonomy and equality. The autonomy strain sees democratic elections as a form of self-expression and self-rule. As individuals, we all have a stake in making decisions that affect our interests. Only we know what is in our best interests.[18] Democracy allows us to participate in choices that affect our lives and define who we are and the kind of society we live in. Popular sovereignty therefore (allegedly) makes us masters of our own fate.[19]

Democracy also accords with concerns about equality. These concerns are articulated in various ways. One version holds that one should not simply impose one's values or ideas on others.[20] In important matters requiring collective decision-making, each person should be treated equally.[21] More specifically, each person's interests or conception of the good life should be given equal weight.[22] One way to treat each person equally is to allow everyone one vote.

Critics, both in China and abroad, raise a number of objections to arguments that assert that democracy is an intrinsic good and justified on the basis of autonomy and equality concerns.[23] As noted in Chapter 2, Chinese political theory on the whole has been hostile to the claim that individuals know best what is in their interest, at least when it comes to complicated issues such as running a huge country in the midst of a major economic transition. On the contrary, Confucian and Party leaders alike have claimed to know what is in the best interests of the people, at least as a whole if not individually. Similarly, there has been relatively little support for the notion that to treat someone with equal respect requires that one allow that person to make his or her own choice. In the hierarchical Confucian world, the emphasis was on showing each person the respect due them given their particular role in society and position in the relationship. Rather than discounting or ignoring manifest differences, such differences are factored into the notion of due consideration.[24] Treating someone with respect does not mean simply allowing that person to pursue his or her own path, no matter how ill-informed and self-destructive.[25] Treating with equal respect has meant that it is the ruler's duty to ensure the well-being and safety of its citizens. More specifically, the ruling regime is obligated to create the material, social, and spiritual conditions for a harmonious society in which each person is able to flourish in a way consistent with the flourishing of others. To that end, the government has taken the lead in defining the substantive moral agenda for society rather than endorsing the principle of a neutral state.

Advocates of democracy counter that the claim of Chinese leaders, particularly today's CCP leaders, that they know what is in the best interests of Chinese citizens is unsustainable. Certainly the disasters of the Great Leap Forward and the Cultural Revolution ought to raise doubts among those who believe that the leaders always know best. Moreover, as market reforms have progressed and society has become increasingly pluralistic, it is doubtful that CCP leaders have the capacity to address many of the technical issues that have arisen or that any group of leaders could resolve the increasing social tensions.

A second line of critique, however, points out that even if democracy, autonomy, and equality are intrinsic goods, when such intrinsically valuable goods may be traded off to secure other goods and instrumental gains is a contentious philosophical issue. Although all societies attach some importance to autonomy, the value of autonomy in the normative hierarchy of societies differs.[26] No doubt Chinese citizens, like everyone else, find the opportunity to express their preferences valuable. But how much importance is attached to the opportunity may vary, particularly given the realities of democratic elections. Democratic elections allow individuals to express their preferences, but each person only has one vote, and there is no guarantee that one's personal preferences will prevail. Democracy is not an exercise in self-rule in that sense but in group-rule. Democracy by itself can hardly ensure that each individual is master of his or her own individual fate. Allowing individuals one vote is equal only in a formal sense, and is consistent with considerable inequality in opportunities and outcomes.[27] Without evaluation of the likely consequences of what the results of implementing democracy would be, it is difficult to determine how much weight to assign to the values of autonomy and equality or to draw any conclusions about the desirability and value of democracy.

There are a number of instrumental or consequentialist justifications for democracy. One pragmatic advantage of democracy is that it provides a procedural mechanism for regulating interest group conflicts and for smoothing over social cleavages. Further, democracy allows for more open debate and greater expression of diverse viewpoints, thus arguably facilitating better decision-making. At minimum, the emphasis on open discussion provides a more accurate feedback mechanism, as evidenced by the fact that there have been fewer famines in democracies than in authoritarian states.[28] Democracies arguably are also less likely to go to war with each other.[29] In addition, democracy provides for greater, albeit still limited, government accountability because citizens can vote out those in office if they so choose. Interestingly, one common instrumental justification for democracy in China and Asia is that democracy will help strengthen the nation. In the West, democracy advocates generally emphasize the potential conflict between the state and citizen and therefore portray democracy as a way of limiting the power of the state. In contrast, the emphasis on harmony in China has led advocates of democracy, from Kang Youwei and Liang Qichao in the late Qing to Deng Xiaoping and Jiang Zemin today, to portray democracy as a tool of nation-building.[30] By far the most powerful instrumental justification for democracy, however, is that democracy allegedly promotes economic growth.

Again, critics remain unpersuaded by these consequentialist arguments, countering that the benefits of democracy are illusory or insufficient. The assumption that democracy will result in greater human happiness has not always been borne out in practice. The late 1980s and early 1990s were a watershed period for democracy, with more than fifty nondemocratic states becoming democratic. However, many of these fledgling democracies have encountered serious difficulties. Democratic governments frequently have not been able to deliver on their promises to improve the material standard of living of the people. Even when there is economic growth, it is often accompanied by unequal wealth distribution, mismanagement of state assets, and widespread corruption. A 1996 poll of seventeen Latin-American countries found that only 27 percent were happy with the way democracy worked.[31] In some states, such as Poland, disenchanted voters reinstated the Communist Party, whose removal had only been won a short time earlier after years of struggle. In other states, decidedly unhappy citizens have taken to the streets to protest the lack of growth, increasing gaps between the rich and poor, corruption, social disorder, and the rise of criminal gangs. Others, giving in to a sense of impotence, simply waive their hard-won right to vote.

In China, some Statist Socialists believe, no doubt genuinely (although the views of some are surely influenced by their own personal stake in maintaining the status quo), that the Party knows best, and that democratic centralism is needed to navigate through the rough and uncharted waters of reform. Neoauthoritarians may favor rule by a technocratic elite rather than the Party, but they do not support democracy. Moreover, even many Communitarians and some liberals who believe that democracy is desirable in the long run still question whether China needs democracy now. Many Chinese citizens of whatever political orientation believe that economic development is more important than democracy and that implementing democracy will lead to instability and impede economic growth. Indeed poll after poll shows that most people are more concerned about stability and economic growth than democracy and civil and political liberties.[32] To be sure, one could object that Chinese citizens are skeptical about democracy and fearful that the process of democratizing could lead to chaos because the government controls the media. Had citizens access to more information, they would hold different beliefs. Yet it is presumptuous and somewhat condescending to assume that the only or main reason Chinese citizens disagree on issues such as democracy and human rights is because they are being manipulated or brainwashed by the government's propaganda machine, particularly given that Chinese citizens have access to much more information than in the past. Clearly, many Chinese academics and intellectuals, including those living abroad, all of whom have ample access to information and who well appreciate that linking democracy with chaos serves the regime's interest, also fear that democratization may be destabilizing. Nor is such a belief unreasonable, given how often democratic transition has led to upheaval and turmoil in other countries.[33]

Whether authoritarian or democratic governments are better able to foster growth has been the subject of intense theoretical debate. Supporters of authoritarian governments argue that politicians in democracies will succumb to public pressure for immediate consumption, thereby lowering investment and growth. They are also likely to give in to the majority's calls to redistribute income by imposing taxes on the wealthy minority, thus discouraging more productive and profitable firms and entrepreneurs. Further, they may not be able to impose tough policies to restrict the money supply to curb runaway inflation, or to push through painful SOE reforms that will result in rising unemployment. To make matters worse, democracy may exacerbate ethnic or religious tensions, with the majority trampling on the rights of the minority, leading to civil unrest, and thus undermining the stability needed for growth.[34]

Conversely, advocates of democracy argue that a market economy requires freedom of economic association, the free flow of information, and transparency in rule-making and in the application of rules, all of which are hallmarks of a (liberal) democracy. In their absence, authoritarian regimes are likely to adopt misguided policies that undermine economic growth. Moreover, without democratic elections, there is no way of holding authoritarian regimes accountable. Accordingly, such regimes are likely to be prone to rampant rent-seeking, undermining the security of property rights and depriving investors of the needed predictability and certainty. The lack of accountability also leads to corruption and waste, with government officials siphoning off state assets and engaging in self-dealing.

As an empirical matter, the relation between regime type and economic development is simply not clear.[35] However, the weight of the evidence seems to suggest that those who believe democracy will lead to growth are putting the cart before the horse. One study employing sophisticated statistical techniques has concluded that economic development *causes* democracy but democracy does not cause economic development.[36] Supportive of that conclusion, several studies have found that economic development is a prerequisite to democracy in that at a relatively low level of development, democracy hinders growth.[37]

As for whether economic growth will result in a transition to sustainable democracies, again, the evidence is at best mixed. Authoritarian regimes are relatively stable at low levels of development, become unstable at medium levels, and then become more stable at higher levels.[38] A number of authoritarian regimes, including Singapore, Malaysia, Spain, Argentina, East Germany, Hungary, Argentina, and Mexico were able to survive for many years even after they became relatively wealthy.

Admittedly, only Singapore and Malaysia remain authoritarian regimes today. But it is not clear that economic development explains the transition to democracy.[39] What is clear is that economic wealth is a good indicator of the sustainability of democracy: poorer democracies are much more likely to collapse than wealthy ones; once per capita income reaches a certain level, democracies rarely fail.[40] What is also clear is that poor democracies are extremely vulnerable to downturns in the economy, regardless of past performance.[41] In the long run, however, the number of stable democratic regimes is likely to grow as countries become richer because once authoritarian regimes in wealthy states fall, for whatever reason, and become democracies, they will remain democracies.

There are a number of plausible explanations why a certain level of development is needed to sustain a stable democracy and why the demand for democracy is likely to increase as a country becomes wealthier.[42] As noted, democratic regimes face pressure to redistribute income from the wealthy minority to the poor majority. Affluence reduces the intensity of distributional conflicts by increasing the resources available for redistribution and decreasing the number of people at or below the poverty line. Development also generates the education and communications networks needed to support democracy. In addition, development increases the ranks of middle class who may seek to protect their growing property rights through political channels, including the electoral process. Thus it is not surprising that economically developed countries tend to be stable democracies, whereas there are few stable democracies in developing countries.

Has China reached the minimum level of development required to sustain democracy? Some scholars claim it has.[43] Others disagree. Among the latter, the liberal PRC political scientist Liu Junning concedes that there is considerably more support for rule of law than for democracy and civil and political rights. His explanation is that rule of law is necessary to protect people's property rights, rights that have increased as a result of economic reform. However, there is still not a large enough middle class demanding protection of political rights to support political reforms and democracy.[44] Supportive of his view, one survey found that while 50 to 60 percent of those polled would be highly resentful if the fruits of their labor were seized by government officials, only 15 percent had considerable or strong resentment of not being able to voice their opinions on policy and law.[45]

The World Bank's estimate of China's Gross National Income (measured in terms of purchase power parity) is $3550.[46] According to Przeworski and Limongi, the cutoff point at which a regime is more likely to be democratic than authoritarian is $4115.[47] At China's current level, the probability of a transition to democracy is 0.0161, which implies a life expectancy of some sixty-two years for the current regime.[48] Indeed, authoritarian regimes are particularly stable in the $3000 to $4000 range, more so than any other range except where per capita income is less than $1000. Furthermore, even assuming China did become democratic, at this level of wealth, the probability of democratic regime failure is 0.0333, equating to a life expectancy of approximately thirty years.[49] Interestingly, the likelihood of a transition to democracy increases when per capita income is between $4,000 and $6,000 and then tapers off. Thus, given China's rapid growth rate, the regime will soon be facing a period when it is most vulnerable to democratic transition.

Reaching the same end point by a different route, Susan Ravich has argued that looking at the level of economic wealth alone is not enough. More important is the level of marketization, which leads to the development and maturation of a civil society and a process of democratic learning on the part of citizens.[50] According to her econometric model, further marketization and economic reforms are required before Chinese citizens will enjoy even the limited political freedoms enjoyed by Indonesian citizens during the Suharto era.

Given the high value attached to stability and economic growth by PRC citizens as indicated in numerous polls,[51] it bears noting that some scholars have argued that the stability of the regime is as important to economic growth as the regime type. The reason is that regimes that are about to fall, whether authoritarian or democratic, are likely to seize assets or engage in acts that undermine the security of property rights.[52] Clague et al. tested empirically the effect of regime duration and found that property rights are more likely to be secure in stable regimes, whatever their type.[53] They also found that a shift from democracy to autocracy is favorable to property rights, but that a shift to democracy is unfavorable to property rights, at least in the short term. They explain this result by noting that autocracies almost never replace democracies unless the economy is performing poorly, which implies that property rights are not adequately protected. In the long term, however, democracies tend to protect property rights better than authoritarian regimes.

Notwithstanding the competing theoretical arguments and the conflicting empirical evidence, several conclusions are possible. First, even allowing that democracy, autonomy, and equality are intrinsic goods (albeit disputed in their particulars), how much weight to attach to them will turn on context-specific issues, including most importantly how likely democracy is to lead to economic development. Second, when it comes to economic development, regime type is not as important as the stability of the regime and variations within regimes.[54] In particular, regimes that are market-oriented, dominated by technocrats, and relatively free from corruption are more likely to be successful. Third, and a corollary of the second, although some authoritarian regimes have been successful at promoting economic growth, not all have. Conversely, although some democracies have been successful at promoting economic growth, not all have. Fourth, all else being equal, authoritarian regimes tend to outperform democratic regimes at low levels of economic development. Fifth, China may not yet have reached the level of development that makes it likely that there will be a transition to democracy, and even if there were, that democracy would be sustainable.[55] Sixth, when the conditions for a durable or stable democracy are not present – which I shall argue shortly is the case in China – the transition to democracy often impedes economic development, at least in the short term. Seventh, economic development is not sufficient for political reform and the emergence of democracy. Countries may develop economically and not become democratic, at least for a considerable period. Hong Kong and Singapore are good examples. Eighth, higher levels of prosperity and economic development are likely to lead to growing demand for democracy – Taiwan, South Korea, Thailand, and Indonesia are good examples. Whether or not economic development is the cause of democratization, in the long term, economically advanced countries are likely to be and to remain democracies.

The long-term need for democracy

Although China may not yet be at the point where it is possible to implement democracy, in all likelihood China will need to adopt democracy at some point in the future for at least three reasons: to overcome what is likely to become a growing legitimacy deficit, to address accountability problems, and to ameliorate intensifying social cleavages.

Without democracy, the ruling regime's claim to legitimacy is primarily performance-based rather than consent-based. In particular, its claim to legitimacy is predicated to a large extent on its ability to sustain economic growth. As has often been pointed out, regimes that rely on performance-based legitimacy are vulnerable to downturns in the economy. China has enjoyed a remarkable run of rapid economic growth. However, the current growth rates cannot be sustained indefinitely. When growth rates dip, the Party is likely to lose the support it has obtained as a result of its ability to improve the standard of living for most people.[56]

To be sure, the legitimacy of the ruling regime turns on more than just growth rates. How the increased wealth is distributed, and who benefits and who loses, are also important. The absence of democracy leads to accountability problems and the perception that the reform process is unjustly benefiting some at the expense of others. Simply put, authoritarian regimes have problems with accountability, particularly during a period of economic transition. In the Soviet Union, economic reforms and premature privatization led to massive plundering of state assets. In Indonesia, the lack of transparency and the inability of citizens to vote out Suharto resulted in crony capitalism. In China, government officials siphon off state assets; impose unauthorized fees on farmers, private businesses, foreign enterprises, and state-owned enterprises alike; and steer valuable business opportunities to the princelings, sons and daughters of senior leaders who have become fabulously wealthy, while those disadvantaged by reforms have been left without medical treatment and in some cases, without food or shelter. As we have seen, the Party and government is plagued by corruption. Without greater public participation in the law-making processes and ultimately democracy, accountability in China will remain an issue. By controlling the law-making process, those in power are able to legalize corruption by passing laws to favor the elite few. Under the guise of various privatization schemes, state assets are siphoned off and end up in the hands of private parties.

Even if China's lawmakers really were genuinely public-minded officials who always put the interests of society first, the lack of accountability would still threaten the legitimacy of the system and lead to greater calls for more participation by groups that felt their interests were slighted. Economic reforms have produced a more pluralistic and deeply divided society in China. In a pluralistic society, individuals inevitably will disagree about what is fair and just and judge laws in terms of their own interests. A political process is needed to work out the conflicts. Democracy provides a procedural mechanism for reducing social tensions and dealing with social cleavages.

Social cleavages already exist in China and are likely to increase over time. One major fault line runs along the rural–urban divide. Huge differences in wealth between Eastern coastal and inner regions have already led to sharp conflicts and political infighting. The issue of Taiwan looms ever larger, and will eventually require a political solution. The future of Hong Kong and Macau, not to mention Tibet and Xinjiang, also pose potentially thorny resource allocation, legal, and political issues. Generational conflicts are likely to become more acute as the effects of the one-child policy force later generations to devote more of their income to supporting the elderly. SOE reform and the need to honor the implicit social contract between the Party and soon-to-be unemployed and unemployable elderly state workers will exacerbate tensions. A viable social welfare system has yet to be established – but whatever the final form, any such system will inevitably produce winners and losers. Similarly, although there are environmental laws on the books, they frequently go unenforced, in part because of the lack of political will to enforce them if that means slowing down economic growth. Yet the failure to deal with pollution now simply means that the unavoidably higher costs of cleaning up the environment later are passed on to future generations. The most divisive cleavage of all, however, is between the haves and the have-nots. Economic reforms have increased income inequality. While many have become extremely rich, others have been left with literally nothing.

Some commentators have suggested that the ruling regime will be able to hold off the demands for democracy in the face of greater social diversity and increased interest group conflicts by implementing rule of law and cleaning up the government.[57] But that is not likely to be sufficient. At minimum, the ruling regime must also be able to sustain economic growth and continue to raise everybody's living standards, even if at somewhat different rates. Hong Kong and Singapore are illustrative in this regard. The Hong Kong government in the 1960s and '70s was able to overcome growing popular discontent and a challenge to its legitimacy without introducing democratic reforms by promising to implement rule of law *and* by buying off the populace through a series of welfare reforms.[58] Similarly, Singaporeans apparently are willing to tolerate limitations on civil and political freedoms in part because of their rising living standards and considerable benefits such as subsidized housing. Yet it is unlikely that in China the ruling regime has the economic resources to buy off a disgruntled populace.

Moreover, in the long run, disputes over how to divide the pie, even assuming the pie continues to grow, are likely to lead to greater demands for democracy. Implementing rule of law will not be sufficient because law alone cannot mediate conflicts between increasingly disparate interest groups and segments of the populace who have been affected in radically different ways by reforms. Law-making, interpretation, and implementation are not simply technical processes; they are inherently value-laden. As the stakes grow, the public will demand a greater say in choosing the people who make the law and more opportunities to participate in the process of making laws. They are also likely to oppose turning over important decisions to the judiciary, even were that possible. At present, the PRC judiciary lacks the independence, authority, and legitimacy to play the role that judiciaries in countries such as the USA have played in mediating social conflicts and deciding contentious social issues. Nor is the PRC judiciary, given the limitations inherent to judiciaries in the civil law system, likely to emerge as a major player in the battle among competing social groups. Nor should it attempt to do so. Relying on the judiciary rather than democratic political organs to resolve social cleavages politicizes the judiciary. Even if the PRC judiciary were more independent and enjoyed wider powers and more legitimacy, it could quickly lose whatever gains it made were it to be asked to assume such a role.[59] Given the inevitable democracy deficit of an unelected judiciary, reformers in China and other countries undergoing transition have emphasized the need to strengthen the legislature.[60]

The forces for and against change

Even assuming China should implement democracy, whether it will do so is another matter. There is no single model for authoritarian states to become democratic. Some states have become democratic through a process of gradual evolution, others as the result of a traumatic "big bang" event.[61] Among the former, in Spain, Brazil, and Taiwan the main driving forces for democratization were internal, whereas in Poland, Czechoslovakia, South Africa, and South Korea external factors played a greater role. Some observers have spotted signs of creeping democratization in China, pointing out that norms, practices, and institutions are slowly changing, often in a bottom-up fashion in response to local concerns.[62] Others doubt that the gradual approach will work. As one skeptic puts it, the gradual approach has relied on reform without reformers, at least at the top levels of power. Yet there are likely to be limits to how far the ruling regime will let creeping reforms creep.[63]

One point on which there is a general consensus is that no one can predict with any reasonable degree of assurance whether China or any other country will democratize and if so, how. The sudden fall of the Berlin wall and the breakup of the Soviet Union caught even the experts by surprise, as did Jiang Jingguo's deathbed support for democracy and the recent fall from power of Suharto in Indonesia.

While it is impossible to predict whether China will democratize and if so when, it is possible to analyze the forces for and against change. Democratization in China is likely to depend on a variety of factors, including support or resistance within the Party; the attitudes of non-Party elites; the views of the citizenry; the level of economic development; the development and orientation of civil society; China's political culture; institutional development, including the extent to which the legal system is able to support the requirements of a democratic order; and exogenous events, some of them foreseeable, such as international pressures arising from globalization in the economic, cultural, legal, and political spheres, and some of them unforeseen, including perhaps wars and new financial crises.[64] A survey of the foreseeable factors suggests that China is not likely to become democratic in the near future.[65]

Although the Party's role in governing society has diminished as a result of economic, social, cultural, political, and legal changes, the Party's retreat from the daily operations of running the state does not mean that democracy is imminent. Naturally, Party leaders want to remain in power, and they are likely to oppose genuine democratic elections for national-level positions. The relentless attacks on any social organization or individual that challenges the Party's right to rule or that constitutes even the remotest of threats to the Party suggests that the Party will fight to hold on to power. Given the ethnic conflicts and territorial conflicts that have accompanied democratization in the former

Soviet republics, senior Party leaders no doubt fear that democratization in China could similarly exacerbate ethnic tensions and embolden separatist movements in Tibet and Xinjiang.

On the other hand, just as the fate of rule of law in China turns on more than the intentions and desires of Party leaders, so too does the fate of democracy. Existing institutions and practices are increasingly insufficient to handle the social, cultural, economic, and legal problems that have arisen as a result of reforms. Farmers in the countryside and laid-off SOE employees and migrant workers in urban areas continue to demonstrate. Corruption seems to be spreading. Predatory officials go on gouging companies. Local governments refuse to toe the line laid down by the central government. Citizens complain of the breakdown of law and order.[66] The Party has responded by trying to build up other political institutions, including the NPC and local people's congresses, the Political Consultative Committee, and the legal system. It has even tolerated the growth of certain social organizations. The government has also experimented with more democracy within the Party, choosing members for important posts through multiple candidate elections with secret ballots. It is possible that the Party would conclude that it is in its own interests to make a transition to democracy. As noted, the Party has begun to study how other authoritarian regimes were able to transform themselves into social democratic parties. Moreover, democratic development may occur when factions in the ruling regime split, and some factions see it as in their self-interest to promote democracy. Notwithstanding such possibilities for reform, however, it is unlikely that the Party will emerge as a strong force for democracy in the near future.

Political scientists have highlighted the role of elites in promoting the transition to democracy.[67] In some countries, the first phase of the transition involved competition among elites, which introduces important democratic values such as competition with civility, tolerance, trust, cooperation, restraint, and accommodation. In the second phase, these values are disseminated to the general populace. The elites are instrumental in the dissemination process as they can model the proper behavior and values. Yet it is unlikely that elites will emerge as a force for democracy in China. Liberal intellectuals have been silenced or marginalized since 1989.[68] More fundamentally, it is far from clear that the elites support democracy. To the contrary, some clearly support the Party, while others support an authoritarian regime, though not necessarily the Party. Many elites are wary and disdainful of the masses, and recoil at the thought of allowing illiterate peasants to decide the fate of China.[69] As urbanites, intellectuals no doubt understand perfectly well that democracy would result in rural voters reversing longstanding policies whereby rural areas subsidize the cities. Not surprisingly, to the extent that the urban elites favor democracy at all, it is frequently an elitist form designed to ensure that intellectuals rule.[70]

Another line of scholarship emphasizes the importance of political culture and the attitudes and values of the general populace.[71] The cultural approach, which fell out of favor during the 1960s and 1970s, reemerged in the 1980s and '90s.[72] Although there is no general consensus as to just what is needed in the way of social requisites or cultural traits to support democracy, typical suggestions include such features as toleration of opposing political beliefs and positions, pragmatism and flexibility as opposed to a rigid ideological approach to politics, a willingness to compromise, trust in other political actors and one's fellow citizens, a civility of political discourse, an intelligent and reasonable suspicion of authority, a public-spiritedness and participatory civic culture, and a commitment to the procedures of democracy and the legitimacy of the results of those procedures.[73]

In contrast, Lucian Pye has portrayed Chinese culture as exhibiting a psychological yearning for authority and a reluctance to criticize, a tendency to personalize authority that leads to factionalism and intolerance, a preference for order over conflict, and a willingness to put the interests of the collective ahead of one's personal interests. He also points out the historical lack of institutional restraints on authority.[74] Along the same lines, whole forests have been felled debating whether Confucianism is or is not compatible with democracy.[75]

Clearly we must be careful not to essentialize cultures or to treat them as stagnant. The success of Taiwan and other Asian countries in implementing democracy demonstrates that change is possible. Moreover, whether any or all of the listed traits are really prerequisites, and in any event whether China has the necessary requisites to support democracy, are open to debate.[76] Tianjian Shi, for instance, suggests that China's mass political culture may have sufficient democratic orientation to sustain democracy.[77] However, he acknowledges weaknesses in some areas, including the tendency to defer to authority. Similarly, other studies have found Chinese citizens to be intolerant of opposing political beliefs and not very supportive of free speech.[78] Most importantly, as we have seen, there appears to be little demand for democracy, with most people fearing that democracy will undermine stability and hinder economic development. Moreover, to the extent that there is support for democracy, it appears to be for a form of democracy that emphasizes meritocracy and good governance by a technocratic elite, and thus is consistent with a leading role for the state.[79] In short, although cultural arguments are easily overstated and less persuasive in light of the success of Taiwan and other Asian countries in implementing democracy, it is possible that democracy will be slower in coming to the PRC as a result of the prevailing political culture.

One of the assumptions of the evolutionary convergence theory is that economic development will give rise to a middle class and a vibrant civil society that will demand political reforms and ultimately democracy. In China, the middle class remains small in numbers, and civil society limited in size.[80] Moreover, the rise of a middle class and civil society is clearly not sufficient for democracy. As important as the size of the middle class and civil society is their political orientation and their relationship with the state. Many of the commercial and social groups that have emerged in China are often not very supportive of democracy.[81] On the contrary, they are often bound to the state by clientelist ties, and thus may see it in their interest to oppose political reforms that would lead to more transparency and accountability and threaten their privileged positions. For the most part, the newly rich seem more interested in maintaining the status quo and hanging on to their newly acquired possessions and income streams than in running the risk of social instability by promoting political reform.

Daniel Lynch paints a grim picture of what might happen if China were forced to embark on political reforms in the absence of a more robust and democratically oriented civil society.[82] In his view, the Party's loss of control over "thought work" combined with an economic recession could generate a genuine political crisis. At the same time, the absence of open political discussion and the failure to develop a liberal public sphere suggest that an imminent transition to democracy is not likely. Accordingly, the demise of the authoritarian propaganda state could result in public-sphere "praetorianism" – that is, uninstitutionalized and chaotic patterns of political participation in which groups activated by economic reforms "compete nakedly in politics by using whatever form of participation in which they have a comparative advantage: business people pay bribes, workers strike, military officers stage coups."

Whatever the likelihood of this scenario actually occurring, it does highlight the importance of institutions. Even if Party leaders were prepared to sanction genuine democracy at all levels, democracy would not be possible at this point because China currently lacks the necessary institutions to make it work.[83] Although proponents of creeping democratization see village elections, the strengthening of the people's congresses, and legal reforms as harbingers of political reform, democratization in China is currently hindered by the lack of sufficient experience with elections and the public's unfamiliarity with the likely candidates for top positions, the low level of competence of the legislatures, and the weakness of the legal system.

Local elections in Taiwan contributed to the gradual evolution of democracy by demonstrating to Guomindang leaders that they stood a good chance of being reelected provided they were able to perform adequately while in office and satisfy the demands of their constituents.[84] Local elections also provided valuable experience in the mechanics of how to hold an election and to campaign for office. Will experiments in the PRC with village elections prove to be a catalyst for greater democratization, as in Taiwan? At present, democratic elections have been held only at the grass-roots level – primarily in villages and more recently for positions on urban neighbor committees.[85] Moreover, skeptics note that the village elections were a response to the breakdown of Party control in the countryside and justified primarily on instrumental grounds. Indeed, some Party leaders supported village elections as a way of strengthening the Party. Elections would enhance the legitimacy of local cadres, and be a way of recruiting talented new members, thus rejuvenating the Party. In practice, local Party officials have resisted village elections, and often have sought to determine the outcome by hook or by crook. Ironically, recent studies suggest that as villagers become more affluent, they show less interest in elections.[86]

Of course, citizens might take more interest in elections were they fairer and more meaningful. One would expect people to be more interested in electing higher-level officials who exercise real power than in electing village committee members who may have little power and in practice answer to the Party secretary and county leaders. Also on the positive side, village elections have provided valuable experience in how

to carry out elections in a country in which many of the citizens are illiterate. In the long run, it is possible that local elections will give rise to
expectations among the citizenry that they should be able to choose
their own leaders. Meanwhile, the ruling regime may come to perceive
elections as less of a threat, or at least see the benefits in meeting citizen
demand for increasingly higher-level elections. Over time, therefore, a
practice of genuine elections might evolve.

Similarly, over time the NPC and people's congresses may provide
an institutional basis for promoting democratization. The experiences
of other authoritarian states such as Poland, Hungary, Taiwan, and the
former Soviet Union demonstrate that legislatures may become an alternative source of normative authority to challenge the Party even in
the absence of democracy.[87] Indeed, the NPC already has achieved some
degree of normative authority, as evidenced by its increasing willingness to oppose Party intervention in the legislation process and reject or
criticize Party-approved candidates.[88] According to some analysts, the
NPC has even become a force for a budding constitutionalism in China
by legitimating new forms and norms of public participation, which
have begun to spill over to other political institutions.[89] There are even
signs of increasing elite tolerance for diverse viewpoints and dissenting
views, suggesting that pluralism may be becoming more accepted and
institutionalized.

On the other hand, the independence and the authority of the NPC
and local people's congresses should not be overstated. The normative
authority of people's congresses is limited by the Party's control of the
process of selecting delegates. The NPC still rarely votes down laws, and
has yet to reject a key appointee. Moreover, local people's congresses have
chosen to trade off their independence and autonomy for effectiveness by
aligning themselves with higher-level people's congresses.[90] And despite
the efforts to raise the level of competence, people's congresses are still
oversized and unwieldy and dominated by part-time legislators who
meet infrequently.

The efforts to build up the legal profession, strengthen the legal system, and implement rule of law provide for a form of political reform
without democracy by limiting the arbitrary acts of the state. They also
may provide the basis for further political reforms. On the other hand,
the legal profession, like the rising middle class more generally, seems
more preoccupied with making money than political reforms, as noted

in Chapter 8. Meanwhile, at present, the judiciary lacks the minimal independence and authority required to ensure that candidates and citizens are able to exercise those rights needed to participate effectively in democratic elections.

Liberal democracy and human rights

The experiences of other countries demonstrates that democracy need not lead to greater protection for human rights, and may even be antithetical in some cases to extensive protection of rights for everyone. Democracy simply provides majoritarian rule. Majorities may happily and willingly trample on the rights of minorities and individuals who espouse different ideas, choose alternative lifestyles, or deviate from the views and practices of the majority. Accordingly, one of the central functions, if not the central function, of rights as conceived in the Western liberal democratic tradition is to prevent the tyranny of the majority. In this view, rights function like trumps in a card game: that is, as trumps, rights impose limits on the interests of others, the good of society, and the will of the majority. In Dworkinian terms, "a right is a claim that it would be wrong for the government to deny an individual even though it would be in the general interest to do so;"[91] in Nozickian, "individuals have rights and there are things no person or group may do to them";[92] in Rawlsian, "each person possesses an inviolability founded on justice that even the welfare of society as a whole cannot override."[93]

Although China has signed numerous international human rights treaties, including recently the International Covenant on Civil and Political Rights, the government continues to promote an interpretation of human rights that challenges the universality of certain rights and exposes fundamental differences in the way rights are conceived and the purposes they are meant to serve. China's human rights policy rests on several pillars.[94] First, although some rights are universal, their interpretation and implementation depends on local circumstances, including the level of economic development, cultural practices, and fundamental values that are not the same in all countries. Second, rights must be prioritized, and the international human rights community and Western countries inappropriately privilege civil and political rights over other rights, including economic, social, and cultural rights, and collective rights such as the rights of countries to development. In China, given its current level of economic development and huge population, subsistence is the most fundamental right. Moreover, stability is a prerequisite for the enjoyment of all rights. The need to ensure economic development and stability justifies limitations on the exercise of civil and political rights. Third, the international human rights regime assumes a liberal democratic framework and emphasizes implicitly, and in some cases explicitly, individual autonomy to a degree not found in other traditions. Greater weight should be placed on the interests of groups within society, of the society as a whole, and of the state. Moreover, the emphasis on rights should not obscure the importance of duties and the responsibilities of individuals toward others. Fourth, countries often use human rights as an excuse for strong-arm politics and to interfere in China's domestic affairs. Fifth, and related, international human rights and the ability of the international community to raise claims based on such rights are limited by sovereignty. Sixth, many of the countries that criticize China for human rights violations have their own problems with human rights at home.

It is important to note that the PRC government is not rejecting rights wholesale. Rather, the debate is over a broad range of more specific issues, including what should be considered a right; how different rights are to be prioritized; the importance of rights as a way of ordering society relative to other means such as relying on virtue-based character-building; how rights are to be interpreted and implemented in practice; what remedies should be available if rights are violated; and when and how other countries and international rights organizations may encroach upon state sovereignty in the name of addressing alleged rights violations. These are difficult issues. Reasonable people can and do disagree, both in China and abroad. At the same time, not all of Beijing's positions are tenable. There are many human rights violations occurring in China that simply cannot be justified.

Two wrongs don't make a right: strong-arm politics and the limits of sovereignty

In recent years, Asian countries have denounced what they considered to be self-righteous preaching by Western states. Every year, for instance, the US State Department issues a report on the human rights record of many countries, including China. In response, China has begun to issue its own report on human rights violations in the USA. One report observed that there are more than 2 million cases of criminal violence in the USA every year, five times as many per capita as in China; that there are 180,000 rapes per year in the USA, eighteen times as many as in China; that there are five times as many Americans incarcerated on a per capita basis; that there are 7 million homeless in the USA; and that in one of the richest countries of the world, eighty people died from the cold during one winter storm.[95]

China and other Asian governments are right to point out that Western countries have committed atrocities in other countries in the past and have their own human rights problems. On the other hand, two wrongs do not make a right. That the USA or any other country has problems of its own does not justify human rights violations in China or excuse China from meeting its obligations under PRC and international law. Each country must be held accountable for their human rights violations and take the necessary steps to stop such violations.

At the same time, foreign governments and rights advocates should appreciate the fact that many Chinese view the human rights policies of Western countries, particularly the USA, as hypocritical and a form of strong-arm politics.[96] Many Chinese today are particularly sensitive about infringements on China's national sovereignty in part because of the decades of bullying by foreign imperial powers. Furthermore, they feel that China is being treated by a double standard. The USA sits idly by while gross violations of human rights occur in Rwanda and East Timor, and yet is quick to criticize China even though most Chinese enjoy more extensive freedoms and a better standard of living than ever before.[97] Behind the double standard, they suspect, lies the desire of the USA and other developed countries to contain China and prevent it from emerging as a rival superpower. Even Chinese rights advocates view with suspicion, if not derision, the attempts to link commercial issues such as renewal of China's Most Favored Nation status, market access concerns, and entrance to the WTO, to improvement on certain human rights issues, especially those involving civil and political rights. The USA's credibility is further undermined when business interests win out and China's MFN status is renewed or its accession to the WTO supported, despite the State Department's acknowledgment that the human rights situation in China did not improve and may even have worsened.

Having stirred up nationalist sentiments, Chinese leaders cannot afford to be seen as toadying to foreigners or succumbing to foreign pressure. Accordingly, Beijing is quick to declare any attempt to censure China for its human rights record a violation of sovereignty and an affront to the dignity of the Chinese people. China is not the only country to claim that foreign countries and international human rights bodies are permitted to intervene in another country's affairs only when there is a consistent and systematic practice of gross violations.[98] Nor is China alone in viewing international human rights as a threat to sovereignty.[99] Nor is China's position wholly without legal basis. In support, Beijing points to Article 2 of the Charter of the United Nations, which states: "Nothing contained in the present Charter shall authorize the United Nations to intervene in matters which are essentially within the domestic jurisdiction of any state."[100]

China's appeals to sovereignty, however, are undermined to a considerable extent by its membership in the UN, its accession to various international human rights treaties, general customary international law principles that do not rely on the consent of states, and its own participation in the UN's imposition of sanctions on South Africa as well as its support of resolutions condemning human rights violations in Afghanistan and the Israeli Occupied Territories.[101] It would be hypocritical for China to participate in the condemnation and penalization of other states for violating human rights and yet assert that the UN and other countries are interfering in China's domestic affairs when they do the same. On the other hand, allowing that China's sovereignty defenses fail in some circumstances does not mean that China's sovereignty concerns are never justified. Nor does it resolve all or even most of the more specific hotly contested issues such as whether the content, interpretation, and implementation of rights will vary depending on cultural values and practices or whether China may limit civil and political rights to secure economic growth and social stability.

"Asian values" and the significance of culture

The PRC government argues that human rights turn to some extent on cultural values and traditions, and that while the human rights movement emphasizes the universality of rights, cultural differences cannot and should not be ignored.[102] Human rights norms are inevitably subject to cultural mediation.[103] Without local support, legally prescribed rights are a dead letter. One need only reflect on the experience in the USA with enforcement of Supreme Court desegregation rulings in the South in the 1960s to appreciate that point.

To allow that culture is important is not to claim that there is something essentialistic about a culture or that culture is monolithic or unchanging. Nor is it to claim that cultures need be preserved. Jack Donnelly, a well-known advocate for the universality of rights, puts the point succinctly and bluntly: "Cultural traditions are socially created legacies. Some are good. Some are bad. Still others are simply irrelevant."[104]

While culture is clearly important from a pragmatic perspective in that cultural beliefs and practices may aid or impede the promotion and protection of rights, whether culture is *morally* relevant in determining what rights there should be or how they should be interpreted or implemented remains contested. Again, reasonable people will disagree, as they will over many other related issues. For instance, how does one justify the superiority of contemporary rights over traditional values? Does it matter whether one is arguing from within the particular tradition or from outside of it? Is there some neutral or objective moral standard to which one may appeal?[105]

There is good reason to be skeptical about Beijing's recourse to the self-serving rhetoric of "Asian values" to justify limitations on the exercise of civil and political liberties that could lead to the downfall of the ruling regime. Yet one should not be too quick to dismiss Beijing's attempt to play the cultural card as merely a cynical strategy seized upon by an authoritarian regime to deny its citizens their rights. There are also legitimate differences in values at stake and legitimate differences of opinion over key issues.

The criticism that the PRC government uses culture as an excuse to deny citizens their rights speaks to the motives of the government, but tells us little about the substantive merits of its position. No Asian government would appeal to "Asian values" unless such values resonated with the attitudes of its constituency. The government's invocation of culture may be politically motivated and yet still accurately reflect the views of the majority of the people. There are, of course, many voices in the PRC, including a liberal democratic one. Yet the liberal democrats are the minority. Empirical studies show at present a population illiberal

in attitudes and more concerned about economic growth than civil and
political liberties.

The economics of rights

Although the Asian values debate is often depicted as a clash of civi-
lizations and cultures, many disputes turn on claims about economic
issues. Asian governments, including China, regularly argue for the so-
called *liberty tradeoff*: civil and political freedoms must take a back seat
to economic development.[106] Although usually not as expressly stated,
there is also tacit acceptance of an *equity tradeoff*: economic growth
will not benefit all equally, and may in the short term actually increase
inequality and make some of the least well off even worse off.[107] Nevertheless, growth continues to be pursued in the belief that the immediate
task is to make the pie bigger, with redistribution of the pieces to come
later.

Donnelly denies that any country needs to make either tradeoff.[108] He
notes that denying civil and political rights has its costs. Officials who
are not held accountable by a free press and disciplined by genuinely
contested elections are easily corrupted. Other critics argue that if any
rights are to be compromised in the process of development, it should
be economic rights rather than civil and political rights as the former
can only be satisfied in reasonably wealthy states whereas even poor
states can provide the latter.[109] Amartya Sen points out that the debate
about tradeoffs assumes an instrumental view of rights (or a utilitarian
or consequentialist view) as opposed to one where rights have intrinsic
value (a deontological view). But as with the arguments for democracy,
whether rights should be conceived of as intrinsic goods, and even if
they are, when intrinsically valuable rights may be traded off to secure
other goods and instrumental gains, are deeply disputed philosophical
issues both in China and abroad.[110]

Although the empirical evidence regarding the relationship between
democracy, civil and political rights, and economic development is
mixed, it is doubtful that more empirical studies will be of much use because China, like other Asian governments, typically presents "*narrower*
justifications for curbing *particular* rights in *particular* contexts for
particular economic or political purposes."[111] As Bauer and Bell

remark, "trade-off arguments for rights violations cannot be refuted solely by appealing to general principles." Each time Beijing attempts to justify a repressive policy as necessary for stability – whether the crackdown on Falungong, the restrictions on the religious practice of Tibet an monks, or the limitations placed on the freedom of speech, assembly, and association of individual academics, democracy advocates, or political organizations – a context-specific examination is required to determine whether the social crisis is real and the government is employing the least restrictive (or at least a proportionate) means to overcome it.

In some cases, such an examination may lead to the conclusion that the government has not acted appropriately. Needless to say, the desire for stability does not give the government free license. No government is free to engage in genocide or to murder or torture its citizens. Even in times of crisis, governments must meet certain minimal standards with respect to due process and fair trials.[112] Neither has Beijing nor any other Asian government evoked Asian values to justify torture or genocide. Agreement on such issues, however, still leaves considerable room for disagreement and variation on other issues.

Overlapping consensus? From theory to practice

It would not be necessary to sort out the limits of acceptable differences and the proper response to unacceptable differences were it possible to obtain a genuine, unforced overlapping consensus on rights issues.[113] The likelihood of obtaining a consensus on rights turns largely on whether one is referring to a consensus as to the content of a wish list of rights that are considered, all else being equal, good things to have; the justifications for such rights; the correct interpretation of such rights; or the proper implementation of such rights. Unfortunately, at present a meaningful consensus on human rights remains more of a hope than a reality, particularly when one turns away from generalizations about the value of rights to actual practice and the way rights are implemented in the real world.

The so-called International Bill of Rights – the Universal Declaration of Human Rights, International Covenant on Economic, Social and Cultural Rights, and the International Covenant on Civil and Political

Rights – sets out a lengthy and impressive bill of rights. These rights include, among many others, the right to: life, liberty, and security of person; protection against torture, protection against arbitrary arrest and detention; the presumption of innocence; access to legal remedies for rights violations; social security, work under favorable conditions, rest and leisure; food, clothing, and housing; health care and social services, special protection for children; protection of minority cultures; self-determination; and a social and international order needed to realize all of these rights.

This lengthy list of rights raises numerous problems for anyone claiming an overlapping consensus. First, even though it is already quite a long list, it is by no means the entire list of rights included in the International Bill of Rights. Nor does the even longer list exhaust all of the rights advocated by rights proponents. To take a few examples suggested by participants from Asian countries in the 1993 Bangkok workshop, there are the rights of the elderly, the rights accorded to the dead in Islam, and the rights of cultural communities to their ancestral domains. The ever-expanding list of rights reflects the tendency in modern society to translate every possible good into the language of rights. This unchecked inflation of rights discourse threatens to rob rights of their value and to undermine any possibility of a meaningful consensus on rights. If rights are considered legal entitlements possessed primarily by individuals vis-à-vis the state and nonstate actors, then the longer the list the more controversial it will be, particularly with respect to positive rights as opposed to negative rights, i.e. those rights that require the government not just to refrain from doing something but to provide some particular benefit, such as the right to food, clothing, and housing.[114] Even if rights are considered to be moral entitlements as opposed to legal entitlements, something to which one should be entitled in an ideal world, many of the rights listed in the International Bill of Rights will be controversial. Libertarians, for instance, might question whether individuals have rights to social security and housing, especially if these rights are given a broad interpretation. Others might question whether all minority cultures deserve to be protected regardless of the nature of the culture, and whether any such right implies that all of the particular practices of a culture must be protected.

Even assuming some broad consensus with respect to the general desirability of most of the items on the list, all else being equal, there is little reason to expect that there will be a consensus with respect to the justifications for such rights. Aristoeleans would justify rights in one way, Platonists another, Kantians another, utilitarians, Buddhists, Muslims, Confucians, Neo-Confucians, New Confucians, Statist Socialists, Neoauthoritarians, Communitarians, liberals, libertarians, civic republicans, postmodern postegalitarian new age yet-to-be-discovered sects in still other ways. While it is possible that there will be some common ground with respect to some rights, one should not be too optimistic about resolving such philosophically contentious issues as the justification for rights in general or for many specific rights any time soon.

One might argue that *how* one justifies a right is not important so long as the rights are realized in practice. That different traditions ground rights in different ways not only does not undermine a meaningful consensus on rights, it makes such a consensus more likely. People may disagree about what makes a right important but still agree that it is important. By leaving rights incompletely theorized, different individuals, traditions, and schools of thought are free to support rights for their own reasons.[115]

The problem with leaving rights incompletely theorized and ignoring justifications for rights by shifting the focus to the pragmatic issue of whether rights are realized in practice is that it doesn't work.[116] Rights must be interpreted to be implemented. The broad language of international human rights documents leaves considerable room for interpretation. Taken together, the various international rights agreements may be internally incoherent and at minimum permit widely divergent interpretations and great flexibility in implementation, in part precisely because they were the result of a negotiated process. For instance, Article 29(2) of the Universal Declaration of Human Rights provides:

> In the exercise of his rights and freedoms, everyone shall be subject only to such limitations as are determined by law solely for the purpose of securing due recognition and respect for the rights and freedoms of others and of meeting the just requirements of morality, public order and the general welfare in a democratic society.

This article alone permits such wide latitude in interpretation and implementation as to challenge any claim to an overlapping consensus. If anything, it points to a lack of a meaningful consensus, an inability to say anything terribly meaningful about the circumstances in which a government is justified in restricting the rights of individuals. What exactly are these "just requirements of morality, public order and the general welfare" to which one's rights are subject? Even allowing that such terms may over time come to have more definite meanings as cases are adjudicated and an international practice begins to emerge, there will always be considerable room for differences of opinion over their interpretation and application in particular contexts.[117]

Interpretation will depend on a number of factors, including international practices and one's own values, beliefs, and worldview, as well as contingent, context-specific factors such as the current level of economic development and existing political and legal institutions. Assuming one accepts that everyone has a right to food, clothing, and housing, exactly what type of food, clothing, and housing are required? Does it matter if the annual per capita GNP of the country is $100 or $10,000? And what exactly is required by way of protection against arbitrary arrest and detention? Miranda warnings? May the police and immigration officers compel anyone who behaves suspiciously to give a urine sample, and if the sample turns up positive for drug use compel them to undergo treatment?[118] May the government require citizens to attend monthly neighborhood meetings to receive government directives and discuss community affairs?[119] May the state in the name of strengthening the family impose a duty on children to support their parents?[120] Does religious freedom extend to sects that advise people to refrain from obtaining medical treatment and rely instead on meditation and breathing exercises to cure themselves? In what circumstances can free speech be restricted in the name of public order and national stability? What is the proper standard – clear and present danger? How clear and imminent must the danger be? And who gets to decide —the regime in control or some international rights commission?

To be sure, there may be consensus on some interpretive issues. Clearly some interpretations are not reasonable by any standard, whether the standards of the international rights community or the standards of the country that is violating the right. Moreover, whatever the initial scope of consensus on particular issues, that scope can be expanded by engaging in intra- and inter-cultural discussions about rights. Such discussions will be more successful if they are based on mutual respect and carried out with sensitivity to the views of others.

Conclusion

Those who think democracy and human rights may not be the answer to a particular country's problems at a particular time often accuse their liberal universalist counterparts of being ethnocentric, suggesting that the universalist's views are the product of a misguided, hegemonic imperialism – images of the ugly American impervious to cultural differences spring to mind. Although the description may fit in some cases to some extent, it tends to focus the discussion on the motives of the party rather than the substance of the arguments – the empirical and normative issues that underlie the claim that democracy and human rights in some form and to some degree are universally applicable goods. Given the prima facie appeal of democracy and human rights around the world and the evils of the more popular alternatives, liberals need not apologize for their suggestion that other countries would do well to adopt some form of democracy and rights. Nor need liberals shy away from confronting dictators bent on genocide, in the name of some misguided notion of liberal tolerance. At the same time, liberals need to bear in mind that the world is a big place and people have different values and ways of doing things. Not everyone shares the predilection for liberal values: for diversity, autonomy, and authority-challenging individuals.

Many Western political theorists, politicians, and citizens simply assume that everyone wants to be like the West.[121] All too often the preliminary questions of whether China needs democracy, and if so whether it needs *liberal* democracy, are simply rejected out of hand as heresy. Indeed, many universalists and ethnocentric liberals are quick to criticize those who do not share their fondness for one-size-fits-all-made-in-America solutions for serving, perhaps unwittingly, as apologists for corrupt tyrants. Again, the criticism should not be dismissed out of hand. In many cases, to a lesser or greater extent, the accusation may be accurate. We must always ask what are the alternatives to democracy and liberal human rights? What are the weaknesses of the proposed alternatives?[122] Who benefits and who loses? In this case, motives seem somewhat more relevant simply because political systems that deny people the right to vote are often dominated by elitist groups whose self-interest is a major obstacle to the realization of democracy. Surely there is no need to accept at face value the self-serving claims of leaders in Beijing that authoritarian rule is necessary to prevent China from degenerating into social chaos. Nor is it necessary to accept uncritically the worried cries of elites that China's rural peasants are not educated or sophisticated enough to vote. Similarly, we should be wary of the claims of China specialists whose careers have been built largely on finding interesting differences between the traditions, philosophies, and political systems of China and the West. Countries are not locked into their past. Democracy was alien to Western countries too. Our forefathers also had reservations about giving the vote to the masses. Meanwhile many Asian countries, for their part, have broken out of the fetters of their authoritarian pasts to adopt some version of democracy and human rights.

Clearly we want to avoid becoming the apologist of dictators. But what separates apologia from genuine disagreement? Again, focusing too much on the motives of the parties may detract from important substantive issues. PRC leaders who worry about disorder may be motivated by self-interest – but they may be right to worry. Elites who fear the dramatic changes that might result from giving the vote to China's rural majority may be thinking of their own place in society – but their fears may be legitimate. Only a context-specific examination of the arguments pro and con will tell. Liberals often claim that whether China would be better off with democracy and human rights is just an empirical question. Just as aspirin is effective in curing our headaches and thinning our blood, so democracy is effective at producing greater human happiness.[123] As we have seen, however, the empirical record is ambiguous with respect to the merits of democracy.[124] And in any event, even if some form of democracy and human rights may be desirable, liberals champion a particular liberal version that goes beyond support for the medicinal effects of a generic drug to favor one particular brand over various competitors. Just as different brands of headache medicine may work better for different individuals, so may different versions of democracy and human rights suit different countries.

Any claim about the applicability and desirability of democracy and human rights is both an empirical and a normative claim. Promoting democracy and human rights inevitably raises important normative issues that implicate our most fundamental values and our views about the relationship between the individual and the state and the proper balance between the individual and the group. Taking rights seriously means that in some cases the rights of the individual will trump the will of the majority and perhaps even what is in the interest of society as a whole. Liberals concede these and other costs but are willing to accept them. Others may reasonably disagree.

On the whole, rights may be more destabilizing in China than elsewhere.[125] Undoubtedly, civil and political rights are more of a threat to the regime's ability to maintain social order than in some other more stable countries. Moreover, the ruling regime has yet to develop political institutions for adequately addressing rights claims. Nor is there a reasonably coherent theoretical framework that incorporates rights and yet is consistent with the regime's norms.

But if we are to make any headway in addressing the normative issue of the value of democracy and human rights we need to draw a distinction between the core institutions of democracy and basic human rights and the liberal values that undergird one particular version of democracy and human rights. There most likely will be more agreement as to the merits of certain institutions and some basic rights than over a particular liberal version of democracy and rights. Liberals favor autonomy, diversity, self-realization, and individuals who constantly challenge authority. Even assuming most Chinese come to support certain democratic institutions and the basic rights necessary to make these institutions work – a free press, a free judiciary, free universities, an apolitical civil service, and nongovernmental organizations – they are still unlikely to support the more contentious litany of liberal values.

Yet the main point of contention is over the values that support democracy and human rights and give it a different shape and feel in different countries. Values are important because they will affect the choice of institutions or particular institutional arrangements as well as where a society draws the line on specific issues. Even if Chinese citizens accept the principles of a free press and free speech, they must still decide how those principles are to be interpreted and implemented in practice.

At the end of the day, it is hard to imagine that in the long run, China will not adopt the basic institutions of democracy. But it is equally hard to imagine that the purpose of democracy in China will be to create the widest possible range of diversity and defiant individuals who challenge authority at every turn. It is precisely because of such fundamentally different goals and orientations that we will be able to enjoy diversity on a global scale. China is obligated to provide political dissidents with the rights conferred on them by the PRC constitution and various international treaties to which China is a signatory and under international customary law. Yet Chinese citizens may not want to see China become just another France or Germany, much less the USA, with its inner city war zones populated by gun-toting teenagers not likely to see their twenty-first birthday.[126] They may rightly believe that such "diversity" is not useful in China, or for that matter anywhere. In some respects, it may be too late for Western liberal democracies and the USA in particular to turn back the clock and avoid some of the extremes of radical diversity, autonomy, and individualism. But it may not be too late for China. As a late bloomer, China may be able to take some lessons from its liberal predecessors and avoid some of the dysfunctional practices of the USA or other liberal democracies. In any event, it is not unreasonable for Chinese citizens to aspire to such an alternative vision of democracy and human rights. Accordingly, it is not unreasonable for China to pursue an alternative to a liberal democratic conception of law. For now, rule of law is a desirable alternative in that it allows for political reform without democracy and provides the ideological basis and institutional means for limiting the government. While law cannot by itself resolve all social tensions resulting from deep social cleavages, the implementation of rule of law is a feasible intermediate point along the way to an as yet undetermined form of Chinese democracy.

Notes

1 As the political scientist Judith Shklar wryly remarked about the elements of a thin rule of law: "As a legal ideal for us there is little to either accept or reject in this conventional list of lawyerly aspirations. It is its moral status that...seems unsure." Shklar (1987: 13).

2 Lipset (1959); see also Dahl (1971).

3 See, for example, McCormick and Kelly (1994); He (1996); Ravich (2000).

4 For a recent statement of this view, see Ravich (2000).

5 As incomes rise, citizens are likely to increasingly see democracy as intrinsically valuable. See Trebilcock (1997). See also Inglehart (1997).

6 See Diamond (1996) for a discussion of the problems with the third wave of democratization.

7 See Fukuyama (1992).

8 See Huntington (1991).

9 Some pragmatic liberals, including Richard Rorty, share the end-of-history liberal's belief in the superiority of liberal democracy and liberal values, but are more cautious about declaring them to be the end of history. Realizing that

many other political theories claiming to transcend space and time turned out to be nothing more than the contingent narrative of a particular people at a particular time, Rorty readily acknowledges the contingency of liberal democracy on what he calls our culture of rights and bourgeois freedoms. Nevertheless, he remains unabashedly ethnocentric, championing on pragmatic grounds liberal democracy and liberal values as the best alternative available for all countries at this time. See Rorty (1989; 2000). For a critique of Rorty's ironic liberalism as a basis for Chinese democracy and human rights, see Peerenboom (2000b; 2000c).

10   As freedom of association, assembly, speech, and press are generally articulated in terms of rights, this dimension could be referred to as the (participatory) rights dimension. However, a polity could provide for these practices without conceiving of them in terms of rights. For instance, although these practices existed in classical Athens, they were not conceived of as rights. These participatory rights are of course only a limited subset of civil and political rights and of rights more generally, which include social, economic, cultural, and collective rights.

11   Schumpeter (1943) emphasized the first two dimensions in his influential conception of democracy. In discussing the reasons why China's repeated experiments with democracies since the turn of the twentieth century have failed, Nathan (1997: 64) discusses the first two dimensions but not the third. This is all the more striking in that he discusses shortcomings in China's institutions as one possible explanation yet does not mention the problems caused by a weak legal system.

   The Universal Declaration of Human Rights (UDHR) and the International Covenant on Civil and Political Rights (ICCPR) do not expressly require democracy in their operative clauses regarding political participation (though both restrict limitations on certain rights to those necessary in a democratic society). Rather the ICCPR, art. 25, provides: "Every citizen shall have the right and the opportunity, without any of the distinctions mentioned in article 2 and without unreasonable restrictions: (a) To take part in the conduct of public affairs, directly or through freely chosen representatives; (b) To vote and to be elected at genuine periodic elections which shall be by universal and equal suffrage and shall be held by secret ballot, guaranteeing the free expression of the will of the electors." These provisions are vague in several respects. They do not explicitly require contested elections at all levels of government between multiple parties. Nor do they define what is required by way of political participation beyond elections, if anything. See Steiner (1988).

12   Although the ICCPR assumes a legal system capable of protecting rights, there is no mention of rule of law. In contrast, the UDHR declares in the preamble that "human rights should be protected by the rule of law." Barro (1997) notes that there is little empirical evidence that rule of law promotes political freedom. That is, rule of law is consistent with nondemocratic, nonliberal forms of government.

13   I prefer rights-based democracy to the more common *liberal democracy* because the latter is ambiguous; it may refer to any form of rights-based

democracy where rights place limits on the majority or to a particular liberal version of rights-based democracy that emphasizes individual rights and autonomy. Thus, rights-based democracy is consistent with Communitarian and Liberal Democratic rule of law, whereas liberal rights-based democracy is only consistent with Liberal Democratic rule of law.

Further, although some (for example, Zakaria: 1997; Diamond: 1996) characterize any democracy that does not adopt liberal values as "illiberal" democracy, I refer to forms of rights-based democracy that do not adopt liberal values as nonliberal democracies because the term "illiberal" seems unduly prejudicial and pejorative. A nonliberal democracy might include for instance a nonneutral understanding of the state, an emphasis on a rationalistic and legal technocracy that manages the state, and the development of a managed rather than a critical public space and civil society. See Bell *et al.* (1995). While offering a defense of such regimes, Bell refers to such regimes as illiberal rather than nonliberal.

14   The distinction between majoritarian democracy and rights-based democracy should not be overdrawn. While conceptually distinct, in practice they exist on a continuum. Most majoritarian democrats recognize some instances where individual rights trump majority rule while, conversely, rights-based democrats and even liberal rights-based democrats recognize instances where the will of the majority prevails over the claims of individuals. Put differently, there are very few if any pure majoritarian democrats.

Conservatives, communitarians, and liberals – as those terms are used in the USA – are all rights-based democrats in the sense that they all believe at least in certain circumstances that the rights of the individual override the democratic majoritarian decision-making process. But conservatives, communitarians, and liberals differ as to how often and for what reasons the rights of the individual should trump the will of the majority. Liberals tend to side with the individual more often, casting a broader and more impenetrable web of protective rights around the individual, than their fellow conservative or communitarian rights-based democrats.

15   Diamond and Myers (2000).

16   Even the participatory process rights could be interpreted in a variety of ways. See Bell (2000: 108); Steiner (1988).

17   Cross (1999) claims that researchers have focused on such factors as national wealth and civil unrest as keys to human rights while ignoring the role of law and legal institutions. Accordingly, he conducted a cross-national test of the effects of codification of a right in the constitution, judicial independence, federalism, separation of powers, and the relative number of lawyers on the protection of political rights and on the right against search and seizure. He found that judicial independence and the number of lawyers were significantly associated with greater protection of political rights, though the number of lawyers was not significant with respect to protection against search and seizure.

18   Dahl (1989: 100) calls this Presumption of Personal Autonomy: in the absence of a compelling showing to the contrary everyone should be assumed to be

the best judge of his or her own good or interests. In Chapter 2, I referred to this as the epistemic equality premise and noted that this premise has been rejected by Confucians and the CCP.

19   For a critique of the justification of democracy on grounds of popular sovereignty and self-government, see Rubin (2001).

20   In Chapter 2, I referred to this view as the normative equality premise: to treat someone with respect and dignity and equal concern requires that we not impose our views on that person. As noted, the rejection of the epistemic equality premise calls into question the normative equality premise.

21   Derived from Locke, Dahl (1989: 85) refers to this notion as the Idea of Intrinsic Equality.

22   This is often referred to as the Principle of Equal Consideration of Interests. See Dahl (1989: 85).

23   Among the critiques relating to China, see Bell (2000); Pan Wei (2001).

24   Hall and Ames (1987).

25   See the discussion of criminal behavior in Chapter 8.

26   A survey of academics, think tank experts, officials, businesspeople, journalists, and religious and cultural leaders found significant differences between Asians and Americans. The former chose an orderly society, harmony, and accountability of public values, in descending order, as the three most important societal values. In contrast, the Americans chose freedom of expression, personal freedom, and the rights of the individual. See Sim (1995). See also Chan (2002); Bell *et al.* (1995); Bell (2000); Peerenboom (1998a).

27   Whether it is even equal in a formal sense is debatable. Pan Wei (2001) points out that inequality of votes is often deliberately designed through "electoral engineering," such as the division and size of electoral districts, the number of candidates in each district, and in "winner takes all" systems.

28   Dreze and Sen (1989).

29   The so-called theory of democratic peace has come under attack recently, however. See, for example, Layne (1994); Farber and Gowa (1995).

30   Nathan (1986a).

31   Wright (1997).

32   See, for example, Yali Peng (1998). See also Minxin Pei (1997b), who cites polls showing that two-thirds of the people thought that the economic situation was improving while half thought their own living standards were improving, and that the majority of respondents (54%) placed a higher priority on economic development than democracy. Over two-thirds of those polled supported the government's policy of promoting economic growth and social stability, and 63% agreed that "it would be a disaster for China to experience a similar change as that in the former Soviet Union." Even 10% of non-CCP member respondents said they voluntarily supported the same political position as the CCP. Similarly, a poll by Lollar (1997) found that 60% of respondents assigned highest priority to maintaining order, while another 30% chose controlling inflation, whereas only 8% chose giving people more say in political decisions and free elections, and only 2% chose protecting free speech. See also Wan

Ming (1998), who cites survey data showing growing support for the Party and concludes that a development consensus that emphasizes stability has emerged. Still another study showed Chinese to be the least tolerant of diverse viewpoints among all of the countries surveyed. It also found little support for a free press and the publishing of alternative views. See Nathan and Shi (1993).

Granted, polling results must be used with caution. Often, the design of the question influences the outcome, as may be the case when people are simply asked to choose between economic growth and democracy. Moreover, respondents may feel inhibited, and provide what they feel are safe answers or the answers desired by the pollsters. On the other hand, as Bell notes (2000: 179), some surveys are designed to minimize the feeling of inhibition on the part of the respondent by asking them to comment on what they believe to be the values or views of others in society, while other studies rely on an analysis of a culture's heroic figures. Further, as Wan Ming (1998) observes, PRC nationals living abroad often make similar arguments about democracy and economic growth and exhibit similar values. Nor are such views limited to mainland PRC citizens. When asked to choose between democracy and economic prosperity and political stability, 71% of Hong Kong residents chose the latter, and only 20% chose democracy. In addition, almost 90% preferred a stable and peaceful handover to insisting on increasing the pace of democracy. Cited in Bell (2000: 119).

33   It is much easier to be bold in proposing reforms when it is someone else that will suffer the consequences. The USA is a stable place; China is much less stable. People in the USA have a comfortable life; many in China are living precariously on the edge. The Cultural Revolution provides a relatively recent reminder of the capacity for China to erupt into violence. Pursuing reforms in a way least likely to lead to chaos strikes me as prudent. What does not seem prudent is for the regime to stick its head in the sand and not move forward with political reform, because the failure to reform is likely to lead to regime collapse and chaos.

34   For a summary of these arguments, see generally, Przeworski and Limongi (1993); Trebilcock (1997); Chua (1998).

35   Based on the Gastil ranking of seventy countries for political rights and civil liberties, including rule of law and the independence of the judiciary, Scully (1991) found that from 1950–85, politically open societies grew at a rate of 2.5% per year compared to a 1.4% rate for politically closed societies, and that societies that comply with "rule of law" grew at a 2.8% rate compared to 1.2% for societies where state rights take precedence over individual rights.

Przeworski and Limongi (1993), however, reviewed eighteen surveys that produced twenty-one results, and found that eight favored democracy, eight authoritarianism, and five discovered no difference. More recently, Burkhart and Lewis-Beck (1994) and Barro (1996) found that democracy does not lead to economic development. Inglehart (1997) observes that economic development alone will not lead to democracy and that cultural factors are also important.

36   Burkhart and Lewis-Beck (1994: 903).

37   See Barro (1996); Burkhart and Lewis-Beck (1994). Barro (1997) found that at extremely low levels of development, introducing greater political freedoms contributes to growth. That is, in the worst dictatorships the lack of limitations on government power deters investment and growth. However, once a moderate amount of political freedom has been attained, democracy inhibits growth. At higher levels of development, the demand for democracy rises.

38   When per capita income is below $1000, authoritarian regimes generally survive or are succeeded by another authoritarian regime; they are somewhat more likely to give way to democracy between $1001 and $4000 and even more likely between $4001 and $6000. Authoritarian regimes become more stable at levels above $6000. Przeworski and Limongi (1997).

39   Przeworski and Limongi (1997: 165) note: "Few authoritarian regimes satisfy the premise of modernization theory; that is, few developed over a long period. And even if most of those that did develop eventually became democracies, no level of income predicts when that would occur."

40   When per capita income (measured in purchase power parity or PPP) is $1000, a democracy's life expectancy is eight years; when per capita income is between $2001 and $3000, the life expectancy increases to twenty-six years; when per capita income exceeds $6000, democracies almost without exception last forever. Argentina is the only democracy among thirty-three that collapsed once per capita income exceeded $6000. Przeworski and Limongi (1997: 170).

41   In countries with a per capita income of $2000 or less, of the 107 years during which a decline of incomes occurred, twelve democracies fell the following year.

42   Przeworski and Limongi (1993).

43   Nathan (1997: 71) claims that China's GNP per capita is above the minimum level required to sustain democracy in some other countries. Przeworski and Limongi (1997) conclude that while democracy may be established at any level, the chances for survival depend on the wealth of the country and its ability to sustain economic growth.

44   Liu Junning (1998: 41).

45   Wan Ming (1998).

46   IBRD World Bank (2001: 12).

47   Przeworski and Limongi (1997: 160).

48   Przeworski and Limongi (1997: 160).

49   Przeworski and Limongi (1997: 161, table 1).

50   See Burich (2000: 50). Burich's study is based on a statistical analysis of the relation between democracy and marketization in seven East Asian countries along with qualitative comparative studies of Korea, Taiwan, Indonesia, and China.

51   See the polls cited above.

52   Olson (1997).

53   Clague *et al.* (1997b).

54 See Przeworski and Limongi (1993); Maravall (1994).

55 Some countries may be able to sustain democracy at lower levels of development than others. However, China is not a likely candidate given all of the
obstacles to democracy discussed below.

56 Although citizens would be more likely to blame the ruling regime for a downturn in growth if they felt that the slowdown was due to the regime's mistaken
policies rather than exogenous events, they might very well blame the ruling
regime regardless of the cause. In the USA, in recent decades, presidents have
been reelected for a second term when the economy was performing well and
rejected when it was not, even though most people would acknowledge that
the fate of the economy turns on many factors beyond the president's control.
Moreover, it bears noting that democracies in developing countries are also
vulnerable to downturns in the economy, suggesting that their legitimacy is
also to a large extent performance-based.

57 Pan Wei (2001).

58 Carol Jones (1999). Bell (2000: 124) notes that the Hong Kong government
spent 47 percent of its public expenditure on social services, more than
Singapore and Taiwan and only slightly less than Great Britain.

59 Bugaric (2001) points out that courts in Eastern European countries frequently
have squandered whatever goodwill they enjoyed and compromised their
legitimacy by intervening aggressively in contentious social issues. He also
notes that the courts have adopted positions based more on ideological faith
than on well-supported empirical studies.

60 See Holmes (1993); Dowdle (1999). On the other hand, in many cases the
legislatures are too weak, incompetent, and plagued by their own democracy
deficit to assume the burden thrust on them when an authoritarian regime falls.
Moreover, the judiciary may serve the important function of establishing new
principles of governance that distinguish the new regime from its predecessor.
See Teitel (1997). Ideally, of course, both the legislature and the judiciary
should be strengthened and struggles for power between them minimized to
avoid plunging the new regime into a political crisis.

61 Dickson (1997).

62 Pei (1995). See also White (1994).

63 O'Brien (1999b); see also Friedman (1989).

64 While history may serve as a guide to some extent in predicting whether and
how China might democratize, globalization, the increasing interdependence
of economies, and the diffusion of technologies and information argue for
caution in relying too heavily on prior examples of authoritarian regime democratization.

65 Solinger (2001) identifies six structural features present in the transition to
democracy in South Korea, Taiwan, and Mexico: (i) decades of elections at
least at the local level; (ii) the presence of at least one opposition party, even if
permitted to exist to shore up the legitimacy of the ruling party; (iii) electoral
reforms to bolster the ruling regime's legitimacy and stifle internal and external
criticism; (iv) an unsustainably high level of corruption; (v) split-offs within
the dominant party resulting in the formation of at least three significant
parties; and (vi) a charismatic opposition leader. Although some of these

criteria are present in China, others are not. Nevertheless, it is not hard to imagine that these elements could coalesce in the future. To be sure, Solinger notes that many other factors played a role in the transition to democracy in the three countries. Needless to say, the presence of these factors is no guarantee that China will become democratic.

66   Pei (1997b).

67   Dahl (1971); Rustow (1970).

68   See Goldman (1999).

69   As Nathan (1991) puts it, China's elite want democracy without the demos. Yali Peng's survey (1998) found that all four groups agreed that giving the vote to the masses would lead to stalemate and factionalism, though the support for that view was not intense. Tianjian Shi (1999: 388) points out that many democracy activists and liberal intellectuals opposed village elections on the grounds that it was wrong to begin reform in rural China and that reforms could perpetuate authoritarian rule.

70   Gu (1997); see also Bell (2000).

71   Diamond (1994: 7–8) defines political culture as a people's predominant beliefs, attitudes, values, ideals, sentiments, and evaluations about the political system of its country, and the role of the self in that system.

72   Diamond (1994). Almond (1994) notes that the growing importance of dependency theory, Marxism, and rational-choice theory all contributed to the reduced importance attached to culture.

73   These elements are drawn from Diamond's (1994) survey of the literature.

74   Pye (1985).

75   Those who see Confucianism as inhospitable to democracy call attention to the authoritarian aspects of the tradition, including the emphasis on harmony rather than conflict, the promotion of unity of thought and the intolerance of heterodox views, the privileging of collective interests over individual interests, the lack of a tradition of rights, the view that power emanates from above and that power must be centralized and monopolized and autonomous groups tightly controlled, the paternalistic nature of government in which all-knowing, benevolent rulers determine the moral agenda for society, the reliance on the discretionary decisions of virtuous rulers rather than generally applicable laws applied by an autonomous judiciary, the hierarchical nature of society, and the expectation of deference to authority. Conversely, others find evidence in the vast Confucian tradition of ideas and values supportive of democracy and even liberalism, including the requirement that the ruler must be just and serve the interests of the people, the attention paid to the ordinary person's responsibility for the state and the duty of intellectuals to remonstrate and protest abuses of power, the importance of education and the practice of meritocratic civil service examinations, an openness to religions, and a respect for the dignity of individuals. See Pye (1985); He Baogang (1996); Fukuyama (1995); de Bary (1998); Peerenboom (1998a).

76   He Baogang (1996), for example, distinguishes between hard and soft constraints.

77   Tianjian Shi (1997; 2000).

78 Nathan and Shi (1993); Yali Peng (1998).
79 Yali Peng (1998). Others have portrayed democracy in Taiwan in similar terms.
    L.H.M. Ling and Chih-Yu Shih, for instance, suggest that in Taiwan, democracy
    was a way of installing and legitimizing a virtuous, benevolent ruling elite.
    They point out, for example, that once Lee Teng-hui was elected and had
    consolidated power, he sought to forge a moral consensus that would lead to
    social harmony and strengthen the state. Rather than being constrained by
    law, he sought to change the law and legal institutions to reflect and better
    serve his moral agenda. Similarly, few Koreans apparently opposed at the time
    President Kim Young Sam's extralegal measures to attack corruption. See Bell
    (2000: 153).
80 See Pei (1998b).
81 See Pearson (1997); Wank (1999); Chamberlain (1998). See also White et al.
    (1996: 216–17).
82 Lynch (1999a: 5).
83 White (1994).
84 Diamond and Myers (2000).
85 See Macleod (2000). In 1998,one township in Sichuan experimented with
    direct elections at the township level. See Manion (2000). Voters also elect
    township and county people's congress delegates. Manion notes that while
    candidates for people's congresses are preselected by Party organs, the Party-
    selected delegates must still be elected by majority vote. Accordingly, Party
    organs are constrained in their choices and must select candidates that will
    appeal to voters.
86 Choate (1997); Oi and Rozelle (2000).
87 Tanner (1999: 9).
88 On one occasion, the NPC even rejected a draft constitutional amendment
    tendered directly by the Party. See Dowdle (1997).
89 Dowdle (2001b).
90 O'Brien (1999b).
91 Dworkin (1977). However, Dworkin does allow that consequences may trump
    rights in certain extreme situations.
92 Nozick (1974: ix).
93 Rawls (1971).
94 See Human Rights in China (1991). See also the Statement by Liu Huaqiu in
    Vienna on June 17, 1993, in Tang (1995: 213–17).
95 "US Human Rights Record Not So Rosy" (1996). The report was prepared by
    Professor Yu Quanyu, vice-president of the China Society for Human Rights
    Studies. See also the Information Office of the State Council (2000).
96 In a survey of 547 students from 13 universities in China, 82 percent claimed
    that for other countries to initiate anti-China motions before the UN Com-
    mission on Human Rights constituted interference in China's internal affairs;
    71 percent believed that the true aim of the United States and other countries
    in censuring China was to use the human rights issue to attack China and im-
    pose sanctions on it, with 69 percent maintaining that this constituted a form

of power politics. See "Student's Attitudes toward Human Rights Surveyed" (1999).

97   Bell (2000: 59) notes criticism of the USA for "the passive acquiescence, if not active support for, gross human rights violations" in the case of East Timor under Suharto and cooperating with the Burmese military junta to fight drug trafficking.

98   See Steiner and Alston (2000: 589–90).

99   The USA has not signed a number of human rights treaties, including a treaty to protect the rights of migrant workers and the first protocol to the ICCPR that would give individuals the right to lodge complaints based on the ICCPR. The USA has signed a number of other treaties but failed to ratify them, including the Convention on the Elimination of All Forms of Discrimination against Women and the International Covenant on Economic, Social and Cultural Rights. When it has ratified them, it has precluded them from having any significant domestic effect through a series of reservations. The USA has also opposed the establishment of the International Criminal Court. A number of scholars have portrayed the rapid expansion of customary international human rights law as a threat to US sovereignty. See, for example, Goldsmith (2000).Of course, others disagree. See Roth (2000).

100 Beijing also relies on the Declaration of the Inadmissibility of Intervention in the Domestic Affairs of States and the Protection of Their Independence and Sovereignty, which provides that "no State or group of States has the right to intervene, directly or indirectly, for any reason whatsoever, in the internal or external affairs of any other State," and various other documents and arguments in support of sovereignty. See Human Rights in China (1991).

101 See, generally, Steiner and Alston (2000: 588–91). The PRC has also recently protested violations of the rights of ethnic Chinese in Indonesia.

102 In contrast, others have argued that culture ought to be contained as much as possible in international relations. For a discussion, see Peerenboom (2000b).

103 An Naim (1999: 148) observes that "because cultural context is integral to the formulation and implementation of all state policies, including those that have clear human rights consequences, detailed and credible knowledge of local culture is essential for the effective promotion and protection of human rights in any society."

104 Donnelly (1999: 87).

105 *Multiculturalism* (Gutman, 1994) contains a number of thoughtful essays that address such issues as: the benefits to individuals of identifying with a particular culture, as well as its disadvantages; how liberal states are to reconcile neutrality with support for particular cultural groups; whether liberal tolerance extends to illiberal cultural groups; and the standards by which some cultures are to be promoted while others are suppressed or simply left to wither and die.

106 Donnelly (1999).

107 In announcing that it was acceptable for some to get rich first, Deng Xiaoping acknowledged that economic reforms would result in greater inequality.

Whether he also accepted that reforms would necessarily make some of the least well off even less well off is not clear.

108   Donnelly (1999).

109   Inoue (1999). For the contrary view that democracy and rule of law are costly, and that first generation rights can be just as expensive as some second and third generation rights, see Shue (1980).

110   I have argued elsewhere that human rights in China have been and continue to be understood primarily in instrumental/consequentialist rather than deontological terms. See Peerenboom (1995).

111   Bauer and Bell (1999: 8). Bell provides a number of examples to illustrate this point. For instance, the Singaporean government claimed that the threat of communism combined with possible ethnic conflict between the majority Chinese and minority Malays could have plunged the country into civil strife in the 1960s. Accordingly, the government used emergency powers to detain suspected subversives without trial. Similarly, post-World War II land reform in Japan, South Korea, and Taiwan might not have been possible had these countries been democratic at the time in that landed interests might have captured the political process. A third example is the right of the hearing disabled to political participation, which is impaired by the inability of many of the poorer Asian countries to afford sign language interpreters and subtitles for all televised political speeches. See Bell (1996).

112   See, for example, UN Human Rights Commission (2000).

113   For the concept of an overlapping consensus, see Rawls (1987). See also Rawls (1993), where he attempts to work out an international political conception of rights and justice.

114   The International Bill of Rights also recognizes the rights of groups, peoples, and states. Some have challenged whether such collective rights should be considered human rights. See, for example, Donnelly (1989: 145).

115   See, for example, Twiss (1998).

116   See Peerenboom (2000b).

117   Kiss (1981) analyzes the meaning and origin of each of these terms. While it is clear that these terms are meant to be interpreted strictly and in a way consistent with the purpose of the treaty, there is still considerable room for disagreement.

118   This is the practice in Singapore. See Chan (1998).

119   This practice occurs in South Korea.

120   See Constitution, art. 49. The Mongolian constitution has a similar requirement. According to one recent survey, 88 percent of Koreans agreed that it was necessary to maintain the tradition of ancestor worship in the face of modernization and 83 percent believed that filial piety will be recognized as a virtue in the future. See Bell (2000: 93).

121   See Bell (2000: 4–6) for a discussion of this phenomenon and relevant references to the political science literature. McCormick and Kelly (1994: 805–96) correctly note that many of the arguments against liberal democracy are variations on a universal stock of arguments and in no way unique to China, including that an ill-educated society is not ready for democracy, liberal democracy

leads to disorder, freedom corrodes social morality, and human rights interfere with sovereignty. But that observation does not tell us anything about whether these concerns are well-grounded in this particular instance.

122   In many cases, the proposed alternatives are based on hopelessly vague attempts to chart a third way between socialism and capitalism or between China's traditional philosophies, political systems, and legal institutions, and the institutions and values of contemporary Western liberal democracies. Or else they are based on overly idealistic accounts of what a properly revisioned Confucian society would be like that fail to take into account the negative aspects of Confucianism or to adequately explain how the negative aspects that are an integral part of the conceptual cluster of Confucianism can be hived off or combined with modern democratic institutions and fundamental rights to form a coherent whole. Their appeal is often based more on their telling critique of the realities of contemporary Western liberal democracies than from the plausibility of their own alternative normative vision. But that need not be the case. One need only look at Japan, Taiwan, or Singapore to see a range of possibilities for a political system that accepts the basic democratic institutions and some version of human rights and yet is colored by the infusion of traditional non-Western (and in particular, Confucian) values. Liberals may prefer the USA – but it is not hard to imagine that others would prefer Japan, Taiwan, or Singapore. The contingent fact of being born in a particular society and shaped by its norms and narratives goes a long way toward determining our preferences as to the kind of society we want to live in.

123   See Rorty (2000).

124   It is particularly important to distinguish between the pros and cons associated with the process of democratization and the benefits of mature democracies that have completed the transition and consolidation phases. Although mature democracies tend to be stable, the process of democratizing is often destabilizing. Of course, even if it is *generally* true that democracy leads to greater human happiness, that would not prove that democracy would necessarily lead to greater happiness in the particular case of China at this particular historical moment.

125   Ghai (1994); Chan (1998). At the same time, we do well to remember that rights have been destabilizing in Western countries as well.

126   The USA is in many ways extreme even among Western liberal democracies. Chinese citizens may find moderate European versions of liberal democracy more appealing, though even then there are likely to be significant areas of disagreement.

12

Conclusion: the future of legal reform

Twenty years ago few would have predicted that China's legal system would have developed to the degree that it has. Given the remarkable progress, skeptics who deny any fundamental change in the basic nature of China's legal system seem unduly pessimistic or cynical.[1] On the other hand, liberals who think that China is on the way to establishing a liberal legal system of the kind found in Western democracies seem at once overly optimistic and underappreciative of differences in fundamental values that have led many Asian countries to resist the influence of liberalism in favor of their own brand of "Asian values" (differences which remain even after we discount the self-interested claims of leaders of authoritarian governments).[2]

I have suggested a middle ground. While the footprint of the system's instrumental rule-by-law heritage remains visible, there is considerable evidence of a shift from a legal regime best characterized as rule by law toward a system that complies with the basic elements of a thin rule of law. Despite numerous obstacles, the legal regime will most likely continue to develop toward some form of rule of law that meets the requirements of a thin rule of law. Yet there is little evidence of a shift toward a rule of law understood to entail democracy and a liberal version of human rights that gives priority to civil and political rights. Accordingly, we need to take seriously alternative conceptions to a Liberal Democratic rule of law. China is more likely to adopt a Statist Socialist, Neoauthoritarian, and Communitarian version of rule of law than it is to adopt a Liberal Democratic one.

In many ways, legal reforms today are in a similar state to that of economic reforms ten years ago. After Tiananmen in 1989 and before Deng's trip south in 1992, when he threw his considerable political weight behind further reforms, the economy stood poised between a centrally planned economy and a market economy. Conservative forces opposed further reforms, and hoped, against all odds, to turn back the tide. Nevertheless, reformers have on the whole prevailed. Even though the future path of reforms was not clear at the time, and reforms have progressed in an incremental, context-specific, step-by-step fashion, there has been steady progress toward a market economy, notwithstanding some setbacks along the way and enduring problems.

China's long march toward rule of law is likely to proceed in much the same way as has the transition to a market economy. Despite opposition and the occasional setback, China's legal system will continue to converge toward some form of rule of law. To the extent possible, the ruling regime will rely on incremental changes, testing the waters first in a series of local experiments. While not ignoring the lessons to be drawn from the experiences of other countries, reformers will be driven primarily by domestic factors and considerations in determining the pace and content of reforms.

Of cups half full

To link China with rule of law will strike some as overly optimistic, if not foolhardy and naïve, or perhaps simply as a category mistake. When I told my research assistant, a very capable and distinguished member of the *UCLA Law Review*, that I was working on a book on the legal system and the role of law in China, she asked "what law?" Indeed, one still reads with alarming frequency articles by consultants claiming that what really matters is *guanxi*, not law, and that as long as one has the proper connections, anything is possible.[3] But it is not only nonlegal specialists or those unfamiliar with China that hold a dim view of the legal system. Many long-time observers of China's legal system, while acknowledging that the legal system has changed considerably from the days of Mao and that law can no longer be ignored, doubt whether there has been any fundamental change. In particular, many legal scholars claim that the legal system remains in essence a system of rule by law rather than rule of law.[4] Admittedly there is wide variation in views among legal scholars, with many significant and subtle differences over important issues. Nevertheless, the dominant views regarding the future of the legal system in China tend to range from extreme cynicism and skepticism to cautious pessimism, even among those who acknowledge considerable progress in institution-building.[5]

A few words are perhaps in order to account for the negative portrait of China's legal system in the Western popular press and academic literature, and to explain why I am somewhat more optimistic about the future of legal reform in China.[6] As documented in the preceding chapters, China's legal system has come a long way in just over twenty years. Two decades of reform have produced remarkable changes with respect to institutions, laws, and practices. It is true that there are still many problems with the legal system. But this is widely acknowledged in China, and systematic efforts are being made to address the many shortcomings. Establishing a well-functioning legal system is a monumental task, one made all the more difficult by the particular obstacles confronting legal reformers in China.

What accounts then for the wide discrepancy between the remarkable progress that China has made in establishing a viable legal order and the exceedingly negative portraits of the legal system? The role of the media is one factor. The Western media's coverage of the PRC legal system (and arguably China more generally) is overwhelmingly negative. The focus tends to be on human rights violations and the plight of individual dissidents, victims of torture, and other injustices.[7] In reporting on such events in China, Western journalists often impose their own values, and are quick to assume violations of international human rights law.[8] As pointed out in the last chapter, while clear violations of international human rights law and China's own domestic laws are occurring in China, international human rights law is much less definitive on many important issues than generally assumed by nonlawyers. Needless to say, there is a crying need to report violations of human rights and other injustices whether or not they amount to a violation of international law, but not to the exclusion of other important developments. Violations of civil and political rights concern only one aspect of the legal system, and probably not the most important aspect for many people within China who are more concerned with such issues as whether courts will protect their property rights or grant them a divorce over the objections of their spouse.

Yet even in reporting on commercial law, the popular media tends to highlight shortcomings in the system and to give prominent play to problematic cases rather than those in which the legal system performed as designed. For instance, while there have been numerous articles lamenting the sorry state of arbitral award enforcement in China based primarily and in some cases exclusively on a single infamous case, I found no article in the foreign press prior to 2000 describing particular cases where CIETAC awards have been enforced, even though at least one widely circulated 1997 survey turned up over one hundred such cases.[9] Man bites dog is news; dog bites man is not. Journalists tend to report the sensational, and businesspeople are more likely to raise a hue and cry over nonenforcement than enforcement. Routine enforcement of an award in accordance with law is simply less newsworthy than a major brouhaha over the refusal to enforce an award.[10]

As suggested by the arbitration cases, the foreign business community has played an important role in shaping the negative image of the legal system. The foreign business community consists of foreign business executives and their trusty sidekick, the expatriate lawyer, as well as many others who do business in China or advise those doing business in China.[11] Foreign businesspeople and their lawyers tend to focus on more immediate practical issues than do legal academics. Whereas the latter are interested in issues such as the compatibility of rule of law with socialism and the continuity of the contemporary legal system with the legal system in Imperial and Mao China, the former are interested primarily in concrete operational issues and obstacles to turning a profit. The more micro-level focus of those in the business community often reveals ways in which China's legal system differs from the legal system of their home countries, usually, in their eyes, for the worse.[12] While on good days they will acknowledge that China's legal system has made considerable progress in the last twenty years, the dominant theme is that the system remains so riddled with problems that it is questionable whether it makes sense to even speak of the system in terms of rule of law.[13] Again, businesspeople and lawyers are more likely to turn to the media to complain when the system fails to function as they expect it to, or at least hope it would. Conversely, when all goes smoothly, they are likely to take it for granted.[14] Furthermore, the views of lawyers are likely to reflect their own experiences. The billing rates of lawyers working in major international firms are very high. Given the high rates, companies are not likely to seek the advice of outside counsel except on cutting edge projects or with respect to complicated issues where the law is unclear or there are other obstacles involved. Thus, lawyers are likely to encounter on a daily basis the tough cases rather than the easy ones.

Within the academic world, political scientists on the whole have paid little attention to legal reforms.[15] Much of the political-scientist literature is devoted to high-level Party maneuvering, elite politics, and geopolitical issues. Nor have sociologists, anthropologists, or economists devoted much time to exploring developments in the legal system, even when they are directly relevant to their research topics.[16]

In part, China specialists in fields other than law may simply be following the lead of legal scholars. After all, if specialists on Chinese law dismiss the importance of legal reforms or the role of law, surely nonspecialists can be excused for doing the same. Why have legal specialists been so critical and suspicious of China's efforts to reform the legal system?[17] The impact of Tiananmen may be one factor. Prior to 1989, many foreign legal scholars were relatively bullish about the path of legal reforms. The brutal crackdown resulted in considerable hand-wringing and soul-searching as legal specialists sought to explain why they did not see the crackdown coming.[18] Having been burned once, some appear to have swung to the other side and adopted a cautious, even jaded, perspective.[19] Whatever the reason, there is a tendency to impute the worst motives to any development and to interpret phenomena in their worst possible light, often by suggesting that the real reason behind some problematic feature of the legal system is the Party and its unbridled lust for power and domination. For instance, some commentators suggest that one of the main functions, if not the main function, of the adjudicative committee is to provide the Party with a channel to influence the court.[20] Yet even many reform-minded PRC legal scholars support the adjudicative committee as a response to rampant judicial corruption and the low level of training of many judges. Similarly, the invocation of stability in association with rule of law may be a coded reference to the continued dominance of the Party, but rule of law is regularly portrayed as pivotal to stability even by Western liberal democrats.[21] And it is possible that the last twenty years of wide-sweeping legal reforms are just an elaborate scheme to hoodwink foreign investors into transferring capital and technology, but it is doubtful.

Granted, complex social phenomena can rarely be reduced to single causes. Rather they are the product of various overlapping, sometimes reinforcing, sometimes contradicting, forces. Because life seldom can be confined to neat analytical boxes, it may not be possible to rule out alternative hypotheses in every instance. Nevertheless, in many cases it is possible to assess the relative merits of the various alternative explanations. Thus, the fact that there are currently a number of proposals to limit or do away with the adjudicative committee because it has not been an effective means of rooting out corruption and ensuring just decisions suggests that the Party's desire to have its way was not the main reason for the practice. Along the same lines, some have argued that PRC laws are deliberately vague and broadly drafted so that the Party can continue to rule by policy.[22] Yet as we have seen in Chapter 6, there are numerous reasons why laws are broadly drafted that have nothing to do with the Party. At minimum, an evenhanded account requires consideration of all of the various relevant explanations.

For instance, in support of the claim that China's legal system is incompatible with WTO rule-of-law requirements, one commentator notes that PRC negotiators wanted to qualify the requirement that administrative decisions in trade disputes be subject to judicial review by adding "except as otherwise provided in relevant laws."[23] He concludes that "this qualification would, of course, eviscerate the general rule" and that the request reflects a "recognition of the relative unimportance of the courts." While it is possible that China could pass laws that would preclude judicial review on trade issues or give final decision-making authority over such cases in general to administrative agencies, it is hardly apparent that that was the reason for insisting on the qualification. In fact, the requirement under PRC laws that only the NPC and the NPCSC may confer final decision-making authority on agencies is intended to ensure more expansive judicial review.[24] Moreover, in practice, final decision-making authority has been conferred on agencies in only a few areas, mainly patent, trademark, and immigration, and even in many of those areas, China has amended its laws to provide for greater review in anticipation of entry into the WTO. Indeed, one could conclude that the PRC side's insistence on the qualification demonstrated respect for rule of law. Given that China, like all countries, precludes certain acts from judicial review and confers final decision-making authority on agencies in a limited number of areas, an unqualified commitment to judicial review in all cases would have been at odds with PRC laws.[25]

China and its legal system have changed considerably since 1989. These changes are readily apparent to those currently practicing law in China, particularly PRC lawyers who deal with a much wider range of issues than foreign lawyers. Indeed, there is little resemblance between the practice of law in the early 1990s and the practice of law today. Even for those in China, it is difficult to keep abreast of the latest developments given the rapid pace of change, and to assimilate the changes and form a reasonably comprehensive and accurate picture. Viewing China today through the lens of the events of Tiananmen more than a decade ago will produce a grossly distorted picture.

Of course, a certain amount of caution is in order. There are a number of obstacles to the implementation of rule of law in China. But even allowing for a healthy dose of prudence, existing accounts of the legal system seem to discount the considerable progress that has been made and to present an unduly negative view of the legal system and its future prospects. In some cases, it may be just a matter of emphasis. Given that there have been improvements and yet there are still many problems, much turns on the interpretive spin.[26] One could either highlight the improvements, and then turn to the problems, or one could make the shortcomings the center of the analysis, reserving acknowledgment of the improvements for later.

At times, however, it seems the PRC legal system has been subject to particularly scathing criticism, in part because foreign legal scholars are measuring the legal system against the standards of a Liberal Democratic rule of law, and indeed often an idealized version of Liberal Democratic rule of law that does not exist in reality anywhere. Some scholars have participated personally in legal reform projects and the training of PRC judges and lawyers, apparently in the belief that the projects would bring about a legal system similar to ours in the West and that those trained in our finest institutions would carry back our values and lead the charge to implement a Liberal Democratic rule of law. When legal reforms do not lead to a liberal democratic order and those who return to China busy themselves with making money rather than pressing for political reforms, the foreign legal scholars are disappointed, and may feel betrayed. Harvard Chinese law professor William Alford, for example, is extremely critical of the PRC legal profession for not being a force for liberal democracy, without addressing the underlying (and contested) assumption that the proper role of the PRC legal profession is to be an advocate for liberal democracy.[27] As we have seen, there is little support for liberal democracy in China at present. It is premature to assume that the end of legal reforms is likely to be a Liberal Democratic rule of law. Nor does it seem reasonable to hold PRC lawyers to some idealized version of what lawyers should be that is not even applicable to the legal profession in the USA or any country. Lawyers everywhere are often more interested in making money than in agitating for political reform.

To cite just one more example, although Stanley Lubman in his deservedly much-praised book *Bird in a Cage: Legal Reforms in China After Mao*[28] repeatedly emphasizes the need to avoid measuring China against the standards of a Liberal Democratic rule of law, and expressly endorses a thin rule of law as a more appropriate benchmark, he nevertheless appears to fall into the trap of measuring China's legal system against an idealized standard when he makes the rather startling claim that China does not even have a legal system. Surely this will come as a surprise to those in China who have spent the last twenty years rebuilding the legal system. It will surely also come as a surprise to the judges, lawyers, legislators, and administrative officials who have been making, interpreting, and implementing law. Clearly, Lubman must mean something in particular by "legal system" and be using the term as a technical term of art. While he does not expressly define the term or attempt to defend some minimal theoretical conception of a legal system, he does state his reasons for claiming that China lacks one.[29] First, China suffers from "considerable fragmentation of authority." Second, China lacks a "unifying concept of law." In particular, there is a conflict between the view that "law must serve the Party-state" and the view that "China must be governed by law and aim to attain the rule of law." In addition, China's institutions and especially the judiciary remain weak, despite considerable progress in judicial reform and institution-building more generally. Accordingly, Lubman cites as further support of his assertion that China lacks a legal system:

> the weak differentiation of the courts from the rest of the Chinese bureaucracy, organizational methods in the courts, and a cast of mind among judges that distinguish the courts little from the rest of the bureaucracy. Structural weakness, ideology, rigidity, entrenched interests, localism, and corruption limit the functions and autonomy of the courts and undermine their legitimacy ... [Moreover,] the difficulties of the courts in applying Chinese law and enforcing their judgments raise an issue of the very capacity of the Chinese state.

China's legal system undoubtedly suffers from fragmentation of authority. Yet so do many other systems, even in advanced countries known for

rule of law. In the USA, for example, there are often conflicts between
the powers of the national government and state governments, and between state governments and local governments. Authority is even more
fragmented in some other countries, particularly those going through a
transition, and yet we still refer to their legal systems as legal systems,
albeit weak or imperfect ones. Accordingly, further specification of the
nature or degree of fragmentation sufficient to render a legal system no
longer a legal system is required to distinguish between weak or imperfect legal systems and nonsystems.

As for the second criterion, it is not clear how the lack of a unifying
concept undermines the notion of a legal system. Clearly, there are many
different views of the legal system in the USA among legal realists, CRITS,
critical race theorists, feminists, law and economics scholars, liberals,
conservatives, postmodernists, and so on. What degree of consensus
is necessary? Over what issues? Who must share the unifying concept –
everyone in society? State leaders? Judges, lawyers, legislators, and others
within the system?

As for the weakness of China's legal institutions and in particular
the judiciary, surely many countries have weak institutions, including
weak judiciaries, some of which are plagued by fragmentation of authority, ideological conflicts, limited independence and authority, and
corruption. Similarly, while China's judiciary is no doubt bureaucratic,
so are the judiciaries in many civil law countries. Again, it is not clear
what makes China's institutions so different or deficient to enable one
to conclude that China lacks a legal system. To be sure, Lubman makes
much of the fact that China's judiciary is embedded within a "socialist
Party-state," rather than a liberal democratic state. But this merely suggests that despite his disclaimers, he is measuring China against the
standards of a Liberal Democratic rule of law and the role of the judiciary within such a system.

Lubman and other scholars are of course free to use "legal system"
as a technical term of art that does not comply with ordinary usage in
order to distinguish between different legal regimes or to call attention
to certain shortcomings in China's legal regime. Thus, some comparative law scholars might wish to reserve "*legal* system" for a particular type of legal regime, such as that found in modern Western liberal
democracies (just as some scholars would define rule of law as a Liberal
Democratic rule of law). A country in which "law" (or to avoid begging

the question – certain kinds of rules) was meant to serve a significantly different purpose and the various state institutions such as "courts" and "government agencies" played a significantly different role from that in some modern Western liberal democracies would then be described as a different type of order. Taking this approach, Stephens has described China's Imperial system as a disciplinarian system rather than a legal system.[30] Other scholars, noting the very different purposes of law, courts, legislatures, and administrative agencies in a Leninist socialist system, might claim that the system in the Soviet Union was not a legal system at all. And, as we have seen, Donald Clarke has questioned whether China's institutions should be understood as legal institutions and challenged the teleological assumption that China's system is converging toward the implementation of "the Western rule of law ideal."[31]

Of course, an alternative, and more common, approach is to refer to the Imperial, Soviet, and contemporary PRC regimes as legal systems, given their significant structural similarities and the internal view among those working within such a system that they are part of a legal system, and then distinguish between different types of legal systems. As in the case of rule of law, which of these strategies one adopts will depend on theoretical considerations such as whether there is sufficient common ground to justify reference to a single term or concept – with variations then constituting different conceptions of the core concept – and on pragmatic considerations such as the rhetorical impact of declaring dramatically that China lacks a legal system (or rule of law).

Lubman's approach, however, is somewhat different from the approach of those who argue that Imperial China and the Soviet Union lacked, and contemporary China lacks, a *legal* system in the sense of institutions that serve the same purposes as institutions in modern liberal democracies. Rather than arguing that China lacks a *legal* system, Lubman claims that China lacks a legal *system*. Accordingly, he focuses on shortcomings in China's legal institutions. But for this approach to be useful for comparative purposes, we would need to know more about the minimal conditions that must be satisfied to qualify as a legal system even if a defective one.[32]

Whatever the theoretical advantages or disadvantages of Lubman's approach, as a practical matter provocative claims such as China lacks a legal system are likely to fuel misconceptions about the role of law in China today and obscure the progress China has made in developing its

legal institutions. Ignoring Lubman's nuanced position, some commentators have picked up and repeated, in soundbite fashion, the assertion
that "China lacks a legal system," without qualification or specification
of Lubman's intended meaning, thus inadvertently or perhaps not so
inadvertently dismissing China's achievements in establishing a legal
system that increasingly meets the standards of a thin rule of law. I was
surprised, for instance, to hear a former senior judge from Hong Kong,
when questioned about the Court of Final Appeal's ill-fated decision
in the illegal immigration cases to challenge the authority of the NPC,
acknowledge in a public forum that he knew little about PRC law. I was
even more surprised when he then blithely dismissed the role of law in
China on the grounds that, as far as he understood, China "lacked a legal
system."[33]

On grand and not so grand theories

The history of foreign scholarship on law in China is filled with the attempts of non-China specialists from Weber to Unger to use China as a
test case for their pet theories. The imposition of preconceived theories
and theoretical models to China by non-China specialists has led to a
cottage industry of articles correcting their mistakes, and often eschew-
ing attempts to theorize about Chinese law in favor of Geertzian thick
descriptions.[34] There is much to be said in favor of thick description.
There is also much to be said in favor of avoiding the assumption that
one size fits all and that a Liberal Democratic rule of law of the type
found in some modern, economically advanced Western countries will
necessarily be appropriate for China. On the other hand, thick description by itself is blind, to adapt an observation of Kant. Indeed, we are
arguably just as likely to impose our own values when we studiously try
to avoid making our theoretical assumptions and values explicit as we
are when we approach China with a preconceived theoretical framework
for what a proper legal system is supposed to be already in hand.

All too often, commentators assume that rule of law means their
own liberal democratic conception of it, and then fault China for failing
to implement "the rule of law." By relying implicitly on the limited
theoretical framework of (socialist) rule by law or Liberal Democratic
rule of law, with no other theoretical alternatives, legal scholars are
forced to the conclusion that there has been no fundamental change.

Although some do allow that China is in transition, they are unable to say in transition from what to what because of the limited conceptual framework and the lack of alternative theoretical conceptions to Liberal Democratic rule of law.[35]

In contrast, I have chosen to make my theoretical presuppositions explicit (to the extent possible). At the same time, I have tried to remain open to the possibility that not all in China (or anywhere, including in the USA) will share my theoretical assumptions or values. Accordingly, I have suggested alternative thick conceptions of rule of law that are consistent with PRC discourse, traditions, and practice. These alternative thick conceptions of rule of law are not grand theories in the sense that they are meant to be universally applicable to all countries. Nor are they grand theories in the sense that they purport to be a complete social and political philosophy. Rather, they are more limited heuristic categories designed to facilitate the task of understanding legal developments in China and possible future trajectories for the legal system.

A frequent objection to my approach is that while it is possible conceptually to distinguish between these different types of rule-of-law legal systems, in reality rule of law is only sustainable in countries that adopt liberal democratic institutions and values. One preliminary response is to suggest that Singapore and Hong Kong, among others, are examples of nondemocratic, nonliberal countries that have enjoyed rule of law,[36] and that contemporary Japan, Taiwan, and South Korea to some extent seem to be examples of a Communitarian rule of law. While an adequate discussion of whether or not these categories do in fact apply to these countries and if so whether they are the best way to characterize the legal systems would take us far afield, a few further comments may help clarify some of the main issues.

Critics suggest that the use of the legal system to harass opposition politicians demonstrates that the Singaporean legal system does not merit the label of rule of law. Naturally, all systems fall short of the ideal of rule of law, and Singapore is no exception. At times judiciaries reach decisions that reflect a degree of politicization that is hard to reconcile with rule of law. Many would argue that the US Supreme Court's intervention in the Gore–Bush election controversy in Florida was one such instance. Moreover, in the USA, former presidents and congressmen receive pardons for their crimes while countless nameless less affluent individuals are sent to jail for much less serious offenses.

As noted in Chapter 4, legal systems will differ both in the degree to which law limits the state and state actors and in the manner in which it does so. Accordingly, reasonable people will disagree about what constitutes "meaningful restraints" on government actors. For some, certain kinds of shortcomings such as the inability of the legal system to ensure political dissidents and opposition party candidates a fair trial will in and of itself be sufficient to demonstrate that there is no rule of law, whereas the ability of the Supreme Court to determine the outcome of elections, the legal use of pardons to set free congressmen convicted of crimes, and the run-of-the-mill injustices that occur when poor criminal defendants unable to afford a decent lawyer accept a plea bargain merely show that the legal system falls short of the ideal of rule of law and thus is an imperfect rule of law, but still a rule of law nonetheless. Thus some may conclude that the nature of executive interference with the judiciary in Singapore arguably constitutes a difference in kind rather than simply degree, and therefore Singapore does not merit the honorific "rule of law" at all. Others, emphasizing all of the ways in which the Singaporean legal system does meet the standards of rule of law, may conclude that such shortcomings simply demonstrate that Singapore's legal system falls short of the ideal and yet on the whole may still be characterized as a rule of law, albeit an imperfect one. For those in the latter camp, Singapore will be an example of a sustainable non-liberal democratic rule of law. For the former group, Singapore will be further proof of the limited ability of law to limit state actors in non-liberal democratic states.

Of course, even if Singapore is not a good example of a nondemocratic, nonliberal rule of law, Hong Kong would still seem to be. Granted, Hong Kong may be a special case, having had the benefit, as it were, of colonial rule by the British. Nevertheless, while many commentators predicted that Hong Kong's reversion to PRC control would result in the demise of rule of law, most now agree that Hong Kong has continued to enjoy rule of law even after the handover.[37] Undeniably, there have been bumps in the road, attributable in part to the differences between Hong Kong's common law system and the more civil law system of the PRC, as well as the sheer complexity of operating a legal system based on the historically unprecedented principle of one country, two systems. Moreover, some of the developments since reversion reflect the more conservative policies of the new administration (though it bears noting that Hong Kong was hardly a bastion of liberal democracy under the colonial rule of the British). Yet the judiciary remains independent. Beijing has been reluctant to intervene, doing so only when forced to by the arguably rash actions of the Court of Final Appeals and Chief Executive Tung Chee-hwa in the infamous illegal immigration case.[38]

It goes without saying that Hong Kong differs from the mainland in many ways. Skeptics could still claim that as a general rule establishing and maintaining rule of law requires democracy.[39] Indeed, one could argue that whatever the general practice, China is an unlikely candidate to implement and sustain rule of law without democracy given the limits of socialist ideology and the Party's commitment to single party socialism and to maintaining its grip on power.

Only time will tell whether China will be able to establish and sustain a non-Liberal Democratic rule of law in China. Although the general direction of likely development seems clear, any prediction of the precise path of future development of the legal system must be taken with a grain, if not chunk, of salt. That said, one plausible path might be as follows. Assuming, as appears to be the case, that the Party will not fall from power in the near future, it will continue to play a key role in defining the nature of the legal system. Statist Socialism is likely to continue to serve as the Party's guiding ideology for future reforms. The Party will support those reforms that serve its interests. Indeed, the legal system already evidences considerable signs of a Statist Socialist rule of law. Moreover, the Party may be compelled to accept additional reforms, for reasons discussed in Chapter 5, that would push the legal system farther in the direction of rule of law, albeit a Statist Socialist version. In the short term, therefore, the legal system may resemble most closely a Statist Socialist version, although it will undoubtedly contain elements of other forms as well.

It is unlikely, however, that Statist Socialist rule of law will prove to be a stable equilibrium state. Having embarked on economic and legal reforms, the Party has unleashed forces that have diminished its control over the economy, society, and legal system. Whether the Party's grip on power has loosened to the point where it has lost the ability to control future reforms and maintain its monopoly on political power remains to be seen. However, as discussed throughout this book, the need for deeper institutional reforms to address urgent problems such as corruption and local protectionism will put pressure on the ruling regime to endorse reforms that are likely to result in a transformation in the nature of the legal system from a Statist Socialist to a Neoauthoritarian or Communitarian rule-of-law regime. Attacking corruption will require a more independent judiciary, a more honest and professional civil service, and a more robust civil society. Tackling legislative inconsistency will require stronger courts and more public participation in the law-making process. Addressing problems in the administrative law regime will require a greater role for interest groups and a freer press as well as stronger courts. As the NPC and local people's congresses, the judiciary, and administrative agencies become more competent, they will gain in stature, and be able to demand more power and authority.[40] As state institutions become more authoritative and rule-of-law norms become more widely diffused and more firmly entrenched in society, the legal culture will change, and people will come to expect more of people's congresses, the judiciary, administrative agencies, and other state organs. With more competent institutions to rely on, and greater expectations on the part of citizens that state organs will handle day-to-day operations, the Party will be pushed to retreat further from daily governance to maintain legitimacy. While single party rule would continue, the Party's role could be reduced to one of nominal leadership. Although the Party could still from time to time offer some basic policy guidance, its policies would have to be transformed into laws and regulations by the legislature and the executive to have any legal effect, and the legislature and executive would be free to disregard the Party's suggestions. Similarly, the courts would reject interference by the Party in deciding particular cases. The result would be a Neoauthoritarian rule of law along the lines envisioned by Pan Wei.[41]

In the end, however, a transition to democracy is likely to be necessary to overcome the Party's legitimacy deficiencies, to address accountability issues, and to reduce growing social cleavages, as discussed in Chapter 11. It is possible that over time the Party could stave off extinction by transforming itself into a social democratic party. The Party could very well gain the support of the citizenry if in the next decade it is able to reduce corruption to a tolerable level and to sustain economic growth while dealing with such pressing problems as SOE reforms, reform of the banking and financial sectors, and the need to establish a social security system and clean up the environment.[42] It could further broaden its appeal by gradually relaxing its grip on society and allowing citizens greater, albeit still limited, freedom of speech, assembly, and association. In short, it could adopt a more communitarian approach. If it does not, and elections are held, it could very well lose out to the party that does adopt such an approach, all else being equal.

Assuming then that in the long run democracy will prevail and that the majority of Chinese citizens will prefer a form of communitarianism to liberalism, the legal system will then come to approximate most closely a Communitarian rule of law. Chinese citizens will enjoy democracy and rule of law but forego the extremes of liberalism in favor of a more balanced form of rule of law in which law both strengthens and limits the state, and the rights of individuals are weighed against the interests of others in the community and in society as a whole. That is, the PRC would come to resemble other Asian countries such as Taiwan, Japan, and South Korea.

To be sure, there are many other possible scenarios besides a gradual transition toward democracy.[43] For instance, buoyed by the success of economic reforms, the Party might try to recentralize control, relying in the process on the strengthened legal system. However, that is unlikely for the reasons discussed in Chapters 4 and 5. Alternatively, the Party could fall from power and be replaced by a nonsocialist authoritarian regime headed by elite intellectuals who oppose democracy, resulting in a Neoauthoritarian rule of law or simply the breakdown of the legal system, at least for a period. Yet the latter too seems unlikely. Even assuming regime collapse, whatever group assumes power is likely to appreciate the advantages of a well-developed legal system for promoting economic growth, implementing central policies, and facilitating governance. That assumes, of course, that one group is able to gain control relatively quickly. If China fell into an extended period of factionalism and power struggles, or even civil war, then efforts to reform the legal system and implement rule of law would be adversely affected, just as war and domestic turbulence undermined the first wave of legal reforms at the turn of the twentieth century.

Still another possibility, although less likely for the reasons stated in the last chapter, is that China could suddenly democratize, perhaps as a result of the emergence of a Chinese Gorbachev, or more likely as a result of regime collapse. If so, the likelihood of establishing a Communitarian rule of law would increase. However, it is also possible that an illiberal form of democracy with many elements of soft authoritarianism could arise. Moreover, the transition to democracy will not cure many of the institutional problems that affect the legal system and undermine implementation of rule of law. A sudden transition to democracy, if accompanied by a weak state or social chaos, could actually impede legal reforms. A weak state might lack the resources to push through controversial reforms that alter the balance of power between state organs or different levels of government. A weak state, facing social chaos, might also have its attention diverted from legal institution-building to crisis management and maintenance of social order.

A general reform agenda

In the preceding chapters, I offered a number of specific suggestions as to how each of the main institutions relevant to the implementation of rule of law could be strengthened and improved. Here I divide the reform agenda into four phases and provide a general overview of the main components of each phase, both to tie together the piecemeal reform proposals offered previously, and to fill in the scenario that I have just sketched leading to a Communitarian rule of law. As we have seen, legal reforms are interdependent. The successful reform of one institution frequently requires complementary reforms in other institutions. Given the interdependence of reforms, a successful reform agenda requires a timetable, with reforms sequenced to take into account the level of development of different institutions and general considerations such as the state of the economy, the level of legal consciousness among the citizenry and state actors, the growth of civil society and the number and strength of interest groups, and the Party's willingness to support institutional reforms. A first step would be to establish a legal reform commission, perhaps under the NPC, and/or an NGO consisting of academics, lawyers and representatives from the courts, people's congresses, procuracy, and police acting in their private capacity to oversee reforms, collect and disseminate information on local reform experiments, and to mediate conflicts of interest among different entities and interest groups.

The dual focus of the first phase is on raising the technical competence of state institutions and mounting a campaign to explain the virtues of rule of law.[44] As I have argued throughout the book, many of the problems with respect to the daily operation of the legal system are due to the lack of adequate training and competence on the part of legislators, judges, lawyers, government officials, police, and procuratorates. The level of competence of all of these actors must be raised before they can be granted significantly greater independence, authority, and responsibility. The government might consider reducing the size of people's congresses and doing away with part-time delegates in the hope that full-time representatives would be more dedicated to their legislative tasks and more committed to raising their level of professionalism. The efforts to improve the quality of the judiciary should continue. Entry-level judges must not only score as high as would-be lawyers and prosecutors on the national examination; they should also be required to undergo special training before taking up their post. In general, new judges should be required to start off in lower courts, except for prominent academics and lawyers. Current judges who are unable to pass the examinations should be terminated or shifted to nonadjudication work. As for lawyers, efforts should be made to raise the bar, as it were, by shifting toward a requirement where students must study law at a four-year college, and improving legal education. Although market forces will force lawyers to raise the level of their skills and improve the quality of their services, the MOJ and bar associations should impose tough penalties on lawyers who violate their professional responsibilities and in particular bribe judges or engage in other corrupt practices. The MOJ and bar associations should also educate citizens about their right to sue lawyers for malpractice. Similarly, procuratorates and police should be held to higher standards, and those who violate their codes of professional responsibility should be subject to administrative sanctions, terminated, or prosecuted for crimes, as has begun to happen. Training of government officials is also essential. A clean and honest administration requires government officials who know and respect the law. Government officials should be required to attend sessions introducing key laws and the requirements of the WTO.

The government should expand its efforts to instill respect for law and promote a rule-of-law culture. The state has the resources to mobilize a campaign to support rule of law. However, the Party must support the campaign by ensuring that government officials and Party members who violate the law are held accountable in accordance with law. The efforts to educate people about their rights should continue. But simply educating people about their rights will not be enough if those rights are not protected in practice. Moreover, citizens should be made aware of the limits of law and the inability of courts to rectify every social and economic problem. All too often, citizens expect the court to decide cases not based on the rights of the particular parties as provided by law but with a view to some grander vision of justice, as for example when employees petition courts not to enforce a judgment against their company because the company will be pushed into bankruptcy and the employees will lose their jobs. Efforts should also be made to explain that rule of law has its costs. Protecting the rights of individuals will sometimes mean that guilty parties go free because their confession was coerced or evidence was illegally gathered.

The focus of the second phase would be to strengthen state institutions by granting them increasing authority and independence as they become more competent. Admittedly, some measures to increase the authority and independence of the institutions could be taken immediately. For instance, public participation in the law-making and administrative rule-making processes could be increased. People's congresses and administrative agencies could hold more hearings to ensure better feedback on proposed legislation. Along the same line, some commentators have proposed the establishment of social consultative committees to monitor administrative agencies and participate in the rule-making process.[45] During this second stage, a Supervision Law might be passed, and a constitutional review body could be created, most likely under the NPC. At first, appointments to the review body would presumably be subject to the nomenklatura system. Some seats might also be reserved for Political–Legal Committee members. Constitutional issues often arise out of a conflict between state organs. The Party's backing of the review committee would provide the necessary authority to sort out the conflicts. Meanwhile, the authority of the judiciary would be greatly enhanced by centralizing funding and appointments. As discussed in Chapter 6, courts could also be given the right to strike down lower-level legislation that is inconsistent with higher-level legislation, beginning with normative documents. Over time, courts could be given the right to strike down increasingly higher levels of legislation. The right of the procuracy to supervise the court could be eliminated or limited. To gain the support of the procuracy and avoid potential layoffs, the procuracy's role might be expanded. Rather than relying on private lawyers to take up public interest litigation (which has not been effective for a variety of reasons), the procuracy could be charged with handling class action suits in some circumstances.[46] As the efforts to address corruption begin to pay dividends and judges become more competent, the adjudicative committee could be eliminated. Other possible institutional developments might include the establishment of an anticorruption commission similar to the one in Hong Kong.[47]

Once the level of competence of state actors is raised and institutions strengthened, the Party could withdraw even more from daily governance. Party cells in courts and other state organs would be eliminated. Courts would decide even the most politically sensitive cases without interference from the Political–Legal Committee or other Party organs. The nomenklatura system would be dismantled. There would be higher-level elections for people's congress delegates and other government positions.[48] Citizens would enjoy greater freedoms of speech, assembly, and association. The fourth stage, which goes beyond the scope of thin rule-of-law reforms, would involve establishing genuine multiparty democracy.

Putting a timetable to this agenda is even more problematic than charting possible trajectories for the legal system.[49] Many of the reforms will be ongoing processes that last for generations. It will take at least a generation to rid the judiciary of unqualified former military officers and for the more highly educated younger judges to assume positions of power within the courts. Similarly, most partners in PRC firms are still in their thirties, while better-trained recent graduates are still cutting their teeth as junior associates. Stable, well-managed firms are only beginning to emerge. Changing the way administrative agencies operate and inculcating rule-of-law values in administrative officials will also not happen overnight. Indeed, developing a culture of legality may be the most time-consuming aspect of all. It will also be decades before the economy reaches a relatively stable equilibrium state.

Nevertheless, the ranks of qualified judges, lawyers, officials, and legislators are growing. Within ten years, there should be enough qualified personnel to justify granting greater authority and responsibility to people's congresses, the judiciary, bar associations, and the civil service. Within twenty to thirty years, these institutions should be capable of adequately carrying out functions similar to their counterparts in other countries. During the first ten years, the Party would preside over a Statist Socialist rule of law. Perhaps within twenty or thirty years, the Party, assuming it still exists in some form, will have retreated to the point where a Neoauthoritarian rule of law is possible or even have transformed itself into a social democratic party and endorsed genuine elections.[50]

Policy implications for foreign governments, development agencies, and NGOs

What can foreign governments, international development agencies, and NGOs do to support and expedite the development of rule of law in China? First of all, it merits reiterating that the reform process will be driven primarily by domestic actors responding to domestic concerns. While foreign actors can play an important role in the process, they should bear in mind that rule of law is an ideology.[51] Implementation of rule of law will directly challenge not only the Party but other vested interests in society. It will alter the balance of power between the Party and the state, among state organs, and between the state and society. It will also lead to changes within society, and require a new cultural orientation that assigns a much higher place to reliance on universally applicable laws and dispute resolution by impartial and autonomous courts than in the past. What may seem on the surface to be merely technical suggestions for tinkering with legal rules or modifying institutions to cope with pressing commercial issues such as local protectionism frequently implicate much broader political and normative concerns.

That said, taking a particular thick conception of rule of law as the basis for reforms raises more ideological issues than basing reforms on a thin version. By focusing on the more technical features of a functional legal system, a thin theory of rule of law increases the likelihood that people of fundamentally different political persuasions will be able to find sufficient common ground to carry out meaningful reforms of the legal system. Accordingly, governments, multilateral agencies, and NGOs that are interested in taking advantage of whatever political space is available to pursue concrete legal reforms are more likely to be effective if they base their discussions with PRC authorities on the core elements of the thin version. Not surprisingly, many donor institutions such as the World Bank have chosen to emphasize the technical aspects of legal reforms rather than the broader normative dimensions and the potential of reforms to lead to social and political changes.[52] To insist on first reaching agreement over which thick conception of rule of law is normatively superior would divert attention away from the significant virtues of even a thin rule of law and result in missed opportunities to realize concrete changes in the legal system that would significantly improve the quality of life for many PRC citizens.

Even in a relatively authoritarian state such as China, the establishment of a legal system that meets the requirements of a thin rule of law promises individuals greater protection from the arbitrary acts of the state. China's current laws and regulations often provide individuals with important rights that cannot be realized because of basic thin rule-of-law problems like a poorly trained and undersized legal profession and a weak judiciary. Focusing on more specific issues such as the institutional changes necessary to ensure the existing rights of criminal defendants to a fair trial or the right of someone arbitrarily denied a license to challenge the decision through impartial administrative procedures may be more important than spending time and energy debating the relative merits of liberal values versus Asian values or whether China needs an authoritarian or democratic government at this stage of its economic and political development. As we have seen, many individuals are more concerned about their ability to obtain consistent and fair application of laws than with larger political issues such as the right to choose their leaders.

Significantly, when the USA and China agreed on a project aimed at improving China's legal system during the 1997 Jiang–Clinton summit, the Chinese side rejected the label "rule of law" in favor of "legal cooperation."[53] Presumably PRC representatives rejected "rule of law" because of its vagueness and the potentially broad implications for political reform. Clearly, the government did not want to be perceived as endorsing a Liberal Democratic conception of rule of law. Nevertheless, even though the PRC government's Statist Socialist rule of law differs from a Liberal Democratic conception of rule of law, both sides were able to find common ground when it came to many concrete programs aimed at strengthening the legal system. For instance, they agreed to judicial exchange and training programs aimed at improving the quality of PRC judges; programs to assist in the development of a legal aid system; exchanges to strengthen the securities regulatory system and the administrative law system; seminars on electronic commerce, corporate law, and the enforcement of arbitral award and court judgments; as well as a symposium to discuss the legal aspects of protecting human rights, including issues such as China's legal responsibilities under international rights agreements, the rights of the criminal defendants, and the legal protection of religious freedom.

This is not to deny that issues such as democracy and human rights or the normative basis for laws are important. Rather, the point is simply to suggest that while such issues should be discussed, they need not be the focus of conversation every time legal reformers meet to consider how to improve China's legal system.

Foreign governments and international development agencies are differently situated than NGOs, however. The mandate of some NGOs is to promote democracy and human rights. Given their more overtly normative agenda, they may conclude that focusing on technical changes at the expense of such basic issues as democracy and freedom (especially expansive civil and political liberties) is wrongheaded if not morally perverse. If so, they will be inclined to favor a particular thick conception of rule of law that accords with their own normative beliefs. NGOs can play, therefore, a valuable role in ensuring that the larger normative issues are not neglected and that the focus on the more technical aspects of reforms does not end up arming authoritarian regimes with more powerful weapons for repressing society and denying individuals their rights.

On the other hand, many NGOs are aware that reforms that are not grounded in the values of the local community are likely to be ineffective. Yet there is little likelihood of NGOs persuading many within China, not to mention Jiang Zemin, Li Peng, or Zhu Rongji, to become liberals. Thus, even for NGOs, it makes sense for purely strategic reasons to begin with common ground, and to take advantage of the opportunities presented by a consensus on the basic requirements of a thin rule of law. Of course, some NGOs may see their mandate in terms of a narrower agenda of promoting legal development. If so, they too would be well served by basing reforms on the thin version of rule of law.

In suggesting reforms or commenting on reform proposals, foreign actors should be attuned to differences in ideology, values, and institutions. For instance, China's legal institutions were modeled to a considerable extent on the civil system. Rather than relying solely on the experiences and advice of American professors or lawyers, the US government or US-based aid agencies should try to include on their team of legal reform advisors experts from around the world and in particular from Germany, France, and Japan. Foreign actors should also make sure that they have sufficient local knowledge to ensure that their reform proposals are appropriate and feasible given the current level of institutional development, existing cultural attitudes, and the current political limits.

Unfortunately, it is very difficult for most foreign actors to gain an accurate picture of what is happening in China and to assess what the possibilities for reform are, for a whole host of reasons including language barriers, lack of access and transparency, and the speed with which China is changing. Accordingly, there is a danger that the prescriptions offered by foreign experts will not be implementable. As we have seen, many of the more successful reform initiatives have been bottom-up proposals from those in the trenches who are confronted with practical problems in their daily work.[54] Although foreign actors frequently may not have sufficient local knowledge to propose context-specific solutions, they serve a useful purpose when they provide a menu of alternative approaches. They also play a valuable role in working with those in China to adapt approaches from the general menu to China's own circumstances or in bringing their own experiences to bear on proposals generated by those in China.

There is no single path of development, and foreign advisors should not adopt a one-size-fits-all approach to rule of law, economic development, or political reform. Similarly, they should be attuned to differences with respect to the controversial issue of human rights. One does not have to be an apologist for Beijing to appreciate that many Chinese are likely to be offended by academics, scholars, and pundits who believe they know what is best for China even though they have never been there and remain blissfully ignorant of China's traditions, its current level of economic development, the state of its institutions, and the values of its citizens. As the Hong Kong-based philosopher Joseph Chan has pointed out, Western rights advocates often launch into a lengthy denunciation of the appalling human rights records of some Asian countries, as if their listeners were unaware of the violations in question or would want to defend them.[55] They then quickly dismiss Asian values as an excuse for authoritarian regimes to commit atrocities and claim that Asian states must adopt the practices and values of Western states.

Chan rightly cautions against throwing the baby out with the bath water. There may be legitimate differences in values and opinions at stake, and reasonable people may reach different conclusions over some issues.

Whatever their position on particular rights issues, foreign actors should make sure that they are well-informed about the local situation. In making proposals, they should tailor their recommendations to fit the context or at least demonstrate that they appreciate the concerns of those within China. One cannot help but wonder, for instance, if Hillary Clinton would have insisted on attacking the one-child policy and advocating the right of women "to determine freely the number and spacing of the children they bear" at the Women's Conference in Beijing in 1995, if she had spent more time wandering through the poor neighborhoods where the effects of poverty resulting from China's huge population are most apparent.[56] Even rights advocates applying US standards are likely to find a compelling state interest in limiting the number of births, though surely there is ample evidence that the least restrictive means have not always been employed.[57] All too often US politicians are more interested in sound bites that play well in the USA than in articulating nuanced positions that are most likely to result in positive changes in China.

Although foreign rights advocates have an important role to play in standard-setting and consciousness-raising, foreign governments and NGOs need to bear in mind that the successful implementation of rights requires support from Chinese citizens. Advocates run the risk of alienating their constituency within China if their proposals are too far out of step with the attitudes of their potential supporters. As we have seen, support for civil and political rights remains weak. Thus, there is likely to be little immediate improvement in this area even if China ratifies the International Covenant on Civil and Political Rights. Whether foreign governments or others concerned about human rights in China should spend what little political capital they have on pressuring China to ratify the ICCPR is questionable.

As Susan Shirk, the former Deputy Assistant Secretary for East Asian and Pacific Affairs at the US State Department, acknowledged, the USA has tried a variety of approaches from linking human rights to trade to delinkage combined with dialogue to public shaming through speeches and resolutions at the UN. However, as she rightly points out, "basically, nothing has worked."[58] External pressure has led to resentment, even among reformers in China.

The USA and other governments must deal with China on a number of issues, from missile nonproliferation and national missile defense to the WTO, drug trafficking, carbon emissions and other environmental issues, the Korean peninsula, Taiwan, and regional stability. Governments should not let human rights issues undermine progress in all of these other areas. Rather, they should seize the opportunities presented by these issues to build up trust and a working relationship that will allow all sides to address human rights issues frankly and in a constructive manner.

The PRC government favors a pragmatic approach of seeking common ground while reserving differences on contentious issues such as human rights, democracy, and rule of law. Consider the government's official position on human rights set forth in 1991 in response to the Tiananmen crisis and foreign criticisms of China's human rights record:[59]

> China is in favor of strengthening international cooperation in the realm of human rights on the basis of mutual understanding and seeking a common ground while reserving differences. However, no country in its effort to realize and protect human rights can take a route that is divorced from its history and its economic, political and cultural realities ... It is also noted in the resolution of the 46th conference on human rights that no single mode of development is applicable to all cultures and peoples. It is neither proper nor feasible for any country to judge other countries by the yardstick of its own mode or to impose its own mode on others ... Consideration should be given to the differing views of human rights held by countries with different political, economic and social systems, as well as different historical, religious and cultural backgrounds. International human rights activities should be carried on in the spirit of seeking common ground while reserving differences, mutual respect, and the promotion of understanding and cooperation.

There is no need to accept at face value everything the PRC government says to appreciate that trying to force China to admit that the West got it right and that China must adopt human rights on Western terms is not likely to be the most efficacious way to bring about liberal democracy in China. On the other hand, to the extent foreign actors can put themselves in the shoes of China's policy-makers, start from the Chinese side's perspective, build on common ground, and persuade those in China that they share the same interests, the likelihood of success increases appreciably.

While the pragmatic approach gives Chinese leaders face, at the same time it helps bring into focus what the real issues are. The makers of China's official human rights policy now hide behind the true assertion that human rights are the product of a particular historical era, Enlightenment Europe. While true, this fact in and of itself is irrelevant. Other non-European countries have accepted the concept of human rights and developed a rights culture, at times even a liberal rights culture. Similarly, in China the size of the population may justify some restrictions on the right to give birth, but the government should do more to ensure that the means employed to achieve that goal are proportional, and that forced abortion and sterilization are curtailed. Even if Falungong does represent a threat to national stability, the government should put an end to arbitrary detentions and torture.

Emphasizing persuasion rather than coercion is also likely to prove a more productive strategy in that foreign governments have very few effective coercive mechanisms at their disposal. The mechanisms for enforcing violations of international human rights law are notoriously weak. The Security Council has been reluctant to impose sanctions for human rights violations and only does so in extreme situations such as South Africa, Kosovo, or Rwanda where there is a consistent pattern of massive human rights violations.[60] In any event, there is no chance of the Security Council ordering sanctions or forceful intervention in China given China's veto power as one of the five permanent Council members. The International Court of Justice rarely hears human rights cases, and is hampered by the need for states to consent to the court's jurisdiction. Many states either refuse or give only a limited consent that excludes from the court's jurisdiction cases involving national defense or security or where the subject matter is within the domestic jurisdiction of the state as determined by that state. Standing is also limited to member states, which excludes individual victims of rights violations. The First Protocol to The International Covenant of Civil and Political Rights creates a mechanism for individual complaints, but many states – including the USA and China – have yet to ratify the Protocol. Signatory states may also raise complaints under the First Protocol, though in practice they never have. In any event, complaints will be taken up by a committee that can only issue non-binding views on the matter. In general, international rights agreements require that signatory states provide periodic reports, and authorize various committees to monitor the rights situation and issue reports censuring renegade states. While such shaming tactics do have some effect, they are not likely to cause PRC leaders to alter domestic policy in any dramatic way.

In the absence of effective legal remedies, rights supporters may turn to political channels. Some rights advocates suggest that because human rights are a legitimate matter of international concern, sovereignty "requires only that states refrain from the threat or use of force in trying to influence the human rights practices of other states."[61] Short of force, governments are free to use any and all of the other foreign policy tools at their disposal, including censure, sanctions, and foreign trade and aid policies that tie preferential treatment, market access, soft loans, and government aid to a country's human rights performance.

The USA and other governments should be careful, however, about spending their limited resources on battles they cannot win. Aid conditions and sanctions may be useful in sending a message to China that human rights violations will not be tolerated, and in some cases have produced positive results, such as in China's periodic release and exiling of high-profile prisoners. However, they often backfire and do more harm than good.[62] The debate about sanctions may be held hostage by domestic politicians, or opposition by the business community may result in a change of policy and the removal of sanctions, which then sends the message that human rights issues may be traded off for short-term domestic economic and political benefits. The selective imposition of sanctions on a few countries, and not always the countries with the worst rights records, gives rise to cries of a double standard and calls into question the fairness of the sanctions and the motives of the country imposing the sanctions. Moreover, whether such sanctions help or hurt the people within the target country is often unclear. Economic sanctions may worsen the living conditions for many people who are already living on the edge of subsistence. In recent years, sanctions have fallen out of favor among many in the human rights community.[63] To the extent that sanctions remain an option, the call is for "smart" sanctions that would minimize the adverse consequences experienced by innocent citizens in the target state. Nevertheless, many critics question the wisdom and feasibility of smart sanctions.[64]

As noted in the preceding chapter, the USA lost credibility when it linked Most Favored Nation status to improvements in human rights and then renewed the status even though the human rights situation arguably deteriorated in some years, at least with respect to civil and political rights which are the main focus of the State Department reports. The USA also runs the risk of appearing like a bullying superpower out to contain China when it repeatedly initiates resolutions to condemn China in Geneva, even though such resolutions fail year after year, and when it imposes sanctions only to find itself isolated as its allies rush to take advantage of the opportunity to sign big ticket commercial deals that would have gone to US companies.

Admittedly, the USA and other countries have the right to stand up for their principles, and should protest violations of human rights under both international law and PRC law. Yet in adopting coercive measures, including public shaming and condemnation, foreign governments should rely on the standards of international law and PRC law rather than their own domestic legal standards or values. When the US State Department prepares its annual report on human rights in China, it should make sure that it gets its facts straight and cites sources for its factual claims and relevant international law for its legal conclusions.[65]

At the same time, governments should avoid treating every issue as a legal matter, particularly given the weak enforcement mechanisms. Rather, they should explore ways to address issues that do not rely on enforcement by international organs or even domestic courts. In the end, the best hope for realization of an overlapping consensus both in theory and practice is continued dialogue and the eradication of the economic conditions that make it difficult for states to comply with their obligations to provide their people with the material conditions within which they can flourish as human beings. Rather than simply condemning China for violating civil and political rights, other countries should seek ways to cooperate with China to promote economic development.[66] They should also pursue ways to strengthen the legal system to ensure that as the demand for rights grows in China, the legal system is able to meet the challenge.

Given the US government's harsh criticism of China on human rights issues and the feeling within China that the USA is applying a double standard to China because it wants to prevent China from assuming its rightful place as a superpower, it is particularly important that the USA back up its rhetoric with action and allocate funding to support the development of rule of law in China. Although Presidents Clinton and Jiang signed their agreement to cooperate in 1997, Congress did not take the necessary actions that would allow for the USA to allocate funds for the purpose of promoting rule of law in China until 2000. Even then, Congress allocated only a miniscule amount of funding that fell far short of what is required to actually carry out the proposed agenda.

More generally, the USA and other countries should seek to engage rather than contain China. China today is far from the threat portrayed in the alarmist accounts of the so-called Blue Team in Washington. The greater risk at present is not that a stronger China will oppose US policies around the world but that a strategy of containment aimed at keeping China weak and subservient will strengthen the hand of hard-liners and slow reforms within China. The gravest threat to stability in China is the increasing discrepancy between the economic structure and the political structure. The failure of political reforms to keep pace with economic reforms is the most likely path to regime collapse. Should the ruling regime collapse and China descend into chaos and perhaps even civil war, the consequences would reach far beyond China's own borders. For the sake of regional peace and global stability, the USA and other countries should seek ways to promote further reforms rather than seeking ways to contain China. The opportunities for engagement and for mutual benefit and learning are unlimited, provided all sides proceed with open minds. There is no reason to assume that China will develop in exactly the same way as have some Western countries. Economic development need not lead to the endorsement of liberal democracy or a liberal interpretation of human rights that privileges civil and political rights over other rights, seeks to maximize individual autonomy and freedom, and tips the scales in the direction of the individual when individual rights conflict with the collective interests of the majority or society as a whole. Notwithstanding the advance of global markets and the encroachment of a global culture, East Asians on the whole continue to draw a different balance than liberals when it comes to conflicts between individual autonomy and freedom versus social stability and the interests of the majority. Even if we take with a grain of salt the claims of authoritarian governments who profess to speak for all citizens when they offer up Asian values as an alternative to liberal values, and recognizing that liberalism is hardly universally endorsed even in Western countries, there is ample evidence to support a difference in values.[67]

We do not all share the same values. We do not all have the same vision of the good life. Nor need we. A certain amount of diversity within the general framework of human rights is valuable in that it allows for social experimentation while making the world a more interesting place.[68] The challenge is for Chinese and other Asians to draw on the diversity within Asia and elsewhere to fashion their own version of a just society that respects human rights and allows individuals to flourish, and for Westerners to learn from Asian countries and incorporate what is useful in improving the lives of people in their countries.

Notes

1   Of course many commentators acknowledge significant change and yet are still extremely critical of the PRC legal system and skeptical of the likelihood of implementing any credible version of rule of law. The issue then becomes what constitutes "fundamental" change. Lubman (1999), for instance, acknowledges significant improvement with respect to the creation of rights via legislation, the establishment of a judicial hierarchy and a more professional judiciary, a reconstituted bar, better legal education, and an increasingly assertive legislature, all of which are steps away from Maoism. Moreover, in a recent article, Lubman (2000) allows that "China is in transition." However, he does not say in a transition from what to what. Presumably it is not from rule by law to rule of law. Though he allows that law plays a more important role than in the past and that there has been considerable progress in institution-building, and even acknowledges certain "fragile harbingers" of a possible rule-of-law future for China, Lubman (1999) denies that China even has a legal system because of the incoherence he perceives in current institutions. He also highlights the instrumental aspects of PRC law and the primacy of policy, claims that there is an "inescapable contradiction between the avowed goal of attaining rule of law and the ideological limits" of the ruling regime, suggests that the Party's emphasis on stability is shorthand for Party control, sides with those who see the development of the NPC not in terms of an evolution to rule of law but as serving the purpose of a heavily instrumental law, and, as a result, remains cautiously pessimistic about the future of legality in China.

Although Lubman does not characterize his own position in terms of rule by law, in my view, an instrumental law in which law is a tool for the Party and is not meant to impose meaningful limits on the CCP because there remains a deep contradiction between rule of law and the leading role of the Party is still (i) a rule by law, and (ii) not consistent with any fundamental change, and in particular a shift toward rule of law. See also in this regard Chen Jianfu

(1999a), who describes the legal system as just a better tool for carrying out Party policies.

In contrast, I have argued that there has been a fundamental shift away from a purely instrumental view to the official position that the law also binds Party organs and state actors and protects the rights and interests of citizens. Moreover, law increasingly plays that role in practice, even though the legal system remains weak in various respects. I have also argued that the primacy of policy is overstated. As in other countries, Party policies must not be translated into law. Furthermore, in all systems, policies and law are complementary tools of governing, although policy may play a somewhat different and greater role in a Statist Socialist rule of law than a Liberal Democratic one. Nor, as argued in Chapter 5, is there an inescapable contradiction between socialist ideology and rule of law. Indeed, I have argued that commentators tend to overstate the importance of ideology as an obstacle to legal reforms and implementation of rule of law. As for stability, it is one of the common purposes for implementing rule of law. Finally, as discussed below, China's legal system, while like many other legal systems far from perfect, is nonetheless a legal system. Where Lubman sees in China's much-strengthened legal institutions at best the tender sprouts of rule of law, I see sturdy young saplings in their prime growth years.

2 Dezalay and Garth (1996), the latter President of the American Bar Association, provide one of the more extreme statements of the liberal convergence assumption: "Law may begin to rival Communism – perhaps more precisely, the legal profession may rival the Party – as the leading legitimating authority. Law may provide a kind of neutral ground between competing national elites. As we shall see, there is also evidence that the US version of law and legal practice is of particular importance." On the Asian values debate, see the preceding chapter and the works cited in Chapter 1.

3 See, for example, Seligman (1999). I have heard similar eternal "truths" repeated time and again at business seminars, often but not always by those who are quick to offer their services for those in need of the right connections.

4 See Chapter 1 for citations to those who characterize China in terms of an instrumental rule by law. See also note 1 above.

5 See note 1, above. For an extremely skeptical view bordering on bitter disappointment over the role of the legal profession in supporting and promoting social and political change, see Alford (2001). See also Alford (1990; 1999). Not all are pessimistic of course. Jerome Cohen, for instance, remains one of the more optimistic. See also Dowdle (1999). Moreover, even those that are skeptical allow that implementation of rule of law is possible. See, for example, Corne (1996; 2001); Lubman (1999).

6 Inevitably, we are all influenced by our experiences. I first went to China in 1981, when the memories of the Cultural Revolution were fresh. China was still very much a closed, authoritarian state. Economic and legal reforms were only in their infancy. There was little civil society to speak of. Over the next two decades, I returned to China many times. From 1994 to 1998, I practiced law with a major international firm in Beijing, which provided a valuable perspective on the important role of law in contemporary China. Since taking up an academic

position at UCLA in 1998, I have been Of Counsel at a Chinese law firm, which has provided a very different but equally valuable perspective from the one gained by working in a foreign firm.

7   The Western media's negative coverage has led to numerous books and articles protesting the "demonization" of China. Although some such works or particular arguments within such works are marred by excessive nationalism and hyperbole, many of the arguments and accusations ring true.

8   Perhaps the best example of interpreting events in China through the filter of American values was the widespread depiction of the events in 1989 as a democracy movement. While a few students and intellectuals called for democracy and human rights (and even fewer could state what they meant), the vast majority of the demonstrators were motivated by other concerns, with inflation, corruption, and for the students, better dormitory conditions and more freedom in choosing jobs, topping the list.

9   See the study by the 1997 Arbitration Research Institute, which was discussed in various articles by foreign lawyers and academics prior to 2000. See Peerenboom (2001a). Harer (1999: 414, 419) claims that Chinese courts "do as they please" when it comes to enforcement of arbitral awards. He cites in support an article in *Business China* that makes a similar claim without citing any empirical evidence other than the Revpower case. See "China's Rocky Road to Dispute Resolution: Rough Justice" (1998). Similarly, one report quotes a foreign lawyer as saying that China "might as well have not bothered signing" the New York Convention. See "Swedish Arbitral Award Enforced in Beijing" (1998). See also Rushford (1999); Zirin (1997).

10 In fact, there was a 55 percent rate of enforcement for the cases where I obtained information directly from lawyers as opposed to a 25 percent enforcement rate for cases drawn from written sources, including academic articles. The difference may be attributable to the small number of such cases. But it may also be due to bias in the cases that get reported. Just as reporters are more likely to report cases of nonenforcement, academics are more likely to analyze decisions not to enforce an award. As a result, more nonenforcement cases end up getting reported. See Peerenboom (2001a).

11 As someone who practiced law in China for a number of years and who continues to practice commercial law on a consulting basis, I would consider myself to have at least a few toes in the business community camp.

12 Sometimes the differences are attributable to generic differences between civil and common law countries. Given their common law training and lack of experience with civil law systems, many American lawyers will often find odd, and criticize, aspects of the PRC legal system that are well-accepted by French and German lawyers. The comments of the foreign legal community on the draft PRC contract law were interesting in that common law lawyers raised concerns about certain features borrowed from civil law systems, while civil law lawyers objected to certain features adopted from common law countries.

13 See, for example, Gordon Chang (1999).

14 Some foreign businesses have taken out articles praising local governments or the courts for upholding their intellectual property rights or enforcing arbitral

awards, both to show their support and to send a warning to possible offenders. However, the practice is rare.

15 For instance, in his deservedly much-praised book *Governing China*, Lieberthal (1995) barely mentions the legal system, even though the legal system would appear to be central to the topic of governing China. See also Alford (1990), who first raised years ago the issue of the relative neglect by political scientists of legal system developments. There are of course notable exceptions. Rick Baum (1986), Minxin Pei (1997a; 2001a), and Murray Scot Tanner (1999) are among those political scientists who have written on legal developments. The relative neglect of legal reforms by many political scientists may be due to their belief that developments in the legal system are likely to be more of a reflection of changes in the economic and political order rather than the cause of any such changes. To focus on legal reform as a driving force for political reform is to put the cart before the horse.

16 For example, the impressive team assembled by Oi and Walder (1999) to examine the issue of property rights and economic reform in China included political scientists, sociologists, and economists but no legal scholars. Again, there are notable exceptions, including the work of David Zweig (2000) and Douglas Guthrie (1998; 1999).

17 One possible explanation is simply differences in personalities. Some people are more optimistic than others. For instance, one China law specialist expressed anxiety and concern over his daughter's pregnancy, noting that she was at the age where there was a 10 percent chance of problems occurring. While the risk was of course worrisome, I could not help but point out that there was a 90 percent chance that all would be fine. Nevertheless, differences in personalities are not the whole story.

18 See Alford (1990).

19 For instance, writing just after the crackdown in Tiananmen, Alford (1990: 181) stated: "From 1978 onward, the leadership's principal objective in initiating and supporting law reform has not been to foster a rule of law. Rather it has been to legitimate the leadership's own power while erecting the edifice of technical guidelines believed necessary to facilitate economic reform and reassure anxious prospective foreign transferrers of sorely needed capital and technology."

20 Woo (1991).

21 See Lubman (1999) and the discussion in Chapter 3.

22 See, for example, Corne (1996), who does consider a variety of alternative explanations.

23 Clarke (1999).

24 Article 12(4) of the ALL states that such authority must be provided by Law (*falu*). The SPC's 1991 Interpretation of the ALL stated unequivocally that "Law" refers to the legislation enacted by the NPC or the NPCSC. In an abundance of caution, it added that while administrative agencies may provide that agency decisions are final, such decisions are still subject to review and courts must accept such cases. Opinion of the Supreme People's Court on Some Issues Relating to the Implementation of the Administrative Litigation Law (adopted May 29, 1991), art. 3.

25   Although some critics have objected to the PRC laws delegating final decision-making authority to agencies, that is a common feature of most administrative law systems. The real issues are how often are agencies granted such powers and to what extent do courts review agency decisions notwithstanding the delegation of final decision-making authority. In practice, delegation of final decision-making authority is rare. As noted, agencies cannot claim such authority for themselves. PRC laws have conferred final decision-making authority on the agencies extremely rarely, the major areas being certain patent, trademark, and immigration issues. Preclusion in these cases is due to the technical nature of the subject matter. The individual still has the right to challenge the decision through other channels, including legislative oversight, administrative reconsideration, or administrative supervision. Ying Songnian *et al.*, eds. (1994: 89–90). In a few cases, a party may choose either administrative reconsideration or litigation in court. However, if the party chooses administrative reconsideration, the decision will be final and not reviewable in court. Ying Songnian *et al.*, eds. (1994). Laws and regulations regarding demonstration and social organizations also allow the agency to make the final decision. See, for example, the PRC Assembly, March and Demonstration Law Implementing Regulations, issued by the State Council on June 16, 1992, art. 14. However, judicial review apparently is not possible because of lack of standing rather than issue preclusion (though admittedly the distinction may not mean much to those denied the right to appeal). The interests implicated are political interests rather than personal or property rights.

26   For example, Lubman (2000: 392), presents a fairly critical view of administrative litigation. In so doing, he states that the number of administrative litigation cases has risen "although plaintiffs lost in more than 50% of the cases," suggesting that the rise of litigation is hard to understand given the low success rate. Yet as noted in Chapter 9, the success rate for administrative litigation plaintiffs in the USA is 12 percent, and just 8 percent in Japan and Taiwan. Thus, another way of describing the same phenomenon is that the number of administrative litigation suits rose because of the high rates of success enjoyed by plaintiffs in the PRC relative to plaintiffs in other countries.

27   Alford (2001a). Ironically, Alford (2000) has taken to task those who would uncritically export liberal democracy for their chauvinism in assuming the superiority of democracy and liberal values and for failing to provide adequate justifications for their faith that liberal democracy and rule of law will take hold and flourish in a very different context like that of China. He has also on numerous occasions warned his readers about the difficulty of transplanting democracy and rule of law to China given the different historical traditions, political system, and level of institutional development. See Alford (2001a; 2001b; 1999). Yet at the end of the day, he remains personally committed to democracy and liberal values, and thus, it seems to me, torn between his more critical intellectual position and his normative commitments. I should perhaps note that I do not mean to single out my friends and colleagues Professors Alford, Clarke, and Lubman. I have gained immeasurably from conversations

with each of them over the years, and all were kind enough to provide constructive comments on my work. However, the field is small and their writings have been extremely influential, and deservedly so for the many insights they contain. Given the impact of their writings, it is crucial that we critically examine their assumptions and conceptual frameworks.

28 For my own favorable review, see Peerenboom (2000e).
29 Lubman (1999: 317–18).
30 Stephens (1992).
31 See Clarke (1998–99) and Chapter 4 for a discussion of his views.
32 In Chapter IV, I discussed the problem of stating the kind or degree of deficiencies sufficient to deprive a legal system of the label "rule of law." Lubman faces similar difficulties with respect to his claim about a "legal system." As noted in Chapter 4, reasonable people can, will, and do disagree about such issues with respect to rule of law, and the same is true with respect to a legal system. Nevertheless, there are important differences. Most notably, whereas rule of law in ordinary usage is an honorific term that implies a certain degree of achievement, legal system in ordinary usage implies a much lower standard. Moreover, the basic elements of a thin rule of law are well accepted, and provide a fairly detailed standard in and of themselves. In contrast, to the extent that there is a common understanding of the elements of a legal system – laws, courts with judges that decide cases by applying the law, administrative agencies that make rules and implement them, lawyers who advise clients and draft contracts – China's legal regime would seem to qualify as a legal system.

   According to the influential account of the legal philosopher H.L.A. Hart (1961: 113), the two necessary and sufficient minimum conditions for a legal system to exist are: (i) the populace must generally obey laws valid in accordance with the rule of recognition and (ii) officials must effectively accept the rule of recognition and its rules of change and adjudication as common public standards of official behavior. Tamanaha (1997: 135) argues that even these two conditions are not necessary: rather, "the *only* condition necessary for the existence of a legal system is the presence of a co-ordinated complex of actors adhering to a shared set of secondary rules who do things *in the name of law*" (emphasis in original). Thus, state actors need not "accept" the secondary rules as long as they adhere to them. Nor does it matter whether citizens actually accept or obey the laws.

   Tamanaha supports his argument by appealing to two examples. The first was a study that showed "substantial aspects of the Austrian Civil Code dealing with social behaviour were generally disregarded." Tamanaha (1997: 136). The second example is based on Tamanaha's own study of law in Yap, Micronesia, where he found that "most portions of the Code were never applied, few lay people have any knowledge of the content of the laws or of the nature of the legal system, a large proportion of social problems were dealt with through traditional means without participation of the legal system, and indeed on most of the islands there is no legal presence at all." Tamanaha (1997: 136). These examples raise two distinct types of questions. The first is a theoretical issue about the degree and nature of acceptance necessary to satisfy Hart's minimal conditions for a legal system: how many people must reject or ignore or be ignorant of how many laws (and how much of the laws) before the system lacks the requisite acceptance to count as a system? This kind of question does not lend itself to a precise answer, or perhaps any answer. The second question is more of a practical/empirical one: at what point will such problems simply render the legal system dysfunctional (and what are the standards for measuring dysfunctionality)? The two questions are often elided. At some point, a legal system becomes so dysfunctional one may not even want to describe it as a legal system. On the other hand, even a very imperfect legal system can still be considered a legal system, albeit a dysfunctional one.

Tamanaha is probably correct that most people would allow that Austria had a legal system, even if a substantial number of people failed to follow certain laws. The Yap case is more difficult. Having been an Assistant Attorney General in Micronesia, Tamanaha is eager to describe the system as a legal system (much as having practiced law in China, I find the claims that China lacks a legal system hard to swallow). Surely he felt like he was part of a legal system. Yet to describe the system as a legal system he must further lower Hart's already fairly minimal conditions. Having done so, he is left with a legal system whose reach, scope, and practical importance in the daily lives of citizens is severely limited. In response, Hart could have argued that "the legal system" proper still refers to that part of the social order where enough people actually accept and obey the laws sufficiently for it to have some practical significance. The remaining sphere of social activity is not governed by a legal system but rather by other systems based on social norms and practices. More relevantly for present purposes, Hart or others might also claim that there is no legal system because there is no area in which sufficient people obey the law. But the claim that there is a legal system, albeit a weak one, seems to better accord with ordinary usage, which is one reason for preferring Tamanaha's even more minimal theory.

Having chosen to use "legal system" in a way contrary to its ordinary usage, and having appealed to types of problems such as fragmentation of authority and lack of a unifying concept of law that are not unique to China though they may differ in degree from similar problems faced by other systems, Lubman would seem, given the controversial and counterintuitive nature of his claim, to owe the reader a more detailed account of (a) why his chosen criteria (fragmentation of authority, unifying concept) rather than the more commonly accepted criteria (existence of legislature that makes rules, implemented by administrative agencies and enforced by courts with the assistance of the legal profession) should be the standard for defining a legal system and (b) the degree at which the shortcomings are sufficient to constitute system failure. Given the difficulties of this approach, it would appear that Lubman would be better off setting a minimal threshold for what constitutes a legal system and then describing existing systems along a continuum from dysfunctional to functional to some ideal.

33   For a variety of perspectives on the illegal immigration cases, see Chan (2000).

34 See Alford (1986; 1990). In fact, until recently, most writing on PRC law was limited to doctrinal analysis, with little concern for how laws were actually implemented. Fortunately, as the number of people with the requisite language skills and experiences in China has grown, more articles have appeared that describe not only what the rules are but how they are implemented in practice. Often these articles are by legal practitioners and graduate students, who may not have the time, inclination, or perspective to construct broader theories.

35 See Lubman (2000). Of course, one may simply not wish to speculate about how China is likely to develop in the future. My point, however, is that were one inclined to speculate about the future of legal reforms in China, one would need to develop theories to guide one's predictions. In so doing, relying exclusively on a Liberal Democratic conception of rule of law would foreclose consideration of many more likely paths of development.

36 See Bell (2000); Pan Wei (2001). Minxin Pei (2001b: 31) cites as further examples in addition to Hong Kong and Singapore, Kaiser Germany, pre-1945 Japan, Pinochet's Chile, Franco's Spain, and "nearly all Western European countries before they became democratic in the mid-1800s." To be sure, full implementation of rule of law generally goes hand in hand with democracy. For instance, it was only after Taiwan and South Korea democratized that the judiciary acquired enough independence and authority to handle virtually all politically sensitive cases in an impartial manner according to law. Nevertheless, rule of law and impartial treatment in politically sensitive cases do not necessarily require democracy, as evidenced by Hong Kong. Pei argues that the key to autocracies maintaining rule of law is the existence of political constraints that oblige rulers to exercise political moderation. These restraints may come from an independent aristocracy, the church, a rising urban capitalist class, or external threats.

37 For an evenhanded, detailed account of important cases and legal developments in Hong Kong since the handover, see Albert Chen (2002). See also the Report of the Joseph & Crowley Program (1999); US State Department Report on Hong Kong (2001). The Crowley report, which clearly assumes a liberal democratic orientation, was more critical of Hong Kong with respect to democracy than rule of law.

38 See Chen (2002). The actions of Elsie Leung, Secretary of Justice, in handling the Sally Aw case are arguably even more objectionable from a rule-of-law perspective than the way the illegal immigration cases were handled. In the Sally Aw case, Leung decided not to prosecute Aw, the head of a newspaper and a friend of Tung Chee-hwa. When asked to explain her decision not to prosecute, she at first limited her comments to general policy considerations, refusing to go into detail as the case was still pending regarding other parties. In response to a public uproar, she then sought to clarify her position and justify her decision in part by appealing to public interest. Aw was in negotiations to sell her newspaper, and Leung did not want to influence the sale. This broad interpretation of public interest provoked a hailstorm of criticism, leading to a no-confidence vote, which Leung survived.

39 Admittedly, the absence of any example of a nondemocratic rule-of-law state would not prove that such a state is not possible or that the PRC could not become one, though it certainly would give pause to those who believe it possible.

40 There is evidence that this is already occurring. NPC delegates challenged Zhu Rongji's right to rely on executive decisions to carry out the develop-the-West program. Others have sought to take over some of the powers of the State Council's Auditor-General's Office, which oversees the annual inspection of the performance and integrity of government officials. See Lam (2001). See also Dowdle (2001b).

41 The five pillars of Pan Wei's (2001) Neoauthoritarian rule of law, which he refers to as consultative rule of law, are a neutral civil service; an autonomous judiciary; extensive social consultative institutions; an anticorruption body similar to Hong Kong's Independent Commission Against Corruption; and more extensive, but still limited, freedoms of speech, press, assembly, and association.

42 As Rose-Ackerman (1999) notes, corruption exists in all states to one degree or another, and it would not be efficient to expend the resources needed to wipe out corruption completely.

43 Oksenberg (2001) sketches five alternatives facing Party leaders ranging from attempting to return to totalitarian rule and class struggle; fighting to maintain the status quo; transforming the Party into a highly nationalistic and assertive party; becoming a force for democracy; or simply sticking their heads in the sand and postponing choices.

44 I follow Pan Wei (2001) in dividing the reform agenda into stages. Although we differ over some of the details, I agree with the basic thrust of his three stages. However, I add a fourth stage, the transition to democracy.

45 Pan Wei (2001).

46 This idea was first raised by Zhu Suli, Dean of Beijing University Law School, during a conversation on future legal reforms and the need to think of creative solutions that fit China's circumstances.

47 Pan Wei (2001).

48 There are already experiments in Guangdong, Shenzhen, and other areas to choose senior government and even Party officials through open competition. Guangdong for instance has relied on open competition to select the vice-director of the general office of the Provincial CCP Committee, as well as vice-directors of the provincial Economic and Trade Commission, Administration Industry and Commerce Bureau, and Foreign Affairs office. See *Guangdong to Choose Senior Officials Through "Open Competition"* (2000).

49 Pan Wei (2001) suggests that the first two stages will take five years each while the third stage will take ten years.

50 I have sketched a scenario leading toward fuller implementation of the rule-of-law ideal because my basic supposition is that China is moving in that direction, and will continue to do so, for the reasons discussed throughout this work. As noted, there are other possible scenarios, including regime collapse, that might not lead to rule of law, or at least not in such a smooth and timely way as I have suggested. My goal is not to sketch in detail all possible paths of development

but to focus on what seems more likely. Although regime collapse is a possibility, it is by no means inevitable or even probable. See the essays in Shambaugh (2000). Accordingly, it is important that one devise reform strategies that could lead to rule of law, particularly given that implementing rule of law may help stave off regime collapse.

Alternatively, one could try to spin out various paths that lead to regime collapse and perhaps the return to rule by law, or that lead to rule of law but assume a more dysfunctional system or difficult transition period. As for the former, the return to rule by law seems unlikely. As for the latter, the end result is the same, as sooner or later the dysfunctional elements will be addressed. It is just a matter of how smooth the transition is and how long the process will take.

Still another approach, discussed in Chapter 4, would be to argue that China is so different from other countries that it is likely to develop a sustainable alternative to rule of law – a (legal) system that does not comply with the requirements of a thin theory. See Clarke (1998–99). That no one has yet even begun to sketch what such an alternative would be suggests how unlikely it is.

51 See Lubman (1999).

52 See, for example, The World Bank Legal Department (1995). However, McAuslan (1997: 121) notes that the World Bank is at odds with Scandinavian, Dutch, and German donors that tend to emphasize not just efficient markets and governance but human rights and administrative justice.

53 Gewirtz (1999).

54 See also Dowdle (2001a).

55 Chan (1998).

56 See UNDP (1995).

57 While the standard under US law for restricting fundamental rights requires a compelling state interest and use of the least restrictive means, the standard under international human rights law would be whether the restriction was prescribed by law, served a legitimate state interest, and was proportional given the purpose.

58 Asia Comment (2001).

59 "Human Rights Situation in China" (1991: 8).

60 For a list of Security Council sanctions, see http://www.un.org/News/ossg/sanction.htm.

61 Donnelly (1999: 71).

62 The 1993 Bangkok Declaration at the center of the Asian values controversy objects to "any attempt to use human rights as a conditionality for extending development assistance."

63 UN Committee on Economic, Social and Cultural Rights General Comment No. 8 (1997) UN Doc. E/1998/22, Annex V.

64 See Gordon (1999).

65 One of Beijing's favorite ploys is to discredit the report by seizing on factual mistakes. The State Department report often cites unidentified sources such as "the Western press," or "a domestic publication" or an "overseas human rights group." The report will also conclude that there has been a violation of

international law or internationally accepted norms, without providing legal authority for these conclusions. As we have seen, there is considerable debate over what the law is with respect to many issues. Having references to the legal authority therefore would be more persuasive.

66   The Bangkok Declaration stressed the right to development and asserted that the main obstacle to realization of the right to development is the widening gap between North and South and rich and poor countries. It called for international cooperation to narrow the income gap and eliminate poverty, which it declared to be one of the major obstacles to the full enjoyment of human rights. The Vienna Declaration was even more explicit: "The World Conference on Human Rights reaffirms that least developed countries committed to the process of democratization and economic reforms, many of which are in Africa, should be supported by the international community in order to succeed in their transition to democracy and economic development."

67   Bell (2000) and Chan (1998) make similar arguments regarding general differences in values.

68   Kausikan (1995–96), Singapore representative to the United Nations, notes the irony in the fact that the liberals are threatened and upset by a more pluralist approach to rights as advocated by some in Asia. Kausikan suggests that the vitriolic attack on Asian values in the West is overblown and disproportionate, and reflects the West's parochialism and fears arising from a crisis of confidence in the economy and social order. Even allowing that the West's reaction may have been overblown, the concern that there must be limits to diversity remains valid. But to sort out these limits it would be necessary to consider a host of context-specific issues such as the particular right at stake, the reasons for limiting the right or interpreting it in a particular way, the source of the obligation (treaty, customary law) and the precise nature of that obligation, the remedy or penalty being suggested for breach of that right (censure, sanctions, military intervention), and arguably the nature of the entity that decides the issue and the remedy (e.g., whether an international court or another state).

REFERENCES

Abel, Richard. 1995. *Politics by Other Means: Law in the Struggle against Apartheid, 1980–1994.* New York: Routledge.

———. 1989. *American Lawyers.* New York: Oxford University Press.

Abel, Richard, and Phillip Lewis, eds. 1988a. *Lawyers in Society.* Vol. I, *The Common Law World.* Berkeley: University of California Press.

———. 1988b. *Lawyers in Society.* Vol. II, *The Civil Law World.* Berkeley: University of California Press.

Academics Discuss Spiritual Civilization. FBIS-CHI-98-131, May 11, 1998.

Addis, Adeno. 1992. "Individualism, Communitarianism, and the Rights of Ethnic Minorities." *Notre Dame Law Review* 67: 615.

Ajani, Gianmaria. 1992. "The Rise and Fall of the Law-Based State in the Experience of Russian Legal Scholarship." In *Toward the "Rule of Law" in Russia?: Political and Legal Reform in the Transition Period,* edited by Donald D. Barry. Armonk, NY: M.E. Sharpe.

Alan, Andre, ed. 1992. *Treatise on Belgian Constitutional Law.* Boston: Kluwer Law and Taxation.

Alford, William. 2001. "Of Lawyers Lost and Found: Searching for Legal Professionalism in the People's Republic of China." (Unpublished manuscript presented at the Rule of Law and Group Identities Embedded in Asian Traditions and Cultures Conference, UCLA School of Law, January 19–20).

———. 2000. "Exporting 'The Pursuit Of Happiness' (Reviewing Thomas Carothers, Aiding Democracy Abroad: the Learning Curve)." *Harvard Law Review* 113: 1677.

———. 1999. "A Second Great Wall? China's Post-Cultural Revolution Project of Legal Construction. *Cultural Dynamics* 11. 193.

———. 1995. "Tasseled Loafers for Barefoot Lawyers: Transformation and Tension in the World of Chinese Legal Workers." *The China Quarterly* 141: 22.

———. 1993. "Double-Edged Swords Cut Both Ways: Law and Legitimacy in the People's Republic of China." *Daedalus* 122: 45.

1990. " 'Seek Truths From Facts' – Especially When They Are Unpleasant: America's Understanding of China's Efforts at Law Reform." *Pacific Basin Law Journal* 8: 177.

1986. "The Inscrutable Occidental? Implications of Roberto Unger's Uses and Abuses of the Chinese Past." *Texas Law Review* 64: 195.

1984. "Arsenic and Old Laws: Looking Anew at Criminal Justice in Imperial China." *California Law Review* 72: 1180.

Alford, William, and Shen Yuanyuan. 1997. "Limits of the Law in Addressing China's Environmental Dilemma." *Stanford Environmental Law Journal* 16: 125.

Allee, Mark A. 1994. "Code, Culture, and Custom: Foundations of Civil Case Verdicts in a Nineteenth Century County Court." In *Civil Law in Qing and Republican China*, edited by Kathryn Bernhardt and Philip C.C. Huang. Stanford: Stanford University Press.

Almond, Gabriel. 1994. "Foreword: a Return to Political Culture." In *Political Culture and Democracy*, edited by Larry Diamond. Boulder: Lynne Rienner.

Alsen, Jonas. 1996. "An Introduction to Chinese Property Law." *Maryland Journal of International Law and Trade* 20: 1.

Amnesty International. 2000. "People's Republic of China: the Crackdown on Falun Gong and Other So-Called 'Heretical Organizations.'" ASA 17/011/2000. 23 March. http://www.web.amnesty.org/ai.nsf/Index/ASA170112000.

1997a. "The Death Penalty in China: Breaking Records, Breaking Rules." ASA 17/038/1997. 1 August. http://www.web.amnesty.org/ai.nsf/Index/ASA170381997.

1997b. "People's Republic of China: Law Reform and Human Rights." ASA 17/014/1997. 1 March. http://www.web.amnesty.org/ai.nsf/Index/ASA170141997.

Amsden, Alice. 1989. *Asia's Next Giant: South Korea and Late Industrialization.* New York: Oxford University Press.

An Naim, Abdullahi. 1999. "The Cultural Mediation of Rights." In *The East Asian Challenge for Human Rights*, edited by Joanne Bauer and Daniel Bell. Cambridge: Cambridge University Press.

Annibale, Robert. 1997. "The Need for a Regulatory Framework in the Development and Liberalization of Financial Markets in Africa." In *Good Government and Law*, edited by Julio Faundez. New York: St. Martin's Press.

Another Self-Immolation. Associated Press/Xinhua. February 16, 2001.

Aristotle. 1984. "Nicomachean Ethics." In *The Complete Works of Aristotle*, translated by Jonathan Barnes. Princeton, NJ: Princeton University Press.

Article on Truth of Falungong Gatherings. FBIS-CHI-1999-0809, August 4, 1999.

Asia Comment. 2001. "Remarks of Susan Shirk at the the Asia Pacific Executive Forum." January 16–19. http://www.asiamedia.ucla.edu/ASIAComment 2001/EastWestCenter01.19.2001.htm.

Background of Foreign Investment in China's Economy. FBIS-CHI-2000-0908, September 8, 2000.

Bainbridge, Stephen M. 2000. "Mandatory Disclosure: a Behavioral Analysis." *University of Cincinnati Law Review* 68: 1023.

——— 1998. "Privately Ordered Participatory Management: an Organizational Failures Analysis." *Delaware Journal of Corporate Law* 23: 979.

Barro, Robert. 1997. *Determinants of Economic Growth.* Cambridge: MIT Press.

——— 1996. "Democracy: a Recipe for Growth?" In *Current Issues in Economic Development: an Asian Perspective,* edited by M.G. Quibria and J. Malcolm Dowling. New York: Published for the Asian Development Bank by Oxford University Press.

Bauer, Joanne R., and Daniel A. Bell, eds. 1999. *The East Asian Challenge for Human Rights.* Cambridge: Cambridge University Press.

Baum, Richard. 1986. "Modernization and Legal Reform in Post-Mao China: the Rebirth of Socialist Legality." *Studies of Comparative Communism* 19: 69.

Baum, Richard, and Alexei Shevchenko. 1999. "The 'State of the State' in Post-Reform China." In *The Paradox of China's Post-Mao Reforms,* edited by Merle Goldman and Roderick MacFarquhar. Cambridge: Harvard University Press.

Becker, Gary S. 1983. "A Theory of Competition among Pressure Groups for Political Influence." *Quarterly Journal of Economics* 98: 371.

"Beijing's Anxiety." http://www.stratfor.com/SERVICES/giu2000/080800.ASP.

"Beijing Claims Victory against Sect." 1999. *The Straits Times,* 9 August, at 2.

Beijing's Political–Legal Organs Cut Business Ties. FBIS-CHI-98-358, December 24, 1998.

Beijing Restructures Police Department in Institutional Reform. FBIS-CHI-2000-1123, November 23, 2000.

Bell, Daniel. 2000. *East Meets West: Human Rights and Democracy in East Asia.* Princeton: Princeton University Press.

——— 1996. "The East Asian Challenge to Human Rights: Reflections on an East West Dialogue." *Human Rights Quarterly* 18: 641.

Bell, Daniel, *et al.* 1995. *Towards Illiberal Democracy in Pacific Asia.* New York: St. Martin's Press.

Berger, Mark. 2000. "Reforming Confession Law British Style: a Decade of Experience with Adverse Inferences from Silence." *Columbia Human Rights Review* 31: 243.

Berger, Suzanne. 1996. "Introduction." In *National Diversity and Global Capitalism*, edited by Suzanne Berger and Ronald Dore. Ithaca, NY: Cornell University Press.

Berkman, Jeffrey. 1996. "Intellectual Property Rights in the PRC: Impediments to Protection and the Need for the Rule of Law." *UCLA Pacific Basin Law Journal* 15: 1.

Berman, Harold. 1993. *Faith and Order: the Reconciliation of Law and Religion*. Atlanta: Scholar's Press.

____. 1992. "The Rule of Law and the Law-Based State (Rechtsstaat)." In *Toward the "Rule of Law" in Russia?: Political and Legal Reform in the Transition Period*, edited by Donald D. Barry. Armonk, NY: M.E. Sharpe.

____. 1983. *Law and Revolution*. Cambridge.: Harvard University Press.

____. 1963. *Justice in the USSR*. Cambridge: Harvard University Press.

Bermeo, Nancy. 1997. "Civil Society, Good Governance and Neo-Liberal Reforms." In *Good Government and Law*, edited by Julio Faundez. New York: St. Martin's Press.

Bernhardt, Kathryn, and Philip Huang, eds. 1994. *Civil Law in Qing and Republican China*. Stanford: Stanford University Press.

Bernstein, Thomas. 2000. "Instability in Rural China." In *The Paradox of China's Post-Mao Reforms*, edited by Merle Goldman and Roderick MacFarquhar. Cambridge: Harvard University Press.

Bernstein, Thomas, and Xiaobo Lu. 2000. "Taxation without Representation: Peasants, the Central and Local States in Reform China." *The China Quarterly* 163: 742.

Bindman, Geoffrey. 1988. *South Africa: Human Rights and the Rule of Law*. New York: Pinter Publishers.

Black, Bernard. 1996. "Company Law for Emerging Markets: the Case of Russia." *American Society of International Law Proceedings of the 90th Annual Meeting*, American Society of International Law.

Black, Bernard, Reinier Kraakman, and Anna Tarassova. 2000. "Russian Privatization and Corporate Governance: What Went Wrong?" *Stanford Law Review* 52: 1731.

Blake, Richard Cameron. 2000. "New Development: The World Bank's Draft Comprehensive Development Framework and the Micro-Paradigm of Law and Development." *Yale Human Rights and Development Law Journal* 3: 159.

Bodde, Derk. 1963. "Basic Concepts of Chinese Law: The Genesis and Evolution of Legal Thought in Traditional China." *Proceedings of the American Philosophical Society* 107: 375.

Bodde, Derk, and Clarence Morris. 1967. *Law in Imperial China*. Philadelphia: University of Pennsylvania Press.

Bohannan, J. 1967. "The Differing Realms of the Law." In *Law and Warfare*, edited by P. Bohannan. Garden City, NY: Natural History Press.

Bourchier, David. 1999. "Between Law and Politics: the Malaysian Judiciary since Independence." In *Law, Capitalism and Power in Asia*, edited by Kanishka Jayasuriya. London: Routledge.

Boyer, Robert. 1999. "The Convergence Hypothesis Revisited: Globalization but Still the Century of Nations." In *Contemporary Capitalism: the Embeddedness of Institutions*, edited by J. Rogers Hollingsworth and Robert Boyer. New York: Cambridge University Press.

Brown, Ronald. 1997. *Understanding Chinese Courts and the Legal Process: Law with Chinese Characteristics*. Boston: Kluwer Law International.

Brunetti, Aymo, Gregory Kisunko, and Beatrice Weder. 1998. "How Businesses See Government." IFC Discussion Paper No. 33. Washington, DC: IFC.

Bugaric, Bojan. 2001. "Courts as Policy-Makers: Lessons from Transition." *Harvard International Law Journal* 42: 247.

Building the Socialist Legal System. FBIS-CHI-98-071, March 12, 1998.

"Bureaucratic Mergers and Acquisitions; Chinese Government's Restructuring Initiatives." 1998. *China Business Review*, 15 May, at 36.

Burg, Elliot. 1977. "Law and Development: a Review of the Literature and a Critique of 'Scholars in Estrangement.'" *American Journal of Comparative Law* 25: 492.

Burkhart, Ross E., and Michael S. Lewis-Beck. 1994. "Comparative Democracy: the Economic Development Thesis." *American Political Science Review* 88: 903.

Burns, John. 2000. "The People's Republic of China at 50: National Political Reform." *The China Quarterly* 159: 580.

———. 1994. "Strengthening Central CCP Control of Leadership Selection: the 1990 *Nomenklatura*." *The China Quarterly* 138: 458.

———. 1993. "Administrative Reform in China." *International Journal of Public Administration* 16: 1345.

Burton, Steven J. 1994. "Particularism, Discretion, and the Rule of Law." In *Nomos xxxvi: the Rule of Law*, edited by Ian Shapiro. New York: New York University Press.

Buscaglia, Edgardo, and Pilar Domingo. 1997. "Impediments to Judicial Reform in Latin America." In *The Law and Economics of Development*, edited by Edgardo Buscalgia, *et al*. Greenwich, CT: JAI Press.

Buscaglia, Edgardo, William Ratliff, and Robert Cooter, eds. 1997. *The Law and Economics of Development*. London and Greenwich, CT: JAI Press.

Butler, W.E. 1991. "Perestroika and the Rule of Law." In *Perestroika and the Rule of Law*, edited by W.E. Butler. New York: St. Martin's Press.

Cabestan, Jean-Pierre. 2000. "Administrative Law-Making in the People's Republic of China." In *Law-Making in the People's Republic of China*, edited by Jan Michiel Otto, *et al.* The Hague: Kluwer Law International.

Cai, Dingjian. 2002. "The Function of the People's Congress of China in the Process of Law Implementation." In *Implementation of Law in the People's Republic of China*, edited by Chen Jianfu *et al.* The Hague: Kluwer Law International.

    1999. "Development of the Chinese Legal System since 1979 and Its Current Crisis and Transformation." *Cultural Dynamics* 11: 135.

    1995. "Constitutional Supervision and Interpretation in the People's Republic of China." *Journal of Chinese Law* 9: 219.

Cai, Shangyi. 1994. "Dangqiang Xingzheng Fuyi Shao de Yuanyin ji qi Duice" ("Reasons for and Responses to the Low Number of Administrative Reconsideration Cases Today"). *Jingji yu Fa (Economy and Law)* 5: 24.

Cao, Lan. 1997. "Law and Economic Development: a New Beginning?" *Texas International Law Journal* 32: 545.

Cao, Siyuan. 1997. "Shinian Lai Zhongguo Pochanfa de Lifa yu Shishi" ("Legislation and Implementation of China's Bankruptcy Law during the Last Ten Years"). *Dangdai Zhongguo Yanjiu (Modern China)* 2: 55.

Chamberlain, Heath. 1998. "Civil Society with Chinese Characteristics." *China Journal* 39: 69.

Chan, Johannes M.M., *et al.*, eds. 2000. *Hong Kong's Constitutional Debate: Conflict over Interpretation.* Hong Kong: Hong Kong University Press.

Chan, Joseph. 2002. "Moral Autonomy, Civil Liberties, and Confucianism." 52 *Philosophy East and West.*

    1998. "Thick and Thin Accounts of Human Rights: Lessons from the Asian Values Debate." In *Human Rights and Values in East Asia*, edited by Edmund Ryden. Taiwan: John Paul II Peace Institute.

    1995. "The Asian Challenge to Universal Human Rights: a Philosophical Critique." In *Human Rights and International Relations in the Asia–Pacific Region*, edited by James T.H. Tang. New York: Pinter.

Chang, Gordon. 1999. "What Does the Rule of Law Mean in China?" *China Law and Practice* 13(6): 33–35. August.

Chang, Seung Wha. 2000. "The Role of Law in Economic Development and Adjustment Process: the Case of Korea." *International Lawyer* 34: 267.

Chang, Wejen. 2000. "Foreward." In *The Limits of the Rule of Law in China*, edited by Karen Turner, *et al.* Seattle: University of Washington Press.

Che, Jiahua, and Yingyi Qian. 1998. "Institutional Environment, Community Government, and Corporate Governance: Understanding China's Township–Village Enterprises." *Journal of Law, Economics and Organization* 14: 1.

Cheetham, Simon. 1996. "Strategies for IP Protection." In *Intellectual Property Protection in China*, edited by Michael Fawlk. Hong Kong: Asia Law and Practice.

Chen, Aimin. 1999. "Inertia in Reforming China's State-Owned Enterprises: the Case of Chongqing." *World Development* 26: 479.

Chen, Albert. 2002. "Hong Kong's Legal System in the New Constitutional Order." In *Implementation of Law in the People's Republic of China*, edited by Chen Jianfu *et al*. The Hague: Kluwer Law International.

——— 1999a. "Toward a Legal Enlightenment: Discussion in Contemporary China on the Rule of Law." *UCLA Pacific Basin Law Journal* 17: 125.

——— 1999b. "Rational Law, Economic Development and the Case of China." Social and Legal Studies 8: 97.

Chen, C., L. Chang, and Y. Zhang. 1995. "The Role of Foreign Direct Investment in China's Post-1978 Economic Development." *World Development* 23: 691.

Chen, Chunlai. 1999. "The Impact of FDI and Trade." In *Foreign Direct Investment and Economic Growth in China*, edited by Yanrui Wu. Northhampton, MA: New Horizons in International Business.

Chen, Guangzhong, and Yan Duan, eds. 1996. *Zhonghua Renmin Gongheguo Xingshi Susongfa Shiyi yu Yingyong (Explanation and Application of the Criminal Procedure Law of the People's Republic of China)*. Jilin: Jilin Renmin Chubanshe.

Chen, Jianfu. 2002. "Mission Impossible: Judicial Efforts to Enforce Civil Judgments and Rulings in China." In *Implementation of Law in the People's Republic of China*, edited by Chen Jianfu, *et al*. The Hague: Kluwer Law International.

——— 1999a. "Market Economy and the Internationalisation of Civil and Commercial Law in the People's Republic of China." In *Law, Capitalism and Power in Asia*, edited by Kanishka Jayasuriya. London: Routledge.

——— 1999b. "Enforcement of Civil Judgments and Rulings." *CCH China Law Update*. July.

Chen, Tsung-fu. 2000. "The Rule of Law in Taiwan." In *The Rule of Law: Perspectives from the Pacific Rim*, edited by The Mansfield Center for Pacific Affairs. Washington, DC: The Mansfield Center for Pacific Affairs. http://www.mcpa.org/rol/perspectives.htm.

Chen, Weidong. 2001. *Xingshi Susongfa Shishi Wenti Diaoyan Baogao (Survey Report on the Problems in Implementation of Criminal Procedure Law)*. Beijing: Zhongguo Fangzheng Chubanshe.

Chen, Yanni. 1998. "Legal Sector Opening Wider." *China Daily*, 21 February.

Cheng, Li. 2000. "Jiang Zemin's Successors: the Rise of the Fourth Generation of Leaders in the PRC." *The China Quarterly* 161: 1.

Cheung, Carmen. 2001. "French Law Basis for Likely Move to Outlaw Sect." *WorldSources Online.* 27 April.

Chibundu, Maxwell. 1997. "Law in Development: on Tapping, Gourding and Serving Palm-Wine." *Case Western Reserve Journal of International Law* 29: 167.

Ch'ien, Tuan-Sheng. 1950. *The Government and Politics of China.* Cambridge: Harvard University Press.

China Announces Largest Judicial Cooperation Program with EU. FBIS-CHI-2001-041, April 11, 2001.

China Economic Quarterly. 2000. "The Economy." *China Economic Quarterly* 4: 4.

"China Holds More Members of Banned Meditation Group." 1999. *Los Angeles Times,* 25 July, at A18.

China: Justice Ministry Opens Website for China's Lawyers. FBIS-CHI-98-223, August 11, 1998.

China Offers More Judicial Assistance to Citizens. FBIS-CHI-2001-0409, April 9, 2001.

"China Offers Reward in Sect Crackdown." 1999. *Los Angeles Times,* 4 August, at A13.

"China – Open Recruitment to Select Best Judges." 1999. *China Daily,* 2 March.

"China Opens Sectors to Foreign Investment." 1998. *China Business Information Network,* 10 July.

China Selects SPC "Presiding Judges" through Public Competition. FBIS-CHI-2000-0921, September 21, 2000.

China to Hold First Televised Lawyers' Debate Contest. FBIS-CHI-2001-0321, March 21, 2001.

China to Test 300,000 Prison Guards for "Quality." FBIS-CHI-2000-1120, November 20, 2000.

China: 20 Years of Legal System Developments. FBIS-CHI-990016, January 16, 1999.

"China's Rocky Road to Dispute Resolution: Rough Justice." 1998. *Business China,* 2 February.

China's Supreme Court Concludes 4-Month Reorganization. FBIS-CHI-2000-1207, December 7, 2000.

"China's Township Enterprises Face Changes." 2001. *Asia Pulse,* 5 February.

"Chinese Premier's Government Work Promises Reduction of Ministries." 1998. *BBC Monitoring Asia Pacific,* 11 March.

Choate, Allen C. 1997. "Local Governance in China: an Assessment of Villagers Committees." San Francisco, CA: The Asia Foundation. http://www.asiafoundation.org/publications/rpt_work.html.

Chow, Daniel C.K. 2000. "Counterfeiting in the People's Republic of China." *Washington University Law Quarterly* 78: 1.

Chu, Henry. 1999a. "Crackdown on Chinese Sect Continues." *Los Angeles Times*, 26 July, at A8.

———. 1999b. "Sect's Extent Caught China off Guard." *Los Angeles Times*, 29 July, at A1.

———. 1999c. "New York-Based Leader of Banned Group Targeted for Arrest Crackdown." *Los Angeles Times*, 30 July, at A4.

Chu, Henry, and Anthony Kuhn. 1999. "Sect's Outlawing Shows Beijing's Fear of Protest." *Los Angeles Times*, 23 July, at A1.

Chu, T'ung-tsu. 1961. *Law and Society in Traditional China*. Paris: Mouton and Co.

Chua, Amy. 1998. "Markets, Democracy and Ethnicity." *Yale Law Journal* 108: 1.

Clague, C., P. Keefer, S. Knack, and M. Olson. 1997a. "Institutions and Economic Performance: Property Rights and Contract Enforcement." In *Institutions and Economic Development*, edited by C. Clague. Baltimore: Johns Hopkins University Press.

———. 1997b. "Democracy, Autocracy, and Institutions Supportive of Economic Growth." In *Institutions and Economic Development*, edited by C. Clague. Baltimore: Johns Hopkins University Press.

Clarke, Donald. 2001. "Puzzling Observations in Chinese Law: When Is a Riddle Just a Mistake?" Unpublished manuscript.

———. 1999. "China and the World Trade Organization." In *Doing Business in China*, edited by Freshfields. Yonkers, NY: Juris Publishing, Inc.

———. 1998–99. "Alternative Approaches to Chinese Law: beyond the 'Rule of Law' Paradigm." *Waseda Proceedings of Comparative Law* 2.

———. 1998. *Wrongs and Rights*. New York: Lawyers Committee on Human Rights.

———. 1997. "State Council Notice Nullifies Statutory Rights of Creditors." *East Asian Executive Reporter*, April, at 9–15.

———. 1996. "Power and Politics in the Chinese Court System: the Enforcement of Civil Judgments." *Columbia Journal of Asian Law* 10: 1.

———. 1992. "Regulation and Its Discontents: Understanding Economic Law in China." *Stanford Journal of International Law* 28: 283.

———. 1991a. "What's Law Got to Do with It? Legal Institutions and Economic Reform in China." *Pacific Basin Law Review* 10: 1.

———. 1991b. "Dispute Resolution in China." *Journal of Chinese Law* 5: 245.

Clinton, William J. 2000. "Remarks on China Trade Status." 8 March. http://www.state.gov/www/regions/eap/2000_eap_speeches.html.

"Clinton Administration's Deal with China on WTO." 1999. *Human Rights for Workers, Bulletin* IV(21), 19 November.

Cohen, Jerome Alan. 1978. "China's Changing Constitution." *The China Quarterly* 76: 794.

—— 1968. *The Criminal Process in the People's Republic of China, 1949-63: an Introduction.* Cambridge: Harvard University Press.

—— 1966. "Chinese Mediation on the Eve of Modernization." *California Law Review* 54: 1201.

Cohen, Jerome, and Adam Kearney. 2000. "The New Beijing Arbitration Commission." In *Doing Business in China*, edited by Freshfields. Yonkers, NY: Juris Publishing, Inc.

Cohen, Paul. 1970. "Ch'ing China: Confrontation with the West, 1850–1900." In *Modern East Asia*, edited by James B. Crowley. New York: Harcourt, Brace and World.

Committee on Economic, Social and Cultural Rights. 1977. *General Comment No. 8.* UN Doc. E/1998/22 Annex V.

Conner, Alison. 1998. "Confucianism and Due Process." In *Confucianism and Human Rights*, edited by Wm. Theodore de Bary and Tu Weiming. New York: Columbia University Press.

—— 1996. "Lawyers and the Legal Profession during the Republican Period." In *Civil Law in Qing and Republican China*, edited by Kathryn Bernhardt and Philip Huang. Stanford: Stanford University Press.

—— 1991. "To Get Rich Is Precarious: Regulation of Private Enterprise in the People's Republic of China." *Journal of Chinese Law* 5: 1.

Cooney, Sean. 1999. "A Community Changes: Taiwan's Council of Grand Justices and Liberal Democratic Reform." In *Law, Capitalism and Power in Asia*, edited by Kanishka Jayasuriya. London: Routledge.

Cooter, Robert. 1997. "The Rule of State Law Versus the Rule-of-Law State: Economic Analysis of the Legal Foundations of Development." In *The Law and Economics of Development*, edited by Edgardo Buscalgia, *et al.* London: JAI Press.

Corne, Peter. 2001. "Creation and Application of Law." In *Doing Business in China*, edited by Freshfields. Yonkers, NY: Juris Publishing, Inc.

—— 1997. "China's Legal Structure." In *A Guide to the Legal System of the PRC*, edited by Chris Hunter. Hong Kong: Asia Law and Practice.

—— 1996. *Foreign Investment in China: the Administrative Legal System.* Hong Kong: Hong Kong University Press.

Corne, Peter, and Andrew Godwin. 1997. "Allocated or Granted Land? New Rules Blur the Boundaries." *China Joint Venturer*, February, at 11.

Court President on Ranks of Judges, Police. FBIS-CHI-98-264, September 21, 1998.

Craenen, G. 1996a. "Legislators." In *The Institutions of Federal Belgium*, edited by G. Craenen. Leuven: Acco.

1996b. "General Background and Legal Characteristics." In *The Institutions of Federal Belgium*, edited by G. Craenen. Leuven: Acco.

Craig, P.P. 1994. *Administrative Law*. 3rd edn. London: Sweet and Maxwell.

Crest, Sed. 2000. "Inside the CSRC: Gao Xiqing." *China Law and Practice*, March, at 35–39.

Cross, Frank. 1999. "Shattering the Fragile Case for Judicial Review of Rule-making." *Virginia Law Review* 85: 1243.

Crowell, Todd, and David Hsieh. 1999. "A New Upheaval?" *Asia Week*, 4 June.

Cua, A.S. 1978. *Dimensions in Moral Creativity*. University Park: Pennsylvania State University Press.

Dahl, Robert. 1989. *Democracy and Its Critics*. New Haven: Yale University Press.

1971. *Polyarchy: Participation in Opposition*. New Haven: Yale University Press.

David, René. 1984. "Source of Law." In *International Encyclopedia of Comparative Law*. Vol. II, ch. III. The Hague: Martinus Nijhoff Publishers.

Davis, Kenneth Culp. 1969. *Discretionary Justice: a Preliminary Inquiry*. Baton Rouge: Louisiana State University Press.

Davis, Kevin, and Michael Trebilcock. 1999. *What Role Do Legal Institutions Play In Development?* Washington, DC: International Finance Corporation.

Davis, Michael. 1998. "Constitutionalism and Political Culture: the Debate over Human Rights and Asian Values." *Harvard Human Rights Journal* 11: 109.

de Bary, Wm. Theodore. 1998. *Asian Values and Human Rights: a Confucian Communitarian Perspective*. Cambridge: Harvard University Press.

1993. *Waiting for the Dawn*. New York: Columbia University Press.

1960a. *Sources of Chinese Tradition*. Vol. I. New York: Columbia University Press.

1960b. *Sources of Chinese Tradition*. Vol. II. New York: Columbia University Press.

deLisle, Jacques. 1999. "Lex Americana?: United States Legal Assistance, American Legal Models, and Legal Change in the Post-Communist World and beyond." *University of Pennsylvania Journal of International Economic Law* 20: 179.

deLisle, Jacques, and Kevin Lane. 1997. "Hong Kong's Endgame and the Rule of Law (II)." *University of Pennsylvania Journal of International Economic Law* 18: 195.

Demirguc-Kunt, Asli, and Vojislav Maksimovic. 1998. "Law, Finance and Firm Growth." *Journal of Finance* 53: 2107.

Deng, Xiaoping. 1994. *Selected Works of Deng Xiaoping*. Vol. III (*1982–1992*). Beijing: Foreign Language Press.

1984. "Emancipate the Mind, Seek Truth from Facts and Unite as One in Looking into the Future." In *Selected Works of Deng Xiaoping (1975–1982)*. Beijing: Foreign Language Press.

1941. "The Party and the Anti-Japanese Democratic Government." In *Selected Works of Deng Xiaoping (1938–1965)*. Beijing: Foreign Language Press.

"Deng's Theory Incorporated." 1999. *China Daily*, Feb. 1.

Dezalay, Yves, and Bryant Garth. 1996. *Dealing in Virtue: International Commercial Arbitration and the Construction of a Transnational Legal Order*. Chicago: University of Chicago Press.

Dhavan, Rajeev. 1994. "Law as Concern: Reflecting on 'Law and Development.' " In *Law and Development in the Third World*, edited by Yash Vyas. Nairobi: Faculty of Law, University of Nairobi.

Diamond, Larry. 1996. "Is the Third Wave over?" *Journal of Democracy* 7: 20.

1994. "Introduction: Political Culture and Democracy." In *Political Culture and Democracy*, edited by Larry Diamond. Boulder: Lynne Rienner.

Diamond, Larry, and Raymond Myers. 2000. "Introduction: Elections and Democracy in Greater China." *The China Quarterly* 162: 365.

Dicey, Albert Venn. 1959. *Introduction to the Study of the Law of the Constitution*. 10th edn. London: Macmillan.

Dicks, Anthony. 1995. "Compartmentalized Law and Judicial Restraint: an Inductive View of Some Jurisdictional Barriers to Reform." *The China Quarterly* 141: 82.

Dickson, Bruce. 2000. "Political Instability at the Middle and Lower Levels: Signs of a Decaying CCP, Corruption and Political Dissent." In *Is China Unstable?*, edited by David Shambaugh. Armonk, NY: M.E. Sharpe.

1997. *Democratization in China and Taiwan*. Oxford: Clarendon Press.

Dieng, Adama. 1997. "Role of Judge and Lawyers in Defending Rule of Law." *Fordham International Law Journal* 21: 550.

"Dispute Slows Passage of Securities Law." 1997. *China Securities Bulletin*, 24 September.

Dodds, Robert, Jr. 1996. "State Enterprise Reform in China: Managing the Transition to a Market Economy." *Law and Policy in International Business* 27: 695.

Dong, Hua. 2000. "Guanyu Woguo Faguan Zhidu Gaige de Sikao" ("Reflections on the Reform of the PRC Judges System"). *Faxue Zazhi* 3.

Dong, Yuyu. 1998. "Tongguo Tizhi Zhengzhi Gaige de Fazhi Zhi Lu" ("The Rule of Law Road to Political System Reform"). In *Zhengzhi Zhongguo (Political China)*, edited by Dong Yuyu and Shi Binhai. Beijing: Jinri Zhongguo Chubanshe.

Donnelly, Jack. 1999. "Human Rights and Asian Values." In *The East Asian Challenge for Human Rights*, edited by Joanne Bauer and Daniel Bell. Cambridge: Cambridge University Press.

1989. *Universal Human Rights in Theory and Practice*. Ithaca, NY: Cornell University Press.

Dorf, Michael, and Charles Sabel. 1998. "A Constitution of Democratic Experimentalism." *Columbia Law Review* 98: 267.

Dowdle, Michael. 2001a. "Preserving Indigenous Paradigms in an Age of Globalization: Pragmatic Strategies for the Development of Clinical Aid in China." *Fordham Journal of International Law* 24: 56.

2001b. "The NPC as Catalyst for New Norms of Public Political Participation in China." In *Changing Views of Citizenship in China*, edited by Merle Goldman and Elizabeth Perry. Cambridge: Harvard University Press.

1999. "Heretical Laments: China and the Fallacies of 'Rule of Law.'" *Cultural Dynamics* 11: 285.

1997. "The Constitutional Development and Operations of the National People's Congress." *Columbia Journal of Asian Law* 11: 1125.

Dreze, Jean, and Amartya Sen. 1989. *Hunger and Public Action*. Oxford: Clarendon Press.

Dworkin, Ronald. 1978. "Liberalism." In *Public and Private Morality*, edited by Stuart Hampshire. New York: Cambridge University Press.

1977. *Taking Rights Seriously*. Cambridge: Harvard University Press.

Economist Intelligence Unit. 1997. *Multinational Companies in China: Winners and Losers*. Hong Kong: The Economic Intelligence Unit.

Editorial Office. 1998. "Yifa Zhiguo yu Lianzheng Jianshe Yantaohui Jiyao" ("Excerpts of Main Points of Conference on Establishing Good Governance and a Country Ruled in Accordance with Law"). *Faxue Yanjiu (Jurisprudence Studies)* 20(4): 3.

Edley, Christopher F., Jr. 1990. *Administrative Law: Rethinking Judicial Control of Bureaucracy*. New Haven: Yale University Press.

Edwards, R. Randle. 1986. "Civil and Social Rights: Theory and Practice in Chinese Law Today." In *Human Rights in Contemporary China*, edited by R. Randle Edwards, *et al.* New York: Columbia University Press.

"Elusive Falungong Leader Says Mass Following Rattles China." 1999. *Inside China Today*, 23 July. www.insidechina.com/features.php3.

Epstein, Amy. 1997. "Village Elections in China: Experimenting with Democracy." In *China's Economic Future: Challenges to US Policy*, edited by Joint Economic Committee. Armonk, NY: M.E. Sharpe.

Epstein, Edward. 1994. "Law and Legitimation in Post-Mao China." In *Domestic Law Reforms in Post-Mao China*, edited by Pitman Potter. Armonk, NY: M.E. Sharpe.

Fa, Jyh-Pin, and Shao-chun Leng. 1991. "Judicial Review of Administration in the People's Republic of China." *Case Western Reserve Journal of International Law* 23: 447.

Fallon, Richard. 1997. "'The Rule of Law' as a Concept in Constitutional Discourse." *Columbia Law Review* 97: 1.

"Falun Gong Practitioners Arrested for Suing Beijing Leaders." 2001. *CNA Hong Kong*, 9 October.

Fan, Mingxin. 1980. "Women Yinggai Paoqi Fazhi he Renzhi de Tifa" ("We Should Abandon the Formulations of Rule of Law and Rule of Man"). *Faxue Yanjiu* 4: 64.

Fang, Ning, *et al.* 2001. *Lixing de Huhuan: Zhongguo Xingzheng Susong Fa Shishi Xianzhuang Diaocha Baogao (A Call for Rationality: a Survey of the Status of Implementation of China's Administrative Litigation Law)*. Dongwu Faxue Chubanshe.

Fang, Shirong. 1996. *Lun Juti Xingzheng Xingwei (Discussion of Specific Administrative Acts)*. Wuhan: Wuhan Daxue Chubanshe.

Farber, Henry, and Joanne Gowa. 1995. "Common Interests or Common Politics? Reinterpreting the Democratic Peace." Working Paper #342, Industrial Relations Section, Princeton University.

Faundez, Julio. 1997. "Introduction: Legal Technical Assistance." In *Good Government and Law*, edited by Julio Faundez. New York: St. Martin's Press.

Favoreau, Louis. 1990. "Constitutional Review in Europe." In *Constitutionalism and Rights: the Influence of the United States Constitution Abroad*, edited by Louis Henkin and Albert J. Rosenthal. New York: Columbia University Press.

Feinerman, James. 1998. "The Give and Take of Central Local Relations." *China Business Review*, January–February, at 16.

Feng, Jianping. 1996. "Woguo Lüshifa de Tedian" ("The Distinguishing Features of Our Country's Lawyers Law"). *Faxue Zazhi* 5: 39.

Fewsmith, Joseph. 2001. "The New Shape of Elite Politics." *The China Journal* 45: 21.

Finder, Susan. 2001. "The Courts." In *Doing Business in China*, edited by Freshfields. Yonkers, NY: Juris Publishing, Inc.

⸺ 1993. "The Supreme People's Court of the People's Republic of China." *Journal of Chinese Law* 7: 145.

⸺ 1989. "Like Throwing an Egg against a Stone? Administrative Litigation in the People's Republic of China." *Journal of Chinese Law* 3: 1.

Finder, Susan, and Fu Hualing. 1997. "Tightening up Chinese Courts' 'Bags' – the Amended PRC, Criminal Law." *China Law and Practice* 11: 35.

Fingarette, Herbert. 1972. *Confucius: the Secular is Sacred*. New York: Harper and Row.

Finnis, John. 1980. *Natural Law and Natural Rights*. Oxford: Clarendon Press.

Forney, Matt. 1996–97. "Outside the Law: Reform Reversals Hit Foreign Law Firms in China." *Far Eastern Economic Review*, 26 December–2 January, at 18.

1996. "Patriot Games." *Far Eastern Economic Review*, 3 October, at 22.

Fox, William F. 1997. *Understanding Administrative Law*. Albany, NY: Matthew Bender.

Francis, Corinna-Barbara. 1999. "Bargained Property Rights: the Case of China's High-Technology Sector." In *Property Rights and Economic Reform in China*, edited by Jean C. Oi and Andrew G. Walder. Stanford: Stanford University Press.

Franck, Thomas. 1972. "The New Development: Can American Law and Legal Institutions Help Developing Countries?" *Wisconsin Law Review* 1972: 767.

Freedman, James O. 1978. *Crisis and Legitimacy: the Administrative Process and American Government*. New York: Cambridge University Press.

Freeman, Jody. 2000. "The Private Role in Public Governance." *New York University Law Review* 75: 543.

Friedman, Edward. 1989. "Theorizing the Democratization of the Leninist State." In *Marxism and the Chinese Experience*, edited by Arif Dirlik and Maurice Meisner. Armonk: M.E. Sharpe.

Friedman, Lawrence. 1969. "Legal Culture and Social Development." *Law and Social Review* 4: 29.

Frischtak, Leila. 1997. "Political Mandate, Institutional Change and Economic Reform." In *Good Government and Law*, edited by Julio Faundez. New York: St. Martin's Press.

Fu, Hualing. 2002. "The Shifting Landscape of Dispute Resolution in Rural China." In *Implementation of Law in the People's Republic of China*, edited by Chen Jianfu, *et al*. The Hague: Kluwer Law International.

1994. "A Bird in the Cage: Police and Political Leadership in Post-Mao China." *Policing and Society* 4: 277.

1992. "Understanding People's Mediation in Post-Mao China." *Journal of Chinese Law* 6: 211.

Fukuyama, Francis. 1995. "Confucianism and Democracy." *Journal of Democracy* 6: 20.

1992. *The End of History and the Last Man*. New York: Free Press.

Fuller, Lon. 1976. *The Morality of Law*. New Haven: Yale University Press.

Galligan, D.J. 1986. *Discretionary Powers: a Legal Study of Official Discretion*. New York: Oxford University Press.

Gao, Xiqing. 1996. "Developments in Securities and Investment Law in China." *Australian Journal of Corporate Law* 6: 228.

Gardner, James. A. 1980. *Legal Imperialism*. Madison: University of Wisconsin Press.

Gaus, Gerald F. 1994. "Public Reason and the Rule of Law." In *The Rule of Law*, edited by Ian Shapiro. New York: New York University.

Gelatt, Timothy. 1991. "Lawyers in China: the Past Decade and beyond." *New York University Journal of International Law and Politics* 23: 751.

——. 1989. "Recent Development: the New Chinese State Secrets Law." *Cornell International Law Journal* 22: 255.

Gelb, Alan, Gary Jefferson, and Inderjit Singh. 1993. "Can Communist Economies Transform Incrementally? The Experience of China." In *NBER Macroeconomics Annual 1993*, edited by Olivier Blanchard and Stanley Fischer. Cambridge: MIT Press.

Gewirtz, Paul. 1999. "Comments at Law in Contemporary China Conference." *Harvard University* (March).

Ghai, Yash. 1994. "Human Rights and Governance: the Asia Debate." *Asia Foundation's Center for Asian Pacific Affairs Occasional Paper* 4.

——. 1993a. "The Rule of Law and Capitalism: Reflections on the Basic Law." In *Hong Kong, China and 1997: Essays in Legal Theory*, edited by Raymond Wacks. Hong Kong: Hong Kong University Press.

——. 1993b. "Constitutions and Governance in Africa: a Prolegomenon." In *Law and Crisis in the Third World*, edited by Sammy Adelman and Abdul Paliwala. London: Hans Zell Publishers.

——. 1987. "Law, Development and African Scholarship." *Modern Law Review* 50: 750.

Gillespie, John. 1999. "Law and Development in 'the Market Place': an East Asian Perspective." In *Law, Capitalism and Power in Asia*, edited by Kanishka Jayasuriya. London: Routledge.

Ginsburg, Tom. 2000. "Does Law Matter for Economic Development? Evidence from East Asia." *Law and Society Review* 34: 701.

Glendon, Mary Ann, Michael Wallace Gordon, and Christopher Osakwe. 1994. *Comparative Legal Traditions*. 2nd edn. St. Paul, MN: West Publishing Company.

Gluck, Carol. 1994. "The Call for a New Asian Identity: an Examination of the Cultural Arguments and Their Implications." *Japan Programs Occasional Papers, No. 5*. New York: Japan Programs, Carnegie Council on Ethics and International Affairs.

Goldman, Merle. 2000. "The Potential for Instability among Alienated Intellectuals and Students in Post-Mao China." In *Is China Unstable?*, edited by David Shambaugh. Armonk, NY: M.E. Sharpe.

——. 1999. "Politically-Engaged Intellectuals in the 1990s." *The China Quarterly* 159: 700.

Goldman, Merle, and Roderick MacFarquhar, eds. 1999. *The Paradox of Post-Mao Reforms*. Cambridge: Harvard University Press.

Goldman, Sheldon. 1993. "Bush's Judicial Legacy: the Final Imprint." *Judicature* 76: 282.

Goldsmith, Jack. 2000. "Should International Human Rights Law Trump US Domestic Law?" *Chicago Journal of International Law* 1: 327.

Goldstein, Leslie Friedman. 2001. "The Rule of Law: Do We Know It When We See it?" Unpublished manuscript presented at the Law and Society Conference, Budapest, 2001.

Gong, Xiangrui, ed. 1993. *Fazhi de Lixiang yu Xianshi (The Ideal and Reality of the Rule of Law)*. Beijing: Zhongguo Zhongfa Daxue Chubanshe.

Goodman, David S. 1987. "Democracy, Interest and Virtue: the Search for Legitimacy in the People's Republic of China." In *Foundations and Limits of State Power in China*, edited by Stuart Schram. Hong Kong: The Chinese University Press.

Gopal, Mohan Gopalan. 1996. "Law and Development: toward a Pluralist Vision." *American Society of International Law Proceedings* 1996: 231–37.

Gordon, Joy. 1999. "A Peaceful, Silent, Deadly Remedy: the Ethics of Economic Sanctions." *Ethics and International Affairs* 13: 123.

Gore, Lance. 1999. "The Communist Legacy in Post-Mao Economic Growth." *The China Journal* 41: 25.

Graham, Angus. 1989. *Disputers of the Tao*. La Salle, IL: Open Court.

Gray, Cheryl, and Kathryn Hendley. 1997. "Developing Commercial Law in Transition Economies: Examples from Hungary and Russia." In *The Rule of Law and Economic Reform in Russia*, edited by Jeffrey Sachs and Katharina Pistor. Boulder: Westview Press.

Great Britain. 1957. *Committee on Administrative Tribunal and Enquiries (Franks Committee Report)*. Cmnd. 218. London: HMSO.

Greenberg, David. 1980. "Law and Development in Light of Dependency Theory." *Law and Society* 3: 129.

Gu, Edward X. 1998. " 'Non-Establishment' Intellectuals, Public Space, and the Creation of Non-Governmental Organizations in China: the Chen Ziming–Wang Juntao Saga." 39 *China Journal*.

———. 1997. "Elitist Democracy and China's Democratization." *Democratization* 4: 84.

Gu, Peidong. 1999. "Zhongguo Lüshi Zhidu de Lilun Jianshi yu Shizheng Fenxi (xia)" ("A Theoretical Examination and Positivist Analysis of China's Lawyer System [Part B])," *Zhongguo Lüshi (China Lawyer)* 12: 51.

Guangdong to Choose Senior Officials through "Open Competition." FBIS-CHI-2000-116, November 16, 2000.

"Guangdongsheng Gong'anting Qiangdiao yao Baozhang Lüshi Yifa Luxing Zhize" ("Guangdong Province Public Security Bureau Emphasizes Need to Guarantee Lawyers Can Carry out Duties in Accordance with Law"). 1997. *Zhongguo Lüshi Bao*, 6 December, at 1.

Guo, Daohui. 1999. "Shixing Sifa Duli yu Xiezhi Sifa Fubai" ("Implement Judicial Independence and Eliminate Judicial Corruption"). In *Yifa Zhiguo yu Sifa Gaige (Ruling the Country According to Law and Judicial Reform)*, edited by Xin Chunying and Li Lin. Beijing: Zhongguo Fazhi Chubanshe.

———. 1996a. "Shixian Fazhi de Siyao" ("On the Four Requirements for the Realization of the Rule of Law"). In "Zhongguo Fazhi Shixian Fanglue (Bitanhui)" (Strategy for the Realization of the Rule of Law [Written Exchange of Ideas]). *Falü Kexue* 3: 3.

———. 1996b. "Enlightenment on Law and Rule of Law in China: Comments on Certain Recent Theoretical Views in the Study of Jurisprudence in China." *Journal of Chinese and Comparative Law* 2: 1.

Guo, Songjie. 1996. "Lun Xingzheng Heli Linian yu Sifa Shencha de Fanwei" ("Discussion of the Concept of Administrative Reasonableness and the Scope of Judicial Review"). *Xingzheng Fazhi (Administrative Rule of Law)* 4: 38.

Guthrie, Douglas. 1999. *Dragon in a Three-Piece Suite*. Princeton: Princeton University Press.

———. 1998. "The Declining Significance of Guanxi in China's Economic Transition." *The China Quarterly* 154: 255.

Gutman, Amy. 1994. *Multiculturalism*. Princeton, NJ: Princeton University Press.

Habermas, Jürgen. 1996. *Between Facts and Norms*. Translated by William Rheg. Cambridge: MIT Press.

———. 1979. *Communication and the Evolution of Society*. Boston: Beacon Press.

———. 1975. *Legitimation Crisis*. Boston: Beacon Press.

Habermas, Jürgen, and N. Luhmann. 1971. *Theorie der Gesellschaft oder Sozialtechnologie*. Frankfurt: Suhrkamp.

Hager, Barry. 2000. "The Rule of Law." In *The Rule of Law: Perspectives from the Pacific Rim*. Washington, DC: Mansfield Center for Pacific Affairs. http://www.mcpa.org/rol/perspectives.htm.

Hall, David, and Roger Ames. 1999. *Democracy of the Dead: Dewey, Confucius and the Hope for Democracy in China*. Chicago: Open Court.

———. 1987. *Thinking through Confucius*. Albany: State University of New York Press.

Hall, Peter. 1999. "The Political Economy of Europe in an Era of Independence." In *Continuity and Change in Contemporary Capitalism*, edited by Herbert Kitschelt, Peter Lange, Gary Marks, and John D. Stephens. New York: Cambridge University Press.

Hamilton, Gary, ed. 1991. *Business Networks and Economic Development in East and Southeast Asia*. Hong Kong: Centre of Asian Studies, University of Hong Kong.

Hamrin, Carol Lee. 2001. "Inching toward Open Politics." *The China Journal* 45: 123.

Hansard Society Commission. 1993. "Making the Law: the Report of the Hansard Society Commission on the Legislative Process." London: Hansard Society for Parliamentary Government.

Hansen, Chad. 1992. *A Daoist Theory of Thought.* New York: Oxford University Press.

Hao, Yufan, and Michael Johnson. 1995. "Reform at the Crossroads: an Analysis of Chinese Corruption." *Asian Perspectives* 19: 117.

Harer, Charles Kenworthy. 1999. "Arbitration Fails to Reduce Foreign Investors' Risk in China." *Pacific Rim Law and Policy Journal* 8: 393.

Hart, H.L.A. 1961. *The Concept of Law.* Oxford: Clarendon Press.

Hayek, Friedrich A. 1944. *The Road to Serfdom.* Chicago: University of Chicago Press.

He, Baogang. 1996. *The Democratization of China.* New York: Routledge.

He, Sheng. 1998. "Lawyers Need to Be Defended Too." *China Daily,* 11 August.

He, Weifang. 1995. "Tongguo Sifa Shixian Shehui Zhengyi: Dui Zhongguo Faguan Xianzhuang de Yi Ge Toushi" ("Realization of Social Justice through the Judiciary: One Perspective of the Current Situation of PRC Judges"). In *Zou Xiang Quanli de Shidai (Toward an Age of Rights),* edited by Xia Yong. Beijing: Zhongguo Zhengfa Daxue Chubanshe.

Hecht, Jonathan. 1996. *Opening to Reform: an Analysis of China's Revised Criminal Procedure Law.* New York: Lawyer's Committee for Human Rights.

Hendley, Kathryn. 1996. "Law and Development in Russia: a Misguided Experiment?" *American Society of International Law Proceedings,* March, at 237.

Hintzen, Geor. 1999. "The Place of Law in the PRC's Culture." *Cultural Dynamics* 11: 167.

Hirst, Paul, and Grahame Thompson. 1996. *Globalization in Question.* Cambridge, MA: Blackwell Publishers.

Hollingsworth, J. Rogers, and Robert Boyer. 1999. "Coordination of Economic Actors and Social Systems of Production." In *Contemporary Capitalism: the Embeddedness of Institutions,* edited by J. Rogers Hollingsworth and Robert Boyer. New York: Cambridge University Press.

Holmes, Stephen. 1993. "Back to the Drawing Board: an Argument for Constitutional Postponement in Eastern Europe." *East European Constitutional Review* 2: 21.

Hong, Joon-Hyung. 2000. "The Rule of Law and Its Acceptance in Asia." In *The Rule of Law: Perspectives from the Pacific Rim.* Washington, DC: Mansfield Center for Pacific Affairs. http://www.mcpa.org/rol/perspectives. htm.

Hong Kong Trade Development Council. 2000. "Market Profile on Chinese Mainland." http://www.tdctrade.com/main/china.htm.

Horwitz, Morton J. 1992. *The Transformation of American Law, 1870–1960: the Crisis of Legal Orthodoxy.* New York: Oxford University Press.

Howson, Nicholas. 1997. "Flood of Legislation Clears the Way for New Corporate Forms – but Are They Worth It?" *China Joint Venturer,* July–August, at 7.

Hu, Jianmiao. 1992. "Youguan Xingzheng Lanyong Zhiquan de Neihan Je he Biaoxian de Xueli Tantao" ("Theoretical Inquiry Relating to the Connotation and Manifestation of Abuse of Authority"). *Faxue Yanjiu* 3: 8.

Hu, Weixi. 1998. "Sixiang Ziyou yu Minzhu Zhengzhi" ("Freedom of Thought and Democratic Government"). In *Zhengzhi Zhongguo (Political China),* edited by Dong Yuyu and Shi Binhai. Beijing: Jinri Zhongguo Chubanshe.

Hu, Yuhong. 1996. "Quanli Kongzhi: Fazhi de Zongzhi yu Guisu" ("Controlling Power: the Goal and End of Rule of Law"). In *Zhongguo Fazhi Shixian Fanglue (Bitanhui) (Strategy for the Realization of the Rule of Law [Written Exchange of Ideas]). Falü Kexue* 3: 18.

Hu, Yunteng. 2002. "Application of Death Penalty in Chinese Judicial Practice." In *Implementation of Law in the People's Republic of China,* edited by Chen Jianfu, *et al.* The Hague: Kluwer Law International.

1999. "Sifa Gaige – Wenti, Mubiao he Silu" ("Judicial Reform – Issues, Target and Conceptual Approach"). In *Yifa Zhiguo yu Sifa Gaige (Ruling the Country According to Law and Judicial Reform),* edited by Xin Chunying and Li Lin. Beijing: Zhongguo Fazhi Chubanshe.

Huang, Daqiang. 1993. "China's Administrative Reform and the Teaching of Administrative Science." *Asian Review of Public Administration* 5: 1.

Huang Lao Boshu. 1980. *Mawangdui Hanmu Boshu.* (Mawangdui Han Tomb Huang-Lao Silk Manuscripts). Vol. I. Beijing: Wenwu Press.

Huang, Philip. 2001. *Code, Custom, and Legal Practice in China: the Qing and the Republic Compared.* Stanford: Stanford University Press.

1996. *Civil Justice in China.* Stanford: Stanford University Press.

1994. "Codified Law and Magisterial Adjudication in the Qing." In *Civil Law in Qing and Republican China,* edited by Kathryn Bernhardt and Philip Huang. Stanford: Stanford University Press.

Huang, Yasheng. 1996. *Inflation and Investment Controls in China.* Cambridge: Cambridge University Press.

Hubbard, Michael. 1999. "Bureaucrats and Markets in China: the Rise and Fall of Entrepreneurial Local Government." *Governance* 8: 335.

Hulsewe, A.F.P. 1955. *Remnants of Han Law.* Leiden: E.J. Brill.

Human Rights in China. 2000. *Impunity for Torturers Continues Despite Changes in Law: Report on Implementation of the Convention against Torture in the People's Republic of China.* April. www.hrichina.org/reports/cat2000. html.

"Human Rights Situation in China." 1991. *Beijing Review* 34: 8. 4–10 November.

Human Rights Watch World Report 1998: China. 1998. 8 December. www. hrw.org/hrw/campaigns/china-98/chn-wr98.htm.

Huntington, Samuel. 1991. *The Third Wave: Democratization in the Late Twentieth Century.* Norman: University of Oklahoma Press.

Hutchinson, Allan C., ed. 1989. *Critical Legal Studies.* Totowa, NJ: Rowman and Littlefield.

Hyde, Alan. 1983. "The Concept of Legitimation in the Sociology of Law." *Wisconsin Law Review* 1983: 379.

IBRD World Bank. 2001. *World Development Indicators 2001.* Washington, DC: World Bank.

Information Office of the State Council. 2000. "US Human Rights Record in 1999." *China Daily*, 27 February.

Inglehart, Ronald. 1997. *Modernization and Postmodernization: Cultural, Economic and Political Change in 43 Societies.* Princeton, NJ: Princeton University Press.

Inoue, Tatsuo. 1999. "Liberal Democracy and Asian Orientalism." In *The East Asian Challenge for Human Rights*, edited by Joanne Bauer and Daniel Bell. Cambridge: Cambridge University Press.

Integration of Confucian Ethics, Socialism. FBIS-CHI-98-035, February 4, 1998.

International Commission of Jurists. 1988. *South Africa: Human Rights and Rule of Law*, edited by Geoffrey Bindman. New York: Pinter Publishers.

International Finance Corporation. 2000. *China's Emerging Private Enterprises.* Washington, DC: IFC.

Jacob, Herbert. 1996. "Courts and Politics in the United States." In *Courts, Law and Politics in Comparative Perspective*, edited by Herbert Jacob, *et al.* New Haven: Yale University Press.

Jayasuriya, Kanishka. 1999a. "Introduction: Framework for the Analysis of Legal Institutions in East Asia." In *Law, Capitalism and Power in Asia*, edited by Kanishka Jayasuriya. London: Routledge.

   1999b. "Corporatism and Judicial Independence within Statist Legal Institutions in East Asia." In *Law, Capitalism and Power in Asia*, edited by Kanishka Jayasuriya. London: Routledge.

   ed. 1999c. *Law, Capitalism and Power in Asia.* London: Routledge.

Jefferson, Gary, and Thomas Rawksi. 1995. "How Industrial Reform Worked in China: the Role of Innovation, Competition and Property Rights." *Proceedings of the World Bank Annual Conference on Developing Economies* 1994: 129.

Jennings, M. Kent. 1997. "Political Participation in the Chinese Countryside." *Political Science Review* 91: 361.

Ji, You. 1998. "China's Administrative Reform: Constructing a New Model for a Market Economy." *Issues and Studies* 34: 69.

Jiang, Lishan. 1998a. "Zhongguo Fazhi Daolu Chutan (shang)" ("Preliminary Examination of China's Rule of Law Road: Part A"). *Zhongwai Faxue* 3: 16.

——— 1998b. "Zhongguo Fazhi Daolu Chutan (xia)" ("Preliminary Examination of China's Rule of Law Road: Part B"). *Zhongwai Faxue* 4: 21.

——— 1997. "Zhongguo Fazhi Gaige he Fazhihua Guocheng Yanjiu" ("Study of the Process of China's Legal System Reform and Rule of Law Development"). *Zhongwai Faxue* 6: 35.

Jiang, Mingan. 1998. "Zhongguo Xingzheng Fazhi Shinian de Huigu yu Zhangwang" ("Ten Years of Administrative Rule of Law in China: Retrospect and Prospect"). In *Xingzheng Susongfa (Administrative Rule of Law)*, edited by Jiang Mingan. Beijing: Falü Chubanshe.

——— ed. 1998. *Xingzheng Susongfa (Administrative Rule of Law)*. Beijing: Falü Chubanshe.

——— ed. 1993. *Xingzheng Susongfa Xue (Study of Administrative Litigation Law)*. Beijing: Beijing Daxue Chubanshe.

Jiang, Ping. 1995. "Xingzheng Xiangduiren de Quanli Jiuji" ("The Rights and Remedies of Parties to Administrative Acts"). In *Zouxiang Quanli de Shidai (Toward an Age of Rights)*, edited by Xia Yong. Beijing: Zhongguo Zhengfa Daxue Chubanshe.

Jiang, Xianfu. 1997. "Fazhi de Wenhua Lunli Jichu ji qi Goujian" ("The Cultural Normative Basis of the Rule of Law and its Structure"). *Falü Kexue* 6: 3.

Jiang Zemin's Congress Report. FBIS-CHI-97-266, September 23, 1997.

Jin, Baicheng. 2001. "*Falun Gong* Causes Deaths of More Than 1,660 People." *China Daily*, 28 February.

Johnson, Ian. 2000a. "Death Trap: How One Chinese City Resorted to Atrocities to Control Falun Dafa." *Wall Street Journal*, 29 December, at A1.

——— 2000b. "Chinese Retiree: Practicing Falun Gong Was a Right." *Asian Wall Street Journal*, 4 April, at A1.

Jolly, Richard. 1997. "Profiles in Success." In *Development with a Human Face: Experiences in Social Achievement and Economic Growth*, edited by Santosh Mehrota and Richard Jolly. Oxford: Clarendon Press.

Jomo, K.S. 2001. "Rethinking the Role of Government Policy in Southeast Asia." In *Rethinking the East Asian Miracle*, edited by Joseph Stiglitz and Shahid Yusuf. New York: Oxford University Press.

Jones, Carol. 1999. "Politics Postponed: Law as a Substitute for Politics in Hong Kong and China." In *Law, Capitalism and Power in Asia*, edited by Kanishka Jayasuriya. London: Routledge.

1994. "Capitalism, Globalization and Rule of Law: an Alternative Trajectory of Legal Change in China." *Social and Legal Studies* 3: 195.

Jones, Thomas, and Susan Finder. 1999–2000. "PRC Law: a Millenium Retrospective." *China Law and Practice*, December–January, at 53.

Jones, William. 1994. *The Great Qing Code.* Oxford: Clarendon Press.

1985. "The Constitution of the People's Republic of China." *Washington University Law Quarterly* 63: 707.

Josephs, Hilary. 2000. "The Upright and the Low-down: an Examination of Official Corruption in the United States and the People's Republic of China." *Syracuse Journal of International Law and Commerce* 27: 269.

Judge Xiao: Legal Reform Should Proceed Gradually. FBIS-CHI-2000-0601, June 1, 2000.

"Judges – a Case of Misunderstanding." 1999. *China Daily*, 6 August, at 1.

Justice Official on China Mulling Higher Salary to Improve Quality of Judges. FBIS-CHI-2000-1213, December 13, 2000.

Kahan, Marcel, and Michael Klausner. 1996. "Path Dependence in Corporate Contracting: Increasing Returns, Herd Behavior, and Cognitive Biases." *Washington University Law Quarterly* 74: 347.

Kairys, David, ed. 1998. *The Politics of Law.* 3rd edn. New York: Basic Books.

Kamuwanga, Mwangala. 1987. "The Teaching of International Trade and Investment Law in a 'Law and Development' Context: a View from Zambia." *Third World Legal Studies* 1987: 131.

Kausikan, Bilhari Kim Hee P.S. 1995–19. "An East Asian Approach to Human Rights." *Buffalo Journal of International Law* 2: 263.

Keith, Ronald C. 1994. *China's Struggle for the Rule of Law.* New York: St. Martin's Press.

Keith, Ronald C., and Zhiqiu Lin. 2001. *Law and Justice in China's New Marketplace.* New York: Palgrave.

Keller, Perry. 1994. "Sources of Order in Chinese Law." *American Journal of Comparative Law* 42: 711.

1989. "Legislation in the People's Republic of China." *University of British Columbia Law Review* 23: 653.

Kelliher, Daniel. 1997. "The Chinese Debate over Village Self-Government." *China Journal* 37: 63.

Kelman, Mark. 1987. *A Guide to Critical Legal Studies.* Cambridge, MA: Harvard University Press.

Kennedy, Duncan. 1979. "The Structure of Blackstone's Commentaries." *Buffalo Law Review* 28: 205.

1976. "Form and Substance in Private Law Adjudication." *Harvard Law Review* 89: 1685.

Key Falungong Members Face Trial in September. FBIS-CHI-1999-0816, August 16, 1999.

Khan, Mushtaq, and Jomo K.S. 2000. "Introduction." In *Rents, Rent-Seeking and Economic Development: Theory and Evidence in Asia,* edited by Mushtaq Khan and K.S. Jomo. Cambridge: Cambridge University Press.

Khoo, Boo Teik. 1999. "Between Law and Politics." In *Law, Capitalism and Power in Asia,* edited by Kanishka Jayasuriya. New York: Routledge.

King, Ambrose Y.C. 1991. "Kuan-Hsi and Network Building: a Sociological Interpretation" in "The Living Tree: the Changing Meaning of Being Chinese Today." *Daedalus* 20: 63.

Kipnis, Andrew B. 1997. *Producing Guanxi.* Durham, NC: Duke University Press.

Kiss, Alexandre Charles. 1981. "Permissible Limitations on Rights." In *The International Bill of Rights,* edited by Louis Henkin. New York: Columbia University Press.

Klap, Arnout. 1994. "Administrative Law, The Netherlands." *REDP/ERPL* 6: 221.

Klein, Chris. 1997. "China Relents on Its Law Firm Rules." *National Law Journal,* 30 December–6 January, at A7.

Knack, Stephen, and Philip Keefer. 1997. "Why Don't Poor Countries Catch up? A Cross-National Test of an Institutional Explanation." *Economic Inquiry* 35: 590.

    1995. "Institutions and Economic Performance: Cross-Country Tests Using Alternative Institutional Measures." *Economics and Politics* 7: 207.

"Knowledge of Law Tested in Beijing." 2000. *China Daily,* 16 October, at 2.

Koekkoek, A.K. 1987. *Administrative Law and the Constitution in Ireland and the Netherlands.* Deventer: Kluwer.

Kolender, Eric. 1994. "Religious Rights in China: a Comparison of International Human Rights Law and Chinese Domestic Legislation." *Human Rights Quarterly* 16: 455.

Kothari, Rajni. 1988. *Rethinking Development: in Search of Humane Alternatives.* Delhi: Ajanta Publications.

Kritzer, Herbert. 1996. "Courts, Justice, and Politics in England." In *Courts, Law and Politics in Comparative Perspective,* edited by Herbert Jacob, *et al.* New Haven: Yale University Press.

Kuhn, Anthony. 1999. "More China Sect Members Arrested in Protests: Hundreds Are Rounded up for the Third Straight Day as the Meditation Group Continues Demonstration." *Los Angeles Times,* 22 July, at A20.

Kung, James Kai-sing. 1999. "The Evolution of Property Rights in Village Enterprises: the Case of Wuxi County." In *Property Rights and Economic Reform in China,* edited by Jean C. Oi and Andrew G. Walder. Stanford: Stanford University Press.

Kung, James Kai-sing, and Liu Shouying. 1997. "Farmers' Preferences Regarding Ownership and Land Tenure in Post-Mao China: Unexpected Evidence from Eight Counties." *The China Journal* 38: 33.

Kuo, Cheng-Tian. 1994. "Privatization within the Chinese State." *Governance* 7: 387.

Kwang, Mary. 2000. "CCP Raises Profile of Local Parliaments." *The Straits Times*, 9 December.

Kynge, James. 2001. "China Rejects Labour Camp Abolition." *Financial Times*, 28 February.

La Porta, Rafael, Florencio Lopez-de-Silanes, Andrei Shleifer, and Robert Vishny. 1997. Working Paper 5879. *Legal Determinants of External Finance.* National Bureau of Economic Research, January.

Lam, Willy Wo-Lap. 2001. "New Generation Pushes China Democracy." *CCN.com*, 13 February.

       2000. "Not All the President's Men." *South China Morning Post*, 25 October.

Lan, Yisheng. 1999. "FDI and Economic Development in Guangdong." In *Foreign Direct Investment and Economic Growth in China*, edited by Yanrui Wu. Northhampton, MA: New Horizons in International Business.

Landis, James. 1938. *The Administrative Process.* New Haven: Yale University Press.

Lardy, Nicholas. 2000. "Fiscal Sustainability: between a Rock and a Hard Place." *China Economic Quarterly* 4: 36.

       1998. *China's Unfinished Economic Revolution.* Washington, DC: Brookings Institute Press.

       1995. "The Role of Foreign Trade and Investment in China's Economic Transformation." *The China Quarterly* 144: 1064.

Larson, Magali. 1977. *The Rise of the Professions.* Berkeley: University of California Press.

Lawyer Qualification Exam Draws 142,500 Applicants. FBIS-CHI-98-283, October 10, 1998.

Lawyers Committee for Human Rights. 1993. *Criminal Justice with Chinese Characteristics.* New York: Lawyers Committee for Human Rights.

"Lawyers' Test Draws Increasing Numbers." 2000. *China Daily*, 23 October.

Layne, Christopher. 1994. "Kant or Cant: the Myth of the Democratic Peace." *International Security* 19: 5.

Lee, David. 2000. "Legal Reform in China: a Role for Nongovernmental Organizations." *Yale Journal of International Law* 25: 363.

Legal System Building Reviewed. FBIS-CHI-98-359, December 25, 1998.

Legge, James. 1985. *The Chinese Classics.* Vol. V. Taibei: Southern Materials Center, Inc.

Leng, Shao-Chuan. 1967. *Justice in Communist China*. Dobbs Ferry, NY: Oceana Publications.

Leng, Shao-Chuan, and Hungdah Chiu. 1985. *Criminal Justice in Post-Mao China*. Albany: SUNY Press.

Leung, Conita S.C. 1998. "Chinese Law-Making: a Case of Legislative Disorder." *China Legal News*, 27 February, at 1.

Levine, Ross. 1999. "Law, Finance and Economic Growth." *Journal of Financial Intermediation* 8: 8.

Li, Buyun. 1998a. "Fazhi Gainian de Kexuexing" ("The Scientific Nature of the Concept of Rule of Law"). In *Zouxiang Fazhi (Toward the Rule of Law)*, edited by Li Buyun. Changsha: Hunan Renmin Chubanshe.

   1998b. "Shixing Yifa Zhiguo Jianshe Shehui Zhuyi Fazhi Guojia" ("Establish a Socialist Rule of Law State by Implementing Ruling the Country in Accordance with Law"). In *Zhonggong Zhongyang Fazhi Jiangzuo Huibian (Collected Symposia of the Central Politburo on the Legal System)*, edited by Ministry of Justice. Beijing: Ministry of Justice.

   1998c. "Xianzheng yu Zhongguo" ("Constitutionalism and China"). In *Zouxiang Fazhi (Toward the Rule of Law)*, edited by Li Buyun. Changsha: Hunan Renmin Chubanshe.

   1997. "Guanyu Qicao Zhonghua Renmin Gongheguo Lifafa (Zhuanjia Jianyigao) de Ruogan Wenti" ("Several Problems in the Expert Opinion Draft of the PRC Law on Legislation"). *Zhongguo Faxue* 1: 11.

Li, Buyun, and Zhang Zhiming. 1997. "Kuashiji de Mubiao: Yifa Zhiguo, Jianshe Shehuizhuyi Fazhi Guojia" ("The Cross-Century Target: Ruling the Country According to Law, Establishing a Socialist Rule-of-Law State"). *Zhongguo Faxue* 6: 18.

Li, David. 1996. "A Theory of Ambiguous Property Rights in Transition Economies: the Case of the Chinese Non-State Sector." *Journal of Comparative Economics* 23: 1.

Li, Hanchang. 2000. "Sifa Zhidu Gaige Beijing xia Faguan Suzhi yu Faguan Jiaoyu Zhi Toushi" ("A Perspective of the Quality of Judges and Legal Education against the Background of Judicial Reform"). *Zhongguo Faxue* 93: 1.

Li, Ji. 1966. *[Book of Rites]*. Taibei: Chinese Materials and Research Aids Service Center.

Li, Lianjiang, and Kevin O'Brien. 1996. "Villagers and Popular Resistance in Contemporary China." *Modern China* 22: 1.

Li, Linda Chelan. 2000. "The 'Rule of Law' Policy in Guangdong: Continuity or Departure? Meaning, Significance and Processes." *The China Quarterly* 161: 199.

Li Peng on Implementation of Criminal Procedure Law. FBIS-CHI-2000-1120, November 20, 2000.

Li Peng Speaks on PRC Judicial Reform. FBIS-CHI-2000-1026, October 26, 2000.

Li, Shaoping. 1990. "Gai 'Xianding Houshen' wei 'Xianshen Houding'" (Change 'Decision First, Trial Later' to 'Trial First, Decision Later'). *Faxue Yanjiu* 2: 39.

Li, Shenzhi. 1998. "Ye Yao Tuidong Zhengzhi Gaige" ("Push Ahead with Political Reforms Too"). In *Zhengzhi Zhongguo (Political China)*, edited by Dong Yuyu and Shi Binhai. Beijing: Jinri Zhongguo Chubanshe.

Li, Shuguang. 1998. "Zhengzhi Tizhi Gaige de Fazhi Quxiang" ("The Rule-of-Law Orientation of Political System Reform"). In *Zhengzhi Zhongguo (Political China)*, edited by Dong Yuyu and Shi Binhai. Beijing: Jinri Zhongguo Chubanshe.

Li, Victor H. 1978. *Law without Lawyers: a Comparative View of Law in China and the United States.* Boulder: Westview Press.

Li, Weidong. 1996. "Mianxiang Ershiyi Shiji de Fa yu Shehui" ("Toward Law and Society in the 21st Century"). *Zhongguo Shekexue* 3: 3.

——— 1971. "The Evolution and Development of the Chinese Legal System." In *China: Management of a Revolutionary Society*, edited by John M.H. Lindbeck. Seattle: University of Washington Press.

Li, Yuwen. 2002. "Court Reform in China: Problems, Progress and Prospects." In *Implementation of Law in the People's Republic of China*, edited by Chen Jianfu, *et al.* The Hague: Kluwer Law International.

Li, Zhongjie. 1998. *Theories and Practice of the Building of Legal System over the Past 20 Years.* FBIS-CHI-98-359, December 25.

Liang, Zhiping. 2000. "Fazhi: Shehui Zhuanxing Shiqi de Fazhijiangou" ("Rule of Law: Institutional Reconstruction in Social Transformation in China"). *Dangdai Zhongguo Yanjiu* 2: 18.

Liao, Jingye. 1980. "Fazhi he Renzhi Meiyou Juedui Jiexian" ("There Is No Absolute Boundary between Rule of Law and Rule of Man"). *Faxue Yanjiu* 4: 63.

Liaowang Assails "Local Protectionism." FBIS-CHI-1999-0406, March 22, 1999.

Lieberthal, Kenneth. 1995. *Governing China: from Revolution to Reform.* New York: W.W. Norton.

Lieberthal, Kenneth, and Michel Oksenberg. 1988. *Policy Making in China: Leaders, Structures and Processes.* Princeton, NJ: Princeton University Press.

Liebman, Benjamin. 1999. "Legal Aid and Public Interest Law in China." *Texas International Law Journal* 34: 187.

"Life after the WTO Honeymoon: Theory and Practice." 2000. *China Economic Quarterly* 4: 17.

Lin, Feng. 1996. *Administrative Law Procedures and Remedies in China.* Hong Kong: Sweet and Maxwell.

Lin, Pao-an. 1991. "The Social Sources of Capital Investment in Taiwan's Industrialization." In *Business Networks and Economic Development in East and Southeast Asia,* edited by Gary Hamilton. Hong Kong: Centre of Asian Studies, University of Hong Kong Press.

Lin, Yimin, and Zhanxin Zhang. 1999. "Backyard Profit Centers: the Private Assets of Public Agencies." In *Property Rights and Economic Reform in China,* edited by Jean C. Oi and Andrew G. Walder. Stanford: Stanford University Press.

Lipset, Seymour Martin. 1959. "Social Requisites of Democracy: Economic Development and Political Legitimacy." *American Political Science Review* 53: 69.

Liu, Cuixiao, and Wang Jianrong. 1998. "Xingzheng Faxue Yanjiu Shuping" ("Critical Commentary on Administrative Law Research"). *Faxue Yanjiu* 20: 102.

Liu, Cuixiao, and Xie Pengcheng. 1999. "1998 Zhongguo Faxue Yanjiu Huigu" ("Retrospective of Legal Research in China in 1998"). *Faxue Yanjiu* 21: 85.

Liu, Hainian. 1998. "Beilun Shehuizhuyi Fazhi Yuanze" ("General Discussion of Socialist Rule of Law Principles"). *Zhongguo Faxue* 1: 5.

——— 1996. "Yifa Zhiguo: Zhongguo Shehuizhuyi Fazhi Jianshe de Lichengbei" ("Ruling the Country According to Law: a New Milestone in the Con-struction of China's Socialist Legal System"). *Faxue Yanjiu* 18(3): 24.

Liu, Jiachen. 1999. "Yikaizhan 'Sanxiang Huodong' wei Dongli Da Li Jiaqiang Jiceng Jianshe" ("Taking the Development of 'The Three Activities' as the Driving Force, Go All out in Strengthening Basic Construction"). *Supreme People's Court Gazette* 61.

Liu, Jinghuai, and Guo Chunyu. 2000. "Jiceng Fayuan Zouxiang Gaige Xuqu" ("Basic People's Courts Strike up the Reform Overture"). *Liaowang,* 17 July.

Liu, Junning. 1998. "Cong Fazhiguo dao Fazhi" ("From Rechtsstaat to Rule of Law"). In *Zhengzhi Zhongguo (Political China),* edited by Dong Yuyu and Shi Binhai. Beijing: Jinri Zhongguo Chubanshe.

Liu, Nanping. 1991. "'Legal Precedents' with Chinese Characteristics: Pub-lished Cases in the Gazette of the Supreme People's Court." *Journal of Chinese Law* 5: 107.

Liu, Renwen. 1999. "Sifa Tizhi Gaige de Fanwei, Mubiao yu Yuanze" ("The Scope, Purpose and Principle of Systemic Judicial Reform"). In *Yifa Zhiguo yu Sifa Gaige (Ruling the Country According to Law and Judicial Reform),* edited by Xin Chunying and Li Lin. Beijing: Zhongguo Fazhi Chubanshe.

Liu, Shouying, Michael Carter, and Yang Yao. 1998. "Dimensions and Diversity of Property Rights in Rural China; Dilemmas on the Road to Further Reform." *World Development* 10: 1789.

Liu, Yongping. 1998. *Origins of Chinese Law*. Hong Kong: Oxford University Press.

Liu, Zheng. 1998. "Shilun Sheding Xingzheng Susong Yuangao Zege yu Xingzheng Susong Shouan Fanwei de Hodong Luoji Guanxi" ("Discussion of the Interactive Logical Relationship between the Establishment of Standing to Sue and the Scope of Administrative Review Cases"). *Fazhi Yu Shehui Fazhan (Law and Social Development)* 54: 58.

Liu, Zuoxiang. 1996. "Zhongguo Fazhi Shixian Fanglue (Bitanhui)" (Strategy for the Realization of Rule of Law [Written Exchange of Ideas]). *Falü Kexue* 3: 3.

Livshits, R.Z. 1991. "Jus and Lex: Evolution of View." In *Perestroika and the Rule of Law*, edited by W.E. Butler. New York: St. Martin's Press.

Lo, Carlos Wing-hung. 1995. *China's Legal Awakening, Legal Theory and Criminal Justice in Deng's Era*. Hong Kong: Hong Kong University Press.

Locke, John. 1960. *Two Treatises of Government*, edited by Peter Laslett. Cambridge: Cambridge University Press.

Lollar, Xia Li. 1997. *China's Transition toward a Market Economy, Civil Society and Democracy*. Bristol, IN: Wyndham Hall Press.

Lowi, Theodore. 1994. "The Welfare State, the New Regulation and the Rule of Law." In *Nomos XXXVI: the Rule of Law*, edited by Ian Shapiro. New York: New York University Press.

Lubman, Stanley B. 2000. "Bird in a Cage: Chinese Law Reform After Twenty Years." *Northwestern Journal of International Law and Business* 20: 385.

1999. *Bird in a Cage: Legal Reforms in China after Mao*. Stanford: Stanford University Press.

1967. "Mao and Mediation: Politics and Dispute Resolution in Communist China." *California Law Review* 55: 1284.

Luo, Haocai, ed. 1997. *Xiandai Xingzhengfa de Pingheng Lun (The Balance Theory of Modern Administrative Law)*. Beijing: Beijing University Press.

et al., ed. 1997. *Xingzheng Faxue (Study of Administrative Law)*. Beijing: Beijing Daxue Chubanshe.

Luo, Qizhi. 1998. "Autonomy, Qualification and Professionalism of the PRC Bar." *Columbia Journal of Asian Law* 12: 1.

Lynch, Daniel. 1999a. *After the Propaganda State: Media, Politics, and "Thought Work" in Reformed China*. Stanford: Stanford University Press.

1999b. "Dilemmas of 'Thought Work' in Fin-de-Siecle China." *The China Quarterly* 157: 173.

Ma, Huaide. 1998. "Jiang Chouxiang Xingzheng Xingwei Naru Xingzheng Fuyi de Fanwei" ("Bring Administrative Abstract Acts into the Scope of Administrative Reconsideration"). *Zhongguo Faxue* 6: 39–44.

Ma, Shu-yun. 1994. "The Chinese Discourse on Civil Society." *The China Quarterly* 138: 180.

Macaulay, Stewart. 1963. "Non-Contractual Relations in Business: a Preliminary Study." *American Sociological Review* 28: 55.

Macauley, Melissa. 1998. *Social Power and Legal Culture: Litigation Masters in Late Imperial China*. Stanford: Stanford University Press.

MacCormack, Geoffrey. 1990. *Traditional Chinese Penal Law*. Edinburgh: Edinburgh University Press.

Macedo, Stephen. 1994. "The Rule of Law, Justice and the Politics of Moderation." In *Nomos XXXVI: the Rule of Law*, edited by Ian Shapiro. New York: New York University Press.

Macey, Jonathan. 1986. "Promoting Public-Regarding Legislation through Statutory Interpretation: an Interest Group Model." *Columbia Law Review* 86: 223.

MacFarquhar, Roderick. 1998. "Reports from the Field: Provincial People's Congresses." *The China Quarterly* 155: 656.

Macleod, Calum. 2000. "China Introduces Some Democratic Elections." *United Press International (via Clarinet)*, 24 May.

Magazine Reviews Jiang Zemin's Efforts on Governing by Law. FBIS-CHI-2000-032, March 24, 2000.

Magnier, Mark. 2001. "Japan Revamps, Reduces Ministries." *Los Angeles Times*, 7 January.

Majone, Giandomenico. 1997. "From the Positive to the Regulatory State: Causes and Consequences of Changes in the Mode of Governance." *International Public Policy* 17: 139.

Malinowski, B. 1926. *Crime and Custom in Savage Society*. New York: Harcourt, Brace and Company.

Manion, Melanie. 2000. "Chinese Democratization in Perspective." *The China Quarterly* 163: 742.

1996. "The Electoral Connection in the Chinese Countryside." *American Political Review* 90: 736.

Mao, Tsetung. 1977. "On the Correct Handling of Contradictions among the People." In *Five Selected Works of Mao Tsetung*. Beijing: Foreign Language Press.

Maravall, Jose Maria. 1994. "The Myth of the Authoritarian Advantage." *Journal of Democracy* 5: 17.

Markel, Douglas, and Randy Peerenboom. 1997. "The Technology Transfer Tango." *China Business Review*, January–February, at 25.

Maslen, Susan. 1998. "Japan and the Rule of Law." *UCLA Pacific Basin Law Journal* 16: 281.

Mauro, Paulo. 1995. "Corruption and Growth." *Quarterly Journal of Economics* 110: 681.

McAuslan, Patrick. 1997. "Law, Governance and the Development of the Market: Practical Problems and Possible Solutions." In *Good Government and Law*, edited by Julio Faundez. New York: St. Martin's Press.

McCormick, Barret, and David Kelly. 1994. "The Limits of Anti-Liberalism." *Journal of Asian Studies* 53: 804.

McKnight, Brian. 1992. *Law and Order in Sung China.* Cambridge: Cambridge University Press.

———. 1987. "From Statute to Precedent: an Introduction to Sung Law and Its Transformation." In *Law and the State in Traditional East Asia*, edited by Brian McNight. Honolulu: University of Hawaii Press.

McKnight, Brian, and James Liu, translated. 1999. *The Enlightened Judgments Ch'ing Ming Chi.* Albany: SUNY Press.

Meng, Yan. 2001a. "Marriage Law Attracts Public Attention." *China Daily*, 2 March.

———. 2002b "New Local Traffic Rules Cause Outcry." *China Daily*, 19 March.

Merryman, John Henry. 1977. "Comparative Law and Social Change: on the Origins, Style, Decline and Revival of the Law and Development Movement." *American Journal of Comparative Law* 25: 457.

Mill, John Stuart. 1885. *On Liberty.* New York : J.B. Alden.

Miyazaki, Ichisada. 1980. "The Administration of Justice during the Sung Dynasty." In *Essays on China's Legal Tradition*, edited by Jerome Cohen, *et al.* Princeton: Princeton University Press.

Moon, Myung-Jae, and Patricia Ingraham. 1998. "Shaping Administrative Reform and Governance: an Examination of the Political Nexus Triads in Three Asian Countries." *Governance* 11: 77.

Moore, Wilbert. 1970. *The Professions: Roles and Rules.* New York: Russel Sage Foundation.

Morgan, Thomas, and Ronald Rotunda. 2000. *Selected Standards on Professional Responsibility.* New York: Foundation Press.

Moser, Michael, J. 1982. *Law and Social Change in a Chinese Community: a Case Study in Rural Taiwan.* New York: Oceana.

Mullerson, Rein, *et al.*, eds. 1998. *Constitutional Reform and International Law in Central and Eastern Europe.* Boston; Kluwer Law International.

Munro, Robin. 2000. "Judicial Psychiatry in China and Its Political Abuses." *Columbia Journal of Asian Law* 14: 1.

Munzer, Stephen. 1982. "A Theory of Retroactive Legislation." *Texas Law Review* 61: 425.

Nagel, Thomas. 1991. *Equality and Partiality.* New York: Oxford University Press.

Name List of Deputies to 9th NPC Published. FBIS-CHI-98-060, March 1, 1998.

Nathan, Andrew. 1997. *China's Transition.* New York: Columbia University Press.

——— 1991. "Tiananmen and the Cosmos." *New Republic,* 19 July.

——— 1986a. *Chinese Democracy.* New York: Knopf.

——— 1986b. "Sources of Chinese Rights Thinking." In *Human Rights in Contemporary China,* edited by R. Randle Edwards, *et al.* New York: Columbia University Press.

Nathan, Andrew, and Tianjian Shi. 1993. "Cultural Requisites for Democracy in China: Findings from a Survey." *Daedalus* 122: 2.

Needham, Joseph. 1956. *Science and Civilisation in China.* Vol. II. Cambridge: Cambridge University Press.

Neville, Robert. 2000. *Boston Confucianism.* Albany: SUNY Press.

Neville-Brown, L., and John Bell. 1993. *French Administrative Law.* 4th edn. New York: Oxford University Press.

"New Duty Exemptions Conceal Tighter Investment Control." 1998. *China Joint Venturer,* January–February, at 3.

"New Private Banks to Enhance Competition in Financial Industry." 2000. www.chinabiz.org. 12 November.

Nichols, Philip. 1997. "The Viability of Transplanted Law: Kazakhstani Reception of a Transplanted Foreign Investment Code." *University of Pennsylvania Journal of International Economic Law* 18: 1235.

Nolan, Peter, and Wang Xiaogang. 1999. "Beyond Privatization: Institutional Innovation and Growth in China's Large State-Owned Enterprises." *World Development* 27: 169.

North, Douglass C. 1990. *Institutions, Institutional Change, and Economic Performance.* New York: Cambridge University Press.

——— 1981. *Structure and Change in Economic History.* New York: Norton.

Nozick, Robert. 1974. *Anarchy, State and Utopia.* New York: Basic Books.

NPC Deputies, CPPCC Members Inspect Supreme Court. FBIS-CHI-98-144, May 24, 1998.

NPC Standing Committee Examines Draft Review Law. FBIS-CHI-98-302, October 29, 1998.

NPC Standing Committee to View Administrative Appeals Law. FBIS-CHI-98-300, October 27, 1998.

O'Brien, Kevin. 1999a. "The Two-Ballot System in Shanxi." *The China Journal* 42: 103.

——— 1999b. "Hunting for Political Change." *The China Journal* 41: 159.

——— 1994a. "Implementing Political Reform in China's Villages." *Australian Journal of Chinese Affairs* 32: 33.

1994b. "Chinese People's Congresses and Legislative Embeddedness: Understanding Early Organizational Development." *Comparative Political Studies* 27: 80.

1990. *Reform without Liberalization.* New York: Cambridge University Press.

O'Brien, Kevin, and Lianjiang Li. 2000. "Accommodating 'Democracy' in a One-Party State: Introducing Village Elections in China." *The China Quarterly* 162: 465.

1999. "Selective Policy Implementation in Rural China." *Comparative Politics* 31: 167.

Ocko, Jonathan. 2000. "Using the Past to Make a Case for the Present." In *The Limits of the Rule of Law in China*, edited by Karen Turner, *et al.* Seattle: University of Washington Press.

1997. "A Review of Geoffrey MacCormack, the Spirit of Traditional Chinese Law." *McGill Law Journal* 42: 733.

1988. "I'll Take It All the Way to Beijing: Capital Appeals in the Qing." *Journal of Asian Studies* 47: 291.

Oda, Hiroshi. 1984. "Judicial Review of the Administration in the Countries of Eastern Europe." 1984: 112.

Official on Laws Violated by Falungong. FBIS-CHI-1999-0809, August 7, 1999.

Official on Problems in Judicial Practice. FBIS-CHI-1999-0423, April 1, 1999.

Oi, Jean. 1999. *Rural China Takes off.* Berkeley: University of California Press.

1989. *State and Peasant in Contemporary China: the Political Economy of Village Government.* Berkeley: University of California Press.

Oi, Jean, and Scott Rozelle. 2000. "Elections and Power: the Locus of Decision-Making in Chinese Villages." *The China Quarterly* 162: 513.

Oi, Jean, and Andrew Walder, eds. 1999. *Property Rights and Economic Reform in China.* Stanford: Stanford University Press.

Oksenberg, Michel. 2001. "China's Political System: Challenges of the Twenty-First Century." *The China Journal* 45: 21.

1971. "Policy Making under Mao, 1949–68: an Overview." In *China: Management of a Revolutionary Society*, edited by John M.H. Lindbeck. Seattle: University of Washington Press.

Olson, Mancur. 1997. "The New Institutional Economics: the Collective Choice Approach to Economic Development." In *Institutions and Economic Development* edited by C. Clague. Baltimore: Johns Hopkins University Press.

O'Neil, Mark. 2001. "China Auditor in Shock Report." *South China Morning Post*, 8 January.

Opinions on Draft for Supervising Cases. FBIS, FTS-1999-0208, February 4, 1998.

Orts, Eric. 2001. "The Rule of Law in China." *Vanderbilt Journal of Transnational Law* 34: 43.

Oshimura, Takashi. 2000. "In Defense of Asian Colors." In *The Rule of Law: Perspectives from the Pacific Rim*. Washington, DC: Mansfield Center for Pacific Affairs. http://www.mcpa.org/rol/perspectives.htm.

Otto, Jan Michiel, *et al.*, eds. 2000. *Law-Making in the People's Republic of China*. The Hague: Kluwer Law International.

"Overhaul of Foreign Investment in China's Retail Sector." 1998–99. *China Law and Practice*, December–January, at 66.

Palmer, Leslie. 1996. "Party and Law in China." In *State and Law in Eastern Asia*, edited by Leslie Palmer. Aldershot: Dartmouth Publishing Co. Ltd.

Pan, Philip. 2001. "Human Fire Ignites Chinese Mystery." *Washington Post Foreign Service*, 4 February.

Pan, Wei. 2001. "Democracy or Rule of Law? – China's Political Future" (unpublished manuscript presented at the University of Denver Center for China, United States Cooperation Conference on China's Political Options, May 19–20, Vail, Colorado).

Parris, Kristen. 1999. "The Rise of Private Business Interests." In *The Paradox of Post-Mao Reforms*, edited by Merle Goldman and Roderick MacFarquhar. Cambridge: Harvard University Press.

Parsons, Talcot. 1968. "Professions." In *International Encyclopedia of the Social Sciences, XII*, edited by David Sills. New York: The Free Press.

"Party Stresses Ethical, Cultural Progress." 1996. *China Daily*, 14 October, at 3.

Pastor, Robert, and Qingshan Tan. 2000. "The Meaning of China's Village Elections." *The China Quarterly* 162: 490.

"Path to Profit." 1998. *Business China* 24: 12.

Pearson, Margaret. 2000. "China's Track Record in the Global Economy." *China Business Review*, January–February, at 48.

1997. *China's New Business Elite: the Political Consequences of Economic Reform.* Berkeley: University of California Press.

Peerenboom, Randall P. 2002a. "Law Enforcement and the Legal Profession in China." In *Implementation of Law in the People's Republic of China*, edited by Chen Jianfu, *et al.* The Hague: Kluwer Law International.

2002b. "A Government of Laws: Democracy, Rule of Law and Administrative Law Reform in the PRC." In *Rule of Law and Democracy: Political Reform in China*, edited by Tom Farer. Boulder: Lynne Reiner.

2002c. "Law and Religion in Early China." In *Religion, Law, and Tradition*, edited by Andrew Huxley. London: Taylor and Francis.

2001a. "Seek Truth from Facts: an Empirical Study of Enforcement of Arbitral Awards in the PRC." *American Journal of Comparative Law* 49.

2001b. "Globalization, Path Dependency and the Limits of Law: Administrative Law Reform and the Rule of Law in the People's Republic of China." *Berkeley Journal of International Law* 19: 161.

2000a. "The Evolving Regulatory Framework for the Enforcement of Arbitral Awards in the PRC." *Asian Pacific Law and Policy Journal* 1: 13.

2000b. "The Limits of Irony: Rorty and the China Challenge." *Philosophy East and West* 50: 56.

2000c. "Beyond Apologia: Respecting Legitimate Differences of Opinion While Not Toadying to Dictators (Response to Richard Rorty)." *Philosophy East and West* 50: 92.

2000d. "Human Rights and Asian values: the Limits of Universalism." *China Review International* 7: 295.

2000e. "Review of *Bird in a Cage: Legal Reform in China after Mao*, by Stanley Lubman." *China Review International* 7: 135.

1999a. "Ruling the Country in Accordance with Law: Reflections on the Rule and Role of Law in China." *Cultural Dynamics* 11: 315.

1999b. "A Missed Opportunity? China's New Contract Law Fails to Address Foreign Technology Providers' Concerns." *China Law and Practice* 83.

1999c. "Approvals for Establishing a Wholly Foreign-Owned Enterprise." In *Obtaining PRC Approvals*, 2nd edn., edited by Clark T. Randt. Hong Kong: Asia Law and Practice.

1998a. "Confucian Harmony and Freedom of Thought: Right Thinking Versus the Right to Think." In *Confucianism and Human Rights*, edited by Wm. Theodore de Bary and Tu Weiming. New York: Columbia University Press.

1998b. *Lawyers in China: Obstacles to Independence and the Defense of Rights.* New York: Lawyers' Committee for Human Rights.

1998c. "Law and Ritual in Chinese Philosophy." In *Routledge Encyclopedia of Philosophy*. New York: Routledge.

1995. "Rights, Interests and the Interest in Rights in China." *Stanford Journal of International Law* 31: 359.

1993a. *Law and Morality in Ancient China: the Silk Manuscripts of Huang-Lao.* Albany: State University of New York Press.

1993b. "The Victim in Chinese Criminal Theory and Practice: a Preliminary Study." *Journal of Chinese Law* 7: 63.

1990. "Confucian Jurisprudence: beyond Natural Law." *Asian Culture Quarterly* 36: 12.

Peerenboom, Randall and Zhou Lin. 1997. "Mixed Messages in the Agricultural Industry: China's Plant Protection Regulations Undermined by Agriculture Ministry Power Grab." *China Law and Practice*, December, at 22.

Pei, Minxin. 2001a. "Legal Reform and Secure Commercial Transactions: Evidence from China." In *Assessing the Value of Law in Transition Economies*, edited by Peter Murrell. Ann Arbor: University of Michigan Press.

2001b. "Political Institutions, Democracy and Development." In *Democracy, Market Economics and Development*, edited by Farrukh Iqbal and Jong-Il You. Washington, DC: The World Bank.

2000. "Rights and Resistance: the Changing Contexts of the Dissident Movement." In *Chinese Society: Change, Conflict and Resistance*, edited by Elizabeth Perry and Mark Selden. London: Routledge.

1998a. "Constructing the Political Foundations of an Economic Miracle." In *Behind East Asian Growth*, edited by Henry S. Rowen. New York: Routledge.

1998b. "Chinese Civic Associations." *Modern China* 24: 285.

1997a. "Citizens v. Mandarins: Administrative Litigation in China." *The China Quarterly* 152: 832.

1997b. "Racing against Time: Institutional Decay and Renewal in China." In *China Briefing: the Contradictions of Change*, edited by William A. Joseph. Armonk, NY: M.E. Sharpe.

1995. "'Creeping Democratization' in China." *Journal of Democracy* 6: 65.

Peng, Guicai. 1999. "Guanyu Xingzheng Susong Kunjing de Falü Sikao" ("Legal Reflections on the Difficult Areas of Administrative Litigation"). *Fazhi Yu Shehui Fazhan (Law and Social Development)* 3: 14.

Peng, Yali. 1998. "Democracy and Chinese Political Discourses." *Modern China* 24: 4.

Perkins, Dwight. 2001. "Industrial and Financial Policy in China and Vietnam: a New Model or a Replay of the East Asian Experience." In *Rethinking the East Asian Miracle*, edited by Joseph Stiglitz and Shahid Yusuf. New York: Oxford University Press.

Perry, Amanda. 2000. "An Ideal System for Attracting Foreign Direct Investment? Some Theory and Reality." *American University International Law Review* 15: 1627.

Perry, Elizabeth, and Mark Selden. 2000. "Introduction: Reform and Resistance in Contemporary China." In *Chinese Society: Change, Conflict and Resistance*, edited by Elizabeth Perry and Mark Selden. London: Routledge.

Perry, Michael J. 1988. *Morality, Politics, and Law*. New York: Oxford University Press.

Pi, Chunxie, and Li Yuji. 1998. "1997 Nian Xingzheng Faxue Yanjiu de Huigu yu Zhanwang" ("Retrospect of 1997 Administrative Law Studies and Future Prospects"). *Faxuejia (Legal Scholar)* 1: 36–42.

Pistor, Katharina, and Philip A. Wellons. 1999. *The Role of Law and Legal Institutions in Asian Economic Development 1960–1995*. New York: Oxford University Press.

Platteau, Jean-Phillipe. 1994. "Behind the Market Stage Where Real Societies Exist: Part I." *Journal of Development Studies* 30: 553.

Pomfret, John. 2001. "A Foe Rattles Beijing from Abroad." *Washington Post Foreign Service*, 9 March.

———. 2000. "China's Poor Fear Cost of Free Trade." *Washington Post*, 24 September.

Potter, Pitman, B. 2000. "PRC Contract Law". In *Doing Business in China*, edited by Freshfields. Yonkers, NY: Juris Publishing, Inc.

———. 1999. "The Chinese Legal System: Continuing Commitment to the Primacy of Power." *The China Quarterly* 159: 673.

———. 1995a. *Foreign Business Law in China: Past Progress and Future Challenges*. South San Francisco: 1990 Institute.

———. 1995b. "Foreign Investment Law in the People's Republic of China: Dilemmas of State Control." *The China Quarterly* 141: 155.

———. 1994a. "The Administrative Law of the PRC." In *Domestic Reforms in Post Mao China*, edited by Pitman Potter. Armonk: M.E. Sharpe.

———. 1994b. "Riding the Tiger: Legitimacy and Legal Culture in Post-Mao China." *The China Quarterly* 138: 325.

PRC Development Commission Reports on 5-Yr Growth in Foreign-Funded Firms. FBIS-CHI-2000-1006, October 6, 2000.

PRC Envoy: Falungong Ban Aimed at Defending Human Rights. FBIS-CHI-1999-0818, August 17, 1999.

"PRC Government Restructuring Continues." 1998. *China Business Review*, 1 September.

PRC People's Congress' Rejection of Report Said "Landmark Event." FBIS-CHI-2001-0216, February 16, 2001.

PRC State Commission Says Township Enterprises Maintaining "Strong Growth." FBIS-CHI-2000-1006, October 6, 2000.

PRC Supreme Court Restructuring Outlined. FBIS-CHI-2000-0808, August 8, 2000.

PRC to Amend Laws for WTO Entry. FBIS-CHI-2000-0309, March 9, 2000.

PRC to Establish "Modern" Trial System in Preparation for WTO Membership. FBIS-CHI-2000-01027, October 27, 2000.

PRC to Reform Judge Selection System. FBIS-CHI-1999-1022, October 22, 1999.

Procurator General Delivers Supreme People's Procuratorate Work Report. FBIS-CHI-2001-0321, March 21, 2001.

Prosterman, Roy, Brian Schwarzwalder, and Ye Jianping. 2000. "Implementation of 30-Year Land Use Rights for Farmers under China's Land Management Law." *Pacific Rim Law and Policy Journal* 9: 3.

Provine, Doris Marie. 1996. "Courts, Justice, and Politics in France." In *Courts, Law and Politics in Comparative Perspective*, edited by Herbert Jacob, *et al.* New Haven: Yale University Press.

Przeworski, Adam, and Fernando Limongi. 1997. "Modernization: Theories and Facts." *World Politics* 49: 155.

———. 1993. "Political Regimes and Economic Growth." *Journal of Economic Perspectives* 7: 51.

Putterman, Louis. 1997. "On the Past and Future of China's Township and Village-Owned Enterprises." *World Development* 25: 1639.

———. 1995. "The Role of Ownership and Property Rights in China's Economic Transition." *The China Quarterly* 144: 1047.

Pye, Lucian W. 1985. *Asian Power and Politics.* Cambridge, MA: Belknap Press.

Qian, Cuihua, *et al.* 1997. "Chouxiang Xingzheng Xingwei Nengfou Tiqi Susong de Tantao" ("Investigation of Whether Abstract Acts Are Justiciable"). 2 *Zhengzhi yu Falü (Politics and Law)* 2: 20.

Rabban, David. 1981. "The First Amendment in Its Forgotten Years." *Yale Law Journal* 90: 514.

Radin, Margaret Jane. 1989. "Reconsidering the Rule of Law." *Buffalo University Law Review* 69: 781.

Rahn, Patsy. 2000. "The Falung Gong: beyond the Headlines." 17 *Cultic Studies Journal: Psychological Manipulation and Society.*

Rakoff, Todd. 2000. "The Choice between Formal and Informal Modes of Administrative Regulation." *Administrative Law Review* 52: 159.

Ramseyer, Mark, and Minoro Nakazato. 1999. *Japanese Law: an Economic Approach.* Chicago: University of Chicago Press.

Rapacynski, Andrzej. 1996. "The Role of the State and the Market in Establishing Property Rights." *Journal of Economic Perspectives* 10: 87.

Rapp, Phillip. 1999. "FIE Holding Companies." In *Doing Business in China,* edited by Freshfields. Yonkers, NY: Juris Publishing, Inc.

Ratliff, William, and Edgardo Buscaglia. 1997. "Judicial Reform: Institutionalizing Change in the Americas." In *The Law and Economics of Development,* edited by Edgardo Buscalgia, *et al.* London: JAI Press.

Ravich, Samantha. 2000. *Marketization and Democracy: East Asian Experiences.* Cambridge: Cambridge University Press.

Rawls, John. 1993. "The Law of Peoples." In *On Human Rights: the Oxford Amnesty Lectures 1993,* edited by Steven Lukes and Susan Hurley. New York: Basic Books.

———. 1987. "The Idea of the Overlapping Consensus." *Oxford Journal of Legal Studies* 7: 1.

———. 1971. *A Theory of Justice.* Cambridge: Harvard University Press.

Rawski, Thomas. 1999. "Reforming China's Economy: What Have We Learned?" *China Journal* 41: 139.

Raz, Joseph. 1979. "The Rule of Law and Its Virtue." In *The Authority of Law,* edited by Joseph Raz. Oxford: Clarendon Press.

Redding, Gordon, S. 1990. *The Spirit of Chinese Capitalism*. New York: W. de Gruyter.

"Renmin Fayuan Wunian Gaige Gangyao" ("Outline of the Five-year Plan for Reforming the People's Courts"). 1999. *Fazhi Ribao*, 20 October, at 2.

Renmin Ribao on Stability, Law Enforcment. FBIS-CHI-98-331, November 27, 1998.

Renmin Ribao Views Jiang Zemin's Exposition of Rule by Law, Virtue. FBIS-CHI-2001-0222, February 22, 2001.

Report of the Joseph R. Crowley Program. 1999. "One Country, Two Legal Systems?" *Fordham International Law Journal* 23: 1.

Reynolds, Noel. 1989. "Grounding the Rule of Law." *Ratio Juris* 2: 1.

Rheinstein, Max. 1954. *Max Weber on Law in Economy and Society*. New York: Simon and Schuster.

RMRB Article Lists Laws Violated by Falungong. FBIS-CHI-2001-0321, March 21, 2001.

Rodrick, Dani. 1997. "Sense and Nonsense in the Globalization Debate." *Foreign Policy* 107: 19.

Rorty, Richard. 2000. "Response to Randall Peerenboom." *Philosophy East and West* 50: 90.

  1989. *Contingency, Irony and Solidarity*. Cambridge: Cambridge University Press.

Rose, Carol V. 1998. "The New Law and Development Movement in the Post-Cold War Era: a Vietnam Case Study." *Law and Society Review* 32: 92.

Rose-Ackerman, Susan. 1999. *Corruption and Government*. Cambridge: Cambridge University Press.

Rosemont, Henry. 1998. "Against Relativism." In *Interpreting across Boundaries*, edited by Gerald James Larson. Princeton: Princeton University Press.

Rostow, W.W. 1960. *Stages of Economic Growth*. Cambridge: Cambridge University Press.

Roth, Kenneth. 2000. "The Charade of US Ratification of International Human Rights Treaties." *Chicago Journal of International Law* 1: 347.

Rowen, Henry S. 1998. "The Political and Social Foundations of the Rise of East Asia." In *Behind East Asian Growth*, edited by Henry S. Rowen. New York: Routledge.

Rubin, Edward. 2001. "Getting Past Democracy." *University of Pennsylvania Law Review* 149: 711.

  1997. "Administrative Law and the Complexity of Culture." In *Legislative Drafting for Market Reform*, edited by Robert B. Seidman, Ann Seidman, and Janice Payne. New York: St. Martin's Press.

Ruf, Gregory. 1999. "Collective Enterprise and Property Rights in a Sichuan Village: the Rise and Decline of Managerial Corporatism." In *Property*

Rights and Economic Reform in China, edited by Jean C. Oi and Andrew G. Walder. Stanford: Stanford University Press.

Rule of Law Foundation. *Rule of Law Principles*. http://www.rol.org/htmfiles/what.htm. (Now extinct.)

Rushford, Greg. 1999. "Chinese Arbitration: Can It Be Trusted?" *Asian Wall Street Journal*, 29 November, at A1.

Rustow, Dankwart. 1970. "Transitions to Democracy: toward a Dynamic Model." *Comparative Politics* 2: 337.

Sachs, Jeffrey. 1998. "International Economics: Unlocking the Mysteries of Globalization." *Foreign Policy* 110: 97.

Sachs, Jeffrey, and Katharina Pistor. 1997. "Introduction: Progress, Pitfalls, Scenarios and Lost Opportunities." In *The Rule of Law and Economic Reform in Russia*, edited by Jeffrey Sachs and Katharina Pistor. Boulder: Westview Press.

Saich, Tony. 2000. "Negotiating the State: the Development of Social Organizations in China." *The China Quarterly* 161: 124.

Sajo, Andras. 1993. "The Role of Lawyers in Social Change: Hungary." *Case Western Journal of International Law* 25: 137.

Sandel, Michael. 1996a. "Dewey Rides Again, Review of *John Dewey and the High Tide of American Liberalism*, by Alan Ryan." *New York Review of Books*, 9 May, at 35.

   1996b. *Democracy's Discontent: America in Search of a Public Philosophy.* Cambridge: Belknap Press of Harvard University Press.

Sargeson, Sally, and Jian Zhang. 1999. "Reassessing the Role of the Local State: a Case Study of Local Government Interventions in Property Rights Reform in a Hangzhou District." *The China Journal* 42: 77.

Sarkar, Rumu. 1998. "The Legal Implications of Financial Sector Reform in Emerging Capital Markets." *American University International Law Review* 13: 705.

Sautman, Barry. 1992. "Sirens of the Strongman: Neo-Authoritarianism in Recent Chinese Political Theory." *The China Quarterly* 129: 72.

Schmitter, Philippe. 1974. "Still the Century of Corporatism?" In *The New Corporatism*, edited by Frederick Pike and Thomas Stritch. Notre Dame: University of Notre Dame Press.

Schoenhals, Michael. 1992. *Doing Things with Words in Chinese Politics: Five Studies.* Berkeley: Center for Chinese Studies.

Schuck, Peter, and E. Donald Elliot. 1990. "To the Chevron Station: an Empirical Study of Federal Administrative Law." *Duke Law Journal* 1990: 984.

Schumpeter, Joseph. 1943. *Capitalism, Socialism, and Democracy.* London: Allen and Unwin.

Schusselbauer, Gerhard. 1999. "Privatisation and Restructuring in Economies in Transition: Theory and Evidence Revisited." *Europe–Asia Studies* 51: 1.

Schwartz, Benjamin. 1957. "On Attitudes toward Law in China." In *Government under the Law and Individual*. Washington: American Council of Learned Societies.

Schwartz, Bernard. 1991. *Administrative Law*. 3rd edn. Boston: Little, Brown.

Scogin, Hugh T., Jr. 1990. "Between Heaven and Man: Contract and the State in Han Dynasty China." *Southern California Law Review* 63: 1325.

Scully, Gerald. 1991. "Constitutional Economics: the Framework for Economic Growth and Social Progress." *The Heritage Lectures*. Washington, DC: The Heritage Foundation.

Segal, Gerald. 1999. "Does China Matter?" *Foreign Affairs*, September–October, at 24.

Segal, Jeffrey A., and Harold J. Spaeth. 1993. *The Supreme Court and the Attitudinal Model*. New York: Cambridge University Press.

Seidman, Robert, and Ann Seidman. 1994. *State and Law in the Development Process*. New York: St. Martin's Press.

Seligman, Scott. 1999. "*Guanxi*: Grease for the Wheels of China." *The China Business Review*, September–October.

Shambaugh, David, ed. 2000. *Is China Unstable?* Armonk, NY: M.E. Sharpe.

Shan, Jordan, Gary Tian, and Fiona Sun. 1999. "Causality between FDI and Economic Growth." In *Foreign Direct Investment and Economic Growth in China*, edited by Yanrui Wu. Northhampton, MA: New Horizons in International Business.

Shanghai Legal Scholars Criticize Falungong. FBIS-CHI-1999-0809, August 9, 1999.

"Shanghai Revises 534 Business Regulations." November 13, 2000. http://www.chinabiz.org.

Shao, Cheng. 1996. "Jiaqiang Lianzheng Fazhi de Jianshe" ("Strengthen the Establishment of Good Governance Rule of Law"). In "Zhongguo Fazhi Shixian Fanglue (Bitanhui)" (Strategy for the Realization of the Rule of Law [Written Exchange of Ideas]). *Falü Kexue* 3: 8.

Shapiro, Martin. 1993. "The Globalization of Law." *Global Legal Studies* 1: 37.

Shen, Bailu. 1996. "Lüshifa de Lifa Guocheng ji Zhuyao Neirong" ("The Legislative Process and Main Content of the Lawyers Law"). *Beijing Lushi*, March.

Shen, Hongwei. 2000. "Lun Woguo Peishenzhi de Foudingxing Sikao" ("A Contrarian Perspective on China's System of Assessors"). *Hebei Faxue* 1: 81.

Shen, Yuanyuan. 2000. "Conceptions and Receptions of Legality: Understanding the Complexity of Law Reform in Modern China." In *The Limits of the Rule of Law in China*, edited by Turner, *et al.* Seattle: University of Washington Press.

Shen, Zongling. 1998. "Yifa Zhiguo yu Jingji" ("Ruling the Country According to Law and the Economy"). *Zhongwai Faxue* 3: 1.

Shetreet, Shimon, and Jules Deschenes. 1985. *Judicial Independence: the Contemporary Debate.* Boston: Martinus Nijhoff Publishers.

Shi, Steven, and Anne Stevenson-Yang. 1998. "Retail Roundabout." *China Business Review*, January–February, at 43.

Shi, Tianjian. 2000. "Cultural Values and Democracy in the People's Republic of China." *The China Quarterly* 162: 540.

1999. "Village Committee Elections in China: Institutional Tactics for Democracy." *World Politics* 51: 385.

1997. *Political Participation in Beijing.* Cambridge: Harvard University Press.

Shi, Yuping. 1996. "Shilun Xingzheng Lanyong Zhiquan ji qi Falü Zhiyue" ("Administrative Abuse of Power and Its Legal Restraint"). *Fashang Yanjiu (Commercial Law Studies)* 1: 81.

Shiga, Shuzo. 1974. "Criminal Procedure in the Ch'ing Dynasty." *Memoirs of the Research Department of Tokyo Bunko* 32: 1.

Shih, Chih-yu. 1999. *Collective Democracy: Political and Legal Reform in China.* Hong Kong: The Chinese University Press.

Shirk, Susan. 1993. *The Political Logic of Economic Reform in China.* Berkeley: University of California Press.

Shirley, Mary, and Lixin Colin Xu. 2001. "The Empirical Effects of Performance Contracts: Evidence from China." *Journal of Law, Economics and Organization* 17: 1.

Shklar, Judith. 1987. "Political Theory and the Rule of Law." In *The Rule of Law: Ideal or Ideology*, edited by Allan C. Hutchinson and Patrick Monahan. Toronto: Carswell.

Shue, Henry. 1980. *Basic Rights: Subsistence, Affluence, and US Foreign Policy.* Princeton: Princeton University Press.

Sim, Susan. 1995. "Human Rights: Bridging the Gulf." *The Straits Times*, 21 October.

Singapore Court Imprisons Seven, Fines Eight Falungong Activists. FBIS-CHI-2001-0329, March 29, 2001.

Singer, Joseph William. 1988. "Legal Realism Now." *California Law Review* 76: 465.

Slobodzian, Joseph. 2000. "Russian Win in Chinese Court Encourages Critics." http://www.2001law.com, 24 October.

Smith, Hannah Clayson. 2000. "*Liberté, Egalité et Fraternité* at Risk for New Religious Movements in France." *Brigham Young University Law Review* 2000: 1099.

So, Irene. 1996. "Justice Ministry Keeps Control of Legal Reforms." *South China Morning Post,* 20 June.

"SOEs to Work under 'Code' to Improve." 2000. *China Daily,* 28 October, at 1.

Solinger, Dorothy. 2001. "Ending One-Party Dominance: Korea, Taiwan, Mexico." *Journal of Democracy* 12: 30.

——— 1999. "China's Floating Population." In *The Paradox of Post-Mao Reforms,* edited by Merle Goldman and Roderick MacFarquhar. Cambridge: Harvard University Press.

"State Will Strengthen Supervision of Taxation." 1998. *China Daily,* 30 March, at 1.

Steinberg, Richard. 1998. *Institutional Implications of WTO Accession for China.* Institute of Global Conflict and Cooperation Policy Paper No. 41.

Steiner, Henry. 1988. "Political Participation as a Human Right." *Harvard Yearbook of International Law* 1: 77.

Steiner, Henry, and Alston, Philip. 2000. *International Human Rights in Context.* Oxford: Oxford University Press.

Steinfeld, Edward. 1998. *Forging Reform in China: the Fate of State-Owned Industry.* New York: Cambridge University Press.

Stephens, Thomas. 1992. *Order and Discipline in China.* Seattle: University of Washington Press.

Stephenson, Matthew. 2001. "A Trojan Horse behind Chinese Walls? Problems and Prospects of US-Sponsored 'Rule of Law' Reform Projects in the People's Republic of China." *UCLA Pacific Basin Law Journal* 18: 64.

Stiglitz, Joseph. 2001. "From Miracle to Crisis to Recovery: Lessons from Four Decades of East Asian Experience." In *Rethinking the East Asian Miracle,* edited by Joseph Stiglitz and Shahid Yusuf. New York: Oxford University Press.

Strauss, Peter. 1991. "An Introduction to Administrative Justice in the United States." In *Administrative Law: the Problem of Justice,* edited by William Wade *et al.* Milan: Giuffre.

Streeton, Paul. 1996. "Governance." In *Current Issues in Economic Development: an Asian Perspective,* edited by M.G. Quibria and J. Malcolm Dowling. Hong Kong: Oxford University Press.

Strengthening PRC's Legal, Judicial Work. FBIS-CHI-1999-0725, June 16, 1999.

"Students' Attitudes toward Human Rights Surveyed." 1999. *BBC Summary of World Broadcasts,* 4 May.

Studwell, Joseph, and Zhong Jiyin. 1999. "The Private Economy." *China Economic Quarterly* 3: 2.

Su, Li. 1998. "Ershi Shiji Zhongguo de Xiandaihua he Fazhi" ("Twentieth Century China's Modernization and Rule of Law"). *Faxue Yanjiu* 20(1): 3.

———. 1996. "Houxiandai Sichao yu Zhongguo Faxue he Fazhi" ("Postmodern Thought and Chinese Jurisprudence and Legal Institutions"). In *Fazhi ji qi Bentu Ziyuani*. Beijing: Zhongguo Zhengfa Daxue Press.

———. 1995. "Bianfa, Fazhi Jianshe ji qi Bentu Ziyuan" ("Change of Law, Establishment of the Rule of Law and Its Native Resources"). *Zhongwai Faxue* 5: 1.

"Summary of the 2000 Work Report of the Beijing Lawyer's Association." 2001. *Beijing Lushi* 1: 6.

Summary of US–China Bilateral WTO Agreement, http://www/uschina.or/public/991115a.html.

Summers, Robert. 1993. "A Formal Theory of Rule of Law." *Ratio Juris* 6: 127.

———. 1988. "The Ideal Socio-Legal Order: Its 'Rule of Law' Dimension." *Ratio Juris* 1: 154.

Sun, Guohua. 1996. "Cong Zhongguo de Shiji Chufa, Zou Ziji de Daolu" ("Start from China's Actual Circumstances, Take Our Own Road"). In "Zhongguo Fazhi Shixian Fanglue (Bitanhui)" (Strategy for the Realization of the Rule of Law [Written Exchange of Ideas]). *Falü Kexue* 3: 7.

Sun, Guolian. 1999. "Lükao Re, Rechu Gaochao" ("Bar Examination Craze, Fever Reaches Peak"). *Zhongguo Lüshi* 5: 18.

Sun, Haishun. 1999. "FDI, Trade and Transfer Pricing." In *Foreign Direct Investment and Economic Growth in China*, edited by Yanrui Wu. Northhampton, MA: New Horizons in International Business.

Sun, Xiaoxia. 1998. "Fazhi Guojia ji qi Zhengzhi Jiegou" ("The Rule-of-Law State and its Political Structure"). *Faxue Yanjiu* 20(1): 16.

———. 1996. "Zhongguo Fazhi de Xianshi Mubiao Xuanze" ("Choosing the Target for the Realization of the Rule of Law in China"). In "Zhongguo Fazhi Shixian Fanglue (Bitanhui)" ("Strategy for the Realization of Rule of Law [Written Exchange of Ideas]"). *Falü Kexue* 3: 12.

Sun, Yatsen. 1990. *The Three Principles of the People*, translated by Frank W. Price. Taipei: China Cultural Service.

Sunstein, Cass. 1996. *Legal Reasoning and Political Conflict*. New York: Oxford University Press.

———. 1995. "Problems with Rules." *California Law Review* 83: 953.

Supreme Court Appoints 10 Judicial Superintendents. FBIS-CHI-98-303, October 30, 1998.

Supreme Court Training Staff on Contract Law. FBIS-CHI-1999-0414, April 14, 1999.

"Swedish Arbitral Award Enforced in Beijing." 1998. 31 *International Commercial Litigation*, 1 June.

Tamanaha, Brian Z. 1997. *Realistic Socio-Legal Theory: Pragmatism and a Social Theory of Law*. Oxford: Oxford University Press.

_____. 1995. "The Lessons of Law-and-Development Studies." *American Journal of International Law* 89: 470.

Tan, Justin. 1996. "Regulatory Environment and Strategic Orientations in a Transitional Economy: a Study of Chinese Private Enterprise." *Information Access Company* 21: 31.

Tang, James T. H., ed. 1995. *Human Rights and International Relations in the Asia–Pacific Region*. New York: Printer.

Tanner, Murray Scot. 1999. *The Politics of Lawmaking in China*. Oxford: Clarendon Press.

_____. 1994. "The Erosion of Communist Party Control over Lawmaking in China." *The China Quarterly* 138: 381.

Tao, Rong. 1999. "Employee's Property Rights in China's State-Owned Enterprise Reorganization." *Columbia Journal of Asian Law* 13: 12.

Tay, Alice Erh-Soon. 1990. "Communist Visions, Communist Realities, and the Role of Law." *Journal of Law and Society* 17: 155.

_____. 1987. "The Struggle for Law in China." *University of British Columbia Law Review* 21: 562.

Taylor, Lance, Santosh Mehrota, and Enrique Delamonica. 1997. "The Links between Economic Growth, Poverty Reduction and Social Development." In *Development with a Human Face: Experiences in Social Achievement and Economic Growth*, edited by Santosh Mehrota and Richard Jolly. Oxford: Clarendon Press.

Teitel, Ruti. 1997. "Transitional Jurisprudence: the Role of Law in Political Transformation." *Yale Law Journal* 106: 2009.

Teiwes, Frederick. 2001. "Normal Politics with Chinese Characteristics." *The China Journal* 45: 255.

Thireau, Isabelle, and Linshan Hua. 1997. "Legal Disputes and the Debate about Legitimate Norms." In *China Review*, edited by Kuan Hsin-chi and Maurice Brosseau. Hong Kong: Chinese University Press.

"Three-Pronged Purge" of Falungong Cited. FBIS-CHI-1999-0728, July 28, 1999.

Timmermans, Wim. 1996. "Constitutional Developments in the Ukraine." In *Constitutional Reform and International Law in Central and Eastern Europe*, edited by Rein Mullerson *et al*. Boston: Kluwer Law International.

Trebilcock, Michael. 1997. "What Makes Poor Countries Grow?" In *The Law and Economics of Development*, edited by Edgardo Buscalgia, *et al*. London: JAI Press.

Trubek, David. 1996. "Law and Development: Then and Now." *American Society of International Law Proceedings*, March, at 223.

    1974. "Scholars in Self-Estrangement: Some Reflections on the Crisis in Law and Development Studies in the United States." *Wisconsin Law Review* 1974: 1062.

    1972a. "Max Weber on Law and the Rise of Capitalism." *Wisconsin Law Review* 1972: 720.

    1972b. "Toward a Social Theory of Law: an Essay on the Study of Law and Development." *Yale Law Journal* 82: 1.

Tsao, King K., and John Abbot Worthley. 1995. "Chinese Public Administration: Change with Continuity during Political and Economic Development." *Public Administration Review* 55: 169.

Tu, Weiming. 1993. *Way, Learning, and Politics.* Albany: SUNY Press.

Turner, Karen. 2000. "Introduction: the Problem with Paradigms." In *The Limits of the Rule of Law in China*, edited by Karen G. Turner, James V. Feinerman, and R. Kent Guy. Seattle: University of Washington Press.

    1989. "The Theory of Law in the *Ching-fa*." *Early China* 14: 55.

Twiss, Sumner. 1998. "A Constructive Framework for Discussing Confucianism and Human Rights." In *Confucianism and Human Rights*, edited by Wm. Theodore de Bary and Tu Weiming. New York: Columbia University Press.

Tyler, Tom. 1990. *Why People Obey the Law.* New Haven: Yale University Press.

UN Human Rights Commission. 2000. *Impunity for Torturers Continues Despite Changes in the Law; Report on Implementation of the Convention against Torture in the People's Republic of China.* http://www.hrchina.org/reports/ cat2000.html.

UNDP. 1995. *First Lady Hillary Rodham Clinton Remarks for the United Nations Fourth World Conference on Women.*

Unger, Jonathan, and Anita Chan. 1999. "Inheritors of the Boom: Private Enterprise and the Role of Local Government in a Rural South China Township." *China Journal* 42: 45.

    1995. "China, Corporatism, and the East Asian Model." *Australian Journal of Chinese Affairs* 33: 29.

Unger, Roberto Mangabeira. 1996. *What Should Legal Analysis Become?* London: Verso.

    1976. *Law in Modern Society: toward a Criticism of Social Theory.* New York: Free Press.

"Unprecedented" Internal Shakeup of Judiciary Noted. FBIS-CHI-98-257, September 14, 1998.

Upham, Frank. 1994. "Speculations on Legal Informality: on Winn's 'Relational Practices and the Marginalization of Law.'" *Law and Society Review* 28: 223.

US Department of State Country Reports on Human Rights Practices for 1999 – China. Released February 25, 2000. Washington, DC: US GPO. http://www.state.gov/www/global/human_rights/1999_hrp_report/china.html.

US Department of State Country Reports on Human Rights Practices for 1996. 1997. Washington, DC: US GPO.

US Department of State. United States Report on Hong Kong. Released August 7, 2001. Washington, DC: US GPO. http://www.usconsulate.org.hk/ushk/pi/20010731.htm.

US Embassy Report. 2000. *China's Top Worries: Lagging Political Reform, Corruption, Environment.* May.

"US Human Rights Record Not So Rosy." 1996. *China Daily*, 25 March.

"USTR Says China Agrees Not to Restrict Financial News Wires." 1997. *Extel Examiner*, 24 October.

Van der Sprenkel, Sybille. 1962. *Legal Institutions in Manchu China.* London: University of London, Athlone Press.

Vermeer, Eduard. 1999. "Shareholding Cooperatives: a Property Rights Analysis." In *Property Rights and Economic Reform in China*, edited by Jean C. Oi and Andrew G. Walder. Stanford: Stanford University Press.

von Mehren, A., and J. Gordonly. 1977. *The Civil Law System.* 2nd edn. Boston: Little, Brown.

von Mehren, Philip, and Tim Sawers. 1992. "Revitalizing the Law and Development Movement: a Case Study of Title in Thailand." *Harvard International Law Journal* 33: 67.

"Vote of Disapproval Prompts Campaign to Clean up China's Courts." 1997. *Agence France-Press*, 2 April.

Vyas, Yash, ed. 1994. *Law and Development in the Third World.* Nairobi: Faculty of Law, University of Nairobi.

Wade, Robert. 1996. "Globalization and Its Limits: Reports of the Death of the National Economy Are Greatly Exaggerated." In *National Diversity and Global Capitalism*, edited by Suzanne Berger and Ronald Dore. Ithaca, NY: Cornell University Press.

Wade, Sir William. 1991. "Administrative Justice in Great Britain." In *Administrative Law: the Problem of Justice: Anglo-American and Nordic Systems*, edited by Aldo Piras. Milan: Giuffre.

Walder, Andrew G. 1998. "The County Government as an Industrial Corporation." In *Zouping in Transition*, edited by Andrew G. Walder. Cambridge: Harvard University Press.

1995. "The Quiet Revolution from within: Economic Reform as a Source of Political Decline." In *The Waning of the Communist State*, edited by Andrew G. Walder. Berkeley: University of California Press.

1986. *Communist Neo-Traditionalism: Work and Authority in Chinese Industry.* Berkeley: University of California Press.

Walder, Andrew, and Jean Oi. 1999. "Property Rights in the Chinese Economy: Contours of the Process of Change." In *Property Rights and Economic Reform in China,* edited by Jean C. Oi and Andrew G. Walder. Stanford: Stanford University Press.

Waldron, Jeremy. 1989. "Rule of Law in Contemporary Liberal Theory." *Ratio Juris* 2: 79.

Walker, Geoffrey De Q. 1988. *The Rule of Law.* Carlton, VT: Melbourne Press.

Wan, Ming. 1998. "Chinese Opinion on Human Rights." *Orbis* 42: 3.

Wang, Chenguang. 1998. "Falü de Kesuxing: Xiandai Fazhi Guojia Zhong Falü de Tezheng Zhiyi" ("Justiciability of Law – One Characteristic of a Modern Rule of Law Country"). *Faxue (Jurisprudence)* 8: 18.

Wang, Guixiu. *Political System Reform as New Revolution.* FBIS-CHI-98-236, August 24, 1998.

Wang, Jiafu. 1998. "Guanyu Yifa Zhiguo Jianshe Shehui Zhuyi Fazhi Guojia de Lilun he Shijian Wenti" ("On Governing the Country in Accordance with Law: Theoretical and Practical Issues in Establishing a Socialist Rule-of-Law State"). In *Zhonggong Zhongyang Fazhi Jiangzuo Huibian,* edited by Ministry of Justice. Beijing: Falü Chubanshe.

Wang, Jiafu, *et al.* 1996. "Lun Yifa Zhiguo" ("On Ruling the Country in Accordance with Law"). *Faxue Yanjiu* 18(2): 3.

Wang, Liming. 2000. *Sifa Gaige Yanjiu (Research on Judicial Reform).* Beijing: Falü Chubanshe.

Wang, Renbo, and Liaoyuan Cheng. 1989. *Fazhi Lun (On Rule of Law).* Jinan: Shandong Renmin Chubanshe.

Wang, Yong. 2000. "China's Domestic WTO Debate." *China Business Review,* January–February, at 54.

Wang, Zucai. 1997. "Faguan Lüshi Qianyue Baolian" ("Judges and Lawyers Sign Pact to Guarantee Integrity"). *Fazhi Ribao (Legal Daily),* 19 June.

Wank, David. 1999. *Commodifying Communism: Business, Trust, and Politics in a Chinese City.* New York: Cambridge University Press.

Warren, Kenneth F. 1982. *Administrative Law in the American Political System.* St. Paul, MN: West Publishing Co.

Watson, Alan. 1993. *Legal Transplants.* Athens: University of Georgia Press.

1976. "Legal Transplants and Law Reform." *Law Quarterly Review* 92: 79.

Weber, Max. 1968. *Economy and Society: an Outline of Interpretive Sociology.* Vol. III. New York: Bedminster Press.

Wei, Ke. 1997. "Importers Keep Tax Break: Extend JV Tariff-Free Regulation." *China Daily,* 9 April, at 5.

Wei, Shangjin. 1995. "Attracting Foreign Direct Investment: Has China Reached Its Potential?" *China Economic Review* 6: 2.

Weitzman, Martin, and Chenggang Xu. 1994. "Chinese Township and Village Enterprises as Vaguely Defined Cooperatives." *Journal of Comparative Economics* 18: 121.

Westen, Peter. 1982. "The Empty Idea of Equality." *Harvard Law Review* 95: 537.

White, Gordon. 1994. "Democratization and Economic Reform in China." *Australian Journal of Chinese Affairs* 31: 73.

White, Gordon, Jude Howell, and Shang Xiaoyuan. 1996. *In Search of Civil Society: Market Reform and Social Change in Contemporary China.* Oxford: Clarendon Press.

Whiting, Susan. 2001. *Power and Wealth in Rural China.* Cambridge: Cambridge University Press.

———. 1999. "The Regional Evolution of Ownership Forms: Shareholding Cooperatives and Rural Industry in Shanghai and Wenzhou." In *Property Rights and Economic Reform in China*, edited by Jean C. Oi and Andrew G. Walder. Stanford: Stanford University Press.

"Why Falun Gong Has the Chinese Government So Nervous." *Talk of the Nation*, August 2, 1999 (transcript of remarks of Yu Shuning, spokesperson for the PRC Embassy).

Wiarda, Howard J. 1997. *Corporatism and Comparative Politics: the Other Great "Ism."* Armonk, NY: M.E. Sharpe.

———. 1971. "Law and Political Development in Latin America: toward a Framework for Analysis." *American Journal of Comparative Law* 19: 434.

Wiersbowsk, Marek, and Stephen C. McCaffrey. 1984. "Judicial Controls of Administrative Authorities." *International Lawyer* 18: 645.

Wilensky, Harold. 1964. "The Professionalization of Everyone?" *American Journal of Sociology* 70: 137.

Winn, Jane Kaufman. 1994. "Relational Practices and the Marginalization of Law: a Study of the Informal Financial Practices of Small Buinesses in Taiwan." *Law and Society Review* 28: 193.

Winn, Jane Kaufman, and Yeh Tang-chi. 1995. "Advocating Democracy: the Role of Lawyers in Taiwan's Political Transformation." *Law and Social Inquiry* 20: 561.

Womack, Brantly, 1989, "Party-State Democracy: a Theoretical Exploration." *Issues and Studies* 25: 37.

Woo, Margaret. 1991. "Adjudicative Supervision in the PRC." *American Journal of Comparative Law* 39: 95.

Woo, Wing Thye. 1999. "The Real Reasons for China's Growth." *The China Journal* 41: 115.

The World Bank. 1999. *Entering the 21st Century: World Development Report 1999/2000.* New York: Oxford University Press.

——. 1997. *China's Management of Enterprise Assets: the State as Shareholder.* Washington, DC: The World Bank.

The World Bank Legal Department. 1995. *The World Bank and Legal Technical Assistance: Initial Lessons.* Policy Research Working Paper 1414.

Wright, Robin. 1997. "Democracy: Challenges and Innovations in the 1990s." *The Washington Quarterly* 20: 23.

"WTO Will Promote Rule of Law in China." http://www.uschina.org/public/wto/ruleoflaw.html.

Wu, Jialin. 1996. "Deng Xiaoping de Fazhi Sixiang" ("On Deng Xiaoping's Rule-of-Law Ideas"). *Zhongguo Faxue (PRC Legal Studies)* 2: 7.

Wu, Yanrui, ed. 1999. *Foreign Direct Investment and Economic Growth in China.* Northhampton, MA: New Horizons in International Business.

Wu, Zheng. 1997. "Shanghai Survey Finds More Red Tape to Cut." *China Daily,* 9–15 November, at 5.

Xia, Yong. 1999. "Fazhi shi Shenme" ("What is the Rule of Law?"). *Zhongguo Shehui Kexue* 4: 18.

——. 1995. "Xiangmin Gongfa Quanli de Shengcheng" ("The Formation of Chinese Rural Citizen's Rights in Public Law"). In *Zouxiang Quanli de Shidai (Toward an Age of Rights),* edited by Xia Yong. Beijing: Zhongguo Zhengfa Daxue Chubanshe.

Xiao, Hongming. 2000. "The Internationalization of China's Legal Service Market." *Perspectives,* 1 June.

Xiao, Shengxi, ed. 1996. *Zhongguo Lüshifa Duben (The PRC Lawyers Law Reader).* Beijing: Xinhua Press.

Xiao, Yang. 2000. "Zhenfen Jingshen, Zhenzhua Shigan, ba Renmin Fayuan Jiceng Jianshe Tuixiang Xinjieduan" ("Lift up Spirits, Work Genuinely and Sincerely, Push the Development of Basic People's Courts to a New Stage"). 66 *Supreme People's Court Gazette.*

——. 1999. "Renzhen Shishi Yifa Zhiguo Jiben Fanglue, Jiji Tuijin Renmin Fayuan Gaige" ("Earnestly Implement Government According to Law, Aggressively Promote Reform of the Courts"). 61 *Supreme People's Court Gazette.*

——. 1998. "Wanggu Fazhan Jioayu Zhengdun Chengguo" ("Consolidate and Develop the Results of Educational Rectification"). 55 *Supreme People's Court Gazette.*

Xiao Yang Discusses Court Reforms. FBIS-CHI-1999-0812, August 12, 1999.

Xie, Hui. 1998. "Quanwei Tuijin yu Quanwei Zhuanhua" ("Authority as Progressive Force and the Evolution of Authority"). *Faxue* 2: 4.

——. 1992. "Lun Xingzheng Yuequan Li" ("On Administrative Excess of Authority") *Falü Kexue* 6: 15.

Xie, Pengcheng. 1996. "Lun Dangdai Zhongguo de Falü Quanwei" ("On the Authority of Law in Contemporary China"). *Zhongguo Faxue* 6: 6.

Xin, Chunying. 1999. *Zhongguo de Falü Zhidu ji qi Gaige (Chinese Legal System and Current Legal Reform)*. Beijing: Falü Chubanshe.

Xinhua Reports Family Background of Tiananmen Suicides. FBIS-CHI-2001-0131, January 31, 2001.

Xinhua Reports on Self-Immolation, Blames Falungong. FBIS-CHI-2001-0130, January 30, 2001.

Xinhua Views Harms Done by "Local Protectionism." FBIS-CHI-2000-0727, July 27, 2000.

Xu, Xianming. 1996. "Lun 'Fazhi' de Goucheng Yaojian" ("On the Constitutive Elements of Rule of Law"). *Faxue Yanjiu* 18(3): 37.

Xu, Yang. 1999. "Road Bill Negation Written in History." *China Daily*, 30 April.

Yahuda, Michael. 1999. "China's Foreign Relations: the Long March, Future Uncertain." *The China Quarterly* 159: 650.

Yan, Cunsheng. 1996. "Yao Queli Zhengque de 'Fazhi' Guannian" ("We Must Establish a Correct Concept of Rule of Law"). In "Zhongguo Fazhi Shixian Fanglue (Bitanhui)" (Strategy for the Realization of the Rule of Law [Written Exchange of Ideas]). *Falü Kexue* 3: 11.

Yan, Shujie, and Liu Jirui. 1998. "Economic Reforms and Regional Segmentation in Rural China, Regional Studies." *Regional Studies* 32: 8.

Yan, Yunxiang. 1996. *The Flow of Gifts: Reciprocity and Social Networks in a Chinese Village*. Stanford: Stanford University Press.

1995. "Everyday Power Relations: Changes in a North China Village." In *The Waning of the Communist State*, edited by Andrew Walder. Berkeley: University of California Press.

Yang, Cheng, and Liu Jingzhu. 1997. "Dui Xingzhengfuyi Xingtong Xushe Wenti de Tiaozheng yu Fenxi" ("Investigation and Analysis of Problem of Administrative Reconsideration Becoming an Empty Form"). *Xingzheng Pian* 2: 31.

Yang, Jiejun. 1997. "Lifa Zhiliang de Shizheng Fenxi: Tan 'Xingzheng Fuyi Tiaoli' do Qianque ji qi Wanshan" ("Positivist Analysis of Legislative Quality: Discussion of the Deficiencies and Improvements of the Administrative Reconsideration Regulations"). *Nanjing Shehui Kexue: Jingji Fazhihan (Nanjing Social Studies: Economic Law Office)* 3: 53

Yang, K. 1993. "Judicial Review and Social Change in the Korean Democratizing Process." *American Journal of Comparative Law* 41: 1.

Yang, Mansong. 1980. "Fazhi wei Wuchan Jieji Zhuanzheng Suo Bixu" ("The Necessity of Rule of Law for the Proletariat"). *Faxue Yanjiu* 4: 61.

Yang, Mayfair. 1994. *Gifts, Favors, and Banquets: the Art of Social Relationships in China*. Ithaca, NY: Cornell University Press.

Yatsko, Pamela. 1998. "New Owners: Privatization Comes to China's Township Enterprises." *Far Eastern Economic Review,* 5 February.

Yeung, Desmone, and Jane Chen. 1997. "Grace Period Extension on Import Duty and Import VAT Exemption." *China Tax Alert,* 7 January, at 1.

"Yifa Zhiguo Jianshe Shehuizhuyi Fazhi Guojia Xueshu Yantaohui Jiyao" ("Excerpts from the Academic Conference on Ruling the Country According to Law, Establish a Socialist Rule-of-Law State"). 1996. *Faxue Yanjiu* 18(3): 3.

Ying, Songnian, *et al.,* eds. 1994. *Xingzheng Susongfaxue (Study of the Administrative Litigation Law).* Beijing: Beijing Zhengzhi Daxue Chubanshe.

—— *et al.,* eds. 1993. *Xingzheng Xingwei Fa (Law of Administrative Acts).* Beijing: Renmin Chubanshe.

You Ji. 1998. "China's Administrative Reform: Constructing a New Model for a Market Economy." *Issues and Studies* 34: 69.

Yu, Keping. 1998. "Zouchu 'Zhengzhi Gaige – Shehuiwending' de Liangnan Jingdi" ("A Way out of the Two Trouble Areas: 'Political Reform–Social Stability'"). In *Political China,* edited by Dong Yuyu and Shi Binhai. Beijing: Jinri Zhongguo Chubanshe.

Yu, Xingzhong. 1989. "Legal Pragmatism in the People's Republic of China." *Journal of Chinese Law* 3: 29.

Yuen, Ada. 1996. "Lawyers Law Effect Doubted." *South China Morning Post,* 11 November.

Yusuf, Shahid. 2001. "The East Asian Miracle at the Millenium." In *Rethinking the East Asian Miracle,* edited by Stiglitz & Yusuf. New York: Oxford University Press.

Zakaria, Fareed. 1997. "The Rise of Illiberal Democracy." *Foreign Affairs* 76: 22.

Zhang, Geng, ed. 1997. *Zhongguo Lüshi Zhidu de Lichengbei: "Zhonghua Renmin Gongheguo Lüshifa" Lifa Guocheng Huigu (A Milestone in the Development of the PRC Lawyers System: a Look Back at the Legislative Process of the PRC Lawyers Law).* Beijing: Legal Press.

Zhang, Geng, and Hu Kangsheng, eds. 1996. *Zhonghua Renmin Gongheguo Lüshifa Quanshu (Compendium of the PRC Lawyers Law).* Beijing: Blue Sky Press.

Zhang, Jiansheng. 1998. "Youguan Xingzheng Susong Shouan Fanwei de jige Lilun Wenti Tanxi" ("Examination of Several Theoretical Problems Relating to the Scope of Administrative Litigation"). *Zhongguo Faxue* 2: 45.

Zhang, Naigen. 1997. "Intellectual Property in China." *Annual Survey of International and Comparative Law* 4: 4.

Zhang, Pufan. 1996. "Wanshan Shehuifazhi de Diandi Sikao" ("Some Accumulated Reflections on the Perfection of a Socialist Legal System"). In

"Zhongguo Fazhi Shixian Fanglue (Bitanhui)" ("Strategy for the Realization of the Rule of Law [Written Exchange of Ideas]"). *Falü Kexue* 3: 6.

Zhang, Qi. 1998. "Fazhi de Lixiang yu Xianshi" ("The Ideal and Reality of Rule of Law"). *Zhongwai Faxue* 2: 128.

Zhang, Wenxian. 1996. "Lun Lifazhong de Falü Yizhi" ("On the Legal Transplant of Legislation"). *Faxue* 1: 6.

Zhang, Wusheng, and Wu Zeyong. 2000. "Sifa Duli yu Fayuan Zuzhi Jigou de Tiaozheng (shang)" ("On Judicial Independence and the Adjustment of the Organization and Structure of the Courts, Part A"). *Zhongguo Faxue* 2: 55.

Zhang, Xiaoguang. 1999. "Foreign Investment Policy, Contribution and Performance." In *Foreign Direct Investment and Economic Growth in China*, edited by Yanrui Wu. Northhampton, MA: New Horizons in International Business.

Zhang, Xingzhong. 1989. "Zhuozhong Tiaojie Yuanze zhi Wojian" ("My Opinion about the Principle of Emphasizing Mediation"). *Fazhi Ribao (Legal Daily)*, 22 May.

Zhao, Ziyang. 1987. *Advance along the Road of Socialism with Chinese Characteristics.* FBIS-CHI, 26 October, pp. 10–34.

Zheng, Shiping. 1997. *Party vs. State in Post-1949 China.* Cambridge: Cambridge University Press.

"Zhongguo Minzhu yu Fazhi Jianshe de Kua Shiji Gongcheng" ("The Cross-Century Project of the Construction of China's Democracy and Legal System"). 1997. *Zhongguo Lüshi* 3: 6.

Zhu, Guobin. 1995. "Reform or Reorganization: Constructing and Implementing the New Chinese Civil Service." *International Review of Administrative Sciences* 61: 91.

Zhu, Jingwen. 2000. "Public Participation in Law-Making in the PRC." In *Law-Making in the People's Republic of China*, edited by Jan Michiel Otto, et al. The Hague: Kluwer Law International.

Zhu, Liyu, and Wan Qigang. 2000. "Lun Dang de Zhizheng Fangshi Xiang Fazhiguo de Genbenxing Zhuanbian" ("On the Fundamental Transition of the Party's Mode of Governing in the Transition to Rule of Law"). *Zhongguo Renmin Daxue Xuebao* 5: 74.

Zhu, Suli. 1997. "Houxiandai Sichao yu Zhongguo Faxue he Fazhi" ("Postmodern Thought and the Jurisprudence and Legal System of China.") *Faxue* 3: 11.

Zhu, Xinli. 1996. "Lun Xingzheng Chaoyue Zhiquan" ("Administrative Excess of Authority"). *Faxue Yanjiu* 2: 112.

Zhuang, Huining. 2000. "Faguanfa he Jianchaguanfa conhe Chugai?" ("How to Amend the Judges Law and Procuracy Law"). *Liaowang*, 24 July.

Zimmermann, Rheinhard. 1996. "An Introduction to German Legal Culture." In *Introduction to German Law*, edited by Werner F. Ebke and Matthew W. Finkin. Boston: Kluwer Law International.

Zirin, James D. 1997. "Confucian Confusion." *Forbes*, 24 February.

Zou, Rong. 1998. "Xingzheng Susong de Yuangao Zige Yanjiu" ("Study of Standing to Sue in Administrative Litigation"). *Faxue* 7: 61.

Zou, Weimin. 2000. *Bianqian yu Gaige: Fayuan zhi Xiandaihua Yanjiu (Change and Reform: Research on the Modernization of the Judiciary)*. Beijing: Falu Chubanshe.

Zweig, David. 2000. "The 'Externalities of Development': Can New Political Institutions Manage Rural Conflict?" In *Chinese Society: Change, Conflict and Resistance*, edited by Elizabeth J. Perry and Mark Selden. London: Routledge.

1996 Supreme People's Court Work Report. In *1996 Law Yearbook*. 1997: Falu Chubanshe.

"1996 Zhongguo Faxue Yanjiu Huigu" (Retrospective of Legal Research in China in 1996). 1997. *Faxue Yanjiu* 19(1): 3.

1996 Zhongguo Tongji Nianjian (1996 China Statistical Yearbook). 1997. Beijing: China Statistical Information & Consultancy Service Centre.

"1997 Zuigao Renmin Fayuan Gongzuo Bagao" ("1997 Supreme People's Court Work Report"). *Renmin ribao (People's Daily)*, 21 March.

1999 Supreme Court Work Report. FBIS-CHI-1999-0323, March 20, 1999.

1999 Supreme People's Procuratorate Work Report. FBIS-CHI-1999-0323, March 20, 1999.

2000 Supreme People's Court Report to NPC. FBIS-CHI-2000-0319, March 19, 2000.

INDEX

accountability
  charitable donations, 363
  corruption, 133, 234
  government officials, 131, 132, 140, 425
  National People's Congress (NPC), 243
adjudicative supervision committees
  abolition proposed, 18, 324
  appointments, 46
  approval of judgments, 281, 286
  Communist Party (CCP), 302, 306, 324
  composition, 284
  judgments challenged, 18
  major/difficult cases, 284, 286–87, 324
  petitions, 287, 313–14
  quality control, 84, 284
  regulations, 305
  Supreme People's Court (SPC), 191
administrative agencies
  bribery, 407
  budgets, 414
  commercial activities, 408–09
  courts, 403
  directly deliberative polyarchy, 425–26
  inconsistent legislation, 421
  legislative powers, 73, 117, 216, 239, 241, 409
  legislative supervision, 414–15
  litigation see administrative litigation
  Mao era, 408
  neutrality/expertise, 424–25
  officials see government officials
  protectionism, 261–62
  reining in bureaucracy, 414–24
administrative discretion
  abuse, 123, 137
  certainty/predictability, 411
  Communist Party (CCP), 85
  corruption, 18–19
  efficiency, 411
  equity, 411, 412, 444
  financing, 196
  flexibility, 394, 455
  hot-line networks, 19, 155

legal limits, 74, 132, 452, 453
Liberal Democrats, 84
licensing, 196, 413, 433, 472
regimes, 4–5, 394
rule of law, 410–14
administrative law
  abstract acts, 260, 261, 267, 438
  abuse of authority, 90, 121
  administrative supervision, 16, 260, 261, 395, 398, 415–17, 435, 436, 576
  agencies see administrative agencies
  balance theory, 137
  central policies, 16, 395
  Communitarians, 90, 433
  deregulation, 396
  draft laws, 13, 17, 90, 110, 240, 243, 263–64, 269, 398, 424, 433
  efficiency, 85, 137, 138, 403, 404, 408
  evolution, 397–399
  file and review system, 261
  Imperial era, 400–1
  interest groups, 396, 430
  legislative oversight committees, 16
  letters and petition system, 19, 132, 419–20
  local courts, 398
  Mao era, 395, 397
  Neoauthoritarians, 90, 433
  officials see government officials
  path-dependent reform, 399–10, 431–38
  post-Mao reforms, 57, 74, 89–90, 136–37
  postmodernism, 396, 424–31, 439
  rational governance, 85
  reconsideration see administrative reconsideration
  regime, 4–5, 16–17, 394–449
  State Council, 243–44, 421
  Statist Socialism, 90, 433
  systemic problems, 12, 395, 399–10
administrative litigation
  Administrative Litigation Law (ALL), 160, 307, 380, 398, 403, 404, 405, 406, 418, 420, 421, 422, 430, 436

administrative litigation (*cont.*)
  authority exceeded/abused, 422, 423
  avoidance, 403
  citizenship, 206
  constitutional law, 397–398
  costs, 405
  evidence, 422
  excluded entities, 420
  expansion, 404, 418
  interest groups, 420
  judicial independence, 307
  judicial review, 16, 17, 264–68, 395, 417,
    420, 421, 424, 438, 494, 563
  legal profession, 352, 362, 405–6, 442–43
  legitimate rights and interests, 420
  mediation, 406
  outcomes, 90, 121, 132, 400, 405, 420,
    435, 440, 445
  political cases, 207, 399, 400
  private attorney-general theory, 420, 436
  private enterprise, 196–97, 478
  procedural violations, 423–24, 432
  public security, 420
  United States, 400
administrative reconsideration
  advantages, 417
  courts, 422
  ex parte communication, 419, 435
  incidence, 404, 418
  inconsistent legislation, 260, 261, 417–18
  law (ARL), 398, 430, 435
  legal profession, 355–56, 357
  local protectionism, 418
  plaintiff uninformed of rights, 403, 418
  procedures, 16, 260, 261, 398, 403, 404,
    417–19
  regulations (ARR), 398, 418
  retaliation, 357, 418
agriculture, privatization, 192
Alford, William, 564
All China Lawyers Association, 235, 349,
  372, 385, 387
Allee, Mark, 40
American Bar Association (ABA), 350, 385
Amor, Abdelfattah, 95
antirightist movement (1957), 44, 81, 170,
  212, 289, 347, 397
arbitration, 58, 163, 296, 561
Asia
  dispute resolution, 184
  economic growth, 466, 468, 469
  financial crisis, 2, 19, 76, 118, 456, 457,
    458, 460, 461, 474
  government intervention, 75–76, 118, 455
  values, 3, 4, 72, 78, 115–16, 152, 536–38,
    539, 558, 579
Asia Foundation, 350

Austin, John, 128
authoritarian regime
  civil society, 168–69
  corporatism, 470–71
  power relinquished, 219, 528
  rule of law, 166–69, 185–86, 378
autonomy
  democracy, 516
  judges *see* judicial independence
  legal profession, 15, 84, 120, 137, 149,
    374, 382, 451, 452, 453
  Liberal Democrats, 84
  local government, 210–11
  rule of law, 78, 79, 83, 219
  social groups, 201
  state-owned enterprises (SOEs), 195, 197,
    409

banking
  bail out, 477
  competition, 496
  state-owned enterprises (SOEs), 194, 198,
    496
  township and village enterprises (TVEs),
    195
Baogang He, 117
Barro, Robert, 458–59
Basic People's Courts (BPC), 44, 155, 283,
  292, 293
Beijing Bureau of Justice, 100, 101, 352, 357,
  358, 387
Beijing Women's Centre, 381
Berman, Harold, 69
Bohannan, Paul, 127–28
bourgeoisie, 43, 44, 59, 171, 183, 217,
  457–58
bribery
  administrative agencies, 407
  government officials, 403
  judicial corruption, 295, 296, 322, 368,
    371
broadcasting
  Cultural Revolution, 199
  investigative reporting, 206, 484
  legal content, 7, 289
Buddhism, 70, 91
Business Environmental Risk Intelligence
  (BERI), 459, 460

cadres
  corruption, 483
  evaluation system, 19, 210
  local government, 196, 203–4, 231, 232
  princelings, 363, 389
capitalism
  businesses *see* private enterprise
  Chinese capitalism, 19, 20, 466

economics *see* market economy
law and development, 151, 453
liberalism, 171
varieties, 75, 456, 457
central government
centralization of power, 81–82, 191
down-sizing, 203, 204–5, 257, 429
market economy, 205
officials *see* government officials
Party groups, 191, 226
Year of Enforcement (1999), 312
Central Military Commission, 214
certainty
administrative discretion, 411
economic growth, 80, 82, 221,
456, 462
rule of law, 80, 82, 221, 411, 462
charitable giving, 363
Chen Guangzhong, 155, 243
China Democratic Party, 207
China Securities Regulatory Commission
(CSRC), 154, 356
Chinese Academy of Social Sciences (CASS),
59, 63, 82, 112, 182, 381, 382
Chinese capitalism, 19, 20, 466
Chinese International Economic and Trade
Arbitration Commission (CIETAC),
296, 561
Chu, Henry, 39, 40
Cisneros, Henry, 133
civil society
authoritarianism, 168–69
bottom-up solutions, 396, 428, 429, 431
Communitarians, 75, 77, 431
corporatism, 471
democracy, 530
interest groups, 428
Liberal Democrats, 77, 201, 202
Neoauthoritarians, 202, 374, 431
post-Mao reforms, 168, 173, 189
social contract theory, 201
social groups, 46, 201, 230
Statist Socialism, 202, 374, 431
civil/political rights, 3, 62, 78, 86, 135, 173,
469, 514
Clarke, Donald, 142–45, 148, 178
classical legal theories, 28–36
classicalism
companies/businesses, 20, 75, 76,
196, 480
connections (*guanxi*), 402, 470, 472–73,
475
corruption, 430, 472
cultural factors, 19
disadvantages, 473
economic growth, 470
horizontal, 470, 473

legal profession, 15, 85, 356, 357, 378,
379, 406
social groups, 201
state-owned enterprises (SOEs), 410
Statist Socialism, 77
township and village enterprises (TVEs),
487
vertical, 470, 471, 473
Clinton, Hilary, 582
Clinton, William Jefferson (Bill), 2, 133, 385,
587
commercial law, role, xii
Communist Party (CCP)
adjudicative supervision committees, 302,
306, 324
administrative discretion, 85
campaigns, 208, 303
Central Committee, 398
connections (*guanxi*), 307
constitutional law, 6, 10, 213–14
corruption, 210, 234, 398, 407
dictatorship of the proletariat, 77
discipline, 162, 210, 214, 234, 303, 318,
415–17, 435
four cardinal principles, 77, 86, 88, 191,
217, 300, 373
groups *see* Party groups
instability, 81
interference, 8, 11, 134, 197, 214, 307
judiciary, 46, 134, 216, 220–21, 224,
302–9, 328–30
leading role *see* leadership
legal system, 211–16
legislation, 84
legitimacy, 61, 169–74, 189, 209, 220, 223,
224–25
Mao era, 84
market economy, 220
membership, 11, 91, 209, 210, 306
National People's Congress (NPC), 62
nomenklatura *see* nomenklatura system
normative agenda, 77, 86
Organization Department, 291, 302,
305
PLC *see* Political-Legal Committee
policy formulation, 213, 214–15
post-Mao reforms, 84, 218
propaganda, 200, 205, 530
retreat, 188–238
rule by law, 8, 10–12, 24
rule of law, 56, 61, 161–62, 169–74
scientific correctness, 46, 170
socialist rule-of-law state, ix, x, 58, 59–60,
62, 219
symbolic influence, 217–18
thin theories, 129
thought *see* thought control

Communitarians
  administrative law, 90, 433
  Asian values, 72, 78
  Chinese tradition, 27
  civil society, 75, 77, 431
  Confucianism, 116
  constitutional law, 89
  democracy, 4, 519
  distinct forms, 72, 116
  elections, 77, 89, 212
  ideal type, 71–75, 104–5, 117
  judicial independence, 86, 300
  justice, 70
  legal profession, 120, 374
  Liberal Democrats, 116, 117
  market economy, 3–4, 76
  morality/virtue, 78–79
  neutral state, 86
  New Conservatives, 72
  normative agenda, 77, 86, 300, 401
  pragmatism, 78, 79
  rights, 78, 79, 86
  rules, 87
  single party socialism, 188, 212
  social groups, 94
  social order, 115
  social solidarity, 79
  stability, 80–81, 82
  state bound/limited, 129
  strengthening state, 80, 167
comparative law
  imperfect realization of an ideal (IRI),
    142–43, 145, 178
  law and development, 152
competition
  banking, 496
  fair rules, 453
  foreign-invested enterprises (FIEs), 198
  legal profession, 369, 371
  market economy, 195, 196, 198
  township and village enterprises (TVEs),
    486
  World Trade Organization (WTO), 196,
    198, 458, 496
Comprehensive Development Framework,
  461
confidential information, legal profession,
  351, 368, 375
conflict of interest
  government officials, 205
  recusal system, 296–97, 322
Confucianism
  Communitarians, 116
  criminal procedure, 28
  customary norms, 31
  dao (Way), 32–33

de (virtue), 32
  democracy, 516, 529
  dispute resolution, 31, 39
  ethics, 176, 363, 402, 407, 466
  harmony, 30–31, 32, 33, 288, 345
  Imperial era, 36, 38, 39, 40, 161,
    345, 401
  legalist response, 33–34
  li zhi, 28–33, 39, 41, 42, 43
  normative system, 170
  particularized justice, 251
  post-Mao reforms, 161, 170, 171
  promulgated laws, 29–30
  sages, 33, 50, 176, 316
  shi (literati) class, 31, 33
  society, 28–29, 516
  terminology, 49
  wuwei (rulers), 31–33, 42, 50
connections (guanxi)
  administrative challenges, 405, 406
  clientelism, 402, 470, 472–73, 475
  Communist Party (CCP), 307
  government officials, 402–3, 417
  human feeling (renqing), 315–16, 402
  judiciary, 290
  legal profession, 7, 15, 296, 366–67, 371,
    379–80, 387, 473
  Mao era, 402
  market economy, 402, 441
  relationships/networks, 19, 165,
    315–16, 402, 408, 418, 456, 466,
    477, 478
constitutional law
  1954 constitution, 44, 88
  1978 constitution, 88
  1982 constitution, 6, 57, 61, 88, 136, 194,
    397
  1988 amendment, 194
  1993 amendment, 194
  1999 amendment, 1, 61, 62, 89, 137, 195
  administrative litigation, 397–398
  basic principles, 57, 61
  Communist Party (CCP), 6, 10, 213–14
  Communitarians, 89
  courts, 280
  Cultural Revolution, 88
  economic growth, 88
  first constitution, 43
  interpretation of laws, 317, 325–26
  judicial independence, 280
  justiciable constitution, 89, 121, 397
  Liberal Democrats, 87
  Mao era, 44
  market economy, 88, 194–95, 478
  Neoauthoritarians, 89
  policy formulation, 61, 62, 63

procuracy, 312
programmatic nature, 61
rule of law, 120, 137
separation of powers, x, 73, 85, 215
socialism, 87, 88
socialist rule-of-law state, 1, 6, 89, 219
Statist Socialism, 89
consumer protection, 467
contract-intensive money (CIM), 459
contracts
dispute resolution, 163, 456, 467
due diligence, 456, 464
enforcement, 459, 462, 464, 473
land use, 481, 483
legislation, 58, 242, 243
market economy, 20, 348
corporatism
civil society, 471
Communitarians, 78
companies/businesses, 20, 75, 76, 196
cultural factors, 19, 26
disadvantages, 473
economic growth, 470–73
legal profession, 15
local government, 471, 472, 475,
478, 487
social groups, 201, 202
societal/neocorporatist version, 470–71
Statist Socialism, 77, 78
statist/authoritarian version, 470–71
theories, 176, 470
corruption
accountability, 133, 234
administrative discretion, 18–19
bribes see bribery
cadres, 483
clientelism, 430, 472
Communist Party (CCP), 210, 234, 398,
407
consultative committees, 18
destabilization, 21
discontent, 11
economic growth, 459–60
government officials, 18, 85, 133, 205,
234, 406–8, 416–17, 484
guanxi see connections
judges see judicial corruption
legal profession, 7, 15, 296, 297, 356–58,
367–69
local government, 222
post-Mao reforms, 60, 158, 159, 162, 172,
205, 406–8
procuracy, 325
rent-seeking, 15, 85, 356–57, 407, 472,
488, 501
systemic, 322

Council of Grand Justices (Taiwan), 221
courts
administrative agencies, 403
administrative divisions, 284, 398, 399
administrative reconsideration, 422
appeals, 287, 288, 294
authority, 316–30, 323–27
cases see litigation
collegiate panels, 281, 286, 287, 297
computers, 294, 295
constitutional law, 280
economic growth, 301, 304
enforcement, 287–88, 290, 315, 327
fees, 154, 281, 285, 295
funding, 280–81, 294–95, 328
Imperial era, 36–38, 160–61
inconsistent legislation, 325–26, 421
incorrect decisions, 290, 294, 296
inefficiency, 285
inquisitorial/adversarial methods, 282,
286, 293, 359
intellectual property, 13, 283, 284, 293
interpretive powers, 317, 326, 421
judges see judiciary
lay assessors, 286, 297
local government, 295, 307, 310–12, 316
macroeconomic policies, 301
Mao era, 44, 212
market economy, 319
mediation, 163, 288–89
money-making enterprises, 295, 296
National People's Congress (NPC), 44, 46,
84, 85, 309–10
open trials, 289, 294, 322
Party cells, 284, 302, 329
Party Committee, 302, 305, 306
Party groups, 191, 284, 302, 303, 305
Party Institutional Organ, 284, 302
people's congresses, 280, 294, 299, 305,
306, 309–10, 325, 327
personnel, 281, 283, 284, 292–93, 327
PLC see Political-Legal Committee
police, 293, 327
Political Department, 302, 303
post-Mao reforms, 155, 182, 285–89,
318–30
presidents, 284–85, 292, 293, 297, 305,
318, 321
presiding judges, 286, 297, 321
published judgments, 287
reasoned judgments, 287, 293–94
responsible judge, 286, 288
rural sector, 484
single party socialism, 302
structure, 44, 283–85
substantive, 283–84

courts (*cont.*)
  summary procedures, 155, 285, 286
  supervision *see* adjudicative supervision
    committees
  transparency, 18, 281
crime
  corruption *see* corruption
  Strike Hard campaign, 9, 24, 303, 375, 385
  violent crime, 129–30, 385
criminal procedure
  confessions, 349, 377
  Confucianism, 28
  dissidents, 90–91, 131, 134, 135, 137, 140,
    214
  fair trial, 91, 131, 134, 135, 214
  heretical organizations, 92, 93, 95, 123
  Imperial era, 36–38, 160–61, 376
  Japan, 122
  legal aid, 160, 252, 350, 362–64
  legal profession, 349, 352, 362–64, 372,
    375–77
  legal research, 155, 182
  Liberal Democrats, 90–91
  Neoauthoritarians, 90
  police, 330, 359
  post-Mao reforms, 9, 15, 57, 160, 207,
    208, 223, 234–35, 243, 359–60
  presumption of innocence, 376
  procuracy, 359, 361
  public security, 318, 325, 377
  speculation, 252
  state secrets, 377
  Statist Socialism, 90
  torture, 101, 330, 539
  United States, 375, 391
Critical Legal Scholars (CRITs)
  administrative law, 424–25
  law and development, 149, 152, 454, 455
  law and oppression, 126, 164, 165
  politics and law, 83, 164–65
  professions, 378
  rationality, 149
critical race theorists, 152
Cui Jianyuan, 243
cultural chauvinism/imperialism, 127, 146,
  153
cultural factors
  clientelism, 19
  corporatism, 19, 26
  human rights, 536–38
Cultural Revolution *see also* Mao era
  constitutional law, 88
  judiciary, 289
  legal profession, 347, 348
  legal system, ix, x, 6, 45–46, 49, 56, 74, 83,
    118

leisure, 199
procuracy, 312
public security, 312
Red Guards, 55
rough justice, 57
rule of man, 118
unlimited government, 398
upheaval, 81, 169, 170, 220, 240, 517
customary norms
  codification, 451
  Confucianism, 31
  dispute resolution, 128

Daoism, 34, 35, 70, 91, 94, 170,
  176, 407
Davis, Kenneth Culp, 410, 411
Defoort, Carine, xi
democracy
  absence, 20–21
  alternate paradigm, 543–46
  autonomy, 516
  China-specific issues, 516–33
  civil society, 530
  Communitarians, 4, 519
  Confucianism, 516, 529
  deliberative, 72–73
  elections *see* elections
  elitist, 116–17
  equality, 516
  evolutionary theory, 514, 521
  forces of change, 526–33
  legitimacy, 524
  long-term need, 523–26
  majoritarian, 515
  minimum requirements, 514–15
  Neoauthoritarians, 4, 117
  neutral state, 72
  public opinion, 117, 519, 521
  rights-based, 515
  rule of law *see* Liberal Democrats
demonstrations, 91, 93, 206, 207, 208, 420,
  458, 492
Deng Xiaoping
  connections, 402
  decentralization, 210
  democracy, 518
  economic growth, 55, 88, 397
  ideology, 24, 321
  leadership, 42, 214
  legal profession, 347, 348, 349, 361
  market economy, 88, 224, 347–48
  overcentralization, 190, 209
  pragmatism, 53, 217, 427
  provisional laws, 57
  reform programme, ix, 1
  riches, 406, 407

theory of socialism, 60, 120
trip south (1992), 58, 62, 112, 183, 361, 558
dependency theory, 149
developing countries
  foreign direct investment (FDI), 149, 453, 454, 456–57
  globalization, 453–54, 457
  intellectual property, 457
  judiciary, 150
  law and development see law and development
  modernization, 452
  rights, 150
  trade barriers, 149
development states, 22
devolution, 137, 138, 189, 209, 210, 221
Deweyean civic republicanism, 72
dispute resolution
  administrative law see administrative litigation
  arbitration, 58, 163, 296, 561
  Asia, 184
  Confucianism, 31, 39
  contracts, 163, 456, 467
  customary norms, 128
  Imperial era, 38–39
  informal mechanisms, 20, 38–39, 162, 456, 466–68, 477, 478
  Mao era, 47, 83
  market economy, 159
  mediation see mediation
  thin theories, 163
  World Trade Organization (WTO), 183, 495
dissidents
  China Democratic Party, 207
  criminal procedure, 90–91, 131, 134, 135, 137, 140, 214
  national security, 82
  prosecution see political cases
  reeducation see reeducation through labour
  rule of law, 166
Dong Yuyu, 70
Donnelly, Jack, 537, 538

economic growth
  Asia, 466, 468, 469
  certainty, 80, 82, 221, 456, 462
  China-specific issues, 450, 462–75
  civil/political rights, 78
  clientelism, 470
  constitutional law, 88
  convergence, 20, 454, 456, 457
  corporatism, 470–73

  corruption, 459–60
  courts, 301, 304
  critical theory, 454–58
  environment, 9, 461, 467
  generalist critics, 450
  globalization, 457, 527
  growth impeded, 474–75
  legal system, 463–64
  legitimacy, 61, 172, 189, 209
  litigation, 162–63, 468
  local government, 18, 81, 211, 220
  managed capitalism, 75
  market economy, 151
  Neoauthoritarians, 86
  neoclassical theory, 452
  political change, 151–52
  predictability, 80, 82, 221, 456, 462
  private enterprise, 193–94
  productivity improvements, 475
  property rights, x, 19, 452–53, 459, 462
  religion, 171–72, 451
  rights, 538–39
  rule of law, 19–20, 166, 450–512
  Statist Socialism, 3, 86
  testing theories, 458–60
  theories, 451–62
  World Trade Organization (WTO), 492–96
education and training
  approved curriculum, 87
  CCP leadership, 209
  government officials, 205
  judiciary, 13, 14, 44, 155, 182, 282, 285, 290–93, 320, 321, 436
  legal profession, 15, 44, 45, 343, 346, 347, 348, 350, 356, 357–58, 364–66, 371
  Liberal Democrats, 86
  reeducation see reeducation through labour
efficiency
  administrative discretion, 411
  administrative law, 85, 137, 138, 403, 404, 408
  businesses, 20, 198, 472–73
  courts, 285
  rule of law, 10, 66, 137–38, 166
elections
  boycotts, 206
  Communitarians, 77, 89, 212
  legitimacy, 82–83
  Liberal Democrats, 76, 82, 212
  limitations, 204, 206, 207, 231
  Neoauthoritarians, 74, 76, 77, 85, 172
  normative agenda, 76–77
  people's congresses, 206, 415
  political reform, 20, 21, 22

elections (*cont.*)
    rule of law, 514–15
    Statist Socialism, 77, 85, 172
    village level, 172, 203–4, 208, 230–31, 428,
        482, 484, 531–32
    work units, 206
enforcement
    coercion, 66, 127
    contracts, 459, 462, 464, 473
    fairness/impartiality, 13
    judgments/awards, 154, 162, 218, 287–88,
        290, 304, 307, 315, 327, 463–64, 561
    local protectionism, 307, 311, 327, 464,
        472, 488
    mediation, 467
    Political-Legal Committee (PLC), 303
    practicality, 66
    property rights, 4, 463
    unpopular policies, 204
Engels, Friedrich, 44
Enlightenment, xi, 42, 87
environment
    clean up costs, 477
    economic growth, 9, 461, 467
    pollution/degradation, 159, 454, 461, 467
equality
    democracy, 516
    epistemic/normative, 41, 42, 52
    equality before the law, 6, 65, 128, 130,
        132–33, 161, 177
ethics
    Confucianism, 176, 363, 402, 407, 466
    judiciary, 323
    legal profession, 346, 350, 354, 364, 367,
        371
    market economy, 161, 171
ethnocentrism, 148, 153
European Union (EU), Legal and Judicial
        Cooperation Program, 2, 22
evolutionary theory
    democracy, 514, 521
    law and development, 148, 149, 150
    liberal democrats, xi, 514
    modernization, 452
ex parte communication
    administrative reconsideration, 419, 435
    judicial corruption, 13, 288, 289, 295, 297,
        322

fair trial, 91, 131, 134, 135, 214
Falungong, 89, 91–102, 122–25, 137, 201,
        207, 208, 352, 485, 539
family businesses, 466, 468–69, 477
family law
    birth control policy, 204, 357, 582
    domestic violence, 9
    family planning decisions, 402

Fan Gang, 207
Fascism, 470
feminism, 152
flag burning, 87, 121
Ford, Gerald, 133
Ford Foundation, 151, 182, 202, 350
foreign aid agencies, 151, 152, 180
foreign investment
    approval processes, 246
    business risk, 465, 476–77
    FDI, 58, 110, 149, 222, 453, 454, 456–57,
        458, 474–75
    import duty exemptions, 253–54
    intellectual property, 222, 463, 464
    law and development, 151
    legal opinions, 365
    local government, x, 154, 222, 429, 464
    national security, 458
    open-door policy, 457, 463
    overseas Chinese, 477, 486
    post-Mao reforms, 55, 154, 158
    rule of law, ix, 1, 19–20, 154, 162, 223,
        462, 474–77
    screening, 149
foreign technology, 55, 256, 464, 474
foreign trade, 149, 247, 456
foreign-invested enterprises (FIEs)
    competition, 198
    deficient information, 465
    equipment imports, 253
    equity pledges, 249
    holding companies, 255
    industrial output, 193, 477
    investment decisions, 476–77
    provision of security, 247, 248
    tax advantages, 227, 229
formalism, 164, 165, 451, 455
freedom of speech, 4, 87, 121, 205–6, 373,
        420, 515, 530, 539
Fu Zitang, 160
Fuller, Lon, 3

General Agreement on Tariffs and Trade
        (GATT), 223
globalization
    developing countries, 453–54, 457
    economic growth, 457, 527
    forces of change, 208
    law and development, 151, 453–54, 456
    rule of law, xi, 43, 159–60
government officials
    accountability, 131, 132, 140, 425
    appointments, 415
    bribery, 403
    complaints, 416
    conflict of interest, 205
    connections (*guanxi*), 402–3, 417

corruption, 18, 85, 133, 205, 234, 406–8, 416–17, 478, 484
 deference, 9, 12, 421, 529
 discretion *see* administrative discretion
 downsizing, 205
 education and training, 205
 Mao era, 401
 nomenklatura system, 205
 political winds, 401
 press/public monitoring, 85, 132
 professionalization, 85, 120, 205, 216, 222
 risk aversion, 401
 rule of law, xii, 7–8, 157, 403
 state-owned enterprises (SOEs), 197, 198, 228, 472, 473, 489, 490
 supervision committees, 16
 township and village enterprises (TVEs), 479
Great Leap Forward, 81, 170, 517
Guangdong, 222, 295, 315, 355, 359
Guo Daohui, 329
Guo Mingrui, 243
Guomindang, 44, 52, 168, 200, 225, 346, 531

Habermas, Jürgen, 130, 187
Han dynasty, 34, 41, 52
Han Fei, 34, 42
Hart, H.L.A., 66, 127, 128, 175
He Xi, 243
Heavenly Soldiers Fraternal Army, 94
High People's Courts (HPC), 44, 191, 283, 291, 292, 293, 297, 305, 318, 326–28
High People's Procuracy, 191
Hobbes, Thomas, 66, 81, 128
Hong Kong, 22, 75, 95, 436, 466, 469, 525, 569, 570, 571
household registration (*hukou*), 193
household responsibility, 194, 196
Huang, Phillip, 40, 51–52
Huang-Lao, 34–36, 48
human rights *see also* rights
 alternate paradigm, 543–46
 Asian values, 78, 115–16, 536–38, 539
 cultural factors, 536–38
 international law, 115, 208, 223, 533, 539, 40, 541
 legal profession, 373
 Liberal Democrats, 533–42
 margin of appreciation, 97
 overlapping consensus, 539–42
 post-Mao reforms, 171, 217
 religion, 95–97
 rule of law, 1, 62
 thick theories, 3
 United States, 534–35, 586

ideology
 legal system, 217
 market economy, 171–72, 189, 217
 Political-Legal Committee (PLC), 303
 rule of law, 24–25, 170, 171, 172, 223
 thick theories, 74
imperfect realization of an ideal (IRI), 142–43, 145, 178
Imperial era
 administrative law, 400–1
 appeals, 37–38, 40, 41
 Bureau of Punishments, 36–37
 complaints, 36, 37
 confessions, 37, 161
 Confucianism, 36, 38, 39, 40, 161, 345, 401
 courts, 36–38, 160–61, 165, 345
 criminal procedure, 36–38, 160–61, 376
 dispute resolution, 38–39
 edicts, 36
 emperor, 36, 38, 41, 52, 128
 fact-finding, 37, 160
 filial piety, 38
 hierarchy, 38
 Kadi justice, 165, 185
 legal system, 36–43, 140, 160–61
 legalism, 38, 161
 li (substatutes), 36, 39, 40
 litigation brokers, 345
 litigation costs, 39, 51, 162
 lu (codes), 36, 38, 40, 41, 43, 51
 magistrates, 36, 37, 39–41, 47, 165
 neutral state, 400
 punishment, 34, 36, 38
 scriveners, 37
 tianli (heavenly principles), 41, 48
 tianming (mandate of heaven), 41, 48, 440
 torture, 37, 38, 39, 161, 162
 trials, 37, 39
 xian (district), 36, 37
 zhou (prefect), 36
inconsistent legislation
 administrative agencies, 421
 administrative reconsideration, 260, 261, 417–18
 battling chaos, 256–68
 complexity, 241
 conflict resolution, 259–62
 courts, 323–26, 421
 institutional reform, 262–64
 local government, x, 18, 19, 81, 131–32, 154, 211, 240, 241–42, 258–59, 421
 rectification, 13
India, 468
Indonesia, 168, 200, 222, 238, 461, 470, 522, 523, 527
informal law, 127

institutions
    autonomy, 134
    imperfect realization of an ideal (IRI),
        142–43, 145, 178
    institution-building, 24, 137, 138
    institutional approach, 9–10
    institutions and practices, 83–86,
        103–8
    law and development, 453
    legal institutions, 128, 144
    norms, 127–28
instrumentalism, 8, 23, 167, 219
intellectual property
    courts, 13, 283, 284, 293
    developing countries, 457
    foreign investment, 222, 463, 464
    foreign technology, 55, 256, 464
    market economy, 58, 463
    private enterprise, 480
interest groups, 396, 420, 428, 430, 470
Intermediate People's Court (IPC), 44, 45,
    283, 292, 293
International Country Risk Guide (ICRG),
    178, 458, 459, 460
International Covenant on Civil and
    Political Rights, 533, 582, 584
international law, 94, 95, 115, 208, 223, 533,
    539–40, 541
International Monetary Fund (IMF), 151
investment
    foreign see foreign investment
    rationality, 46–48, 462
Islam, 48, 68

Japan, 43, 95, 122, 132, 400, 468, 469, 569,
    573
Jiang Jingguo, 219, 527
Jiang Mingan, 63, 155
Jiang Ping, 243
Jiang Xianfu, 161
Jiang Zemin
    accountability, 133
    campaigns, 303
    civil/political rights, 62
    constitutional law, 89
    democracy, 518
    Falungong, 97, 99, 207
    human rights, 62
    judicial independence, 319
    local government, 81, 220
    market economy, 120, 194–95
    policy formulation, 213
    political reform, 203, 580
    rule of law, 2, 6, 60, 61, 111–12, 120, 170,
        173, 220
    socialist rule-of-law state, 60, 62, 76, 219

socialist spiritual civilization, 53, 60, 170,
    171, 186, 224
Statist Socialism, 3, 81, 173, 224
Jie, 34
joint ventures (JVs), 244, 247, 248, 250–51,
    409, 465, 476
Jones, Carol, 466
Josephs, Hilary, 133
Judaism, 48, 172
judicial corruption
    adjudicative supervision committees, 18
    bribery, 295, 296, 322, 368, 371
    complaints, ix–x, 220, 296
    ex parte communication, 13, 288, 289,
        295, 297, 322
    Political-Legal Committee (PLC), 303
    scale, 281, 295–96, 408
    Supreme People's Court (SPC), 295,
        296–97
    unfairness, 13, 289
judicial independence
    administrative litigation, 307
    collective, 299
    Communitarians, 86, 300
    constitutional law, 280
    external, 299
    higher/lower courts, 314–15
    internal, 299
    Liberal Democrats, 86, 100, 299–1
    limitations, 84
    local protectionism, 14, 17, 218,
        220, 288, 307, 308, 311–12,
        327, 328
    Mao era, 45, 47, 212
    Neoauthoritarians, 85, 300, 301
    personal, 298, 299
    political cases, 220, 298
    post-Mao reforms, 156, 328–30
    rule of law, 5, 13–14, 60, 137
    Statist Socialism, 85, 99, 300–1
    substantive/decisional, 298, 299
judicial review see administrative litigation
judiciary
    administrative rank, 319, 321, 324
    appointment/tenure, 46, 84, 134, 214,
        216, 282, 291–92, 293, 298, 299–300,
        305–6, 320, 327, 328–29
    authority, 323–27
    categories, 284–85, 286
    Communist Party (CCP), 46, 134, 216,
        220–21, 224, 302–9, 328–30
    competence, 281, 289–298, 320–22
    courts see courts
    Cultural Revolution, 289
    developing countries, 150
    dismissal, 292–93, 294, 298

education and training, 13, 14, 44, 155, 182, 282, 285, 290–93, 320, 321, 436
ethics, 323
examinations, 290, 291
future reform, 318–20
Judges Law (1995), 13, 58, 214, 291, 294, 298, 304, 305
Legal and Judicial Cooperation Program, 2, 22
legal research, 156
Liberal Democrats, 73, 84
Mao era, 44, 45, 47, 212, 289, 318
military officers, 14, 290, 293
nomenklatura system, 8, 14, 77, 191, 214, 284
political affiliation, 300, 306
procuracy, 280, 298, 312–13, 323, 325
professionalism, 222, 290, 320, 323
promotion, 292, 298, 299, 320, 321
qualifications, 290, 292, 293
relations with legal profession, 291, 296, 320, 360, 361
salaries, 288, 294, 298, 321, 322, 324
sanctions against, 285, 288, 291, 294, 298
social pressures, 315–16, 325
stability, 99, 100
weakness, 9, 12, 162, 281–82, 301, 367, 399–400
justice
Huang-Lao, 35
rule of law, 70
substantive/procedural, 37, 161, 376, 424

Kang Youwei, 518
Kong Fansen, 171

law
binding rules, 127
normative authority, 137
system see legal system
law and development
capitalism, 151, 453
comparative law, 152
Critical Legal Scholars (CRITs), 149, 152, 454, 455
evolutionary theory, 148, 149, 150
feminism, 152
foreign investment, 151
globalization, 151, 453–54, 456
institutions, 453
legal profession, 343
new movement, 150–53, 343, 453
old movement, 148–50, 158, 167, 185, 343, 460
states, 152–53, 158, 167, 185, 343
Law and Society scholars, rationality, 149

lawlessness, 129–30
leadership
CCP role, 10–12, 45, 61, 77, 82, 120, 165, 211–12, 217, 226
charismatic leadership, 168, 209
constraints see state bound/limited
education and training, 209
future leaders, 209–10
insights, 42
villages, 204
work units, 206, 207
legal academics
legislation, 212, 243, 381
post-Mao reforms, 155–56, 182, 212, 243
rule of law, 380
salaries, 320, 369
legal aid, 160, 252, 350, 362–64
legal consciousness/awareness, 7, 12, 17, 18, 23, 60, 382, 395, 405, 418, 421, 483
legal norms, 127
legal pluralism, 127
legal profession
access to advice, 353, 361–69
administrative litigation, 352, 362, 405–6, 442–43
administrative reconsideration, 355–56, 357
analytical skills, 366, 369
annual reviews, 355, 357
autonomy, 15, 84, 120, 137, 149, 374, 382, 451, 452, 453
bar associations, 346, 348, 349, 350, 354, 355, 363, 368–69, 372, 378, 575
barefoot lawyers, 362
clientelism, 15, 85, 356, 357, 378, 379, 406
Communitarians, 120, 374
competence, 364–67
competition, 369, 371
confidential information, 351, 368, 375
connections (guanxi), 7, 15, 295, 366–67, 371, 379–80, 387, 473
cooperatives, 353, 386
corporatism, 15
corruption, 7, 15, 296, 297, 356–58, 367–69
criminal procedure, 349, 352, 362–64, 372, 375–77
Cultural Revolution, 347, 348
discipline, 350, 354, 355, 366, 371
dual management system, 353–54
education and training, 15, 30, 44, 45, 343, 346, 347, 350, 356, 357–58, 364–66, 371
ethics, 346, 350, 354, 364, 367, 371
expansion, ix, 7, 14, 346, 361–62, 369
Falungong, 100, 101, 352

legal profession (*cont.*)
fees, 353, 362
foreign law firms, 245, 358, 365, 369–70, 373
future prospects, 369–71
historical overview, 345–50
hotline networks, 155, 361, 368
human rights, 373
independence, 15, 84, 120, 343–93
interests served, 377–83
justice bureaux, 100, 101, 352, 357, 358, 372, 373, 387, 388, 406
law and development, 343
law firms, 58, 154, 347, 348, 351, 352–53, 366, 369, 372, 373, 378, 386
law journals, 7, 44, 45, 346, 348, 371, 382
Lawyers Law (1996), 58, 154, 160, 234, 252, 255, 304, 349–54, 362, 364–65, 368, 374
legal advisory offices, 346–47, 348
legal consultants, 368
legal opinions, 365
Liberal Democrats, 73–74, 84, 373, 374
licensing, 356, 357, 364, 387
limited independence, 371–83
Mao era, 44, 45, 47, 84, 346–47
market economy, 347–48, 353
Ministry of Justice (MOJ), 15, 58, 84–85, 155, 245, 255, 344, 346, 349–50, 353–58, 361, 368, 370, 372–74, 378, 575
Neoauthoritarians, 120, 374
partnerships, 58, 154, 353, 386
Party groups, 351
physical attacks, 360–61, 371
political cases, 15, 100, 101, 352, 356, 370, 378–79
post-Mao reforms, ix, 14–16, 58, 154, 222, 347–50
practicing certificates, 355, 364
professionalism, 343–93
Provisional Regulations, 345–46, 347, 348–49, 351, 353–54, 364
qualifications, 348, 350, 355, 362, 364, 365, 369
redefining lawyers, 351–52
Regulations, 345–46
regulatory compliance, 371
relations with judiciary, 291, 296, 320, 360, 361
remuneration, 357, 366
rule of law, 7, 16, 343–45
scriveners, 37
securities regulation, 356
social change, 377–83
socialist rhetoric, 348, 351–52, 364
sole practitioners, 255

state secrets, 351, 368
state-owned firms, 353, 372
Statist Socialism, 373–74
tax evasion, 357, 373
technical capacity, 343–44, 369–71
Township Legal Services Stations (TLSS), 388, 484
UN Basic Principles, 343, 373, 384, 390
websites, 357, 372
"workers of the state", 15, 84, 348
World Trade Organization (WTO), 369–70, 373
Legal Realists, 164, 165
legal system
civil law, 73, 251–52, 281, 317, 380, 381
common law, 73
Communist Party (CCP), 211–16
convergence, 4, 301
Cultural Revolution, ix, x, 6, 45–46, 49, 56, 74, 83, 118
culture of legality, 437
economic growth, 463–64
ideology, 217
Imperial era, 36–43, 140, 160–61
institution-building, 24, 137, 138
logic, 451
Mao era, 6, 8–9, 43–47, 48, 136, 140, 165
post-Mao reforms, xi, 55–125
rule of law compared, 63–64
traditional culture, 158, 160, 400–5
transplantation, 148, 158–63
legalism
equality before the law, 161
fa zhi, 28, 33, 41, 42, 43
Imperial era, 38, 161
response to Confucianism, 33–34
rulers, 34, 42, 161
legislation
administrative agencies, 73, 117, 216, 239, 241
Communist Party (CCP), 84
contracts, 58, 242, 243
dispersed authority, 241–42
drafting quality, 240, 244, 247–53
electronic databases, 246–47
excessive generality/vagueness, 251–52
frequent change, 240, 253
implementation, 58
inconsistency *see* inconsistent legislation
inexperienced drafters, 249–51
internal directives, 7, 245–46
Law on Legislation, 12, 240–42, 246, 259, 262–65, 313, 495
law-making, 241–45
legal academics, 212, 243, 381
legislative explosion, 6, 239

legislative hierarchy, 241, 271
legislative system, 12–13, 239–79
  market economy, 58, 412, 463, 478–79
  nonexistent regulations, 252–53
  Normative Documents, 241, 246, 247,
    260, 263, 266, 268, 421–22
  NPC *see* National People's Congress
  people's congresses, 239, 241, 263, 265,
    412
  problem areas, 240
  provisional regulation, 255
  publication/accessibility, 245–47
  retroactive laws, 65, 130
  rules/regulations, 244–45
  stability, 253–55
  State Council, 241, 242, 262
  Supreme People's Court (SPC), 304
  thin theories, 240
  trade regulations published, 247
  transparency, 242–45
legitimacy
  Communist Party (CCP), 61, 169–74, 189,
    209, 220, 223, 224–25
  democracy, 524
  economic growth, 61, 172, 189, 209
  elections, 82–83
  people's congresses, 414–15
  rule of law, 82–83, 169–74, 187,
    223, 224
  Statist Socialism, 224, 225
Lei Feng, 171
leisure, 199, 200
Leninism, 10, 61, 77, 88, 165, 170, 200, 201,
  230, 567
letters and petition system, 19, 132, 419–20,
  484
Levine, Ross, 459
Li Buyun, 59, 63–64, 113
Li Fan, 243
Li Hongzhi, 92, 97, 99, 100, 124
Li Peng, 60, 119, 329, 424, 580
Li Shenzhi, 82, 207
Liang Huixin, 59, 243
Liang Qichao, 43, 518
Liberal Democrats
  administrative discretion, 84
  autonomy, 84
  civil society, 77, 201, 202
  civil/political rights, 3, 62, 78, 86, 135
  Communitarians, 116, 117
  constitutional law, 87
  criminal procedure, 90–91
  cross-cultural dialogue, 68, 147
  education, 86
  elections, 76, 82, 212
  evolutionary theory, xi, 514
  human rights, 533–42

  ideal type, 71–75, 103, 117
  judicial independence, 86, 100, 299–1
  judiciary, 73, 84
  justice, 70
  legal profession, 73–74, 84, 373, 374
  market economy, 3, 4, 75
  neutral state, 76, 86, 119, 304, 401
  parliamentary supremacy, 73
  predictability, 82
  rules, 86
  separation of powers, 73
  single party socialism, 188, 212
  social groups, 94
  social order, 116
  stability, 80–81
  state bound/limited, 80, 129
  unlikely outcome, 48
  Western tradition, 2, 5, 27, 73, 116, 145
liberalism, 171, 471
licensing
  administrative discretion, 196, 413, 433,
    472
  foreign technology, 256
  legal profession, 356, 357, 364, 387
Lipset, Seymour Martin, 513
litigation *see also* dispute resolution
  administrative law *see* administrative
    litigation
  costs, 281, 285, 455–56
  economic growth, 162–63, 468
  expansion, 7, 162, 382
  Imperial era, 39, 51, 162, 345
  precedents, 286, 380
  representation rates, 352, 362
  women's issues, 380
Liu Jiachen, 99
Liu Junning, 64, 69, 115, 207, 521
local government
  arbitration commissions, 58
  autonomy, 210–11
  cadres, 196, 203–4, 231, 232
  central/local relations, 12, 81, 210–11,
    220, 312
  commercial involvement, 409, 410, 471,
    472
  corporatism, 471, 472, 475, 478, 487
  corruption, 222
  courts, 295, 307, 310–12, 316
  economic growth, 10, 61, 211, 220
  foreign investment, x, 154, 222, 429, 464
  inconsistent legislation, x, 18, 19, 81,
    131–32, 154, 211, 240, 241–42, 258–59,
    421
  legislative powers, 241
  regional variation, 18
  township and village enterprises (TVEs),
    192–93, 471, 485, 486, 487

local protectionism
  administrative reconsideration, 418
  economic growth, 18, 81, 307
  enforcement, 307, 311, 327, 464,
    472, 488
  judicial independence, 14, 17,
    218, 220, 288, 307, 308, 311–12,
    327, 328
  regionalism, 472, 488
Locke, John, 112, 128, 129, 149
Lubman, Stanley, xi, 120, 565, 567
Luhmann, Nicolas, 130
Lynch, Daniel, 530

Macau, 525
Malaysia, 468, 520, 521
Malinowski, Bronislaw, 127
Mao era *see also* Cultural Revolution
  administrative agencies, 408
  administrative law, 395, 397
  antirightist movement (1957), 44, 81, 170,
    212, 289, 347, 397
  arbitrariness, 171
  class struggle, 44, 45, 347
  Communist Party (CCP), 84
  connections (*guanxi*), 402
  constitutional law, 44
  courts, 44, 212
  dispute resolution, 47, 83
  government officials, 401
  Great Leap Forward, 81, 170, 517
  hundred flowers movement (1956), 45,
    212, 347
  internal directives, 245
  judicial independence, 45, 47, 212
  judiciary, 44, 45, 47, 212, 289, 318
  legal profession, 44, 45, 47, 84, 346–47
  legal system, 6, 8–9, 43–47, 48, 136, 140,
    165
  mass line, 44
  policy formulation, 23, 213
  rule by law, 74, 75, 79, 395
  socialist theory of law, x, 43–44
  thought control, 46, 80
  work units, 199
Mao Zedong
  leadership, 42, 224
  Marxism-Leninism, 77
  revolutionary beliefs, 53, 120
market economy *see also* capitalism; private
    enterprise
  central government, 205
  Communist Party (CCP), 220
  Communitarians, 3–4, 76
  competition, 195, 196, 198
  connections (*guanxi*), 402, 441

constitutional law, 88, 194–95, 478
contracts, 20, 348
courts, 319
deregulation, 396
dispute resolution, 159
economic growth, 151
ethics, 161, 171
ideology, 171–72, 189, 217
incomplete separation, 408–10
intellectual property, 58, 463
intermediary organizations, 353
legal profession, 347–48, 353
legislation, 58, 412, 463, 478–79
Liberal Democrats, 3, 4, 75
market failure, 75, 152
market mechanisms, 456
mergers and acquisitions, 356
Neoauthoritarians, 76
normative basis, 120
regulation, 150
retreat of party/state, 192–199, 216
rule of law, 55, 221
socialist rule-of-law state, 3, 59
Statist Socialism, 71, 76
Marx, Karl Friedrich, 44
Marxism, 88, 165, 171, 470
Marxism-Leninism, 77, 470
mediation *see also* dispute resolution
  administrative litigation, 406
  commercial transactions, 162–63, 456
  courts, 163, 288–89
  enforcement, 467
  Imperial era, 38–39, 184
  judicial corruption, 296
  Mao era, 47
Mencius, 49, 50
microanalysis, 145
migrant workers, 193, 202
Ming dynasty, 37
Ministry of Agriculture, 244, 409, 443
Ministry of Civil Affairs, 92, 200
Ministry of Foreign Trade and Economic
    Co-operation (MOFTEC), 110, 154,
    244, 245, 248–50, 253–57, 269, 421,
    441, 477
Ministry of Justice (MOJ)
  budget, 355
  corruption, 85
  created, 44
  dismantled, 45, 212, 347
  hotline network, 155, 361, 368
  legal profession, 15, 58, 84–85, 155, 245,
    255, 344, 346, 349–50, 353–58, 368,
    370, 372–74, 378, 575
  reestablished, 6–7
Ministry of Public Security, 330

Ministry of Supervision, 212, 415
modernization, 148–49, 151, 452, 455
money-worshipping, 367, 371
moral conduct, 78–79, 130, 170–71, 173, 175, 407
Most Favored Nation (MFN) status, 535, 586
multinational companies, 161, 222, 453, 457, 465, 476, 477

National Judges Institute/Training College, 13, 155, 182, 293, 321
National People's Congress (NPC)
  see also legislation
  accountability, 243
  Communist Party (CCP), 62
  courts, 44, 46, 84, 85, 309–10
  delegates, 239, 269–70
  inconsistent legislation, 259
  independence, 203, 215
  Legal Affairs Committee, 234
  Legislative Affairs Commission, 191, 239, 381
  meetings, 269
  normative authority, 532
  Office of Legislative Affairs, 155
  post-Mao reforms, 60, 144, 203, 219, 222
  proposals voted down, 215, 532
  public hearings, 243
  Standing Committee (NPCSC), 6, 191, 215, 234–35, 239, 243, 259, 264–65, 304, 317, 421, 563
  transparency, 242–43
  work reports, 414, 444
National Seed Group Corporation (NSC), 409
nationalism, 61, 171, 173, 535, 536
natural law
  Huang-Lao, 34–36, 48
  normative foundation, 69
  thick theories, 127
Nazi Germany, 64, 69, 114
Neo-Confucians, 49, 50, 70
Neoauthoritarians
  administrative law, 90, 433
  Chinese tradition, 27
  civil society, 202, 374, 431
  constitutional law, 89
  criminal procedure, 90
  democracy, 4, 116
  economic growth, 86
  elections, 74, 76, 77, 85, 172
  ideal type, 71–75, 103–4, 117
  judicial independence, 85, 300, 301
  justice, 70
  legal profession, 120, 374
  market economy, 76

morality/virtue, 78–79
New Conservatives, 72, 117
nomenklatura system, 216
normative agenda, 77, 86, 300
  pragmatism, 79
  rights, 78, 79
  rule by law, 74
  rules, 87
  single party socialism, 188, 212
  social groups, 94
  social order, 115
  social solidarity, 79
  stability, 80–81, 82
  state bound/limited, 129
  strengthening state, 80, 167
  technocratic elite, 519
neoinstitutionalists, 75, 457
neutral state
  Communitarians, 86
  democracy, 72
  Imperial era, 400
  Liberal Democrats, 76, 86, 119, 304, 401
  Statist Socialism, 77, 120
New Confucians, 3, 49, 70, 72
New Conservatives, 70, 72, 117
Nixon, Richard, 133
nomenklatura system
  government officials, 205
  judiciary, 8, 14, 77, 191, 214, 284
  Neoauthoritarians, 216
  no legal basis, 214
  people's congresses, 8, 12
  post-Mao reforms, 191, 192, 576, 577
  Statist Socialism, 216
normative agenda, 76–77, 86, 300, 306, 401
normative equality, 41, 42, 52
North, Douglass C., x, 452–53

Oi, Jean, 471
Old Conservatives, 70

Pan Wei, 4, 70, 117
Party groups
  central government, 191, 226
  courts, 191, 284, 302, 303, 305, 306
  law firms, 351
  state-owned enterprises (SOEs), 210
  Supreme People's Court (SPC), 191
paternalism (*fumu guan*), 9, 12, 40, 42, 46, 400, 408, 419–20
path-dependent reform, 17–19, 153, 158, 399–10, 431–38
Pearson, Margaret, 471
Peng Zhen, 60, 219
People's Bank of China, 247

people's congresses
  assertiveness, 215
  courts, 280, 294, 298, 305, 309–10, 325,
    327
  elections, 206, 415
  legislation, 239, 241, 263, 265, 412
  legitimacy, 414–15
  nomenklatura system, 8, 12
  NPC *see* National People's Congress
  rebuilt, 220
  work reports, 414, 444
People's Liberation Army, 91
People's Tribunals, 283, 484
Philippines, 470
pluralistic society, 159, 200, 202, 319, 452
police, 293, 327, 330, 359
policy formulation
  Communist Party (CCP), 213, 214–15
  constitutional law, 61, 62, 63
  Mao era, 23, 213
  socialist rule-of-law state, 6, 27
political cases *see also* dissidents
  administrative litigation, 207, 400
  judicial independence, 220, 298
  legal profession, 15, 100, 101, 352, 356,
    370, 378–79
  Political-Legal Committee (PLC), 306–7
  Supreme People's Court (SPC), 99, 100
Political Consultative Committee, 197, 528
political reform, rule of law, 20–21, 513–33
political succession, 81, 119–20
Political-Legal Committee (PLC)
  composition, 302–3
  court president, 285
  enforcement, 303
  ideology, 303
  influence, 302–3, 306
  judicial corruption, 303
  judicial recruitment, 290
  legislation, 235
  Mao era, 212
  no legal basis, 133
  political cases, 306–7
  public security, 312
  reform, 329, 576, 577
politics and law
  Critical Legal Scholars (CRITs), 83,
    164–65
  Statist Socialism, 84, 133–34
positive law, thin theories, 66, 69, 127
post-Mao reforms
  adaptation, 158–63
  administrative law, 57, 74, 89–90, 136–37
  civil society, 168, 173, 189
  Communist Party (CCP), 84, 218
  Confucianism, 161, 170, 171

corruption, 60, 158, 159, 162, 172, 205,
    406–8
  costs of reform, 156–58
  courts, 155, 182, 285–89, 318–30
  criminal procedure, 9, 15, 57, 160, 207,
    208, 223, 234–35, 243, 359–60
  devolution, 137, 138, 189, 209, 210, 221
  economic *see* market economy
  forces of change, 208–11
  foreign investment, 55, 154, 158
  future prospects, 558–598
  gradualism, 157
  grass-roots initiative, 154
  human rights, 171, 217
  implementation of legislation, 58
  judicial independence, 156, 328–30
  legal academics, 155–56, 182, 212, 243
  legal profession, ix, 14–16, 58, 154, 222,
    347–50
  legal system, xi, 55–125
  native resources, 158, 160, 161, 183
  nomenklatura system, 191, 192, 576, 577
  outcomes, 87–91
  path-dependent reform, 17–19, 153, 158,
    399–10, 431–38
  policy implications, 578–88
  property rights, 60
  reform agenda, 574–78
  top-down nature, 153–56
  unemployment, 81, 91, 97, 321
postmodernism
  administrative law, 396, 424–31, 439
  indeterminacy of language, 454–55
power
  centralization, 81–82, 191, 218, 219
  devolution, 137, 138, 189, 209, 210, 221
  relinquished, 219, 528
  separation of powers, x, 73, 85, 215
pragmatism
  Communitarians, 78, 79
  Neoauthoritarians, 79
  socialism, 53, 79, 217, 251, 255
  Statist Socialism, 79
predictability
  economic growth, 80, 82, 221, 456, 462
  Liberal Democrats, 82
  rule of law, 67, 74, 80, 82, 131, 164, 411,
    462, 463
  thin theories, 67, 74
private enterprise *see also* market economy
  administrative litigation, 196–97, 478
  discriminatory treatment, 479, 480
  economic growth, 193–94
  intellectual property, 480
  rule of law, 478–81
  taxation, 480

privatization
  agriculture, 192
  Russia, 460, 461
  state-owned enterprises (SOEs), 196, 198,
    489, 490–91
  township and village enterprises (TVEs),
    193, 194, 227, 486, 488
procuracy
  constitutional law, 312
  corruption, 325
  criminal procedure, 359, 361
  Cultural Revolution, 312
  High People's Procuracy, 191
  judiciary, 280, 298, 312–13, 323, 325
  petitions, 287, 313–14
  Supreme People's Procuratorate, 98, 295,
    317
project finance, 248–49
promulgated laws, xiii, 7, 29–30, 128–29
propaganda, 98, 200, 205, 530
property rights
  economic growth, x, 19, 452–53, 459, 462
  enforcement, 4, 463
  post-Mao reforms, 60
  state-owned enterprises (SOEs), 410
  township and village enterprises (TVEs),
    485, 488
public ownership, 76, 171
public security
  administrative litigation, 420
  criminal procedure, 318, 325, 377
  Cultural Revolution, 312
  Political-Legal Committee (PLC), 312
punishment
  capital punishment, 375, 377
  harm to society, 376–77
  Imperial era, 34, 36, 38
  reeducation see reeducation through
    labour
  vengeance, 377
Pye, Lucian, 529

Qiao Shi, 60
Qigong, 92, 93
Qin Shi Huang, 34, 35, 48
Qing dynasty, 1, 37, 40, 43, 49, 52, 81, 184,
  345, 384, 518

rationality, 85, 149, 451, 455, 462, 464–66
Raz, Joseph, 67, 113
Rechtsstaat, 69
reeducation through labour
  administrative sanction, 90, 208, 214, 330
  challenges/appeals, 400, 404, 440
  Liberal Democrats, 91, 135–36
  social stability, 91, 325

religion
  Buddhism, 70, 91
  Daoism, 34, 35, 70, 91, 94, 170, 176, 407
  divine law, 48, 69
  economic growth, 171–72, 451
  Falungong, 89, 91–102, 122–25, 137, 201,
    207, 208, 352, 485, 539
  human rights, 95–97
  Islam, 48, 68
  Judaism, 48, 172
  mandate of heaven, 41, 48, 440
  Republican era, 43, 52, 81
retroactive laws, 65, 130
rights
  civil/political rights, 3, 62, 78, 86, 135,
    173, 514
  Communitarians, 78, 79, 86
  developing countries, 150
  economic growth, 538–39
  Enlightenment, 42
  human see human rights
  Neoauthoritarians, 78, 79
  property see property rights
  Statist Socialism, 78, 79, 173
Rostenkowski, Daniel, 133
Rostow, Walt Whitman, 452, 455
rule by law
  Communist Party (CCP), 8, 10–12, 24
  dissidents, 131, 141
  fazhi, 33, 64
  fair trial, 131
  instrumentalism, 8, 23, 167
  Mao era, 74, 75, 79, 395
  regime pronouncements, 129
  rule of law compared, 8–9, 23, 24, 64–65,
    74, 75, 106–7, 137–40
  Statist Socialism, 74, 77, 167
rule of law
  administrative discretion, 410–14
  alternate paradigm, 543–46
  alternatives, 466–74
  authoritarian regime, 166–69, 185–86,
    378
  autonomy, 78, 79, 83, 219
  bourgeois law, 43, 44, 59, 183
  certainty, 80, 82, 221, 411, 462
  Communist Party (CCP), 56, 61, 161–62,
    169–74
  consistency, 65, 130, 131–32
  critics, 126–87
  dissidents, 166
  economic growth, 19–20, 166, 450–512
  economic regime, 75–76, 101–6
  efficiency, 10, 66, 137–38, 166
  enlightenment, xi, 87
  evolution, 27–54

rule of law (*cont.*)
    eyeball test, 135–36
    fazhi, 63–5
    foreign investment, ix, 1, 19–20, 154, 162, 223, 462, 474–77
    globalization, xi, 43, 159–60
    government officials, xii, 7–8, 157, 403
    human rights, 1, 62
    ideology, 24–25, 170, 171, 172, 223
    institutional approach, 9–10
    institutions/practices, 83–86, 101–6
    judicial independence, 5, 13–14, 60, 137
    legal profession, 7, 16, 343–45
    legal system compared, 63–64
    legislative system *see* legislation
    legitimacy, 82–83, 169–74, 187, 223, 224
    liberal *see* Liberal Democrats
    meaning, 2–6, 63–71, 102
    minimal conditions, 130–41
    moral conduct, 130, 175
    Neoauthoritarian
        see Neoauthoritarians
    normative appeal, 146, 170, 171
    political reform, 20–21, 513–33
    political regime, 76–78, 103–8
    power, 218
    predictability, 67, 74, 80, 82, 131, 164, 411, 462, 463
    private enterprise, 478–81
    procedural rules, xiii
    progress towards, 6–8
    promulgated laws, xiii, 7, 128–29
    property *see* property rights
    purposes, 80–83, 103–8, 146–47
    repression, 1, 2
    retreat of party/state, 217–23
    rights, 78–80, 103–8
    rule by law compared, 8–9, 23, 24, 64–65, 74, 75, 108–9, 137–40
    rules, 86–87, 103–8
    rural sector, 481–89
    sectoral benefits, 475–96
    single party socialism, 188, 211–12
    sliding scale, 136, 140, 178
    stability, 80–82, 119, 173, 220
    state-owned enterprises (SOEs), 489–92
    states *see* state bound/limited
    statist *see* Statist Socialism
    thick description *see* thick theories
    thin description *see* thin theories
    toward rule of law, 56–63
    transplantation/adaptation, 158–63
    typology, 71–75, 103–9, 117
    viable alternatives, 141–45
    Western ideal, 141–45

World Trade Organization (WTO), 492–96, 563
rule of man (*ren zhi*), 33, 43, 56, 58, 118, 161, 212, 237
rule of virtue (*de zhi*), 237
rulers
    Confucianism, 31–33, 42, 50
    Huang-Lao, 35–36
    legalism, 34, 42, 161
    rural sector, 192, 481–89
Russia, privatization, 460, 461

sages
    Confucianism, 33, 50, 176, 316
    Huang-Lao, 35
Saich, Tony, 202
securities regulation
    CSRC, 154, 356
    drafting, 247–51
    equity pledges, 249–50
    immature markets, 159
    legal profession, 356
    listing requirements, 491
    substitutes, 469
Sen, Amartya, 538
separation of powers, x, 73, 85, 215
shareholdings
    joint ventures (JVs), 250–51, 356
    regulation *see* securities regulation
    shareholders rights, 455
    state-owned enterprises (SOEs), 195, 197
Shi Qinfeng, 120
Shirk, Susan, 582
Shu Xiang, 30
Shun, 32, 34, 42
Singapore, 42, 138, 152, 466, 469, 520, 521, 525, 526, 569, 570
single party socialism
    courts, 302
    rule of law, 188, 211–12
    supremacy of law, 61, 211, 212–13
social democracy, 217, 219, 225
social groups
    autonomy, 201
    civil society, 46, 201, 230
    clientelism, 201
    Communitarians, 94
    corporatism, 201, 202
    economic reform, 202
    Liberal Democrats, 94
    Neoauthoritarians, 94
    pluralism, 200, 202
    registration, 69, 86, 87, 92, 93, 94, 201
social/cultural sphere, 199–2

socialism
  constitutional law, 87, 88
  justice, 70
  nationalism, 171
  normative order, 172
  pragmatism, 53, 79, 217, 251, 255
  spiritual civilization, 53, 60, 170, 171, 186, 208, 224, 407
  statist *see* Statist Socialism
socialist rule-of-law state
  Communist Party (CCP), ix, x, 58, 59–60, 62, 219
  constitutional law, 1, 6, 89, 219
  economy, 3
  market economy, 3, 59
  policy formulation, 6, 27
  public ownership, 76
Song dynasty, 36, 37
South Korea, 62, 133, 134, 168, 222, 238, 466, 468, 469, 523, 527, 569, 573
sovereign authority, 128, 129, 536
speculation, 252
stability
  Communitarians, 80–81, 82
  instability, 21, 81
  judiciary, 99, 100
  legislation, 253–55
  Liberal Democrats, 80–81
  rule of law, 80–82, 119, 173, 220
  Statist Socialism, 80–81, 82, 173, 300–1
State Administration for Industry and Commerce, 250
State Administration of Foreign Exchange (SAFE), 247–48, 254, 357
state bound/limited
  Communitarians, 129
  elites, 167
  equality before the law, 65, 128
  Liberal Democrats, 80, 129
  litigation *see* administrative litigation
  meaningful restraints, 65, 74, 131, 132, 136, 148, 218
  normative commitment, 136, 138, 139, 140
  rule by law compared, 74
  skepticism, 137, 138–39
  Statist Socialism, 139
  supremacy of law, 61, 65, 112, 128
State Council
  administrative law, 243–44, 421
  Administrative Regulations, 241, 243, 246, 267, 268, 271, 421
  constitutional law, 318
  FIE exemptions, 253
  interpretive powers, 317

Legislative Affairs Office, 239, 381
legislative powers, 241, 242, 262
State Planning Commission, 248
state strengthening, 80, 167
state-owned enterprises (SOEs)
  1988 law, 489
  1992 regulations, 489
  accountancy, 491
  asset stripping, 491
  autonomy, 195, 197, 409
  banking, 194, 198, 496
  clientelism, 410
  corporate governance, 195, 490
  debt/equity swaps, 196
  government officials, 197, 198, 228, 472, 473, 489, 490
  inefficiency, 20, 198
  insolvency, 198, 229, 252, 353, 490
  lay-offs, 303, 489
  listing requirements, 491
  management, 490
  Party groups, 210
  party-state control, 195–96, 197–198, 210
  privatization, 196, 198, 489, 490–91
  property rights, 410
  rule of law, 489–92
  shareholdings, 195, 197, 356
  wages/salaries, 196, 200, 490
  welfare obligations, 196, 229, 489
states
  government intervention, 75–76, 118, 153, 455
  law and development, 154–55, 158, 167, 185, 343
  neutral *see* neutral state
  socialist rule-of-law *see* socialist rule-of-law state
Statist Socialism
  administrative law, 90, 433
  Chinese tradition, 27
  civil society, 202, 374, 431
  constitutional law, 89
  criminal procedure, 90
  economic growth, 3, 86
  elections, 77, 85, 172
  ideal type, 71–75, 106–8, 117
  judicial independence, 85, 99, 300–1
  legal profession, 373–74
  legitimacy, 224, 225
  local government, 81
  market economy, 71, 76
  morality/virtue, 78–79
  neutral state, 77, 120
  New Conservatives, 72
  nomenklatura system, 216
  normative agenda, 77, 86, 300

Statist Socialism (*cont.*)
  politics and law, 84, 133–34
  pragmatism, 79
  public ownership, 76
  public participation, 166
  rights, 78, 79, 173
  rule by law, 74, 77, 167
  rules, 87
  single party socialism, 188, 212
  social order, 115
  social solidarity, 79
  stability, 80–81, 82, 173, 301–3
  state bound/limited, 129
  strengthening state, 80, 167, 519
  thought control, 79
Strike Hard campaign, 9, 24, 303,
    375, 385
Summers, Robert, 68
Sun Yatsen, 19, 43, 436
supremacy of law
  constitutional law, 6
  morality, 130
  single party socialism, 61, 211, 212–13
  state bound/limited, 61, 65, 110, 128
Supreme People's Court (SPC)
  Adjudicative Committee, 191
  administrative law division, 398
  branches, 328
  civil law, 317–18
  constitutional law, 44, 318
  contract law, 242, 304
  court reform, 155, 283–84, 324
  deadlines, 285
  enforcement of judgments, 154, 304,
    315
  Falungong, 98, 99, 100, 101
  interpretive powers, 317, 326
  judicial appointments, 291, 292, 293
  judicial corruption, 295, 296–97
  jurisdiction, 283
  legislation, 304, 316
  nomenklatura system, 191
  Party groups, 191
  policy guidelines, 301, 304
  political cases, 99, 100
  propaganda, 98
  published judgments, 287
  recusal system, 296–97, 322
Supreme People's Procuratorate (SPP), 98,
    295, 317

Taiwan, 62, 132, 134, 168, 200, 219,
    221–22, 225, 238, 379, 380, 393,
    400, 466, 468, 469, 523, 526,
    529, 531, 569, 573, 583
Tanner, Murray Scot, 219, 220, 236

taxation
  charitable donations, 363
  foreign-invested enterprises (FIEs), 227,
    229
  legal profession, 357, 373
  private enterprise, 480
Thailand, 523
theories
  economic growth, 451–62
  incompletely theorized arguments, 130,
    175
  law reform, 568–74
  theoretical issues, 127–38
thick theories
  different conceptions, 5, 21, 74
  economic beliefs, 101
  forms of government, 3
  Geertzian sense, xii
  human rights, 3
  ideology, 74
  moral/political philosophy, 3, 67, 94, 173
  natural law, 127
  sensitive topics, 146
  substantive theories, 68
  theoretical issues, xiii, 144
  threshold criteria, 4
thin theories
  advantages, 67–69
  alternatives, 144
  Communist Party (CCP), 129
  convergence, 74
  core concept, 5
  dispute resolution, 163
  economic growth, 3, 26, 469
  formal/instrumental aspects, 3, 22
  forms of rule of law, 4
  legislation, 240
  minimum standards, 22, 27, 65, 115, 136
  moral order, 173
  narrow focus, 68
  normative issues, 66–67, 69, 114–16
  objections, 69
  positive law, 66, 69, 127
  predictability, 67, 74
  procedural rules, xiii, 68, 69
  promulgated laws, xiii
  socialist rule-of-law state, 60
  validity/efficacy of laws, 66
thought control
  breakdown, 207, 208
  Mao era, 46, 80
  rule by law, 75
  Statist Socialism, 79
  thought work, 79, 119, 202, 530
"three representatives", 224, 237, 303
"three stresses" (*sanjiang*), 303

Tiananmen Square
  incidents (1989), 58, 111, 160, 170, 191,
    206, 207, 208, 458, 558, 562, 564
  suicides (1999), 93, 122–23
Tianjian Shi, 529
Tibet, 72, 525, 528, 539
tifa (1996), 21
toleration, 41
township and village enterprises (TVEs)
  banking, 195
  clientelism, 487
  competition, 486
  government officials, 479
  initial success, 485, 486
  local government, 192–93, 471, 485, 486,
    487
  privatization, 193, 194, 227, 486, 488
  property rights, 485, 488
  rural economy, 485–88
  salaries, 486, 487, 488
transparency
  courts, 18, 281
  law-making, 242–45
  National People's Congress (NPC),
    242–43
  World Trade Organization (WTO), 76,
    222
triads, 130
"Trojan Horse" strategy, 237, 238
Tung Chee-hwa, 571

unemployment, 81, 91, 97, 321, 457, 458,
  486, 487, 520
United Nations, 153, 345, 375, 386, 392, 538
United States
  administrative litigation, 400
  corruption, 135
  criminal procedure, 375, 391
  human rights, 534–35, 586
  political activists, 135
urbanization, land values, 482
US-Asia Law Institute, 350

villages
  committees, 204
  elections, 172, 203–4, 208, 230–31, 428,
    482, 484, 531–32
  leadership, 201
  Party cells, 203
  protests, 483
  rural sector, 192, 481–89
  TVEs *see* township and village enterprises
  unpopular policies, 204, 206–7

violent crime, 129–30, 385

Wade, William, 215
Walker, Geoffrey, 66, 113
Wang Jiafu, 59
Wang Liming, 243
Wank, David, 402
Warring States period, 42
Way (*dao*)
  Confucianism, 32–33
  emperor, 41
  Huang-Lao, 35
Weber, Max, x, 127, 149, 165, 168, 171, 185,
  450, 452, 455, 466
wholly foreign-owned enterprises (WFOEs),
  227, 247, 248
Wittgenstein, Ludwig, 184–85
work units, 199, 205–7
World Bank, 151, 180, 181, 450, 454, 461,
  475, 522
World Trade Organization (WTO)
  competition, 196, 198, 458, 496
  dispute resolution, 183, 495
  economic growth, 492–96
  GATT requirements, 223
  globalization, 160
  international legal regime, 198, 208,
    454
  legal profession, 369–70, 373
  MFN status, 535
  preferential arrangements, 222
  rule of law, 492–96, 563
  trade regulations published, 247
  transparency, 76, 222

Xia Yong, 59, 117
Xiao Gongqin, 117
Xiao Yang, 292, 302, 309, 314, 319, 355
Xinhua, 254
Xinjiang, 72, 525, 528
Xun Zi, 49, 50

Yang Jinguo, 372
Yao, 34, 42

Zhang Guangxing, 243
Zhang Wenxian, 158, 183
Zhao Ziyang, 116, 190–91, 329
Zheng Shiping, 308
Zhongnanhai, 91, 97, 98
Zhou, 34
Zhu Rongji, 60, 97, 98, 204, 580
Zhu Suli, 158, 166, 183, 439